SECURITY INTERESTS IN MOBILE EQUIPMENT

Security Interests in Mobile Equipment

Edited by
IWAN DAVIES
Centre for Instalment Credit Law
University of Wales, Swansea

Routledge
Taylor & Francis Group
LONDON AND NEW YORK

First published 2002 by Dartmouth Publishing Company, Ashgate Publishing

Reissued 2018 by Routledge
2 Park Square, Milton Park, Abingdon, Oxon OX14 4RN
711 Third Avenue, New York, NY 10017, USA

Routledge is an imprint of the Taylor & Francis Group, an informa business

Publisher's Note
The publisher has gone to great lengths to ensure the quality of this reprint but points out that some imperfections in the original copies may be apparent.

A Library of Congress record exists under LC control number: 2002101562

ISBN 13: 978-1-138-73879-9 (hbk)
ISBN 13: 978-1-138-73874-4 (pbk)
ISBN 13: 978-1-315-18456-2 (ebk)

Contents

Notes on Contributors *vii*

Foreword
Mr Justice John Thomas *viii*

Introduction *ix*

PART I: THE CONCEPT OF SECURITY AND REMEDIES FROM MISUSE OF CHATTELS

1 The Development of the Contract of Hire or Lease in Scots Law
R Bruce Wood 3

2 Twenty-Five Years of *Romalpa*
J R Bradgate 29

3 Rights of Ownership in Goods
Pip Giddins 95

4 Mortgages of Aircraft
J A M Edmunds 145

5 The Rights of a Ship's Mortgagee in English Law
Gotthard M Gauci 155

6 Remedies Available From Misuse of Chattels
Paul Todd 181

7 Purchase Money Security Interests under the Revised Article Nine of the Uniform Commercial Code
Keith Meyer 251

PART II: CHOICE OF LAW RULES

8 International Insolvency, Security Interests and Creditor Protection
Paul Omar 293

9 Retention of Title Clauses and Non-Possessory Security Interests: A Secured Credit Regime within the European Union?
Iwan Davies 335

PART III: UNIFORM LAW

10 The Characterisation of Interests and Transactions Under the Convention of International Interests in Mobile Equipment, 2001
Ronald Cuming 377

11 From Ottawa to Cape Town: Unidroit's Role in the Modernisation of the Law governing Leasing and the Taking of Security
Martin Stanford 397

APPENDIX I Unidroit Convention on International Financial Leasing 1988 451

APPENDIX II Convention on International Interests in Mobile Equipment 2001 465

APPENDIX III Protocol to the Convention on International Interests in Mobile Equipment on Matters Specific to Aircraft Equipment 2001 509

Index *539*

Notes on Contributors

J R Bradgate is Professor of Commercial Law at the University of Sheffield.

Ronald Cuming is Professor of Law at the University of Saskatchewan, Canada.

Iwan Davies holds the Sir Julian Hodge Chair of Asset Finance Law at the University of Wales, Swansea and is Director of the Centre for Instalment Credit Law.

J A M Edmunds is a partner with Beaumont and Son, London.

Gotthard M Gauci is a Lecturer in Maritime Law at the University of Wales, Swansea.

Pip Giddins is Assistant Director of the Centre for Instalment Credit Law, University of Wales, Swansea and a consultant solicitor with DLA.

Keith Meyer is the Hampton Professor of Law at the University of Kansas, USA.

Paul Omar is a Lecturer in Company and Commercial Law at the University of Wales, Swansea.

Martin Stanford is the principal research officer at Unidroit, Rome.

Paul Todd is a Senior Lecturer in Law at the University of Wales, Swansea.

R Bruce Wood is a partner with Morton Fraser, Solicitors, Edinburgh.

Foreword

Traditionally lawyers in different disciplines have considered security over movables predominantly in relation to the discipline with which they are familiar. The shipping lawyer would have learnt the intricacies of ship mortgage finance in the few firms and chambers that dealt with that work largely by tradition and unaided by texts; in my first days of practice, there were little more than rare copies of Constant's book already more than half a century old to add to the learning that was handed down within my chambers. Although within that discipline there are now texts available, it has been high time for a treatise that has as its focus the law relating to security interests in all movables.

By bringing together the law relating to security interests in movables, this work is a major contribution to a more systematic and structured approach to the subject which should lead to a greater synthesis of the law. It traces the development of different strands of the law from *Romalpa* clauses to consumer credit transactions, finance leases and mortgages on ships. But no one can examine this area of the law without close attention to comparative law and in particular Article 9 of the UCC and developments within the European Union. Not only does the work cover these matters, but also the steps being taken towards the creation of uniform laws, the most important of which is the recent Convention on the secured financing and leasing of high value mobile equipment.

As legal scholarship has again become an important driving force in the development of commercial law, this book is a timely contribution to a more structured and purposive approach to the future development of commercial law in this area which is significant to innovative economic and financial activity. Commercial law has always tried to keep pace with such innovation; the contribution of the scholar is, in these day of much more rapid change, vital to that task. This work should therefore be widely welcomed by the financial community and lawyers alike.

MR JUSTICE JOHN THOMAS
Judge in Charge of the Commercial Court
Royal Courts of Justice
Strand
London

Introduction

This collection of essays marks the formal launch of the Centre for Instalment Credit Law at the University of Wales Swansea. The book is divided into three parts: The first part examines the general concept of security and the remedies available from misuse of chattels within domestic personal property law; the second considers the choice of law rules in respect of mobile assets subject to security interests which move between frontiers; finally, the development of uniform law particularly a body of international substantive law that addresses the central legal elements of secured financing and leasing of high-value mobile equipment is considered.

The traditional approach to the legal treatment of security concentrates upon the extent of the financier's capability, as a matter of law, to effectively lend on a gone concern as distinct from a going concern basis. From the financier's point of view, the taking of security is considered to be axiomatic of a model financing transaction. By no means is this a new phenomenon. Thus, under classical Roman law, for example, security was intimately connected with property as the tender of goods was made a condition of the buyer's duty to pay.[1] Herein also lies the reason for the distinction drawn under the later common law between the conditional sale and hire purchase.[2]

It is too narrow to define security simply in terms of a right in another's property which gives the creditor a right of preference and a right to follow. Such an approach fails to deal with manipulation of title mechanisms through contractual provisions such as leasing, hire purchase and retention of title clauses which are functionally equivalent to a security device, that is, where the security interest arises out of a retention of title by the creditor rather than the granting by the debtor of a *jus in re aliena*. However, in a dynamic commercial setting, it is artificial to try and distinguish between a sale of goods from a finance lease because what

[1] This reflects the Compilation of Justisian where the effect of the suspensive *lex commissoria* was to protect the seller on the buyer's insolvency by giving him the right to recover his property.
[2] *Helby* v *Matthews* [1895] AC 471; *Lee* v *Butler* [1893] 2 QB 318.

is involved in both is an allocation of risks and benefits in respect of economic assets.[3] As Kripke has colourfully put it:

> The man from Mars with a clear eye undistorted by training in law, accounting or taxation, would find in the installment purchase a device by which the user of property acquired the right to use it in return for installment payments which cover the costs advanced by someone else (the secured party or lender) plus a charge for the use of money. If a man from Mars looked at the long term lease with the same clear eye he would find precisely the same thing except that installment payments by the user are limited, and at the end of a limited contracted period of use, the remaining use life of the property belongs either to the supplier of the funds or to the passive third-party lesser who occupies that position to receive the benefit of the tax manna. The similarities are so great that the differences should fade into insignificance.

A better analytical approach in evaluating any legal institution which is intended to function as a security device is to focus upon criteria associated with the intended effect of the security. In this respect the first criterion is satisfaction since a secured creditor will wish the most expeditious remedies for realising against his debtor upon default; second, a secured creditor will want to obtain priority against third party interests; last, a secured creditor will seek to monitor or control how his debtor deals with and disposes of the secured asset(s). Such criteria will be important for the creditor's choice of a security device in so far as the law allows him to choose with regard to specific assets.

The conventional wisdom concerning the need for a system of secured credit has been put by Riesenfeld as follows:[4]

> The availability of a properly functioning system of legal devices to secure credit is one of the main prerequisites of economic growth. While in days long past land was the main basis of security for lenders, modern conditions have greatly enlarged the range of assets which *may and must* be utilised in order to afford adequate sources of security for members of the commercial community who are willing and able to supply

---

[3] See Davies, "The Trade Debtor and the Quest for Security" *Insolvency Law Theory and Practice* ed Rajak (1993) Chapter 3.

[4] Riesenfeld SE, *The Quagmire of Chattels Security in New Zealand* (1970) Occasional Paper 1 (emphasis added).

manufacturers or distributors with capital needed for modernisation, expansion, or steadiness of operation.

The application of categorical terminology referred to above embraces two factors: first, the idea of security as a bargained for right which justifiably, in the absence of fraud, supersedes the *pari passu* principle of distribution; second, security is conceived as being desirable *per se* as it stimulates economic growth and the modernisation of business. In order to facilitate these factors, legislation, it has been argued,[5] should promote the low-cost granting and taking of security by, for example ensuring that accurate information is available about the status of the asset to be secured, by increasing the pool of assets available to be secured,[6] by allowing ease of documentation for the transaction and also enabling the creditor to enforce his security as cheaply as possible. If all this is achieved then, it is maintained, transaction and monitoring costs are reduced thereby enabling the debtor to enjoy the maximum interest rate reduction for the secured loan which efficiency allows.[7] As Cuming has pointed out:

> ...there is a direct inverse relationship between legal risk and the availability of credit facilities: the lower the risk, the greater is the willingness to grant credit.[8]

---

[5] Jackson and Kronman, "Secured Financing and Priorities Among Creditors" (1979) 88 *Yale LJ* 1143.

[6] For example, after-acquired property interests. The difficulty with the recognition of an after-acquired property clause is that it can lead to a situational monopoly for the primary/first creditor. It is for this reason that the Uniform Commercial Code, recognises the purchase money security interest on the basis that it represents "new money" to the commercial enterprise. See below Meyer, "Purchase Money Security Interests under the Revised Article Nine of the Uniform Commercial Code" Chapter 7.

[7] The difficulty is to determine precisely the lowering of risk as a result of the security which should then be reflected in the interest charged. The taking of security as a means for reducing uncertainty should not be considered in isolation from other means which achieve the same end such as, for example, restrictive contents.

[8] See Cuming, "Modernising the Secured Financing and Lease Financing Laws of Developing Nations with Particular Focus on the West Bank and Gaza" *New Developments in International Commercial and Consumer Law* ed Ziegel (1998) Chapter 9 at p 185.

The argument here is that an integrated priority structure giving effect to an efficient public registration mechanism can increase the accuracy of the legal risk assessment.

It is probably true to say that commercial law where this is defined as a legal regime facilitating the creation and enforcement of security interests came of age with the publication of Article 9 of the Uniform Commercial Code. Whilst there is no evidence to suggest that the draftsmen of Article 9 were consciously laying down principles which could form cornerstones for the harmonisation of secured financing legal regimes outside of the USA, nevertheless, the influence of Article 9 has been immense.[9] A possible explanation for this influence is that Article 9 presents reformers with a system of law which focuses upon the economic function of transactions as distinct from narrow legal conceptualism.[10] More recently, the collapse of the Soviet Bloc and the transition from one economic regime to another has allowed the opportunity for fresh examination of the basic assumptions of other systems which are often taken for granted, notably the need to facilitate or otherwise the creation and enforcement of security interests.[11] In this respect the European Bank for Reconstruction and Development (EBRD) *Model Law on Secured Transactions* (1994) is designed to provide a guide to the emerging states of central and eastern Europe who were intent to modernise their secured financing law and this model law clearly draws its inspiration from Article 9. Similarly, the World Bank has linked many of its lending provisions to the reform of secured transactions laws in debtor countries[12] where the legal regimen does not facilitate the use of movable property as security for loans. The argument is that the consequence for the local economy of a legal regime in which producers cannot borrow to expand or purchase

---

[9] Article 9 has been adopted throughout the Anglophone Provinces in Canada. It has also inspired reform in Australia and New Zealand.

[10] See below Bradgate, "Twenty-Five Years of *Romalpa*" Chapter 2.

[11] See Drobnig, "The Conversion of a Socialist Economic System to a Market Economy: Legal Implications" *Commercial and Consumer Law* ed Cranston (1993) Chapter 15.

[12] The World Bank has financed projects to reform secured transaction law in Argentina, Bolivia, Brazil, Honduras, Peru, El Salvador and Uruguay. At the same time, the World Bank is collaborating with the Inter-American Development Bank in Mexico in respect of the development of a modern secured transactions law. For a general overview see www.ceal.org.

equipment on credit by using this equipment as security is that there is insufficient equipment, thereby, there is lower production and from this it follows lower incomes.[13] In expanding the legal framework for secured credit the reforms are again inspired by Article 9 of the Uniform Commercial Code.

In international transaction insolvency involving assets subject to security interests moving between national frontiers, the differences in principles which apply to secured credit in various jurisdictions is staggering. Whilst in North America Article 9 provides a unified treatment, in Europe, there are separate regimes for particular transactions. The ability of the debtor to grant a security interest in after-acquired property will differ whilst the priority regime is not consistent ranging from first-in-time to order of notice, order of registration or publicity of the secured interest. These differences cause uncertainty especially in a commercial context where financiers are risk averse and this can prejudice the extension of credit or increases the cost of it through higher interest charges.[14] Furthermore, the uncertainty augments transactional costs through higher level fees as well as other internal costs of time and effort.[15]

Significantly during the course of the last decade of the twentieth century a great change can be seen in the attitude of legal policy makers towards the issue of harmonisation of credit and security law. The traditional approach was to focus upon contract whilst the proprietary effects of a transaction were often ignored.[16] With this in mind, the work of Unidroit in sponsoring the International Interests in Mobile Equipment Convention which was completed in Cape Town in November 2001 is innovative because the Convention is designed to provide a body of

[13] As World Bank Studies have demonstrated, the absence of an efficient legal regime governing secured transactions significantly diminishes the economic output of developing nations. See Office of the Chief Economist, Latin America And Caribbean Region, *How Legal Restrictions on Collateral Limit Access to Credit in Bolivia* (World Bank Report No 13873 - BO, 1994). For a general discussion see De la Pena, "Reforming the Legal Framework for Security Interests in Mobile Property" [1999] *Unif LR* 347.

[14] See Cohen, "Harmonising the Law Governing Secured Credit: The Next Frontier" (1998) 33 *Texas International LJ* 173.

[15] *Ibid.*

[16] See below Davies, "Retention of Title Clauses and Non-Possessory Security Interests: A secured Credit Regime within the European Union" Chapter 9.

international substantive law including an international registry for interests in certain specified high-value goods that are taken across national frontiers. As such, it is not a conflicts of law convention but rather constitutes a form of international substantive law with its own default remedies including provisions for speedy interim judicial relief.[17] From this it appears that an international legal framework, a new *lex mercatoria,* presenting a transnational system for securing loans is now emerging.[18]

This volume is dedicated to the memory of the late Professor Peter Kaye, a distinguished scholar and colleague. Professor Kaye was the Morgan Bruce Professor of European Union Law at the University of Wales, Swansea from 1994-2000.

IWAN DAVIES
CENTRE FOR INSTALMENT CREDIT LAW
UNIVERSITY OF WALES, SWANSEA

---

[17] See below Stanford, "From Ottawa to Cape Town: Unidroit's Role in the Modernisation of the Law governing Leasing and the Taking of Security" Chapter 11. See also especially Appendices II and III.

[18] See below Cuming, "The Characterisation of Interests and Transactions under the Convention of International Interests in Mobile Equipment 2001" Chapter 10.

PART I: THE CONCEPT OF SECURITY AND REMEDIES FROM MISUSE OF CHATTELS

1 The Development of the Contract of Hire or Lease in Scots Law

R BRUCE WOOD

The Legal Context

Scots law is a very different legal system from English law; it is not just English law with a few variations, but rather comes from completely different sources and rests on a different basis. English law is a common law system, indeed the original common law system, to which over the years has been added a system of equity. Scots law by contrast, like most European legal systems, is a civil law system derived from Roman law. As such, its historical background is to be inductive rather than deductive. However, given the dictates of geography, Scots law has inevitably been more influenced of late by English law than its cousin European systems have been, so that when Napoleonic codification came to European systems in the nineteenth century it was English common law's influence which came to Scots law instead. As a result, in comparative law terms, Scots law is now one of the so-called mixed systems of law like those of South Africa, Quebec and Louisiana, to name but three. I give this brief introduction to a significant topic in comparative law, because it has direct relevance to an understanding of the contract of hire in Scots law in two ways. First, it follows from what is written above that the civil law elements of Scots law will be found to be very similar to those of the pre-Napoleonic code European systems. Given the antiquity of the contract of hire (it is not a modern type of relationship; it was known in Roman times and doubtless before then), it will come as no surprise to learn that the Scots contract of hire can clearly be traced to its Roman law roots and then forward through European developments into modern times. Second, Scots law does not have a system of equity, with the result that certain recent English decisions in this area, which depend on concepts of equity, would not have the same result if litigated in Scotland. Given the ease with which parties in the United Kingdom can often choose between Scots and English law as the basis of their contract, this is an issue which can have significant commercial effects.

The original sources of Scots law are quite different from those of English law. Of course, nowadays our principal sources are statute law and case law. Particularly significant in this latter context is the plethora of cases decided in the second half of the 19th century when much of what is modern Scots law was worked out by a number of judges whose decisions remain highly regarded today. But such cases are not the starting point. Rather that starting point consists of the writings of the so-called institutional writers, the founding fathers of Scots law, whose texts remain authoritative and are still cited both in court and academic writings. These institutional writers are such luminaries as Erskine, Bankton, Bell and many others but above them all stands Viscount Stair, whose *Institutions of the Law of Scotland* was first published in 1693. These institutional writers took Roman law as their source and set out to explain in a comprehensive form what was then the whole of Scottish private law as it had been adapted through the Middle Ages from that Roman law background. Of course, although pre-eminent in today's terms, in their own day they wrote their works against a background of influence from other nations, but in this context England was of less relevance due to its very different legal system (and perhaps also for political reasons) and so education and cross fertilisation were sought in Continental Europe, where many Scots lawyers studied their law. And in a few cases, as a result, the writings of foreign institutional writers came to be recognised as having authority in Scots law as well. One of the most prominent examples of this is the French writer Pothier, whose *Contrat de Louage* remains perhaps the seminal influence on the Scots contract of hire. Pothier was writing on French law pre-codification and his text considerably influenced the Scottish institutional writers (other than Stair, whom he post-dates).

So if the contract of hire can be traced back to Roman law, what sort of goods were hired by Romans? The principal answer is slaves. It does not take much study of the old Roman texts to realise that slaves were amongst the most important of commercial goods, and much law was worked out with regard to contracts relating to slaves at a time when chattels were not otherwise of great commercial significance. Horses were also the subject matter of contracts of hire, of course, as were land and services. All of these four types of things were regarded as being capable of being hired and the contract of hire which was developed was the same contract for all of them. To quote from Stair: "... location and conduction is a contract, whereby hire is given for the fruits, use or work of persons or things".[1] As this indicates, the Latin name for this contract was *locatio conductio*, which has been translated into Scots as the contract of location. Such a term is still used today interchangeably for the, to us, more obvious contract of hire. The hire of a thing, whether land or chattels, is the Roman law contract *locatio conductio rei*; the hire of services is the *locatio conductio operarum*. These Latin tags remain valid for use in Scottish courts to this day, and serve as useful reminders that decisions handed down in relation to contracts for the lease of land or for the hire of services can also be regarded as authoritative in relation to a dispute concerning the contract of hire or lease of goods. This can have present day significance. Thus a contract for the lease of land or buildings and a contract for the hire or lease of goods are, in legal principle, one and the same contract. They may not often be thought of in modern practice in this light, but there can be important consequences. For example, until recently there were few recent cases involving the contract of hire of goods (though there was a plethora of cases in the 19th century concerning the hire of horses). But with the overweening importance of land as a source of wealth throughout most of the 20th century there were many cases through that century relating to leases of land. As the significance of the hire of goods in commerce increased in the last part of the 20th century, it became possible to look at cases relating to the lease of land as a guide to how the courts would determine disputes relating to the lease of goods.

The contract of hire of goods and the contract of hire of services are at root the same contract. In very recent times this has taken on potential significance in relation to private finance initiative contracts (PFI). To be comfortable within public sector accounting rules it will be necessary, under FRS 5, to be able to treat the contract as being attributable to the public sector's revenue account rather than to capital account, but yet to preserve the security of the equipment financier in the goods financed the financier may wish to retain title to the goods. This will look like a contract of hire to which accounting rules under SSAP 21 may also apply, leading to treatment of the finance as capital expenditure in certain circumstances. But a contract for the provision of services may be treated as revenue expenditure because of the ongoing maintenance obligations accepted by the lessor (who also provides the relevant asset) and the terms of SSAP 21 may not be applied because there is no lease of goods, but

---

[1] Stair, *Institutions* I, 15, 1.

merely a hire of services making use of goods. In Scots law it is a very simple step to slide from a contract of hire, which might be treated as capital expenditure, to a contract for services, which might be treated as revenue expenditure, because in effect you are just moving from one facet of the same contract to another facet of the same contract, namely, the contract *locatio conductio*.

To return to the historical basis of this contract: in its simple form in Roman times the contract of hire was common and well established. As a result it came to be, as it still is in Scots law today, what is called a "nominate" contract. Nominate contracts can be distinguished from innominate contracts, the distinction in effect being between types of contract which have fixed legal consequences on the one hand and more unusual types of contract where the consequences may be more variable on the other. Thus the nominate contract is blessed with attributes which are referred to, using the Latin tags, as the *essentialia* and the *naturalia*. That is to say, the *essentialia* are those things which are essential for the nominate contract (in our case, of hire) to exist; the *naturalia* are the consequences which flow in respect of the relationship between the parties once it has been established that the contract between them is a contract of hire. The *naturalia* in effect are the rights and duties of the parties which flow from the existence of the contract. By looking at Pothier's *Contrat de Louage*[2] and a whole host of 19th century cases in the Scottish courts, we can establish how this Roman contract was brought into the modern world in Scots law. We now therefore have to look briefly at the *essentialia* and then in more detail at the *naturalia* of this contract. Having then discovered the *naturalia*, we must then look at how the courts have applied and adapted the law to the modern commercial world of leasing.

Essentialia

In determining the *essentialia* of the contract of hire, the later institutional writers all quote copiously from Pothier. They agree that there are four simple essentials for a contract of hire to be established, namely a thing which is let, rent which is agreed, a duration of the let and consent of the contracting parties. The thing in question cannot be of such a nature that it is consumed by its use and it has to be identifiable. The rent can take any form, that is to say, it does not require to be money. In the case of *Wilson* v

---

[2] All references to Pothier are to the English translation contained in Pothier, *Traité de Louge* (trans GA Milligan 1953).

Orr[3] it was sufficient that the rent was the cost of keeping the leased horse in question. It is probably the case that the duration must be fixed, though extendable - for example, it is probably not the nominate contract of hire if the lease is for the natural life of the goods without further explanation. To establish the consent of the parties, writing is not required; the contract can be proved by oral evidence.

Naturalia

Having established that a contract of hire exists, let us now look at the implied terms of that nominate contract which apply unless the parties take steps to exclude or vary them. Once that is done we can then consider how such concept has been or requires to be adapted to cope with the modern finance lease. The *naturalia* fall into two categories, the lessee's implied duties and the lessor's implied duties (subject always of course to any express contrary provision).

The Lessee's Duties. There are five of these: to take delivery of the goods; to pay the rent; to use the goods for the intended purpose; to take proper care of them, and to restore them to the lessor at the end of the contract.

1. Taking Delivery. It is the lessee's duty to uplift the goods from the lessor and take them into his possession.[4] Therefore, if he fails to do so, he has breached his obligations with the result that the lessor can terminate the contract and either claim damages for that breach or seek from the court a decree of specific implement (specific performance in English legal terminology).

2. Paying Rent. Unless provided otherwise, rent is due in arrears, not in advance, though it can be otherwise in relation to particular goods if there is a custom of trade to that effect. The rent however is payable for the use and enjoyment of the goods and therefore, if he cannot have that use and enjoyment, the lessee is entitled to a rebate of rent.[5] This of course ties in with the duties which we shall examine below concerning the lessor's obligation to deliver a hire-worthy thing. There is a relatively strong presumption in favour of the lessee being entitled to abatement of rent if he cannot make use of the goods and

3 (1879) 7 R 266.

4 Pothier *op cit* fn 2 paras 53-74; Bell, *Commentaries* I, 482.

5 Pothier *op cit* fn 2 paras 134 ff and 178.

therefore, where the contract seeks to exclude such right of abatement, the wording will have to be clear to achieve the exclusion and the court will have to be satisfied that the exclusion clearly applies to the circumstances which have in fact happened.

3. Use for the intended purpose. The leading case here is *Seton* v *Paterson*[6] where the defender hired a horse for the purpose of making a journey which would take him one day. Somewhere along the way the defender paused in his journey and took the horse for a gallop in a field. The gallop caused the horse to break its pastern bone and some days later it died. The court held that taking the horse for a gallop was not the intended use of the animal under the contract and the lessee therefore had to compensate the lessor for the value of the horse.

4. Take proper care of the goods. The lessee is responsible for taking ordinary proper care of the goods but is not responsible for fair wear and tear. But if the goods are destroyed or damaged without the lessee's fault then the loss is the owner's, not the lessee's, that is, *res perit domino*.[7] However, if the goods are destroyed or lost it is for the lessee to show what the cause was, so that it can be determined that this was not the lessee's fault. If he cannot show the cause, then the risk will fall on the lessee. The leading case is *Wilson* v *Orr*,[8] where a hired horse died as a result of a blow on the shoulder. If the lessee had been able to show that the blow on the shoulder happened in the normal course of events and without any fault on the part of the lessee, then the problem would have been the lessor's. But the lessee could not prove this and therefore he was held liable for the death of the horse arising as a consequence of the unexplained injury. However, once he has paid the damages to the lessor the lessee is then subrogated to any rights the lessor has to recover damages from a third party or to claim restitution from a third party of the value which the lessee has had to pay the lessor.

---

6 (1880) 8 R 236. As with many of the 19th Century cases, if you substitute "car" for "horse" it is not hard to see the law in modern terms.

7 Stair, *Institutions* I, 15, 5; *Jacksons (Edinburgh) Ltd* v *Contractors John Brown Ltd* [1965] SC 796.

8 *Loc cit* fn 3.

5. Obligation to restore. The lessee has an obligation to restore the goods, fair wear and tear excepted, to the lessor at the end of the contract period. This is a consequence of the duty to take proper care of the goods set out above.[9] It has been suggested that this duty can override, in certain circumstances, the duty to take proper care set out above; that is to say, the duty to restore the goods may in some circumstances impose liability on the lessee even where the inability to restore is not the lessee's fault. This suggestion has been made consequent upon an English case, *British Crane Hire Corporation Limited* v *Ipswich Plant Hire Limited*,[10] which cited the leading Scottish text of Gloag's *Law of Contract*[11] among the authorities for its decision. In that case, a crane on hire sunk in marshy ground without fault on the part of the lessee. It was still stuck there when the hire contract came to an end and the court held that it was the lessee's duty to re-deliver the goods and therefore pay the cost of extracting the crane from the mud. The better view, despite the citation of Professor Gloag as authority, is that this is not a case which should be followed in Scots law, as it appears to clash with the clear view of the institutional writers and with the decision in *Wilson* v *Orr*[12] that if loss is suffered without the fault of the lessee then the risk is with the lessor.

The Lessor's Duties. The obligations implied on the lessor under the nominate contract of hire are similar to those implied in the old nominate contract of sale, but in saying this we must bear in mind that we are talking about the pre-1893 Scots common law of sale, not the new statutory regime which the Sale of Goods Act of that year introduced, and in a sense the implied obligations in the contract of hire are wider because some of them relate to the whole period of the hire. There are four implied obligations: To deliver the goods; to warrant that they are free from defects; not to interfere with the lessee's enjoyment of the goods; and to keep them in repair. We shall consider each in turn:

1. Delivery. The four implied obligations on the part of the lessor are interlinked. The fundamental basis of the contract is that the lessee has the use and enjoyment of the goods. Therefore to have such use

---

[9] *Wilson* v *Orr, supra.*

[10] [1975] QB 303.

[11] Gloag, *The Law of Contract* (2nd ed 1929).

[12] Pothier *op cit* fn 2 paras 197-201; *Wilson* v *Orr, supra.*

and enjoyment the starting point must be that they are delivered in such a condition that this use and enjoyment is possible.[13] Whilst the condition of the goods at delivery is important and is the lessor's responsibility, there is not much else onerous included in this obligation of the lessor. It is the lessee's duty to come and uplift the goods at the lessee's expense from the lessor. So all the lessor has to do is make them available for delivery at some reasonable location. Also, if the goods are destroyed before they are uplifted then the contract is frustrated (in Scottish terms that is to say, *rei interitus* applies) so that the lessor cannot be sued for failing to make the goods available nor can the lessee be sued for failing to pay the rent.[14] However, the obligation of delivery includes the obligation to deliver the goods with the accessories which are necessary to make the goods usable.[15] The example which used to be given was the bit and bridle of a horse, but nowadays the equivalent might be the keys of a car and possibly this could extend in some cases to operating software for equipment which cannot be used without it.

2. Warranty that the goods are free from defects. The leading case is *Wilson* v *Norris*,[16] where a mill engine was let by the lessor to the lessee. It was proved that it was inevitable that mill engines would suffer from downtime and the contract provided that the machine could be worked extra hours where such downtime was suffered. However it was also proved that the downtime on this machine was more than could reasonably have been expected. The lessor was found liable in damages as the machine had to be "sound and fit for the implied or avowed use intended". However it should be noted that this is not the same as warranting that the machine is of merchantable or satisfactory quality, since the lessee is not becoming the owner. The machine only has to be capable of carrying out its purpose. However, the obligation that it is so fit for its purpose continues throughout the whole of the period of hire so that in one respect the obligation is more onerous and in another respect less onerous than the equivalent obligation in the common law contract of sale.

---

[13] Pothier *op cit* fn 2 paras 53-74.
[14] *Duff* v *Fleming* (1870) 8 M 769.
[15] Pothier *op cit* fn 2 para 54.
[16] 10 March 1810 FC.

3. Not interfere with the lessee's enjoyment. Again, this is a corollary of the essential nature of the contract being to provide the lessee with the use of the goods hired for the period of the lease. The obligation therefore extends to preventing third parties disturbing the lessee's possession. This is also a familiar concept in leases of heritable property where it is not just the loss of possession which has to be indemnified but also any diminution of the use and enjoyment. Again, as the two contracts are by historical derivation one and the same, it follows that cases involving, for example, claims against a landlord where the lessee suffers from an undisclosed servitude (in English law terms, an easement) can be used by way of analogy in a lease of moveables. The obligation cannot found a claim, however, if the lessee were aware of the third party rights or the third party has acted delictually (in English law terms, tortiously).[17]

4. To keep the goods in repair. It is the lessor's duty throughout the period of hire to maintain the goods in good order and repair so that the lessee can have their use and enjoyment. However, normal running repairs are the lessee's responsibility, for example to keep a horse shod or to keep a car with tyres which meet legal requirements.[18] All this however varies according to circumstances. Therefore if a car is leased on short-term hire, it will be the lessor's duty to ensure that it is fit for its purpose throughout the short-term hire. If, on the other hand, there is a long-term hire, then there will be assumed to be a need for normal running repairs which, unless otherwise stated, will be the lessee's responsibility. Likewise, if a vehicle breaks down on short-term hire the lessee will be entitled to an abatement of rent. If repairs are required to a vehicle on long-term hire, rent will not be abated unless the repairs are out of the ordinary. Again, if the vehicle is a total loss during the contract the contract will be frustrated (*rei interitu*) and neither party will have any further liability.

This completes our discussion of the *naturalia*, the implied rights and obligations in the nominate contract of hire. All of these have been established for a long time. All can be varied by contractual provisions between the parties. We have seen how easy it is to apply provisions about

---

[17] Pothier *op cit* fn 2 paras 74-105 and 86; Erskine, *Institutes* III 3, 15.
[18] Pothier *op cit* fn 2 paras 106-108; *Wilson* v *Norris, loc cit* fn 16.

horses to the hire of cars, so, despite its antiquity, the basic contract appears fit for use in the modern world. But then in the last quarter of the twentieth century modern commerce and tax laws turned this relative legal backwater into a contract which had to bear the weight of millions of pounds of commercial investment. Suddenly the contract of hire found itself in the limelight as a financing tool, a role for which it had never been developed. This is a common problem, noted in other jurisdictions as well. German commentators have, for example, considered for many years the question of whether finance leasing should be introduced into their code as a separate category of contract. The Americans, having recognised the problem, introduced the concept of requiring registration under the Uniform Commercial Code so that the security aspects could be properly dealt with.[19]

The following might be regarded as the principal areas of difficulty in seeking to apply and adapt the old contract of hire to the new field - to what extent can the duties of the lessor be fully excluded; what happens if the goods become fixtures; on termination of the contract is it possible to seek future rentals by way of lessor compensation, and can the lessor simply forfeit the goods and keep their benefit; what happens to a sublease contract if a head lease contract terminates; is the arrangement truly one involving the grant of security so that it can be open to challenge if not documented as such?

The Modern Finance or Operating Lease Under Scots Law

In general over recent years Scots law has dealt with these issues quite well, but sometimes the old legal principles have been twisted beyond recognition. In this process Scots law's difficulties with having welded an English-style common law deduction-based system on top of the old civil law induction-based system can be clearly seen. Another difficulty has been the modern obsession with obtaining a result which is apparently just to all parties at the expense of legal principle, that is to say at the expense of a legally certain or predictable result. Relative legal certainty was always one of the great benefits of a principle-based system and perhaps the resulting tension between that principle-based system and a common law or equitable justice-based overlay can be observed in the rules and

[19] Uniform Commercial Code (ucc) Article 9. See also the *Report of the Committee on Consumer Credit (the Crowther Report)* Cmnd 4596 (1971) para 5.2.7.

cases relating to unfair contract terms. It is not always commercially desirable that there be justice in any particular case at the expense of future certainty or predictability.

We shall now consider the above areas of difficulty, choosing those areas where there is perhaps the most contrast with the results which have been obtained under English law.

The Exclusion of the Lessor's Duties

The Sale of Goods Acts 1893 and 1979 (as amended) specified implied conditions or duties incumbent on a seller in a sale of goods. The conditions were the same north and south of the border. The Supply of Goods (Implied Terms) Act 1973 did the same for hire purchase. But whereas in England the Supply of Goods and Services Act 1982 specified similar implied conditions or duties on the lessor in a contract of hire, for a long time there was no equivalent legislation in Scots law imposing duties in a hire contract. Why not? Perhaps this was oversight; perhaps it was because it was felt that Scots law, as derived from the institutional writers, quite clearly imposed implied duties on the lessor, all as set out above, so that no legislation was required.

There being no statutory background of implied duties, it followed, so it was thought, that in Scots law there was freedom of contract to exclude the implied common law duties subject only to the Unfair Contract Terms Act 1977, which applies in both jurisdictions (albeit with separate provisions). Then came the landmark case, in the Inner House, of *G M Shepherd Ltd* v *North West Securities Ltd.*[20] This case related to a finance lease of a printer processor which proved defective. The lessee contended that under the old Scots common law there was an implied term that the equipment was hireworthy and that the exclusion of that term in the contract was of no effect by virtue of the Unfair Contract Terms Act. The Court held that while in the ordinary contract of hire there was such an implied term of hireworthiness, this new form of finance lease with which they were faced was not a normal contract of hire, that the lessor did not have the same type of connection with the goods as he would have in a normal contract of hire and therefore that there were no implied terms as to the hireworthiness of the goods in the contract nor as to their being kept by the lessor in such a condition so as to be available for the lessee's use and enjoyment. As there were no implied terms of hireworthiness, there was

[20] [1991] SLT 499.

nothing to be excluded and therefore there was no need to look at whether any exclusion would or would not have been fair under the Unfair Contract Terms Act. In effect the Court was deciding that the modern form of finance lease is a different type of contract from the nominate contract of hire, which was the subject of development in Roman law and by the institutional writers. According to this decision it is, as it were, an innominate contract so it has no *naturalia* and there are, therefore, no implied duties at all. So now apparently we have two types of contract of hire in Scots law. One is the traditional contract of hire which has existed since time immemorial; the other is the modern finance lease (or presumably operating lease) where there are no implied rights and duties and therefore where the contract itself will be the sole measure of the parties' obligations.

The above benign situation for finance lessors subsisted only until 1994, when Parliament passed the Sale and Supply of Goods Act 1994, which for the first time brought Scots Law in relation to the lessor's implied duties in the contract of hire fully into line with English law. The implied conditions in a contract of hire in Scots law now track exactly the same conditions as are implied in English law under the Supply of Goods and Services Act 1982. Furthermore, these implied terms affect all Scots contracts of hire, whether a finance lease which would otherwise be free of implied duties as a result of the *G M Shepherd* decision, or a traditional contract of hire in which as we have seen there are already many implied duties, some of them more onerous than those contained in the statutory format. The statute preserves the validity of the old implied duties in the common law contract (except conditions relating to the quality or fitness of the goods) and the result is therefore something of a hotchpotch, so far as the traditional contract of hire is concerned where both sets of implied conditions will apply (other than in the excepted area).[21]

In the light of the above, Scots lawyers are now just as interested in English Court decisions on the reasonableness of exclusion clauses as they are in Scottish precedent. As is well known, English precedent has gone both ways, sometimes for the lessor, sometimes for the lessee, in an area where any hope of legal certainty has gone by the board. Perhaps the high water mark of lessees' rights was the Court of Appeal decision in *Lease Management Services Ltd* v *Purnell Secretarial Services Ltd*,[22] which can be contrasted with some cases which have turned out more favourably to a

---

[21] Supply of Goods and Services Act 1982, s 11L (as inserted by the Sale and Supply of Goods Act 1994).

[22] [1994] CCLR 127.

finance lessor who has had no involvement with the goods themselves, as, for example, in the cases of *Photoprint*[23] and *Winther Brown*.[24] Whatever the decision, these cases have been struggling to deal with a simple problem. This is that as the lessor is the one who has purchased the goods from the supplier, it follows that the lessee may have no contractual rights against the supplier and therefore, if he does not have a claim against the lessor for deficient goods, he may be deprived of a remedy. Accordingly, in cases where the exclusion clause has been found invalid in favour of the lessee, the Courts have been struggling to do justice by giving the lessee a remedy, in other words they have struck down the exclusion clause and imposed the statutory duty on the lessor. This has included some striking, almost emotional, statements. For example, in the *Purnell* case, where there was a simple total exclusion of liability for the condition of the goods, the Court said:

> One would like to think the days of such blanket exclusion clauses, daunting to anyone and incomprehensible to an ordinary customer, are past. One would hope that finance companies and suppliers of expensive equipment no longer use small-print standard conditions as a means to avoid liabilities otherwise attaching to them for breach of resale representations or breach of implied warranties. It was to meet conditions of this sort that Parliament enacted the Unfair Contract Terms Act 1977.[25]

A detailed critique of the Court of Appeal decision in the *Purnell* case is beyond the scope of this chapter, but suffice it to say that in terms of the application of logic it is a poor decision. To take just the one instance of the words quoted above, Parliament did not enact the 1977 Act to outlaw blanket exclusion clauses. What it said was that blanket exclusion clauses, like any other exclusion clauses, should only be enforceable if they were reasonable. Lessors, of course, contend that they are reasonable because of their lack of knowledge of, or contact with, the goods, but this leaves the problem outstanding of the fact that it is the lessors who have the remedies against the suppliers for the goods being defective. In this light it is significant that in the *Photoprint*[26] and *Winther Brown*[27] cases the Court attached weight to the fact that the lessors promised in the lease contract to

---

23 *W Photoprint Ltd* v *Forward Trust Group Ltd* (1993) 12 Tr L 146.

24 *Anglo Group PLC* v *Winther Brown & Co Ltd* [1997] TCC 413.

25 *Loc cit* fn 22 at p 129.

26 *Supra.*

27 *Supra.*

make available to the lessees the rights which those lessors had against the suppliers should the goods prove defective. One wonders, however, how much use these rights will be to lessees in the face of opposition from an astute supplier, who could aver that the lessor's rights are of no value to the lessee if the lessor himself has suffered no loss, because the lessee is bound by the terms of the lease contract to continue paying rent notwithstanding defects in the goods. It may be therefore that the comfort which the Court has found in such clauses, whereby the lessor promises to make available to the lessee its rights against the supplier, is in truth cold comfort, and it would have been better instead to have focused on the need for a lessee to ensure that it obtains a collateral contract with the supplier, whereby the supplier gives warranties in respect of the goods direct to the lessee notwithstanding that the supply contract is now with the lessor. This of course is what happens in many transactions.

All of which leads to a new Scottish solution which has been found for this problem. In truth this solution has always been there, but it did not see the light of day until the Outer House decision in the 1988 case of *North Scottish Helicopters Ltd* v *United Technologies Corporation Inc.*[28] That case however obviously pre-dates the 1994 Act, and given the decision in the case, it can be argued that the 1994 Act was otiose and unnecessary, that the Scots common law was perfectly adequate to deal with the situation and gave a more certain and a fairer result than that which eventuates from denying the lessor the right to exclude liability in situations where he has no connection with the goods. The facts in *North Scottish Helicopters Ltd* were simple. A finance company leased a helicopter, excluded its obligations in respect of the condition of the helicopter and required the lessee to keep it maintained. The helicopter was destroyed by fire as a result of a defect for which it was claimed the manufacturers of the helicopter (its suppliers) were to blame. The Court held that the lessees had a possessory right to the helicopter as a result of which they had title to sue the suppliers for the suppliers' negligence which caused them loss. This was not a right which arose in contract but rather in delict (in English law terms, tort). There was a duty of care by the suppliers to the lessees which gave title to sue. This is delightfully simple. The lessee has a direct right of action against the supplier based on negligence. Indeed one can go further and suggest that in a Scottish context by simple wording in the lease contract this right can also be made contractual, that is to say, the lessee by virtue of the lease contract can be

[28] [1988] SLT 77.

given a *ius quaesitum tertio* to sue the supplier under the sale contract. A *ius quaesitum tertio* is the old Scots law remedy allowing third parties to sue in respect of a contract between others which is of concern to them. Admittedly there are restrictions on what can be recovered under the *ius quaesitum tertio* but this has always been a right available in Scots law where there has never been an equivalent of the old English rule of privity of contract. Of course the Contracts (Rights of Third Parties) Act 1999 in England has now introduced similar concepts into English law. It will be interesting to see if the English Courts are readier to uphold the validity of exclusion clauses in the future where lessors have sought to extend the benefit of supply contract liabilities to the lessee by virtue of that Act.

Termination

There are some interesting parallels and distinctions to be drawn with English law and practice in the context of early termination of lease contracts.

Where the Lessor Seeks a Termination Payment. Giving the leading judgment in the case of *Bell Brothers (HP) Ltd* v *Aitken*[29] in 1939, Lord President Normand said:

> It appears to me that the mode of assessing damages prescribed by the clause in the contract here at issue very much resembles the method by which damages would be assessed by a court in the case of breach by the hirer, if there were no special contractual provisions. It is simply taking the total sum due under the contract on the one hand and the sum actually received together with the value of the thing actually returned on the other, and treating the difference between them as damages.[30]

Although *Bell Brothers* was a hire purchase case, this judgment does, of course, express exactly the type of termination payment which a lessor is likely to provide for in contractual terms in his finance lease. Thus such termination payment provision has the benefit of judicial blessing. The case itself however is a confusing one in other respects, in particular, in that it fails to draw a distinction between the enforceability of liquidated damages clauses where the termination event is breach of contract by the lessee on the one hand, from the enforceability of a contractual payment

[29] [1939] SC 577.

[30] *Supra* p 587.

stipulation where the termination event is not a breach event on the other. This lack of distinction in the *Bell Brothers* case was quite deliberately stated in the judge's opinion - he in effect was stating that the normal termination payment type of provision was exactly what the Court would award by way of actual damages on a breach and that there was no difference between actual damages, liquidated damages and stipulated termination sums in relation to non-breach events. In subsequent cases it has not always been so clear.

Lest there be any doubt, however, the position in the case of stipulated termination payments on non-breach events was put beyond doubt by the Inner House in its 1992 decision in *EFT Commercial Limited* v *Security Change Ltd (No 1)*.[31] In that case the ground of termination of a finance lease was the insolvency of the lessee and the Court held that, as this was not a breach event, the stipulated termination payment could not be attacked as being a penalty. It was not liquidated damages but was simply a termination payment and was enforceable as a contractual stipulation between the parties. They confirmed what had always been thought, namely, that a liquidated damages clause could only be attacked as a penalty where the termination event was breach of contract. Prior to the decision in *EFT Commercial* there had been doubt expressed in various decisions as to whether it was possible to construe the same clause as being penal in a breach situation but enforceable in a non-breach situation. However, such comments appear against a long background of authority to represent only muddled thinking, and there have been various decisions now where a court has drawn a distinction between the enforceability of a termination payment clause in breach and non-breach situations[32] Despite the decision in *Bell Brothers*,[33] there have been Scottish cases where the normal calculation of a termination payment has been doubted as being penal. *Granor Finance* itself is an example of a case where a payment of two-thirds of total rentals caused concern as to whether it might be a penalty. It is generally believed, however, that a carefully constructed termination payment clause which allows for the value of the returned goods as well as discounting on a reasonable basis the future rentals will be upheld and that *Bell Brothers* continues to be good law.

But there is one further complication. Unlike what has possibly been regarded as the position in England, in Scotland it has been well established for some time that a liquidated damages clause survives repudiation by the

[31] [1993] SLT 128.
[32] See *Granor Finance Ltd* v *Liquidator of Eastore Ltd* [1974] SLT 296.
[33] *Loc cit* fn 29.

lessee and termination of the contract. Yet even this rule has recently been doubted in the *Eurocopy Rentals*[34] case where, apparently influenced by the English rule and the case of *Lombard North Central plc* v *Butterworth*,[35] a single judge in the Outer House refused to treat as valid a liquidate damages clause following repudiation of contract accepted by the lessor. Because of this it is undoubtedly currently correct practice in Scotland as it is in England to make it clear in the contract that the liquidated damages / termination payment provision does survive its repudiation and termination.

Where the Lessor Does Not Seek a Termination Payment. With some technical differences, much of what is written above will be familiar to readers to English lawyers. The next very much related topic, however, does exhibit a greater divergence between the two systems. Suppose on early termination for breach or other default the goods are worth more than the outstanding amounts under the contract. Is it possible for the lessor to terminate the contract, recover possession of the goods, sell them and keep the proceeds without (a) ever seeking a termination payment from the lessee or (b) contemplating sharing the benefit of the proceeds with the lessee? In England in a hire purchase context, the *Transag*[36] case caused a ripple of excitement through the asset finance industry when it was held that the lessor could not forfeit goods under a hire purchase contract, terminated at a relatively late stage of its hire period, because to do so would deny the lessee vindication of his equitable interest in the goods hired. Very recently, and to the dismay of the same asset finance industry, it has been accepted by the Court of Appeal in the *Gerson*[37] case that the same rule can be applied to a finance lease, although in that case sale of the goods prevented relief from forfeiture being granted. But for that, again the Court would have been prepared to uphold equitable rights which had vested in the lessee.

As mentioned earlier, there is no separate equitable jurisdiction in Scots law. The basis in equity of the judgments in the *Transag* and *Gerson* cases has no equivalent in Scotland. It is submitted that there is no impediment in Scots law to a lessor terminating an agreement and keeping the value of the goods for himself. By not seeking a termination payment from the lessee, he is treating the contract as being at an end, is seeking no

[34] *Eurocopy Rentals Ltd* v *Tayside Health Board* [1996] SLT 1322.

[35] *Lombard North Central plc* v *Butterworth* [1987] All ER 267.

[36] *Transag Haulage Ltd* v *Leyland DAF Finance plc* [1994] 2BCLC 88.

[37] *On Demand Information plc* v *Michael Gerson (Finance) plc* [2000] 4 All ER 734.

further performance under the contract from the lessee and is therefore not obliged to give any further performance under the contract himself - and further performance under the contract in the lessor's case would be making the goods available in some further way to the lessee. Although at first glance there appears to be no direct authority for this proposition in Scots law, other than just the absence of concepts of equity, on further thought, by making reference to the concept stressed at the beginning of this chapter, namely, that the contract of hire, derived as it is from Roman law, is the same contract whether it relates to land, services or goods, a compelling authority can be found. This is the House of Lords decision in *Dorchester Studios (Glasgow) Limited* v *Stone*.[38] This was a case about the forfeiture of let subjects, but the subjects in question consisted of land and buildings in Glasgow. The case was an extreme one. A tenant was a few days late in paying his rent and had received no notice requiring payment from his landlord nor any notification that he was late with payment. However, the lease agreement required payment without demand on the due date. The Court held that this lease contract, like any other lease contract, had to be enforced strictly in accordance with its terms, there was no concept of there being relief against forfeiture, and therefore the landlord won his action, the tenant was evicted and the property vacated. Such was the discomfort felt with the decision that Parliament was prevailed upon to legislate to require landlords to allow tenants of real estate an opportunity to remedy the situation which could lead to such forfeiture, but the legislation relates to real estate only. It is thus clear that, except where the statutory dilution is operative, in the contract of hire, no matter what it is that might be hired, the contract is interpreted strictly according to its terms and there is no relief from forfeiture.

Landlords and Fixtures

A lessor may have to take steps to protect himself against the landlord of the premises where the leased goods are situated, not only where the leased goods have become fixtures, which is also a common problem in England, but also where the leased goods clearly remain moveable. This arises due to the existence in Scotland of a security implied by law in favour of landlords, namely, the landlord's hypothec. The landlord's hypothec is a form of security for rent which extends to goods situated on leased premises, even in some circumstances where those goods belong to a third

---

[38] [1975] SC (HL) 56.

party and not to the tenant/lessee. These landlord's rights do not flow from any concept of reputed ownership, but rather are based on the assumption, which a landlord is entitled to make, that a tenant will secure the landlord's rent by carrying on business from the premises let and thus bringing on to them furnishings and equipment to enable that business to be carried on. The theory is that the lessor has consented to his goods being situated on the let premises and therefore is presumed to understand and accept that there is a risk of their attachment in a sequestration for rent (that is, the process by which the hypothec is enforced).

Accordingly in the normal case a lessor in Scotland will seek a waiver from a landlord even in respect of goods which remain moveable. The question then arises as to what the lessor ought to do if the landlord refuses to grant a waiver. There are two ways in which the lessor's position can be improved. First, the presumed consent to goods being brought on to let premises can be negated in the lease agreement itself. There can be a covenant in the lease to the effect that the goods may not be taken onto let premises and may not be made subject to sequestration for rent. It is open to debate whether this will be effective against a sequestrating landlord, particularly if it could be shown that the lessor was in fact aware that the goods had been taken onto tenanted premises, but the point is at worst arguable. The second possibility, which builds on the first, is to rely on the decision in the *Ditchburn*[39] case. That case is authority for the proposition that if the landlord has been notified that the goods are the property of the lessor and may not be attached in a sequestration for rent, then the landlord may not attach them. Thus even if a waiver were not signed by a landlord, the fact that the waiver had been sent to him would constitute notice to the landlord that he could not take action against the goods. This result seems conceptually sound given the basis of the hypothec, namely, that the landlord is entitled to presume that the goods are there to enable business carried on from the premises to help pay his rent. If he is told that his presumption is incorrect in relation to certain of the goods, then it follows that his hypothec should be unenforceable in relation to such third party goods.

Let us turn now to fixtures. The rule in Scots law is quite clear that if moveable property is affixed to heritage in such a way as to become a fixture, then the moveable property becomes part of the heritage and title to it is lost in favour of the owner of the heritage.[40] Unlike in England, where

---

[39] *Ditchburn Organisation (Sales) Ltd* v *Dundee Corporation* [1971] SLT 218.

[40] For examples of Scottish cases involving finance leases, see *Cliffplant Ltd* v *Kinnaird* [1981] SC 9; *Scottish Discount Co* v *Blin* [1986] SLT 123.

some equitable right may in some circumstances be retained by or granted to the original owner of the moveables so that on severance from the heritage the original owner's title can resurrect, in Scotland, there being no divisibility of ownership, severance of the moveables from the heritage gives no benefit to the former owner. Therefore if a lessor is to be restored to ownership of his moveable goods, which have become fixtures, at the end of a lease, then, in theory at least, steps have to be taken by way of reconveyance of the title from the owner of the heritage to the lessor. If the lessee is the owner of the heritage, this can be provided for as a contractual stipulation in the lease and causes no difficulty, provided the lessee remains solvent.

Problems of course arise where the lessee becomes insolvent. Accordingly it is common practice among lessors to take waivers from the holder of a floating charge granted by the lessee or from the holder of a standard security (the Scottish equivalent of a legal mortgage) secured over the property and granted by the lessee. Such waivers are personal contracts only and therefore can be of limited efficacy if the identity of the creditor in the security were to change. Likewise, such a waiver does not avail the lessor against the insolvent lessee himself, who owns the property. The lessee may be bound to recognise the lessor's title in the moveables by contract, presumably on the basis of provisions contained in the lease agreement, but such contractual provisions will not bind the lessee's trustee in bankruptcy or liquidator. The lessor cannot take a waiver from the lessee, because that too is a simple contractual arrangement and takes him no further forward. The lessor is undoubtedly therefore in an invidious position in competing against an insolvency practitioner appointed to the lessee where the goods have become fixtures and the lessee owns the premises, even if the lessee has bound himself to reconvey affixed goods to the lessor on expiry or termination of the lease. Of course if securities have been granted, whether by floating charge or standard security, then the lessor may be able to overcome this problem by the terms of the waiver which he has negotiated with the security holder. However the only safe route for the lessor is himself to have taken some form of security over or other interest in land in respect of the premises to which the goods are affixed.

By a curious paradox this exposed position of the lessor can be more readily overcome where the lessee is merely a tenant of, rather than the owner of, the premises. The lessor may take a waiver from the landlord in respect of the lessor's interest in the goods which have become fixtures. Again such a waiver is a personal contract with the landlord only and it may fall on the landlord transferring his interest or becoming insolvent. But the lessor has one other simple route open to him here. In relations between landlords and tenants the law recognises that a tenant may, in terms of his lease of heritage, have the right to remove his own trade fixtures from the premises, notwithstanding that they have indeed become fixtures. This right to remove trade fixtures is a right arising under the heritable lease which can be assigned to the moveables' lessor. If the heritable lease is drawn properly and if a tripartite arrangement is entered into amongst the lessor, lessee and landlord, whereby the right of removal of trade fixtures is assigned to the lessor with the agreement of the landlord, then such arrangement should be sufficient to protect the lessor's interest. The important point is that this arrangement is part of the heritable lease contractual document and therefore should be binding on successors of the landlord, even if he takes no steps to bind them to it. Of course the circumstances in which the right of removal can be exercised will still have to be negotiated with the landlord and the heritable lease may need amending accordingly.

Disguised Security

Scots law, like most civilian based systems and unlike common-law based systems, takes a strict view of what is required to create a valid security. The taking of a valid security is something which should be a public act and it is the policy of the law to take a prejudiced view of a device which is intended to operate as a concealed security, not obvious to third parties dealing with the ostensible owner of the property. Accordingly, creating a trust over property as a security for borrowings has been regarded as invalid under Scots law.[41] However, while the Uniform Commercial Code in the United States may treat moveables financing by way of lease or hire purchase as security transactions which require to be registered for validity,[42] there is no doubt that Scots law over many years now has accepted that hire purchase transactions are not disguised securities and are valid. Similarly the finance lease, being a development of the contract of hire, has never been questioned on the grounds of it being some form of security. However this is an area where there can be difficulties. Thus, for example a chattel mortgage is not recognised in Scots law, except in relation to ships and aircraft, where statute has established a specific

---

41 *Clark Taylor & Co Ltd* v *Quality Site Development (Edinburgh) Ltd* [1981] SC 111.

42 See Article 9 UCC *op cit* fn 9.

regime. These exceptions apart, the general rule remains that where moveables are concerned, the creditor must have possession (this being the necessary public act) to have a valid security - for example, the pawnbroker's pledge. As a matter of policy there is no doubt that this causes difficulties in financial practice, with the increased emphasis in modern company balance sheets on the value of moveable property. Indeed a Uniform Commercial Code type arrangement for the registration of such financing interests would be a welcome reform in many people's view in Scots law. It should also be noted that the validity of a chattels mortgage at the time of enforcement is tested according to the law of the country in which the chattel is situated. It is not unknown for a creditor who thought he was comfortable with a chattels mortgage in England to find to his consternation on the liquidation of his debtor that the chattels mortgage had flown off and ceased to be effective because the chattel in question had been removed by the debtor to Scotland prior to insolvency.[43]

With the foregoing by way of background, let us now turn to the relevant problem issue so far as asset financiers are concerned. This concerns sale and hire-purchase back transactions, and, while the notion of a problem in that area is entirely familiar to English and Welsh readers, the issue in Scotland comes from a different source. In the pre-1893 Scots common law of sale, a purchaser could only acquire title to goods by delivery. The Sale of Goods Act 1893 was a revolutionary measure in Scotland (and ill-thought out in the context of Scots law). It introduced the new rule that title passed when the parties intended it to pass. There was however, and remains, a carve-out from this new rule which is currently contained in section 62 (4) of the Sale of Goods Act 1979 (as amended). This tells us that the Act does not apply "to a transaction in the form of a contract of sale which is intended to operate by way of mortgage, pledge, charge or other security". In the landmark case of *Scottish Transit Trust* v *Scottish Land Cultivators*[44] the Court held that where there was a sale of goods by a seller to a finance company followed by a hire purchase back of those goods by the finance company to the original seller, then the original sale was a transaction by way of security, as a result of which a valid title in the goods had not passed to the purchaser because of this carve-out in the Sale of Goods Act. The Court accepted however that the hire purchase

---

[43] For example, see *Re Anchor Line (Henderson Bros) Ltd* [1937] Ch 483 and *Carse* v *Coppen* [1951] SC 233, applying this rule in relation to floating charges, which were not recognised in Scots law at the time.

[44] [1955] SC 254.

contract remained valid as a document of debt between finance company and hirer.

It is the author's view that such transactions by way of sale and hire purchase back can still validly be entertained, provided that prior to the hire purchase back the goods sold are actually delivered to the finance company. The logic for this derives from the fact that section 62 (4) is quite clearly a saving section and it must therefore be assumed that, where the Act is excluded from applying by that savings provision, then the old Scots common law in its pre-1893 form must revive. Under that common law, title passed on delivery and therefore if there has been delivery (actual or constructive) the problem of the otherwise disguised security will have been solved. This leads to some very cumbersome transaction settlements in which artificial measures are resorted to whereby finance companies take some form of temporary possession of the goods in question. However, the current topic is not hire purchase, it is finance and operating leases, and of course the question which then arises is whether a sale and finance lease back could possibly be attacked on the same grounds as being a disguised security? The analogy with hire purchase is obvious. Upon expiry of the primary period of a finance lease the lessor's financial interest in the goods has been amortised and, upon a sale of the goods thereafter, virtually all of the sale proceeds will be passed on by the lessor to the lessee. The difference between this arrangement and a hire purchase arrangement therefore, it can be argued, is one of form rather than substance. Nevertheless, as we have seen, Scots law in this field pays considerable attention to form and is quite prepared to prefer it to substance. There is a crucial distinction between a hire purchase contract and a finance lease, namely, that the title in the goods, admittedly only for tax reasons, never reverts to the lessee. He may get the benefit of the value of the goods, but not of title to the goods itself. How then could the arrangement be truly regarded as a security when even with perfect performance of the obligation the title to the asset does not return to the supposed security granter?

Attractive though the above argument may be to lessors, it has to be admitted that the only case which has considered the issue appeared to assume that sale and lease back could be subject to the rule in section 62 (4).[45] However this case involved complex facts and this particular issue was only noted in passing, was not properly argued and does not form part of the *ratio decidendi* of the decision. Moreover it has undoubtedly become

---

[45] *Ladbroke Leasing (South West) Ltd* v *Reekie Plant Ltd* [1983] SLT 155.

common practice in Scotland over the last ten or fifteen years for sale and lease-back transactions to be entered into, with perhaps only the caveat that the lessor takes care to document the transaction properly and to use a sale agreement rather than simply an invoice from the seller to record the transaction. It is also of course true that the more the lease arrangement moves towards being an operating lease with true residual value risk being taken by the lessor, similarly the more impossible is it to regard the arrangement as a security.

In all of this there is a significant competing authority, namely *Gavin's Trustee* v *Fraser*,[46] a much earlier case. In that Inner House decision (also involving sale and hire purchase back) attention was focused on the legal effect which the transaction was intended to have rather than on any question of the underlying purpose or motive for which the transaction was entered into. In the hire purchase arrangement (as in that case) there was no specific sum which could be said to be advanced as a loan and to be repayable as such, nor did there exist a personal obligation antecedent to or independent of the transaction in question. It was thus felt that the transaction was in truth a real sale rather than a disguised security for a loan and weight was attached to the fact (a) that a realistic price, not an inflated price, was being paid for the asset, and (b) that the sale had been documented properly as a sale prior to the hire purchase contract being entered into. It is this case which gives encouragement to parties in sale and lease-back transactions to rely on clearly structured documentation as additional support to rebut any argument which might be brought under section 62 (4).

This remains an interesting area for academic discussion and of course commercial parties usually wish to avoid their transactions being regarded as interesting. Nevertheless, for the reasons set out above, this author is firmly of the view that sale and lease-back transactions should not be caught by section 62 (4), but nevertheless has to admit that in commercial advising he proceeds cautiously!

---

[46] [1920] SC 674.

Conclusion

The contract of hire is just one example of a legal concept which the Romans developed and refined to such an extent that it can still be applied quite satisfactorily today to produce just, or at least certain, results. Of course, their basic concepts have been much expanded over the last three hundred years beginning with the writing by Stair of his *Institutions*, but the Roman kernel remains. The judgment in the *G M Shepherd*[47] case in 1991 tells us that a finance lease (and presumably an operating lease), however, are contracts of a slightly different nature, so that implied duties in the traditional contract of hire cannot be imported into such contracts. Since then modern statute has rendered this distinction more or less irrelevant and supervened for the first time to adjust the old concepts for the modern world and, in doing so, may or may not have improved matters - depending on where the correct emphasis should be between consumer protection on the one hand and the desire for certainty of legal effect in commercial contracts on the other.

The similarity of the resultant legal effects which the Scots contract of hire achieves, when compared with the English equivalent, will be striking. Equally striking is the very different legal background which produces these results. I hope to have exemplified at least some areas where that background can produce a different analysis from that which would obtain south of the border and hence some results which might come as a surprise, pleasant or unpleasant, to the English or Welsh finance or operating lessor. Indeed, where a pleasant surprise can be produced, perhaps such lessors might consider adopting Scots law as the governing law of their contract?

---

[47] *Loc cit* fn 20.

2 Twenty-Five Years of *Romalpa*

J R BRADGATE

Introduction

It is now twenty-five years since the landmark decision of the Court of Appeal, affirming that of Mocatta J, in the *Romalpa* case, *Aluminium Industrie Vaasen* v *Romalpa Aluminium*.[1] Initial reaction to the decision was mixed. The Court of Appeal thought that the case raised, in the words of Goff LJ, a "short question of construction",[2] albeit according to Megaw LJ, "by no means an easy one"[3] and that the case had little precedent value. Leave to appeal to the House of Lords was refused and the case was never reported in the official Law Reports. Commentators however recognised the significance of the decision. Professor Goode famously commented that: "It is doubtful whether any case decided this century has created a greater impact on the commercial law".[4] Commercial people, "knew a good thing when they saw one"[5] and the incorporation in commercial contracts for the sale of goods of so-called "*Romalpa* clauses" quickly became common practice. By 1979 Slade J was able to comment that such clauses were "in quite common use".[6] Today, although the wording of clauses may vary considerably, making different types of claim, the use of

[1] [1976] 2 All ER 552.

[2] [1976] 2 All ER 552 at p 565 *per* Goff LJ.

[3] [1976] 2 All ER 552 at p 568.

[4] (1977) *Times*, 11 May. Similarly Professor Schmitthoff described the decision of Mocatta J as "of considerable importance" and observed that its affirmation by the Court of Appeal would be "welcomed by businessmen engaged in the international sale of goods": see [1975] *JBL* 85 at p 86 and [1976] *JBL* 209.

[5] Burke (1979) *NLJ* 1183.

[6] *Re Bond Worth Ltd* [1980] Ch 238 at p 241; [1979] 3 All ER 919 at p 923.

such clauses is commonplace if not universal.[7] Moreover, having infiltrated the UK, the *Romalpa*/retention of title phenomenon has spread around the common law world, including to Ireland, Canada, New Zealand and Australia. In its turn this growth has generated a significant body of case law and, in consequence, an extensive academic and practitioner literature.[8]

In *Romalpa* S supplied aluminium foil to B on 14 days' (later 75 days') credit. As S knew, B would use the foil to manufacture new products, which would themselves in all likelihood be sold before B paid for the foil. The parties therefore must have anticipated that, in the ordinary run of things, the foil would cease to exist before the buyer paid for it, and that in the event of non-payment the seller would be unlikely to recover all, if any, of the foil supplied. The contract anticipated and expressly provided for the possibility that the buyer might use the foil to manufacture new products and resell the products made from it. Thus it provided that S retained title to unprocessed foil until payment and for ownership of products manufactured from the foil and, on demand, claims for payment for such products, to be transferred to S. S, however, had not anticipated that its customer might resell unprocessed foil, and the contract was silent about the effects of resale of unprocessed foil. B became insolvent but prior to its insolvency did indeed sell some unused aluminium foil. After its insolvency the receiver received payment for that foil. S claimed the proceeds of sale, amounting to some £35,152. Both parties agreed that B was impliedly authorised to resell the unprocessed foil. S however claimed the proceeds of sale "on the basis of the principle of *re Hallett's Estate,* entitling them to trace the proceeds of sale their property sold by [B] into the receiver's bank account".[9] Mocatta J sitting in the Queen's Bench Division, and confessing himself to be "in a most unfamiliar field", upheld that claim. The Court of Appeal consisting of Roskill, Goff and Megaw LJJ, two common lawyers and one chancery

---

[7] In a survey in 1991 Wheeler found that ninety two per cent of the companies she surveyed incorporated retention of title clauses in their contracts of sale: see Wheeler, *Reservation of Title Clauses: Impact and Implications* (Oxford, 1991); see also Spencer, [1989] *JBL* 220. In the receivership of Leyland Daf in the early 1990s there were over 400 retention of title claims: see *Lipe Ltd* v *Leyland Daf Ltd* [1993] BCC 385.

[8] See especially McCormack, *Reservation of Title* 2nd ed (1995) and Wheeler, *op cit* fn 7. For consideration of the position in Europe see Davies (ed), *Retention of Title Clauses in Sale of Goods Contracts in Europe* (1999).

[9] *Per* Mocatta J at p 555.

lawyer, affirmed that decision, enabling the sellers to take the proceeds of sale of the unmixed foil in priority to the secured and unsecured creditors of the buyer.

The concept that a supplier of goods on credit terms could reserve property in the goods until payment as security for payment, was nothing new. Conditional sale and hire purchase had been established since at least the late 19th century and the Sale of Goods Act 1893 expressly provided that under a contract of sale "the seller may, by the terms of the contract or appropriation, reserve the right of disposal of the goods until certain conditions are fulfilled", in which case "the property in the goods does not pass to the buyer until the conditions imposed by the seller are fulfilled".[10] Two years after the Act was passed the House of Lords held, in *McEntire* v *Crossley Bros*,[11] that, notwithstanding that their purpose and effect was to provide the seller with security against non-payment, conditional sale and hire purchase agreements were not chattel mortgages registrable under the Bills of Sale Acts: if the contract by its terms prevented property passing to the "buyer", the buyer had nothing to mortgage or charge. Such an arrangement is therefore not registrable under the company charges or bills of sale registration regimes, and yet takes priority over the claims of secured creditors including, most importantly, the claim of a bank or other lender under a floating charge.

Conditional sale and hire purchase were developed to finance the supply of fixed items such as machinery, railway wagons, pianos and furniture, items which might be expected to be retained *in specie*. The terms of a traditional hire purchase or conditional sale agreement would normally prohibit the hirer/buyer reselling the goods before paying for them.[12] In *Romalpa* however, the contract expressly anticipated that the goods would be used in a manufacturing process and the products be sold

---

[10] SGA 1893 s 19. The same provision appears, with only minor changes to punctuation, in the Sale of Goods Act 1979.

[11] [1895] AC 457. The case concerned a hybrid agreement under which the goods were leased to the lessee but property would pass on payment in full of the price. Unlike the modern form of hire purchase there was no separate option to purchase. The reasoning in the case applies equally to conditional sale and hire purchase.

[12] As in *McEntire* v *Crossley Bros* itself. Resale of goods supplied on conditional sale terms would destroy the seller's security by passing good title to the goods to the buyer's customer, pursuant to s 25 Sale of Goods Act. Section 25 does not apply to hire purchase agreements (see *Helby* v *Matthews* [1895] AC 471) but in the case of motor vehicles let on hire purchase Pt III of the Hire Purchase Act 1964 offers similar protection to private purchasers.

before payment. Moreover it provided for the seller to continue to enjoy property rights in products manufactured from "its" foil and for those rights to continue through to the proceeds of sale of the products made from the foil. *Romalpa* therefore made the security of the conditional sale form available to a seller of goods intended for resale or use or consumption in a manufacturing process. Moreover the decision of the Court of Appeal that the seller was entitled to claim the proceeds of sale of foil sold by the buyer enabled the seller to transfer his security into the proceeds of sale and suggested that the provisions relating to manufactured goods would also be effective.

The response to *Romalpa* was however not entirely positive. Many commentators saw in the decision the potential for abuse. Views were expressed that the retention of title device was contrary to the central policy of insolvency of *pari passu* distribution of assets. Whilst some saw the device as a welcome way for suppliers of goods to improve their position as unsecured creditors, others anticipated that its widespread use might lead to a depletion of the assets available for distribution either to secured creditors such as banks,[13] or to the general pool of unsecured creditors unprotected by retention of title. Because the retention of title clause created a security which escaped the registration requirements of the companies charges and bills of sale regimes there was no way for another intending creditor to discover that a portion of the assets of a potential debtor would not be available to satisfy its claims in the event of the debtor's insolvency.[14] The view was even expressed that banks and other lenders might themselves make use of the device, for instance by establishing purchasing arms which would provide finance to customers by buying goods on their behalf and then re-selling them to the customers on retention of title terms, thus obtaining a security functionally equivalent to a floating charge without the publicity provided by registration.

Now, a quarter of a century later, retention of title is ubiquitous but neither the hopes nor the fears expressed in the immediate aftermath of *Romalpa* have been realised. Banks have continued to lend on the security of fixed and floating charges. Law reform proposals have been made but come to nothing.[15] Instead, the development of the law has been left to the

---

[13] See, for example, Chapman, (1977) 1221 *Sol Jo* 682, who observed that "the decision in *Romalpa* has taken us to a commercial precipice".

[14] See Pennington, (1977) 121 *Sol Jo* 294.

[15] Proposals were made by the Cork Committee, *Insolvency Law and Practice* (1982) Cmnd 8558 and by Professor A L Diamond in his *Review of Security Interests in Moveables* (1989) DTI.

courts which have drawn back from the position apparently adopted in *Romalpa* and, ignoring appeals to policy, have developed the law in a typically pragmatic fashion. As a result, in England at least, retention of title clauses have only limited effect. The objective of this chapter is to examine how this has come about.

Equity and Commercial Law

One aspect of the *Romalpa* decision which attracted particular comment [16] was its reliance on equitable principles and, in particular, what Mocatta J referred to as the "equitable remedy" of tracing[17] and "the principle of *re Hallett's Estate*". The basis of the decision was that, as the buyers held foil as the sellers' bailee, and sold as their agent, the sellers were entitled to "trace" their property into the proceeds of sale, which the buyers held in the same capacity. Mocatta J quoted at length from the judgments in *re Hallett's Estate*[18] and his approach, and those quotations, were expressly adopted by the members of the Court of Appeal in their judgments. Thus Roskill LJ found "no difficulty in holding that the principles in *re Hallett's Estate* ... are of immediate application, and ... that the plaintiffs are entitled to trace these proceeds of sale and to recover them."[19] and Goff LJ (rather more accurately) found that the sellers "must, on the principle of *re Hallett's Estate*, be entitled to trace their aluminium into the proceeds of sale".[20] Subsequent cases saw attempts by sellers to invoke the same principles in order to claim proceeds of sale of goods supplied, products manufactured from such goods and proceeds of sale of such products. Clauses were drafted so as to enable those principles to be invoked, in some cases making express reference to *re Hallett's Estate* in the words of the retention of title clause itself.[21]

The courts have traditionally been suspicious of admitting equitable doctrines into commercial law for fear that their emphasis on conscience

---

[16] See especially Goodhart and Jones, (1980) 43 *MLR* 489; see also Burke, (1979) *NLJ* 1183.

[17] At p 555.

[18] *Knatchbull* v *Hallett* (1880) 13 Ch D 696.

[19] *Loc cit* fn 1 at p 564.

[20] *Loc* cit fn 1 at p 565.

[21] See notably the clause in *In re Peachdart Ltd* [1984] Ch 131, [1983] 2 All ER 304 which stated that "the seller shall have the right to trace the proceeds [of sale of goods supplied] according to the principles in *In re Hallett's Estate*".

and discretion would be "inconsistent with the certainty and speed which are essential requirements for the orderly conduct of business affairs".[22] There is therefore no place in commercial law for the equitable doctrine of constructive notice,[23] and the courts have refused to accept that an ordinary commercial contract for the sale of goods, unlike a contract for the sale of land, gives rise to any equitable interest in the buyer[24] or to admit trust concepts into commercial transactions. Recognition of equitable property interests might mean that "a businessman who has entered into transactions relating to or dependent on property rights could find that assets which apparently belong to one person in fact belong to another; that there are 'off balance sheet' liabilities of which he cannot be aware".[25]

Of course, equity has long had a role to play in commercial transactions. The charge and, particularly, the floating charge, the basis of much secured lending to limited companies, are creations of equity. Nor is it correct that equitable principles are necessarily unpredictable. As Lord Browne-Wilkinson has pointed out, equitable proprietary interests are not discretionary or based on some vague notion of "fairness":

> The rules establishing equitable proprietary interests and their enforceability against certain parties have been developed over the centuries and are an integral part of the property law of England. It is a fundamental error to think that, because certain property rights are equitable rather than legal, such rights are in some way discretionary.[26]

More recently there has been an increased willingness to recognise that equitable concepts may have a role to play in the commercial sphere.[27] The invocation of equitable principles in *Romalpa* and subsequent cases seemed, however, to run contrary to the tradition of treating equitable principles with caution in the commercial context. The cases which

[22] Lord Browne-Wilkinson in *Westdeutsche Landesbank Girozentrale* v *Islington LBC* [1996] AC 669 at p 704, [1996] 2 All ER 961 at p 987.
[23] Per Lindley LJ in *Manchester Trust Ltd* v *Furness, Withy & Co Ltd* [1895] 2 QB 539 at p 545.
[24] See, for example, *Re Wait* [1927] 1 Ch 606, [1926] All ER Rep 433, CA; *Re Goldcorp Exchange Ltd* (*in receivership*) [1994] 2 All ER 806, [1995] 1 AC 74.
[25] Lord Browne-Wilkinson in *Westdeutsche Landesbank Girozentrale* v *Islington LBC* [1996] AC 669 at p 704, [1996] 2 All ER 961 at p 987.
[26] *Foskett* v *McKeown* [2000] 3 All ER 97.
[27] Thus it has recently been held that the equitable jurisdiction to grant relief against forfeiture may be exercised in respect of a finance lease: see *On Demand Information plc* v *Michael Gerson (Finance) plc* [2000] 4 All ER 734.

introduced the retention of title phenomenon were therefore seen as exemplifying a novel, and potentially destabilising, introduction of equitable concepts into the commercial law arena.

Tracing, Claiming and Property Rights

Prior to the House of Lords' decision in *Foskett* v *McKeown*[28] it was generally accepted[29] that the rules of equitable and common law tracing differed in several respects. In particular (a) only equitable tracing could follow funds through a mixed bank account; (b) in order to trace in equity it was necessary to establish a fiduciary relationship between the parties; and (c) only equitable tracing resulted in a proprietary claim. No distinction was drawn between the process of tracing and the claim in which it might result. *Re Hallett's Estate* was seen as an authority on equitable tracing. The case concerned a solicitor who held investment bonds on behalf of a client. Having sold the bonds he paid the proceeds into his bank account, thus effectively mixing the proceeds with his own money. It was held that the client was entitled to trace the bonds into their proceeds and to a charge on the bank account. The case is, or has been regarded as, authority for several "principles", in particular the propositions that equity can trace property into funds mixed with others in a bank account, and that, where a fiduciary wrongfully mixes his beneficiary's money with his own, withdrawals from the mixed fund are appropriated first to the defaulting fiduciary's share of the fund.[30] It is for this second proposition that the case is perhaps best known.

The court in *Romalpa* was primarily concerned to determine whether there was a fiduciary relationship between seller and buyer, which would enable "the principle of *re Hallett's Estate*" to be invoked. *Romalpa* was therefore seen as a case on "equitable tracing" which were necessary in order to trace through a mixed bank account. There was, however, no question in *Romalpa* of a need to trace through a mixed fund. The funds claimed by the seller had been received after the appointment of the receiver and were therefore identifiable. The rules relating to mixed funds would only be relevant where S claimed proceeds of sale received *prior* to

[28] [2000] 3 All ER 97.

[29] This view was not universal and there were cogent expressions of contrary views: see Goode, (1976) 92 *LQR* 360; Pearce, (1976) 40 *Conv (NS)* 272.

[30] Rather than in accordance with the "first in, first out" rule derived from *Clayton's Case* (1816) 1 Mar 572 which applies where the moneys of two beneficiaries are mixed.

B's insolvency and mixed with other funds in B's bank account. Such claims are unlikely. Any claim would be limited by the "lowest intermediate balance" rule according to which the ceiling to a claim over a mixed fund is fixed by the lowest balance standing to the credit of the account between the date of receipt of the misappropriated payment and the date of the claim.[31] In a retention of title context S will normally only assert his rights where B is insolvent, in which case B's bank account will generally be overdrawn and there will be no fund into which to trace proceeds received prior to insolvency.

The modern understanding of the law of tracing, as adopted by the majority of the House of Lords in *Foskett* v *McKeown*, requires that a distinction be drawn between *tracing* and *claiming*. *Tracing* is the process by which a claimant identifies particular assets as representing his property and enables the claimant to "trace" the value derived from his property into an asset substituted for it. It is not, of itself, a claim, or a remedy.[32] The rules of identification are the same in equity and at law: in other words there are no separate rules of "equitable" and "common law" *tracing*. There is therefore no need to identify a "fiduciary relationship" in order to invoke the rules of "equitable tracing". Once the claimant has traced his property into its proceeds, the tracing exercise can provide the basis for a claim based on the appropriation of the property so identified, which claim may be either legal or equitable, personal or proprietary. In other words the tracing process allows the claimant to assert a proprietary right over a particular asset at law or in equity, and thus provides a basis for a claim to vindicate that right. It is at *this* point that the distinction between law and equity becomes significant. Property rights are vindicated at common law by personal actions, either in tort or restitution, for money had and received. Equity, however, is capable of giving proprietary remedies and, in particular, after a tracing claim, of protecting the claimant's interest in the traced asset by way of the grant of a charge or lien or a declaration of trust. The existence of a fiduciary relationship, although not necessary to invoke the rules of *tracing* or to make a proprietary *claim*, is a pre-requisite to a claim for an equitable proprietary *remedy* in respect of the proceeds of disposition. The seller in *Romalpa* needed to claim a proprietary remedy, and therefore had to establish a fiduciary relationship in order to claim equitable remedies. The "principle of *re Hallett's Estate*" invoked was therefore simply the proposition that where a fiduciary disposes of property

---

[31] *James Roscoe (Bolton) Ltd* v *Winder* [1915] 1 Ch 62.

[32] [2000] 3 All ER 97 at p 120 *per* Lord Millett.

of his beneficiary, he receives and holds the proceeds of the disposition in the same capacity, as is clear from the passages from the judgment of Jessel MR in *Hallett* cited by Mocatta J[33] and approved by Roskill and Goff LJJ.

Equitable Liens: and Contracts of Sale

The willingness of the court to apply equitable principles in *Romalpa* was perhaps all the more surprising in view of the received attitude to another equitable security device in commercial transactions. It is well established that the unpaid vendor of real property, and of certain types of personalty, is entitled to an "equitable lien" over the property to secure sums due to him from the buyer. The accepted view, however, is that no such lien is available to the unpaid seller of goods.

The commercial purpose of all title retention devices, including conditional sale and hire purchase, is to secure the credit supplier of goods against the risk of the buyer's failure to pay. The Sale of Goods Act in fact provides an unpaid seller[34] with a measure of protection against such default, giving him a lien over the goods whilst in his possession and a right of stoppage in transit, enabling him to recover possession of the goods if, before they reach the buyer, the buyer becomes insolvent. Moreover the Act gives the seller a right to enforce his security by resale in certain circumstances, effectively where the time of payment is initially (expressly or impliedly) or is subsequently made of the essence.[35] Significantly if the seller exercises his right of resale the sale contract is brought to an end, the seller sells on his own behalf and is therefore entitled to retain any surplus over the original contract price but without prejudice to any claim for damages against the buyer in the event of a shortfall. The security afforded by these provisions is, however, of limited practical value, for the seller's rights to retain or recover possession end as soon as the goods come into the buyer's possession and are therefore not available where goods are supplied on credit terms for use or consumption prior to payment. The "equitable lien", however, does not depend on possession for its effectiveness.

---

[33] *Loc cit* fn 1 at p 555.

[34] "Unpaid seller" is defined for these purposes in s 38 of the Act.

[35] The right of resale is available where (a) the goods are perishable in nature; (b) the seller serves notice of his intention to resell the goods and the buyer fails to pay for them within a reasonable time; and (c) the right is expressly reserved by the terms of the contract.

The precise nature and scope of the equitable lien is in fact somewhat unclear.[36] It has been described as an equitable property right which arises "as part of a scheme of equitable adjustment of mutual rights and obligations"[37] which entitles the lienee to apply to the court to have property of the lienor applied in satisfaction of a claim. Unlike a true common law or statutory lien it does not depend on the lienee having possession of the property affected so that, for instance, the unpaid vendor of land can claim an equitable lien over the property after completing the sale and allowing the buyer into possession. In fact it operates rather more like a charge than a lien,[38] but unlike a charge it arises by operation of law and is therefore not registrable under Companies Act s 395 or the Bills of Sale Acts. Indeed, an attempt to create an "equitable lien" over property by agreement is likely to be construed as a charge created by the parties and therefore requiring registration.[39]

Equitable liens can arise in a range of situations.[40] Essentially, however, it seems that an equitable lien is recognised to guard against unconscionability, so that a lien will arise over property where the relationship between the property and the lienee's claim is such that it would be unconscionable to allow the lienor to dispose of the property and enjoy its fruits without satisfying the claim.[41] As noted, it is well established that the unpaid vendor of land is entitled to an equitable lien on the property to secure payment. Similarly the pre-paying buyer of land is entitled to a lien on the property to secure repayment of sums paid. It seems, too, that liens may arise in favour of both vendors and purchasers of

---

[36] See, generally, Phillips, "Equitable Liens - A Search for a Unifying Principle" *Interests in Goods* Palmer and McKendrick (eds) 2nd ed (1998); Worthington [1994] *CLJ* 234.

[37] *Davies* v *Littlejohn* (1923) 34 CLR 174 at p 185 *per* Isaacs J.

[38] The words "lien" and "charge" are sometimes used interchangeably: see for instance *Lord Napier and Ettrick* v *Hunter* [1993] 1 All ER 385 at p 397 *per* Lord Templeman.

[39] See, for example, *Care Shipping Corp* v *Latin American Shipping Corp* [1983] QB 1005; *re Welsh Irish Ferries Ltd* [1986] Ch 471; *Annangel Lory Cia Naviera SA* v *M Golodetz Ltd* [1988] 1 Lloyd's Rep 45; *Care Shipping Corp* v *Itex Itagrani Export SA* [1992] 1 All ER 91; but see the comments of Lord Millett in *Agnew* v *Commissioner of Inland Revenue* [2001] UKPC28 at para 39-41, doubting these cases.

[40] See, generally, Phillips, *op cit* fn 36.

[41] See *Hewett* v *Court* (1983) 149 CLR 639 at p 668 *per* Deane J.

certain categories of personalty.[42] There is clear English authority, however, that no equitable lien arises under a contract for the sale of goods in favour either of a pre-paying buyer[43] or an unpaid seller.[44] Various reasons have been offered for this. Thus it has been said that the Sale of Goods Act's provisions concerned with the transfer of property from seller to buyer contain a complete statement of the relations between seller and buyer arising out of the contract[45] and, more specifically, that "it would be quite inconsistent with what I think is intended to be an exhaustive statement of the law in the Sale of Goods Act to say that, in the case of an ordinary sale of a commercial article under a commercial agreement, there can be any vendor's lien other than that which the statute itself provides".[46] Alternatively it has been said that the availability of the equitable lien depends on the contract being specifically enforceable[47] and that since commercial contracts for the sale of goods are not normally specifically enforced, an equitable lien is therefore not available to either party under a sale contract. Both these reasons have, however, been doubted[48] and the High Court of Australia has held that a lien may arise in favour of the buyer under a contract for work and materials.[49] Nevertheless it seems to be settled that in English law an unpaid seller of goods is not entitled to an equitable lien over the goods once they have left his possession. The decision in *Romalpa* thus enables the seller to obtain by contract the security which is not available as a matter of law.

---

[42] See, for example: *Barker* v *Cox* (1876) 4 Ch D 464 (stock); *Imperial Ottoman Bank* v *Trustees, Executors and Securities Insurance Corporation* (1895) 13 R 287 (debentures).

[43] *Re Wait* [1927] 1 Ch 606.

[44] *Transport and General Credit Corporation Ltd* v *Morgan* [1939] Ch 531; *re Bond Worth Ltd*.

[45] *Per* Atkin LJ in *re Wait* [1927] 1 Ch 606 at p 636.

[46] *Per* Simonds J in *Transport and General Credit Corporation Ltd* v *Morgan* [1939] Ch 531 at p 546; [1939] 2 All ER 17 at p 25. The reference to an "ordinary sale of a commercial article" seems to leave open the possibility that an equitable lien might be recognised in an exceptional case - for instance on a sale of a particular, unique item.

[47] See *Capital Finance Co Ltd* v *Stokes* [1969] 1 Ch 261, [1968] 3 All ER 625; see also *per* Lord Browne-Wilkinson in *Lord Napier and Ettrick* v *Hunter* [1993] 1 All ER 385 at p 409.

[48] See Phillips and Worthington, *op cit* above fn 36. The requirement of specific performance for the recognition of an equitable lien was specifically rejected by Murphy and Deane JJ in *Hewett* v *Court* (1983) 149 CLR 639 at pp 651 and 665.

[49] *Hewett* v *Court* (1983) 149 CLR 639.

Classification of Transactions

Romalpa caused consternation to receivers and other insolvency practitioners who saw the possibility of the pool of assets available for satisfaction of the claims of secured (and unsecured) creditors being depleted by extensive retention of title claims. They therefore sought to challenge such claims and in the cases which immediately followed *Romalpa*, *Borden (UK) Ltd* v *Scottish Timber Products Ltd*[50] and *re Bond Worth Ltd*,[51] receivers successfully resisted the sellers' claims by invoking another equitable concept, that of the charge. This has become the principle argument advanced against retention of title claims, that they give the seller, at most, not full property in the asset claimed, but a charge over it, which is required by s. 395 of the Companies Act 1985[52] to be registered and, in default of registration, is void against a liquidator or creditor of the company. Invocation of this argument requires the court to consider not only whether the seller has a proprietary interest in a particular asset but also to determine the nature of that interest, which may be full legal ownership or an equitable interest arising under a trust, a charge or a lien. Nor is it enough to establish that a claim gives rise to a charge. Section 395 does not apply to all charges, but only to certain types of charge created by the chargor company. A person wishing to challenge a retention of title claim on this basis must therefore establish not merely that the agreement gives rise to a charge but also that it falls within a category of charges required to be registered *and* that it is created by the company.

There is in fact little difficulty distinguishing between an equitable charge and an equitable lien. Confusion is sometimes causes because, in certain contexts, the terms "charge" and "lien" are used more or less interchangeably. As noted above, however, an equitable lien arises automatically, as a matter of law, whereas a charge is created by agreement, and it seems likely that an attempt to create a non-possessory lien by contract will be regarded as giving rise to a charge. Thus in a line of cases concerned with charterparties it has been established that a contract term giving the ship-owner a "lien" over sub-freights to be received by the charterer operates as an equitable assignment of future debts and thus gives

---

50 [1981] Ch 25; [1979] 3 All ER 961.

51 [1980] Ch 238; [1979] 3 All ER 919.

52 Replacing s 95 of the Companies Act 1948. S 395 only applies to charges created by a limited company but similar securities created by individuals will require to be for example registered pursuant to the Bills of Sale Acts.

rise to a registrable equitable charge.[53] In contrast the equitable property right which arises after a successful tracing exercise under the principle of *re Hallett's Estate*, as described above,[54] being a right arising by operation of law rather than created by consent, is perhaps better categorised as an equitable lien rather than a charge. The distinction between a charge and a trust, and even between a charge and a retained property interest may, however, be more difficult to draw. Various attempts have been made to define, or identify the essential characteristics of a charge. According to Lord Hoffman:

> An equitable charge is a species of charge, which is a proprietary interest granted by way of security. ... A proprietary interest provided by way of security entitles the holder to resort to property only for the purpose of satisfying some liability due to him ... and, whatever the form of the transaction, the owner of the property retains an equity of redemption to have the property restored to him when the liability has been discharged.[55]

Of course, the objective of a retention of title is to provide the seller with security for the unpaid price of the goods (and possibly for other debts). It has been settled since *McEntire* v *Crossley Bros*, however, that the classification of a transaction is not determined by its purpose, and it is possible to achieve a security effect without creating a charge. If it were otherwise, hire purchase and conditional sale arrangements would be registrable under the Bills of Sale and Companies Acts. Transactions are classified according to their substance. "Substance", however, means *legal*, not *commercial* substance, to be derived from the terms used in the agreement. Thus if an agreement purporting to be a sale contains terms inappropriate to a sale but consistent with the creation of a charge, the agreement will be classified as a charge. But provided that the agreement contains terms appropriate to a sale, and no terms inappropriate to a sale, a sale it will be. The terms of the agreement will only be disregarded where they are a "sham" designed to mask the true nature of the agreement. It is rarely found that this is the case. As appears from Lord Hoffmann's definition, one crucial characteristic of a charge is the chargor's right to redeem the charged property by discharging the secured debt. Another essential characteristic was identified by Romer LJ in *Re Geo Inglefield*

[53] See the cases cited above at fn 39.

[54] See text accompanying fns 32-33.

[55] *Re BCCI No 8* [1997] 4 All ER 568 at p 576.

Ltd,[56] when he observed that under a charge the chargee's interest in the property is limited to the amount of the secured debt. Thus if he enforces his security by realising the charged property, he may retain only so much of the proceeds as is required to discharge his debt and is accountable to the chargor for any surplus. Conversely, if the sale realises insufficient to discharge the debt, the chargor remains liable for the outstanding debt.

The distinction between a charge and a transaction having similar effect is nevertheless often elusive, and since the test of "substance" depends on the terms used in the agreement, it is possible, by careful drafting, to produce an agreement with the effects and function of a charge, which in law is a sale or some other transaction falling outside the statutory registration requirements.[57] Thus, for instance, a provision in a conditional sale agreement providing for the seller to recover the goods on default and have power to sell them, subject to accounting to the buyer for any surplus if the sale realises more than is required to discharge the debt is not inconsistent with the contract being a genuine conditional sale.[58] This does not mean that the contract drafter has *carte blanche*. The court retains a considerable degree of control. The approach of the court to classification was explained by Lord Herschell in *McEntire* v *Crossley Bros:*

> The agreement must be regarded as a whole - its substance must be looked at. The parties cannot, by the insertion of any mere words, defeat the effect of the transaction as appearing from the whole of the agreement into which they have entered. ... [I]f, although the parties have inserted a provision to that effect, they have shewn in other parts of the agreement, by the language they have used or the provisions they have made, that they intended the property to pass, you must look at the transaction as a whole.[59]

More importantly, if classification of an agreement depends on identifying its substance from its terms, classification is a two stage process.[59a] The first stage requires the court to identify and construe the terms of the contract, to determine the rights of the parties. The second requires the court to determine as a matter of law the nature of the interest created by a contract granting those rights. There is therefore scope for the court to

---

[56] [1933] 1 Ch 1 at p 27.

[57] For a striking example see *Welsh Development Agency Ltd* v *Export Finance Co Ltd* [1992] BCLC 148.

[58] *McEntire* v *Crossley Bros* [1895] AC 457 where the contract included such a provision.

[59] [1895] AC 457 at pp 462-3.

exercise control through the processes of term implication and contract construction. A term will not be implied unless it is "necessary to give business efficacy to the contract" but the court decides what is "necessary" in the interests of business efficacy. The modern approach to construction of commercial agreements, which requires contract terms to be interpreted "purposively", in accordance with "commercial common sense" and with regard to the context in which they appear, gives further latitude to the court. Although this approach has only been articulated in these terms in recent years,[60] its roots go back at least to the 1970's.[61] It requires the court first to give words their ordinary, literal meaning, but in the event of ambiguity or lack of clarity, to interpret them in context and in the light of the parties' commercial purpose. It too, therefore, provides the court with a wide discretion, first whether to adopt a literal or a purposive approach, and, if a purposive approach is adopted, to determine the purpose of the parties.[62]

Claims to the Original Goods

The effectiveness of the retention of title to the aluminium foil itself was not considered in *Romalpa*. In *re Bond Worth Ltd* contracts for the supply of fibres for use in the manufacture of carpets provided that "the equitable and beneficial ownership" of the fibre was to "remain" with the seller until the price was paid; that if the fibre was re-sold prior to payment, the seller's "beneficial entitlement" was to attach to the proceeds of resale "or to the claim for such proceeds"; and that if the fibre was used as a constituent of or converted into a new product, the seller should have the "equitable and beneficial ownership" of the new product. After a careful and detailed analysis, in a judgment running to some forty-two pages and involving the

---

[59a] See *per* Lord Millett in *Agnew* v *Commissioner of Inland Revenue* [2001] UKPC 28, [2001] 3 WLR 454, at para 32.

[60] See especially *Charter Reinsurance Co Ltd* v *Fagan* [1997] AC 180; *Mannai Investment Co Ltd* v *Eagle Star Life Assurance Co Ltd* [1997] 3 All ER 352; *Investors Compensation Scheme Ltd.* v *West Bromwich Building Society* [1998] 1 All ER 98.

[61] It is said to have its origins in the decisions of in the speeches of Lords Wilberforce in *Prenn* v *Simonds* [1971] 3 All ER 237 and Lord Reid in *Schuler* v *Wickman Machine Tool Sales Ltd* [1974] AC 235, [1973] 2 All ER 39.

[62] See McMeel, [1998] *LMCLQ* 382.

citation of twenty-five cases,[63] Slade J sitting in the Chancery Division, concluded that the effect of this provision was to allow property in the fibre to pass to the buyer, subject to the grant back to the seller of an equitable charge, which was void for non-registration pursuant to s 95 Companies Act 1948. It was clear on the face of the contract that the seller did not purport to retain legal property in the goods. The crucial question was therefore to identify the nature of its equitable interest. Slade J explained his task thus:

> The court is not entitled to discard the plain, ordinary meaning of the phrase "equitable and beneficial ownership" unless there can be found in the relevant contracts other language and stipulations which necessarily deprive it of its ordinary meaning. The court, however, is entitled and indeed bound to look at the substance of the transactions as appearing from the wording of the whole of the retention of title clause, and indeed the other provisions of the relevant contracts of sale, for the purpose of deciding whether the essence of the transactions which the clause embodied was on the one hand a bare trust or on the other hand a trust by way of equitable mortgage or charge.[64]

On this basis he concluded that the seller's rights in the goods were not those of an equitable owner under a trust. For instance, the seller had no right to call for the delivery of the goods. Nor was the seller's interest one by way of equitable lien. Slade J was prepared to accept that an equitable lien could arise over personalty but doubted that one could arise under a contract for the sale of goods, and took the view that the availability of the lien depends on the availability of specific performance. He concluded, however, that any equitable lien arising by operation of law would in any case be excluded by the parties' express agreement for the seller to have security by means of the retention of title clause, and that security interest, being created by contract, could not be an equitable lien. The interest possessed the characteristics of a charge or mortgage identified in the classic description given by Romer LJ in *re George Inglefield Ltd.*[65] The buyer was entitled to redeem the seller's interest by discharging the debt. If the seller enforced its rights under the clause by repossessing the goods and

---

[63] A further 62 cases were cited by counsel. Reactions to *re Bond Worth* differ. Goodhart and Jones described it as "a full and closely reasoned judgment". In contrast Parris wrote that the judgment "contained more errors in law than any other judgment before or since" (*Effective Retention of Title Clauses* (1986) p 11).

[64] [1980] Ch 228 at p 248; [1979] 3 All ER 919 at p 938.

[65] [1933] Ch 1 at pp 27-28.

selling them, and the proceeds of sale were less than the outstanding debt, the buyer would remain liable for the balance, whereas if the goods were sold for more than the debt, the parties must have intended that the buyer would be entitled to the surplus. Slade J observed that:

> In my judgment, any contract which, by way of security for the payment of a debt, confers an interest in property defeasible or destructible on payment of such debt, or appropriates such property for the discharge of the debt, must necessarily be regarded as creating a mortgage or charge, as the case may be.[66]

This dictum was relied on in *Clough Mill Ltd* v *Martin*[67] by the receiver who challenged a supplier's claim to goods supplied which remained in their original form. Yarn was supplied for use in the manufacture of fibre. Both parties knew that much of the yarn would, in the ordinary run of things, be used in the manufacturing process before being paid for, and the contract made express provision for this eventuality, including a claim to goods manufactured from the yarn supplied in identical terms to the claim to the yarn itself. The receiver argued that the retention of title to yarn supplied should not be taken at face value because (a) the grant to the buyer of such extensive rights to use and otherwise deal with the yarn was inconsistent with the seller's continued ownership and (b) as the seller could not be owner of new products manufactured by the buyer, which had no existence at the time of the contract, it could at best have only a charge on them, the seller's rights to yarn, which were expressed in the same terms, must also be by way of a charge.[68] The retention clause should therefore be given a purposive construction, and since its purpose was clearly to provide the seller with security, it should be construed as a charge.

These arguments were accepted at first instance.[69] A strong Court of Appeal[70] however, unanimously rejected the receiver's arguments. Adopting a literal approach to the construction of the retention clause the court concluded that the buyer could not grant a charge unless it had

---

[66] [1980] Ch 228 at p 248; [1979] 3 All ER 919 at p 939.

[67] [1984] 3 All ER 982; [1985] 1 WLR 111.

[68] An argument canvassed by Goodhart and Jones in relation to *re Bond Worth*: see (1980) 43 *MLR* 489 at p 510.

[69] By His Hon Judge O'Donoghue sitting as a Deputy Judge of the Chancery Division of the High Court: [1984] 1 All ER 721, [1984] 1 WLR 1067.

[70] Lord Donaldson, MR, Robert Goff and Oliver LJJ.

property in the goods out of which to grant a charge. The clause provided that property did not pass to the buyer until payment and therefore it had nothing to charge.

The same approach was adopted by the House of Lords in *Armour* v *Thyssen Edelstahlwerke AG.*[71] A, a German company, supplied steel strip to C, a Scottish company, on terms that the steel was to remain the suppliers' property "until all debts owed to us including any balances existing at relevant times - due to us on any legal grounds - are settled. ... Debts owed to companies, being members of our combine, are deemed to be such debts." It was argued that the effect of the clause was to permit property in the steel to pass to C subject to the grant back to A of a security interest which, according to the law of Scotland, which was the applicable law, would be ineffective. The House of Lords, in a brief and unanimous decision, rejected that interpretation and, overturning the decisions of the Lord Ordinary and of the Second Division of the Inner House of the Court of Session, held that the clause should be taken at face value. On its face it stated that property remained in the seller. Sections 17 and 19 of the Sale of Goods Act 1979 permitted the imposition of a condition on the passing of property. According to Lord Keith:

> The parties in the contract of sale clearly expressed their intention that the property in the steel strip should not pass to Carron until all debts due by them to the appellants had been paid. In my opinion there are no grounds for refusing to give effect to that intention. ... Here the appellants, by the terms of the contract of sale, have in effect reserved the right of disposal of the steel strip until fulfilment of the condition that all debts due to them by Carron have been paid. By virtue of [s 19], that has the effect that the property in the goods did not pass to Carron until that condition had been fulfilled.[72]

The result was that C never acquired ownership of the steel and were therefore never in a position to grant A a security interest in it.

The reasoning in both *Clough Mill* and *Armour* can be criticised as circular. In essence the argument that the clause constituted the grant of a charge (*Clough Mill*) or a security without possession (*Armour*) was rejected on the basis that the buyer could not grant a charge or other security over the goods unless he had property in the goods and, since the contract in each case said, in terms, that property would not pass until the

---

[71] [1991] 2 AC 339, [1990] 3 All ER 481, HL; see Bradgate (1991) 54 *MLR* 726. Compare Mance, [1992] *LMCLQ* 35.

[72] [1991] 2 AC 339 at p 352; [1990] 3 All ER 481 at p 485.

stipulated condition was fulfilled, the buyer had no property and therefore could grant no charge. But this is to avoid the issue. The essential question in both cases was whether the contract *was* effective to prevent property passing or whether, notwithstanding its terms, its effect was to allow property to pass subject to, at most, the grant back of a security interest to the seller.

It may be argued that the approach in these cases is consistent with that to other title retention arrangements such as hire purchase or conditional sale, or that a simple retention of title to the goods supplied is sanctioned by the provisions of ss 17 and 19 of the Sale of Goods Act. A sale subject to retention of title differs from hire purchase and conditional sale, however, precisely in that it grants extensive rights of dominium over the goods to the buyer which, it is argued, are inconsistent with the seller's continued ownership.[73] A hire purchase, or traditional conditional sale, contract will normally impose strict controls on the hirer/buyer's rights to deal with the goods.[74] In particular it will normally prohibit resale of the goods and will require them to be retained *in specie* until completion of the contract by payment of the price. In contrast a sale subject to retention of title will not only anticipate the resale and/or use of the goods but will generally, expressly or impliedly, permit such acts. In *Clough Mill*, for instance, the clause permitted the buyer to use the goods in a manufacturing process which would effectively consume them, and to sell the products of that process. Indeed, almost *ex hypothesi*, wherever a seller retains title it will be anticipated that the buyer will need to deal with the goods, either by reselling them or by using them in a manufacturing process, before paying for them. A retention of title will only be required where the seller supplies goods on credit terms. In most cases the buyer's purpose in seeking credit will be to buy time to earn money to pay for the goods, and the most obvious way to do that will be by selling the goods themselves, or products made from them. In *McEntire* v *Crossley Bros* the House of Lords emphasised the need to classify the agreement by reference to *all* of its terms. The point is made in the passage from the speech of Lord Herschell quoted earlier.[75] Lord Watson observed that although the contract provided that the owner retained property in the goods, words used elsewhere in the contract might show that the literal meaning of the language of the contract did not reflect the parties' true intentions, as, for instance, if they had

---

[73] See Bradgate, (1987) *Conv* 434; Everett, (1994) 68 *ALJ* 404.

[74] See, for instance, the restrictions imposed by the contract in *McEntire* v *Crossley Bros*.

[75] See text accompanying fn 59.

"given power to the purchaser to exercise a right of implied dominium before the contractual term for the passing of the property arrived".[76] This approach is reflected in s 17 of the Sale of Goods Act, which provides that under a contract of sale property in the goods is transferred when the parties intend it to be transferred, and that "for the purpose of ascertaining the intention of the parties regard is to be had to the terms of the contract, the conduct of the parties, and the circumstances of the case." (section 17(2)).

The willingness of the courts in *Clough Mill* and *Armour* to accept at face value claims to original goods, without reference to the language of s 17(2), suggests a positive desire to uphold such claims. This is apparent in the courts' approach to a particular problem. In *Clough Mill* the seller retained title to all goods supplied in a particular consignment until the whole price of that consignment was paid. In *Armour* the clause reserved property in each consignment of steel until payment of not only the price of that particular consignment but also other debts owed to the supplier (and related companies). Property in any particular consignment of steel would therefore not pass even on payment of its price if other debts were at that time due to the seller or its related companies.[77] Such clauses raise the possibility that the seller may repossess goods for which he has received payment, and whose value exceeds the amount of the unpaid debt and it had therefore been argued that, in order to prevent the seller obtaining a windfall, whilst giving effect to the intentions of the parties, they would have to be construed as creating charges.[78] The House of Lords in *Armour* found it unnecessary to consider the point. In *Clough Mill*, however, the Court of Appeal did consider the problem and tentatively concluded that, at least during the subsistence of the contract, the seller's retention of title should be qualified by an implied term, pursuant to which the seller would be entitled to repossess only sufficient goods to discharge the amount of the buyer's outstanding debt and be accountable to the buyer for any surplus.[79] The result is that, by virtue of an implied term, the retention of title operates in much the same way as a charge, allowing the seller to look to a pool of assets for satisfaction of a debt, and being accountable to the buyer for any surplus, but without actually creating a charge.

---

[76] [1895] AC 457 at p 468.

[77] It should be noted that the clause in *Romalpa* was in similar form.

[78] See Goodhart and Jones, *op cit* fn 16 at p 508.

[79] Robert Goff LJ concluded that any such term would cease to apply on termination of the contract, but that restitutionary principles would then require the seller to refund the price received for any goods actually repossessed. For discussion see Bradgate, (1991) 54 *MLR* 726.

It must be conceded that some of the reasoning in *Bond Worth* is open to the same charge of circularity. In particular, the assertion that the buyer would be entitled to any surplus on resale, which gave the clause one of the characteristics of a charge, was based on no more than an unreasoned inference that "the parties' intention surely was that Bond Worth rather than Monsanto would be entitled to receive the surplus".[80] The reasoning is circular: if we conclude that the seller has retained property, the seller will be entitled to any surplus on resale; if we conclude that the parties intend the buyer to receive any surplus the seller's interest is likely to be by way of charge.[81] *Bond Worth* was however not questioned in either *Clough Mill* or *Armour*. The court in *Clough Mill* distinguished it on the grounds that since the seller only claimed to have an equitable interest in the goods its interest must arise either under a trust or a charge. The decision in *Bond Worth* has however been questioned in the light of later decisions. The receiver's argument was that the retention of title clause created a charge which was registrable under s 95 of the Companies Act 1948. A charge is only registrable under this provision (or now its successor, s 395 of the 1985 Act) if it is created by the company. The clause in *Bond Worth* provided that the seller *retained* equitable and beneficial ownership of the goods. It was therefore argued that even if the seller's interest was by way of equitable charge, it was not a charge created by the company. Slade J concluded, however, that the effect of the contract was that property in the goods passed to the buyer with an instantaneous grant back of a charge over the goods. He was reinforced in this view by the fact that the clause purported to give the seller the same rights over manufactured goods and proceeds of sale as it enjoyed over the original fibre, and, since the new goods and proceeds of sale did not exist at the time of the sale contract, those rights, he concluded, could only arise by way of grant by the buyer rather than by reservation.

Slade J relied on the decision of the Court of Appeal in *Capital Finance Co Ltd* v *Stokes*[82] and distinguished the decision in *re Connolly Bros Ltd (No 2)*.[83] In *Connolly* a company, A, which had already granted a

[80] [1980] Ch 228 at 249; [1979] 3 All ER 919 at p 939.

[81] Significantly in *Clough Mill* v *Martin* the Court of Appeal were all of the opinion that if the seller were to repossess and sell goods covered by a simple retention of title clause, the seller would be entitled to retain any surplus realised on the sale, but that if the sale produced a shortfall the buyer would remain liable for the outstanding portion of the price. See below.

[82] [1969] 1 Ch 261.

[83] [1912] 2 Ch 25.

floating charge over its property, wished to purchase property from B, and entered into an agreement with C whereby she agreed to provide a loan to finance the purchase and the company agreed to grant her a charge over the property to secure her advance. It was held that C's charge took priority over the pre-existing floating charge because the company was contractually committed to grant her charge before it acquired any interest in the property purchased. According to Cozens Hardy MR "all the company in equity obtained was the equity of redemption in the property subject to [C's] charge".[84] The reasoning in *Connolly* was adopted by the House of Lords in *Abbey National Building Society* v *Cann.*[85] Their Lordships there held that where a person acquired property with the assistance of a loan from a building society to be secured by a charge on the property there was no *scintilla temporis* between the completion of the purchase and the grant of the charge to the building society - no "gap" in the proceedings during which the buyer was unencumbered owner of the property. Although conceptually the buyer must become owner of the property in order to grant a charge over it, all that he acquires is an equity of redemption subject to the building society's charge. The result was that where a third party was in occupation of the premises at the time of completion (s)he could not acquire an overriding interest in the property having priority over the building society's charge because there was no moment in time when the buyer/chargor was unencumbered owner of the property. In reaching this conclusion their Lordships overruled the earlier case of *Church of England Building Society* v *Piskor.*[86] *Piskor* was not cited in *Bond Worth,* but was relied on in *Capital Finance Co Ltd* v *Stokes* on which Slade J relied. It has therefore been argued that, whether originally correct or not, *Bond Worth* should now be regarded as incorrect.[87] *Bond Worth* was, however, followed in *Stroud Architectural Systems Ltd* v *John Laing Construction Ltd*[88] and although the point here under consideration was not considered it is submitted that the decision in *Laing,* was correct and that *Bond Worth* remains good law. *Cann,* like *Connolly,* concerned a three party situation and a question of priority. The question raised in *Bond Worth* and *Laing,* by contrast, concerns only the relationship between seller and buyer and is concerned with the mechanism of creation of the seller's interest. Their Lordships in *Cann* recognised that,

[84] At p 31.
[85] [1990] 1 All ER 1085.
[86] [1954] Ch 553.
[87] See Gregory, (1990) 106 *LQR* 550.
[88] [1994] BCC 18.

conceptually, the buyer in the three-party situation must acquire property before granting a charge and there is nothing in the decision to suggest that it is conceptually possible for a seller to *retain* an equitable interest in property. A legal interest in property normally carries with it the equitable interest which, until the moment of separation has no independent existence.[89] *Cann* rejected the notion that there is an instant - a *scintilla temporis* - between the completion of the purchase financed by a mortgage and the grant of the mortgage during which a third party can acquire rights. Slade J in *re Bond Worth*, however, spoke of the grant of the seller's equitable charge occurring at the same moment - *eo instanti* - as the transfer of property to the buyer. In both *Connolly* and *Cann* the borrower had contracted to grant a security before acquiring the property. Equity, looking on as done that which ought to be done, perfects that contract. This is entirely consistent with the charge being one granted by the chargor.[90]

The Need for Identification and the Application of "Tracing Rules"

Provided only, therefore, that the seller retains full property in the goods, and not merely "equitable and beneficial ownership" a simple retention of title to the goods supplied will be effective so long as the goods remain identifiable in the buyer's hands and in their original form. Receivers, however, often seek to resist retention of title claims on the basis that in order to recover any particular item the seller must prove that it is in fact

---

[89] Conversely there is support for the line taken in *re Bond Worth* in the speech of Lord Browne Wilkinson in *Westdeutsche Landesbank Girozentrale* v *Islington LBC* [1996] AC 669 at p 706, [1996] 2 All ER 961 at p 989 where his lordship observed that "A person solely entitled to the full beneficial ownership of money or property, both at law and in equity, does not enjoy an equitable interest in that property. The legal title carries with it all rights. Unless and until there is a separation of the legal title and equitable estates, there is no separate equitable title. Therefore to talk about [the owner] 'retaining' its equitable interest is meaningless".

[90] Acceptance of the argument that *Cann* overrules *Bond Worth* would seriously undermine the policy of the Company charges for legislation. If we were to accept the argument that where money is lent to be secured by a charge pursuant to a prior agreement for the grant of the charge, the buyer never owns the unencumbered property but acquires only an "equity of redemption", and that there is therefore no grant of a charge to the lender, a charge granted in such circumstances, to secure money lent to finance the purchase of specific property, would not be registrable, driving the proverbial coach and four through the company charges registration regime. See de Lacy, (1994) *Conv* 242.

his property - that is, that he supplied it, subject to a retention of title, and that property in that particular item has not yet passed to the buyer. It is not enough for the seller to prove that he supplied the item and that the price for an identical, but not necessarily the same item, remains unpaid: he must prove that the particular item claimed remains his property.

In some cases, particularly of higher value items, such as motor vehicles and electrical or mechanical items, individual items may be specifically identifiable, for example, by serial number. If the serial numbers of items supplied under particular contracts are identified on the appropriate invoice it will be a relatively simple task for the seller (or buyer) to identify individual items and determine whether an item in stock is the seller's or buyer's property. Such identification may not be possible, however. Lower value items may simply not be identifiable in this way. Other items may be so identified but the identifier may appear on, say, packaging rather than on the goods themselves, so that it is lost on unpacking. Or again even if the goods have an identifier it may not be referred to on the relevant invoice.

Of course, the precise moment when property in a particular item passes to the buyer will depend on the terms of the particular retention of title clause. Where a single item is supplied subject to retention of title until its price is paid, the position is relatively simple. Where several items are supplied together under a single contract on terms that no property in any of the goods will pass until the whole of the price is paid the position is more difficult: no property in any items will pass so long as any part of the price due under that particular contract is outstanding. However, once the contract price for that consignment is paid, all of the items supplied under that contract will become the buyer's property. Where there is continuous trading between seller and buyer the need for the seller to be able to identify a particular item as not paid for and therefore his property will often pose huge difficulties. Over a period of time the buyer may buy many identical items. There may be continuous movements of goods into and out of the warehouse. If they are stored together it may be difficult, or even impossible, to identify individual items and connect them to particular contracts so as to determine whether a particular item in stock after the buyer's insolvency is the seller's property (not paid for) or the buyer's (paid for). The seller may seek to avoid this difficulty by requiring the buyer to store goods separately until payment, so that those which are the seller's property are readily identifiable as such, but such provisions may well be included more in the hope than the expectation of compliance and if the goods are confused in the buyer's warehouse the practical problem of identification will remain. As an alternative the seller may therefore seek to avoid the problem by including an "all sums" retention of the type used in *Armour*. However, even such a clause does not wholly negate the need for identifiability. Its effect is that so long as there is money outstanding from buyer to seller, no property in any goods supplied subject to the term will pass to the buyer. But if the account between the parties is at any time clear, property in all goods supplied prior to that time will pass to the buyer, and if the seller subsequently seeks to enforce his retention of title claim he will be called upon to identify the goods claimed as his property by proving that they were supplied after the date when the account was last clear.

The argument that the seller must identify goods as his property in order to claim them was accepted, without detailed consideration, by Deputy Judge David Neuberger, sitting in the Chancery Division, in *Ian Chisholm Textiles Ltd* v *Griffiths*.[91] The result is counter to one's sense of justice especially where, as is often the case, the clause requires separate storage of the seller's goods prior to payment, to enable them to be identified as the seller's property. *Ex hypothesi* in such a case if the goods *cannot* be identified it must be because the buyer has failed to comply with his contractual undertaking to keep the seller's goods separate.[92] To require the seller to identify the goods as his property in such a case allows the buyer - or more accurately, the buyer's creditors - to profit from his breach of contract.[93] Recent cases suggest, however, that it is in fact not necessary for the seller to identify particular items as his property in order to enforce his retention claim. We are not here concerned with the case where goods supplied have been used in the manufacture of some new product and have thus ceased to exist, as where resin was used to manufacture chipboard.[94]

---

[91] [1994] BCC 96.

[92] Although it must be conceded that separate storage provisions are rarely likely to be policed and in many cases the seller will be well aware that the buyer is unlikely to comply.

[93] In an insolvency it is of course often the case that the insolvent's general creditors benefit from breaches of contract by the insolvent. Thus, for instance, where a buyer pays in advance for unascertained generic goods to be supplied by the seller from stock and the seller becomes insolvent before the goods are appropriated to the buyer's contract so as to pass property to the buyer, the buyer will become merely a general creditor of the seller, and his payment will go to swell the fund available for distribution amongst creditors generally. This is the mirror image of the case currently under consideration.

[94] *Borden* v *Scottish Timber Products Ltd* [1981] Ch 25.

We are concerned with a loss of identifiability rather than with a loss of identity, as where three identical items are stored side by side so as to make it impossible to tell one from another.

In *Indian Oil Corp* v *Greenstone Shipping, The Ypatianna*[95] oil of two different owners was mixed when carried on a vessel where the cargo and fuel tanks were so connected as to result in the mixture of the two. Older cases were cited as authority for the rule that in cases of wrongful mixing of goods of two owners the innocent party should own the whole of the resulting mixture. Staughton J, an experienced commercial judge, reviewed the law and concluded than even if that had once been the rule it was no longer justified. Instead he concluded that in cases of wrongful - that is non-consensual - mixing, the contributing owners should own the resulting mixture as tenants in common on the basis that the innocent party should be entitled to receive out of the mixture a quantity equal to the amount he contributed to it, and to be compensated for any reduction in quality or shortfall in quantity of the goods received. The older, penal, rule would only apply where it was impossible to determine the quantity of goods contributed by the innocent party.[96] The reasoning of *Indian Oil* appeared to be capable of application in the retention of title context. *Indian Oil* was, however, a case of a liquid mixture, and, adopting a distinction derived from Roman law,[97] doubts were expressed as to whether the same

---

[95] [1988] 1 QB 345; [1987] 3 All ER 893.

[96] The decision in *Indian Oil* produces a result very similar to that now produced by s 20A of the Sale of Goods Act 1979 where a pre-paying buyer contracts to buy a specified quantity of goods from an identified bulk source. Under s 20A the buyer in such a case becomes a tenant in common of the bulk, the size of his share being determined by reference to the ratio of the quantity he has paid for to the overall quantity of the bulk from time to time. In other words (subject to the possibility of shortfall in the bulk) he is entitled to receive from the bulk the quantity for which he has paid and any loss from the bulk is borne by the seller.

[97] Roman law developed relatively sophisticated rules for dealing with this sort of problem. It drew a distinction between *confusio*, where mixing resulted in a loss of identity, and *commixtio* where items were "mixed" without loss of identity. *Confusio* covered so-called "fluid" mixtures such as oil or wine; *commixtio* "granular" mixtures, of items such as grain. A case of *confusio* of the goods of two owners would result in them having joint ownership of the mixture. The effects of *commixtio* would depend on whether the mixing was consensual or wrongful. In the case of consensual mixing the result would be co-ownership; in the case of non-consensual mixing the original ownership would survive. The rationale of these distinctions was that in cases of *confusio* of liquid mixtures it was thought to be impossible to separate the goods of the two owners, whereas in a

reasoning could apply to cases of "granular" mixtures. *Ian Chisholm Textiles*, referred to above, was decided after, but without citation of, *Indian Oil* and the point was not considered. Moreover, it was powerfully argued that, in any case, in order to claim anything from the mixture the seller would have to prove not only that his goods went into it, but also that they remained in the mixture.[98] Where there has been continuous trading by the buyer with his stock such a requirement would often defeat the seller's claim.

The essential problem is one of evidence: who should bear the burden of proof where the means of identifying goods as the seller's property have been lost? Equity developed powerful rules for resolving such problems in the context of claims to money which had been mixed in a bank account, in the forms of the rules in *Clayton's Case*,[99] *re Hallett's Estate*,[100] *re Oatway*,[101] and *Roscoe* v *Winder*.[102] In particular the rule in *Clayton's Case*, "first in, first out" might be invoked so that, where there had been continuous trading between seller and buyer, it would be presumed that the buyer would use his own goods first, and that therefore any goods left in stock in the event of insolvency would be presumed to include those belonging to the seller. The obstacle to applying this reasoning in the present context, however, was that the rules in *Clayton's Case, re Hallett's Estate* and so on were seen as aspects of the rules of "equitable tracing", capable of being invoked only in relation to claims to

---

case of *commixtio* separation was possible, albeit difficult, and therefore unless mixing were consensual there was no reason to deprive the contributing owners of their property. Such distinctions are, it is submitted, too subtle for modern commercial practice. First, whilst separation may be *theoretically* possible in cases of *commixtio*, in practice it may be impractical to the point of impossibility to separate my grains of corn from yours. Second, the distinction is scientifically unsound: in cases of liquid mixtures there is no loss of identity at the molecular level. In other words, the difficulty in cases of both liquid and granular mixtures is the practical one of identifying the goods of the individual owners and effecting a separation. A solution which requires microscopic examination of the facts to identify the goods of individual owners and the assistance of atomic physicists to effect a separation is of no use in the real world of practical commercial problems.

98 Goode, *Proprietary Rights and Insolvency in Sale Transactions* 2nd ed (1989) p 91; compare Birks, "Mixtures" *Interests in Goods*, Palmer and McKendrick (eds) 2nd ed (1998).

99 (1816) 1 Mer 572.

100 (1880) 13 Ch D 696.

101 [1903] 2 Ch 356.

102 [1915] 1 Ch 62.

money mixed in a bank account and where there was a fiduciary relationship between the parties. In *Foskett* v *McKeown*, however, the majority of the House of Lords held that the rules of tracing are neutral as between common law and equity, that is, that the same rules apply in both cases. Moreover Lord Millett observed that:

> The tracing rules are not the result of any presumption or principle peculiar to equity. *They correspond to the common law rules for following into physical mixtures* (though the consequences may not be identical). Common to both is the principle that the interests of the wrongdoer who was responsible for the mixing and those who derive title under him otherwise than for value are subordinated to those of the innocent contributors.[103]

Thus as against the wrongdoer the innocent contributor is entitled to "locate his contribution in any part of the mixture and to subordinate their claims to share in the mixture until his own contribution has been satisfied".[104]

This reasoning was applied in a context closely analogous to that of retention of title by Moore-Bick J in *Glencore International AG* v *Metro Trading Inc.*[105] D had commingled oil supplied to it for storage by various suppliers and had used the commingled bulk as its trading stock, selling oil from stock and buying in more to replace it. Moore-Bick J concluded that a supplier of oil in these circumstances could retain title to the oil supplied notwithstanding its being stored in a commingled bulk, and that provided a particular supplier could show that it had supplied oil to D and had not withdrawn its entitlement it did not have to trace the remaining bulk to a particular cargo in order to claim. In other words, it was not necessary for a supplier to prove that "its" oil remained in the bulk in order to establish a claim. In a lengthy judgment he referred specifically to Lord Millett's speech in *Foskett* v *McKeown* and the cases on "tracing in equity into mixed funds" and held that analogous rules would apply in the present situation.

---

[103] [2000] 3 All ER 97 at p 124, emphasis added. The analogy with homogenous mixing and tracing had been recognised by Buckley LJ in *Borden* v *STP* [1981] Ch 25 at p 41.

[104] *Ibid.* Again we may note that the result is similar to that achieved under s 20A of the Sale of Goods Act in relation to pre-paying buyers: the claim of the "innocent" party in this case the seller - must be satisfied before that of the "wrong-doer".

[105] [2001] 1 All ER Comm 103.

The result would appear to be that where goods supplied subject to an unsatisfied retention of title have been mixed with other similar goods of the buyer, it will no longer be necessary for the supplier to identify his goods in order to claim them. Provided that the sale contract requires separate storage of the supplier's goods he will be entitled to rely on a series of presumptions. In particular it will be presumed that, given the choice between acting properly and improperly, the buyer will choose the former and will therefore use his own goods first. The seller will therefore be entitled to remove from the "mixed bulk" a quantity equivalent to the quantity he contributed to it - in effect the quantity for which he has not been paid - subject only to the possibility that the buyer may affirmatively prove that the goods in the "bulk" are *his* rather than the seller's property. The only other limitation on the seller's right is that it will be subject to the "lowest intermediate balance" rule.[106] This means that if the quantity of goods in the bulk has at any time been reduced to less than the quantity "contributed" by the seller, that lower quantity fixes the ceiling of the seller's recovery. Subsequent additions to the bulk will not be available to satisfy the seller's claim unless it can be established that in making the addition to the bulk the buyer intended to replace the seller's goods. The result is more in accord with one's sense of justice: the seller is entitled to have his debt satisfied out of the pool of assets - rather as if, instead of retaining property in goods supplied, he were to be given a charge on the mixed bulk.

Processing and Manufacturing

As we have seen, even the grant to the buyer of extensive rights of resale, use and consumption will not be considered inconsistent with the seller's retention of ownership.[107] More difficult, however, is the question of the effect on the seller's security of such resale or use.

Leaving aside for the moment the possibility of resale, goods could be used in a range of different ways including as raw materials in the manufacture of a new item (for example, plastic used to make plastic bottles); components in the assembly of a larger product (for example, body panels, engine parts, wheels, tyres, lights, radio, nuts, bolts and so on used

[106] See fn 31 and accompanying text.

[107] See *Clough Mill* v *Martin*; *Armour* v *Thyssen*. The point is made expressly in the New Zealand case of *New Zealand Forest Products* v *Pongakawa Sawmill Ltd* [1991] 3 NZLR 112, [1992] 3 NZLR 304 (CA).

in the assembly of a motor vehicle); raw materials in a process (for example: coke used to fire a furnace used to produce steel). Where raw materials are used to produce a finished item they might be the sole or principle ingredient – for example, grapes used to make wine or olives pressed to make oil - or one of several "ingredients", as where resin is mixed with solvents and wood chip to produce chipboard, or eggs, fat, sugar, flour and milk are mixed to make a cake. The process might be reversible, as in the case of the plastic used to make plastic bottles, or irreversible, as in the case of the wine, chipboard or cake. Items bought for consumption might be used directly in the production of a finished product, as, for instance, where coke is used in furnaces to produce steel, or only indirectly and remotely, as where coke is burned in boilers to heat the manufacturer's factory.

In this type of case three issues must be considered: (a) what is the effect of the manufacturing process on the seller's property in the original goods supplied; (b) can the seller claim any rights in the manufactured product; (c) what is the nature of any such rights? The issue was first considered in the retention of title context in *Borden* v *Scottish Timber Products Ltd.*[108] S supplied resin which was mixed with various other substances to produce a glue which, in turn, was combined with wood chip to manufacture chipboard. The process was irreversible so that once it had been used to make chipboard the resin ceased to exist as such. As S knew, B had storage facilities at its premises for, at most, sufficient resin for two days' manufacture, so that resin supplied would normally be consumed in the manufacturing process before being paid for. On B's insolvency S claimed to be entitled to an interest in the chipboard manufactured from its resin by tracing its property in the resin into the manufactured product. This claim succeeded at first instance, his Honour Judge Rubin QC, sitting as a deputy judge of the Chancery Division, holding that S was entitled to trace according to the principle of *re Hallett's Estate* as applied in *Romalpa*. S's claim was, however, unanimously rejected by the Court of Appeal. All three judges - Bridge, Templeman and Buckley LJJ - assumed, in accordance with the prevailing wisdom, that in order to trace it would be necessary for S to establish a fiduciary relationship between itself and B.[109] All three found that there was no such relationship, distinguishing *Romalpa* on the grounds that (*inter alia*) it was there conceded that the buyer held the

---

[108] [1981] Ch 25.

[109] Bridge LJ quoted at length at [1981] Ch 25 pp 39-40 from the judgment of Jessel MR in *re Hallett's Estate.*

seller's goods as bailee, whereas here B manufactured chipboard for its own benefit, rather than in any fiduciary capacity.

This part of the reasoning can no longer stand after *Foskett* v *McKeown*. There is no separate concept of "equitable tracing" and a fiduciary relationship is not necessary in order to trace. The explanation for the decision in *Borden* must therefore be sought elsewhere. Bridge LJ noted that there was no previous case in which tracing had been applied in this context, where different goods of more than one owner were combined in a manufacturing process to produce a new product. He was prepared to countenance the possibility that tracing might apply in a case of homogenous mixing - as, say, where oil of two different owners is mixed[110] - but "a mixture of heterogeneous goods in a manufacturing process wherein the original goods lose their character and what emerges is a wholly new product is in my judgment something entirely different".[111] He offered as examples cases of cattle cake supplied to a farmer being fed to cattle, or coal supplied to a steel maker being used to power furnaces used to manufacture steel. It was conceded that in these cases the supplier would have no interest in the cattle or steel and he found it "impossible to draw an intelligible line of distinction in principle which would give the sellers a right to trace the resin into the chipboard in the instant case".[112] For good measure he added that were a tracing right to be recognised, it would give rise to "intractable" practical difficulties: how would the supplier's share of the finished product be quantified? Templeman LJ, although preferring to base his reasoning on the absence of any fiduciary relationship between the parties, referred to the same difficulties when he observed that recognition of a tracing claim would require the court to "unearth the unearthable, trace the untraceable and calculate the incalculable."[113] For Buckley LJ, too, the resin's loss of identity was crucial to the denial of a right to trace. He concluded that any interest S enjoyed in the chipboard must be by way of transfer of ownership or grant of a charge by B.

There are powerful arguments in favour of this analysis, and yet it cannot be correct that the fact that property ceases to exist is a bar to tracing. Tracing is a process by which value inherent in property is identified in other property substituted for it. If money is withdrawn from

---

[110] As noted above this situation is resolved by the common law rules governing ownership of mixtures, analogous to the identification rules of tracing.

[111] [1981] Ch 25 at p 41.

[112] *Ibid.*

[113] [1981] Ch 25 at p 41.

my bank account and used to buy a painting, I can trace my "money" into the painting. Closer analysis, however, reveals that my original property has ceased to exist. The original property in this case is the credit balance on my bank account - a debt. Assuming that the whole credit balance is withdrawn, that particular item of property ceases to exist, and yet its value can be traced into its substitute, the painting. A better explanation of the outcome in *Borden* would, it is submitted, be simply that on the proper construction of the contract the intention of the parties was that when the buyer used the seller's resin in its manufacturing process to produce chipboard, it did so on its own behalf. As Templeman LJ noted, there was no requirement in the contract for the buyer to provide substitute security on consumption of the resin, and the difficulties referred to by all three judges in quantifying the seller's share of any manufactured product are powerful arguments against the implication of any term to that effect.

Borden therefore decided that where goods are consumed in a manufacturing process the seller of the goods cannot claim an equitable property interest in the manufactured product by tracing. In *Hendy Lennox v Grahame Puttick Engines Ltd*[114] S supplied diesel engines which were used by B in the manufacture of generator sets. Part of the claim related to engines which had been incorporated into generator sets by a process of "doing up bolts and other connections, which could later be undone".[115] The engines were at all times identifiable by means of serial numbers and could be detached from the generator sets without damage to either, albeit that disconnection would take a little time. Having quoted a passage from Crossley Vaines on *Personal Property*, citing Bracton and Blackstone on the ownership of new items produced "when a thing is changed into a different species, as by making wine, oil, bread or malt out of grapes, olives, wheat or barley", Staughton J concluded that the situation before him was different and that the incorporation of S's engines into the generator sets had no effect on their ownership: "They just remained engines, albeit connected to other things".[116]

It is clear that items incorporated into larger items may lose their identity so as to become part of the larger item, in accordance with the doctrine of accession. Whether or not that happens depends on the degree and purpose of the annexation. This, of course, is a matter of fact and degree. There are no hard and fast rules. Other factors which may be relevant will be the relative size and value of the connected items and the

---

114 [1984] 2 All ER 152, [1984] 1 WLR 485.

115 [1984] 2 All ER 152 at p 159; [1984] 1 WLR 485at p 493.

116 [1984] 2 All ER 152 at p 159; [1984] 1 WLR 485 at p 494.

commercial and practical value of effecting the separation. The test is similar to that for determining whether an item affixed to land becomes a fixture and thus loses its separate identity and becomes part of the land. If goods supplied by S are so affixed to B's goods that they lose their separate identity, they become part of B's goods. S's property in the goods supplied will be extinguished and any attempt to claim property in the item to which they are affixed will be regarded as constituting a charge.[117] In this type of case no new item is produced. Prior to the incorporation of the accessory the item in which it is incorporated is owned by the buyer. The contract therefore purports to effect a transfer of ownership of the buyer's goods by way of security for payment of the debt due to the seller.[118]

Rather more difficult is the situation where the buyer uses the seller's goods to produce a wholly new item so that the seller's goods lose their identity. This, of course, is the situation considered in *Borden*. According to Bracton[119] and Blackstone[120] English law adopted the Roman law doctrine of *specificatio* and gave ownership of the manufactured item to the manufacturer where the manufacturing process was irreversible and resulted in the original goods' losing their identity, as in the cases cited

---

[117] In *Specialist Plant Services Ltd* v *Braithwaite* [1987] BCLC 1 S supplied a part to be used in repairing machinery belonging to B. The contract provided that "if the ... goods or materials [supplied]... become a constituent of another article or articles the [supplier] shall be given ownership of this (these) new article(s) as surety of the full payment ..." The Court of Appeal held that S's property in the component had been lost on incorporation and the interest it claimed in B's machine was by way of a registrable charge.

[118] The principle of "accession" may, of course, work in favour of, as well as against, the seller. In general where one item is annexed to another, the accessory item becomes part of the dominant, as in *Braithwaite*. If, therefore, the buyer affixes an item to a larger, dominant item belonging to the seller and the affixation is such that the buyer's item becomes part of the seller's goods, the seller will take property in the whole. It is possible to extend the general rule by contract so that an accessory becomes part of the dominant item even if the degree of annexation is not sufficient to satisfy the common law test for accession - See *Akron Tyre Ppty Ltd* v *Kittson* (1951) 82 CLR 471 where tyres fitted to a vehicle let on hire purchase became part of the vehicle as a result of a contract term to the effect that "Any accessories or goods supplied with or for or attached to or repairs executed to the goods shall become part of the goods." - but not to reverse the principle that the accessory becomes part of the dominant chattel.

[119] *On the Laws and Customs of England* (v) II.

[120] Blackstone *Commentaries* 14th ed pp 404-5.

above, of the manufacture of wine from grapes, oil from olives and so on.[121] The doctrine of *specificatio*, however, only applies where the manufacturing is wrongful. Where goods are supplied on retention of title terms for use in a manufacturing process it will normally be an implied, if not an express, term of the contract that the buyer is permitted to make use of them in that process. The case law shows that the first question then is to determine when the original goods lose their identity in that process so as to become a new item. In *re Peachdart Ltd*[122] S supplied leather which was used by B in the manufacture of handbags. On B's insolvency S claimed, *inter alia*, stocks of finished and unfinished handbags made from its leather. The retention of title clause included a claim to products manufactured from S's leather in the following terms:

> If any of the products are incorporated in or used as material for other goods before ... payment the property in the whole of such other goods shall be and remain with the seller until ... payment is made ... and all the seller's rights hereunder in the products shall extend to those other goods.

The clause continued with a statement that until payment the buyer should hold the seller's goods - original leather and manufactured products - as a fiduciary and that in the event of their being sold the seller should be entitled to trace the proceeds "according to the principles in *re Hallett's Estate*".

There was no problem of physical identification: evidence was given that an expert in the trade would be able to identify a piece of leather as coming from a particular parcel and that the leather would remain thus identifiable throughout the manufacturing process. It was argued that the situation was analogous to that where a "sportsman" supplies a skin or hide to a craftsman to make into a bag, and the skin remains the "sportsman's" property throughout. Vinelott J however rejected this analogy, finding it "impossible to suppose that ... the parties intended that ... [the buyer] would remain a bailee of each piece of leather ... throughout the whole process of

[121] A dictum to the contrary in *re Oatway* [1903] 2 Ch 356 at p 359 that "whatever alteration of form any property may undergo, the true owner is entitled to seize it in its new shape if he can prove the identity of the original material" probably misstates the common law position: see Webb [2000] *JBL* 513 at pp 518-9. See also the discussion in *Glencore International* v *Metro* [2001] 1 All ER Comm 103 at pp 162-3.

[122] [1983] 1 WLR 873.

manufacture".[123] Two factors were significant. First, although each parcel of leather would remain identifiable throughout the manufacturing process, so that it would be possible to relate any particular handbag to a particular parcel, and thus identify it as the seller's or buyer's property, there was no requirement to keep separate the proceeds of sale of finished handbags so as to identify which were the proceeds of the seller's bags. Second, the value of the finished bags would derive mainly from the skill of the buyer and its workforce in design and manufacture. Whilst admitting that his construction did "some violence to the language" of the retention of title clause, Vinelott J therefore concluded:

> It seems to me that the parties must have intended that at least after a piece of leather had been appropriated to be manufactured into a handbag and work had started on it (when the leather would cease to have any significant value as raw material) the leather would cease to be the exclusive property of [the seller] and that the seller would thereafter have a charge on handbags in the course of manufacture and on the distinctive products which would come into existence at the end of the process of manufacture.[124]

In the search for the intention of the parties Vinelott J was therefore prepared to disregard the literal meaning of the contract. There was no detailed consideration of the effect of the express claim to title to manufactured products. Nevertheless, it is submitted that the learned judge's conclusion was correct. First, the "sportsman" analogy was rightly rejected. In that case there is little doubt that the craftsman works on the hide as the "sportsman's" agent and holds the hide as his bailee. It is never intended by either party that the craftsman should become owner of the hide or the finished bag.[125] Second, it is surely correct that a finished handbag is something fundamentally different from the leather from which it is made. Even if the leather is the principle "component" and the value of other items used in manufacture - thread, clasp and so on - is minimal in comparison, common sense tells us that the finished item is a "handbag", not "leather". The key features are, it is submitted, those identified by Vinelott J: first, that the value of the finished bag (which considerably

---

[123] [1983] 1 WLR 873 at p 885.

[124] *Ibid.*

[125] Although such an arrangement could be construed as involving a sale of the hide to the craftsman with a sale back of the finished bag, the two prices being set off against each other: see *Dixon* v *London Small Arms Co Ltd* (1896) 1 App Cas 632.

exceeds that of the leather used in its manufacture) derives primarily from the design and workmanship of the buyer (so that, although this point is not made in the judgment, to give the seller ownership of the bag would be to give it a "windfall" profit); and, second, that once it had entered the manufacturing process and been cut into shape, the leather would cease to have any real value as leather.

A similar approach is discernible in *Clough Mill* v *Martin*. The court in that case was not directly concerned with a claim to manufactured products, but the seller's clause provided that if yarn supplied by S was used in the manufacture of new products, S's rights should extend to the products. It was argued that (a) S's rights in new products could only be by way of charge and (b) therefore that its rights to the original yarn must be of the same nature. The Court of Appeal rejected this argument but considered the effect of a claim to manufactured products. The yarn, it will be recalled, was used to manufacture fabric. All three members of the Court of Appeal agreed that that part of the clause which referred to newly manufactured products probably had the effect of creating a charge on such products. Robert Goff LJ cited Blackstone for the proposition that "it is no doubt true that where A's material is lawfully used by B to create new goods, whether or not B incorporates other material of his own, the property in the new goods will generally vest in B, at least where the goods are not reducible to the original materials".[126] He considered, however, that it would, at least in principle, be possible for the parties expressly to agree that the property in such new goods should vest in A. Nevertheless, having recognised this possibility, he concluded that that could not have been the intention of the parties here. In construing the clause the court had to take account of the possibility that the buyer might not only have paid some of the price but also have provided some of the component parts of the new product and borne the costs of manufacture. The contract made no provision for the seller to make any refund or allowance in such circumstances. His lordship found it "impossible to believe that it was the intention of the parties that the seller would thereby gain the windfall of the full value of the new product, deriving as it may well do, not merely from the labour of the buyer, but also from materials that were his, without any duty to account to him for any surplus of the proceeds of sale above the outstanding balance of the price due by him to the seller".[127] This analysis seems to leave open the possibility that were the contract to include

---

[126] [1984] 3 All ER 982 at p 989.
[127] [1984] 3 All ER 982 at p 990.

appropriate terms requiring the seller to pay the buyer an allowance for his contribution to the enhanced value of the manufactured product, a provision giving the seller property in the manufactured product might be effective. His Lordship rejected this possibility on the grounds that on repossession the seller would terminate the contract and therefore be "uninhibited by any terms of the contract, which had then ceased to apply", but there seems no reason why, if suitably drafted, such terms should not be construed as continuing to apply after termination of the contract. It seems, however, that even were such terms included the court would be unlikely to recognise the seller as outright owner of manufactured products, for they might contain not only components provided by the buyer, to whom an allowance might be paid under the contract, but also components supplied by other suppliers, possibly on similar retention of title terms. This possibility also led his lordship to reject the possibility that the clause should be construed as creating a trust over new products. The only possible construction, even if, like that of Vinelott J in *re Peachdart*, it did some violence to the language of the clause, was that it created a charge which required registration. Oliver LJ observed that "English law has developed no very sophisticated system for determining title in cases where indistinguishable goods are mixed or become combined in a newly manufactured item"[128] but indicated his tentative agreement with the reasoning of Robert Goff LJ. Lord Donaldson took a similar line. So long as the yarn remained separate and identifiable, even as a component of a new item, the seller would be able to rely on its retention of title, although any attempt to assert a proprietary interest in the new product as a whole would amount to an attempt to create a charge over the other items included in the new product. Once the manufacturing process led to the yarn's losing its identity and the production of a new product, it would be necessary to consider who initially owned the new product: if the buyer, the clause in the contract would create a charge. He did not, however, consider whether the buyer or the seller would be the first owner of the new product, but merely concluded that in some circumstances the claim to new products would constitute a charge.

The judgments in *Clough Mill* therefore suggested that where goods are used in a manufacturing process which results in the manufacture of a new product, a claim by the seller to property in the manufactured product is likely to be construed as giving rise to, at best, a charge. Nevertheless the comments that it is open to the parties to the sale contract to agree that

---

128 At p 993.

new products shall be the property of the seller, despite the clear inference that this will rarely be found to be the case, leave open the possibility that the seller may be able to establish such a claim. The possibility has subsequently been explored in a series of cases at first instance. In *Modelboard Ltd* v *Outer Box Ltd*[129] M supplied O with cardboard sheets which were used by O to manufacture cardboard boxes. The manufacturing process involved printing the cardboard and cutting it into shapes, before folding it to produce finished boxes. M's retention of title clause provided for O to hold the cardboard as bailee and to store it prior to payment so as to be identifiable as M's property. However, it also expressly licensed O to "process the Goods in such fashion as he may wish and/or incorporate them in or with any other product or products" subject to the condition that such new products "or any other chattel whatsoever containing any part of the Goods" should be separately stored so as to be identifiable as M's property. The clause continued that if the seller's cardboard was mixed in manufacture with any property of the buyer, the resulting new product should be the "sole and exclusive property" of M; if similarly mixed with goods of any other party, then the resulting product should be owned by M in common with the other contributor. This last provision was clearly an attempt to address the problem identified in *Clough Mill*, that manufactured products might include components or ingredients supplied by other suppliers on retention of title terms. Mr Michael Hart QC, sitting as a Deputy Judge of the Chancery Division, nevertheless held that the clause had the effect of creating a charge over completed and partly-completed boxes manufactured from M's card. Apparently differing from the view of Vinelott J in *re Peachdart*, he was prepared to accept that M could retain property in the board even after work on it had started, on the basis that initial processing would not necessarily destroy its character as the board supplied by M, even if such processing had added to its value. Nevertheless he concluded that once processing had resulted in the board losing "all significant value as raw material", the board would cease to be "the goods" supplied by M. At this point M's retained interest would disappear to be replaced by an interest arising under the claim to manufactured products. He further concluded, although without any detailed analysis, that that interest was one by way of charge which required registration. Property in the manufactured boxes would originate with O, the manufacturer, who would then grant an interest to M in accordance with the clause. That interest, granted by way of security for

129 [1993] BCLC 623.

the payment of the price of the original goods supplied, would be defeated on payment of that price and was therefore to be categorised as a charge.

Modelboard was followed almost exactly a year later by the decision of David Neuberger QC, also sitting as a Deputy Judge of the Chancery Division, in *Ian Chisholm Textiles Ltd* v *Griffiths.*[130] C had supplied to R fabric for use in the manufacture of dresses. At the time of R's receivership it had in stock a quantity of such fabric. Some remained uncut, exactly as supplied; some had been cut but subjected to no further processing, whilst a third batch had been cut and had undergone some work or initial processing with a view to its being made up into dresses. C claimed to be entitled to all three categories of fabric. The first two claims were conceded;[131] the third was contested. The case was complicated by the fact that C had used two different retention of title clauses. The first provided that "property in goods sold shall be and remain in the company until the company has received payment in full for them ... *This will include finished garments which have been made up from fabric purchased from our company...*". The second, although more detailed, made no express reference to manufactured products and merely retained "legal and beneficial ownership" to "the goods". It did, however, grant R a licence to sell the goods "as principal in the ordinary course of its business" and required R to hold the proceeds of sale in trust for C, in a separate account, and provided for C to trace such proceeds "according to the principles in *re Hallett's Estate*". Mr Neuberger concluded that once fabric had entered the manufacturing process and had undergone initial processing there were four possible interpretations. First, the retention of title clause would cease to apply. Second, C would retain title to the fabric used but property in attached items such as thread, zips and buttons would remain either in R or in the supplier of those items if supplied on retention of title terms. Third, that title to the manufactured item, including any attached items, would be transferred to C. Fourth, that C's original "unqualified beneficial ownership of the supplied goods becomes at some point transformed to a charge on the manufactured article (and title to which passes to the purchaser) to the extent of the value of the supplied goods".[132] Curiously, neither party contended for either the first or second interpretation - curiously because there would appear to be a good case for the first

---

[130] [1994] BCC 96.

[131] The report states that the parties had reached agreement in relation to the first two categories, but since the claim to fabric in the third category was contested, it seems clear that the first two must have been conceded.

[132] At p 101.

interpretation, at least in relation to goods supplied under the second retention of title clause which did not extend to manufactured products. That left the judge with a choice between the third interpretation, argued for by C, and the fourth, favoured by R's receiver. Having referred to the need to construe the contract, the judge indicated that "there must be a strong presumption, essentially based on commercial common sense, to the effect that in the absence of very clear words, the parties would not have intended the result for which the [seller] contends."[133] The reason for this conclusion is that that result would give the supplier the windfall benefit of R's work, skill and materials. In addition the judge observed that, since the contract only permitted sales of goods in the ordinary course of R's business, only sales of finished products could be permitted. The claim to proceeds of sale must therefore relate to sales of finished products and since, as he concluded (without any analysis), any rights C had in such proceeds were by way of charge, their rights in the products themselves must also be by way of charge. The judge concluded that the charge was one created by an instrument which, if executed by an individual, would require registration under the Bills of Sale Acts, or a floating charge on the company's property, and therefore required registration.

The result, and the reasoning, in *Chisholm* are, as the judge recognised, very similar to those of Vinelott J in *re Peachdart*. In *Peachdart* Vinelott J recognised that his construction of the seller's clause did "some violence" to the language of the contract which provided that property in manufactured goods should "be and remain" in the seller until payment. Here too the contract provided that property in the goods should "remain" in the seller, but the judge found it "difficult ... to impute to the parties an intention that goods other than the cloth, which were never vested in the [seller] ... should nevertheless be transferred and, be it noted, not merely transferred as security but transferred absolutely beneficially, to the [seller]."[134]

The result, then, is that goods supplied subject to a retention of title clause remain the seller's property as such so long as they remain identifiable, but once they lose their identity as a result of a manufacturing or other process, whether through accession by incorporation into other property of the buyer, or use in the production of a new item, the seller's property in the goods will be lost. Where they lose their identity by accession they become part of the item into which they are incorporated

---

[133] *Ibid.*

[134] At p 102.

and the property of the owner of that item. Any interest the seller has in that item must be granted by the owner and is almost certain to be construed as a charge. Where goods are used in a manufacturing process which results in the production of a new item property in that item will normally vest first in the manufacturer - the buyer. Any attempt by the seller to claim an interest in the new product is likely to be construed as a charge. The dicta in *Clough Mill* tell us that it is not *impossible* for the parties to provide for the seller to acquire outright ownership of newly manufactured products,[135] but it seems that the court will require clear wording to achieve that result. The owner of a raw material can employ another to work on it for him to produce a new item, as is illustrated by the example considered in *Peachdart* of the "sportsman" who employs a craftsman to make a bag from hides supplied to him. The hides remain throughout the property of the "sportsman" who employs the craftsman to work for him, supplying labour and, possibly, accessory materials such as thread, clasps and so on. Thus where S has retained property in goods supplied it is, *in theory*, possible to analyse the situation as one in which B works on the materials as S's agent. In the retention of title context, however, this construction is unlikely to be accepted. It depends on finding that the intention of the parties is that the craftsman works on the materials supplied for the benefit of the owner and is rewarded for his labour. Even where it is intended that the finished product should be returned to the original supplier of the raw material it is possible to construe the arrangement as involving a transfer of property in the materials to the manufacturer, with a subsequent sale back of the finished item.[136] Where goods are supplied under a retention of title clause the intention of the parties will surely be that the buyer is entitled to work on them for his own benefit. The objective of the transaction, from the buyer's perspective, is to make a profit by adding value to the goods supplied. That is known to the seller. The seller's objective is to receive the price of the goods supplied. The correct analysis must therefore be that the first owner of the new item will be the buyer who creates it.

Can the seller then claim property in the new item? Assuming that its first owner is the buyer, there is in theory nothing to prevent the parties agreeing that the buyer should transfer property in it to the seller. The cases show, however, that the courts will be reluctant to accept this interpretation. In *Clough Mill*, *Peachdart* and *Chisholm* the courts were

---

[135] Webb, [2000] *JBL* 513 is critical of this view, arguing that original ownership vests in the manufacturer as a matter of law.

[136] See *Dixon* v *London Small Arms Co Ltd* (1896) 1 App Cas 632.

prepared to "do violence" to the language used to give effect to what they perceived as the commercially realistic intentions of the parties. In *Chisholm* the judge proceeded on the basis that it is a presumption, rebuttable only with difficulty, that the parties cannot intend the seller to be sole owner of manufactured products. The new item will be worth more than the value of the supplier's contribution and will include value derived from the buyer/manufacturer, or other suppliers of materials, or both. To give the seller the benefit of the buyer's labour without payment would result in the seller receiving a windfall profit at the expense of the buyer and/or suppliers of other materials used in the process, which is both contrary to policy, in that it over-secures the seller, and contrary to the presumed intentions of the parties. At least where the process involves any significant addition of value, therefore, any interest the seller may claim in the finished item is likely to be construed as a charge. The parties must intend that the seller's interest should be limited to the amount due to him from the buyer, and that that interest should be defeasible on payment of that sum. It might be possible to draft a contract so that on production of a new item manufactured from the seller's property (a) the buyer is released from the obligation to pay for the original goods in return for transferring to the seller property in the new item and (b) the seller agrees to transfer property in the new item to the buyer on payment of the price for the goods from which it was made, but even such a term would not resolve the difficulty caused by the possibility that the finished item might include materials supplied by several suppliers on similar terms.

Resale of Goods and Claims to Proceeds

Where goods are supplied subject to retention of title, it will generally be anticipated that either the goods themselves or products manufactured them will be resold (a) at a profit and (b) before payment is made for the goods supplied. A principle objective of the supply of goods on credit is to allow the buyer to use them to earn the funds with which to pay for them. The effect of such a resale will normally be to extinguish the seller's property, if any, in the goods sold.

Since resale is anticipated, it will be an implied, if not an express, term of the contract between S and B that such resale is permitted. Thus, for instance, in *Romalpa* the buyer was expressly permitted to sell products manufactured from the supplier's foil and it was accepted by all parties that a further implied term permitted sale of unprocessed foil. The capacity in which B resells will depend on the contract. It was accepted in *Romalpa* that resale was effected by the buyer as agent for the seller. However, any such agency must be limited. S will be anxious not to enter into direct privity with B's customers, in order to avoid incurring contractual liability to them for the quality etc of the goods under the Sale of Goods Act implied terms,[137] whilst B will wish to sell in its own name in order to develop its own goodwill and customer base. Against this background Roskill LJ saw:

> no difficulty in the contractual concept that, as between the defendants and their sub-purchasers, the defendants sold as principals, but that, as between themselves and the plaintiffs, those goods which they were selling as principals within their implied authority from the plaintiffs were the plaintiffs' goods which they were selling as agents for the plaintiffs to whom they remained fully accountable.[138]

In subsequent cases the clause has sometimes been specifically drafted to achieve this effect. Thus, for instance, in *Tatung (UK) Ltd* v *Galex Telesure Ltd*[139] the contract provided that "the buyer shall be at liberty to sell the goods in the ordinary course of business in the name of the buyer and as principal not as agent for the company". Similarly in *Compaq Computers Ltd* v *Abercorn Group Ltd*[140] the contract permitted the buyer to deal with goods supplied but provided that "it is mutually agreed that the dealer is and shall be deemed to be an independent contractor and shall have no power, right or authority to bind Compaq or to assume or to create any obligation or responsibility, express or implied, on behalf of Compaq. Nothing stated in the agreement shall be construed as constituting the dealer and Compaq ... principal and agent".

The Effect of Resale: Section 25 Sale of Goods Act 1979 (as amended)

Plainly S will be bound by B's authorised dealings with the goods. The contract may impose limitations on B's authority to deal with the goods: for instance, limiting it to dealings "in the ordinary course of business" or by way of *bona fide* sale. Nevertheless, S's retention of title will generally be

---

137 Sale of Goods Act 1979 ss 12-15. This will be especially important if the buyer's customers are consumers as defined in the Unfair Contract Terms Act 1977, s 12.

138 [1976] 2 All ER 552 at p 563.

139 (1988) 5 BCC 325. See also Farrar and Chai, [1985] *JBL* 160.

140 [1991] BCC 484; see Sealy, [1992] *CLJ* 19.

overridden even by unauthorised dealings with the goods. Although the general rule of English law is *nemo dat quod non habet* - no-one can transfer a better title than he has - persons with whom B deals will generally be able to rely on the exception to the *nemo dat* rule contained in s 25 of the Sale of Goods Act 1979. Section 25 applies where a person who has bought, or agreed to buy, goods and is in possession of them with the consent of the owner, transfers them to another "under any sale, pledge or other disposition". Where goods are supplied by S to B subject to a retention of title clause, B will be in possession with S's consent and have agreed to buy the goods.[141] If before paying for them B then resells the goods to C, C will take a good title, overriding S's retention of title, provided only that the other requirements of s 25 are satisfied. These require that C (a) take delivery of the goods and (b) receive them in good faith and without notice of S's rights.

Like all the exceptions to the *nemo dat* rule, the objective of s 25 is to promote the free circulation of goods in commerce. Although the courts generally adopt a protective attitude to dispossessed owners of property who seek to recover that property from third parties, s 25 has, in this context, been interpreted in a manner broadly favourable to the interests of the buyer in C's position. Thus the requirement that B be in possession of the goods is satisfied if B obtains *constructive* possession of the goods which remain in the physical possession of S, as where S delivered the goods direct to C as B's agent and at B's request.[142] Similarly it is sufficient if C takes constructive delivery of the goods.[143] The traditional reluctance to admit equitable doctrines into commercial transactions means that the equitable doctrine of constructive notice has no role to play here, and C will therefore be deemed to have notice of S's rights only if he has actual notice thereof, or, possibly, if the circumstances are such that any reasonable person would necessarily have been aware of those rights. It will not be enough to deny C the protection of s 25 that retention of title clauses are in common usage. To prevent reliance on s 25 it must be shown that C had actual notice both of the existence of the retention of title clause *and* that pursuant to it the goods remained S's property.[144] The only restriction on the operation of s 25 in this context is that it will not apply unless the transaction between B and C involves a transfer of a property

---

141 The position would be different if S supplied the goods on hire purchase terms, in which case B would not be a person who has "agreed to buy" the goods.

142 *Four Point Garage* v *Carter* [1985] 3 All ER 12.

143 *Forsythe* v *Silvery Shipping, The Saetta* [1994] 1 All ER 851.

144 *Forsythe* v *Silvery Shipping, The Saetta*.

interest. So if S supplies goods to B subject to retention of title and B resells to C on similar terms, s 25 will not apply in favour of C unless and until he satisfies the condition for the transfer of property to him under his contract with B.[145]

The result, then, is that, by virtue either of s 25 of the 1979 Act or of resale being authorised, the seller's property in the goods supplied, or in products manufactured from them, will generally be overridden if the buyer resells them to a good faith purchaser. Nor will it make any difference that S's retention of title clause purports to be enforceable against and allow the goods to be recovered from purchasers from B. It is for this reason that the seller in *Romalpa* sought to establish a proprietary right to the proceeds of B's resale. The seller conceded that the buyer was entitled to sell unprocessed foil and the buyer conceded that it held the foil until resale as bailee for the seller. The Court of Appeal held that in those circumstances the buyer sold the foil and received the proceeds of sale as a fiduciary for the seller, and that the seller was therefore entitled to trace its property in the foil into the proceeds of sale which were therefore its property in equity. It was this decision which was seen as heralding the "infiltration of equitable doctrine into English commercial law".

Claims to Proceeds of Sale

If any retention of title claim going beyond a simple claim to the goods supplied, in their original form, is going to succeed, the claim to the proceeds of their resale surely looks to have the best chance. It involves no more than a transfer of the seller's property interest from the goods to their identifiable proceeds.[146] In fact, however, the bright start of *Romalpa* proved to be a false dawn and despite repeated attempts, no claim to proceeds of sale has succeeded in any reported English case since *Romalpa*.

---

[145] *Re Highway Foods Ltd* [1995] BCC 271, [1995] BCLC 209. A similar exception to the *nemo dat* rule in s 9 of the Factors Act 1889 applies in favour of a person who receives goods under any "sale, pledge or other disposition ... or agreement for sale, pledge or other disposition" but although under this provision S will be bound by B's contract with C, C will acquire no proprietary interest in the goods until the condition of B's retention of title is satisfied.

[146] Significantly in his 1989 Report *Review of Security Interests in Moveables* for the DTI, Professor Diamond recommended favourable treatment of purchase money securities including claims under retention of title clauses to the goods supplied and to the proceeds of their resale. Under the proposals a purchase money security would have priority over a bank's floating charge.

In a series of decisions at first instance the courts have repeatedly distinguished *Romalpa*, to the point where it may today be considered to be a case decided on its own facts, and this notwithstanding that the contracts in the later cases have, apparently been drafted so as to maximise the chances of invoking the principle relied on in *Romalpa*. Thus clauses have expressly referred to the buyer holding the seller's goods as "bailee", selling as "agent", within a defined authority, and holding the proceeds of sale "on trust" as a "fiduciary"; some have required the buyer to pay the proceeds of sale into a separate bank account and even to provide the seller with details of resales; others have expressly referred to the seller's interest being transferred to the proceeds of sale of its goods and required the buyer, if called upon, to assign its claims against its customers. There have even been express contractual references to the "principle in *re Hallett's Estate*". All to no avail: the courts have repeatedly refused to recognise that a retention of title seller has property rights in the proceeds of sale of its goods.

In *Romalpa* all parties agreed that the implication of a power of sale of unprocessed foil was necessary, for to hold otherwise would "stultify the whole business purpose of these transactions".[147] Now, one may question this assumption at the outset. According to normal principles of construction, *expressio unius est exclusio alterius*. The contract made express provision for resale of manufactured products but not for unprocessed foil. That might well be said to indicate that no power of sale of unprocessed foil was intended. The expectation of the parties was, after all, that the buyers would use the foil in their manufacturing process: they were manufacturers of foil products, not dealers in foil. Such an interpretation would have made no difference to the position of buyers who would have been able to rely on s 25 of the Sale of Goods Act. However, the Court of Appeal accepted that a power of sale was to be implied. The question then was to define the scope of the buyer's power of sale. The seller argued that the buyer sold as a fiduciary and received the proceeds of sale in the same capacity. Whether or not it did so depended on the proper construction of the contract. Thus Roskill LJ observed that the question "what implication is to be made ... is the all important issue"[148] and Goff LJ that the proceeds claim "comes down to a short question of construction".[149]

---

[147] Per Roskill LJ at p 563.

[148] *Ibid* at p 559.

[149] *Ibid* at p 565.

Megaw LJ agreed, although adding that the point was "by no means an easy one".[150]

The principle argument for the receiver was that the contract of sale provided for the buyers to have 75 days' credit before paying for the foil. The purpose of this provision was to improve the buyers' cashflow by enabling them to use the foil and its proceeds in their business during that period. A requirement to hold proceeds of sale as fiduciary would stultify that grant of credit - especially because the seller retained title until all sums owing to it were paid. The sellers' proposed interpretation of the clause would therefore mean that the proceeds of sale of foil would never be available for use in the buyer's business: the whole of those proceeds, including any profit element, would be the sellers' property. Roskill LJ recognised that this was a "formidable argument if one looks at the matter solely from the point of view of the [buyers]. But ... the question of business efficacy ... must be answered in the light of what both parties have expressly agreed on and therefore must be taken also to have impliedly agreed on, and not unilaterally from the point of view of one party only".[151] He continued that the purpose of the retention of title clause as a whole was, from the seller's point of view to protect the seller against the buyer's insolvency, and that purpose would be frustrated without the implication argued for by the sellers. The same approach is apparent in the judgment of Goff LJ who observed that "there are two distinct and opposing approaches to 'business efficacy' ... one, looking at the matter from the point of view of the [buyers] ... the other from the standpoint of the [sellers]". The court unanimously preferred the seller's interpretation of the contract.

This is a curious approach to contract interpretation. The general rule is that a term can only be implied in fact if it is necessary to make the contract work (give it business efficacy) and is such that it would have been agreed upon by both parties had it been put to them when the contract was made.[152] Even accepting that the purpose of the retention of title clause was to protect the seller against the buyer's insolvency, one may question whether the implication of a term requiring the buyer to hold proceeds of sale as a fiduciary was necessary in this sense. The seller had an effective security without such implication. So long as the buyer retained the foil *in specie* it could recover it. If, as anticipated, the buyer made products from the foil the seller's clause claimed property in those products and in the proceeds of their sale. Moreover the bifocal approach to business efficacy

---

[150] *Ibid* at p 568.

[151] *Ibid* at p 563.

[152] A point noted by Buckley LJ in *Borden* v *STP* [1981] Ch 25 at p 46.

seems inconsistent with the requirement that the term implied should be one to which *both* parties would have agreed. The term implied would mean that, if the buyers resold the foil at a profit, the whole of the proceeds would be the property of the seller, and be unavailable for use in the buyer's business, and this state of affairs would continue so long as the buyer owed money to the sellers. This last point clearly troubled their Lordships, but only briefly. Both Roskill and Goff LJJ happily accepted that the term implied was one which would not be enforced so long as the buyer remained solvent.

The Court in *Romalpa* therefore found that the seller was able to trace into and assert property rights over the proceeds of sale of its foil. If *Romalpa* represented a triumph for sellers, however, it was short lived. In *Bond Worth* as we have seen Slade J construed a clause retaining equitable and beneficial ownership as allowing property to pass subject to the grant back of a charge over the goods. The clause also contained express claims to proceeds of sale of the original goods, providing that in the event of sale "our beneficial entitlement shall attach to the proceeds of resale or the claim for such proceeds" and products manufactured from them. The adoption of the curious "equitable and beneficial ownership" formula seems to have been intended to reinforce the interpretation of the contract as involving a fiduciary relationship and thus the sellers' chance of claiming proceeds of sale on the basis of *Romalpa*. Nevertheless, Slade J held that the clause gave the sellers no right to trace into proceeds of sale of the goods supplied. *Romalpa* could be distinguished on several grounds. The clause in *Romalpa* had expressly referred to the buyer holding manufactured products "as fiduciary owner"; the existence of a bailment had been conceded; and there was a requirement for the buyer to store products manufactured from the seller's foil so that they would be identifiable as the seller's property. Citing *Henry* v *Hammond*[153] - which had not been considered in *Romalpa* - he observed that not all agents are fiduciaries, and the absence of a duty to keep receipts separate from the agent's own funds is an indicator that there is no fiduciary relationship. Above all, since *Romalpa* was decided on a point of construction of a particular contract, it was of little precedent value. He concluded that the most the sellers had was a charge over proceeds of sale.

Re Bond Worth set the tone for subsequent proceeds cases. In *Hendy Lennox* the sellers sought, *inter alia*, to claim the proceeds of sale of generators sold by the buyers incorporating engines supplied by the sellers.

---

153 [1913] 2 KB 515.

Staughton J distinguished *Romalpa* and rejected the claim. It was argued that *Romalpa* was decided on the basis that *re Hallett's Estate* decided that all agents and bailees are fiduciaries. Staughton J rejected that proposition. If it were correct the court in *Romalpa* would have had no need to examine the facts of the case to decide in what capacity the proceeds were received. It was, moreover, contrary to authority, and he too cited *Henry* v *Hammond* as authority that where an agent employed to sell property was not required to keep the proceeds of sale separate from his own money, he was not a fiduciary of the proceeds. He was prepared to accept that *Romalpa* might be authority that there is a presumption that an agent is a fiduciary, but any such presumption may be rebutted by an indication of a contrary intention. On the facts before him, the absence from the clause of any reference to manufactured products or proceeds of sale, any requirement of separate storage of the goods supplied[154] and any reference to the buyer as a "fiduciary", and the fact that the fiduciary relationship contended for would extend beyond the proceeds of sale of the engines supplied to the proceeds of the generators in which they were incorporated, were all significant differences from the facts of *Romalpa* which enabled the earlier decision to be distinguished. Most significantly of all, he found that no term requiring the buyer to receive sale proceeds as a fiduciary could be implied for some of the very reasons rejected or not considered in *Romalpa*. It was unnecessary to imply such a term because the parties had provided expressly for a remedy in relation to unsold goods and *expressio unius est exclusio alterius*. Moreover, implication of a fiduciary relationship would stultify the grant of credit to the buyer. "It is not easy to reconcile that with an obligation to keep the proceeds of sale in a separate account."[155]

This theme was developed in *re Andrabell Ltd.*[156] S had supplied travel bags to B subject to a simple retention of title until full payment. B became insolvent after selling a quantity of bags and S now sought to claim sums received by the receiver as a result of those sales. The contract made no provision for the proceeds of resale. It was agreed that the contract must include an implied term permitting B to resell the bags and S argued that, on the basis of *Romalpa* and the principle of *re Hallett's Estate*, the contract must also include a further implied term that so long as property in the bags remained in S, B should account to S in respect of the proceeds of resale. Recognising that a claim to the whole proceeds of sale might be

[154] Such a requirement would have been unnecessary since the goods - diesel engines - were all identifiable by serial number.

[155] At p 499.

[156] [1984] 3 All ER 407.

rejected as inconsistent with the commercial purpose of the contract, for it would deprive B of any profit from resales, S argued that the duty to account was limited to the amount owing by B to S. Nevertheless Peter Gibson J in the Chancery Division rejected this claim. Like Staughton J in *Hendy Lennox* he identified the key question as whether B stood in a fiduciary relationship with S. The sellers in *Romalpa* had relied heavily on the judgment of Jessel MR in *re Hallett's Estate* in which he had declared that where goods are deposited with an agent for sale the agent is under the same duty to account to his principal as if he were a trustee disposing of trust property. However, Jessel MR had himself qualified his own remarks later the same year in *Kirkham* v *Peel*[157] where he said:

> My observations in *[re Hallett]* had nothing whatever to do with the case of a commission merchant or agent. They were confined to the case of a bailee, ordinarily called a factor, who sells single articles, and whose duty is to remit the necessary proceeds to his principal.[158]

In *Hallett* itself Thesiger J had expressed much the same view, limiting the duty to account to the case where "a specific chattel is entrusted by one man to another, either for the purposes of safe custody or for the purpose of being disposed of *for the benefit of the person intrusting the chattel*"[159] (emphasis added). Peter Gibson J therefore concluded, like Staughton J in *Hendy Lennox* that not all agents are fiduciaries. Like Staughton J he approached the question of the buyer's fiduciary status as one of construction of the contract but whereas Staughton J had been prepared to accept that there might be a presumption that agents and bailees are fiduciaries, Peter Gibson J doubted that there was any such presumption. The seller's case for there being a fiduciary relationship depended solely on the fact that the buyer was selling the seller's goods, which it held as a bailee. Peter Gibson J did not consider that the categorisation of the buyer as a bailee was crucial to the determination of its fiduciary status. He identified a number of crucial differences between the case before him and *Romalpa*. There was no mention of the buyer acting as a fiduciary, no requirement for separate storage of the seller's goods, no provision for assignment of claims against sub-buyers. Unlike in *Romalpa* property was retained only until payment of the particular contract price. More significantly the seller did not claim to be entitled to

[157] (1880) 43 LT 71.
[158] At p 72.
[159] (1880) 13 Ch D 696 at p 723.

the whole of the proceeds of sale. This concession to the commercial reality of the situation, worked against the seller: if it was not entitled to the whole proceeds of resale, how could it be claimed that the buyer was acting as its agent? Three other factors were significant. First, there was no requirement for B to keep proceeds of resale separate from its own monies. Second, the proposed duty to account would undermine the grant of credit to the buyer. Peter Gibson J acknowledged that this had not been decisive in *Romalpa* but "there were other factors present there".[160] He did not indicate what those factors were. Finally, he concluded, there was no necessity to imply the term sought by S: the contract worked perfectly well without it, and he was not convinced that the parties would have agreed that such a term was practical.

The decisions in *Hendy Lennox* and *Andrabell* sent a clear message that, notwithstanding *Romalpa,* the courts were reluctant to find a fiduciary relationship requiring the buyer to account for proceeds of sale, but suggested, nevertheless, that careful drafting might enable a seller to bring itself within the ratio of *Romalpa.* Subsequent decisions have cast doubt even on this. *In E Pfeiffer Weinkellerei-Weineinkauf GmbH & Co* v *Arbuthnot Factors Ltd*[161] S sold wine to B subject to retention of title. The clause permitted B to resell the wine before payment but continued by requiring B to "pass on" to S "all claims that [B] gets from the sale ... with all rights including his profit amounting to his obligation to [S]". It also required B on demand by S to provide S with details of the sub-sales and to keep the proceeds of sub-sales separate from its own funds. Phillips J rejected the contention that the clause made B a fiduciary of proceeds of resales. Peter Gibson J in *Andrabell* had doubted that there is a presumption that agents are fiduciaries. Phillips J in *Pfeiffer* found a presumption the other way: where a buyer is permitted to resell goods supplied subject to retention of title before paying for them the "normal implication" is that he does so for his own account, not as a fiduciary.[162] A fiduciary relationship would mean that B held the goods in circumstances excluding any right to deal with them for his own account. Such a relationship would therefore only be found where the terms of the contract pointed positively to its existence contrary to the normal situation. Pfeiffer's clause, properly construed, contained an agreement to assign claims against sub-buyers, albeit limited to the amount of B's outstanding

---

[160] *Loc cit* fn 156 at p 416.

[161] [1988] 1 WLR 150.

[162] *Ibid* at p 159.

debt: that was an equitable assignment by way of security for a debt and defeasible on its payment, and as such was void for non-registration.[163]

Phillips J returned to the topic the following year in *Tatung (UK) Ltd* v *Galex Telesure Ltd.*[164] The sellers here had supplied television sets and other electrical goods to the buyer, who supplied them to customers by way of sale and hire. The seller sought to claim hire payments received by the buyer from its customers. The relevant contract terms[165] provided that property in the goods sold remained in the seller until payment of the price for (a) those goods and (b) any other goods sold to the buyer by the seller, but expressly permitted the buyer to "resell or otherwise deal with the goods in the ordinary course of business in the name of the buyer". They further required the buyer:- to hold the goods prior to payment "as bailee" and to store them separately so as to be identifiable as the seller's property; to hold proceeds of dealings with the goods in a separate account as "trustee" for the seller; and, on demand, to deliver up goods in its possession if it failed to pay for them on the due date or entered into liquidation or receivership. The seller claimed therefore to be entitled to the proceeds of sale, again invoking the principle of *re Hallett's Estate*. The receiver argued, however, that any interest the seller had in the proceeds arose from the wording of the contract which required the buyer to hold the proceeds on trust for the seller, and that, properly construed, the seller's interest was by way of equitable charge. Phillips J accepted the receiver's interpretation. Under the contract the sellers had only a limited interest in the proceeds, defeasible upon payment of the contract debt. Such an interpretation was in accordance with "the requirements of business efficacy having regard to the basic relationship between the [parties] of vendors and purchasers",[166] because it avoided the possibility of the sellers making a windfall profit at the expense of the buyers and their creditors. Since the charge derived from the terms of the contract, it was created by the buyer and was therefore registrable under s 95 of the Companies Act 1948 as a charge on future property of the buyer. Phillips J expressly found that the seller's interest did not arise under the principle of *re Hallett's Estate*, but added for good measure that even had it done so he would have categorised it as a charge. Jessel MR in *re Hallett* himself

---

[163] Compare the cases concerned with contractual liens over sub-freights, above at fn 53.

[164] (1988) 5 BCC 325.

[165] There were in fact two different sets of terms used at different times but the case was considered only on the basis of the second set of terms.

[166] *Ibid* at p 333.

observed that where the principle applied "the beneficial owner ... is entitled at his election either to take the property, or to have a charge on the property for the amount of the trust money". Here, where the interest of the sellers was by way of security, it would be proper to protect the seller by recognising a charge in its favour, and since the existence of the relevant fiduciary relationship depended on the terms of the contract, the charge was created by the buyers and was therefore registrable. On this basis Phillips J concluded that, properly construed, the seller's interest in *Romalpa* was by way of a registrable charge. That possibility was rejected by Mocatta J at first instance in *Romalpa* but was not considered by the Court of Appeal.[167]

A proceeds claim was again construed as a charge in *re Weldtech Equipment Ltd.*[168] S supplied welding equipment to B. The contract retained property until payment of all sums due to S but permitted resale prior to payment if the goods were bought for resale "within the framework of [the buyer's] normal business operations",[169] in which case B's rights against its customer under the resale contract were to be transferred to S "automatically upon completion of the sale". The contract required B to notify S of any resale, and to provide details of the sub-buyer, but added (crucially) "this transfer takes place for securing our claims against the purchaser and does not affect his payment obligations". In a short judgment Hoffmann J, in the Chancery Division, concluded that the clause operated by way of assignment of future debts, and, in view of these last words, such assignment was intended to be by way of charge.[170]

By this point the spirit of *Romalpa* is a weak and fading presence. A seller who makes no claim to proceeds is unlikely to persuade a court that such a right arises impliedly under the *Hallett* principle, but an express claim is likely to be construed as giving rise to a charge. The point was re-

---

[167] Phillips J found support for this analysis in the judgments in *Borden*. This conclusion must, however, be open to doubt. The principle of *re Hallett* is normally applicable where a person in a fiduciary capacity misappropriates property, and is intended to protect the beneficiary. The beneficiary will normally be unaware of the default. To require him to register a charge which arises automatically in such circumstances and of which he is almost certainly unaware would be to deprive the principle of all protective value, at least where the fiduciary is a company, in the situation where it is most important, where the fiduciary is insolvent.

[168] [1991] BCC 16.

[169] In all other cases resale was prohibited.

[170] His Lordship expressly cited and approved the reasoning of Phillips J in *Tatung*, although in fact the clause before him would appear to have been closer in language and effect to that considered by Phillips J in *Pfeiffer*.

emphasised by the decision of Mummery J *in Compaq Computers Ltd* v *Abercorn Group Ltd.*[171] C appointed A an authorised dealer for its products and entered into a dealer agreement, described as a "carefully drafted, detailed commercial document".[172] The agreement contained a retention of title to goods supplied to A until payment of sums owed by A to C. It then:-

- provided for A to hold the goods as bailee and agent for C;
- required A to take care of the goods, store them so as to be identifiable as C's property and notify any sub-bailee of C's interest;
- permitted A to dispose of the goods prior to payment in the ordinary course of its business;
- required A to account to C for the whole of any proceeds of such disposals and to keep a separate account of such proceeds; and
- required A to deliver up goods to C on demand, to enable C to sell them for its own account.

The contract further provided that A was to operate as an independent contractor with no power or authority to bind C.

The contest here was between C, the unpaid seller, and K, in whose favour A had discounted sums due to it from its customers. K argued that C's retention of title constituted a charge, void for non-registration. Mummery J considered that the accumulation of case law on retention of title clauses made it "possible to state some well settled principles without the need to refer in detail to the facts and legal discussion in individual cases".[173] A claim to proceeds could not be established simply by showing that the seller had retained title to the goods. It was necessary to establish a fiduciary relationship, the existence of which "depends on whether the parties have agreed terms, either expressly or by implication, which, when construed in the context of the whole agreement and the surrounding circumstances of the individual case, are appropriate to create such a relationship".[174] Unlike Phillips J in *Tatung* and Peter Gibson J in *Andrabell* he took the view that agency and bailment relationships are normally fiduciary but the existence of a fiduciary relationship can be negatived by the terms of the particular contract.

---

[171] [1991] BCC 484; see Sealy, [1992] *CLJ* 19.

[172] *Ibid* at p 490.

[173] *Ibid* at p 492.

[174] *Ibid* at p 493.

Now, if ever a claim to proceeds was to succeed, this looked to be it. Most of the objections raised to the existence of a fiduciary relationship in earlier cases were addressed in the dealer agreement. It was conceded that A could not create a registrable charge over proceeds if they belonged in equity to C, and that, contrary to the view of Phillips J in *Tatung*, a charge arising under the principle of *re Hallett* would not be registrable. Nevertheless, Mummery J held that, on its proper construction the agreement did not give rise to a fiduciary relationship but created a charge over proceeds. C argued that it required that, so long as sums were due to it under the agreement, A had to pay all sums received from its dealings into an account separate from its own funds, on which A could draw only for the purpose of making payments to C. On payment of all sums due to C, however, the balance on the account would become A's property. This analysis was fatal to the existence of a fiduciary relationship. "Once it is accepted that the beneficial interest in the proceeds of sale was determinable on the payment of debts, C is faced with the difficulty that the rights and obligations of the parties were in reality and in substance characteristic of those of the parties to a charge and not those of a trustee/beneficiary or other fiduciary relationship".[175] This is, in effect, the reasoning of Phillips J in *Tatung*: the seller's interest was limited to the amount of its debt and was defeasible on payment of that debt. Its origin is in the passage from the judgment of Slade J in *re Bond Worth* quoted earlier.[176] So long as the goods remained unsold, the retention of title operated according to its tenor. When A sold, however, it did so with C's authority, but for its own benefit, at prices and on terms it determined without reference to C, and with a view to making a profit for itself. A fiduciary relationship would be inconsistent with the terms of the contract.[177]

Claims to proceeds were also made in *Modelboard* and *Chisholm*. In *Modelboard* S claimed the proceeds of sale of boxes made from card it had

---

[175] *Ibid* at p 495.

[176] See text at fn 66.

[177] For good measure Mummery J added that if he were wrong in construing C's interest in proceeds as one by way of charge, K's assignment would still have priority because C's interest would then be by way of equitable assignment of the debts due to A, and as between two equitable assignees of the same debt, priority goes to the first to give notice of the assignment to the debtor, in accordance with the rule in *Dearle* v *Hall* (1828) 3 Russ 1; see also *E Pfeiffer Weinkellerei-Weineinkauf GmbH & Co* v *Arbuthnot Factors Ltd.* C's argument that the rule applied only to assignments of existing equitable interests was rejected.

supplied. The contract expressly permitted the buyer to sell products manufactured from the seller's goods, on condition that such sale take place "as agents and bailees" for the seller "and the entire proceeds thereof are held in trust for the [seller] and are not mingled with any other monies and shall at all times be identifiable as the [seller's] monies]". The clause further provided for the buyer on demand by the seller to assign its rights against its customers arising from such sales. The seller argued that there could be no question of the buyer granting a charge over proceeds for they were never the property of the buyer. The judge observed, however, that the seller's right to proceeds had to be read in light of the buyer's duty to pay the price. What would happen if the buyer sold goods at a profit? Would he remain liable to pay the price? Would the seller be entitled to retain the proceeds of sale and demand payment? He concluded that the only interpretation which made "business sense"[178] was that, in the event of resale, the seller could have recourse to the proceeds "so far as necessary to discharge the outstanding obligation" of the buyer, "subject to which the [seller] must account to the buyer for the balance". Any other solution would require implication of an "elaborate system of implied contractual obligations" in order to meet the "commercial reality"[179] of the parties' relationship. The seller's interest was therefore properly classified as a charge. In *Chisholm* the seller's claim was to products - dresses - manufactured from fabric it had supplied. However, the retention clause included a claim to proceeds of sale and the deputy judge considered the effect of that claim in the course of his construction of the claim to products. The clause permitted the buyer "as principal in the ordinary course of its business to sell the goods by bona fide sale at full market value", the proceeds of such sales to be held by the buyer "in trust for" the seller "to the extent of sums recoverable" by the seller in respect of the goods. Proceeds were to be kept in a separate bank account and for good measure the clause expressly stated that the seller should have "the right to trace such proceeds (according to the principles in *re Hallett's Estate*)" and contained a present assignment by the buyer of its claims against its customers and others in respect of goods sold. The judge concluded that since the clause only permitted sale "in the ordinary course of business" the reference to proceeds must be to the proceeds of sale of manufactured dresses, and that notwithstanding the reference to their being held "in trust", it therefore constituted a charge on the proceeds of sale of each dress

---

[178] [1993] BCLC 623 at p 628.
[179] *Ibid* at p 629.

to the extent of the sums due to the seller in respect of the sums due in respect of the batch of fabric from which the dress was made.

It is difficult to extract clear principles from these cases. As a decision of the Court of Appeal *Romalpa* remains good law but has effectively been confined to its own facts. In theory it remains possible for a seller to draft a contract so as to constitute its buyer a fiduciary of proceeds of sale, but very clear language will be required. It will not be sufficient, as it apparently was in *Romalpa*, to show that the goods sold were the seller's property. Nor will it be sufficient to show that the buyer held the goods as bailee and/or sold them as agent, for agents and bailees are not necessarily fiduciaries. *Hendy Lennox* suggests that there may be a presumption that the relationship is fiduciary, but this is doubted in *Andrabell*, and *Tatung* suggests that the presumption is the other way. Whilst this may not be correct as a matter of strict law, it seems clear that in fact the court will require clear evidence of an intention to create a fiduciary relationship, and if the contract in *Compaq* (where Mummery J was prepared to assume that there was a presumption *in favour* of a fiduciary relationship) was insufficient to achieve this effect it is difficult to see what more the seller can do. The rationale appears to be that a fiduciary relationship is inconsistent with the reality of the relationship between seller and buyer. When the buyer resells goods he does so for his own benefit. He fixes the resale price, and takes the risk of non-payment. His objective in reselling is to make a profit *for himself*. If he is treated as a fiduciary not only must he keep the proceeds separate from his own monies, thus stultifying the grant of credit which necessitated the retention of title in the first place, but, strictly, the buyer is entitled to the whole of the proceeds of sale. This approach is in fact entirely consistent with developments in the general law of agency where an agent who receives money for his principal but is free to mix it with his own monies may be personally accountable to his principal but will not hold the proceeds as a fiduciary.[180]

One may in fact question whether there is an agency relationship between seller and buyer at all. In *Romalpa* the Court of Appeal found that the buyer acted as agent *vis à vis* the seller, but as principal selling on its own behalf *vis à vis* its customers. The contract of sale will generally be drafted so as to achieve this effect. As we have seen, however, in all cases

---

[180] See *Neste Oy* v *Lloyds Bank plc* [1983] 2 Lloyd's Rep 658; *Kingscroft Insurance Co Ltd* v *H S Weavers (Underwriting) Agencies Ltd* [1993] 1 Lloyds Rep 187 at p 191; *re Japan Leasing (Europe) plc* [1999] BPIR 911; *Triffit Nurseries* v *Salads Etc Ltd* [2000] 1 All ER Comm 737.

subsequent to *Romalpa*, the court has refused to find a fiduciary relationship between the parties on the grounds that it would be inconsistent with the reality of their relationship. This is therefore a very bare agency indeed, which gives rise to neither the normal internal, nor external, consequences of agency. The reality of the parties' relationship is, surely, that the buyer resells for its own benefit, as principal, but with the express or implied licence of the seller goods which are, prior to sale, the seller's. Perhaps the intentions of the parties are better accommodated by abandoning notions of agency and treating the buyer as selling his own goods. On this analysis, where resale is contemplated and permitted, the retention of title would be qualified by an implied term that, in the event of resale, property will pass from the seller to the buyer at the moment of resale, and immediately pass from the buyer to his customer, rather as happens where goods supplied on sale or return terms are sold.

There is, of course, nothing to prevent the seller reconstituting the whole relationship as a genuine agency, under which, perhaps, the buyer would be authorised to determine resale terms and prices and be remunerated by a commission equal to the excess of the resale price over the seller's list price. It is possible to draw such a relationship so as to avoid the seller incurring contractual liability to the buyer's customers.[181] But such an arrangement might be disregarded as a sham, and cannot be guaranteed to produce the fiduciary relationship needed to give the seller proprietary rights over resale proceeds. Moreover it might be commercially unacceptable to the parties. Attempts by the seller to avoid these problems may be counter productive. An express claim to proceeds is likely to be construed as creating a charge on the grounds that the true intention of the parties cannot be that the seller is entitled to the whole of the proceeds of any sale. If the seller limits his claim to the amount of his unpaid debt he in effect acknowledges that he is not entitled to the whole of the proceeds, and thus that if he has a proprietary interest in them that interest is a limited one, defeasible on payment of the debt. Moreover, arising from the terms of the contract the charge will be one created by the buyer.

An Australian Alternative

The atmosphere in England is therefore inimicable to retention of title claims to proceeds of sale. In general the courts in Australia have been less

---

[181] See *Welsh Development Agency* v *Export Finance Co Ltd* [1992] BCLC 148 where such an arrangement was used.

hostile to retention of title claims, and the recent decision in *Associated Alloys Pty Ltd* v *Metropolitan Engineering & Fabrications Pty Ltd*[182] suggests that a claim to proceeds of sale may in some circumstances be effective. The case arose out of supplies of steel for use in manufacture. Under the contracts the seller retained title to the steel until payment of the price. The clause provided that until payment the buyer should hold the steel as fiduciary agent and bailee and store the steel separately so as to be identifiable, but could resell the steel before payment as fiduciary agent, albeit without authority to bind the seller, in which case it was to hold the proceeds of sale in trust for the seller in a separate bank account. The case turned, however, on the final part of the clause which related to the proceeds of sale of manufactured goods. The buyer used the steel in a process of fabrication, and sold the manufactured products. Although the products were made entirely from the steel supplied it was held that they were different items and no longer the seller's steel. The relevant part of the retention of title clause provided that:

> In the event that the purchaser uses the goods/product in some manufacturing or construction process of its own or some third party, then the purchaser shall hold such part of the proceeds of such manufacturing or construction process as relates to the goods/ product in trust for the vendor. Such part shall be deemed to equal in dollar terms the amount owing by the purchaser to the vendor at the time of the receipt of such proceeds.

The seller claimed on the basis of this clause to be entitled to the proceeds of sale of the products manufactured from its steel. The receiver argued that the clause should be construed as creating a charge on such proceeds which was void for non-registration. The receiver's argument was accepted at first instance and in the New South Wales Supreme Court, but the High Court of Australia found by a majority of 4 - 1 in favour of the seller. The case deserves attention not only for the authority of the court which decided it, but also because if the reasoning were adopted in England it would enable sellers to claim not merely proceeds of sale of the goods supplied but also of manufactured products. The majority started by observing that in every case the effect of a retention of title clause depends on the proper construction of the particular contract. The key issue here was the distinction between a charge and a trust. If the clause created a

---

[182] [2000] HCA 25, available at http://www.austlii.edu.au/au/cases/cth/high-et/2000/25.html.

trust it would be effective notwithstanding the lack of registration. The court recognised that:

> The distinctions involved here have been seen by some as representing a sterile, overly conceptualist approach to the solution of legal controversies. However, these distinctions serve to identify the various building blocks of the law of property. Moreover distinctions between the two institutions have been adopted by legislatures ... to mark the ambit of various regulatory regimes.[183]

The construction of the clause was not easy, but the court concluded that the reference to "proceeds of such manufacturing ... process" should be read as referring to the proceeds of sale of the products of such process. The Supreme Court of New South Wales had held that the clause related both to book debts and to actual payments received and that it therefore constituted a registrable charge on book debts. The majority of the High Court rejected this interpretation, and, whilst recognising that its interpretation left it open to the buyer to defeat the operation of the clause, for instance by factoring its book debts, construed "proceeds" as limited to actual payments received. It was then necessary to classify the seller's interest in those proceeds as arising either under a trust or a charge. At the time of the contract, there being no proceeds in existence, there was no completely constituted trust. This was however no obstacle to the seller's argument: there being a contract for value to create a trust, equity looking on as done that which ought to be done would regard the trust as completely constituted once proceeds of sale were received.[184] The absence of a requirement to keep the "trust monies" separate from the buyer's own funds was not fatal to the seller's claim: if there is no express trust, a requirement to keep funds separate may be crucial to the finding of a trust, but where there is an express trust an obligation to keep trust funds separate is imposed on the trustee as a matter of law. The key question thus became whether the contract meant what it said, and reflected the parties' true intentions. There was nothing here to suggest that the arrangement was a "sham". The Court recognised that if the contract had purported to require the entire proceeds of sale to be held on trust it might have been open to question whether it reflected the parties' true intentions, for that would

---

[183] [2000] HCA 25, para 5.

[184] If the buyer were to fail to pay the proceeds into a separate bank account as required the court considered that the seller would be able to trace the proceeds, for instance in to a general account into which they were paid.

have given the seller a windfall profit, but since the trust was limited to the amount owing to the seller, there was no such risk. A recurring theme in the English decisions on proceeds claims has been that an interest defeasible on payment of a debt is likely to be categorised as a charge - but if the seller's interest is not defeasible on payment of the debt, there will be a risk of double payment. The court concluded, however, that there was no such risk here: the contract was construed as containing an implied term that on receipt of the proceeds and constitution of the trust the buyer was released from its debt under the contract and the seller's sole interest was in the trust fund. Moreover, the objection that the constitution of a trust would stultify the grant of credit to the buyer was met by interpreting the contract as qualifying the trust so as to prevent the seller calling on the trust during that period. Thus, the court concluded:

> The contractual and trust arrangement with which this appeal is concerned did not involve the creation of ... a charge or an agreement to create one. To treat the Proceeds Subclause as an agreement which falls foul of the Law is to rewrite the statute. It is not for the courts to destroy or impair property rights, such as those arising under trusts, by supplementing the list of those rights which the legislature has selected for such treatment.[185]

The result, like that in the English cases, thus depended on the "flexible interplay of law and equity".[186] Nevertheless, the approach of the court contrasts sharply with that of the English courts in some of the decided cases. In particular the willingness of the court to imply a complex set of terms in order to prevent the trust arrangement producing a windfall for the seller is in sharp contrast with the refusal of Judge Hart in *Modelboard* to recognise a right to proceeds which would require an "elaborate system of implied contractual obligations" in order to make commercial sense.

Conclusion

Despite, or perhaps because of, twenty-five years of case law on retention of title clauses, a number of issues remain wholly or partly unresolved. Broad conclusions can, however, be drawn. A retention of title to the goods in their original form will almost certainly succeed, even if the

---

185 Para 51.

186 *Quistclose Investments Ltd* v *Rolls Razor Ltd* [1970] AC 567 *per* Lord Wilberforce at p 582.

retention is to secure payment not only of their price but also of other debts due from the buyer. Any attempt to extend the security into other property, such as proceeds of sale or products of manufacture, is likely to fail, being construed as giving rise, at best, to a charge. The infiltration of equitable doctrine represented by the *Romalpa* decision has thus been rebuffed. Determining, correctly, it is submitted, that in general the imposition of fiduciary obligations is inconsistent with the commercial reality of the contractual relationship of buyer and credit seller, the courts have denied the seller an equitable interest in proceeds or products merely because of his ownership of the original goods, so that if any such interest arises it is created contractually.[187] The seller may claim an equitable interest in proceeds or products, but the categorisation of that interest depends on the proper construction of the sale contract, and it seems that it is likely to be construed as a charge. In the "flexible interplay of law and equity" on which the cases turn it has therefore been the legal principles of contract interpretation which have exerted the dominant influence.

Sometimes, as in *Romalpa* itself, the approach to contract interpretation may be questioned. In general, however, the approach adopted seems to reflect the modern "commercial" or "purposive" approach. The language of the reports is full of references to the "commercial reality" of the situation and the need to achieve the parties' purpose. Parties are assumed to have drafted their contracts in the light of previous decided cases.[188] Interpretations which would produce unreasonable results are rejected.[189] Contract terms are interpreted against their context or, as we might now say, background matrix of fact. In *Clough Mill* Robert Goff LJ said "In every case, we have to look at the relevant documents and other communications which have passed between the parties, and to consider them in the light of the surrounding circumstances, in order to ascertain the rights and duties of the parties inter se, always paying practical regard to the effect of any conclusion concerning the nature of those rights and duties".[190]

If the issue is treated, as it has been, as one of contract interpretation, it is not surprising that there are inconsistencies in the case law. In any

---

[187] See McMeel, "Retention of title: the interface of contract, unjust enrichment and insolvency" *Restitution and Insolvency*, Rose (ed).

[188] See, for example, *Ian Chisholm Textiles Ltd* v *Griffiths, loc cit* fn 130.

[189] See the comments of Judge Neuberger in *Chisholm* at pp 101-2; compare the comments of Lord Reid in *Schuler* v *Wickman Machine Tool Sales Ltd* [1974] AC 235 at p 251, [1973] 2 All ER 39 at p 45.

[190] *Loc cit* fn 126 at p 987.

particular case everything will turn on the precise wording of the particular contract. Thus the decision in *Bond Worth* can be reconciled with those *Clough Mill* and *Armour* v *Thyssen* as depending on the use of the formula "equitable and beneficial ownership". Similarly, the proceeds cases subsequent to *Romalpa* can be reconciled with that case on the basis that the *Romalpa* case was decided on the wording of the particular contract and the facts of the case. But these explanations are not entirely satisfying, for the differences in approach evident in these cases run deeper than simply matters of construction. In relation to claims to the original goods the contract is taken at face value, the court implying terms, if necessary, to give it efficacy and make it work as the parties "must have intended", even if the effect, as in the cases of all monies clauses and homogenous mixing of goods, is very much like that of a floating charge, effectively appropriating a fluctuating pool of assets for satisfaction of the seller's claims against the buyer from time to time. The approach in relation to claims to proceeds and products is quite different. Here the courts repeatedly adopt a "commercial" approach and conclude that the literal meaning of the contract cannot reflect the parties' true intentions. This difference in approach is sometimes apparent in individual decisions, most notably in *Clough Mill* where the same wording is effective to retain title to original goods but gives rise to a charge over products manufactured from those goods.

Is there some deeper principle underlying the cases which might explain these differences in approach? It is not simply a distinction between common law and equity, for we find in the cases judges from common law and equity backgrounds adopting both approaches. Indeed, it is striking that in the four cases to come before an appellate court in England there has been not one dissenting judgment. Why, then, are the courts willing to uphold retention of title claims to the original goods but deeply reluctant to accept any claim to manufactured products or proceeds of sale? Why refuse to allow the seller an equitable lien over the goods but allow him to achieve much the same effect by contract?

In general the appeal to "purposive interpretation" conceals a judicial sleight of hand. Before interpreting the contract the judge must determine its purpose, but the purpose must be determined primarily from the language of the contract itself. Often the judge will be faced with a choice between two or more "purposes". In the present context, for instance, the parties' purpose may be said to be to provide the seller with security, or to provide the seller with a security having priority over the bank's floating charge without the need for registration. The choice is vividly illustrated in

Romalpa itself and the subsequent proceeds cases, where there is a clash between the objectives of the buyer - to obtain effective credit - and the seller - to obtain an effective security. In *Romalpa* the court gave priority to the seller's purpose; in the later cases to the buyer's. Insofar as the cases depend on classification of transactions they raise the same issue. Purpose, we are told, is not determinative of the classification of a transaction. Classification depends on substance, as reflected in the contract terms. But the construction of the meaning of those contract terms depends on the judge's view of the parties' purpose and thus depends, at least in part, on the classification of the contract. In short the processes of interpretation and classification are closely bound together. There is no obvious right starting point to the process, which must therefore depend to some extent on judicial policy preferences.

The academic's description of a decision as based on "policy" is often a metaphorical shrug, indicating an inability to identify a doctrinal explanation for a decision. If commercial law has a policy it is that it should so far as possible facilitate commercial activity. As the High Court of Australia recognised in the *Associated Alloys* case, upholding retention of title claims may promote such activity:

> The lack of any statutory obligation to register the Proceeds Subclause ... creates commercial incentives for entities, in the position of both the Buyer and the Seller, to incorporate [such clauses] into their purchase agreements. These clauses reduce the risk of non-payment by the buyer. To the extent that this financial, or credit risk is reduced, the commercial viability of the transaction for both parties may be increased. For example the availability of this means of reducing credit risk for the seller may result in the seller accepting a lower cost price [for the goods].[191]

If the protection of the credit seller facilitates commerce, why limit that protection to an interest in the original goods? Why, indeed, deny the seller an equitable lien? The approach to proceeds and products claims might be seen as motivated by a concern to avoid the seller's being over secured and obtaining a "windfall profit". But the seller may also achieve a profit if he repossesses and resells goods on a rising market. That is not seen as a reason to deny effectiveness to a simple retention of title: the seller is entitled to the profit because he is simply repossessing his own property. It may be objected that the difference is that the profit in the case of original goods, unlike that in the case of products or proceeds, is not derived from

---

[191] At para 50.

the efforts or property of the buyer. As the decision in *Associated Alloys* shows, however, implication of appropriate terms might prevent the seller obtaining a windfall under proceeds or products claims. Conversely, if the seller were entitled to an equitable lien over the goods (or their proceeds) there would be no risk of a windfall, for a lienee's interest is limited to the amount of the unpaid debt.

One of the reasons generally given for the commercial law's suspicion of equity is its uncertainty. The truth, however, as the retention of title cases show, is that if all depends on construction, contract law itself is no more predictable. Another objection to equitable interests is that equitable property rights are undiscoverable and thus pose a threat to commercial activity. In *Transport and General Credit Corporation Ltd* v *Morgan* Simonds J explained that recognition of an equitable lien in favour of an unpaid seller of goods would "throw into confusion the law in regard to bankruptcy and in regard to any other matter which has been treated as regulated by the same principles".[192] Similarly, Goodhart and Jones, commenting on the retention of title phenomenon, wrote that "The trust is then a snare for secured and unsecured creditors, for no reasonable investigation may ever reveal that a company holds goods on trust for another".[193] The equitable charge, being registrable, poses no such threat. But if this is an objection to concealed security interests it is an objection to retention of title claims to the original goods - including hire purchase and conditional sale - as well as to claims to proceeds of sale and manufactured products. In each case the seller's interest operates as a security which takes priority over the interests of all other creditors, disturbing the statutory prescribed order for payment of their claims, and yet escapes registration and which can therefore be discovered no more easily than a trust. In the case of an all monies retention it may be impossible to determine precisely what the buyer owns, without detailed examination of its trading records from time to time. And, as we have seen, the courts do not only reject equitable property rights but also seem reluctant to recognise a claim to legal property in manufactured products.

The real objection is to the recognition of any undiscoverable property interest which, being enforceable against third parties, may hinder commerce by undermining the certainty of transactions. Recognition of the seller's interest in the original goods under a simple retention of title creates no such problems. The exception to the *nemo dat* rule in s 25 of the

---

192 [1939] Ch 531 at p 546.

193 *Op cit* fn 16 at p 491.

Sale of Goods Act means that a purchaser of the goods will normally take free of the seller's interest. In contrast the seller's equitable interest in proceeds of sale or manufactured products arising out of a fiduciary relationship would be enforceable against anyone but a bona fide purchaser for value without notice of the seller's interest and, being equitable, would bring with it the doctrine of constructive notice against which commercial law has set its face. The same would be true of the recognition of interests arising under a trust, so that the Australian approach to proceeds claims adopted in *Associated Alloys* would be unacceptable to an English court. On this basis the decision in *re Bond Worth* is explicable and defensible, as is the refusal to recognise an equitable lien over the original goods, their proceeds or products. So, too, is the refusal to recognise the seller as outright legal owner of manufactured products. A legal property interest would be enforceable against the whole world, and a purchaser of the product would be unprotected by s 25, which applies where the purchaser of goods contracts to resell those goods.

There is no reference to these issues in the cases. Nevertheless it would seem that, in determining the effectiveness of retention of title claims, the English courts have drawn the line in the right place, striking a balance between providing the credit seller with effective protection whilst avoiding giving effect to property rights which would hinder commercial activity. The result may not be entirely intellectually satisfying, but it is perhaps typical of the pragmatic approach of English commercial law.

3 Rights of Ownership in Goods

PIP GIDDINS

Overview

In this chapter we shall consider the restrictions on the rights of an owner of goods to retake possession of its goods and keep the sale proceeds of them. This will be in the context where the owner of the goods (a Finance House) supplies the goods to the person who seeks to have use of those goods (the customer) in circumstances where the customer does not buy the goods and pay the purchase price at the outset and the Finance House keeps ownership of the goods.

In practice, the likely legal structures of such a supply are:

(1) sale subject to a *reservation of title* clause.[1] This is often used where a wholesaler supplies stock to a trader. The wholesaler agrees that the retail trader need not pay the purchase price until the retail trader resells the goods to the ultimate retail buyer or expiry of an agreed period if sooner, for example, six months;[2]

(2) sale under a *conditional sale* agreement. The buying customer is committed at the outset to buy the goods and pay the purchase price. However, the purchase price (plus any finance charges) is paid by

[1] The agreement could be: (1) a conditional sale agreement by which the buyer is committed to buy the goods and pay for them; or (2) sale or return by which the buyer has the option (a) to appropriate the goods and acquire title or (b) to return the goods to the supplier and have no further liability.

[2] If the nature of supply is sale or return, and not conditional sale, then the tax point for value added tax (VAT) can be postponed until appropriation.

instalments,[3] and property[4] in the goods[5] does not pass to the buyer until the purchase price is paid;[6]

(3) supply under a *hire purchase* agreement. This is where the customer does not agree to buy the goods. Instead, the customer (the hirer) hires the goods in consideration of rentals and has the option to buy the goods (and so acquire property) at the end of the hire period;

(4) supply under a *lease* or *rental* agreement. This is similar to hire purchase but with no option for the hirer to buy the goods.

In practice, the following terminology is used:

- "**lease**" is used where the relationship is between (1) an owner[7] whose principal interest is financial: to recover the capital cost[8] of the goods;[9] and (2) a hirer whose principal interest is to have use of the goods, usually over a medium term, for example, 1-7 years;
- "**rental**" is used where the relationship is between (1) an owner whose principal interest is to make an income from successive lettings of the goods; and (2) a hirer who wishes to have use of the goods for a short term, for example, one day or one month, or indefinitely from day to day until the hirer no longer needs the goods;
- "**finance lease**" has a special meaning under accounting conventions[10] but in general terms means a hire agreement under which the hirer is committed to pay rentals which cover the capital cost plus "interest";

---

[3] The price does not have to be paid by instalments but usually it is; for example, cash price £3,000 plus finance charges of £600 payable by 36 monthly instalments of £100.

[4] "Property" means "ownership" or "title". See Sale of Goods Act 1979, s 61(1).

[5] It is possible to have a conditional sale of land as well.

[6] It would still be conditional sale if the agreement provided for property to pass before the whole of the purchase price is paid, for example, on payment of the 18th of the 36 instalments. However, this is uncommon.

[7] Strictly a "bailor"; it need not be the owner of the goods. The bailor could itself hire the goods from a "head-lessor".

[8] The purchase price payable by the owner to buy the goods; their "cash price".

[9] Either from the original lease (a finance lease) or partly from the original lease (an operating lease) and partly from subsequent resale or re-letting of the goods.

[10] For example SSAP 21.

- "**operating lease**" likewise has a special accountancy meaning but in general terms means a hire agreement under which (1) the aggregate amount of the rentals that the hirer must pay is less than the capital cost, and so (2) to recover its "investment" in the goods (that is, the cash price) the owner will look to receive (i) additional rental under the operating lease if the hirer chooses to extend the hiring; (ii) rental under a subsequent lease with another hirer; or (iii) proceeds of re-sale of the goods after the end of the hiring.

The Nature of the Respective Interests of the Owner and the Hirer[11]

A person may have the following interests in, or in the context of, goods:

(1) A right *in rem*, or real right: sometimes called a proprietary right. This is a right in the goods: I have ownership of the goods or I have possession of the goods,[12] rather than I have a right against someone else to require delivery of goods or transfer of ownership of the goods.

(2) A right in *personam ad rem.* This is a right to require someone to deliver goods or transfer ownership of them. At such time (if ever) as I have acquired ownership or possession of the goods, I shall have a real right in the goods. Until then, I have only a personal claim.

(3) A right *in personam*: a purely personal right. This is a purely personal claim against someone else to perform some obligation. For example, having bought goods from you on terms that you will make good any defect appearing within one year; I have a personal claim against you to perform your obligation.

In the current context our concern is with the real rights of ownership or possession as opposed to any other right. The main significance of these real rights is that they take priority upon insolvency: the person having the real right can assert it against a liquidator or trustee in bankruptcy.

---

[11] In English Law the correct term is "bailee".

[12] In the context of this chapter we shall not consider rights by way of equitable charge which are real rights, although not proprietary rights.

We have established that the two real rights (rights *in rem*), in goods are ownership and possession. We can call the right of ownership the "legal title" to the goods. The Sale of Goods Act 1979 calls this "property" in the goods. The owner has all the legal rights to the goods subject only to any specific rights in the goods which have been granted to others. For example, if FH is the owner of goods, and FH lets the goods (bails them) to H, then FH is still the owner: but subject to the rights of H. A person in possession of goods is considered to have a legal title to the goods, even though it is not an absolute title. In the example of our equipment lease, H has all the legal rights of an owner against the whole world other than the true owner (FH). If a third party (T) wrongfully converts the goods, H can sue T in the tort of conversion. If a person is the owner of the goods and has possession of them, that person can be said to be the absolute owner with an indefeasible title. It is possible for more than one person to own the legal title to goods, by way of co-ownership: as joint tenants or tenants in common. However, it remains a single legal title. It is not possible to split (divide) a legal title to goods or to grant a subordinate legal interest which will co-exist with the original legal title: other than a separate legal right of possession.

The position of goods can be contrasted with that of land, for example, F owns the freehold of land (fee simple) and grants a lease for a term of 3 years or longer in writing to L. F grants a legal mortgage of the freehold to M1. L grants a charge by way of legal mortgage of the leasehold to M2. All four parties have legal interests in the land: F, L, M1 and M2. In contrast, consider the position where an owner of goods (O) grants a legal mortgage of the goods to M1. Here M1 acquires a legal title and O divests itself of legal title, retaining only an equity of redemption. Of course O may retain possession of the goods and so have a separate coincidental legal title as possessor: but subject to the single legal right of ownership vested in M1. It is for this reason that, if O purports to sell the goods to a third party buyer (T), then M can assert priority over T.[13] If O granted a fixed charge on the goods to M2, then this would be an equitable charge and not create a legal interest. With the legal mortgage to M1 O transferred the legal title to M1: M1 acquired the legal title and O lost it. With the fixed charge, O retains the legal title and M2 does not acquire it.

---

[13] See *The Shizelle* [1992] Lloyds LR 444 (High Court). Note that O is not a seller in possession and so cannot pass good title to T under s 24 of the Sale of Goods Act 1979.

Now consider the position of an agreement by the owner of goods, a Finance House (FH), to let (bail) the goods to a hirer (H). We have already seen that (1) FH has the legal title as owner; (2) if H has possession, then H has the legal title as possessor. Imagine that FH enters into the equipment lease with H, but has not yet delivered the goods to H. The goods remain in the possession of FH. Of course if FH wrongfully refuses to deliver the goods to H, then H has a claim for damages against FH: a purely personal right. If FH sells the goods to a third party (T) then T acquires the legal title as owner. Even if T knew of O's obligation to H, if T refused to deliver the goods to H then H would have only a personal claim against T.[14] H's right is not a derivative interest carved out of the owner's legal title. If H acquires possession of the goods then, by coincidence, H acquires a new separate original legal interest as possessor. If H does not acquire possession, H has no legal interest. Of course it is possible for a person to have a right of possession of goods - and so a legal title to them - other than as a result of a bailment (hiring). For example, the owner of goods (O) may transfer possession of the goods to someone else (P) to hold them as security for a loan to O. This is called a "pledge" or a "pawn" and P is a pawnbroker. O is still the owner of the goods and has a legal title as such. P is the possessor and has a legal title as such. P is entitled to retain possession until O repays the loan.

We have seen that the legal interest of an owner of goods is indivisible: there is only one legal interest of ownership. However, it is possible for the legal owner to grant a subsidiary equitable interest in the goods. For example, O can declare itself trustee of the goods for a beneficiary B: O retains the legal title while B acquires a beneficial (equitable) title. It is possible for more than one person to share the (single) right to possession. FH can let goods to H1 and H2 to enjoy possession jointly. In passing we can note that a legal owner is not able to transfer the legal title to someone else while retaining the beneficial (equitable) title itself. Above we have seen that O can declare itself trustee for B and so transfer equitable trust to B; but O could not transfer legal title to B while retaining equitable title itself. This can be summarised by saying that an equitable interest in goods must be created by grant and not by reservation. This principle was illustrated in *Re Bond Worth.*[15]

---

[14] In tort for wrongful interference with the contract between FH and H.

[15] [1979] 3 All ER 919.

Just as a legal interest as owner is not divisible, so a legal interest as possessor is not divisible: there is only one right of possession. Thus where O is the owner of goods, and H is a hirer (bailee) from O, and H has possession of the goods, each legal title is indivisible: O has the legal title of owner and H the legal title of possessor. On termination of the bailment to H, O becomes entitled to possession: but until O recovers physical possession, O has no right as possessor. In the same context it is suggested that the owner has a right of "constructive possession" even though the goods are in the physical possession of someone else as bailee. The example given illustrates this. Another example is where the owner (O) deposits goods with a warehouseman (W). W is a bailee from O and is in possession. The capacity in which W holds possession of the goods is rather different from that of our equipment lease hirer: unlike H, W does not have any right to use the goods - only a right to retain possession until O pays the storage charge. It can be said that W holds possession to the order of O subject only to W's lien on the goods for payment of warehouse charges. However, it is submitted that, at best, this is confusing. O has only a right to possession, not actual possession. In consequence, O has no legal title as possessor: only O's separate legal title as owner. There is one possessory legal title and that is vested in the possessor: W.

The Use of Security

Where a customer raises money from a Finance House, the Finance House may require security to cover the liabilities of the customer to repay the money with interest and other charges. The principal legal mechanisms available in the context of personal property will now be discussed.

Security in Goods with Transfer of Possession: a Pawn

Under English and Welsh law (and Scottish law) it is possible to create a security interest in goods by the act of transfer of possession of the goods to the mortgagee. This security right is called a "pawn" or a "pledge" (the two terms are interchangeable). Creditors who are willing to grant loans on this basis are called "pawnbrokers". The interest rate is usually high to reflect the ease of access to the loans and the short lending periods. For example, an individual may pawn a watch as security for a loan of £200 on the basis that the loan is to be repaid after three months with interest at 4 per cent per month. The practical disadvantage of a pawn is that the borrower loses possession and use of the pawned asset. In the absence of transfer of possession of the asset, it is not possible to have a pawn. A mortgage of goods without transfer of possession is called a bill of sale.

Mortgage of Goods: a Bill of Sale

To be valid and enforceable the mortgage in the form of a bill of sale must comply with all requirements of the Bills of Sale Acts.[16] These requirements are technical in detail, and the consequences of non-compliance are very serious: the lender may be unable to claim repayment of the loan, let alone enforce the right of security in the goods. The requirements include: (1) the form of the Bill of Sale must follow the statutory form set out in the schedule to the Bills of Sale Act 1878 (Amendment) Act 1882, failing which the Bill is void; (2) execution of the Bill by the borrower must be witnessed; and the witness must make a statutory declaration to confirm that he or she witnessed the execution; (3) the Bill of Sale and statutory decoration must be registered with the Bills of Sale Registry, and a small fee paid, within seven days following execution of the Bill of Sale; (4) the interest rate must be a fixed rate, and not a floating rate linked to an index such as a base rate; (5) the Bill of Sale must be executed before the loan is advanced: a Bill of Sale security for prior advances will be void; (6) upon enforcement, the mortgagee must "seize" the goods but then leave the goods at the premises where they were seized for five days before removing the goods and selling them.[17] In practice with freely moveable goods it is impractical to comply with this requirement: if the goods are left in the possession of the defaulting borrower for five days, then it is likely that the borrower will remove the goods and hide them.

Because of the difficulty in complying with the Bills of Sale legislation, it is uncommon for Bills of Sale to be taken as security. Following the introduction of the Bills of Sale legislation, lenders developed new ways of obtaining security in goods. This led to the development of the hire purchase mechanism.

---

[16] Bills of Sale Act 1878; Bills of Sale Act 1878 (Amendment) Act 1882.

[17] Bills of Sale Act 1878 (Amendment) Act 1882 s 13.

Hire Purchase and Conditional Sale

In practice, it is common for goods to be used as security for credit advanced to finance the purchase of those goods. For example, if an individual buys a motor car then he or she may borrow money to finance that purchase: for example, if a new car costs £12,000, then the buyer may have £3,000 and need to borrow the other £9,000. The motor car will provide good security to the lender provided that its depreciating value exceeds the reducing balance of the loan outstanding. With hire purchase, usually the purchase fee payable on exercise of the option to purchase is substantially less than the value of the goods: for example, £100. On expiry of the (say) 36 months period of hire, the customer has a choice: (1) to buy the car for the purchase fee of £100, or (2) not to buy the car, in which case the hirer delivers up possession to the Finance House with no further right or obligation. The Finance House can then resell or re-let the car, or do whatever it wishes with it.

In the case of conditional sale, the Finance House sells the goods to the individual customer on terms that: (1) the customer may pay the purchase price by instalments for example, 36 monthly instalments, and (2) until all instalments are paid (or some other specified event occurs) property in (title to) the goods remains in the Finance House. The buyer is committed to buy the goods. Unlike hire purchase, conditional sale is not the grant of possession with an option to buy. In practice the instalments are calculated to recover to the Finance House the credit plus finance charges.[18]

If the hire purchase hirer were asked "What is the nature of your credit agreement?" it is likely that he or she would answer as follows: "I buy the goods and pay for them, with interest, by instalments, and the Finance House can take the goods away from me if I fail to pay the instalments". It is unlikely that the hirer would consider that he or she is hiring the goods in return for rental and, as a separate matter, may or may not choose to buy the goods at the end of the hire period for a purchase fee. Can it therefore be said that an agreement for hiring with an option to purchase truly reflects the agreement made between the parties? Is the true position that the Finance House is providing credit to finance purchase of the goods by the individual, taking a security interest in the individual's

---

[18] With hire purchase (usually) there must be a purchase fee payable with the last instalment: *Carlyle Finance Limited* v *Forthright Finance Limited* [1997] 4 All ER 99. With conditional sale there is no need for any fee. It follows that "interest free credit" must be written on conditional sale rather than hire purchase.

goods to cover the risk of non-payment? The courts have considered this question and, in the main, clearly answered it in favour of the validity of hire purchase.[19] It is now clearly established that if parties voluntarily choose to structure the supply of goods as being a hiring, then they are free to do so.

The position may be different where, at the outset, the customer is the owner of the goods. For example if, as a business person, I own a machine worth £10,000, and I need to raise money for my business, then I am entitled to sell that machine on the open market for £10,000 and use the sale proceeds for my funding requirements. If I wish to have continued use of that machine, then I am entitled to sell that machine to an equipment rental company for £10,000 and then agree to hire back that equipment under a hire contract. In England and Wales such a sale and lease back of equipment is permitted. For example, I could: (1) hire the equipment for £300 per month from month to month indefinitely until terminated by either side by one month's notice; or (2) hire the equipment for a minimum period or 36 months at £300 per month, and after then at £1 per month indefinitely until terminated by the hirer (or by either side) by one month's notice. However, what if I wish to hire the equipment for a fixed period of 36 months, and at the end of that 36 months have the right to repurchase the equipment whether for its then value or for a pre-agreed amount? The courts have been ready to conclude that the true intention of the parties was that I am mortgaging my equipment to the Finance House as security for a loan on the basis that I can re-acquire my title by paying off the balance of loan outstanding.[20] If the true nature or the transaction is that I am mortgaging my property as security for a loan, then the consequence is: (1) if I am an individual, then the mortgage should have been documented and registered as a security Bill of Sale, and so the security is void and the loan irrecoverable; while (2) if I am a company, then the mortgage should have been registered in the Mortgages Register with the Registrar of Companies within 21 days following execution, failing which the mortgage is void against a liquidator or another creditor: s 395 of the Companies Act 1985.

---

[19] *Helby* v *Matthews* [1895] AC 471.

[20] For example *Polsky* v *S and A Services* [1951] 1 All ER 102; *Re Watson* (1890) 25 QBD 27.

Right to Proceeds of Resale of the Goods

With hire purchase or conditional sale, if the net sale proceeds of the goods are insufficient to cover the balance of credit owing, then (under the terms of the agreement) the Finance House may reserve a right to claim money damages from the customer. This is not a simple money claim for a debt due. Rather, the Finance House is claiming damages to compensate it for loss suffered. In practice, it is usual for the parties to agree (within the terms of credit agreement) the amount of damages to the paid upon premature termination. Sometimes this is called a liquidated damages clause. Such a liquidated damages clause may not be enforceable following breach of obligation by the hirer in the absence of repudiation as in *Financings Limited* v *Baldock.*[21] If the clause is enforceable in principle, because the hirer has repudiated the agreement, then still it will be valid only if the amount of compensation specified is a genuine pre estimate of the loss likely to the suffered by the Finance House as a consequence of the breach.[22] Conversely, if the net sale proceeds of the repossessed goods exceed the unpaid balance of hire rent then, until recently,[23] it was considered that the Finance House may keep the windfall surplus. The Finance House is the owner of the goods. Subject to any encumbrances that the Finance House has created, the Finance House can do whatever it wishes with the goods. The Finance House created the encumbrances of the hirer's right of possession and the hirer's option to purchase the goods. However, following default by the hirer, the Finance House has validly terminated those rights of the hirer. Those rights cease to exist. Therefore once again the Finance House is the unencumbered owner of the goods and can do what it wishes with them.

Examples of Different Legal Structures Applied to the Same Economic Context

Imagine that a company wishes to acquire a new item of machinery which the dealer will sell for £8,000 (sometimes called "the capital cost"). The company has only £500. The company wishes to acquire immediate exclusive use of the machine under its own control at its own risk. The company is willing to pay the full amount of the capital cost of the machine, plus interest over a period of three years, but - having done so -

---

[21] [1963] 2 QB 104.

[22] *Robophone Facilities* v *Blank* [1966] 3 All ER 128.

[23] See pp 125-142 below.

would wish then to have the right to sell the machine and keep the sale proceeds, and the right to use the machine indefinitely until the company chooses to sell. We shall now consider how this objective can be met by the use of three alternative financing techniques.[24]

Loan secured by a mortgage of the machine. The Finance House will lend £7,500 to the company towards this. The company will repay this £7,500, with interest of £1,500, by 36 monthly payments of £250. As security the company will mortgage the machine to the Finance House: thus title to the machine is vested in the Finance House. The Finance House has the legal interest of ownership while the company has the legal interest of possession. When the last repayment has been made, the Finance House will release the mortgage and the company is the unencumbered owner: the company now has the legal interest of ownership and the legal interest of possession.

Hire Purchase. The Finance House buys the machine from the dealer for £8,000. Thus title to the machine is vested in the Finance House: the Finance House has the legal interest of ownership. The Finance House lets the machine on hire to the company for a fixed period of three years. The machine is delivered to the company which now has the legal interest of possession. On the date of the agreement the company pays an advance payment of £500. At the end of each month, for 36 months, the company pays a rental in arrears of £250. Thus the Finance House recovers its credit advanced of £7,500 plus finance charges of £1,500. On the last day of the period of hire, the company has the option (granted in the original hire purchase contract) to buy the machine for £10. Upon exercise of the option to purchase, the Finance House no longer has any interest and the company is the unencumbered owner: because the legal interest of ownership has passed from the Finance House to the company.

Finance Lease. The Finance House buys the machine from the dealer for £8,000. Thus title to the machine is vested in the Finance House. The Finance House lets it on hire to the company for a period of hire as follows: (1) a fixed Primary Period of three years. The company pays an Initial

---

[24] The treatment in all cases ignores taxation consequences of each financing technique.

Rental of £500 followed by 36 monthly rentals in advance[25] of £250;[26] (2) after the Primary Period, an indefinite Secondary Period from year to year until such time as the company chooses to terminate the hiring by notice. The company pays annual rentals in advance of a nominal £10 p.a. (or a peppercorn);[27] (3) there is no option for the company to purchase the machine. The company can enjoy virtually the same rights of use of the machine as an owner by hiring it indefinitely for a nominal rental. However, how does the company enjoy the "equity" in the machine; having paid off its capital cost, how can the company sell the machine and keep the sale proceeds? The answer is by "agency" and "Residual Value Refund". The company has a right - under the terms of the original lease contract - acting as agent for the Finance House, to sell the machine to a third party;[28] and upon receipt of the sale price by the Finance House, the Finance House will - under the terms of the original lease contract - make a rebate of rentals to the company of an amount equal to 99 per cent[29] of that sale price. Thus, with a Finance Lease, the company has the legal interest of possession but never has the legal interest of ownership.

We have three alternative structures with very different legal content but which achieve the same economic outcome. In the case of the mortgage taken to secure repayment of the loan, it is accurate to say that the purpose of the mortgage is to secure repayment of the loan and interest. In the case of the hire purchase and lease agreements this is not accurate: the Finance House is the owner; and the company has only the legal interest of possession coupled with personal rights against the Finance House.

---

[25] In practice while hire purchase rentals are usually payable in arrears, equipment lease rentals are usually payable in advance. Thus the rental pattern would probably be an Initial Rental of £750 followed by 35 monthly rentals of £250.

[26] Thus the Finance House recovers its "investment" of £8,000 plus "profit" of £1,500.

[27] One assumes a peppercorn because it is physically small and of trivial value which supports the smallness and triviality of the value of the rental. The writer has seen a more attractive alternative of "one white rose to be delivered on Mid-summer's Day".

[28] Alternatively the lease contract may say the hirer can introduce a third party buyer to the Finance House which will then sell to that buyer. This avoids any risk attached to the hirer acting as agent of the Finance House.

[29] The amount of the percentage is subject to negotiation. The Finance House may consider it should keep some part of the sale proceeds to support the fact it is owner of the machine, not a mere mortgagee. In theory the Inland Revenue may argue a 100 per cent refund shows that the Finance House is not the owner and should not receive capital allowances.

However, in a commercial sense it can be said that the Finance House's right to terminate the agreement if default should occur, and then to take possession of the machine and sell it, is to secure payment of the rentals. Once the fixed mandatory rentals have been paid, the Finance House no longer has any real interest in the machine: with hire purchase it actually transfers title to the company, while with a finance lease it no longer has any practical interest.

It is of interest to note that the accounting treatment of the machine will follow the economic reality rather than the legal structure. Under SSP21 the machine will be treated the same whether it is acquired with a loan, hire purchase or finance lease. It will be an asset on the company's balance sheet, and the liability to pay all instalments will be shown as a liability. The tax treatment is a hybrid. First, for value added tax (VAT) purposes hire purchase is similar to a loan: the company pays VAT on the cash price at the outset[30] but no VAT on the finance charges or rentals. In contrast, with leasing the Finance House does not charge VAT on the cash price, but does so on each rental. Second, for capital allowances, again hire purchase is similar to loan: the company claims them and the Finance House does not. With leasing the Finance House claims the capital allowances: although since the Finance Act No2 1997 at a reduced rate with a finance lease. Third, for corporation tax/income tax relief with hire purchase the company claims relief on the finance charges but not the rentals: just as a borrower claims relief on the interest but not repayment of capital. With leasing the company claims tax relief on the rental (subject to limits with a motor car).[31]

The Perceived Unfairness to the Customer

When a hirer enters into a hire purchase agreement, the expectation of both sides is that: the hirer will pay off the balance so that the Finance House recovers its credit and interest; and the hirer will then continue to have possession of the goods with all the rights of an owner, including the right to sell the goods and retain the sale proceeds; but if the hirer fails to repay the credit, then the Finance House may retake possession of the goods and

[30] Strictly the Finance House buys the goods and recovers input VAT on the cash price. Then the Finance House accounts for output VAT on the cash price as suppliers under the hire purchase agreement (which the hirer can recover as input VAT). The Finance House will usually require that the advance payment payable by the hirer should at least equal the VAT.

[31] In the case of a finance lease, the position is more complicated. See SP3/91.

sell them with a view to recovering its loss; and if the net sale proceeds of the goods are insufficient to cover the balance owing, then the hirer must pay the shortfall. The strict legal position is that the Finance House has the legal interest of ownership and on termination of the hiring (for example, because of the hirer's insolvency) the Finance House is entitled to retake possession: upon which the Finance House becomes the unencumbered legal owner. As we have seen, in these circumstances the Finance House has the rights of unencumbered ownership and so may retake possession of its goods, sell them, and keep the whole of sale proceeds.

In the circumstances where the value of the goods exceeds the balance owing, the hirer may perceive it as unfair that the Finance House should be entitled to terminate the agreement for some trivial matter and so deprive the hirer of continued use of the goods. For example, if the hire purchase agreement provides that the hirer must pay each monthly rental on its due date, then (under a right in the agreement) the Finance House is entitled to terminate the agreement if the hirer is one day late in making payment (particularly where the agreement provides that the time of punctual payment is of the essence of the contract).[32] Thus the perceived injustices arise where: (1) the Finance House is able to make a windfall profit upon resale of the goods following premature termination of the hire purchase agreement; and (2) the Finance House is able to terminate the hire purchase agreement prematurely by reason of some trivial matter with no right for the hirer to remedy the position or to pay off the balance owing. It is to meet these perceived injustices that parliament and the courts have imposed restrictions upon the rights of the Finance House owner. It is these restrictions which we shall now consider. In summary, the restrictions are under the Consumer Credit Act 1974, under the Insolvency Act 1986 and at common law under the concept of relief from forfeiture.

The Consumer Credit Act 1974

The Consumer Credit Act 1974 ("CCA 1974") applies to regulate the relationship between: (1) a creditor and a debtor: where the creditor grants credit (in any form) to the debtor including hire purchase;[33] and (2) an owner and a hirer where the owner lets on hire (bails) goods to a hirer with no option to purchase. The CCA 1974 applies where the debtor is an

---

[32] See *Lombard North Central plc* v *Butterworth* [1987] QB 527 (Court of Appeal).

[33] CCA 1974 s 9(3) and s 15(1)(a).

"individual" defined[34] to include a consumer or joint consumer customers; a sole trader an individual carrying on business; and a business partnership. It does not apply to corporate bodies such as a limited company. Most of the provisions of the CCA 1974 apply where the agreement is within a prescribed financial limit: at present £25,000. A consumer credit agreement is one where the amount of credit is £25,000 or less; a consumer hire agreement is one where the minimum amount of the payments which the hirer must pay is £25,000 or less. The consumer credit/hire agreement is regulated unless it is an exempt agreement.[35] Certain provisions apply regardless of the financial limit, for example, an extortionate credit bargain can be an agreement for credit of any amount;[36] the restrictions on advertisements apply to advertising of credit secured on land of any amount.[37]

The Restrictions on Repossession

In the absence of special protection under the CCA 1974 the Finance House may (and in practice does) have the right to terminate the hiring and the agreement upon the occurrence of a specified event. Upon such termination the customer's right of possession comes to an end - and so the Finance House is entitled to possession. The specified events usually include the following: breach by the customer of a contractual obligation owed to the Finance House which may be failure to pay an instalment or breach of an obligation not involving payment: for example, wrongfully parting with possession of the goods; and events which are not breach, for example, the bankruptcy of the customer. The CCA 1974 imposes restrictions to protect the customer from the perceived unfair consequences of an arbitrary termination by the Finance House. It does so by requiring the Finance House to give a written "default" notice to the customer before the Finance House may terminate and enforce repossession.[38] The notice must specify the breach or other event permitting termination and enforcement, specify the steps to remedy the matter (if it is remediable), allow a minimum period of time for such remedy, specify the consequences

[34] Section 8(1) and s 189(1) CCA 1974.
[35] As to which see section 16 and the Consumer Credit (Exempt Agreements) Regulations 1989.
[36] CCA 1974 s 137(2)(a).
[37] CCA 1974 s 43(1)(a) and s 43(3)(a).
[38] CCA 1974 s 87(1).

of failure to remedy, and notify the customer of certain rights that he or she has.[39]

If the customer takes remedial action within the prescribed period then the Finance House is not permitted to terminate and enforce. The agreement carries on as if it had never been in default.[40] The prescribed period for remedy must be at least "7 clear days". This has been construed as meaning that there must be 7 days starting after the day on which the customer receives the default notice, and ending before the first day on which the Finance House may terminate and enforce. For example, if the Finance House produces a default notice on April 1st, it should specify a first date for termination and enforcement of (say) April 11th. This is because the customer may receive the notice in the post on April 3rd, to be followed by 7 days (last day April 10th).

The sections which contain these requirements for notices are as follows:

	Enforcement, for example, repossession	Termination
For breach by the customer	Section 87	Section 87
For some other event	Section 76	Section 98

Note that different notices are required depending upon: (1) the action which the Finance House wishes to take: enforcement (such as repossession or demanding the balance outstanding) or termination; and (2) the nature of the event which entitles the Finance House to take this action: a breach of obligation by the debtor (for example, non payment) or some other event (for example, bankruptcy).[41]

---

39 CCA 1974 s 88(1).

40 CCA 1974 s 89.

41 In the context of an agreement with an individual, in practice the events which a Finance House is likely to specify as grounds for enforcement, which are not breach of obligation, are bankruptcy, voluntary arrangement or death. The writer has seen a regulated agreement which included an undertaking by the debtor "not to become bankrupt". One assumes the Finance House was trying to avoid the need to hold two forms of notice (s 76/s 98 and s 87) by specifying grounds for enforcement/termination which are all breach of obligation: which would require a s 87 notice and not a s 76/s 98 notice.

The debtor cannot consent to a termination and repossession without service of a default notice, or without expiry of the 7 clear day period. If the Finance House enforces without observing these requirements then, it seems, there is a tortious act by the Finance House: that is, a wrongful interference with the debtor's rights in the goods.

Protected Goods

Section 90 provides that the Finance House may not repossess "protected goods" without (1) a court order or (2) the consent of the debtor given at the time of repossession. Section 90 applies to regulated hire purchase and conditional sale, but not to hire. "Protected goods" are goods where the debtor has paid "one third or more of the total price of the goods".[42] "Total Price" is defined in s 189(1) as "the total sum payable by the debtor under a hire purchase or conditional sale agreement, including any sum payable on the exercise of an option to purchase, but excluding any sum payable as a penalty or as compensation or damages for a breach of the agreement". Put simply, it is the "total amount payable". The "total price" does not include default interest or arrears charges.[43]

If the debtor consents to repossession at the time when the repossession takes place, then the Finance House may repossess without a court order. Section 173(3) says that a provision under which a thing may be done in relation to any person (here the debtor) only with a court order does not prevent its being done at any time with that person's consent given at that time. It is not valid to obtain consent in advance: for example, in the terms of the credit agreement. It is arguable that the consent must be an informed consent. The debtor must consent in the knowledge that he/she has a right to withhold consent and so the Finance House must obtain a court order.[44] Section 90 requires a court order or consent where the act is recovery of possession of the goods "from the debtor". If the debtor has abandoned the goods, a court order is not required.[45] If the debtor gives possession of a car to a dealer with a view to the dealer trying to find a buyer, then the Finance House may not repossess from the dealer: because

[42] CCA 1974 s 90(1)(b).

[43] *Julian Hodge Bank Limited* v *Hall* [1998] CCLR 14.

[44] See *Chartered Trust plc* v *Pitcher* [1988] RTR 72; [1999] GCCR 1099 (Court of Appeal). The writer knows of a Finance House which requires the debtor to write a letter (based on suggested wording) in his/her own handwriting.

[45] *Bentinck Limited* v *Cromwell Engineering Co* [1971] 1QB 324.

the dealer holds possession as bailee from the debtor.[46] Likewise if the dealer leaves the car with the dealer for repair.[47]

Section 90(1)(a) provides that the protected goods restriction applies where "the debtor is in breach". This suggests that where the Finance House terminates the agreement for an event which is not breach (for example, bankruptcy) then the Finance House may repossess without regard to s 90.

Restrictions on Repossession from Premises

By s 92 the Finance House is not entitled to enter any premises to take possession of goods subject to a regulated agreement (hire purchase, conditional sale or hire). The policy reason for s 92 is not clear. Why should a Finance House have to obtain a court order to repossess a car from the debtor's driveway, but not where that same car is parked in the road outside the debtor's house? The concept of s 92 suggests that the policy is to impose a restriction where the Finance House would have to enter into private property to retake possession. It seems that the action to be guarded against is trespass to the underlying land rather than trespass to the goods. It is not clear why the owner of the land (who may or may not be the debtor/hirer) needs such protection.

Different Applications of s 90 (Protected Goods) and s 92 (Goods on Premises)

The protected goods rule applies to hire purchase and conditional sale. It does not apply to hire (leasing or rental) or to a bill of sale. On the other hand s 92 applies to regulated hire purchase, conditional sale and hire (but not bill of sale). The policy reason for this additional restriction is not clear. It leads to the arbitrary distinction that if I park my (hire purchased) car in my driveway or in a car park, then the Finance House may not repossess (without my consent or a court order); but if I park that same car in the public road outside my house, then the Finance House may repossess (provided I have not paid one third of the total price). Given that the debtor's statutory right of termination under section 99 also applies to hire purchase and conditional sale, but not to hire or bill of sale, the effect is to make hire and bill of sale more attractive to the Finance House.

---

[46] *Kassam* v *Chartered Trust plc* [1998] RTR 220; [1999] GCCR 2245 (Court of Appeal).

[47] *FC Finance Limited* v *Francis* (1970) 114 Solicitors Journal 568.

Factors in Deciding whether or not to Grant a Return Order

Protected Goods or Goods on Premises. If the Finance House applies to the court for a return order under s 90 or s 92, the grant of the order is in the discretion of the court. The court will take account in particular of its power to make a "time order" under section 129. This is an order which reschedules the payments (arrears and future instalments[48]) so that the debtor/hirer has a right to pay off the balance by instalments. It is common for the court to make a time order coupled with a return order which return order is suspended for so long as the debtor/hirer complies with the time order. The net effect is: (1) the customer has a second chance if he or she pays the revised payments then he/she can keep the goods; but (2) if the customer defaults again then the Finance House can proceed to repossess without having to obtain a further court order: the Finance House files a warrant for delivery up of goods and proceeds to repossess at a time appointed by the court bailiff.

Goods on Premises. It is difficult to answer the question without knowing the purpose behind s 92. If the purpose is to protect the owner/occupier of premises from having a Finance House enter into its premises without consent - then it seems the consent of the owner/occupier is required. Conversely, it is not clear why the debtor/hirer as such should need additional protection (beyond protected goods under s 90) only by reason of the goods being on premises in which the debtor/hirer has no interest.

Consequences of Wrongful Repossession: Protected Goods

Protected Goods. If the Finance House repossesses in breach of s 90 (protected goods) then the consequences are spelt out in s 91. The Finance House may keep the goods; the debtor is released from all liability under the regulated agreement: to pay any arrears, future instalments, or other liability: for example, for lack of good repair; and the Finance House must repay to the debtor all payments already made. The outcome is that the debtor enjoyed free use of the goods (apart from cash flow), while the Finance House will lose if the value of the goods when repossessed is less than the original cash price. However, in some circumstances (perhaps unusual) the allocation of loss is not quite so simple: first, what if the

---

[48] Section 130 (2) CCA 1974 provides that, for hire purchase and conditional sale only the court may reschedule instalments not yet due.

debtor took out payment protection insurance, and other additional services (for example, mechanical breakdown insurance, GAP insurance, maintenance and servicing contract). The debtor may have paid for these in cash or, more likely, borrowed additional credit from the Finance House. Section 91 does *not* say that the Finance House must refund such loan repayments already made, or that the debtor is released from liability to pay the future loan repayments. Second, what if the value of the repossessed goods is greater than the original cash price. This could be because the goods are of a nature that their value appreciates for example, a work of art or classic car,[49] or the debtor has altered the goods so as to increase their value for example, by installing new mechanical parts.[50] Third, it could be that the goods have a special value to the debtor, for example, if the wrongly repossessed equipment is essential to a business thereby causing significant financial loss. Accordingly, we must consider whether the debtor has any other remedy against the Finance House for breach of s 90.

Debtor's Remedy: Contract. If the Finance House validly terminated the hire purchase agreement (or conditional sale or hire) before repossession, and the contract terms entitled the Finance House to retake possession, then it seems that the debtor/hirer has no claim in contract: unless it can be said that there is a statutorily implied term in the contract. The contract terms may say: "Following termination of this agreement, the Finance House may retake possession of the goods (subject to the Consumer Credit Act 1974)". The words in brackets are usually added so that the term does not mislead the customer by saying that the Finance House has a right to repossess. It could be argued that, by addition of the words in brackets the Finance House is agreeing as a contract term "following termination of this agreement, the Finance House may retake possession of the goods provided that it does so in compliance with the CCA 1974, and if it repossesses in breach of CCA 1974 then this is a breach of contract".

Debtor's Remedy in Tort. The alternative course is that the debtor/hirer sues in tort for wrongful interference with the customer's interest in the goods. The consequences of an action in tort, as opposed to an action in

[49] Practitioners will know that in the early 1990s many Finance Houses experienced severe losses as the value of classic cars plummeted. However, it is possible the value could rise.

[50] Generally an accession or improvement by a hire purchase hirer becomes the property of the Finance House: see Goode, *Hire Purchase Law and Practice* 2nd ed (1970) p 746 *et seq.*

contract, include a different test of remoteness (for what loss is the Finance House liable) and a different basis of measure of damages. The possibility of a claim in tort is discussed above in the context of the Finance House's failure to serve a default notice.

Debtor's Remedy for Breach of Statutory Duty. Section 92(3) provides that an entry into premises by the Finance House in breach of s 92 is actionable as a breach of statutory duty. It is not obvious what would be the customer's measure of damages. There is no equivalent provision conferring an action for breach of statutory duty in the context of s 90.

Customer's Right of Voluntary Termination of a Hire Purchase or Conditional Sale Agreement

The Common Law Position. At common law, it is arguable that - with hire purchase - the hirer must have the right to terminate the hiring (rather than the agreement) at any time. This is to ensure that, in substance, the agreement is not conditional sale. The point is this: with hire purchase I am bound to pay rentals which cover the whole of the cash price plus interest. It is true that I am not bound to buy the goods: on expiry I can exercise my option right *not* to purchase the goods and *not* to pay the purchase fee.[51] However, where the purchase fee is a nominal amount - substantially less than the value of the goods - then this can be said to be artificial. In reality I am agreeing to take the goods and pay for them. In contrast, if the hire purchase agreement provides (as it must) that I hire the goods from the Finance House, and that I have a right to terminate the hiring and return the goods to the Finance House, and so avoid having to pay further rentals, then this supports the concept that the agreement is for hire and not sale. In economic terms, the Finance House will not want the hirer to have the right to return the goods and walk away with no further liability. This would render the transaction a form of operating lease[52] where the Finance House takes the risk (that the value of the goods is less than the balance) and reward (that the value is greater). In consequence that hire purchase agreement will usually provide that, as a condition of exercise of the right of termination, the hirer must pay a termination charge of an agreed amount. This could be an amount equal to the balance outstanding. Such a

---

[51] See *Forthright Finance Ltd* v *Carlyle Finance Ltd* [1997] 4All ER 99 (Court of Appeal).

[52] Indeed it is possible for hire purchase to be an operating lease for the purpose of SSAP21: as regards the hirer and (separately) as regards the Finance House.

term would not be subject to the doctrine of penalties as the doctrine does not apply where the hirer terminates the hiring under a contractual right. Of course in practice there would be no reason why the hirer should exercise a right to terminate on such terms: the hirer has to pay the full balance (except the purchase fee) with no rebate for accelerated receipt[53] and loses the car. In consequence it is arguable that such a right is illusory, and in reality the hirer is bound to pay an amount equal to the cash price plus interest.

Sections 99-100 CCA 1974. This provides that: (1) the customer under a hire purchase or conditional sale agreement has a statutory right to terminate the agreement at any time; and (2) upon such termination the customer's money liability is restricted. The hire purchase/conditional sale customer exercises such a right of termination by giving notice to the creditor (that is, the Finance House). The notice must be in writing.[54] Upon termination the customer must deliver up the goods at once. If the customer fails to deliver up then the Finance House may repossess without the restrictions under s 90 (protected goods).[55] Upon termination the customer must pay the following: first, all arrears of instalments; second, such further sum (if any) as will bring the total of the advance payment and instalments paid up to one half of the total price; third, damages for any breach of obligation which existed before termination: for example, failure to keep the goods in a state of repair as required by the terms of the agreement. Until the late 1990s debtors rarely exercised a right of termination under s 99. However, with the substantial reduction in values of second hand motor cars, the option to terminate under s 99 becomes attractive. Consider the position of a customer who wishes to part exchange his old car (held on hire purchase from ABC Finance) when acquiring a new car from a dealer with hire purchase from XYZ Finance. If the settlement figure payable to ABC is more than the value of the car to be part exchanged, and the customer has already paid one half of its Total Price to ABC, the dealer may suggest to the customer that he should terminate the hire purchase agreement with ABC under s 99, return the old car to ABC, and walk away. In consequence the customer does not have to pay off the "negative equity" before acquiring a new car. For Finance Houses it would appear that, regardless of s 99, they should seek a

---

[53] Under CCA 1974 s 94 it seems a rebate of part of the total charge for credit must be allowed.

[54] CCA 1974 s 189 definition of "notice".

[55] CCA 1974 s 90(5).

sufficiently large deposit/advance payment, and a sufficiently short repayment period, in order to ensure that throughout the repayment period the value of the goods will exceed the settlement figure.

Hirer's Right to Terminate a Consumer Hire Agreement after 18 Months: s 101

Section 101 applies to a limited class of regulated hire agreements. Where s 101 applies, the hirer has a right to terminate the agreement (not just the hiring) on or after the expiry of 18 months from the date of the agreement. The hirer must give notice of a length of time equal to the periodicity of the rental subject to a maximum of 3 months: for example, with weekly rentals the notice period is 1 week; with yearly rentals the notice period is 3 months. The notice must be in writing.[56] The effect is that even if the hirer commits to a minimum or fixed period of hire of (say) 2 years, still the hirer can terminate from month 18 onwards. In practice s 101 applies in only a limited number of cases. Section 101 does *not* apply to: (1) any agreement where the hirer must pay at least £900 in any year;[57] or (2) any agreement where the hirer selected the goods from a supplier who is not an associate of the lessor, and then asked the lessor to buy the goods from the supplier for the purpose of letting them to the hirer for the purpose of the hirer's business;[58] or (3) any agreement where the goods are let to the hirer for use in the hirer's business of sub-letting out those goods to sub-hirers.[59] The policy decision behind s 101 appears to be that "true consumers should not be bound to hire small items for more than 18 months".

Statutory Restrictions on Repossession from an Insolvent Person or Company: The Insolvency Acts 1986-2000

Types of Insolvency Procedure

Corporate Insolvency. For corporate bodies there are 4 types of insolvency procedure under English law:

---

[56] CCA 1974 s 189 definition of "notice".
[57] CCA 1974 s 101(7)(a).
[58] CCA 1974 s 101(7)(b).
[59] CCA 1974 s 101(7)(c).

(1) *Liquidation:* the "death" and "burial" of a company. The company ceases to trade. A liquidator is appointed to preside over the burial. The liquidator collects in the company's assets,[60] converts them into cash, and pays off the creditors in the statutory order of priority. Upon completion of the distribution the company is struck off the register of companies. A liquidation may be: (i) Members' Voluntary: where the company is solvent and the shareholders resolve to wind up; (ii) Creditors' Voluntary: where the company is *not* solvent and the shareholders resolve to wind up; (iii) Compulsory: where the court orders liquidation following a petition by someone such as a creditor or member.

(2) *Administration:* designed to achieve one of four statutory purposes the more important being: (i) to enable an insolvent company to trade through its difficulties and emerge as a solvent company; or (ii) to enable a more orderly progress to a winding up, that is, the company is bound to fail but overall the creditors will recover more if its is let down gracefully rather than allowing creditors to tear it apart.

(3) *Voluntary Arrangement:* initiated by the shareholders but requiring the consent of 75 per cent by value of the unsecured creditors. The unsecured creditors agree to accept a percentage of their debts over an agreed period: for example, 50 per cent over 5 years. A supervisor oversees the arrangement. This is colloquially called a "CVA" (Corporate Voluntary Arrangement).

(4) *Receivership:* initiated by a creditor who holds security with a power to appoint a receiver. The receiver usually acts as agent of the company, but in reality exists to recover the money owing to the creditor. The receiver will replace the directors until the receiver resigns when the directors take over again. It is possible to have a receiver and a liquidator working (separately) at the same time; but not a receiver and an administrator.[61]

(5) *Administrative receiver:* A special type of receiver is an "administrative receiver".[62] An administrative receiver is appointed by a creditor who holds charges over all, or substantially all, the

---

[60] A creditor with a mortgage or charge security may still exercise its power of sale, and will pass any surplus to the liquidator. If the liquidator sells, the liquidator will pay off the amount owing to the secured creditor.

[61] Insolvency Act (IA) 1986 s 11(1), 11(2), 11(3)(b).

[62] In June 2001 the Government announced proposals to introduce legislation to abolish the concept.

assets of the company, of which at least one is a floating charge. The main significance of an administrative receiver, as opposed to an ordinary receiver, is that the administrative receiver automatically has the powers set out in Schedule 1 to the Insolvency Act 1986,[63] and automatically is the agent of the company (until it goes into liquidation).[64] However, for an ordinary receiver it is a simple matter for the charge instrument to adopt the schedule 1 powers and say the receiver is agent of the company. The charge holder who is entitled to appoint an administrative receiver may veto an Administration Order.[65]

Personal Insolvency. For individuals, the insolvency procedures are comparable although different:

(1) *Bankruptcy*: comparable with liquidation of a company.[66] The Trustee in Bankruptcy collects in assets and pays off creditors in the statutory order. At the end of a period the bankruptcy order is discharged and the individual is released from the consequences of insolvency;
(2) *Voluntary Arrangement:* colloquially called an "IVA" (Individual Voluntary Arrangement);
(3) *Receivership:* an individual may not grant a floating charge[67] and there is no concept of an administrative receiver; but usually a charge on land or other assets incorporates a power to appoint a receiver.

The Effect of Liquidation on a Finance House

The fact of liquidation does not affect the Finance House's rights. Usually the hire purchase, conditional sale or lease agreement will entitle the Finance House to terminate the agreement if a petition for winding up is presented or a resolution for winding up is passed.[68] Upon termination, the Finance House may repossess its goods. Following disposal, the Finance

---

[63] IA 1986 s 42.
[64] IA 1986 s 44(1)(a).
[65] IA 1986 s 9(3).
[66] Although the individual is not dead and buried.
[67] Except in the case of an Agricultural Holding.
[68] The terms may qualify this: for example, an exception for solvent winding up for reconstruction.

House may claim any shortfall as an unsecured creditor.[69] The position is similar with bankruptcy of an individual.

The Effect of Receivership on a Finance House

Again, the fact of receivership does not affect the Finance House's rights of repossession and to claim any shortfall. An administrative receiver may apply to the court for an order that the administrative receiver may sell assets owned by the company which are subject to a security: a mortgage or a charge.[70] Upon sale the administrative receiver must account to the secured creditor for the net sale proceeds, which must not be less than the market value.[71] The benefit of this power is that the administrative receiver may sell the business of the company as a going concern - including the plant and machinery subject to mortgage or charge security. However, in contrast to an administrator, the administrative receiver does *not* have this power in relation to leased goods.

The Effect of an Administration Order on a Finance House

Here the position is very different. From the time of presentation of the petition to the court asking for the administration order,[72] and from the date of the administration order,[73] the Finance House is prohibited from taking any enforcement action, repossession or otherwise, unless the Finance House obtains a court order permitting this.[74] The logic behind this can be seen if we look at the purpose of an administration order. To achieve the survival of the company as a going concern, it must be able to continue to use its plant and machinery. To achieve a more orderly progress to a winding up, the Finance House must be prevented from diving in and repossessing the equipment: just as secured creditors must be prevented from taking possession of mortgaged assets, and all creditors must be prevented from taking court proceedings against the company. Further, the

[69] Or as a secured creditor if the Finance House holds a charge on the company's assets.

[70] IA 1986 s 43(1). In practice this power is used where the holder of the security is a party which did not appoint the administrative receiver.

[71] IA 1986 s 43(3).

[72] IA 1986 s 10(1)(b): note the prohibition arises on presentation of the petition, not the subsequent order. If the petition is dismissed then the prohibition ends.

[73] IA 1986 s 11(1)(b).

[74] IA 1986 s 11.

administrator has a right (if first a court order is obtained to approve it) to sell property owned by the company which is subject to a security (for example, a mortgage or charge),[75] *and* to sell leased equipment[76] (or equipment held on hire purchase or conditional sale). The administrator must account to the Finance House for the net sale proceeds (which must not be less than the market value).[77] It is of great significance that an administrator, but not an administrative receiver, has a statutory right to convert the goods owned by the Finance House, and to pass good title to those goods to the third party buyer. The combined effect of s 10(1)(b) and s 15(2) is to impose serious restrictions on the Finance House's rights as owner: (1) the Finance House is automatically prohibited from taking possession of its goods; and (2) if the court agrees, the Finance House can be deprived of its ownership of the goods although it must receive the net sale proceeds.

The basis on which the court will decide whether the administrator should be allowed to retain possession and use the equipment, or whether the Finance House should be allowed to repossess and sell the equipment, is the important case of *Re Atlantic Computers Plc.*[78] In this case the court expressed its reluctance to give guidance on the principles to be applied on an application by a Finance House under s 11 to repossess the goods. Section 11 deliberately leaves the matter at the discretion of the court. The circumstances will vary widely from case to case. However, the Court of Appeal recognised the need of administrators and legal advisers for some general guidance. The important guidelines can be summarised as follows, as a non-exhaustive list:[79]

- The role of the administrator is important. In the first instance the Finance House should seek the decision of the administrator. The administrator should then respond speedily and responsibly.
- If the administrator refuses to allow repossession, it is then for the Finance House to make out a case why the court should order otherwise.
- The restriction in s 11(3)(c) & (d) is to assist the company to achieve the purpose for which the administration order was made. In the *Atlantic* case this was a more orderly realisation of assets than by a

[75] IA 1986 s 15(1).
[76] IA 1986 s 15(1)(b).
[77] IA 1986 s 5(5).
[78] [1992] Ch 505 (Court of Appeal).
[79] *Ibid* at p 543.

winding up. It could be to achieve a turn around and so enable the company to continue to trade as a solvent concern. If allowing the Finance House to repossess is unlikely to impede the achievement of this objective, then leave to repossess should normally be given.

- In other cases (where to allow repossession would impede the achievement of the objective of the administration), the court has to carry out a balancing exercise: balancing the legitimate interests of the lessor and those of the other creditors of the company. While the purpose of the restriction in s 11 is to assist the company to achieve the purpose for which the administration order was made, the purpose of the court having the power to overrule the decision of the administrator is to enable the court to relax the prohibition on repossession where it would be inequitable to refuse repossession.
- In carrying out this balancing exercise, great importance is attached to the proprietary interests of the Finance House. The underlying principle is that an administration is for the benefit of the unsecured creditors, but this should not be conducted at the expense of those who have proprietary rights except where this is unavoidable; and even then only to a strictly limited extent.
- It is normally a sufficient ground to allow the Finance House to repossess if refusal would result in significant loss to the Finance House. However, if repossession would cause substantially greater loss to others, then this may outweigh this.
- When assessing the losses arising to the Finance House and other creditors, the court will consider matters such as: the financial position of the company; its ability to pay the arrears of rental and the ongoing rentals; the administrator's proposals; the period for which the administration order has been in force and is likely to continue in force; the effect on the administration if repossession is allowed; the effect on the Finance House if repossession is refused; the objective of the administration and the prospects of that result being achieved; and the history of the administration to date.
- When considering the alternative consequences of granting or refusing leave to repossess, the court must consider the likelihood of these consequences arising in practice.
- The court may attach conditions to an order allowing repossession or an order refusing repossession. The court envisaged that in practice there would be frequent cases where leave to repossess is refused, but on conditions: for example, that the administrator must pay the ongoing current rentals as they arise.

To avoid the adverse implications of a moratorium on enforcement upon grant of an administration order or a CVA,[80] a Finance House may seek to take a floating charge over all the assets of the company as collateral security. The effect of this is that the Finance House, as floating chargee, will have the right to appoint an administrative receiver, and so to veto an administration or CVA. In practice it is likely that the company will already have granted charges on all assets (sometimes called a "debenture") to its clearing bank, and that the consent of that bank will be required to the grant of any further charge. It is for this reason that the Finance House will seek to take a floating charge which is expressed to be fully postponed in priority behind all other charges. In the "priority agreement" between the bank and the Finance House, the Finance House may agree not to appoint an administrative receiver unless (1) an administration order or CVA is proposed and (2) at that time the bank chooses not to appoint its own administrative receiver.

The Effect of an Individual Voluntary Arrangement on a Finance House

An individual voluntary arrangement ("IVA") is available to an individual. A proposal is approved first by the court in an "interim order", and then approved by the unsecured creditors by a 75 per cent majority by value of debts. If approved, the IVA will allow the individual to settle his or her liability by paying the agreed percentage of the debt over the agreed period: for example, 50 per cent over 5 years. Provided the individual keeps to the arrangement, no creditor may seek to enforce immediate payment or to make the individual bankrupt. An IVA is appropriate for individual traders such as solicitors whose only asset to pay off the debt is their future earning power, and who would be unable to work if made bankrupt. During the period for which an interim order is in force, the Finance House may not enforce its rights of repossession;[81] and when the application is pending the court may stay any legal process[82] (including such repossession). However, once the interim order is made there is nothing to prevent the Finance House from repossessing its goods.

---

[80] As to which see pp 124-125 below.

[81] IA 1986 s 252(2)(b).

[82] IA 1986 s 254.

The Effect of a Corporate Voluntary Arrangement on a Finance House

A corporate voluntary arrangement ("CVA") is appropriate for a company. In practice the CVA procedure was used rarely. The probable reasons for this were: first, that a proposal for a CVA can be vetoed by appointment of an administrative receiver - the same as with a proposal for an administration order - which remains the case; and second, the insolvent company received no protection from direct enforcement action by creditors until such time as the court approved the CVA: which was usually too late. The fact that a CVA was proposed usually prompted the suppliers of stock to stop further deliveries and retake stock already supplied (of which the supplier remained the owner under a "reservation of title" clause). The Insolvency Act 2000 sought to remedy the second reason by preventing enforcement by creditors from the time of filing the petition for the CVA. The change made by the Insolvency Act 2000 is likely to result in an increase in the number of CVAs and saved businesses because the company will have protection from enforcement from the time of filing the petition: which can be done at the instigation of the directors and achieved quickly. Further, the costs of a CVA are considerably less than the costs of an administration order.

In the context of hire purchase and equipment leasing, during the period for which a CVA moratorium is in force, no steps may be taken to repossess goods in the company's possession under a hire purchase or lease agreement except with the leave of the court and subject to such terms as the court may impose.[83] However, the restrictions on enforcement will not overcome the appointment of an administrative receiver who is able to prevent a CVA. Even if the CVA is approved, it only has the effect of binding the unsecured creditors to a 'work out' period and to recovery of a limited proportion of the debt: for example, 50 per cent over 5 years. However, once the CVA is approved the restrictions on enforcement by a secured creditor (chargee or Finance House) come to an end: a secured creditor is not bound by the CVA. Thus the Finance House can then proceed to terminate the hire purchase or lease agreement and repossess its equipment; or a creditor holding a charge on an asset of the company can take possession of it and sell it under a power of sale. While creditors cannot enforce repayment of credit already advanced, there is no obligation on anyone to grant further credit: in practice this could prevent the company from continuing to trade.

[83] IA 1986 Schedule 1A paragraph 12(1).

The extended protection, that is the restriction on enforcement introduced by the Insolvency Act 2000, applies only to a "small company": defined as a company with an annual turnover (gross sales income) of less than £2.8 million, and a balance sheet assets of less than £1.4 million, and less than 50 employees.

Relief from Forfeiture

The court will normally give effect to the contract agreed between the parties. If the Finance House and the hirer agreed for a letting of the goods, and that the Finance House could terminate the hiring upon certain events - then the court would uphold this; as well as the inevitable consequence that all the rights of an owner (including possession of the goods and the right to sell them) are vested in the Finance House. However, in some cases this could result in a harsh outcome. In economic substance - as opposed to legal substance - the parties to a hire purchase transaction expect that the hirer must pay an amount equivalent to the cash price plus interest and will then become the unencumbered owner. If the hirer paid all the instalments, and was just about to buy the goods for the agreed purchase fee of £10, it could be considered unfair if the Finance House arbitrarily terminated the agreement for some purely technical reason, and then repossessed the goods and resold them for its own profit. It is in this case that the court has a discretion to grant the equitable remedy of "relief from forfeiture" - to order that the agreement be revived on terms that the hirer pays everything due to the Finance House and then the hirer can exercise the option to purchase.

Jurisdiction to Grant Relief

The leading authority is the judgment of Lord Wilberforce in *Shiloh Spinners Limited* v *Harding*,[84] where it was said that equity will grant relief against forfeiture for breach of condition (or covenant[85]); and that the court has the jurisdiction to do so where:[86] (1) the primary object of the bargain (the contract) is to secure a stated result; (2) that the result can still be effectively attained when the matter is brought before the court for

[84] [1973] AC 691 at p 723.

[85] A covenant is simply a promise made in a deed.

[86] The court also has jurisdiction in a case of fraud, but that is outside the current discussion.

decision; and (3) the forfeiture term was included in the contract by way of security for the attainment of that result. Relief is granted in the context of a hire purchase option to purchase, or a lease hiring. In either case the court is granting relief to a hirer who has a legal interest in the goods *viz* possession.[87] However, can relief be granted in favour of someone who holds only a personal right in contract? It seems not. A leading case is *Scandinavian Trading Tanker Co A B* v *Flota Petrolera Ecuatoriana*: *The Scraptrade*.[88] In that case the owner of the ship "chartered" the ship to the charterer. This is a contract for services where the shipowner provides a ship with crew for an agreed period of time and the crew then sail the ship in accordance with the charterer's instructions. The contract does not grant to the charterer an interest in the ship, or a right of possession of the ship.

In the *Scraptrade* case, the House of Lords said that the charterer paid an agreed rate of hire for the ship and crew - for the services rendered by the shipowner. There was no payment which was in excess of a fair consideration for the services rendered by the shipowner. Further, the contractual right of the shipowner to terminate the charter was not to secure payment of a sum of money (said the court). In consequence, the House of Lords in *Scraptrade* held that the doctrine of relief could not be applied in the context of a purely personal right in contract. Lord Diplock said that relief would not be granted for contracts "not involving any transfer of proprietary or possessory rights".[89] Note that this encompasses a contract for personal property (such as goods) as well as land provided the contract for personalty involves a transfer of title or possession (as does hire purchase and equipment leasing). In a subsequent case,[90] the Court of Appeal went further and said that the doctrine of relief applies only in the context of land. However, the House of Lords in that case did not say that the doctrine was so restricted in application. In the later case of *BICC Plc* v *Bundy Corporation*[91] the Court of Appeal reaffirmed that the doctrine is available only in respect of proprietary or possessory rights, but crucially said the doctrine is not restricted to such rights in land. In the more recent cases concerning hire purchase and equipment leasing agreements, it is

[87] See p 97 above.
[88] [1983] 2 All ER 763 (House of Lords).
[89] [1983] 2 All ER at p 767.
[90] *Sport International Bussum BV* v *Inter - Footwear Limited* [1984] All ER 376; subsequently before the House of Lords [1984] 2 All ER 321.
[91] [1985] 1 All ER 417.

clear that the courts do not restrict the availability of relief to land.[92] However, the courts have continued to hold that relief is not available for a purely personal right in contract. The party seeking relief must have a proprietary or possessory interest in the subject matter.[93]

The "policy" argument in favour of granting relief is based upon "fairness": that is, to apply the terms of the agreed contract could lead to a result which is excessive and harsh where: (1) the damage suffered by the innocent party is slight, and (2) the blameworthy conduct of the guilty party is slight. Applying this argument in the context of relief from termination of a hire purchase agreement for goods, it is arguable that it is excessive and harsh to deprive the hirer of the benefit of the option to purchase the goods for a purchase price which is far less than the value of the goods, and where the hirer has already paid off part of the cash price of the goods and is willing to pay the balance. Further, the damage suffered by the Finance House will be slight and if relief is granted the hirer will pay off the whole balance such that the Finance House will be in no worse a position than if the hirer had not defaulted. Moreover, the blameworthy conduct of the hirer is slight; for example, it may have had a receiver appointed which gave rise to the Finance House's right of termination, at a time when the hirer had paid every instalment of rental promptly and observed all its obligations under the hire purchase agreement.[94]

We shall now consider the cases on application for relief in respect of hire purchase and leasing of equipment.

Goker v *NWS Bank plc*[95]

In this case NWS terminated a hire purchase agreement for a Mercedes car in circumstances where: the hirer was in arrears to the extent of 5 months rental totalling £6340; the car was worth some £10-20,000 more than the balance outstanding; and the hirer sought relief on the basis that he would pay off the arrears and then resume payments at the contractual rate. The court held that it had jurisdiction to grant relief, but the court refused to exercise its discretion mainly on the basis that the hirer was not offering to

[92] For example, On *Demand Information plc* v *Michael Gerson (Finance) plc* [2000] 4 All ER 734 (Court of Appeal) [1999] 2 All ER 811 (High Court); *Goker* v *NWS Bank Plc* [1990] GCCR 1507 (Court of Appeal).
[93] For example, *Crittall Windows Limited* v *Stormseal (UPVC) Window Systems Limited* [1991] RPC 265.
[94] As was the case in *Transag*: see p 128 *et seq*.
[95] [1990] GCCR 1507.

pay off the whole balance at once. To reinstate the hiring - even if the hirer paid off all arrears - would expose the Finance House to an unfair risk that it had not assumed on the date of the contract *viz* the risk that the hirer would default in payment again when his conduct showed that he had defaulted before and so was more likely to do so again.

Transag Haulage Limited v *Leyland DAF Finance plc*[96]

This case concerned hire purchase of three commercial vehicles over a period of 36 months from (respectively) January, March and May 1991. During November 1993 the hirer went into receivership. At that time the hirer was up to date with all payments and not otherwise in breach. The Finance House terminated the hire purchase agreements by reason of the receivership. At that time the balance outstanding under the hire purchase agreements was c£14,000, while the value of the vehicles was between £65,000 and £72,500. The receivers of the hirer wished to tender the balance of £14,000 plus the purchase fee of £5 and acquire ownership of the vehicles. They offered to do so three days after termination, and sent a cheque to the Finance House for the full balance outstanding. The Finance House refused. The receivers applied for "relief from forfeiture" - an order that the vehicles be sold and that the sale proceeds should be applied as to £14,000 to the Finance House, and as to the balance (the "equity") to the receivers. The court accepted that it had jurisdiction to grant relief only for forfeiture of proprietary or possessory rights, but said it could do so for personal property as well as for land. In this case, the owner of the equipment (the Finance House) was asserting its right to recover possession of its goods where the hiring of them had been terminated upon an event agreed by the contract. The hirer had argued that the Finance House was imposing a "penalty", but rightly the court rejected this on the basis that the Finance House was not claiming money, simply return of its own property. The court then moved on to consider the principles of when it could grant relief (jurisdiction) and after this whether on the facts it would grant relief (discretion).[97] We shall consider these in turn.

Jurisdiction. The court has jurisdiction where the primary object of the bargain is to secure a stated result and the provision for forfeiture is added as security for the production of that result. The court said the "forfeiture"

---

[96] [1994] GCCR 1819 (High Court).

[97] Citing with approval passages from Snell *Principles of Equity* 29th ed (1992) at p 541.

concerned was loss of the option to buy the goods for £5. This was forfeiture of a proprietary right, not a mere contractual right. While the court did not say so, it seems that the court assumed that the primary object of the hire purchase contract was to secure that the hirer paid all the instalments, and upon this the hirer could acquire title for a nominal sum, and that the Finance House's rights to terminate the hire purchase agreement existed to secure that the Finance House received payment of all the instalments. The court did not mention the third condition for jurisdiction set down in the *Shiloh* case *viz* that the result (that the Finance House receives all instalments and the hirer can acquire title) can still be attained when the matter is brought before the court.[98]

Discretion. The *Transag* court referred to the *Goker* case with approval and applied its principles as follows:

- The terms on which relief will be granted must confer on the owner (the Finance House) at least as valuable rights as the owner would have enjoyed if the hire purchase agreements had been performed.
- Failure to grant relief would result in a substantial windfall to the Finance House over and above what it would have received if the hire purchase agreements had been performed.
- The conduct of the hirer must not disentitle it to receive relief.

On the facts of the *Transag* case, the court decided as follows: the hire purchase agreements were terminated close to the end of the payment period;[99] the hirer had not been in breach before termination; the Finance House is entitled to protect itself against adverse consequences of receivership; the hire purchase agreements were commercial contracts entered into at arm's length between two significant commercial entities; if relief is not granted the Finance House will receive a windfall of c.£53,000; if the hirer pays off the balances outstanding in full (as it was willing and able to do) the Finance House would not suffer any detriment - it was this last fact which distinguished *Transag* from *Goker*; and to refuse relief would cause significant loss to the hirer. Therefore the court concluded that "this is indeed one of those rare cases where it would be right for the court to grant relief". Of significance the court made it clear that the only "forfeiture" in respect of which it could grant relief was the loss of the

[98] This third condition may still apply: the court will not grant relief if the goods have been sold when the application for relief is made: see pp 132-138 below.

[99] Between six weeks and six months before expiry.

option to purchase. The implication is that the court would not grant relief in the case of a lease agreement as opposed to hire purchase.[100] The form of the relief was that the hirer would forthwith pay off the gross balances, the purchase fees, interest and costs, and the hirer could then exercise its option to buy the vehicles.

In view of the subsequent decisions in the *Alf Vaughan* and *On Demand Information* cases, it is of great importance to note that the Finance House had not repossessed the vehicles, let alone sold them.

Form of relief. In *Transag,* the court said that termination so as to deprive the hirer of the option to purchase for £5 was forfeiture of a proprietary interest of the hirer in the goods. It was not merely termination of a contractual right. Accordingly, the court had the jurisdiction to grant relief. The court held that it would be prepared to grant relief only: (1) if the owner (the Finance House) was in no worse a position than the owner would have been if the hire purchase agreement had been performed; because the receivers had the cash to pay off the whole balance immediately, the Finance House was not taking any risk - it received everything it would have received if the hire purchase agreement had run to maturity; and (2) if failure to grant relief would result in the owner (the Finance House) receiving a windfall which it would not have received if the hire purchase agreement had run to maturity - if Transag had not gone into receivership and the hiring had continued to maturity then Transag would have received the sale price of £65,000-£72,500 rather than Leyland DAF Finance; and (3) if the conduct of the hirer (Transag) did not disentitle it to relief. The court said that the doctrine of penalties is not relevant.

The Concept of Relief from Forfeiture

Relief from forfeiture has existed in various forms by statute[101] and at common law in the context of leases of real property. If a tenant fails to pay rent, or breaches some other covenant, then the landlord can forfeit the lease. This means that the tenant is evicted and the landlord can re-let elsewhere. If the landlord can re-let for a higher rent then that is the landlord's good fortune (windfall). Accordingly, the law allows the tenant to ask the court to order that the tenant should be given a second chance - if

---

[100] *Obiter*. In *On Demand Information plc* v *Michael Gerson (Finance) plc* [2000] 4 All ER 734, it was held that relief can be granted for an equipment lease. See pp 133-139 below.

[101] Law of Property Act 1925 s 146.

the tenant pays off the arrears of rent (or remedies the other breach) then the lease will carry on as if there had been no breach. This involves the tenant re-acquiring the right to continue in possession of the demised premises. The court will not re-write the terms of the lease. All that happens is that the tenant has the chance to make good the default - bring the position up to date - and then carry on under the original lease terms. In the context of an equipment lease agreement, it would be possible for the court to grant relief in a similar form: the hirer re-acquires the right to continue in possession of the goods, the hirer pays off all arrears and remedies and other default, and the lease then carries on in accordance with its original terms. In the context of a hire purchase agreement, the same form of relief could be granted. However, there is the alternative possibility that the form of relief is reinstatement of the option to purchase rather than reinstatement of the hiring: the hirer re-acquires the right to pay the gross balance (which remedies all default) and then exercises its right to buy the goods for the purchase fee. It is notable that in *Transag* the court granted relief on the latter basis: reinstatement of the option to purchase; while in *Goker* the court refused to grant relief on the former basis: reinstatement of the hiring.

The reason that the court in *Goker* refused to grant relief in the form of reinstatement of the hiring was that it would force the Finance House to accept an unforeseen additional credit risk - that the hirer would default again and the Finance House may then be in a worse position because the goods were worth less or had disappeared. It seems that the position of goods is different from that of land: goods depreciate more rapidly and can disappear. It should be noted that the court did not say it would never grant relief in the form of reinstatement of the hiring of goods. The matter remains open. If relief in that form is to be available, at the very least the hirer must be willing and able to pay off all arrears of rental.[102]

In the case of a finance lease there may be provision for the hirer to obtain indirectly continued use of the goods without risk to the Finance House, or the equity value of the goods. This is because once the hirer has paid off the primary rentals, the hiring may continue indefinitely at a peppercorn rental, while the hirer may be able to sell the goods to an independent third party,[103] and receive a residual value refund of rentals equal to 99 per cent of the net sale proceeds.[104] Thus we have the

---

[102] *Barton, Thompson & Co Ltd* v *Stapling Machines Co* [1966] 2 All ER 222.

[103] By selling the goods as agent for the Finance House; or by introducing the third party buyer to the Finance House which is obliged to sell.

[104] See pp 105-106 above.

possibility of alternative forms of relief for an equipment lease by which (1) the hirer pays off the gross balance of rentals and the hiring is reinstated; or (2) the goods are sold to a third party and the hirer receives the bulk of the sale proceeds after payment of the gross balance to the Finance House. This does not mean that relief in the form of reinstatement of the hiring is irrelevant. This would be relevant where: (1) the lease is an operating lease; or (2) the lease is a finance lease but with no secondary period or RVR; or (3) the hirer cannot afford to pay off the whole balance at once.

Alf Vaughan & Co Limited v *Royscot Trust plc*[105]

In this case there were 8 hire purchase and 2 finance lease agreements for vehicles. The gross balances outstanding were £34,000 and the value of the vehicles was £82,000. The hirer went into receivership and Royscot terminated the agreements. The receivers wished to sell the business as a going concern. They offered to pay off the £34,000. Royscot refused and said it would repossess unless the receivers paid the full value of the vehicles being £82,000. The receivers paid the £82,000 under protest and later applied for refund of the "equity" by way of relief from forfeiture. The court held that Royscot was entitled to repossess, and to threaten to do so. This is not illegitimate unless there are exceptional circumstances amounting to unconscionable behaviour. The agreement by the receivers to pay the £82,000 under protest, because they had to acquire the right to pass title to the buyer of Alf Vaughan's business and complete that sale quickly, was not voidable for "duress of goods". The receivers were not entitled to 'relief from forfeiture' because the vehicles had been sold. The receivers should have applied for relief before the sale. The court accepted that it had the jurisdiction to grant relief, but refused to exercise its discretion to do so because the hirer (through its receivers) had not applied for relief before the sale of the vehicles.

On Demand Information Plc v *Michael Gerson (Finance) plc*[106]

In this case the terms of the leases were as follows: (1) there were 4 finance leases for equipment; (2) in each case the primary hiring period ("PHP")

---

[105] [1991] All ER (Comm) 856 Chancery Division: This case was decided after *Transag* after the first hearing in *On Demand Information*, but before the appeal in the latter.

[106] [2000] 4 All ER 734 (Court of Appeal) [1999] 2 All ER 811 (High Court).

was 36 months with an initial rental equal to 3 subsequent monthly rentals and a terminal hiatus;[107] (3) after the PHP there was a secondary hiring period from year to year at an annual rental in advance equal to about 1 per cent of the capital cost;[108] (4) the hirer could terminate the hiring by 60 days notice to the Finance House to expire on the last day of the PHP or any anniversary of that date; (5) the hirer was appointed "sales agent" of the Finance House for the period of 6 months after termination of the hiring by notice as in para (4) above. The Finance House would sell the equipment to a third party buyer and make a rebate of rental to the hirer equal to 95 per cent of the net sale proceeds.

The facts of the 4 leases are summarised below:

		Termination of Lease	**Earliest date of termination of hiring by 60 days notice from ODI to MG to expire on or after end of PHP**	**£p rentals unpaid (in arrears) if the hiring were so terminated**
LEASE NO.1	PHP had ended 04/09/97	19/02/98	04/09/98	Nil[109]
LEASE NO.2	PHP had ended 19/10/97	19/02/98	19/10/98	nil[110]
LEASE NO.3	PHP due to end 30/03/98	19/02/98	30/03/99	?c.£3000 + VAT[111]
LEASE NO.4	PHP due to end 16/05/98	19/02/98	16/05/98	£3308.45 + VAT[112]

---

107 In practice lease rentals are payable in advance. For example, if the Primary Period begins on January 1 2000, it ends on January 1 2003; on 1/1/2000 the hirer pays £300, on 1/2/2000 to 1/10/2002 the hirer pays £100, and no rental is payable on 1/11/2002 or 1/12/2002.

108 For example, if the equipment cost £100,000 then the secondary rental is £1000.

109 PHP ended 04/0/97, so an annual rental had already been paid for the period to 04/09/98. ODI would be able to serve 60 days notice to expire on 04/09/98 at any time before c. 04/07/98. The date of terminate was 19/02/98. Therefore no further rental would have to be paid.

110 As with Lease 1.

111 The PHP would end on 30/03/98: some 40 days after termination. Therefore, to terminate by 60 days notice at the end of the PHP or a SHP, the earliest date by which ODI could terminate would be 30/03/99 being the end of the first SHP. ODI had already paid the final Primary Rental for the quarter 30/12/97 to 30/12/98, but would have to pay one annual Secondary Rental for the year to 30/03/99.

Before the matter came to the Court of Appeal: (1) there had been an exchange of correspondence between the receivers of On Demand Information ("ODI") and Michael Gerson (Finance) Ltd ("MG") promptly after termination, in an attempt to agree a settlement; no settlement was agreed; (2) on 2 March, MG wrote offering to co-operate in a sale of the equipment (to the incoming buyer of ODIs business) on the basis that the sale price would be held in "an escrow account"; with the receivers then being entitled to apply for relief within 60 days paying all costs; MG made it clear it did not accept that ODI was entitled to relief, but it wanted to co-operate in realising a good price for the equipment and saving the jobs of the ODI employees; and (3) the receivers applied to the court with a hearing on 5 March. While not a formal consent order, in practice the parties substantially agreed to the course suggested by MG.

Before we consider what the court decided as to jurisdiction, discretion and form of relief, we should note the general nature of the respective interests of ODI and MG; first, this was a lease rather than hire purchase. In contrast to *Transag* (the only other case where relief was granted[113]) the hirer could not acquire title to the goods; second, it was a finance lease rather than an operating lease. If relief were to be granted, the form of that relief would be as follows: (1) the court could not reinstate the hiring because the equipment had been sold; and so (2) the court would have to reword the terms of the contract (the sale agency term) or interpret that term in a flexible manner. The hiring had not been terminated by 60 days notice by the hirer; indeed with two of the leases this would not yet have been possible because the primary hiring periods had not yet ended.

Jurisdiction. The Court of Appeal referred, with approval, to the principles laid down by the House of Lords in the *Shiloh* case. The court reviewed and approved the various authorities for the principles that: (1) the court does *not* have jurisdiction to grant relief where the subject matter is mere personal contractual rights as opposed to the transfer or creation of proprietary or possessory rights; but (2) the court does have jurisdiction

---

[112] The PHP would end on 16/05/98. The final quarter's rental would be due on 16/02/98. The earliest date by which ODI could terminate by 60 days would be 16/05/98 (the end of the PHP is some 86 days after termination). Therefore, it is likely ODI owed the last quarterly rental due on 16/02/98.

[113] Relief was not granted in the *ODI* case - because the goods had been sold before the application was made - but the court made it clear it was willing to grant relief of an equipment lease.

where the subject matter is chattels (goods) rather than land. Further, the court held it does *not* have jurisdiction where the goods have been sold.

In general, at the time of the application for relief from forfeiture, the following possibilities exist with regard to the existence of goods:

- the equipment is still in the possession of the hirer, and has not been sold - relief is available;
- the equipment has been repossessed by the Finance House, but has not been sold - relief is available;
- the equipment has been repossessed and sold by the Finance House - relief is *not* available;
- the equipment has been sold by the hirer under a court order - relief is *not* available;
- the equipment has been sold by the hirer without a court order - relief is *not* available.[114]

Review of Transag. The court in *ODI* reviewed the *Transag* case. Counsel for MG had argued that *Transag* was wrongly decided as the option to purchase (in respect of which the *Transag* court granted relief) was not a proprietary right but was a mere contractual right. The court held in the other direction: that *Transag* was actually too restrictive in holding that relief could be granted only for the option to purchase.[115] It was held that in *Transag* it would have been possible to grant relief on the basis of the possessory rights as hirer, since these possessory rights are *not* "purely contractual rights".[116] In consequence the court held it could grant relief in the context of a finance lease (sic)[117] provided that the forfeiture provision satisfies one of the following two relevant conditions laid down in *Shiloh*[118] namely, the forfeiture provision must be (1) security for payment of money or (2) security for attaining a specific and attainable result. The court held

---

[114] Relief is on equitable remedy. If the Hirer deliberately acted wrongly by selling the goods then it seems unlikely the court would help. The Third Party buyer of the goods may or may not acquire good title, depending on the existence of an exception to the *Nemo Dat* Rule.

[115] See p 130 above.

[116] [2000] 4 All ER 734 at p 750c.

[117] At p 750c.

[118] See p 125 above.

one or both conditions were satisfied[119] and at the same time the court accepted that MG's real interest in the lease was a financial one.[120]

Form of Relief. The court had to consider: (1) can it accelerate the time at which the sales agency/residual value refund ("RVR") clause could be applied because *ODI* had not served 60 days notice of termination of the hiring and indeed could not have done so with two of the leases; (2) can it vary the terms of the lease contract so that the sales agency/RVR clause could be applied even though the goods had already been sold. The lower court in *ODI* had asked the following hypothetical question: if a receiver had not been appointed of *ODI*, could the hirer (*ODI*) come along before expiry of the primary hiring period ("PHP") and ask the court to authorise a sale of the equipment? It seems not as this would be justified only if the court had a general jurisdiction to rewrite contracts which it does not.[121] However, on the particular facts of the *ODI* case, the court was prepared to order reinstatement of the hiring and the lease agreement, so that then *ODI* could serve the 60 day notice ending the hiring at a future date (the end of the PHP for Leases 3 and 4 and the first anniversary of the start of the SHP for Leases 1 and 2), then sell the equipment as agent, and require MG to make the 95 percent RVR. The judge at first instance had said he would be prepared to grant relief in this situation and by implication the Court of Appeal agreed. Thus the answer to the problem posed above is that the court can accelerate the time at which the sales agency/RVR clause will be applied. Neither the lower court nor the Court of Appeal specified the consequences of such an acceleration. It is arguable that in practice the court will re-write the terms of the contract and allow a hirer to compel a sale of the equipment before the expiry of the PHP.

The majority of Court of Appeal held that the court could not grant relief from forfeiture in relation to a sum of money (the net sale proceeds held in the escrow account) after the goods had been sold and gone: "The object of relief against forfeiture is the continuation of a lease, not its extinction".[122] The court held if it were to allow relief - after sale of the goods - it would introduce unacceptable uncertainty into commercial transactions[123] and approved previous House of Lords decisions that "the

---

[119] It is not clear from the judgment which condition applied in the *ODI* case.
[120] At p 750f.
[121] *Loc cit* fn 116 at p 752d.
[122] Per Dillon LJ in *Fulle* v *Judy Properties* [1991] 64 P&E CR 176 at p 184 cited with approval at p 753g.
[123] *Loc cit* fn 116 at p 754d.

equitable jurisdiction is to relieve against forfeiture of property not to rewrite bargains".[124] The outcome of the Court of Appeal case is: (1) the court has jurisdiction to grant relief in the case of a finance lease with a sales agency/RVR term; (2) little was said specifically about how the court's discretion would be exercised, but it seems - at least where the hirer is insolvent - the facts that the hirer was willing and able to pay off the gross balance due to the Finance House, coupled with the likely result that the Finance House would make a substantial unforeseen windfall profit, were relevant; (3) the form of the relief will be to require that the goods be sold and the RVR made; (4) the court will grant relief even where the effect is to authorise a sale at a time when the hirer could not have required this under the terms of the lease contract; (5) relief is not available (that is, the court cannot grant relief) where the goods have already been sold at the time of the hearing of the application for relief.

In *On Demand Information* v *Michael Gerson*, and in many other cases, the receivers of the hirer will wish to sell the business as a going concern, to include the leased equipment in the sale, and to complete the sale quickly. On the basis of the majority decision in *ODI* it seems that the receivers must make a decision either (1) to apply for an order for sale - and lose the right to relief, or (2) to apply for relief, resisting repossession in the meantime (with the attendant risk of personal liability for conversion) and risk delay with consequential depreciation in value of the goods and loss of the initial buyer. Given that the Finance House may also have an interest in an early sale of the goods, one can foresee negotiation by bluff: *unless* a later decision overturns *ODI* and allows the court to order a sale without prejudice to a subsequent application for relief.

Operating Leases

The *On Demand* case held that a hirer under a finance lease is entitled to apply for relief. This is on the basis that the interest of the Finance House in the right to terminate and repossess and sell is "security" for a financial interest. Could it be argued that a hirer under an operating lease_has a right to claim relief? First consider the nature of the relief that would be granted. While not impossible, it is unlikely that the court will allow the hirer to pay off the arrears and then continue with the hiring for the balance of the original period at the original rental. This would require the Finance House to assume a credit risk of future default by the hirer which is unacceptable.

---

[124] *Ibid* at p 753f.

Perhaps an exception would be made where: (1) the Finance House has terminated the agreement for some arbitrary reason not related to the financial standing of the hirer; and (2) the hirer is able to demonstrate that the risk of future default is no greater than the risk assumed by the Finance House when it first entered into the lease agreement. Normally an operating lease does not grant rights to the hirer to sell the goods as agent for the Finance House, and recover the equity via a residual value refund. However, such a term is possible in an operating lease. If it is then, following the principles in *ODI*, it is arguable that the hirer can apply for relief on the basis that the operating lease has been terminated, but the hirer has a ready buyer willing to pay market value, and so the Finance House should make such a sale, on the basis that after deduction of the gross unpaid rentals and the residual value, the balance of the net sale proceeds (the equity) should go to the hirer.
Multiple Agreements - Can the Hirer Cherry Pick? Consider a position where the hirer has two lease agreements: Lease 1 with £10,000 in unpaid rentals and equipment worth £15,000, and Lease 2 with £10,000 in unpaid rentals and equipment worth £8,000. Can the hirer apply for relief under Lease 1 by tendering the £10,000 leaving the Finance House to exercise its rights in respect of Lease 2? It seems not. The grant of relief from forfeiture is an equitable remedy. It seems unlikely that the court would exercise its discretion if the net effect is to give the hirer a windfall of £5,000, but to leave the Finance House with a net loss of £2,000. Perhaps the court would grant relief on the basis that the hirer must tender the balances on all agreements (£10,000 + £10,000 = £20,000), and so access the aggregate value of the goods (£15,000 + £8,000 = £23,000).

Relief from Forfeiture of Instalments Already Paid

The cases discussed above consider relief in the form of allowing the hirer to pay the total rentals and acquire ownership of the goods or equivalent. An alternative form of relief would be to allow the hirer to recover instalments already paid to the Finance House. For example, under a hire purchase agreement the hirer pays a substantial deposit/advance payment (for example, 50 per cent of the cash price) and one monthly instalment of hire-rent; then the Finance House terminates, repossesses, and resells the goods for more than the original cash price. The hirer had used the goods for only one month. Should it be entitled to recover the deposit and/or monthly instalment? This concept was discussed in *Stockloser* v *Johnson,*[125] where S sold machinery and other assets to B on terms that the sale price was payable by instalments and title passed on final payment and, if B defaulted, then S could retake possession of the machinery and keep instalments already paid. B defaulted in payment, S accepted this as repudiation and recovered possession. B sought relief in the form of an order that S should repay instalments already paid by B to S. It should be noted that the case did not concern a penalty as it was not a case where S seeks to enforce a contract term requiring B to pay a sum which is not a genuine pre-estimate of loss likely to be suffered by S. Rather S was content to let the matter rest and retain money already paid to S. It was B who sought to recover this money already paid that is, to obtain relief.

The court refused to grant relief, but for different reasons: (1) whether or not the contract term was a penalty, B could obtain relief only if it would be unconscionable for S to retain the instalments; (2) all 3 judges held that the contract term entitling S to keep instalments already paid was not a penalty; Rowe LJ held that was the end of the matter; no question of relief arose unless (a) there was a special circumstance such as fraud, sharp practice or unconscionable conduct on the part of S; and (b) B was willing and able to complete; (3) unlike Rowe LJ, the other two judges held that to obtain relief it was not necessary that B should be willing and able to perform B's obligations under the contract; (4) Denning LJ (as he then was) held that, even though the term was not a penalty, the court could grant relief if (a) the term was penal in that the instalments retained by S were out of all proportion to the damage suffered by S and (b) it was unconscionable for S to retain the instalments; on the facts these conditions were not satisfied; (5) Denning LJ referred to the case of *Steedman* v *Drinkle*[126] where V sold land on hire purchase terms to B by which B went into possession at once paying an advance payment with the next instalment due 1 year later and the balance over a further 5 years. On payment of the final instalment V would convey the land to B. B failed to pay the first annual instalment and V accepted this as a repudiatory breach terminating the agreement. V resold the land for a larger sum than the cash price to B. B sought an order that the advance payment should be refunded, which the court granted; (6) when exercising its discretion the court will consider the circumstances applying at the time of termination of the contract, not at the time of creation of the contract. If we revert to our hypothetical example

---

125 [1954] 1 All ER 63 Court of Appeal.

126 [1916] 1 AC 275 Privy Council.

where the hirer paid a 50 per cent advance payment, had the goods for only 1 month, and then the Finance House terminates peremptorily and resells for more than the cash price, it seems the court will grant relief to the hirer by ordering the Finance House to refund the advance payment as (a) otherwise the sums retained by the Finance House would be disproportionate to its loss (indeed, on our hypothetical facts, the Finance House makes a profit), and (b) it would be unconscionable for the Finance House to retain these sums.

The Policy Argument Revisited

It has been suggested that relief from forfeiture should be granted because, otherwise, the Finance House will make a windfall. The court has said that this windfall result will not be conclusive in persuading it to grant relief: "If the law requires the court to reach a conclusion which confers a substantial windfall on the Respondent [Michael Gerson] and this injustice on the Claimant [ODI], so be it".[127] However, is it injustice to the hirer not to grant relief? In the usual case, where the hirer is insolvent, the effect of grant of relief is to transfer the value of the equity from the Finance House to other creditors of the hirer. For example, if the insolvent hirer granted a debenture to its bank, and the other assets of the hirer have not paid off the bank's debt, then the effect of grant of relief is to transfer money from the Finance House to the bank. Alternatively it transfers value to the preferential or unsecured creditors. The practical result of granting relief seems to be that, where one creditor (the Finance House) has been paid off in full, then the windfall should go to another creditor who has suffered a loss. Certainly the bank cannot keep the excess value of the mortgaged assets: the bank must account to the hirer for this excess. That excess will then be available to pay off other creditors (which may or may not include the Finance House). Consider the converse position where the hirer owes £10,000 to its bank, having mortgaged to the bank assets worth £12,000, while the hirer owes £10,000 unpaid rentals to a Finance House where the leased goods are worth £7,000. Here the Finance House has no claim to the £2,000 surplus value of the mortgaged assets other than as an unsecured creditor.

In economic terms the argument for granting relief from forfeiture may be understandable. The criticism is that the court may be allowing the economic justice to override the legal facts. If the insolvent company owes

[127] Per Murray Stuart-Smith *loc cit* fn 92 at p 738.

money to its unsecured creditors, and has been hiring plant on a day to day rental, no-one would reasonably suggest that the plant owner must sell the plant and pay its value to the hirer's receiver. Of course the courts are not suggesting this. The court in *On Demand* was careful to lay down that relief from forfeiture is available only in narrow circumstances: where the Finance House bought the equipment, and let it to the hirer, only with a view to recovering the cash price plus interest in the form of rentals, with the hirer keeping any excess value (equity), or bearing the loss of the equipment being worth less.

The *On Demand* case does represent a significant detraction from the legal substance that the owner of the goods is the owner with all the rights of ownership, subject only to the limited rights of the hirer under the terms of the hire purchase/lease agreement; and if the hire purchase/lease agreement is terminated without the hirer having exercised certain rights (option to purchase or sales agency/RVR) then the owner becomes again the unencumbered owner with all the rights of an owner - to keep the equipment, re-let it, resell it, or destroy it. The hirer chose to acquire the equipment by way of hire. The hirer had the ability to buy the equipment for cash (with or without finance by way of loan). The Finance House entered into the transaction on the basis that it was by way of hire, and not that it was a sale. There must remain a doubt that the court is re-writing the contract and reconstituting a hire arrangement as though it were a loan upon the security of a mortgage. It has long been established that a hire purchase relationship is *not* a loan secured by a mortgage (bill of sale);[128] all the more a hire with no option to purchase. If one of the purposes of the common law is to achieve certainty, so that business people may enter into relationships able to predict the outcome, then this subject must be brought back to the House of Lords for a clear ruling.

Conclusion

Where the economic substance of the relationship is such that the customer must pay off the cash price plus interest, and the customer will acquire ownership or equivalent rights (that is, hire purchase, conditional sale or finance lease) it would be unfair if the Finance House arbitrarily terminated the agreement, repossessed the goods, and kept the proceeds. Where the economic substance of the relationship is one of rental (an operating lease)

128 *Helby* v *Matthews* [1895] AC 471.

then it may be considered unfair if the Finance House arbitrarily terminates the hiring before expiry of the contemplated period of hire. The dilemma arises because in England and Wales, finance for the acquisition of capital equipment is effected through the medium of a contract of bailment. If the finance were provided by way of a loan, secured by a mortgage of the equipment, some of the problems would disappear:

- The customer could exercise all the rights of ownership subject to the security interest. The customer would have a right to sell or enjoy unencumbered ownership at any time by paying off the finance balance.
- The Finance House would have to take possession and exercise a power of sale: for which appropriate safeguards could apply: either a requirement for a court order in all cases (as with a mortgage of a dwelling)[129] or - better - an automatic right for the Finance House to take possession for sale: subject to a default notice period without remedy, and subject to the right for the customer to apply to the court for postponement. There would be no need for such arbitrary factors as whether one third of the total price has been paid or the goods are on (anyone's) premises.
- The Finance House would recover its finance plus interest - no more and no less. If there was a shortfall after sale of the mortgaged equipment then the customer would have to make good the deficit; if there was a surplus then automatically this would go to the customer. There would be no need for the arbitrary right of termination with restriction of liability to one half of the total price.
- If, as a policy decision, it is considered that a company should have a right to a rescue period or orderly winding up, then the mortgage secured creditor would be bound by the administration order: just as it is at present; but the genuine rental company would not be unfairly deprived.

In March 1971 the Crowther Committee[130] undertook a wide ranging review of the laws relating to credit and hire. In summary the Committee made two recommendations: first, that new comprehensive statutory

[129] Administration of Justice Act 1970.

[130] *Report of the Committee on Consumer Credit (the Crowther Report)* Cmnd 4596 (1971).

legislation[131] should be introduced regulating all types of credit and hire, and regulating all stages of the life cycle of a credit or hire agreement; this recommendation was implemented within the Consumer Credit Act 1974; second, that the concept of hire purchase should be abolished and replaced with a loan secured by a mortgage of the goods financed, which mortgage would be registered in a public chattel mortgage register.[132] It is regrettable that this recommendation has not been implemented.

One of the marks of a civilized society is that it has laws which strike a fair balance between interests, which reflect the economic and social reality of the society and which are intelligible and accessible to all. There seems little doubt that - in the context of equipment and vehicle finance - English law falls a long way short of this; but one has to ask whether - despite good intent by legislator and judge - it is possible to be otherwise when the law is built around such structures as we have. One must be cautious before overturning long established law and commercial practice but at some time it may be preferable to revisit the Crowther Committee Report, to introduce a practical method of advancing loans on the security of goods, to introduce an effective chattel mortgage registry (taking advantage of modern technology), to repeal the bills of sale legislation, and to restrict hire purchase to cases where the parties genuinely intend a relationship of bailment.

---

[131] A Consumer Sale and Loan Act.

[132] A Lending and Security Act: see *Crowther Report op cit* fn 130, Chapters 5.3-5.7.

4 Mortgages of Aircraft

J A M EDMUNDS

The Legal Context

Aircraft are personal chattels and as such may be made the subject of security for obligations. Mortgages may be created either as legal or equitable mortgages. A legal mortgage over an aircraft may be created only by a conveyance or assignment of the whole or part of the estate or interest of the mortgagor in the aircraft of which it is the legal owner subject to a proviso that upon payment of the debt or satisfaction of the obligation, the property should be reconveyed. All other mortgages are equitable. Equitable mortgages occur either where there is an agreement to effect a legal mortgage or where it is intended to take a second mortgage over an aircraft. The essential feature of these instruments is that there is no actual transfer of legal title though the mortgagee will have a right to call for such a transfer which right will be enforced in the courts by the application of equity. An equitable mortgage includes the right to redeem the aircraft upon payment of the debt or satisfaction of the obligation secured.

A charge may be created over personal property such as an aircraft as security for the discharge of an obligation which then gives rise to an encumbrance on the aircraft. A charge is the appropriation of real or personal property for the discharge of a debt or other obligation without giving the creditor either a general or special property in or possession of the subject of the security. In such a case the court will enforce the creditor's equitable interest. It should be noted that the provisions of the Law of Property Act 1925 sections 85 and 86 for the creation of a charge by way of legal mortgage subject to a provision for cesser on redemption is restricted to land only.

A mortgage or charge over an aircraft is registerable under section 395 of the Companies Act 1985 and failure to register such a charge within 21 days of its creation renders the charge void as against liquidators, administrators and creditors of the company. Registration under the Act is required in respect of companies incorporated outside the United Kingdom having an established place of business here whether or not the company is registered as an overseas company. Under Section 396(4) of the Companies Act 1985 the word "charge" is defined as including a mortgage. A mortgage created outside England over an aircraft situated outside England by a mortgagor being a UK company or having an established place of business in England is required to be registered at Companies House within 21 days of the date on which the mortgage could have been received had it been remitted by post with due diligence. Non-registration makes the mortgage void against a liquidator administrator or any creditor of mortgagor.[1]

If the mortgage or charge over the aircraft is created by an individual who owns the aircraft as opposed to a company then the mortgage is subject to the provisions of the Bills of Sale Acts 1878 and 1882. The provisions of these Acts as to the formalities required to be observed in documenting the transaction not to mention the restricted rate of interest permitted under those Acts results in lenders seldom offering transactions which require compliance with these Acts. Traditionally hire purchase or leasing was used to finance such aircraft but under the Mortgaging of Aircraft Order 1972 ("MAO") the Bills of Sale Acts do not apply to aircraft not registered on the UK register of aircraft since the MAO provides an alternative method of securing a loan over an aircraft.[2] Mortgages granted by individuals over aircraft registered on the United Kingdom register of aircraft are still subject to the Bills of Sale Acts. Additionally some mortgages or charges will be subject to the Consumer Credit Act 1974 (CCA). If the loan to which the mortgage relates constitutes a personal credit agreement in which the creditor provides the debtor with credit not exceeding £25,000 then it is a regulated agreement.[3] Credit here means a cash loan or any other form of financial accommodation[4] down payments and credit charges being excluded.[5] A regulated consumer credit agreement is subject to the documentary, enforcement, termination and information requirements of the CCA1974.

---

1 Companies Act 1985, s 398.
2 See below.
3 CCA 1974, s 8(2).
4 CCA 1974, s 9(1).
5 CCA 1974, s 9(3).

The Developed Law

The Mortgaging of Aircraft Order 1972 ("MAO") made under Section 16 of the Civil Aviation Act 1968 came into force on 1st October 1972. It created a register of mortgages of aircraft registered in the United Kingdom nationality register maintained by the Civil Aviation Authority. The two registers should not be confused though both are maintained by the Civil Aviation Authority. The United Kingdom nationality register is the internationally recognised register of British aircraft made under Section 8 of the Civil Aviation Act 1949.[6] The Register of Aircraft Mortgages introduced by MAO is quite separate and is open only to mortgages of aircraft registered on the United Kingdom nationality register.

The Subject of the Aircraft Mortgage Register

A mortgage of any aircraft registered in the United Kingdom register of civil aircraft may be registered on the aircraft mortgage register no matter who is the mortgagee (domestic or foreign) or whether it is an individual or a company. Provision is even given under Article 62 for cases where a mortgage is in a language other than English when a translation certified by the applicant as being true must be supplied. Registration of a mortgage over an aircraft is not compulsory. However, the registration creates priority for the registered mortgage over an unregistered mortgage[7] and consequently there is every reason to register and none not to register. Article 16(1) MAO excludes from the operation of the Bills of Sale Acts 1878 and 1882 any mortgage registered under MAO but if the mortgage is created by a company, registration under Section 395 of the Companies Act 1985 is still required. Similarly if the loan to which the mortgage relates is under the limit prescribed by the Consumer Credit Act 1974 the transaction may be regulated by that Act. If an aircraft is not registered under the United Kingdom nationality register then it may still be subject to the Bills of Sale Acts, for instance, if an individual in the UK owns a US registered aircraft which is mortgaged to a bank.

In addition to the aircraft itself, Article 3 of the MAO provides that a registered mortgage may include any store of spare parts for the aircraft the subject of the registered mortgage. Spare parts includes spare engines.

---

6 Now the Air Navigation (No 2) Order 1995.

7 MAO 1972, Article 14(1).

However a mortgage of spare parts taking effect as a floating charge is not registerable nor is a mortgage covering spare parts alone. Schedule 1 Part 1 of the MAO requires details to be provided to the Registrar of the character of the spare parts, approximate numbers and the place or places where they are stored. Parts to be added to the mortgaged aircraft are often expressed to be the subject of the aircraft mortgage. Equity gives effect to this if the goods are sufficiently identifiable when acquired by the mortgagor and terms of mortgages providing for the mortgaging of future parts are allowed by the Register.

Form and Content

The MAO does not prescribe any particular form of mortgage.[8] The form and content of a typical aircraft mortgage are set out below.

1. Details of the aircraft and spares the subject of the mortgage.
2. Representations and warranties relating to the ownership of the aircraft and spares and that it is free from encumbrances (unless stated).
3. An acknowledgement of the loan made and the details of the interest to be charged and the method of repayment of the loan and the payment of interest.[9]
4. Provision for the payment of interest on overdue sums.
5. The charging clause. Generally an assignment by the mortgagor with full title guarantee in favour of the mortgagee with a provision for re-assignment or discharge upon payment of all sums secured by the aircraft mortgage.
6. Mortgagor's covenants:
    - to use the aircraft carefully, properly and legally and to maintain the aircraft;
    - to hangar the aircraft at an agreed location(s);
    - to comply with all laws and regulations relating to the aircraft and its operation and use wherever it may be;

---

[8] It is otherwise if the mortgage is created in Scotland. See below.

[9] To register an aircraft mortgage the applicant is obliged to provide details of the amount of the sum secured and consequently it is common for details of the loan and repayment terms to be within the Aircraft Mortgage rather than in a separate loan agreement.

- to maintain the current registration of the aircraft and to comply with all mandatory airworthiness directives, air navigation orders and alert service bulletins relating to the aircraft;
- to obtain and maintain all necessary licences and authorisations for the use of the aircraft;
- to maintain the manuals relating to the aircraft;
- not to sell, encumber, let, charter or otherwise dispose of the aircraft or to lose control of it;
- not to allow the aircraft to become the subject of any judicial action, lien or right of detention and pay rents for anywhere the aircraft is kept;
- to insure the aircraft hull on an agreed value basis (rather than on a replacement value basis since the mortgagee will always require its financial interest to be secured by insurance) and to insure the mortgagor and the mortgagee for liabilities to third parties arising out of the presence, use or operation of the aircraft. The mortgagor agrees to procure that the payment of insurance money in relation to a claim on the hull policy be made to the mortgagee in the case of a total loss or to pay for repairs in the case of a partial loss;
- to repair all damage suffered by the aircraft;
- to pay all taxes or airport charges relating to the aircraft or its operation;
- to indemnify the mortgagee against any claims, expenses, liabilities, costs relating to the operation or use of the aircraft.

7. Default or Breach and the mortgagee's remedies. On default in payment by the mortgagor, breach of the terms of the aircraft mortgage by the mortgagor, or the insolvency of the mortgagor causes the security created by the mortgage to become enforceable. The powers of the mortgagee are then listed and usually include the following power:
    - to take possession of the aircraft;
    - to sell the aircraft (this is implied at law but invariably included in the aircraft mortgage) and to give a receipt for the purchase money;
    - to appoint a receiver of the aircraft (although it may do so without an express power if the mortgagee has obtained a

judgment against the mortgagor which remains unsatisfied); and

- to operate, let and use the aircraft for so long as it may wish.

The powers of a receiver are generally set out *seriatim*. The order of application of the proceeds of sale are also generally set out namely:

- to pay costs of taking possession or of enforcing the mortgage;
- to pay arrears of interest;
- to repay the loan;
- to pay any other moneys owing under the aircraft mortgage; and
- to pay any surplus to the mortgagor.

8. An aircraft mortgage will also include provisions relating to further assurance, consolidation of mortgages, a notice and a governing law provision.

Although the MAO does not prescribe any form of mortgage in England, Schedule 2 Part 1 (the application of the Order to Scotland) prescribes that a security created in Scotland under Article 3 of the MAO shall be constituted by a mortgage in or as nearly as may be in, the form specified in Part 2 of Schedule 2 of the MAO. The crucial test is where the mortgage is created. However the prescribed form to be used where the mortgage is created in Scotland doesn't include any provisions relating to the loan to be granted the terms of which must be in a separate document. Neither does the MAO prohibit other terms being agreed between the mortgagor and the mortgagee. Consequently any terms which are regarded as desirable may be added to the loan agreement or provided in a separate deed of covenant between the mortgagor and the mortgagee.

Registration

To register a mortgage the form prescribed by Schedule 1 Part 1 of the MAO is used together with a certified copy of the mortgage and fee. The Register will record the following: first, a description of the aircraft including its type, nationality and registration marks and the manufacturer's serial number; second, a description of any store of spare parts including an indication of their character and approximate number and the place or places where they are stored; third, the name and address and where applicable the company registration number of the mortgagor. When an application to enter an aircraft mortgage or priority notice in the Register is duly made the Authority will enter the aircraft mortgage or the priority notice in the Register by placing the application form thereon and by noting on it the date and time of the entry.[10]

The Authority will notify the applicant of the date and time of the entry of the mortgage or the priority notice in the Register and of the register number of the entry and will send a copy of the notification to the mortgagor and the owner of the aircraft appearing in the United Kingdom Nationality Register.[11] A priority notice may be registered where there is an intention to register a mortgage in the future.[12] Priority is only given if the mortgage which is contemplated is made and entered into within 14 days of the entry of the priority notice. Separate applications are required if a mortgage covers more than one aircraft or if more than one mortgage affects a single aircraft.[13] Article 8 provides that changes in the registration particulars may be notified on behalf of the mortgagee and the form prescribed for so doing is given under Schedule 1 Part 3. There is provision for transfer of the mortgage in the form prescribed by Schedule 1 Part 4 and Schedule 2 Part 3 (Scotland) and discharges may be made by filing the form set out in Schedule 1 Part 4 and Schedule 2 (Scotland) duly signed by the mortgagee together with a copy of the document of discharge or any other document which shows to the Civil Aviation Authority's (CAA) satisfaction that the mortgage has been discharged. The form is then entered in the register and the entries are marked "discharged".

There is provision for rectification of the register upon an Order of the High Court.[14] The register of aircraft mortgages is open to the public upon payment of an appropriate fee and inspection may be made in person or by application for a certified copy of the entries in the register.[15] An application may also be made to be notified as to whether or not there are any relevant entries in the register.[16] An entry in the register of mortgages is admissible in evidence if certified as a true copy by the CAA. Removal of an aircraft from the UK nationality register does not affect the rights of

---

[10] MAO 1972, Article 7(1).
[11] MAO 1972, Article 7(4).
[12] MAO 1972, Article 5.
[13] MAO 1972, Article 6.
[14] MAO 1972, Article 10.
[15] MAO 1972, Article 11(2).
[16] MAO 1972, Article 11(3).

any mortgagee under any registered mortgage and entry shall continue to be made in the register as if the aircraft had not been removed.[17]

The Effect of Registration

This can be simply stated: first, the registered aircraft mortgage will take priority over all other mortgages and charges save for prior registered mortgages (or priority notices current in respect of them) and mortgages created prior to October 1972 when the MAO was introduced; second, all persons are deemed to have express notice of all facts appearing on the register although the registration of a mortgage does not contribute evidence of its validity; third, registered mortgages are not affected by or subject to the terms of the Bill of Sale Acts 1878 and 1882; last, the CAA will indemnify any person suffering loss by reason of any error or omission on the register or of any inaccuracy in the copy of an entry in the register supplied by the registree.[18]

With regard to the international recognition of a mortgage registered at the UK Register of Aircraft Mortgages, the Geneva Convention on the International Recognition of Rights in Aircraft[19] may govern the matter but a number of countries have not ratified it (including the United Kingdom, Ireland, Canada and Australia although the concept of aircraft mortgages is established in each of them) and other countries (for example, Belgium and Austria) do not recognise aircraft mortgages at all. Consequently, a UK mortgage of an aircraft may not be recognised or enforceable in other countries. This problem is mitigated since most legal systems regard rights *in rem* over aircraft to be governed by the *lex registri*, that is, the law of the jurisdiction where the aircraft is registered, though difficulties may still occur where, for example, the insolvency law in a country where an aircraft mortgage is not recognised may prevail. A Contracting State (one that has ratified the Geneva Convention) may apply its own laws when considering mortgages of aircraft registered in Non-Contracting States so the closer the form of the aircraft mortgage of the Non-Contracting State is to the form used in the Contracting State in which it is sought to enforce it the easier enforcement is likely to be. However a UK aircraft mortgage will not be

---

[17] MAO 1972, Article 12.

[18] MAO 1972, Article 18.

[19] Signed at Geneva 19 June 1948, 310 UNTS 151.

recognised in, for example, the Netherlands if the aircraft happens to be there when the mortgagor becomes insolvent.

Even between two Contracting States problems may occur as some jurisdictions will not enforce mortgages created under other jurisdictions, for example, when the rights of creditors in an insolvency compete with a mortgagee. The problem is that each situation needs to be addressed individually and there are no general rules. Where the aircraft is located at the time of insolvency or enforcement, the state of registration of the aircraft and the law governing the mortgage as well as whether any of these jurisdictions is a contracting state are all relevant. If the Convention does not apply, certain lien holders may have priority over the mortgagee whilst even if the mortgage is recorded in a contracting state and enforcement is sought in a contracting state certain matters still have priority to the claim of a mortgagee since the Convention provides the following priorities: first, Customs and air navigation charges (Article XII); second, costs of enforcement (Article VII Paragraph 6); third, claims for spare parts (Article X); lastly, salvage and preservation costs (Article IV), damage on the ground caused to third parties (Article VII Paragraph 5) and then purchase options lease rights and mortgage rights (Article I).

Protection against prior rights arising may be possible in a contracting state by the mortgagor prohibiting the mortgagee from registering such rights in the aircraft register or prohibiting sub-letting of the aircraft to a country not being a contracting state. The contractual relationship between mortgagor and mortgagee is governed by the proper law of the contract usually as chosen by the parties but otherwise that relationship is governed by the law of the jurisdiction with which the mortgagee is most closely connected. However it does not follow that this law decides whether title to the aircraft has passed to the mortgagee. Generally the law that governs this is the *lex situs*, (the law of the place where the aircraft is situated at the time of the transfer) but this is difficult to determine in the case of an aircraft so probably the proper law of the contract governs the transfer of title. To be certain in an uncertain situation it is advisable when entering into a mortgage for the mortgagee to ensure that the aircraft is located in the place which contractually is the proper law of the contract so that the proper law and the *lex situs* are the same.

Flying the aircraft to another jurisdiction may adversely affect the enforceability of the mortgage if rights created in it are not recognised by the new jurisdiction, for example, a mortgage in England can be overreached by a sale to a bona fide purchaser in a country which does not recognise the mortgage unless it is registered on that country's mortgage register and an English court may have to recognise this situation even if the mortgage is enforced here when the aircraft returns. An English Court will usually uphold a choice of the governing law by the parties to a mortgage subject to the following exceptions as laid out in the Rome Convention on Contractual Obligations: first, the choice of governing law shall not prejudice the application of the rules of law of the country with which it has connection; second, nothing can restrict the application of the rules of the *lex fori* which are mandatory irrespective of the law governing the contract; third, the rule of the chosen law may be refused only if its application is manifestly incompatible with the public policy of the *lex fori*.

5 The Rights of a Ship's Mortgagee in English Law

GOTTHARD M GAUCI

The Legal Context[1]

Although its real origin is unknown,[2] the ship's mortgage is a widely utilised mechanism included in the process of ship finance. It is also a mechanism which, to a very large and substantial extent, is intertwined with the system of registration of such mortgages, which, although not compulsory, is particularly relevant in relation to priorities and in relation to enforcement against third parties.

The current English law system of ship registration in the Merchant Shipping Act 1995[3] and in the Merchant Shipping (Registration) Regulations 1993[4] abandons the system which had existed up to 1988 in terms of which there was a requirement as distinct from an entitlement for ships which qualified to be British ships to be registered as British ships.[5] Historically there had been an obligation to register a British ship if it qualified as such. This was specified in s 2 of the Merchant Shipping Act

[1] This chapter will address the rights of a ship's mortgagee in terms of English law. Selective reference will be made for comparative purposes to other legal systems, particularly that of Malta, in view of its popularity in ship financing. Unless otherwise stated all references in this article refer to English law. The author wishes to acknowledge the helpful discussions he had with Mr Jonathan Pace of the Malta Maritime Authority, Dr Anne Fenech and Dr Andrew Borg Cardona. Responsibility for any errors remains with the author.

[2] Tetley, *Maritime Liens and Claims* (1985) p 205.

[3] [1995] c 21.

[4] Statutory Instrument No 3138 of 1993. These regulations have been amended by: the Merchant Shipping (Registration of Ships) (Amendment) Regulations 1998 (SI 1998 No 2976).

[5] A system of registration of ships was introduced in the Navigation Act of 1660 [12 Car 2, c 18, s 10 AD 1660]. See Tenterden, *A Treatise on the Law relative to Merchant Ships and Seamen* (1901) p 77 fn D.

1894 which stated in sub-paragraph (1) that "[e]very British ship shall, unless exempted from registry be registered under this Act". Exemptions were specified in s 3: "ships not exceeding fifteen tons burden employed solely in navigation on the rivers or coasts of the United Kingdom, or on the rivers or coasts of some British possession within which the managing owners of the ships are resident", and "ships not exceeding thirty tons burden and not having a whole or fixed deck, and employed solely in fishing or trading coastwise on the shores of Newfoundland or parts adjacent thereto, or in the Gulf of St Lawrence, or on such portions of the coasts of Canada as lie bordering on that gulf". The obligation of registration was repealed by the Merchant Shipping Act 1988, and the registration legislation is now contained in the Merchant Shipping Act 1995, and in the Merchant Shipping (Registration) Regulations 1993. A mortgage on property of a company registered in England and Wales is further subject to s 395 of the Companies Act 1985.[6]

In terms of Part II of the Merchant Shipping (Registration of Ships) Regulations 1993, the Register of British Ships in the United Kingdom is divided into four parts: Part I which is the main register, Part II for fishing vessels, Part III for small ships[7] and Part IV for bareboat registered vessels.[8] The system of registration of mortgages and transfer by a bill of sale is excluded from application to small ships;[9] similarly s 17 of the Merchant Shipping Act 1995, in the case of bareboat charter registration, refers issues

---

[6] Section 395(1) states as follows: "(1) ... a charge created by a company registered in England and Wales and being a charge to which this section applies is, so far as any security on the company's property or undertaking is conferred by the charge, void against the liquidator [or administrator] and any creditor of the company, unless the prescribed particulars of the charge together with the instrument (if any) by which the charge is created or evidenced, are delivered to or received by the registrar of companies for registration in manner required by this Chapter within twenty-one days after the date of the charge's creation".

[7] A "small ship" is defined for the purposes of the Merchant Shipping (Registration of Ships) Regulations 1993 [SI 1993 No 3138] as meaning "a ship which is less than twenty four metres in overall length and is, or is applying to be, registered under Part XI of the Regulations".

[8] The term "bareboat charter term" is defined in s 17(11) of the Merchant Shipping Act 1995 as "the hiring of the ship for a stipulated period on terms which give the charterer possession and control of the ship, including the right to appoint the master and crew".

[9] Paragraph 91 of The Merchant Shipping (Registration of Ships) Regulations 1993.

relating to mortgages to the legal system of the underlying registry.[10] Paragraph 7 of Schedule 1 of the Merchant Shipping Act 1995[11] provides that "[a] registered ship, or share in a registered ship" may be made a security for the repayment of a loan or the discharge of any other obligation, and refers to the instrument creating such security as a mortgage. Section 313 of the same Act defines a "ship" as including every description of vessel used in navigation. This would exclude a ship which is in the process of construction. In contrast to the British Merchant Shipping Act, the Italian *Codice della Navigazione* allows the registration of a hypothec[12] on vessels in the process of being built from the point in time that a note is made of such vessels in the register.[13] It may also be noted that whereas the British ship registration system provides only for the registration of a security interest by way of mortgage, the Maltese Merchant Shipping Act for example, makes provision for the registration of other interests: privileges or charges over any part, appurtenance or accessory of a ship;[14] and reservation of ownership rights on any such part, appurtenance or accessory.[15] Furthermore, a mortgagee is offered further protection under the Maltese registration system in relation to a prohibition of further mortgages and prohibition of transfer where this is agreed between the parties. In such instances, the registrar is required to make a note to this effect in the register, and furthermore, on pain of nullity of the registration, contractually prohibited mortgages and transfers will not be recorded in the register unless the consent of the registered mortgagee is produced; an exception is made in relation to a sale by court order.[16]

The system of registration of mortgages allows for notification to third parties through public access at the registry of shipping. Although this system normally avoids the problems associated with latent mortgages, as will be noted below, in the English legal system, enforceability of a mortgage against third parties does not necessarily depend on registration

---

[10] This is a reference to the legal system from which the registered vessel has been bareboat-chartered out. Regulation 3 of the Merchant Shipping (Registration of Ships) Regulations 1993 provides that there are two types of registration of fishing vessels, that is, simple registration and full registration; registration of mortgages is possible only in relation to the latter category.

[11] [1995] c 21.

[12] See *infra* text at fn 37, in relation to hypothecs.

[13] Article 566.

[14] Chapter 234 of the Laws of Malta, s 40(2).

[15] Section 40(2) and (3).

[16] Section 39(3).

but on whether or not the mortgage is legal as distinct from equitable. It is noteworthy that the contents of the certificate of registry give rise to a rebuttable presumption of the veracity of the statements therein contained,[17] and the same reasoning can be extended *vis-à-vis* the actual entries in the ship's register.

The Legal Framework of a Ship's Mortgage

It has been said that the ship mortgage until 1854 involved a property transfer mortgage.[18] As will be discussed below, the current system retains elements of the old system subject to changes introduced by legislation.

In English Law, the ship's mortgage originated from the common law and not from *the lex mercatoria* or *lex maritime*.[19] In the *lex maritima*, a method of acquiring finance was that of the bottomry bond, which although effectively obsolete,[20] is still referred to in the Supreme Court Act section 20, subsection 2, and in the 1952 Arrest Convention.[21] Bottomry has been said to have been in existence in Greek law in the fourth century BC,[22] and also in Roman law and later Codes.[23] It may be noted that the Admiralty Courts initially did not have jurisdiction over mortgages, as this lay within the ambit of control of the courts of equity and of common law.[24] Jurisdiction was later granted to the Admiralty Courts by statutes in 1840, 1861 and later years.[25]

However, despite the changes effected through legislation, the mortgage still involves a transfer of legal interests and this remains the position between mortgagor and mortgagee. The case of *Keith* v *Burrows*[26] is normally referred to as the authority expounding the traditional view of

---

[17] See *R* v *Bjornsen* [1865] 10 Cox CC 74.

[18] See Clarke A, "Ship Mortgages" *Interests in Goods*, Palmer and McKendrick (ed) 2nd ed (1998) at p 675.

[19] Tetley W, *Maritime Liens and Claims* (1985) p 207.

[20] The need for large amounts of capital in the 19th century shipping industry is said to have rendered the use of bottomry impractical. See Tetley, *supra* p 205.

[21] International Convention for the Unification of Certain Rules Relating to the Arrest of Sea-Going Vessels 1952, Article 1.

[22] Tetley, *Maritime Liens and Claims* (1985) p 205.

[23] *Ibid.*

[24] *Ibid.*

[25] *Ibid.*

[26] [1876] CPD 722 at p 731.

the current British ship's mortgage, that is, "that the ship mortgage transfers ownership to the mortgagee, but that paragraph 10[27] restrains the mortgagee exercising ownership-type rights, except so far as may be necessary to make the ship available as security".[28] Here it was stated:

> The word "mortgagee" is a well-known word, and signifies a transfer of property by way of security:... A mortgage is a transfer of all the mortgagor's interest in the thing mortgaged; but such transfer is not absolute; it is made only by way of security; or, in other words, it is subject to redemption. Unless, therefore, there is any statutory enactment to the contrary, and so far as there is no enactment to the contrary, the plaintiffs in this case acquired by their mortgage the whole of the mortgagor's interest in the ship, or, in other words, the legal title to the ship as security.

Similarly Constant states:

> The effect of a legal mortgage is to pass the mortgagor's interest in the mortgaged property to the mortgagee, subject to the right of the mortgagor to redeem his property by paying off the mortgage debt with interest at any time after the date specified in the mortgage as the date for repayment provided the mortgage has not been foreclosed or the property sold under the mortgagee's power of sale.[29]

This traditional view of a mortgage essentially reflects the position of a common law mortgage. It is only slightly different from the old Roman law mortgage which involved "the transfer of ownership with possession, with an understanding , *fiducia*, for its reconveyance".[30]

The notion of the mortgagee having all the legal interest transferred to him by reason of the mortgage is tempered by the equitable principle of redemption[31] and also by statutory provisions, notably paragraph 10 of Schedule 1 of the Merchant Shipping Act 1995, which provides:

> Where a ship or share is subject to a registered mortgage then -
> (a) except so far as may be necessary for making the ship or share available as a security for the mortgage debt, the mortgagee shall not

[27] See *infra* text at fn 32.

[28] Clarke A, "Ship Mortgages" *op cit* fn 18 at p 674.

[29] Constant B, *The Law Relating to the Mortgages of Ships* (1920) § 21.

[30] Turner RW, *The Equity of Redemption* (1931) p 111.

[31] The equitable principle of redemption is protected by the rule prohibiting "clogging". See Constant *op cit* fn 29 § 16.

by reason of the mortgage be treated as owner of the ship or share; and

(b) the mortgagor shall be treated as not having ceased to be the owner or share.

This provision is derived from the slightly different wording of section 34 of the Merchant Shipping Act 1894 which provided that "[e]xcept as far as may be necessary for making a mortgaged ship or share available as a security for the mortgage debt, the mortgagee shall not by reason of the mortgage be deemed to be the owner of the ship or share, nor shall the mortgagor be deemed to have ceased to be the owner thereof".[32]

One interpretation is that paragraph 10 referred to above effectively modifies the mortgage as an outright property transfer and applies a different rule to the ship's mortgage. According to the 1914 edition of Halsbury's Laws of England: "[t]he result is that while as between the parties to the mortgage the property in the ship has passed, yet so far as regards third parties the mortgagor remains *dominus* with regard to everything connected with the employment of the ship, and the mortgagee is protected from liabilities connected therewith".[33] The position of the English law ship mortgage is thus rendered - in so far as the relationship between mortgagor/mortgagee and third parties is concerned - similar to that of the Roman Law *hypotheca*. Via the mechanism of the *hypotheca*, ownership and possession do not pass - it is purely a security interest. It may be noted that Roman law recognised three related rights in rem as mechanisms for the obtainment of financial security: these were the *fiducia*, the *pignus*, and the *hypotheca*.[34] The *contractus fiduciae*, referred to earlier in this Chapter, was an agreement that "if the purchase-money were repaid

---

[32] This provision is in turn derived from s 43 of the 1823 Act for the Registering of Vessels [4 Geo 4, c 41] which provided: "... the person or persons to whom such transfer shall be made, or any other person or persons claiming under him or them as a mortgagee or mortgagees, ... shall not by reason thereof be deemed to be the owner or owners of such ship or vessel, share or shares thereof, to have ceased to be an owner or owners of such ship or vessel, any more than if no such transfer had been made, except so far as may be necessary for the purpose of rendering the ship or vessel, share or shares so transferred, available by sale or otherwise, for the payment of the debt or debts for securing the payment of which such transfer shall have been made". It may be noted that s 34 of the Merchant Shipping Act of 1894 is obviously the source of the latter part of s 42(1)(a) of the Maltese Merchant Shipping Act.

[33] Vol 26 § 29.

[34] Hunter MA, *Roman Law* 4th ed (1903) at p 430 *et seq.*

by a day named, the lender would re-convey the property to the borrower".[35] A change was effected via praetorial intervention through the creation of the *pignus* regime, in which the lender retained possession, but ownership and rights *in rem* remained with the borrower".[36] Finally, a transition was made through the *actio quasi-Serviana* (or *hypothecaria*) towards the institution of the *hypotheca*, in terms of which the borrower retained ownership, possession and enjoyment until default.[37]

Perhaps it may be time for the legislator to consider altering the British ship mortgage and to bring it fully into line with the *hypotheca* in terms of which the borrower has only a security interest in the property.[38]

Mortgages Distinguished from Bottomry

Bottomry has been described as "a contract whereby in certain circumstances a ship or a ship and her freight, with, if necessary, her cargo, may be charged with the repayment, on safe arrival, of a debt contracted for the ship's preservation or to enable her to continue upon her voyage".[39] Bottomry bears a strong resemblance to a pledge; however, possession is retained by the owner and the privilege or maritime lien[40] arising out of the existence of the bond is enforceable through Admiralty proceedings.[41] The bottomry bond is subject to a number of restrictions for its validity; for instance the master's authority "to raise money from bottomry arises only in case of urgent necessity, and not only must the expenditure in respect of which the charge is given be one which a reasonable and prudent owner, if present, would incur in order to enable the ship to prosecute her voyage, but the money must be incapable of being raised without resorting to bottomry".[42]

The bond becomes void on the total loss - not a constructive total loss[43] - of the vessel or other property which is the object of the bond, in which case the debt will automatically be extinguished. However, the bond

---

[35] Hunter *ibid* p 431.
[36] Hunter *ibid* p 433.
[37] Hunter *ibid* pp 433-434.
[38] See, generally, Clarke A, *op cit* fn 18.
[39] Constant B, *The Law Relating to Mortgages of Ships* (1920) § 71.
[40] See *infra* in relation to maritime liens.
[41] Constant B, *The Law Relating to Mortgages of Ships* (1920) § 80.
[42] Constant B, *ibid* § 74.
[43] For the implications of a constructive total loss under English law, see the Marine Insurance Act 1906 ss 60 *et seq.*

attaches to the last plank.[44] A mortgage is different in the sense that it is an outright security for a debt which, as long as it is not otherwise terminated, survives the destruction of the security.

Mortgages Distinguished from Maritime Liens

The maritime lien, unlike the mortgage, arises *ipso facto* by the operation of the law. It is a creature of the *lex maritima*, and it is authoritatively stated that it arises "automatically without any antecedent formality and simultaneously with the cause of action and confers a true charge on the ship and freight of a proprietary nature in favour of the privileged creditor... [the lien] goes with the ship everywhere even into the hands of a purchaser for value without notice and has a ranking with other maritime liens - all of which take precedence over mortgages".[45]

Mortgages in United States federal law are closely linked to maritime liens and it is possible for a mortgage to be elevated to the status of a maritime lien. The Ship Mortgage Act 1920 provides for a "preferred ship mortgage" which gives rise to a maritime lien against the mortgaged vessel.[46] For the 'preferred' status to be obtained, certain formalities have to be followed.[47]

---

[44] Constant B, *The Law Relating to Mortgages of Ships* (1920) § 79.

[45] *The Tolten* [1946] pp 135, 140, per Lord Scott. A typical maritime lien is that created as a result of damage caused by a ship. It may be noted that maritime liens also arise *inter alia* in the following causes: for money given on the security of a bottomry bond, and funds provided on the security of a *respondentia* bond. In *The Bold Buccleugh* [1851] 7 Moo PC 267, Sir John Jervis commented as follows: "Having its origin in the rule of the civil law, a maritime lien is well defined by Lord Tenterden, to mean a claim or privilege upon a thing to be carried into effect by legal process and Mr Justice Story ... explains that process to be a proceeding *in rem* and adds, that wherever a lien or claim is given upon the thing, then the Admiralty forces it by a proceeding *in rem*, and indeed is the only court competent to enforce it... This claim or privilege travels with the thing into whosoever's possession it may come. It is inchoate from the moment the claim or privilege attaches, and, when carried into effect by legal process, by a proceeding *in rem*, relates back to the period when it first attached".

[46] See Schoenbaum T, *Admiralty and Maritime Law* 2nd ed (1994) § 9-5; 46 U S C § 31322, 31325.

[47] *Ibid.*

Mortgagee's Powers

Registered Mortgagee's Power of Sale

This is dealt with in paragraph 9 of Schedule 1 of the Merchant Shipping Act 1995:

> (1) Subject to sub-paragraph (2) below, every registered mortgagee shall have power, if the mortgage money or any part of it be due, to sell the ship or share in respect of which he is registered and to give effectual receipts for the purchase money.
> (2) Where two or more mortgagees are registered in respect of the same ship or share, a subsequent mortgagee shall not, except under an order of a court of competent jurisdiction, sell the ship or share without the concurrence of every prior mortgagee.

This is a very powerful provision; it may be viewed as an effect of the common law position in terms of which the mortgagee becomes the owner of the vessel for the purposes of the mortgagor-mortgagee relationship.[48] It is available to a registered mortgagee and is subject to the equitable right of redemption; a mortgagee may be liable in damages if he prevents the mortgagor from exercising his right of redemption,[49] and redemption is further protected by the anti-clogging doctrine.[50] There is a right of the mortgagor to redeem the mortgage until the sale or until the mortgage is foreclosed. An equitable mortgagee does not seem to be able to utilise this power of extra-judicial sale as the legislation refers to a registered mortgage; possibly he may have a right to utilise section 101(1) of the Law

---

[48] See *supra* text at fn 33.

[49] The legal justification of this right was referred to in *Fletcher* v *Campbell* [1968] 2 Lloyd's Rep 520. According to Roskill J: "... in my judgment, there is, as a matter of English law, a right in the mortgagor of a ship to recover damages against his mortgagee, if his right to redeem is prevented by the wrongful act of the mortgagee. I do not think it matters whether one makes the necessary implication into the collateral deed as a matter of law or whether one makes the implication therein as arising from the other express terms of the deed or whether one arrives at the same result by the application of basic principles of equity. Basically....the ordinary principles of the law relating to mortgages and their redemption apply and, as I read the cases, have always been applied to mortgages of ships during the 19th century". [pp 538-539].

[50] See Constant B, *The Law Relating to the Mortgages of Ships* (1920) p 16.

of Property Act 1925.[51] Caselaw supports the view that an abuse of the power of sale by the mortgagee would give rise to a claim in damages.[52] According to Constant:

> In the exercise of this power of sale the mortgagee must act *bona fide* for the purpose of realising his security and must take reasonable precautions to secure a proper price. If he does not, the Court may grant an injunction at the instance of the mortgagor or any other person interested in the proceeds to restrain the mortgagee from proceeding with the sale ... and the Court will even set aside a contract of sale by a mortgagee which has been effected by fraud if relief is sought properly .... Again, right of sale may be expressly limited by the mortgage, and where that is so the mortgagee can only sell in accordance with that limitation, so that where a mortgage stipulated that the mortgagee should sell at public auction the sale of the ship by private treaty was held improper and the mortgagee liable in damages to the mortgagor.[53]

Section 42, as recently amended,[54] of the Malta Merchant Shipping Act[55] contains a provision similar to paragraph 9 of Schedule 1 of the British Merchant Shipping Act 1995 to the effect that "[i]n the event of default of any term or condition of a registered mortgage or of any document or agreement referred to therein, the mortgagee shall, upon giving notice to the mortgagor ... have power absolutely to sell the ship or share in respect of which he is registered..." Subsequent mortgagees are afforded a degree of protection. The specific right of redemption, alien to the basic civilian law system applicable in Malta, is not referred to in the Maltese Merchant Shipping Act,[56] and this would make it ideal for protective provisions to be utilised as part of the contractual agreement; there is however protection under the general principles relating to payment under the Maltese Civil Code in relation to the obligation of a creditor to accept payment when this is outstanding.[57]

---

[51] 15 & 16 Geo 5, c 20.

[52] See *Bank of Cyprus* v *Gill* [1980] 2 Lloyd's Rep 51, which related to a mortgage of land. See also *The Jocylene* [1984] 2 Lloyd's Rep 569.

[53] Constant B, *The Law Relating to the Mortgages of Ships* (1920) § 39.

[54] Amendment made by Act XXII of 2000.

[55] Chapter 234 of the Laws of Malta.

[56] Chapter 234 of the Laws of Malta.

[57] See ss 1148, 1149 *et seq*, of the Maltese Civil Code [Chapter 16 of the Laws of Malta]. In the case of a judicial sale, s 256(2) of the Code of Organization and Civil Procedure [Chapter 12 of the Laws of Malta] provides protection for the

When the extra-judicial sale is effected, the right of the mortgagor to foreclose comes to an end.[58] The mortgagee becomes a trustee in relation to any balance from the payment of the mortgage debt and the expenses relating to possession and sale.[59] Constant states the legal position in the following terms: "A mortgagee, therefore, who has sold the mortgaged property and finds himself with a surplus after paying off his own debt is bound to discharge out of that surplus the debt of any subsequent incumbrance of which he has notice and to pay the ultimate balance to the mortgagor, and if he has any difficulty in deciding how to deal with the surplus in his hands, he may pay the money into court for distribution".[60]

The mortgagee may also utilise his right to force a judicial sale. This will be in terms of proceedings started under the jurisdiction provided under section 20(2)(c) of the Supreme Court Act 1981; the court may order the sale of the vessel either *pendente lite*[61] or on judgment.[62] Although there may be commercial disadvantages to a judicial sale,[63] there may be advantages for the claimant in adopting this procedure rather than the extra-judicial sale, because the use of the court procedure protects the claimant from allegations of an abusive sale. Furthermore, under English law, the buyer in a judicial sale will know that he acquires a vessel with a clean title and unencumbranced by maritime liens or other charges.[64]

As stated earlier the mortgagor has a right to redeem; however, this may be blocked by an action for foreclosure.[65] It may be noted however that there is doubt as to whether this procedure can be utilised in relation to a registered ship mortgage.[66]

---

mortgagee by providing that the execution of an executive title cannot be effected before the lapse of two days after a the service of a request of payment by means of a judicial act.

[58] Constant B, *The Law Relating to the Mortgages of Ships* (1920) § 40.

[59] *Ibid.*

[60] *Ibid.* See also *The Glastnos* [1991] 1 Lloyd's Rep 482.

[61] See Meeson N, *Admiralty Jurisdiction and Practice* 2nd ed (2000) § 4-115.

[62] See Meeson N, *ibid* § 4-096.

[63] See Meeson N, *ibid* § 10-212.

[64] See *The Tremont* [1871] 1 Wm Rob 163; *The Acrux* [1962] 1 Lloyd's Rep 405; *The Cerro Colorado* [1993] 1 Lloyd's Rep 58.

[65] Constant B, *The Law Relating to the Mortgages of Ships* (1920) § 37.

[66] Meeson N, *Admiralty Jurisdiction and Practice* 2nd ed (2000) § 10-183: "It is doubtful however whether the remedy of foreclosure is available as regards a registered ship mortgage given the nature of the security as being a form of charge. It could nonetheless be resorted to in the case of an unregistered mortgage of an unregistered ship".

Right to Take Possession of the Vessel

The mortgagee may, in some circumstances, have a right to take possession of the ship. This may well be specified in the deed of covenants.[67] This right is not specified in the Merchant Shipping Act 1995; however, it is well established in English case-law. The legal position is stated in Constant to be that there is a right to take possession where there is default under the express term of the mortgage, and that it also extends to the case where the mortgagor is acting in such a manner as to materially imperil the security.[68] There are various mechanisms for a mortgagee to take possession of the vessel used as security, namely, by physically putting his representative on board; by obtaining a court order for the arrest of the ship, and by constructive possession; this last procedure consists in "giving notice to all parties interested of his intention to take actual possession at the first available opportunity".[69] The effect of taking over possession of the vessel has been said to be that the mortgagee becomes master and owner of it.[70] However, title is not perfected in the sense that the mortgagor still has a right to redeem the object of the mortgage. The mortgagee by taking over possession becomes liable for expenses incurred after that date.[71] It may be noted that the mortgagee is excluded from primary liability *vis-à-vis* the victims of pollution in terms of the International Convention on Civil Liability for Oil Pollution Damage 1992 and the International Convention on Liability and Compensation for Damage in Connection with the Carriage of Hazardous and Noxious Substances 1996. Both these Conventions impose strict primary liability, in the case of a registered ship, on the registered owner of that ship, without prejudice to the right of recourse; in contrast the International Convention on Civil Liability for Bunker Oil Pollution Damage 2001 imposes strict liability

---

[67] Meeson N, *ibid* § 10-130.

[68] Constant B, *The Law Relating to the Mortgages of Ships* (1920) § 26 *et seq*, and case law there cited.

[69] Constant B, *ibid* § 29.

[70] Constant B, *ibid* § 30.

[71] Constant B, *ibid* § 36, where it is stated: "Inasmuch as by the act of taking possession of a mortgaged ship the mortgagee takes the entire dominion of her as his property, it follows that all expenses incurred as from that date in the working of the ship are payable by him, and as from date the master becomes the agent and subject to the orders of the mortgagee. Moreover, the mortgagee is entitled to receive payment of all moneys otherwise payable to the mortgagor in respect of the mortgaged property, and of these he must keep careful account".

inter alia on the "operator" of a ship.[72] It is likely that the term "operator" will be interpreted to include a mortgagee in possession.

The Maltese Merchant Shipping Act[73] provides for the right of taking possession "in the event of default of any term or condition of a registered mortgage or of any document or agreement referred to therein".[74] The provision goes on further to state, on the basis of the obvious British source, that "except so far as may be necessary for making a mortgaged ship or share available as a security for the mortgage debt, the mortgagee shall not by reason of the mortgage be deemed to be the owner of the ship or share, nor shall the mortgagor be deemed to have ceased to be the owner thereof".[75] It is significant to note that the Malta Merchant Shipping Act provides in the same section for a right on the part of a mortgagee which is not specified in the British equivalent, that is: "[I]n the event of default of any term or condition of a registered mortgage, the mortgagee shall, upon giving notice to the mortgagor.... have power to apply for any extensions, pay fees, receive certificates, and generally do all such things in the name of the owner as may be required in order to maintain the status and validity of the registration of the ship".[76]

Right of Mortgagee to Insure their Interest in the Vessel

The mortgagee has a right to insure his interest in the vessel and the same can be said about the mortgagor. Section 14(1) of the Marine Insurance Act 1906[77] provides that "[w]here the subject-matter insured is mortgaged, the mortgagor has an insurable interest in the full value thereof, and the mortgagee has an insurable interest in respect of any sum due or to become due under the mortgage." The mortgagee can insure his interest via three basic mechanisms; firstly he can effect separate insurance to cover his own interest. A mortgagee has to be careful, in this respect, however, because an ordinary hull policy may not provide adequate cover. In the well-known case of *Samuel* v *Dumas*[78], it was held that the wilful casting away of the vessel by the owner of that vessel was not covered within the risk of "perils of the seas" and therefore the mortgagee could not recover. This reasoning

[72] Articles 1 and 3.

[73] Chapter 234 of the Laws of Malta.

[74] *Ibid* s 42, as amended by Act XXII of 2000.

[75] *Ibid.*

[76] *Ibid.*

[77] 6 Edw 7 c 41.

[78] [1924] AC 431.

would apply equally whether the assured is the owner or the mortgagee and for this reason it is customary for mortgagees to obtain further coverage under, for example, the Institute Mortgagee's Interest Clauses [Hulls].[79] Clause 1.1 thereof provides:

> This insurance will indemnify the Assured for loss resulting from loss of or damage to or liability of the Mortgaged Vessel which, in the absence of an Insured Peril set out in Clause 2.1 below, would prima facie be covered by the Owners' Policies and Club Entries, and not excluded therein, but in respect of which there is subsequent non-payment (or reduced payment which is approved in advance by the Underwriters hereon) by any of the underwriters of Owners' Policies and Club Entries as a result of any Insured Peril, *provided always that such Insured peril occurs or exists without the privity of the Assured.*

Moreover, Clause 2.1 includes, under Insured Perils, "any deliberate or fraudulent casting away of or damage to the Mortgaged vessel".

The mortgagee can cover his interest via an assignment of the primary insurance of the mortgagor. Such an assignment would, in English law, be regulated by subsection (2) of section 50 of the Marine Insurance Act 1906 which provides that:

> Where a marine policy has been assigned so as to pass the beneficial interest in the policy, the assignee of the policy is entitled to sue thereon in his own name; and the defendant is entitled to make any defence arising out of the contract which he would have been entitled to make if the action had been brought in the name of the person by or on behalf of whom the policy was effected.

It may also be noted at this point that the assignee does not obtain any more rights than the assignor has.[80] A valid defence would be the fact that the loss was caused by the wilful misconduct of the assured.[81]

A further alternative is that both the mortgagor and mortgagee could be co-assured under the same policy.[82] This may cause problems to a

---

[79] Dated 1/3/1997.

[80] See Lambeth RJ, *Templeman on Marine Insurance* pp 75-76, where reference is made to the case of *Graham Joint Stock Shipping Co Ltd* v *Merchants Marine Insurance Co Ltd* [17] Ll L Rep 44.

[81] See s 55 of the Marine Insurance Act 1906.

[82] It should be noted that the Norwegian Marine Insurance Plan 1996, Version 1999, addresses co-insurance of mortgagees in Chapter 7.

mortgagee if the policy is considered to be joint rather than composite as in such a case the underwriter could utilise the defence of wilful misconduct of one co-assured as a defence against the other co-assured. It is unlikely that the interests of mortgagee and mortgagor will be considered to be joint; support for this view can be found in *Arnould*, where it is stated that "[g]enerally when two or more interests are insured under the same policy, the policy will be construed as a composite insurance, insuring each person interested severally in respect of his own interest" and that "[t]here can only be a joint insurance in the strict sense when the assured have a joint interest in the insured property, as where they are joint owners".[83]

The very nature of the security of the mortgage depends on the survivability of that mortgage, hence the need for assignment of insurance proceeds and other insurance provision. The Maltese Merchant Shipping Act[84] also protects the mortgagee by specifically providing that the "mortgage shall attach to any proceeds from any indemnity arising from collisions and other mishaps as well as any insurance proceeds".[85]

Droit de Suite

In English Law, a ship subject to a legal mortgage is transferable, but when transferred, it is transferred *cum onere suo*, that is, subject to that mortgage.[86] The *droit de suite* attributable to legal mortgages distinguishes mortgages from a number of other statutory rights *in rem* listed in section 20(2) of the Supreme Court Act 1981.[87] In fact, in the majority of cases, with one exception being the mortgage, the right of action *in rem* against a ship depends *interalia* on the premise that the person who would be liable on the claim in an action *in personam* was the owner, or charterer of or in possession or control of the ship when the cause of action arose.[88] However section 21(2) refers specifically to a number of instances - including claims

---

[83] Mustill and Gilman, *Arnould's Law of Marine Insurance and Average*, 16th ed (1981) § 341; see also MacGillivray and Parkington, Insurance Law, 8th ed (1988) where the example of a composite policy relating to the diverse interests of landlord, tenant and mortgagee is referred to. Both extracts are cited in *State of Netherlands* v *Youell* [1997] 2 Lloyd's Rep 440, at p 448.

[84] Chapter 234 of the Laws of Malta.

[85] Section 38(2).

[86] See below.

[87] [1981] c 54.

[88] See The Supreme Court Act 1981, s 21(4).

in respect of a mortgage - where an action *in rem* may be brought in the High Court against the ship, or property in connection with which the claim or question arises irrespective of ownership of the vessel. To this extent, the mortgage is put on a par with a maritime lien. It may be noted that section 20(7) provides that the reference to mortgages is not dependent on registration or the nature - that is, legal or equitable - of the mortgage, and includes a reference to mortgages created under foreign law. However, one must note that the *droit de suite* attaches in English Law only to a legal - registered or unregistered - mortgage.[89] To this extent, and to this extent only, the mortgage is put on a par with a maritime lien. It must be noted also that to a very limited extent statutory rights *in rem* other than mortgages do have an attribute of the *droit de suite*, in the sense that it is not the case that "if there is a change of ownership after action brought but before service or arrest, the right which is given to proceed in rem against the ship is thereupon to lapse".[90]

Specific Problems Caused by Non-registration of Mortgages on Unregistered Ships

The Shizelle[91] is probably the most important case on the law of ship's mortgages to emerge from the English courts in recent years. The facts were briefly the following. The plaintiffs - The British Credit Trust Ltd - lent £40,000 to Mr Martin. A marine mortgage was used as security. The defendants purchased the vessel, at the time unregistered, from Mr Martin. The sale was supported by a bill of sale for an unregistered vessel. Later Mr and Mrs Haddock, the purchasers, registered their ship in the small ships register. As stated above, the small ships register does not make provision for the registration of mortgages as the private law provisions of Schedule 1 of the Merchant Shipping (Registration etc.) Act 1993 - now contained in the Merchant Shipping Act 1995 - do not apply to this part of the register.[92] The plaintiffs proceeded with an action to enforce their mortgage. The specific question of law to be determined by the Court was the following:

---

[89] See below.

[90] *The Monica S* [1968] P 741 at p 773, per Brandon J.

[91] [1992] 2 Lloyd's Rep 444, per Adrian Hamilton QC sitting as Deputy Judge.

[92] The Merchant Shipping (Registration of Ships) Regulations 1993, paragraph 91.

> Is a bona fide purchaser for value of an unregistered vessel liable to mortgagees under an unregistered mortgage of the vessel where he has neither actual nor constructive notice of the mortgage at the time of the purchase of the vessel ?[93]

The court did not specifically answer this question as the answer depended on the effect of the nature of the mortgage, that is, "a legal mortgage at common law is enforceable against such a purchaser, but an equitable mortgage would not be."[94]

The following extract from Constant[95] is cited with approval in *The Shizelle.*[96]

> Little need be said with regard to the mortgaging of ships which are not registered under the Act. Such mortgages require no registration either under the Merchant Shipping Acts or Bills of Sale Acts in order to make them effective as passing the legal interest to the mortgagee.
>
> It should also be observed with regard to a ship which, though exempt under the Act from registration, is, in fact, registered under the Act, that the legal ownership can be transferred without the necessity of a duly registered Bill of Sale, and it would appear that a mortgage of such a ship need not comply with the provisions of the Act in order to create a legal interest in the ship.

The Court effectively decided in this case that the unregistered mortgage - being a legal mortgage - did bind Mr and Mrs Haddock:

> Inevitably I started consideration of this case with sympathy for Mr and Mrs Haddock, which sympathy, of course remains. I also started with a strong feeling that the legislature cannot have intended to allow unregistered and undiscoverable mortgages of small vessels to bind purchasers for value without notice. I have, however, been driven, reluctantly, to the conclusion that this is what they have done. The lacuna between the provisions of the Bills of Sale Act and the Merchant Shipping Acts was pointed out in the Court of Appeal in 1878 (the Union Bank case) and again in 1887 (*Gapp* v *Bond*). The legislature has left out of the Merchant Shipping Acts vessels under a certain size (*Benyon v Cresswell*), without bringing them within the Bills of Sale Act or any other statutory system of registration of mortgages.

---

93 [1992] 2 Lloyd's Rep 444 at p 446.
94 *Ibid* at p 451.
95 *Op cit* fn 68 § 13.
96 [1992] 2 Lloyd's Rep 444 at p 451.

> There is a statutory lacuna, but I do not consider that it is appropriate for the Courts to seek to fill it. Finance companies, like other persons, are entitled and obliged to regulate their affairs according to the law as it is.
>
> I hope that the lacuna can be filled by introducing a system of registration of mortgages for all British ships, possibly under the system for Small Ships registration.[97]

There is no doubt that the decision in *The Shizelle* raises a number of problems, one of which relates to the existence of a mortgage before the registration of a ship. It would seem that, on the basis of *The Shizelle,* that mortgage would be a legal mortgage with priority over later registered mortgages; this is supported by the view, referred to earlier, that once there is a legal mortgage, subsequent mortgages can only be of an equitable nature.[98] This would mean that it would be advisable for a buyer to ensure that his vessel is covered, throughout its life, by continuous registration. The problem seems to have arisen in *The Shizelle* as a result of the distinction between legal and equitable interests under English law, and also, to a lesser extent, as a result of the fact that registration is no longer compulsory under English law. However, the suggestion in *The Shizelle* that the problem would be solved by a system of registration of mortgages under the small ships register would not solve the problem of mortgages in existence prior to registration. The solution should be effectively to make enforceability against third parties dependent on registration. This approach would be in conformity with article 1 of the International Convention for the Unification of Certain Rules Relating to Maritime Liens and Mortgages 1967[99] which states:

> Mortgages and "hypotheques" on sea-going vessels shall be enforceable in Contracting States provided that:
>
> a) such mortgages and "hypotheques" have been effected and registered in accordance with the law of the State where the vessel is registered;

---

[97] *Ibid* at p 451.

[98] Constant B, *The Law Relating to the Mortgages of Ships* (1920) § 46.

[99] As at April 2001, the United Kingdom is not a party to the three International Conventions concerning mortgages, namely: The International Convention for the Unification of certain rules relating to Maritime Liens and Mortgages, Brussels, April 10th 1926; The International Convention for the Unification of certain rules relating to Maritime Liens and Mortgages, Brussels, May 27th 1967; International Convention on Maritime Liens and Mortgages, Geneva, May 6th 1993.

b) the register and any instruments required to be deposited with the register in accordance with the law of the State where the vessel is registered are open to public inspection, and that extracts of the register and copies of such instruments are obtainable from the registrar, and

c) either the register or any instruments referred to in paragraph b) above specifies the name and address of the person in whose favour the mortgage and "hypotheque" has been effected or that it has been issued to bearer, the amount secured and the date and other particulars which, according to the law of the State of registration, determine the rank as respects other registered mortgages and "hypotheques". [100]

Another solution would be the amendment of the Bills of Sale Act[101] to include unregistered vessels. However, in view of the international nature of ship finance, the ideal solution would be on the basis of enforceability being dependent on the registration of the mortgage.

Making enforceability of a mortgage dependent on registration is in accordance with expectations of fairness, and it avoids the utilisation of the English law distinction between principles of law and equity as a mechanism for removing remedies from a party in situations where principles of justice would dictate otherwise. The adoption of such a system would put the buyer of a vessel in a position of reducing his potential exposure and minimising his risk to the possible existence of maritime liens, in relation to which there is no system of registration, and in English law, those claims in respect of which the vessel has been arrested.[102] Continental civil codes as well as specific shipping legislation[103]

---

[100] See also Article 1 of the International Convention on Maritime Liens and Mortgages, 1993, and Article 1 of the International Convention for the Unification of Certain Rules Relating to Maritime Liens and Mortgages 1926.

[101] See *supra* text at fn 96.

[102] *The Monica S* [1968] p 741.

[103] For example, in the Italian *Codice della Navigazione*, s 567 refers to s 2808 of the Civil Code and makes enforcement against third parties dependent on the registration of the hypothec. Section 47 of the Maltese Merchant Shipping Act similarly provides: "A transfer or mortgage of a registered ship or share therein, and a transfer of a registered mortgage, shall have no effect in regard to the ship or share or against any person other than the transferor or mortgagor, or their heirs, unless the transfer or mortgage has been registered under and in accordance with this Act".

render unenforceable the secret hypothec,[104] and it may well be the right time for English law to follow the same system in relation to ship's mortgages.[105]

Prioritisation

Prioritisation of Mortgages in Relation to Other Security Interests[106]

At the end of an action *in rem*, the vessel may be sold under the authority of the Admiralty court. In these instances, issues of prioritisation arise. This is a matter which is within the ultimate discretion of the courts.[107] Mortgages have relatively limited strength in relation to prioritisation. A registered mortgage does not have priority over: claims secured by the issue

---

[104] See Trabucchi, *Istituzioni di Diritto Civile* (1975) p 642, where it is stated: "La funzione essenziale della garanzia ipotecaria si manifesta specialmente nei riguardi dei terzi, sia perche' la preferenza che essa offre si riferisce ai concreditori (*ius prelationis*), sia perche' il vincolo segue il bene nell'eventualita' che questo passi in proprieta' altrui (*ius distrahendi*). Da qui deriva l'esigenza della pubblicita' del vincolo ipotecario. Il diritto moderno non conosce l'ipoteca occulta, che sarebbe profondamente contrario alla sicurezza della circolazione a della tutela del credito."

[105] It may be noted that, in *The Angel Bell* [1979] 2 Lloyd's Rep 491, Donaldson J (as he then was) gave effect to Panamanian Law to the effect that a mortgage not registered within a six-month period did not create rights *in rem* against third parties. The Maltese Merchant Shipping Act [Chapter 234 of the Laws of Malta], in s 49 thereof, makes recognition of a foreign mortgage *inter alia* dependent on registration: "A foreign mortgage shall be recognised as a mortgage with the status and all rights and powers specified in this Act, notwithstanding the fact that it is not entered over a registered ship if:

(a) such mortgage has been validly recorded in the registry of ships of the country under whose laws the ship is documented;
(b) such registry is a public registry;
(c) such mortgage appears upon a search of the registry and
(d) such mortgage is granted a preferential and generally equivalent status as a mortgage under this Act under the laws of the country where the mortgage is registered."

[106] For the position of a mortgagee in relation to insolvency proceedings, see Meeson N, *Admiralty Jurisdiction & Practice* 2nd ed (2000) § 3-064 *et seq.*

[107] See, further, Gauci G, "Liens in English Maritime Law" *Benedict on Admiralty*, Chapter XII.

of an *in rem* writ prior to the time when the mortgage was entered into;[108] the possessory lien of a shiprepairer.[109] And finally it needs to be emphasised that maritime liens - whether later or earlier - have priority over a mortgage; however a mortgagee may apply to the court to pay off a maritime lien and to retain the priority of that claim.[110]

Priorities of Mortgages Inter Se

A registered mortgage does not have priority over earlier registered mortgages.[111] By registration the mortgagee obtains priority over earlier unregistered mortgages, whether he knows of them or not.[112] Obviously, in this respect it is presumed that the unregistered mortgage is an equitable one.[113] An unregistered mortgage on an unregistered vessel would obviously be treated as a legal mortgage.[114] This view is unaffected by subparagraph (1) of paragraph 8 of schedule 1 of the Merchant Shipping Act 1995 which deals with priority as between registered mortgagees[115] which is made dependent on the timing of registration on the principle of *prior in tempore, potior in iure*. Subparagraph (2) further provides for a mechanism for the utilisation of priority notices. This mechanism, in a way, dilutes the strictness of the priority order by allowing the utilisation of priority notices for the purposes of obtaining prioritisation before the actual mortgage itself is registered. Regulations to this effect are contained in the 1993 Regulations.[116] Furthermore, by registration, a mortgagee obtains priority over later registered or unregistered mortgages.[117] Later registered mortgages would have an equitable character as the mortgagor would have

108 Meeson N, *Admiralty Jurisdiction and Practice* 2nd ed (2000) § 6-039.

109 See *Fletcher* v *Campbell* [1968] 2 Lloyd's Rep 520.

110 See *Sameiet* v *The Berostar* [1970] 2 Lloyd's Rep. 403; *The Vasilia* [1972] 1 Lloyd's Rep 51; *The Cape Souion* [1990] 2 Lloyd's Rep 329.

111 Merchant Shipping Act, Schedule 1, paragraph 8.

112 *Coombes* v *Mansfield* [1855] 24 LJ Ch 513.

113 See *The Shizelle* [1992] 2 Lloyd's Rep 444.

114 See *The Shizelle, ibid.*

115 The said paragraph 8(1) provides: "Where two or more mortgages are registered in respect of the same ship or share, the priority of the mortgagees between themselves shall, subject to subparagraph (2) below, be determined by the order in which the mortgages were registered (and not by reference to any other matter)".

116 Statutory Instrument No. 3138 of 1993, paragraph 59.

117 *The Basildon* [1967] 2 Lloyd's Rep 134.

already parted with his legal interest in the creation of the first mortgage.[118] Unregistered debentures of earlier creation rank after registered mortgages, even though known to the mortgagee.[119] By registration, a mortgagee obtains priority in relation to advances made subsequently by virtue of an earlier registered mortgage under which it was agreed that the mortgage was to cover both present and future advances by the mortgagee. Registration in this case is notice to the earlier mortgagee of the creation of a later mortgage.[120] This situation can arise in the case of a mortgage to secure account current, as distinct from a mortgage to secure principal sum and interest, in respect of both of which a specific form is available from the Department of Transport, Local Government and the Regions. It can be said that the former mechanism is more popular as a result of its flexibility.[121]

Tacking is a mechanism whereby a mortgagee may enhance his position *vis-à-vis* other creditors. However, tacking can only occur in certain specific circumstances as illustrated in case law. The problem arises specifically where the mortgage is used to an arrangement like an overdraft facility in terms of which the mortgage is said in the document to extend to an advance made in the future. If tacking is allowed in these instances, obviously other legal mortgagees may find their position prejudiced. The matter is addressed in Constant,[122] where the example is given of the possibility of tacking an advance to a registered mortgage despite the existence of intermediate equitable mortgages. In the case of *Hopkinson* v *Rolt*,[123] it was held that there was no entitlement to tack an advance, on a first mortgage, but subsequent to a second mortgage, as the mortgagee [that is, mortgagee 1] was not bound to provide the advance. In *West* v *Williams*,[124] it was held that the rule in *Hopkinson* v *Rolt* applies even where a mortgage is contractually bound to make the further advance to the mortgagor under the terms of the mortgage, on condition that he has notice of the second mortgage. In *The Benwell Tower*,[125] it was held that the rule applied in relation to registered mortgages despite the provisions of section 33 of the 1894 Act. Bruce J stated that "[t]he case of *Hopkinson* v

[118] Constant B, *The Law Relating to the Mortgages of Ships* (1920) § 46.
[119] *Black* v *Williams* [1895] 1 Ch 408.
[120] *The Benwell Tower* [1895] 8 Asp LMC 13; See *infra* in relation to tacking.
[121] Tetley W, *Maritime Liens and Claims* (1985) p 209.
[122] *Op cit* § 47.
[123] [1861] 9 HLC 514.
[124] [1899] 1 Ch 132.
[125] [1895] 8 Asp 13.

Rolt...establishes the general principle that a first mortgagee, whose mortgage is taken to cover future advances, cannot claim in priority over a second mortgage, the benefit of advances made after he had notice of the second mortgage". It would seem, however, that a first mortgagee will have priority over a second mortgagee in respect of an advance subsequent to the second mortgage if he has no notice of the second mortgage.[126]

The problem of tacking can in theory be addressed in terms of a provision under the Maltese Merchant Shipping Act.[127] Section 45A[128] provides that the mortgage registration may be amended with the consent of the mortgagee. Subsection 1 states that "any such amendment shall form an integral part of the registered mortgage which it amends and such mortgage, as amended, shall continue to have the same priority as it had before the amendment was noted". The interests of mortgagees registered subsequent to the registration of the first mortgage are however protected by subsection (5) of the same provision which states that "[w]here any mortgages other than the mortgage that it is intended to amend are entered in the register of the ship an amendment shall not be noted unless the consent in writing of all the other mortgagees whose interests may be prejudiced by the amendment, is produced to the registrar".[129] It would seem, however, that the amending mortgage does not provide the necessary flexibility to operate in the context of a commercial overdraft facility and is normally only used for the recording of rescheduling of loan agreements.

The Extent of the Security Obtained Through the Mortgage of a Ship

The wording of the mortgages set out in schedule 1 of the Merchant Shipping Act 1894 refers to the ship, and her boats, guns, ammunition, small arms, and appurtenances. *Temperley's Merchant Shipping Acts*[130]

---

[126] See *Liverpool Marine* v *Wilson*, Law Journal (1872) 41 (Chancery) p 798; Meeson N, *Ship and Aircraft Mortgages* (1989) p 119.

[127] Chapter 234 of the Laws of Malta.

[128] Added by Act XXIV 1986 11. The original provision has been amended by: Act XXXVII 1988 26; Act XXII 2000 33.

[129] See also s 45A(6) of the Maltese Merchant Shipping Act which provides: "The consent to an amendment to a mortgage shall be signified by means of a declaration executed by the mortgagee in the presence of, and attested by a witness or witnesses".

[130] Thomas M and Steel D, *Temperley's Merchant Shipping Acts* (1976) § 701.

refers to the case of *Coltman* v *Chamberlain*[131] as authority for the statement that the term "ship" includes everything then on board necessary for the prosecution of the voyage or subsequently brought on board in substitution therefor. Charles J, in that case, stated that he was of the opinion that "those articles, which practically consisted of machinery for working the fishing gear - articles necessary for steering, lights necessary for navigation and sails necessary for sailing - passed to the mortgagee under the mortgage of the ship".[132] The judge stated that in this respect there was no need to look at the meaning of the word "appurtenances" as the meaning of "ship" comprised the objects in question. Furthermore he stated that his reasoning would extend to articles in substitution of the original ones.[133] It may be noted that the new form of mortgage documents issued by the Department of Transport, Local Government and the Regions for the purposes of the Merchant Shipping Act 1995 refers to the ship as well as to its appurtenances.[134] The form utilised by the Merchant Shipping Directorate at the Malta Maritime Authority refers to the ship, her boats, as well as her appurtenances.

In relation to fishing stores, in the case of *Gale* v *Laurie*, Abbott CJ stated:

> The fishing stores were not carried on board the ship as merchandize, but for the accomplishment of the objects of the voyage; and we think, that whatever is on board a ship for the objects of the voyage and adventure on which she is engaged, belonging to the owners, constitutes a part of the ship and her appurtenances within the meaning of this Act, whether the object be warfare, the conveyances of passengers, or goods, or the fishery.[135]

In the case of *The Humorous and The Mabel Vera*,[136] the court dealt with the difficulty of ascertaining appropriation to the vessel at the time of the mortgage as a precondition to the attachment of the mortgage in relation to items used on the vessel. In relation to the *Humorous*, Bateson J, decided that nets, which had been lent or hired by an individual, on board the vessel were not appropriated to her. It was held that she had taken from general stores items without a specific appropriation; later appropriation, that is,

---

[131] (1890) 25 QBD 328.
[132] *Ibid* p 334.
[133] *Ibid*.
[134] Forms ROS 25 and ROS 30.
[135] [1826] 5 B & C 156, p 164.
[136] [1933] p 109.

following the entering into of the mortgage, was held to be irrelevant.[137] In relation to the other vessel, the *Mabel Vera*, it was held that at the time that the mortgage was entered into, a number of nets were appropriated to her, and nets in substitution of the appropriated ones, were held to fall within the ambit of the mortgage.[138]

In *Hull Ropes Company* v *Adams*,[139] a rope purchased under hire purchase by the mortgagor was seized by the same mortgagor after he had taken possession of the vessel. It was held by Grantham J that "the hirer had agreed to buy the rope within the meaning of the Factors Act, 1899, and we have already expressed our opinion that the addition of the rope to the equipment of the mortgaged ship was a sufficient delivery or transfer to the mortgagee under a "disposition" within the meaning of the Act, or at any rate became so when, under and pursuant to the powers of the mortgage, possession was taken by the plaintiffs".[140]

The issue of whether the mortgage extends to the bunkers within the vessel is a point which has arisen on a number of occasions, particularly as a result of the fact that frequently charterers intervene in the judicial sale of a vessel to enforce a mortgage on the basis that the fuel belongs to them and its proceeds should be set apart from the proceeds of the vessel. In *The Eurostar*,[141] the property mortgaged was said to be "sixty-four sixty-fourth shares of which the Owners in the Ship above particularly described and in her boats, guns, ammunition small arms and appurtenances".[142] The judge in this case (Sheen J) stated that the term "ship" does not ordinarily include bunkers and that the only word which arguably covers fuel is "appurtenances"; however "the ordinary meaning of 'appurtenances' is a mechanical accessory or some apparatus or gear which appertains or belongs to the ship".[143] The judge referred to a number of cases including *The Honshu Gloria*[144] and *The Pan Oak*[145] and decided that fuel oil was not an appurtenance.[146]

---

[137] *Ibid* p 115.
[138] *Ibid* pp 115-116.
[139] [1895] 65 LJQB 114.
[140] *Ibid* at p 117.
[141] [1993] 1 Lloyd's Rep 106.
[142] *Ibid* at p 111.
[143] *Ibid.*
[144] [1988] 2 Lloyd's Rep 67
[145] [1992] 2 Lloyd's Rep 36.
[146] [1993] 1 Lloyd's Rep 107 at p 112.

Cargo is not considered to be an appurtenance of the vessel,[147] and it is not considered to be part of the ship even in the case where it is actually owned by the mortgaging shipowner.[148] If the parties mortgage items which are not comprised within the term "ship" or "appurtenances" of the vessel, these would fall within the ambit of application of the Bills of Sale legislation and would therefore require registration to that effect.[149]

Conclusion

A number of legal issues relating to ship's mortgages have been highlighted in this Chapter. It would seem that the most pressing legal issue in the context of British ship's mortgages relates to the enforceability as legal mortgages of some unregistered ship mortgages. This is an issue which distinguishes the British ship mortgage from systems which adhere to the principle, also enshrined in the 1967 International Convention for the Unification of Certain Rules Relating to Maritime Liens and Mortgages, in terms of which enforceability of a mortgage against a third party transferee of a ship depends on the registration of that mortgage. It is submitted that the adoption of this principle in English law would bring the British ship's mortgage in this respect into line with expectations of fairness and would avoid the inequity inflicted by the application of the principles utilised in *The Shizelle.*[150] Furthermore, it may also be opportune to examine the nature of the British ship mortgage, and to consider the introduction of legislative amendments to transform the said mortgage into one which gives the mortgagee exclusively a security interest.

---

[147] *Langton* v *Horton* 5 Beav 9 at p 19. See, further, Meeson, *op cit* fn 126. As to the position in relation to freight earned before the mortgagee enters into possession of the mortgaged vessel, see Meeson, at § 10-075.

[148] Meeson, *ibid* at § 10-074.

[149] The Maltese Merchant Shipping Act provides specifically in a proviso to subsection 1 of section 40 that "provisions, fuel and other consumable goods shall not be considered as appurtenances". See also s 37A (2) of the same statute which provides: "A ship shall include together with the hull, all equipment, machinery and other appurtenances as accessories belonging to the ship, which are on board or which have temporarily been removed therefrom".

[150] *Loc cit* fn 91 and related text.

6 Remedies Available From Misuse of Chattels

PAUL TODD

Introduction

For the purposes of this chapter, it is assumed that misuse of chattels can take one of two forms. The chattel may be wrongfully damaged or destroyed, or the person entitled to its use may be wrongfully deprived of it.

This chapter is concerned entirely with actions in the civil, rather than criminal courts. If the function of civil litigation were purely to compensate, then the law would be relatively easy to state. The person with an interest in the chattel, suffering loss from its misuse, would be entitled to compensation for that loss. All that would be necessary would be to define the interests protected by the law, and notions of misuse, loss and, perhaps, causation.

In reality, however, the position is much more complicated. The civil litigation process has many functions, some of which do not lie well with principles of compensation. Accordingly, a claimant may receive no compensation, or may be under-compensated. There are also arguments for the development of gain-based remedies, which could lead to over-compensation.[1] In reality, the law has not, I suggest, taken this route, but has instead, in some cases, adopted a wide view of loss, for example giving compensation for loss of opportunity to bargain, whether or not the claimant intended to exercise that opportunity.

Much of this chapter is concerned with torts, or breaches of trust, which the law regards as wrong. That being so, another legitimate function of the litigation process is to discourage them. For some types of wrong, equitable remedies, such as injunctions (or in post-Woolf terminology, freezing orders), are available, which are intended to prevent the wrong from occurring at all, but injunctions are rare in chattel misuse cases; at any rate where there is a ready market in the chattel concerned, repair, replacement and loss of use costs can usually be adequately compensated by damages.

[1] See, generally, the discussion *infra* fns 172ff, and text thereto.

Deterrence is still possible with a monetary award, but the aim of preventing or deterring wrongs will nearly always lead to over-compensation of the claimant. In *Rookes* v *Barnard*,[2] Lord Devlin set out the principles for awarding exemplary damages in tort, and in *Cassell* v *Broome*,[3] the House of Lords upheld such an award. The damages, which were intended to punish and deter, over-compensated the plaintiff, who therefore received a windfall. Cases such as these are fairly rare, but although neither case involved chattel misuse, the principles are applicable, in theory at any rate.

It is more difficult to justify deterring breaches of contract, which can occur innocently, and against which monetary compensation is normally sufficient protection for the claimant. In any case, the law does not appear to regard breaches of contract as undesirable in themselves. The principles in *Rookes* v *Barnard* do not apply to breaches of contract, and exemplary damages cannot be awarded. Suppose, for example, Alan agrees to sell a chattel to Belinda but, in breach of contract and on a rising market, sells to Charles. Since the market is rising, Alan should profit from the breach, but compensatory damages will redress the wrong. Belinda will go into the market to buy a replacement, and will have to pay the new, higher market price. She will claim the difference as damages, however, and no harm will have been done.[4] It would be different, of course, if the chattel were a Constable painting, or a vintage Aston Martin, for which there is no ready market. Rarely for chattels, injunctions are awarded preventing breaches of contract, and this might be an appropriate case.[5] In *A-G* v *Blake*,[6] disgorgement damages (which deprive the defendant of his gain) were awarded for a breach of contract, even though the plaintiff had suffered no loss. Like *Cassell* v *Broome*, this resulted in a windfall, but also like *Cassell*, it was an exceptional case; this was a deliberate and cynical breach of contract, for which, exceptionally, deterrence was arguably appropriate.

In these cases, principles of deterrence conflicted with, and indeed overrode, those of compensation. Both *Cassell* v *Broome* and *A-G* v *Blake* were highly exceptional, however. In each, the defendant had acted

---

2 [1964] AC 1129 at pp 1226-1227.

3 [1972] AC 1027. See further the discussion *infra* fn 242 and text thereto.

4 Nor, in this simple example, does Alan keep his gain, but we consider variations, *infra* fns 209-226 and text thereto, where Alan's gain arguably exceeds Belinda's loss.

5 As will become apparent, the availability of an injunction or, to use post-Woolf terminology, freezing order, can also (at least arguably) affect the amount of financial awards: *infra* fn 219 and text thereto.

6 [2000] 3 WLR 625. See further *infra* fn 251 and text thereto.

intentionally, intending to profit from his wrong; the activity was one which the courts wished to discourage, but in *Broome* the criminal law would have been inappropriate,[7] and in *Blake* ineffective.[8] Whether one would wish to extend, or narrow, these developments, depends very much on one's views of the interrelationship between civil and criminal law. As the law stands, however, the factors in these cases will rarely be present in chattel misuse cases, and this type of over-compensation is of marginal relevance.

Another situation, which also arguably gives rise to a type of over-compensation, can arise where the courts protect an interest which would normally be too remote to justify protection. Again, this is done on essentially moral grounds, as an expression of disapproval of the defendant's conduct. As will become apparent, the law accords reasonably strong protection to legal and possessory title, and more limited protection to lesser interests, such as equitable title, and contractual rights. More remote interests are generally unprotected. This can be justified simply on the basis of the type of society in which we live. If I have a contract to purchase, or hire, a chattel, it may be reasonable to expect the law to afford some protection to that right, for example from intentional interference by third parties. If I am merely at the negotiation stage, it would normally be quite unreasonable to expect similar protection, since otherwise a competitor would be unable, knowing of my offer, intentionally to make a better one. For even more remote interests the argument is stronger. The law would not normally protect my "interest" in my neighbour's car, for example, which I hope to service for profit in the summer, since again, it should be quite open for someone deliberately to make a better offer. A competitive capitalist society necessarily places limits on the nature of interests in chattels which the law should protect.

Despite these arguments, sometimes the law will protect even such remote interests, where the defendant is motivated by malice, or (possibly) intends to harm the claimant by unlawful means.[9] The clearest example is the pure tort of conspiracy, which depends not on infringing any legitimate interest of the claimant's, but only on the malice of two or more defendants, in combination. Another example is the tort of intimidation, which depends on an unlawful threat, not to any interest of the claimant, but to that of a third

---

[7] On the assumption that libel should be discouraged but not made criminal. The same view could presumably be taken of the tort of intimidation in *Rookes* v *Barnard*.

[8] Blake having escaped from both prison and the jurisdiction of the English courts.

[9] On the existence of a general tort of causing harm by unlawful means, see, for example, *infra* fn 113.

party, with a view to damaging the claimant. For neither conspiracy nor intimidation, therefore, is it necessary for the claimant to show interference to a contractual or property interest, of the type that the law would normally protect. If the claimant obtains damages, that must therefore, at least arguably, represent over-compensation.

While all the forms of over-compensation so far discussed are possible in relation to chattel misuse, however, it is necessary to invent fairly fanciful situations;[10] in reality, over-compensation, certainly on the moral grounds discussed so far, is of marginal relevance to the content of this chapter.

There are other cases which are possible to analyse in terms of compensation for the claimant's loss, but only on a wide, and arguably artificial notion of loss. Account of profits, for example, appears much more clearly to be a gain-based remedy, although it is possible to analyse it in loss-based terms.[11] There are also deprivation of use cases, where the defendant is required to pay a market rate for the wrongful use of a chattel, even where the claimant would not, apart from the wrongful use, have obtained the market rate himself. These are also sometimes said to be gain-based remedies, although this is not clearly so, since they do not depend on the defendant in fact saving the market rate for use, and if the defendant profits from the wrongful use, he is not required to disgorge the actual profit made. Thus, the damages awarded do not necessarily represent, directly, the defendant's gain. Moreover, though not always easy to analyse in loss-based terms, these cases are nonetheless susceptible to such analysis.

Whether cases such as these more easily fit into a loss or gain-based analysis is not merely an exercise in semantics, but central to the very function of the civil law system. Some might argue that it should be an instrument of restitution as well as compensation, but even restitutionary principles are intended to reverse unjust enrichment at the expense of the claimant,[12] and do not therefore justify over-compensation. The only

---

[10] *Infra* fns 122-123 and text thereto.

[11] See *infra* fn 166 and text thereto.

[12] For example, in *Lipkin Gorman* v *Karpnale Ltd* [1991] 2 AC 548, Lord Goff (at p 572) justifies, in restitutionary terms, a money had and received action on the basis that "the [defendant] cannot in conscience retain the money - or, as we say nowadays, for [him] to retain the money would result in his unjust enrichment at the expense of the owner of the money". It is not enough that the defendant is unjustly enriched; it must also be at the expense of the claimant, in the case itself the (original) owner of the money. The view is also sometimes expressed that a man should not profit from his own wrong. This is essentially a form of the deterrence argument, however, and if the principle leads to over-compensation, I would argue

possible justifications for over-compensation are to punish the defendant, or to deter. It will be rare for either to be appropriate in chattel misuse cases.

Even adopting a loss-based approach, however, the extent of recovery varies in different circumstances, so that not all losses are necessarily recoverable. What we do not have is a claimant-centred scheme, providing full compensation, and nothing more, to a claimant whose chattels have been misused. Certainly, a claimant can be under-compensated, as where the loss is regarded as too remote. There is, also, of course, no remedy at all in the absence of a wrong; claims will be in contract (including breach of bailment contract), tort or breach of trust, but the law does not accord automatic protection to owners of chattels, still less to those with interests less than ownership. It follows that a claimant can suffer misuse to his chattel, without any fault on his part, but be without remedy. The law therefore places an incentive on those with interests in chattels to look after them, and will only attach liability to a third party where there is a good reason for so doing. Of course, a chattel owner will often be able to protect himself by first party insurance.

It is clear, then, that the law performs functions other than compensating the claimant, and that in so doing, has regard to matters other than the claimant's loss. Whether or not it is appropriate for the civil (as opposed to criminal) courts to seek to condemn conduct that is regarded as immoral, they are surely the appropriate forum for a just allocation of losses, and promotion of the efficient functioning of a commercial society. These aims can also conflict with those of compensation *simpliciter*. Indeed, whether a wrong is committed at all, and if so the extent to which the claimant's interests are protected, depend as much on the relationship between the parties, and the defendant's conduct and state of mind, as on the claimant's losses.

Two variables are of fundamental importance in any discussion of misuse of chattels, the relationship between the parties, and the nature of the claimant's interest in the chattel. To take first the relationship between the parties, in commercial societies people make choices, one such choice being the nature of relationships they enter into with others. The law rightly accords consequences to these relationships, especially where voluntarily entered into, so that the duties between the parties are to a large extent defined by such relationships:[13]

---

that it can only be justified where the law regards the wrong as very serious (for example, breaches of fiduciary duty, considered *infra* fns 152-168, and text thereto).

[13] *Per* Diplock LJ in *Morris* v *Martin* [1966] 1 QB 716 at p 731.

> Duties at common law are owed by one person to another only if there exists a relationship between them which the common law recognises as giving rise to such duty.

Thus, for example, those who voluntarily undertake to care for the claimant's property, especially for reward, owe a greater duty than a stranger. Those who enter into other undertakings (for example, of a contractual nature) are also bound by them, and consequences attach to placing oneself in a position of trust. Central to any discussion of chattel misuse, therefore, is the relationship between claimant and defendant.

As to the nature of the claimant's interest, where misuse of a chattel occurs, it is not only the owner who can suffer loss. Hirers, and those with other interests, less than legal ownership, can also suffer, or even (for example where delay is caused by a train or aircraft accident) persons with no interest at all. A lot of this chapter revolves around discussion of lesser interests. The law in general does not accord such interests protection as good as legal ownership, but they can be protected nevertheless, depending on the conduct of the defendant, and his relationship with the claimant. For example, the law protects even limited economic interests in chattels from deliberate attempts to damage the claimant's interests, even if not from mere negligent interference from a stranger.[14]

There is accordingly a relationship between the nature of the interest being protected, the proximity of the relationship between claimant and defendant, and the state of mind of the defendant; the greater the plaintiff's interest in the chattel the better it is protected; the greater the degree of proximity between the parties, the greater the likelihood of liability, and the better the remedies. Conversely, the defendant's state of mind takes on a greater role where the plaintiff's interest in the chattel is remote, and the relationship between the parties distant.

It is convenient to begin with relatively distant relationships between the parties, and to compare liability regimes as the relationship becomes closer. The analysis will therefore begin with actions against strangers, by which I mean persons with whom the plaintiff has no particular connection.[15] Such people owe relatively limited duties to the claimant. As the relationship between the parties becomes closer, the interests of the plaintiff

---

[14] *Infra* fns 112-137 and text thereto.

[15] Lord Atkin uses the term "neighbours" to describe what I am calling strangers: *infra* fn 32. My terminology is intended simply to indicate that there is no special relationship between the parties.

become better protected, and the defendant's state of mind becomes less important.

Before concluding the introduction, I shall adopt the convention in this chapter that claimants and defendants are accorded the pronoun "he". They are often companies, and unlike their biological counterparts, legal persons do not come in two genders. Nor can someone with the legal personality required to sue and be sued reasonably be referred to as "it". "He" seems to be conventional usage, and will therefore be adopted here. Ships, of course (which have sufficient personality to suffer arrest) are female.

Misuse by Strangers

Protection of Property Interests

Strangers do not owe stringent duties to protect the property of others, but can become liable for trespass to goods, and for conversion. Trespass is defined in Salmond & Heuston *The Law of Torts* as follows:[16] "The tort of trespass consists in committing without lawful justification any act of direct physical interference with goods in the possession of another person". This is a relatively limited action, protecting only actual possession, and only against direct interference. A more versatile tort is conversion:[17] "Conversion is a common law action, tortious in form, imposing strict liability for a wrongful interference with the right to possession of a chattel. It consists of any act of wilful interference, without lawful justification, with any chattel in any manner inconsistent with the right of another, whereby that other is deprived of the use and possession of it".

The modern law of conversion (originally based on the action of trover), as implemented by the Torts (Interference with Goods) Act 1977, also encompasses what used to be detinue. There are a number of ways in which the tort can be committed, which arguably fall into three main categories:[18]

[16] Salmond and Heuston, *The Law of Torts,* Heuston & Buckley 21st ed (1996) p 94.

[17] Accepted without dispute by the parties in *MCC Proceeds Inc* v *Lehman Bros International (Europe)* [1998] 4 All ER 675, at p 684. Reference was made to Salmond and Heuston *ibid* at pp 97-98.

[18] *Ibid* at p 97. Winfield and Jolowicz add wrongfully refusing to give them up when demanded: Rogers, *Winfield and Jolowicz on Tort* 15th ed (1998) at p 588. A detailed description of torts relating to interference with goods is beyond the scope of

> There are three distinct methods by which one man may deprive another of his property, and so be guilty of a conversion and liable in an action of trover - (1) by wrongly taking it, (2) by wrongly detaining it, and (3) by wrongly disposing of it. The term conversion was originally limited to the third of these cases.

It is said to be a strict liability tort, but also requires wilful interference with the right to possession of a chattel. The authorities were reviewed by Rix J in *Motis Exports Ltd* v *Dampskibsselskabet AF 1912, Aktieselskab,*[19] where this apparent contradiction was explained. The act of interference must be voluntary, but it is not necessary for there to be an intention to interfere with the rights of the claimant. Rix J adopted Diplock LJ's exposition from *Marfani & Co Ltd* v *Midland Bank Ltd*:[20]

> At common law, one's duty to one's neighbour who is the owner, or entitled to possession, of any goods is to refrain from doing any voluntary act in relation to his goods which is a usurpation of his proprietary or possessory rights in them. Subject to some exceptions which are irrelevant for the purposes of the present case, it matters not that the doer of the act of usurpation did not know, and could not by the exercise of any reasonable care have known, of his neighbour's interest in the goods. The duty is absolute; he acts at his peril.

In *Motis Exports*, forged bills of lading were used to obtain delivery orders, and hence delivery to the fraudsters of goods on board the defendant's vessel. The defendants were held liable in contract and conversion to the holders of the genuine bills of lading, who were entitled to possession of the goods. It mattered not that the shipowners did not know that the bills of lading were forged, and hence that they were interfering with the plaintiff's rights. It was enough to establish the conversion claim only that the delivery was intentional. Another consequence of the irrelevance of ignorance of the claimant's title is that it is possible to have successive conversions of the same chattel, for example by a thief, and a purchaser from the thief, who innocently believes the thief has title; both can be liable in

---

this chapter, but see in general, for example, Salmond and Heuston, *op* cit fn 16, Chapter 6.

[19] [1999] 1 Lloyd's Rep 837, affd [2000] 1 Lloyd's Rep 211.

[20] [1968] 1 WLR 956 at p 971. See also in *Fowler* v *Hollins* (1872) LR 7 QB 616, *per* Cleasby B at p 639: "... persons deal with the property in chattels or exercise acts of ownership over them at their peril".

conversion, although the purchaser is ignorant of the claimant's title.[21] Nonetheless, this is not a strict liability tort in the sense that it could be committed by an automaton, or a sleep-walker.

The interference must also be wrongful. *Glyn Mills Currie & Co* v *East and West India Dock Co*[22] is factually similar to *Motis Exports*, but there the original bills of lading were issued in a set of three, "... one of which bills being accomplished, the others shall stand void." The bills were fraudulently negotiated separately, and the defendant was held by the House of Lords not liable for delivering the goods against an original bill in the set, in ignorance of its presenter's lack of title. A possible explanation of the case is that there was a conversion, but that the plaintiffs must have been aware that there was more than one bill, and were therefore *volenti*,[23] but the view of Lord Selborne LC,[24] depending on mercantile usage, does not appear to depend on notice. A better explanation is that to deliver against production of an original bill, without notice of competing claims, is not wrongful, whereas conversion requires a wrongful act.[25]

Apart from what was originally the separate tort of detinue, the essence of conversion is the exercise of dominion over a claimant's goods, or the deprivation of the claimant's title by the defendant.[26] To destroy goods can be to convert them, but merely to damage them is not. Nonetheless, owners of chattels were also protected, even before the landmark decision in *Donoghue* v *Stevenson* in 1932,[27] from negligent damage to them, at any rate in defined circumstances.[28] For example, owners of ships and cargoes were

---

[21] The authorities were reviewed by the *Court of Appeal in Kuwait Airways Corp* v *Iraq Airways Co* [2001] 1 Lloyd's Rep 161. Aircraft owned by Kuwait Airways were confiscated by the Iraqi government in the invasion of August 1990, and later transferred to Iraq Airways Co. The Court of Appeal, taking the view that neither the confiscation nor subsequent transfer were legal, held Iraq Airways Co liable, as the successive converter.

[22] (1882) 7 App Cas 591.

[23] The views of Lords Blackburn and Watson, *ibid* at pp 606 and 614, are consistent with this view.

[24] *Ibid* at p 596.

[25] For example, Bools, *The Bill of Lading: A Document of Title to Goods* (1997) at p 166.

[26] The authorities are reviewed in *Kuwait Airways Corp* v *Iraq Airways Co, supra* fn 21, paras 414 ff.

[27] [1932] AC 562.

[28] For a full review, see, for example, Winfield, "The History of Negligence in the Law of Torts" (1926) 42 *LQR* 184. Note that "negligence so far as it results in

protected against damage caused by collision with another ship, where the colliding shipowner was negligent.[29] The interests protected were the same as with conversion, however, and those with merely contractual interests in ship or cargo could not sue.[30]

The various forms of negligence liability were generalised into the modern form of negligence in *Donoghue* v *Stevenson* in 1932,[31] so that even persons who have no special relationship with the claimant at least owe a duty of care not to damage his property negligently. As a means of protecting chattels, negligence has its limitations. As Lord Atkin observed in *Donoghue* v *Stevenson*,[32] the defendant is required only to:

> ... take reasonable care to avoid acts or omissions which you can reasonably foresee would be likely to injure [his or her] neighbour. Who, then, in law is my neighbour? The answer seems to be - persons who are so closely and directly affected by my act that I ought reasonably to have them in contemplation as being so affected when I am directing my mind to the acts or omissions which are called in question.

It follows that no duty is owed to a claimant who the defendant might reasonably not have had in contemplation as being affected by his or her acts or omissions. Even if a duty is owed, there will be liability only if the defendant breaches the duty, by failing to take reasonable care. While damages are intended, as far as possible, to reverse the wrong done, another limitation is that remote losses cannot be recovered, even where liability is established.[33]

---

damage to goods or to an interest in goods" is defined as wrongful interference with goods under s 1(c) of the Torts (Interference with Goods) Act 1977.

[29] See further *infra* fns 232-237 and text thereto (in a damages context). These cases were exercises of Admiralty jurisdiction.

[30] For example, *The Charlotte* [1908] p 208, where buyers of cargo, to whom property had not yet passed, for this reason failed before Bargrave Deane J. In the Court of Appeal the sellers were joined, so the issue no longer arose, but no doubt was cast on Bargrave Deane J's decision. Title to sue generally is considered in detail later in the chapter.

[31] [1932] AC 562, Lord Atkin observing at p 580 that "... in English law there must be, and is, some general conception of relations giving rise to a duty of care, of which the particular cases found in the books are but instances".

[32] *Ibid* at p 580. A review of the basic law of negligence is not within the scope of this chapter.

[33] For a situation where remoteness principles were used to restrict recovery, see *The Leisbosch*, *infra* fn 231.

Neither negligence nor conversion therefore give claimants automatic protection against chattel misuse, even where they have legal title to the chattel concerned. Both the wrong and (at any rate in negligence) the remedy to some extent depend on the defendant's fault. It follows that chattel owners should take steps to protect their own property, and it may well be advisable for them to insure against their misuse. The extent of cover required, and hence the cost of first party premiums, will be reduced to the extent that there is third party liability. In the common situation where the third party is also insured, a *de facto* function of the tort system is to allocate risks between first and third party insurers.[34] Though fault-based liability in tort has attracted criticism, albeit more in the context or personal injury than property damage,[35] it makes sense in the present context, at any rate where both plaintiff and defendant have the opportunity to insure. Property-owners should themselves bear the cost of first-party insurance, except for risks created by the fault of third parties.

Title to Sue: General Observations

Historically, conversion was a common law action, the essence of which was denial of the claimant's title. Later, it seems to have developed to protect possession or the immediate right to possession. The legal owner of a chattel will usually enjoy one of these rights,[36] but where there is a bailment, conversion may protect the rights of the bailee, rather than the bailor.[37] Persons with lesser rights, such as equitable title, or contractual rights, will

---

[34] All parties to international trade transactions, for example, will typically be insured, and the issue will therefore come down to whether the loss is borne by the first or third party insurance company. In *The Aliakmon* at first instance (a case considered in detail below), Staughton J thought that the issue was in reality between two insurance companies: [1983] 1 Lloyd's Rep 203 at p 205 (col 1). The Law Commission, in recommending the reforms that led to the enactment of the Carriage of Goods by Sea Act 1992, saw no reason why increased premiums should be borne by the cargo owners, while the shipowners were entitled to rely on a legal technicality: Law Com 196 (1991), para 2.15. The effect of the reforms was to increase the likelihood of (contractual) liability on the part of carriers.

[35] See, for example, Cane, *Atiyah's Accidents, Compensation and the Law,* 6th ed (1999) especially Chapter 7.

[36] But a reversionary owner will not: see *The Mineral Transporter*, [1986] 1 AC 1.

[37] This will depend on the terms of the bailment, and in particular on whether the bailment is terminated by the conversion, thereby re-vesting the immediate right to possession in the bailor.

not, in the absence of either actual possession or an immediate right to possess, be able to sue for conversion.[38]

This was reaffirmed by the Court of Appeal in *MCC Proceeds Inc* v *Lehman Bros International (Europe)*.[39] There a plaintiff with equitable title, but no immediate right to possession of shares, was held unable to sue the recipient, to whom the trustees had wrongfully transferred the shares, in conversion.[40] Indeed, since liability in conversion is strict, to allow the plaintiff to sue could subvert the principle that a *bona fide* purchaser of legal title, without notice of equitable title, takes free of that title. Another justification was the historical one that "conversion is a common law action and the common law did not recognise the equitable title of the beneficiary under a trust. It recognised only the title of the trustee, as the person normally entitled to immediate possession of the trust property."[41]

The first of these justifications has no obvious application outside in the context of wrongful disposal. The second is historical, and depends on the tort of conversion having developed relatively little over time. It is perhaps curious, then, that Mummery L J uses negligence authorities to support his argument.[42] Neither justification has any obvious application to negligence, the first for obvious reasons, the second because negligence is a developing subject, which should not be constrained by history.

Even with the widening (or at least generalising) of negligence liability in *Donoghue* v *Stevenson*, however, and later cases, such as *Home Office* v *Dorset Yacht Co Ltd*,[43] the range of interests protected has arguably not been widened. Just as with conversion, and historically in negligence-based

---

[38] Lesser rights may nevertheless be protected, albeit in fairly limited circumstances, by other actions. See below.

[39] [1998] 4 All ER 675. The case involved a trust of shares. Trusts of chattels are rare, but this case is referred to in a related context *infra* fn 93 and text thereto. In any case, the reasoning would surely apply all the more strongly to mere contractual rights.

[40] *Healey* v *Healey* [1915] 1 KB 938 and *International Factors Ltd* v *Rodriguez* [1979] 1 QB 351 were distinguished, on the basis that in both cases the person with equitable title also had a possessory title.

[41] *Supra* fn 39 at p 690.

[42] Lord Brandon's *dicta* in *Leigh and Sillivan Ltd* v *Aliakmon Shipping Co Ltd* [1986] 1 AC 785 at p 812A, rejecting the proposition that a person who has the equitable ownership of goods is entitled to sue in tort for negligence anyone who for want of care causes them to be lost or damaged without joining the legal owner as a party to the action, were adopted in *Lehman*, at p 688. *The Aliakmon* is discussed further *infra* fns 81ff, and text thereto.

[43] [1970] AC 1004.

actions, persons with an interest less than a legal or possessory title cannot sue, it seems, at any rate without the person with such title being joined. Lesser interests are protected, if at all, only by the economic torts considered later in this chapter.

We end up with a curious situation, then. The same limits are placed on title to sue in negligence as in the old tort of conversion, although negligence is essentially a developing tort and conversion is not. Then the negligence authorities are used to justify a restrictive view of title to sue in conversion. This curious state of affairs, if correct, clearly requires some kind of explanation.

Title to Sue: Economic Loss

Even with the widening of negligence liability, the courts have been reluctant to allow recovery for pure economic loss. In a chattel-misuse context this is relevant to two situations. First, where property is damaged or destroyed, people who have no proprietary interest in it may suffer economic loss, but such loss is not recoverable. In ***Weller & Co* v *Foot and Mouth Disease Research Institute***,[44] for example, the defendants were held to owe a duty of care to cattle owners in the neighbourhood, not to allow the disease they had imported to escape, but not to the plaintiff cattle auctioneers, who were not owners of cattle and had no proprietary interest in anything which could be damaged by the escape of the virus. The *Weller* reasoning has been extended, however, so that persons with mere contractual interests in the chattel concerned, or even an equitable proprietary interest, will not normally be able to sue. Thus, for example, in ***The Mineral Transporter***,[45] the Privy Council held a time charterer of a ship unable to recover in respect of loss of use of the vessel, where the ship had been damaged in a collision caused by

[44] [1966] 1 QB 569.

[45] [1986] 1 AC 1. Unlike a demise charterer, a time charterer does not obtain possession of the vessel, which remains with the shipowner. Indeed, in the case itself, the plaintiff was also shipowner, who had demise chartered the vessel and time chartered it back. It was assumed that only the demise charterer, being in possession, could sue, there having been no damage to the plaintiff's reversionary proprietary interest (as shipowner). The time charterer could presumably have claimed for any bunker fuel, owned by him, lost in the collision. Perhaps also if his fuel had been consumed getting into port for repairs, but arguably use of fuel for its proper purpose would not constitute damage.

the negligence of the defendant shipowners.[46] In *The Aliakmon,*[47] the House of Lords, adopting Roskill J's reasoning in *The Wear Breeze,*[48] held a cif buyer of steel coils unable to sue the shipowner in respect of damage negligently caused to it on board ship, where property had not passed to him by that time, even though risk had passed, and the buyer therefore had no redress against the seller, under the sale contract; thus, the effect of denying his action against the shipowner was to leave the cif buyer entirely without redress.

What is particularly striking about this development is the rigidity with which the courts seem to have adopted it, especially in the light of the flexibility of most propositions in this area of law. For example, in *Caparo Industries plc* v *Dickman,* Lord Bridge accepted without qualification the proposition that:[49]

> In case of a wrong done to a chattel the common law does not recognise a person whose only rights are a contractual right to have the use or services of the chattel for purposes of making profits or gains without possession of or property in the chattel. Such a person cannot claim for injury done to his contractual right.

---

[46] An analogous situation recently occurred in the university where I work. An Internet line was severed by contractors using digging machinery. The line was owned by NTL, and the university would have had a contractual right to use it. Had the issue arisen, the university would have had no action against the contractors in negligence.

[47] *Leigh & Sillivan Ltd* v *Aliakmon Shipping Co Ltd* [1986] AC 785, overruling Lloyd J in *Schiffahrt und Kohlen GmbH* v *Chelsea Maritime Ltd, The Irene's Success* [1982] QB 481. The buyers in *The Aliakmon* alternatively argued, unsuccessfully, that equitable title to the cargo had passed to them, although legal title remained with the sellers. Lord Brandon thought that even if this were correct, equitable property alone would not given them title to sue. Note that unlike the time charterer in *The Mineral Transporter,* a demise charterer can sue, in both negligence and conversion, not however because of his equitable (lease) interest in the vessel, but because he is legally in possession, at least from delivery to redelivery.

[48] *Margarine Union GmbH* v *Cambay Prince Steamship Co Ltd, The Wear Breeze* [1969] 1 QB 219.

[49] [1990] 2 AC 605 at p 618. He cited *Elliott Steam Tug Co Ltd* v *Shipping Controller* [1922] 1 KB 127, 139 *per* Scrutton LJ, *Cattle* v *Stockton Waterworks Co* (1875) LR 10 QB 453, *Candlewood Navigation Corporation Ltd* v *Mitsui OSK Lines Ltd* [1986] AC 1 and *Leigh & Sillivan Ltd* v *Aliakmon Shipping Co Ltd* [1986] AC 785. Acceptance of this statement as an unqualified rule is also implicit in *The Starsin, infra* fn 106.

No exceptions appear to be recognised to this proposition, at any rate by Lord Bridge in *Caparo*. Given the trend in cases such as *Donoghue* v *Stevenson* itself, *Dorset Yacht* v *Home Office*[50] and *Anns* v *Merton LBC*,[51] away from rigid rules towards more general principles, this is remarkable and, if correct, in need of explanation.

It is easier to justify exclusion of recovery for pure economic loss than it is to justify the proposition stated above, but in fact, all the justifications are subject to exceptions, and there is no clear rigid rule against recovery for pure economic loss. However, any justifications against the stronger proposition would clearly apply less forcibly to the weaker.

Beginning, then, with that stronger case, the justification in *Weller* was in terms of duty of care:[52]

> The duty of care arose only because a lack of care might cause direct injury to the person or property of someone, and the duty was owed only to those whose person or property were foreseeably at risk.

Since the plaintiffs' loss was accepted as being a foreseeable result of the defendant's negligent act in importing an African virus onto their premises, and allowing it to escape,[53] this statement amounts to a general exclusion of recovery for economic loss. Since a duty of care is undoubtedly owed to those whose persons and property are at risk, this apparently blanket exclusion requires further justification.

In *SCM (United Kingdom) Ltd* v *WJ Whittall & Son Ltd*, Lord Denning MR justified refusal to allow recovery for pure economic loss as being too remote, and he explained *Weller* in remoteness terms also.[54] He accepted, however, that economic loss would not necessarily be unforeseeable on *Wagon Mound*[55] principles.[56] The problem is the same as with a reasoning

---

[50] [1970] AC 1004.

[51] [1978] AC 728. *Anns* v *Merton* seems to have taken the generalisation a step too far, however, the reasoning having been departed from in (for example) *The Aliakmon*, *infra* fn 85, and *Murphy* v *Brentwood District Council* [1991] AC 398.

[52] *Supra* fn 44 at p 587.

[53] *Ibid* at p 576.

[54] [1971] 1 QB 337 at p 345. See also his explanation in *Spartan Steel & Alloys Ltd* v *Martin* [1973] 1 QB 27 (at p 36) of *Cattle* v *Stockton Waterworks Co* (1875) LR 10 QB 453, *Société Anonyme de Remorquage à Hélice* v *Bennetts* [1911] 1 KB 243, and *King* v *Phillips* [1953] 1 QB 429. Note that the plaintiffs recovered all the losses claimed in *SCM*, so that Lord Denning MR's remarks are technically *dicta*.

[55] [1961] AC 388.

[56] *Supra* fn 54 at p 345.

based on duty of care; if loss is a foreseeable consequence of the defendant's negligent actions, a blanket refusal to allow its recovery on the grounds that it is too remote requires further justification, and such justification must be in terms of public policy.[57]

Turning, therefore, to grounds of public policy, a common fear, expressed in *Ultramares Corporation* v *Touche*,[58] has been that the defendants might otherwise be exposed to: "... a liability in an indeterminate amount for an indeterminate time to an indeterminate class." Indeed, it seems to have been this factor which convinced Widgery J in *Weller* itself:[59]

> It may be observed that if [the plaintiff's] argument is sound, the defendants' liability is likely to extend far beyond the loss suffered by the auctioneers, for in an agricultural community the escape of foot and mouth disease virus is a tragedy which can foreseeably affect almost all businesses in that area. The affected beasts must be slaughtered, as must others to whom the disease may conceivably have spread. Other farmers are prohibited from moving their cattle and may be unable to bring them to market at the most profitable time; transport contractors who make their living by the transport of animals are out of work; dairymen may go short of milk, and sellers of cattle feed suffer loss of business.

This fear is most compelling where (as in *Weller)* a single negligent act, affecting the property of one person, can cause economic loss to many, for example where destruction of an earning chattel, which would be difficult quickly to replace, leads to closure of a business, causing economic loss at the very least to all employees. The problem is multiplication of numbers of potential plaintiffs, causing problems both for the courts and insurance companies, where claims are settled. A similar argument was propounded by Lord Penzance in *Simpson* v *Thomson*, in relation to a personal injury claim:[60]

> An individual injured by a negligently driven carriage has an action against the owner of it. Would a doctor, it may be asked, who had contracted to attend him and provide medicines for a fixed sum by the year, also have a right of action in respect of the additional cost of attendance and medicine cast upon him by that accident? And yet it cannot be denied that the doctor had an

---

[57] As recognised by Lord Denning MR in *SCM* itself, (at p 344) and *Spartan Steel.*

[58] (1931) 174 NE 441 at p 444.

[59] *Supra* fn 44 at p 577.

[60] (1877) 3 App Cas 279 at p 290. This case, and also *Cattle* v *Stockton Waterworks Co* (1875) LR 10 QB 453, were followed in *Weller.*

> interest in his patient's safety. In like manner an actor or singer bound for a term to a manager of a theatre is disabled by the wrongful act of a third person to the serious loss of the manager. Can the manager recover damages for that loss from the wrongdoer? Such instances might be indefinitely multiplied, giving rise to rights of action which in modern communities, where every complexity of mutual relation is daily created by contract, might be both numerous and novel ...

Although the *Ultramares* argument is in terms of liability in an indeterminate amount to an indeterminate class, the real fear appears (from the other passages above) to be of multiplicity of claims, rather than large amounts for each claim. Where there is no likelihood of such multiplicity of claims, therefore, the argument is weakened, and indeed economic loss may be recoverable. This is a possible justification for cases such as *SCM (United Kingdom) Ltd* v *WJ Whittall & Son Ltd* and *Spartan Steel & Alloys Ltd* v *Martin & Co (Contractors) Ltd*,[61] in both of which a plaintiff who had suffered foreseeable physical loss was also held entitled to claim consequential economic loss. There is no possibility of multiplicity of claimants in cases such as these, since the duty of care has already been established towards the particular claimant.

The multiplicity of claims argument is also one reason why, while pure economic loss is not recoverable in *Donoghue* v *Stevenson* based actions, it is under *Hedley Byrne* v *Heller*.[62] There, however, the restricted nature of the action itself limits the number of potential claimants.[63] Indeed, in *Caparo*

---

[61] Respectively [1971] 1 QB 337 and [1973] QB 27. As will appear *infra* fns 227-228, and text thereto, this is not my preferred explanation of these cases. Indeed, it cannot explain the rejection of other economic losses, independent of the physical damage, claimed by the plaintiffs in *Spartan Steel*. Nonetheless, Lord Denning MR regarded multiplicity of claims as a factor in a refusal, generally and in the particular instance, to recognise recovery for economic loss in negligence (at p 39). Another argument (at p 38) was, in effect, that pure economic losses were part of the vicissitudes of life, about which the law should not encourage litigation.

[62] The line of negligent misstatement cases based on *Hedley Byrne & Co Ltd* v *Heller & Partners Ltd* [1964] AC 465, where the only loss suffered was economic.

[63] For example, Craig, "Negligent Misstatements, Negligent Acts and Economic Loss" (1976) 92 *LQR* 213 at p 218: "The very nature of the duty framed by the House of Lords in 1964 has within it certain limiting factors ... which mean that these problems of indeterminate liability are far less likely to arise: the need for some form of relationship between the participants, reasonable reliance leading to loss, knowledge by the representor of some particular transaction for which the information is to be required. The nexus envisaged was far closer than that of

Industries Plc v *Dickman*,[64] the House of Lords expressly rejected the notion that economic loss could be recoverable merely because it was the foreseeable consequence of a negligent misstatement.[65] Though it was foreseeable that the plaintiffs would rely on the defendant chartered accountants' audit of a public limited company, to purchase more shares in the company, the criteria for the imposition of a duty of care were not simply foreseeability of damage, but also proximity of relationship and the reasonableness or otherwise of imposing a duty.[66] Here, no duty of care was owed, the relationship being insufficiently proximate, even if it was foreseeable that the certified accounts would be relied on by those among whom they were circulated. No more in *Hedley Byrne* than in ordinary negligence actions is economic loss recoverable merely because it is the foreseeable consequence of the defendant's negligence. Multiplicity of claims is therefore not a realistic fear in a *Hedley Byrne* action; hence one of the main arguments for refusal to allow recovery for pure economic loss is missing, and pure economic loss is indeed recoverable.

Another ground for the recovery of economic loss on *Hedley Byrne* principles, which would not apply in an ordinary negligence action between strangers, is the assumption of responsibility by the defendant:[67]

> [If] a person assumes responsibility to another in respect of certain services, there is no reason why he should not be liable in damages for that other in

---

reasonable foresight *per se*". Thus the relationship between the participants necessarily limits the number of claimants. In *White* v *Jones infra* fn 74, Lord Mustill (at p 287) noted that whereas in *Donoghue* v *Stevenson* the liability "was derived by the court from the position in which the parties found themselves", in *Hedley Byrne* it "arose internally from the relationship in which the parties had together chosen to place themselves". Unlike his brethren, however, Lord Mustill (who made a strong dissenting speech) was not prepared there to extend the law to allow recovery for economic loss, outside established principles.

[64] [1990] 2 AC 605.

[65] In the light of this decision, it is very difficult to justify the tort reasoning in *Ministry of Housing and Local Government* v *Sharp* [1970] 2 QB 223.

[66] In this regard, *Caparo* was distinguished, and a duty of care owed to the plaintiff, in *Spring* v *Guardian Assurance Ltd* [1995] 2 AC 296. The relationship between the parties was very close in *Spring*, however, and there is nothing in the case to suggest that foreseeability of economic loss is itself sufficient to found an action for negligent misstatement.

[67] *Henderson* v *Merrett Syndicates* [1995] 2 AC 145, *per* Lord Goff at p 181. In *White* v *Jones*, *infra* fn 74 at p 273, Lord Browne-Wilkinson clarifies that it is: "assumption of responsibility for the task not the assumption of legal liability".

> respect of economic loss which flows from the negligent performance of those services.

The defendant in a *Hedley Byrne* action is therefore no longer the stranger we have been assuming up to now, but somebody who has put himself into a much closer relationship with the claimant. Indeed, Lord Goff described the relationship as "equivalent to contract".[68] For both these reasons, therefore, that there is no possibility of a multiplicity of claims, and that the defendant has assumed a particular responsibility towards the claimant, it is possible to argue consistently in favour of recovery for pure economic loss in *Hedley Byrne*, but not in ordinary negligence actions.

Perhaps a more convincing argument than those already advanced, against recovery for pure economic loss under *Donoghue* v *Stevenson*, is that in a competitive capitalist society, the infliction of economic loss, even deliberately, has to be seen generally as justifiable. As Lord Reid observed in *Home Office* v *Dorset Yacht Co Ltd*,[69] after referring to Lord Atkin's speech in *Donoghue* v *Stevenson*:

> ... causing economic loss is a different matter; for one thing, it is often caused by deliberate action. Competition involves traders being entitled to damage their rivals' interests by promoting their own ...

Even in this respect, losses may be recovered in exceptional circumstances, such as in the economic tort actions considered later in this chapter. In such cases, the defendants might perhaps be regarded as having deliberately broken the rules of fair competition. Even relatively remote economic interests ought perhaps to be protected from such intrusion.

Flexibility in the Law

Had I been writing this chapter 15 years ago,[70] I would probably have concluded that whereas personal injury and property damage are, in principle, always recoverable under *Donoghue* v *Stevenson*,[71] economic loss never is. Neither of these statements is any longer possible, the law having developed more flexibly in recent years. It is not clear, however, that this

---

[68] *Henderson* v *Merrett Syndicates*, *ibid.* See also *Hedley Byrne*, *supra* fn 62, *per* Lord Devlin at pp 529-530, and *White* v *Jones*, *per* Lord Browne-Wilkinson, *ibid.*

[69] [1970] AC 1004 at p 1027, referring to Lord Atkin's speech *supra* fn 32.

[70] After *The Aliakmon*, *infra* fn 85, but before *Caparo*, *supra* fn 64.

[71] Property being defined in the same way as in conversion actions.

flexibility has extended to the nature of property interest required to sue in negligence.

Though the arguments rehearsed above might convincingly justify a general exclusion of recovery for economic loss in negligence, in fact the law is not inflexible, but allows exceptions to the principle, where necessary to do justice. The starting point is, paradoxically, *Caparo,* a decision which was against recovery, and in which their Lordships played down the role of underlying general principles in favour of a more traditional categorisation. However, Lords Bridge and Oliver recognised the possibility of developing novel categories of negligence "incrementally and by analogy with established categories",[72] and this flexibility was later adopted, both to extend liability for economic loss, and perhaps more controversially to restrict liability for property damage, in an ordinary negligence action.

In *Caparo*, the criteria for determining liability in negligence included not only the elements of foreseeability and proximity, but also whether it was fair, just and reasonable to impose a duty of care on the defendant.[73] It is the "fair, just and reasonable" requirement which has been used in later cases to import flexibility into the law.

To begin with the extension of liability, in *White* v *Jones*,[74] two intended beneficiaries under a revised will successfully sued the testator's solicitors for negligently failing to make the revisions before the death of the testator, although obviously they did not (precisely because of the solicitor's negligence) obtain any title to the disputed property; hence the only loss that they suffered was (at most) purely economic. Nor was there any special relationship between the plaintiff and the testator's solicitors. Clearly, then, the rule against recovery for negligently caused economic loss, in the absence of a *Hedley Byrne* special relationship, is not set in stone.[75] In *White* v *Jones*, there was nobody, apart from the intended beneficiaries, who were in any position to bring an action. In Lord Goff's view, recovery could be based neither on conventional *Hedley Byrne* principles, nor on those of ordinary negligence, but "it seems to me that it is open to your Lordships' House ... to fashion a remedy to fill a *lacuna* in the law and so prevent the injustice which would otherwise occur on the facts of cases such as the

---

[72] *Supra* fn 67, respectively at pp 618 and 634.

[73] For example, Lord Oliver of Aylmerton *ibid* at p 633.

[74] [1995] 2 AC 207, Lords Mustill and Keith dissenting. The essentially similar case of *Ross* v *Caunters* [1980] Ch 297 was upheld, but on different reasoning.

[75] *White* v *Jones* also extended the law by imposing liability for an omission.

present".[76] Even in cases involving pure economic loss, it seems, the courts are prepared to adopt a degree of flexibility in order to prevent a perceived injustice, the injustice there being that in the absence of recovery, the defendants would have been unaccountable for their admitted negligence, which caused the plaintiffs a clear loss.

Caparo has also been used to restrict liability; even an owner whose chattel is foreseeably damaged by the negligence of the defendant may be unable to claim, if there are policy reasons to the contrary. It is also necessary to determine whether it is fair, just and reasonable to impose a duty of care on the defendant. In *The Nicholas H*,[77] a surveyor negligently passed as satisfactory temporary repairs to a ship. She sailed and sank, with the plaintiffs' cargo on board. Though the plaintiffs had suffered physical loss of their property, as a result of the defendant's negligence, the House of Lords held that they were not entitled to recover; the defendant owed them no duty of care. The reasons were essentially of policy, and in particular that a tort action would allow the cargo owners to avoid the limitations under the Hague or Hague-Visby Rules, to which they would have been subject had they instead sued the shipowner.[78]

In summary, *White* v *Jones* shows that there is no clear rule against recovery of economic loss, and *The Nicholas H* that there is no automatic right to recover, even for foreseeable physical losses, in negligence cases. There is flexibility, and a role for public policy.

---

[76] *Supra* fn 74 at p 268, on analogy with *Linden Gardens Trust Ltd* v *Lenesta Sludge Disposals Ltd* [1994] 1 AC 85. Lord Browne-Wilkinson, at p 270, was prepared to extend liability "using the incremental approach by way of analogy advocated in *Caparo Industries Plc* v *Dickman* [1990] 2 AC 605", referred to *supra* fn 72.

[77] [1996] 1 AC 211. Lord Lloyd dissented. His view was that whereas it was justifiable to use proximity and fairness arguments, as in *Caparo*, to contain liability for pure economic loss, in physical damage cases "proximity very often goes without saying". He would not have used *Caparo*, in other words, as a justification for restricting recovery for property damage.

[78] See further discussion of *The Aliakmon*, *infra* fn 90. This at least was the view of the Court of Appeal ([1994] 1 WLR 1071, *per* Saville LJ at pp 1081-1082). In the House of Lords, Lord Steyn (at p 238) thought that the relevant limitation arose by reason of the tonnage limitation, under the Convention on Limitation of Liability for Maritime Claims 1976. In reality, of course, a tort action against a third party would avoid both limitations.

Title to Sue: Interests in Chattels Less than Full Ownership

Clearly, the arguments rehearsed above, against recovery for pure economic loss, apply where the claimant has no direct interest in any property damaged, but in the context of damage to chattels, the economic loss reasoning has been extended, so as to allow only legal owners, or those entitled to immediate possession, to sue, people who have clearly suffered loss that cannot be regarded as purely economic. However, given the flexibility adopted even in cases of pure economic loss, it is striking how inflexible the law has apparently been in its refusal to allow recovery by persons with an interest in the chattel, less than full legal ownership.

It is true that assumption of responsibility arguments, such as have been used to justify recovery for economic loss in *Hedley Byrne* actions,[79] are unlikely to apply in chattel misuse cases. However, the arguments against recovery for pure economic loss apply, if at all, less clearly where damage is done to property in which the claimant has an interest, albeit not (at the time of the damage) a legal or possessory title.

Arguments based on foreseeability are clearly inapposite, since the claimant's loss is foreseeable.[80] Nor is it immediately apparent that the interests of the time charterers in *The Mineral Transporter*, or the cif buyers in *The Aliakmon*,[81] should be unprotected in the interests of promoting a competitive capitalist society, or that damage to them should be regarded as one of the vicissitudes of life.[82]

It might however be argued that the problem in these cases could have been avoided by the plaintiffs, and that they were in some way, therefore, responsible for their own loss. In *The Mineral Transporter*, for example, part at least of the loss could have been avoided by the inclusion in the time charterparty of a suitably-drafted off-hire clause.[83] In *The Aliakmon,* Lord

[79] For example *supra* fn 67.

[80] This was accepted by all parties, for example, in *The Wear Breeze* [1969] 1 QB 219 at p 233.

[81] *Supra* fns 45-48 and text thereto.

[82] Among Lord Denning MR's justifications (in slightly different language) for refusal to allow full recovery in *Spartan Steel*, *supra* fn 61 at p 38.

[83] The loss was in the form of wasted payments of hire and loss of profits. While a suitable off-hire clause would have prevented hire being payable for the period, it would not have protected the plaintiffs' loss of profits, for example on sub-freights. Many standard off-hire clauses expressly cover accidents (for example, Baltime, clause 11, Shelltime 4, clause 21) or collision (Intertanktime 80, clause 20). In *The*

Brandon observed that had the original c & f contract been performed as contemplated, the buyers would have had a contractual action against the ship, under the Bills of Lading Act 1855, which at that time applied to most ordinary cif and fob contracts, and variations thereon.[84] The buyers were unable to pay when the documents were tendered, however; the contract was renegotiated so as to delay passing of property, and this was really the cause of the problem:[85]

> In the present case ... the variation of the original c & f contract agreed between the sellers and the buyers produced a hybrid contract of an extremely unusual character. It was extremely unusual in that what had originally been an ordinary c. & f. contract became, in effect, a sale *ex warehouse* at Immingham, but the risk in the goods during their carriage by sea remained with the buyers as if the sale had still been on a c & f basis. In this situation the persons who had a right to sue the shipowners for loss of or damage to the goods on the contract contained in the bill of lading were the sellers, and the buyers, if properly advised, should have made it a further term of the variation that the sellers should either exercise this right for their account[86] or assign such right to them to exercise for themselves. If either of these two precautions had been taken, the law would have provided the buyers with a fair and adequate remedy for their loss.
>
> These considerations show ... that the buyers, when they agreed to the variation of the original contract of sale, did not take the steps to protect themselves which, if properly advised, they should have done.

A similar view, that the buyers were in some way at fault for their predicament, had been voiced by Roskill J in *The Wear Breeze*, this time because they had accepted, in place of bills of lading, very inferior documentation:[87]

> The plaintiffs chose to take delivery orders instead of a bill of lading. The documents which they took were not even ship's delivery orders. The bills of

---

Mineral Transporter itself, hire was reduced by approximately 75 per cent while the ship was not operational (see p 14).

[84] It has since been replaced by the Carriage of Goods by Sea Act 1992.

[85] [1986] AC 785 at p 819.

[86] Lord Brandon here refers to *The Albazero* [1977] AC 774. Presumably he had in mind that *Dunlop* v *Lambert* (1839) 6 Cl & F 600 would apply, allowing the seller to claim substantial damages on the buyer's behalf, property (unlike that in *The Albazero* itself) not having passed.

[87] *Supra* fn 80 at p 254.

> lading from which the delivery order derived were not shipowners' bills of lading. They were not even time charterer's bills of lading. They were sub-time charterer's bills of lading. It may be that had proceedings been brought in contract, considerable procedural complexities would have arisen.

The implication appears to be that, had the plaintiffs been fussier over the documentation they would accept, they would have had a contractual action against the shipowner.

Looked at more closely, however, these arguments do not justify the general position adopted in either of these cases. While for a one-off sale, as in *The Aliakmon*, there would have been no particular problem in the buyers taking an assignment of the sellers' rights, or requiring them to sue on their behalf, a buyer at the end of a long chain is in a very different position. He cannot protect himself in this manner, because he does not know what rights the seller himself has.[88] In *The Wear Breeze*, the problem was that property could not pass in part of a bulk cargo, and the position would almost certainly have been no different, whatever documentation the buyers had obtained. The implication that, had the buyers been more careful about their documentation, they would have had a contractual action, was almost certainly unjustified.[89] The reality was that the Bills of Lading Act 1855, triggered as it was by the passing of property from seller to buyer, was inadequate, in many cases, to transfer contractual rights against the shipowner, whether or not the buyers could be regarded as in some sense at fault, in entering into the contractual relations, or accepting the documentation, which they did. The only person with an interest in suing, the buyer at whose risk the goods were during sea transit, often therefore had no contractual action. Buyers tried, unsuccessfully, to use the tort action to remedy the inadequacies of the legislation; in the absence of an action in either contract or tort, a negligent carrier would be unaccountable even to a plaintiff who had suffered a clear loss. In the end, the legislation was

---

[88] Each merchant might have taken an assignment of the rights of the previous seller in the chain, but one break in the chain would destroy it, and the ultimate buyer has no way of checking every link.

[89] They would certainly have been unable to rely on s 1 of the Bills of Lading Act 1855, property in the goods not having passed to them (because of the operation of what was then s 16 of the Sale of Goods Act 1893, the goods being unascertained). Even if they had taken bills of lading, they would also probably have been unable to rely on the principles established in *Brandt* v *Liverpool, Brazil and River Plate Steam Navigation Co Ltd* [1924] 1 KB 575; there is no finding that they paid freight or other charges, and it is in any case unlikely, the contracts being on c.i.f. terms.

replaced by the Carriage of Goods by Sea Act 1992, and the particular problem largely disappeared.

In *The Aliakmon*, there was the additional problem that the shipowners had agreed to carry the goods on the terms of the Hague Rules, which accorded them various protections in the form of excepted perils, package limitations, time bars, etc. The Hague Rules operated by incorporation into the carriage contract, however, and a buyer, by suing in tort in the absence of a contractual nexus between plaintiff and defendant, could, had the decision gone the other way, have avoided the Rules. To an argument that the duty of care in tort could be qualified by the Hague Rules, which were incorporated into the carriage contract between seller and shipowner, Lord Brandon adopted the views of Sir John Donaldson M.R. in the Court of Appeal:[90]

> I have, of course, considered whether any duty of care in tort to the buyer could in some way be equated to the contractual duty of care owed to the shipper, but I do not see how this could be done. The commonest form of carriage by sea is one on the terms of the Hague Rules. But this is an intricate blend of responsibilities and liabilities (art III), rights and immunities (art IV), limitations in the amount of damages recoverable (art IV, r 5), time bars (art III, r 6), evidential provisions (art III, rr 4 and 6), indemnities (art. III, r 5 and art IV, r 6) and liberties (art IV, rr 4 and 6). I am quite unable to see how these can be synthesised into a standard of care.

Even if this was a good argument for not extending tort liability in the particular case,[91] it is an argument that is specific to sea carriage, and from which it is not possible to generalise. In the particular context of sea carriage, it is an argument for extending contractual, rather than tortious liability, and this was indeed done when the Bills of Lading Act 1855 was replaced by the Carriage of Goods by Sea Act 1992.

What appears actually to have happened is that the judges, in contrast to other aspects of the law of negligence, have adopted an essentially conservative approach. The reasoning appears to amount to little more than

[90] [1985] QB 350 at p 368, adopted by Lord Brandon, [1986] AC 785 at p 818.

[91] A similar argument was adopted, in a slightly different context, in *The Nicholas H*, *supra* fn 77 at pp 238-240. There, however, the plaintiffs had suffered physical damage. On traditional principles they would have recovered, but policy reasons, similar to these, were invoked to reduce the normal range of recovery. Here, an extension to the general principle was sought, to allow recovery for economic loss.

that the law has always been thus. An example is the following passage from Roskill J's judgment in *The Wear Breeze*:[92]

> The truth is that English law does not recognise and never has recognised a duty of care on a shipowner to anyone who was not the owner of the goods at the time when the tort was committed.

This conclusion was based on a thorough analysis of earlier cases, but it is noteworthy that the authorities were either pre-1932 negligence, or conversion cases. Title to sue in negligence, in other words, takes as its cue title to sue in conversion, but the conversion arguments that were rehearsed in *Lehman* simply do not apply to negligence,[93] and negligence liability significantly expanded in the early and middle part of the twentieth century.[94] It seems to be exclusively in this area that such conservative reasoning has been adopted.

None of the above, then, I would suggest, represents a convincing argument, capable of generalisation, for the present position.

Nor, at first sight, might it seem that these cases can convincingly be justified on the floodgates argument, since so it seems, the number of potential claimants would be scarcely increased, if at all, by allowing recovery.[95] In *The Aliakmon*, for example, only the buyer had any interest in suing, precisely because the risk had passed to him from shipment. Moreover, although he had no property at the time of the damage, he expected to obtain title eventually, on paying for the goods.[96] Even where there is a long chain of cif sales, and hence potentially a larger number of

---

[92] *Supra* fn 80 at p 254. Roskill J whose views were generally adopted by Lord Brandon in *The Aliakmon, supra* fn 85, especially at p 820.

[93] See *supra* fn 39 and text thereto. In fact, Lord Brandon's rejection in *The Aliakmon* (at p 812) as insupportable the proposition that "a person who has the equitable ownership of goods is entitled to sue in tort for negligence anyone who for want of care causes them to be lost or damaged without joining the legal owner as a party to the action", was adopted by the Court of Appeal in the later case, *supra* fn 39.

[94] An argument that the development of the law after *Donoghue* v *Stevenson* altered the position was rejected in *The World Harmony* [1967] P 341 at p 362. The issue there was essentially similar to that in *The Mineral Transporter*, *supra* fn 45.

[95] This argument appealed to Lloyd J in *The Irene's Success* [1982] QB 481, a similar case to *The Wear Breeze* and *The Aliakmon*, later overruled in *The Aliakmon.*

[96] The reason that property had not passed was because the seller had reserved title against payment, within s 19(1) of the Sale of Goods Act 1979. Property issues were discussed more fully in the Court of Appeal [1985] QB 350.

claimants, only the ultimate purchaser will normally have any interest in suing. In both *The Aliakmon* and *The Mineral Transporter*, the totality that could be recovered would also have been unaffected by allowing the plaintiff to recover, since to the extent that the cif buyer suffers loss, the cif seller does not. In the case of the time-chartered vessel, losses claimed by the charterer would reduce those of the shipowner.

However, in *The Wear Breeze*, Roskill J observed that the plaintiffs were able to avoid floodgates reasoning by artificially limiting their argument, by refusing to extend it beyond cif buyers in the chain:[97]

> [Counsel] sought to limit what I might call the range of foreseeability which a shipowner must be taken to possess in the eyes of the law by saying that it did not extend beyond the last cif buyer who might buy those goods while they were still afloat. He expressly disclaimed any intention of contending that the range of foreseeability went so far as to cover, for example, a buyer who bought *ex ship*. Still less did he suggest that it would extend right down the line so that, for example, a merchant in a small country town who happened to have some cockroach-ridden copra in his warehouse could recover damages from the shipowner notwithstanding that it was the ship's negligence which caused the copra in the warehouse to be riddled with cockroaches.

Clearly, had this disclaimer not been made, there would still have been some force in the floodgates argument, albeit quantitatively less than in the case of pure economic loss.

Perhaps the best argument for the present position is that if it is accepted that recovery for pure economic loss is undesirable, then clearly that must be defined, and a line drawn. In *The Mineral Transporter*, the Privy Council effectively took the view that the traditional line was the best:[98]

> Their Lordships consider that some limit or control mechanism has to be imposed on the liability of a wrongdoer towards those who have suffered economic damage in consequence of his negligence ... The common law limitation which has been generally accepted is that stated by Scrutton LJ in

---

[97] [1969] 1 QB 219 at p 234. In *The Aliakmon*, also, Lord Brandon thought the limited exception to the floodgates argument argued by the buyers artificial: "If an exception to the general rule were to be made in the field of carriage by sea, it would no doubt have to be extended to the field of carriage by land, and I do not think that it is possible to say that no undue increase in the scope of a person's liability for want of care would follow". This seems less convincing than Roskill J's illustration in *The Wear Breeze*.

[98] [1986] AC 1 at p 25.

> *Elliott Steam Tug Co Ltd* v *Shipping Controller*[99] ... Not only has the rule been generally accepted in many countries, including the United Kingdom, Canada, the United States of America and until now Australia, but it has the merit of drawing a definite and ascertainable line. It should enable legal practitioners to advise their clients as to their rights with reasonable certainty, and their Lordships are not aware of any widespread dissatisfaction with the rule.

Effectively, therefore, the argument boils down to this. While a duty of care is generally owed to prevent infliction on one's neighbour of physical loss or damage to his property, no duty is owed to prevent infliction on one's neighbour of economic loss. The law has to decide which is which, and the line has been drawn at legal ownership. The lack of flexibility is justified (in the above passage, for example) on grounds of certainty.

Flexibility in the Law?

All the above discussion has been premised on the assumption that only legal and possessory titles are protected, but it is worth considering at least the possibility that this is incorrect, and that negligence at least is wider in its scope than this.

The weight of authority cited in the previous few paragraphs is substantial, but it is worth observing that the cases pre-date *Caparo,* and the recent developments based upon its supposed flexibility. It is at least possible that Lord Goff in *White* v *Jones*[100] doubted the correctness *The Aliakmon*, and certainly he doubted some of the reasoning. Thus, for example, Lord Goff recognised that there was a *lacuna* in the law in *The Aliakmon*, though denied by Lord Brandon in the case itself, which Lord Goff in the later case suggested the common law might have been flexible enough to fill.[101] It must also surely be the case that a disclaimer of liability in *White* v *Jones*, or a limitation of liability, as between testator and solicitor, would also have affected the duty of care owed to the plaintiffs.[102] If so, the extent of a duty

---

[99] [1922] 1 KB 127 at pp 139-140.

[100] *Supra* fn 74.

[101] At pp 819 and 265, respectively in *The Aliakmon* and *The Wear Breeze*. In the end, the supposed *lacuna* was filled by the Carriage of Goods by Sea Act 1992, and the particular problem largely disappeared. So, of course, did the opportunity to develop the common law.

[102] Lord Goff observed in *White* v *Jones*, *supra* fn 74 at p 268 that: "Such assumption of responsibility will of course be subject to any term of the contract between the solicitor and the testator which may exclude or restrict the solicitor's liability to the testator under the principle in *Hedley Byrne*. It is true that such a term

of care in tort can, in principle, be modified, or even negated, by a contract between the defendant and a third party, precisely the argument that had been advanced unsuccessfully regarding the Hague Rules in *The Aliakmon*.[103]

If Lord Goff doubted two of the main pillars in Lord Brandon's reasoning, it is possible that he also doubted the correctness of the decision itself. Nonetheless, none of the cases cited as authority in this section has been overruled. Moreover, *The Aliakmon* has been applied twice recently by the Court of Appeal, without even a hint of criticism, in *MCC* v *Lehman* and *The Starsin*.[104] The most plausible conclusion, therefore, is that the inflexible face of the common law in this regard has not been put out of joint.

Side Issues: Continuing Damage

In *The Wear Breeze* and *The Aliakmon*, both damage and breach of duty occurred before property passed to the plaintiffs, but it is possible for damage to occur on an ongoing basis, as a result of a single prior breach, in which case the breach, but not the damage, may occur prior to the passing of property. For example, a breach by the shipowner, in failing to provide a seaworthy vessel at the start of the voyage, may allow seawater to leak in gradually, causing incremental damage to the cargo. If the plaintiff can claim only in respect of damage occurring after he becomes owner of the cargo, this can give rise to evidential problems as to apportionment, when property passes from seller to buyer at some time during the voyage, but the damage, caused by exposure to seawater, for example, occurs continuously, some before and some after the passing of property.[105] If on the other hand, in order to claim the claimant must have legal title at the time of the breach of duty, the evidential problems will be reduced, but so will the prospects of successful recovery.

This issue had not been dealt with in either *The Wear Breeze* or *The Aliakmon*, but in *The Starsin*,[106] the Court of Appeal decided that in a case

---

would be most unlikely to exist in practice; but as a matter of principle it is right that this largely theoretical question should be addressed". This implies that the tort duties owed to the plaintiffs could be affected, or indeed negated, by the contract between the solicitor and the testator.

[103] *Supra* fn 90.

[104] Respectively *supra* fn 39; *infra* fn 106.

[105] As in *The Nea Tyhi* [1982] 1 Lloyd's Rep 606. The tort aspects of that decision must now be regarded as wrong, however, in the light of *The Aliakmon*.

[106] *Homburg Houtimport BV* v *Agrosin Private Ltd, The Starsin* [2001] 1 Lloyd's Rep 437.

involving incremental damage, the cause of action arose when (more than negligible) damage was first caused. The allegation was that bad stowage had caused damage to the cargo by condensation, but whereas stowage had occurred at the start of the voyage, most of the damage had occurred during the course of it. Property passed to the plaintiff buyers during the voyage, after the breach, and after some, but not all the damage had occurred. In the event a contract action succeeded,[107] on the bills of lading, but the Court of Appeal also considered the position in tort, the shipowners having argued (unsuccessfully) that the bills of lading were issued on behalf of the charterers, rather than themselves. Had the contract action not succeeded, the tort action would have failed also.

The authorities were fully reviewed, in particular by Rix LJ, who had dissented on the contract issue. In *Weller*, the claim failed because no duty of care was owed. Since the reasoning was in terms of duty of care, the relevant time was arguably the breach of duty, rather than the occurrence of the damage. On the other hand, in many personal injury cases, including *Donoghue* v *Stevenson* itself, the breach preceded the injury, and yet the claim succeeded. The decision in *The Starsin* is effectively to adopt one rule for both personal injury and property damage cases, in line with the decisions in *Cartledge* v *Jopling & Sons Ltd*[108] and *Pirelli General Cable Works Ltd* v *Oscar Faber & Partners*.[109]

Side Issue: What is Damage?

Where the claimant is within the class of persons to whom the defendant owes a duty, in other words in the present context somebody who owns the chattel at the relevant time, he can, in principle, recover for the damage caused.[110] Only damage can be recovered, however, and even the owner of a chattel cannot recover from its manufacturer in respects of defects which reduce its value. Such loss is regarded as economic, and the proper remedy is to proceed against the supplier for breach of contract.[111] It is not damage,

[107] Rix LJ dissenting on this issue.
[108] [1963] AC 758.
[109] [1983] 2 AC 1.
[110] Subject to breach of duty and remoteness of damages rules being satisfied.
[111] *Murphy* v *Brentwood District Council* [1991] 1 AC 398, not adopting *Anns* v *Merton London Borough Council* [1978] AC 728. The case involved a building but it was accepted that similar principles applied to chattels. It is not clear from the report why no contract action was brought against the vendor.

because the chattel has never existed in an undamaged state, whereas the notion of damage implies a change of state from good to bad.

Conclusion

Negligence and conversion protect claimants against chattel misuse even by strangers, with whom they have no particular relationship. Neither requires intention, although a voluntary act is required to sustain a claim in conversion. They protect only a limited range of interests, however; those with lesser interests are relatively ill-protected, unless they enjoy a closer relationship, such as a contract, with the defendant.

Protection of Lesser Forms of Interest

Though the hirer of a chattel, or for example the time charterer of a ship, has no cause of action in negligence or conversion, his or her contract with the owner of the chattel is accorded limited protection by the economic torts. A defendant who deliberately acts so as to interfere with the contractual relationship, or so as to damage the plaintiff, may be liable for interference with contract, or conspiracy. Moreover, a defendant who takes the chattel expressly subject to the plaintiff's contractual rights may be required to hold the chattel on constructive trust for the plaintiff.

It is beyond the scope of this chapter to describe the economic torts in detail, or to consider whether they can be generalised under the umbrella of a super-tort, such as causing harm by unlawful means.[112] The economic torts undoubtedly include interference with contract, conspiracy and intimidation,[113] only the first of which is likely to be of significant relevance

[112] It is worth observing, however, that the umbrella does not appear to fit very well, since the discrete tort actions are very different. The gravamen of interference, at least where direct, is infringement of the claimant's right, or in other words, the very harm that is being complained of. No additional unlawful means are required, so it is artificial to regard this as within the umbrella of causing harm by unlawful means. Neither unlawful means nor harm to any defined right of the claimant is required for conspiracy. An unlawful threat is required for intimidation, but again, no harm to any defined right of the claimant. Only indirect interference with contract, which requires additional unlawful means, clearly falls within the generalised umbrella, therefore.

[113] See, in general, Winfield and Jolowicz *supra* fn 18, Chapter 18.

to chattel misuse. The torts in effect define what is, and what is not, legitimate behaviour in a competitive commercial society. All are intentional torts,[114] and a defence of justification exists.[115] Continuation of each may be restrained by injunction.[116] Damages are also available, and since the only loss is likely to be economic, compensation extends even to pure economic loss.[117]

Of the three torts, only interference with contract protects the claimant's entitlement to a right, namely a contractual right, whether or not the contractual right relates to a chattel. It is necessary only to show interference, however, not that the defendant's actions induced a breach, a development of the tort some 30 years ago to cover cases where the contract excluded liability for damage caused by the defendant's activity.[118] It is still unclear whether interfering with contractual negotiations, at the pre-contractual stage, is also actionable.[119]

The tort of conspiracy can amount to no more than committing an act already unlawful, in combination,[120] but it can also exist in pure form, where

---

[114] Although the intention need not necessarily be to damage the claimant in particular: *Falconer* v *ASLEF and NUR* [1986] IRLR 331. See further on intention, *Emerald Constructions* v *Lowthian* [1966] 1 All ER 1013, *infra* fn 127.

[115] Although the justification is not necessarily the same for each tort. The House of Lords held in *South Wales Miners Federation* v *Glamorgan Coal Co* [1905] AC 239 that advancement of industrial interests is not a justification for inducing a breach of contract, whereas it is for the pure tort of conspiracy. This difference seems reasonable, given that a contractual right is being protected in the former, but not the latter tort.

[116] For example, *Sefton* v *Tophams Ltd* [1965] Ch 1140.

[117] For example, *Falconer* v *ASLEF and NUR* [1986] IRLR 331 (interference with contract); *Rookes* v *Barnard* [1964] AC 1129 (intimidation).

[118] *Torquay Hotel* v *Cousins* [1969] 2 Ch 106, where industrial action interfered with the performance of a contract, which exempted liability for industrial action. *Torquay Hotel* was affirmed by the House of Lords in *Merkur Island* v *Laughton* [1983] 2 AC 570, and *Dimbleby* v *NUJ* [1984] 1 WLR 427.

[119] The Court of Appeal decision in *Acrow Automation* v *Rex Chainbelt* [1971] 3 All ER 1175 is somewhat inconclusive.

[120] For example, *Belmont Finance Corporation* v *Williams Furniture Ltd (No 2)* [1980] 1 All ER 393 (pursuance of an agreement in breach of s 54(1) of the Companies Act 1948); *Lonrho* v *Fayed* [1992] 1 AC 448. In the latter case, the House of Lords held that where the conspirators used unlawful means, their conduct would be tortious even though their primary purpose was to further or protect their own legitimate interests. Compare *infra* fn 122, for pure conspiracies.

the act, performed by one person, would be lawful.[121] As such, it does not necessarily protect any clear entitlement of the claimant, and amounts to making malice itself tortious. It could certainly, for example, cover a combination to prevent acquisition, or hire, of a chattel by the claimant, even in advance of a contract being concluded. It is not easy, I would suggest, to justify actions by claimants who have no interest, recognised by the law, to protect, and it is as well that the courts have later placed significant limits on the development of this tort action.[122]

Intimidation occurs where the rights of a third party are threatened by the defendant, unless some damage is done to the claimant. Like the pure form of conspiracy, therefore, this tort does not necessarily protect any interest of the claimant. Nor, indeed, does it directly protect the interests of the third party, since only if the third party gives into the threat (thereby avoiding any damage) is the tort committed. Application of this tort in the context of this chapter is likely to be quite limited, but it could be committed, for example, where a Luddite threatens destruction of a machine unless the director of the company is removed. Another possibility would be a threat of (unlawful)[123] industrial action by dock workers against their employers, if the claimant's ship is allowed to leave harbour.

An Example

As an illustration of how contractual, but non-proprietary rights to a chattel might be protected, suppose a ship is time chartered to the claimant, and the shipowner sells the ship to the defendant, who proposes to use the ship inconsistently with the claimant's time charter. On the principles already discussed, there is no actionable conversion by either the shipowner or the defendant, since the claimant has neither possession, nor an immediate right to possession of the ship. The shipowner is acting in breach of the charterparty contract, however, by selling the ship to the defendant in these circumstances, and the law protects these contractual rights from interference

---

[121] *Quinn* v *Leathem* [1901] AC 495.

[122] For example, *Crofter Harris Tweed* v *Veitch* [1942] AC 435 and *Lonrho Ltd* v *Shell Petroleum Co Ltd (No 2)* [1982] AC 173. In the latter case, the House of Lords held that injury to the plaintiff, and not the self-interest of the defendants, must be the predominant purpose of the agreement in execution of which the damage-causing acts were done. This effectively excludes from the ambit of the tort all normal competitive business behaviour.

[123] That is, in breach of contract, this requirement being derived from the Court of Appeal decision in *Morgan* v *Fry* [1968] 2 QB 710.

by third parties (here, the defendant).[124] Therefore, there are circumstances where the defendant will be liable.

An issue of this type arose as early as *De Mattos* v *Gibson*, where Knight Bruce LJ said:[125]

> Reason and justice seem to prescribe that, at least as a general rule, where a man, by gift or purchase, acquires property from another, with knowledge of a previous contract, lawfully and for valuable consideration made by him with a third person, to use and employ the property for a particular purpose in a specified manner, the acquirer shall not, to the material damage of the third person, in opposition to the contract and inconsistently with it, use and employ the property in a manner not allowable to the giver or seller.

There, it was accepted that a mortgagee of a vessel, Gibson, with express notice of the plaintiff's charterparty, could in principle be restrained from selling the vessel, in breach of the charterparty. In the particular case, however, it was clear that the shipowner (who was in financial difficulties) could not perform the charterparty in any circumstances, so that Gibson could not be said to be interfering with the charterparty, whatever he did; no causal link could be established between any action of Gibson and any breach of contract by the shipowner. In *Swiss Bank Corporation* v *Lloyds Bank Ltd*,[126] Browne-Wilkinson J interpreted this case as one of interference with contract. Reviewing all the authorities he concluded that (at any rate in the present context) to become liable the acquirer of the vessel would need to have actual knowledge of the charterparty, constructive knowledge not being sufficient,[127] and act in such a way as to cause a breach of it (this last not being made out in *De Mattos* v *Gibson* itself).[128] This is also the most plausible explanation of the decision of the Privy Council in *Lord Strathcona Steamship Co Ltd* v *Dominion Coal Co Ltd*;[129] the purchasers of a vessel had express notice of both the existence and terms of the plaintiffs' time

[124] Of course, the original contract also remains enforceable, and the original shipowner can be sued for damages for its breach.

[125] (1858) 4 De G & J 276 at p 282.

[126] [1979] 1 Ch 548 at pp 569-575.

[127] However, constructive knowledge of its terms should be sufficient: *Emerald Constructions* v *Lowthian* [1966] 1 All ER 1013.

[128] *Swiss Bank Corporation* v *Lloyds Bank Ltd* was reversed on its facts ([1982] AC 584), but no doubt was cast on Browne-Wilkinson J's views. Similar views were expressed by Hobhouse J in *Rickless* v *United Artists Corporation*, partially reported at [1986] FSR 502 (but full transcript on LEXIS), affirmed [1988] QB 40.

[129] [1926] AC 108.

charterparty, refused to perform it, and proposed to use the vessel for other purposes. The Privy Council held that they could be restrained by injunction from using the vessel inconsistently with the terms of the charterparty.[130]

It is important to appreciate the limits of the protection granted, by these means, to someone who, like a time charterer, has only contractual rights in the chattel concerned. There is no suggestion that the acquirer of the vessel would be directly bound to perform the charterparty itself. Certainly, he could be restrained by injunction from acting inconsistently with the charterparty, and could also become liable in damages if he did so act, but would not otherwise come under any positive obligation to perform.[131]

The issue of whether any positive rights could be acquired by a time charterer against a new owner arose in *Port Line Ltd* v *Ben Line Steamers Ltd*,[132] where a time charterer claimed from a purchaser a share of the compensation received by them from the Crown, for the requisition of the vessel during the Suez crisis. The claim was unsuccessful, although Diplock J held that the charterparty had not been frustrated by the requisition. Unlike the cases discussed so far, this was not merely an attempt by the charterers to prevent use inconsistent with the charterparty, but to enforce positive rights under it. They could succeed only if they showed either that they had a positive right to possession of the vessel, or that the defendant was accountable for the compensation as constructive trustee. Not being demise charterers, they could not show the first,[133] and Devlin J. was unimpressed by the trust argument.

It might however be thought that if a vessel is acquired expressly subject to the charterparty, the purchaser becomes a constructive trustee, and hence becomes bound directly to the contractual terms. This is also consistent with reasoning such as that of Lord Denning M R in *Binions* v *Evans*.[134] Indeed, for someone to take property expressly subject to

---

[130] Browne-Wilkinson J interpreted it as an interference with contract case in *Swiss Bank*, *supra* fn 128 at p 574.

[131] Hoffman J concluded in *Law Debenture Trust Corp plc* v *Ural Caspian Oil Corp Ltd* [1993] 2 All ER 355 that there was nothing in the *De Mattos* principle which could impose upon a purchaser a positive duty to perform the covenants of his predecessor, only the negative remedy of the injunction being available.

[132] [1958] 2 QB 146.

[133] If a time charterer had an immediate right of possession, then the decision in *The Mineral Transporter*, *supra* fn 45 would have gone the other way.

[134] [1972] Ch 359 at p 368.

obligations is essentially similar to taking the property on express trusts, so there can be little doubt that this reasoning is, at least in principle, possible.

Constructive trust reasoning appealed to the Privy Council as an alternative basis for the *Strathcona* case.[135] It is a doubtful application of the doctrine, however, because although the purchasers had notice of the charterparty, they did not take subject to it.[136] There may, in any case, be problems with the doctrine in the context of time charterparties in particular, although not necessarily with contractual rights over chattels in general. In *Port Line*, Diplock J concluded that *Strathcona* was wrong, or alternatively, that it should be limited to its facts. Clearly, there would be difficulties with the terms of the trust, since a time charterparty includes the services of the ship's officers and crew, which would not be amenable to specific performance. It is not at all like *Binions* v *Evans*, where Mrs Evans required no more than a defence to a possession action, to remain in occupation of premises. Of course, this objection to the imposition of trusteeship would not apply to a contractual right for the use of a chattel, where (unlike a time charterparty) there were no additional service elements. Demise charterparties, by contrast, have long been held to create equitable property rights in the vessel.[137]

Of *Strathcona* itself, there is no reason why it cannot be explained as an interference with contract case: The same result would have been reached on the basis of the interference with contract doctrine already described.

Closer Relationships

As has been explained above, strangers come under only limited duties not to interfere with the chattels of others, and the law is particularly weak at protecting interests that are less than legal or possessory title.

The position is different where the defendant puts himself into a closer relationship with the claimant. The economic interests of the claimant are now better protected, and indeed in many cases, the defendant's liability is strict. The differences can perhaps be justified on either a defendant or

---

[135] *Supra* fn 129, especially at pp 124-125. However, whether the case actually turned on this reasoning must be open to doubt.

[136] On this distinction, see Fox LJ's judgment in *Ashburn Anstalt* v *Arnold* [1989] Ch 1, where the purchaser also had express notice of a contract, but did not take expressly subject to it, and *Binions* v *Evans* was not applied.

[137] Probably the correct inference to be drawn from *CN Marine Inc* v *Stena Line A/B, The Stena Nautica (No 2)* [1982] 2 Lloyd's Rep 336.

claimant-centred basis. If the defendant has placed himself into a position where the claimant has relied upon his statements or conduct, then certainly there is a case for liability being stricter. If the defendant has made an undertaking to the claimant, which has economic consequences, then there is a case for making him liable even for losses which are purely economic.[138]

Relationships to consider in this section include those created by bailment and contract. Fiduciary relationships are still closer, but are dealt with before contract, so that contractual remedies may be contrasted with them.

Bailment

The duties of bailees are often governed by contract, so that the older law, relating to bailment, is arguably less important. The obligations of bailees form the starting point, however, for interpretation of a contract. Duties of bailees also arise independently of contract,[139] and therefore can govern in the absence of privity of contract between the owner of the goods and the bailee,[140] or where the contract has been repudiated, as for example (arguably) where a shipowner wrongfully deviates on the voyage.[141]

The basis of any bailment is a voluntary taking of possession of goods owned by another, from which the law also assumes a voluntary undertaking of duties towards the owner. In the case of gratuitous bailment, these duties are not particularly onerous, the bailee being required only to keep the

[138] This is essentially similar to the justification for *Hedley Byrne* liability *supra* fn 62.

[139] *Morris* v *Martin*, [1966] 1 QB 716 *per* Diplock LJ at p 732, and also part of the *ratio*. Indeed, the concept of bailment, being derived from Roman law, is much older than modern contractual concepts.

[140] For example, in *Compania Portorafti Commerciale SA* v *Ultramar Panama Inc, The Captain Gregos* [1990] 1 Lloyd's Rep 310, where a shipowner who misdelivered cargo was held liable to the owner in conversion, there being no contractual nexus between plaintiff and defendant.

[141] For example, *Joseph Thorley Ltd* v *Orchis SS Co Ltd* [1907] 1 KB 660, *per* Fletcher Moulton LJ at p 667, who thought that the shipowner might in these circumstances be entitled to freight as a common carrier. It is not clear how far these observations survive the views expressed in the House of Lords, however, in *Hain SS Co Ltd* v *Tate & Lyle Ltd* [1936] 2 All ER 597. For a full review, see, for example, Coote "Deviation and the Ordinary Law", *Lex Mercatoria*, ed Rose (2000) Chapter 2.

property as his own. Bailees for reward are subject to the more stringent duty, to take reasonable care to keep them safe:[142]

> If the goods are lost or damaged, whilst they are in [the bailee's] possession, he is liable unless he can show - and the burden is on him to show - that the loss or damage occurred without any neglect or default or misconduct of himself or of any of the servants to whom he delegated his duty.

The undertaking being both voluntary and for reward, it is appropriate for this is to be more rigorous that the *Donoghue* v *Stevenson* duty of care, primarily in the reversal of the burden of proof. In reality, however, the content of the duty will be modified by contractual provision.[143]

A particularly stringent regime applies to common carriers for reward.[144] As with other bailees for reward, the stringency of the common law position is usually modified by contract, for example a charterparty or bill of lading contract in the case of a sea carrier,[145] but the contract is interpreted in the light of the common law position. It was because carriage contracts were so interpreted that the courts developed the idea of fundamental obligations, out of which the carrier could contract only by the clearest words, and breach of which might prevent the application of contractual excepted perils. In *Paterson Steamships Ltd* v *Canadian Co-Operative Wheat Producers Ltd*,[146] for example, Lord Wright observed:[147]

> At common law, he was called an insurer, that is he was absolutely responsible for delivering in like order and condition at the destination the goods bailed to him for carriage. He could avoid liability for loss or damage only by showing that the loss was due to the act of God or the King's enemies. But it became the practice for the carrier to stipulate that for loss due to

---

142 *Morris* v *CW Martin & Sons*, *supra* fn 139 *per* Lord Denning MR at p 726.

143 The basis upon which sub-bailees can enforce the terms of the sub-bailment against the owner, with whom he is not in privity of contract, were considered by the Privy Council in *The Pioneer Container* [1994] 2 AC 324.

144 Probably for reasons of public policy.

145 I am assuming that a sea carrier is a common carrier, although the authorities are not unequivocal: see, for example, the material collected by Dockray, *Cases and Materials on the Carriage of Goods by Sea*, 2nd ed, Cavendish (1998) at pp 22ff. For present purposes, all that matters is that a strict bailment-based regime was modified by contract, but that in interpreting the contractual provisions, the courts took account of the earlier regime.

146 [1934] AC 538 (Privy Council).

147 *Ibid* at pp 544-545.

> various specified contingencies or perils he should not be liable: the list of these specific excepted perils grew as time went on. That practice, however, brought into view two separate aspects of the sea carrier's duty which it had not been material to consider when his obligation to deliver was treated as absolute. It was recognized that his overriding obligations might be analysed into a special duty to exercise due care and skill in relation to the carriage of the goods and a special duty to furnish a ship that was fit for the adventure at its inception. These have been described as fundamental undertakings, or implied obligations. If then goods were lost (say) by perils of the seas, there could still remain the inquiry whether or not the loss was also due to negligence or unseaworthiness. If it was, the bare exception did not avail the carrier.

This was elaborated on in *Smith, Hogg* v *Black Sea and Baltic General Insurance*:[148]

> In carriage of goods by sea, the shipowner will in the absence of valid and sufficient exceptions be liable for a loss occasioned by negligence. Apart from express exceptions, the carrier's contract is to deliver the goods safely. But when the practice of having express exceptions limiting that obligation became common, it was laid down that there were fundamental obligations, which were not affected by the specific exceptions, unless that was made clear by express words. Thus an exception of perils of the sea does not qualify the duty to furnish a seaworthy ship or to carry the goods without negligence ...[149] From the nature of the contract, the relevant cause of the loss is held to be the unseaworthiness or the negligence as the case may be, not the peril of the sea, where both the breach of the fundamental obligation and the objective peril are co-operating causes. The contractual exception of perils of the seas does not affect the fundamental obligation, unless the contract qualifies the latter in express terms.

In sea carriage at least, therefore, contractual interpretation is still heavily influenced by the bailment duties that existed prior to the development of modern forms of contract.

A bailee will, of course, also be liable for conversion for wrongfully failing to deliver up the goods to the person entitled to them, or for misdelivering them, to someone not entitled. As with all conversion actions, however, the act complained of must be wrongful. This is probably the best explanation of the owner's failure to recover in *Glyn Mills Currie & Co* v

---

148 [1940] AC 997 at p 1004.

149 Reference is made to the *Paterson Steamships* case *supra* fn 146.

East and West India Dock Co,[150] where a defendant in the position of a shipowner delivered to someone who was not entitled to them, but against production of one of the three original bills of lading issued. So to deliver was not to act wrongfully, and therefore no liability in conversion arose.[151]

Misuse by Fiduciaries

The fiduciary relationship is the closest of those considered in this chapter. It is considered next, mostly as a contrast against which lesser forms of relationship are judged. It is also probably the least important in practice; trusts of chattels, and hence misuse by trustees, seem to be relatively rare,[152] but it should be remembered that the fiduciary relationship encompasses agents as well as trustees.[153] Also, of course, if a trustee of money uses it to purchase a chattel, he becomes trustee of the chattel,[154] and it is also possible to become a constructive trustee, on the principles considered above.[155]

Let us suppose, however, that the trustee of a chattel, in breach of trust, uses that chattel in such a way as to make a large profit for himself. The unique feature of fiduciaryship,[156] compared with all the other relationships so far discussed, is that the trustee will be required to account all profits received in his capacity as fiduciary, irrespective of whether the beneficiary has suffered any actual loss.[157] The account will be of actual profit made, and

---

150 *Supra* fn 22 and text thereto.

151 Compare *Motis Exports Ltd* v *Dampskibsselskabet AF 1912, Aktieselskab supra* fn 19 where the carrier was held liable in conversion, for delivery against a forged bill.

152 The courts have shown themselves reluctant to imply trusts in sales of goods: *Re Wait* [1927] 1 Ch 606; *The Aliakmon, supra* fn 47 ; *Re Goldcorp Exchange* [1995] 1 AC 74. Chattels can sometimes form part of an express settlement, as in *Healey* v *Healey, supra* fn 40. Express trusts are also declared in bankers' documentary credit transactions, when the bank releases the documents to the buyer, to enable him to resell the goods (and hence reimburse the bank): for example, *Lloyds Bank* v *Bank of America* [1938] 2 KB 147.

153 For example, *English* v *Dedham Vale Properties Ltd* [1978] 1 WLR 93.

154 On analogy with *Cave* v *Cave* (1880) 15 Ch D 639, where trust money was used to purchase a house.

155 *Supra* fns 134-136 and text thereto.

156 *Halifax Building Society* v *Thomas* [1996] Ch 217 shows that disgorgement damages are generally limited to fiduciary relationships. See however *A-G* v *Blake, infra* fn 251.

157 *Reading* v *Attorney-General* [1951] AC 507; *A-G for Hong Kong* v *Reid* [1994] 1 AC 324.

tracing in equity is also possible, if for example the profits have been converted into other property, which has increased in value.[158]

Damages in general are discussed in the following section, where it will be seen that the principles adopted are compensatory, based on the loss to the claimant. Even in cases such as *Strand Electric* and *Penarth Dock*, which can also be analysed in gain-based terms, there is no enquiry as to the actual, as opposed to objectivised gain made by the defendant. For breach of fiduciary duty, however, the additional remedy of account of profits is available,[159] which appears to be gain-based. It is not easy to justify this distinction merely on the basis that fiduciaryship has to be deliberately undertaken, or at least that the circumstances must be such as to impose on the conscience of the defendant.[160] Nor is it justified, in my view, on the basis that liability is fault-based. These considerations merely show that no injustice is done to the defendant by the imposition of a gain-based remedy. They do not justify what is apparently an unearned windfall to the plaintiff.

A possible justification is deterrence, again given the nature of a fiduciary relationship, under which the fiduciary is expected to act exclusively in the interests of his principal.[161] In ordinary commercial relationships, by contrast, the parties act independently in their own interests, except to the extent that they have contracted otherwise.[162] For example, if an engine supplier contracts to supply engines to a sports car manufacturer, unless the contract otherwise provides, he can also supply to other, even competing manufacturers. Moreover, the manufacturer is free to obtain engines from other, even competing suppliers.[163] The law of contract does not prevent, in principle, supplier to manufacturer A breaking his contract in order to make a greater profit by supplying the same engines to competing

---

[158] As in *A-G for Hong Kong* v *Reid*. Tracing would also be of value, of course, where the defendant were bankrupt, and a proprietary remedy therefore required.

[159] Loss-based damages are also available for breach of trust, on principles similar to damages at common law, as in *Target Holdings Ltd* v *Redferns* [1995] 3 WLR 352.

[160] *Westdeutsche Landesbank Girozentrale* v *Islington London Borough Council* [1996] AC 669.

[161] "The purpose of an account of profits is deterrence." Edelman, "Profits and Gains from Breach of Contract" [2001] *LMCLQ* 9 at p 11.

[162] For a comparison between fiduciary and ordinary commercial relationships, see, for example, *Re Goldcorp Exchange Ltd* [1995] 1 AC 74.

[163] This is not a fanciful example. Rover used to supply engines to Morgan, TVR, Caterham and Westfield. Morgan and Westfield also used Ford as an engine supplier. Caterham still takes engines from both Rover and Vauxhall. Ordinary commercial relationships allow this, whereas fiduciary relationships do not.

manufacturer B, subject only to compensating A for any losses. By comparison, it would be quite inappropriate for a fiduciary to act also for a competitor. One way of discouraging this is to require all profits thereby made to be disgorged.[164]

This only justifies a disgorgement remedy, however, where there is a conflict of interest, or possibility of one, and the law may go further than this, requiring an account of profits in all cases.[165] A better justification, however, is to regard all profits earned by a fiduciary, for example a trustee, as the property of the trust.[166] This also justifies restricting account of profits to fiduciary relationships, where that inference can reasonably be drawn.[167] Moreover, if the profits belong to the trust from the moment they are received by the trustee, any increase in their value also belongs to the trust.[168] It can also be seen, however, that account of profits can be analysed as compensating for the loss of profits that belong to the claimant. On that analysis, it is not a gain-based remedy at all.

---

[164] There is a clear deterrence justification in *A-G for Hong Kong* v *Reid*; the defendant should not be allowed to retain any of the profits of his wrongdoing. In *A-G* v *Blake, infra* fn 251, Lord Nicholls observes (at p 634) that the remedy "ensures that trustees and fiduciaries are financially disinterested in carrying out their duties".

[165] The only possible conflict of interest in *Boardman* v *Phipps* [1967] 2 AC 46, for example, is somewhat artificial (solicitor arguing for variation of trust's investment powers). But the decision can alternatively be justified on the basis that all information obtained in a fiduciary capacity belonged to the trust, for whom the fiduciary was acting. There was no obvious conflict of interest in *Keech* v *Sandford* (1726) Sel Cas Ch 61. See also *dicta* in *Don King Productions Inc* v *Warren* [1999] 2 All ER 218, suggesting that even the possibility of a conflict of interest is unnecessary.

[166] For example, Lord Templeman reasoned in *A-G for Hong Kong* v *Reid*, of a bribe received in breach of fiduciary duty *supra* fn 157 at p 331: "In the present case, as soon as Mr Reid received a bribe in breach of the duties he owed to the Government of Hong Kong, he became a debtor in equity to the Crown for the amount of that bribe". This was also the basis upon which *Lister & Co* v *Stubbs* (1890) 45 Ch D 1 was departed from.

[167] Perhaps also patent infringement cases.

[168] The result in *A-G for Hong Kong* v *Reid, supra* fn 157.

Contract

Almost all chattels are likely to form the subject matter of contracts, for example of sale or purchase, hire, repair, carriage, storage, etc. These contracts will typically involve the parties in mutual undertakings, intended to be enforceable, from which each hopes to profit. The expected profit may be purely economic, for example sub-hire or resale at a higher price, or from sub-contracting carriage or repair obligations. Contracts are generally entered into openly and deliberately, and again it is not therefore surprising that the duties between the parties differ from those of mere strangers. There is an assumption of responsibility by both parties, similar to that of the defendant in *Hedley Byrne* actions, which can similarly be used to justify recovery for pure economic loss.[169]

The most important features of a breach of contract claim are that liability is strict, and that pure economic loss, including expectation damages, can be recovered.[170] Not all aspects of the relationship favour claimants, however. In negligence, for example, remoteness of damage principles depend only on what might reasonably be foreseen by the defendant. In contract, apart from those losses which arise naturally, the test depends on what might be within the reasonable contemplation of both parties at the time the contract is made. This might require, for example, an owner of an especially valuable or sensitive chattel, or one from which an extraordinary profit is expected to be made, so to declare before entering into (for example) a contract for its carriage. This enables the carrier to negotiate either a limit to damages, or a higher rate for the carriage; in other words, unusual risks can be taken account of during the negotiation process. This would normally be inapposite in a negligence case, by contrast, where there is unlikely to be any pre-existing relationship between the parties.[171]

---

[169] *Supra* fn 67 and text thereto. There is also no multiplicity of claims problem, since responsibility is assumed only to the other contracting party.

[170] See in general on damages for breach of contract, for example, Treitel, *The Law of Contract,* 10th ed (1999) Chapter 21.

[171] For a comparison between the tests in contract and tort, and a justification for the difference between them, see, for example, *The Heron II* [1969] 1 AC 350 *per* Lord Reid at pp 385-386.

Assessment of Loss

General Principles

We have seen that for breach of fiduciary duty, account of profits is available as a remedy. This appears most obviously to be a gain-based remedy. However, we saw that it is also possible to analyse it in loss-based terms, and also that a loss-based analysis is arguably easier to justify in principle.

The general principle is that: "Damages for any tort are or ought to be fixed at a sum which will compensate the plaintiff, so far as money can do it, for all the injury which he has suffered."[172] Damages for breach of contract are also loss-based in principle, but in order to protect the expectation losses, are calculated so as to put the claimant, as far as possible, into the position he would have been in had the contract been performed.

There are, however, cases where the plaintiff has been compensated for losses which, arguably, he had not suffered. Sometimes these cases have been analysed in gain-based, rather than loss-based terms. This section will therefore examine how compensation should be assessed in principle, on both gain and loss-based approaches, and then consider the extent to which the law has developed along the lines of either or both of those principles.

Loss-based Compensation in Principle

We can start with the simplest case, where a chattel is destroyed, or disposed of permanently. Obviously, compensation should be sufficient to allow the claimant to replace it. Equally obviously, I would have thought, merely because the owner of a chattel does not use all its attributes should not affect its value; compensation should be sufficient to replace it with the equivalent, even if the claimant does not need all of the features. This seems obvious for most attributes. Like many people, I suspect, I hardly ever use all the features of my video recorder or stereo CD player, but if either were actionably destroyed I would expect compensation to be sufficient to allow me to obtain equivalent replacements.

At the time of writing, a Japanese motor cycle manufacturer manufactures a 400 cc motor scooter. It also manufactures a 250 cc machine, which seems to be identical apart from the engine size; it is built on the same frame, with the same equipment. It is reasonable to suppose that the only advantage of the 400 cc machine is that it is faster, with better acceleration

172 *Cassell* v *Broom, supra* fn 3 *per* Lord Reid at p 1085.

and a higher top speed. In all other respects the 250 cc machine is just as good, possibly better even, since it is lighter, probably cheaper to insure and with better fuel economy. Yet the 400 cc machine retails at several hundred pounds more, and it is reasonable to suppose that this is also reflected in second hand values.

Now, suppose that I own a 400 cc machine, but am a very slow driver, and never exceed speeds of which the 250 cc machine would be easily capable. Surely if my machine is destroyed in an accident, caused by the defendant's negligence, nobody would argue that my compensation should be limited to the value of a 250 cc machine, merely because I never use the additional performance. Quite apart from other considerations, before the accident I had a machine which I could sell, and only the market price of a 400 cc machine will compensate me for that. Thus, the amount of my compensation should not depend on whether I personally used all the attributes of the chattel in question.

Nor, conversely, is the value of a chattel increased merely because the claimant makes unusually great use of it. If, for example, damage is done to the engine of my 400 cc machine, reducing its performance, surely nobody would argue that the damages should be increased on proof that I habitually drove flat out. In any case, I could sell my damaged machine and purchase the equivalent of what I had before in the marketplace. In principle, therefore, the value of a chattel should not depend on the use the claimant makes of any of its attributes.

Yet although this conclusion seems obvious where attributes such as the performance of the machine are at issue, for some reason people are reluctant to adopt similar reasoning where the attribute is the chattel's profit-earning capability. But let us suppose that there has been a loss of use; perhaps the chattel has been wrongly detained, or having been damaged has been unavailable while being repaired, or has been destroyed and will take time to replace. In principle, the compensation should be the cost of hiring a replacement. On the principles argued above, it should not matter whether the claimant actually needs a replacement over that period; if he has a spare which he can readily use, he has lost the comfort of having the spare over the period in question, and it is reasonable to compensate him for that loss. Of course, if the chattel has been damaged, the cost of repair should also be included in the compensation, save that where the claim is for cost of repairs, the mitigation principle should prevent recovery where these costs exceed the value of the repaired chattel, since in such cases the claimant should replace the chattel instead.

This reasoning can be extended to profit-earning chattels. If I lose the use of a profit-earning chattel, I can still normally be compensated by being awarded the cost of hiring a replacement, since I can use the replacement to earn the same profits as previously. This would be so, even if I were previously earning above the market rate with my chattel. Compensation should normally be based on the cost of hiring a replacement, therefore, rather than the actual earnings.

This will be inadequate compensation, however, in two circumstances. The first is where the replacement cannot be obtained immediately. In that event, I have lost the chattel's earning capability in the meantime. On the principles arrived at above, however, that the claimant's loss does not depend on the use actually made of the chattel's attributes, I must have lost the market earning rate for this period, whether or not I actually had a profitable fixture for the chattel. It should not reduce my loss, for example, if I had loaned it to my aunt for a peppercorn.[173]

More interesting is the situation where the fixture was at above the market rate.[174] There are two points of interest about this example. First,

[173] Suppose I had a contractual fixture at below the current market rate. I entered into a contract of affreightment, at the start of 2001, when the market was low, to transport a fixed quantity of cargo over the year at a freight rate of £50 per ton, using my fleet of ships, and one of my ships is wrongfully damaged. Suppose current freight rates are now £100 per ton. Compensation based on £100 per ton will be required to compensate me for chartering in the necessary replacement tonnage to complete the contract, but it might be argued, on the principles of *Ruxley Electronics* considered *infra* fn 198, and text thereto, that it would be unreasonable for me to insist on replacing the vessel at £100 per ton, in order to earn £50 per ton. It is surely questionable, however, whether *Ruxley Electronics* would require me to break a contract, but even if I did, I would lay myself open to a damages claim, based on current market rates. On either basis, therefore, my loss is £100 per ton.

[174] This is probably most likely to occur where the fixture is long term and there has been a decline in market rates. Let us vary the example in the previous note. This time, the contract of affreightment entered into at the beginning of 2001 was to transport a quantity of cargo over the year, but within limits variable at my option. It was also entered into at the top of the market, at a freight rate of £100 per ton. As before, one of my fleet of ships is wrongfully damaged. Suppose current freight rates are now £50 per ton. Compensation based on £50 per ton will allow me to charter in the necessary replacement tonnage to complete the contract, as long as I can obtain the replacement tonnage. If not, my loss is £100 per ton, assuming that I do not go below the contractual quantity limits. Current market rates will under-compensate me. (Note that if the quantity of cargo had been fixed, as in the previous note, I would be in breach of the contract of affreightment, and the other party would

unlike the previous examples, the actual loss depends on my personal circumstances. Second, if the chattel had been wrongfully converted for the period, the defendant's gain would have been the market rate of hire, since he could have obtained an equivalent chattel on the market at that price. Gain-based damages would also seem to under-compensate in this situation, therefore.

To remain with a loss-based analysis, however, one view would be that I should be fully compensated for the earnings that I have actually lost, subject to remoteness of damage rules, and if the claim is contractual, there would seem to be no obvious objection to this. If the claim is in tort, however, we have seen that in neither negligence or conversion actions are mere contractual rights in property protected. Arguably, whereas the market value of a chattel includes a market rent element, any rental over and above the market rate must be purely contractual. On this argument, the principles which restrict title to sue should also limit recovery to the profit normally, as opposed to actually made. All losses which exceed the market value of the chattel could be regarded as economic, and hence irrecoverable in negligence or conversion. Conversely, the view could be taken that this is an over-elaboration of title to sue principles. Moreover, since the claimant is already ascertained, there is no possibility of a floodgates argument here, so that a central tenet of the title to sue argument does not apply here.

The second situation where the cost of hiring a replacement will under-compensate is if I cannot make the same use of the replacement as I could of the original chattel. For example, suppose I have time chartered my ship for five years at £10,000 per day, but a year later the market rate has decreased to £5,000 per day. If the ship is negligently damaged, and put out of use, I cannot use a replacement ship for the remainder of the charter period. Moreover, if the loss of use is likely to be extensive, going to the root of the charter, the charterer would be well-advised to repudiate, obtaining a replacement himself at the new market rate. In that event, I have lost £10,000 per day, and the £5,000 cost of hiring a replacement appears to be inadequate compensation. So, of course, would be gain-based damages, had the vessel been converted for the same period, rather than damaged, since the defendant could have obtained the equivalent vessel at the current market price. The analysis is effectively the same as in the previous example; if the claim is in tort, there is an argument that only £5,000 should be awarded, as

---

rationally repudiate. Then I would be in the same position as in the time charterparty example considered below.)

the market value of the chattel, the remaining £5,000 deriving from my purely contractual rights with the charterer.

The main point that follows from this analysis is that even on a loss-based analysis, compensation should normally depend on market rates, not the actual losses, or lack of them, incurred by the claimant. There is a possible exception where the chattel was earning at above the market rate, and cannot be immediately replaced, or the replacement cannot earn at the same rate, although even there, there is a case, at least in tort, for limiting compensation to the market rate. Actual losses may still be relevant, of course, in the absence of a clear market rate, or where they are themselves the best evidence of the market rate.

It is also worth observing that gain-based principles do not resolve the problem in the last paragraph.

A Footnote on Market Rates

If my chattel is converted and lost, or negligently destroyed, I have lost its market value, whether or not I decide to replace it. Market values can vary from place to place; my loss depends on its value at the place where I was deprived of its use. If I replace the chattel, and have to purchase it from elsewhere, I have also lost the cost of getting it to that place. This loss is in principle compensatable.[175]

Where there are successive conversions, the chattel can move between each conversion. In *Kuwait Airways Corp* v *Iraq Airways Co*,[176] aircraft in Kuwait were converted (in August 1990) by the Iraqi government and taken to Iraq, where a further act of conversion, this time by the defendants, occurred. One of the defendants' arguments was that their value in Iraq was less than that in Kuwait, because of risk of destruction by bombing, and the general difficulty of making any recovery. Yet obviously, the plaintiffs' loss was the market value in Kuwait, and the Court of Appeal assessed compensation on that basis.[177] Interestingly, gain-based damages would have under-compensated, since the defendants' gain was the value of the aircraft in Iraq.

Finally, the market value of a chattel can be lower if it is subject to contractual commitments. It follows that if, for example, a ship with a long-

---

[175] See *The Liesbosch, infra* fn 231 *per* Lord Wright at pp 468-469. If the new chattel (in that case a dredger) required adaptation, the cost of so doing should also be included in the compensation.

[176] *Supra* fn 21.

[177] *Ibid* at paras 606 ff.

term fixture is lost, its market value might be below that of a ship free of charter. If the compensation is to include any loss of freight or hire, therefore, merely to add that to the market value of a ship free of commitments might be to over-compensate. It is difficult to lay down general principles as to how market values should be adjusted in these circumstances, as there can be a wide variation in types of market. This problem was alluded to by Lord Wright in *The Liesbosch*,[178] and all authorities reviewed in *Kuwait Airways Corp* v *Iraq Airways Co*,[179] where no adjustment was made in a market that was very different from the tramp steamer market used in *The Liesbosch* example.

Gain-based Compensation in Principle

Suppose a profit-earning chattel is converted, depriving me of its use for a year. In reality, however, I had not been earning anything from it prior to the conversion, and had no plans to earn from it over the lost year. The argument goes that I have lost nothing, but that the defendant should disgorge his gain, which is the rate he would have had to pay to hire the chattel over the period.[180]

There are two observations that may be made about this argument. First, unlike account of profits considered earlier, it takes no account of any actual gains made by the defendant, for example if he had personally been able to hire an equivalent chattel much more cheaply, or if he had sub-let the converted chattel at above the market hire rate. So this calculation does not take account of the actual gain the defendant has made. We are not talking about disgorgement damages, for these purposes.

The second point is that the argument is based on the fallacy, that because I do not make use of all the attributes of a chattel, I have not lost them. Most people would probably regard that argument as untenable for

---

[178] *Infra* fn 231 at pp 464-465 where Lord Wright expressly declined to lay down any universal formula.

[179] *Supra* fn 21 at paras 599 ff.

[180] For example, *Strand Electric, infra* fn 204 *per* Denning LJ at p 254. But there was no enquiry as to the actual gain made by the defendant, and the loss no more represents that than it does the plaintiff's loss: see Somerville LJ at p 252: "... in considering the measure of damages as raised here I think the actual benefit which the defendants have obtained is irrelevant. The damages could not, in my view, be increased by showing that a defendant had made by his use of the chattels much more than the market rate of hire. Equally they cannot be diminished by showing that he had made less".

any attribute apart from the chattel's ability to earn profits; surely it is equally untenable if the attribute is that ability. The reality is that I have lost that ability, and should be compensated for it, on a loss-based analysis, whether or not I was actually intending to make use of that attribute. Loss-based principles therefore award the market hire rate, and so do gain-based. There is no difference between the two analyses. It might be argued that this loss-based analysis is very artificial, but that is also true of the gain-based version, since no account is taken of the actual gains made by the defendant. They are objectivised, using the market hire rate. If gains can be so objectivised, why not losses? Why is one artificial, the other not?

The other circumstance would be where I am deprived the use of a non-profit-earning chattel, but do not need to replace it immediately. Arguably again, I have lost nothing, but the fallacy is exactly the same as before; merely because I do not need the attributes of a chattel does not mean that I have not lost them.

Since both lead to the same result, one could argue that it does not matter which analysis is adopted, but it goes to the issue whether the tort system is intended to be an engine of compensation or restitution. It is surely difficult to justify depriving the defendant of gains that exceed the claimant's loss, unless it is intended to deter a particular form of behaviour. Generally, therefore, a loss-based analysis is to be preferred. What I have called deterrence damages, which I suggest are not easy to justify in a chattel-misuse context, are dealt with separately later.

Loss-based Compensation in Fact

The law at any rate pays lip service to a loss-based analysis, subject to the exceptions discussed in the deterrence section below. In contract, for example, Lord Haldane said:[181]

> ... I think that there are certain broad principles which are quite well settled. The first is that, as far as possible, he who has proved a breach of a bargain to supply what he contracted to get is to be placed, as far as money can do it, in as good a situation as if the contract had been performed. The fundamental basis is thus compensation for pecuniary loss naturally flowing from the breach; but this first principle is qualified by a second, which imposes on a plaintiff the duty of taking all reasonable steps to mitigate the loss consequent on the breach ...

---

[181] *British Westinghouse Electric and Manufacturing Co Ltd* v *Underground Electric Railways Co of London Ltd* [1912] AC 673 at pp 688-689.

There is no real problem where the chattel is lost,[182] except that damages are determined at the time of the breach of contract, or breach of duty if in tort. In contract, for example, these timing issues can be important, especially in widely-fluctuating markets.[183] In a negligence action, the assessment of loss, at the time of the breach, and this generally poses no problems, since it is unlikely that the breach will be of a continuing nature. For conversion this is not necessarily the case, however, particularly where a chattel is wrongfully detained over a period.[184] In *Bristol and West of England Bank* v *Midland Ry Co*,[185] the Midland Railway had wrongfully disposed of goods prior to the plaintiffs obtaining title to them. On the principles discussed above, this might be thought fatal to the plaintiff's claim. In *The Wear Breeze*, however, Roskill J (using the case to establish those very principles), accepted counsel for the defendants' argument "that the successful cause of action of the Bristol Bank was not the original conversion but the conversion following the inability (and therefore, the refusal) of the defendants to deliver the goods to the Bristol Bank when the Bristol Bank claimed them under the bills of lading after the Bristol Bank had got title thereunder."[186] No doubt, had the goods increased in value over this period, the appropriate time for their valuation would therefore have been at the later time, rather than the time of their wrongful disposal.

Where property is wrongfully detained over a period, the courts are prepared, in appropriate cases, to value it at a time later than the original act of conversion.[187] In *IBL Ltd* v *Coussens*,[188] the defendant had been dismissed

---

[182] In the light of the discussion that follows, it is perhaps worth observing that the claimant is entitled to the market value of the chattel, whether or not he intends actually to buy a replacement: for example, *Southampton Container Terminals Ltd* v *Schiffahrisgesellsch "Hansa Australia" Mgh & Co*, *infra* fn 199 at para 71(2).

[183] For example, *Concordia Trading BV* v *Richco International Ltd* [1991] 1 Lloyd's Rep 475, where an f.o.b. seller of goods had failed to send forward shipping documents, and the sole issue, on a volatile market, was when the breach occurred. Evans J adopted the c.i.f. rule, that shipping documents were required to be shipped within a reasonable time after shipment.

[184] Note that although the damages will normally be the value of the chattel at the time of the conversion, this will be reduced by the value of any interest the defendant has in the same chattel; for example, *Belsize Motor Co* v *Cox* [1914] 1 KB 244, where the defendant had a valuable interest under a hire purchase contract.

[185] [1891] 2 QB 653.

[186] *Supra* fn 48 at p 246.

[187] See, for example, Winfield & Jolowicz *supra* fn 18 at p 614.

as managing director of a company, and refused to return the two company cars he had been using. By the time damages came to be assessed, the cars had significantly increased in value. The Court of Appeal was prepared, in principle, to value them after the initial refusal,[189] and possibly as late as the date of assessment of damages. The case does not establish particularly clear principles, but it is clear that mitigation principles may require the claimant to replace the converted assets soon after their initial detention. This will depend on the availability of a ready market, which there was not for the particular vehicles in *Coussens* (one of the cars had been specially built for the defendant, and the other had an exclusive personal number plate). In most cases, however, the mitigation might require earlier replacement, and hence an earlier date for the assessment of damages.

In contract, as with conversion,[190] an issue of the appropriate calculation time arises where the breach can continue over a period, in particular where there is a failure to perform.[191]

Where the defendant converts and then sells a chattel belonging to the claimant, or exchanges it for something else of value, the sale (or exchange) is of course wrongful. However, the claimant can elect to "waive the tort" and effectively ratify the transaction.[192] If the property is sold, this allows the claimant to claim the proceeds as money had and received, or indeed to claim a proprietary title to the proceeds. In the former case, liability is complete on receipt of the money, and does not depend on retention of the proceeds by the defendant. However, the claimant is limited to the amount received (that is, the amount of the proceeds). Moreover, a money had and received action, being a personal action, is useless if the defendant is bankrupt. If on the

---

[188] [1991] 2 All ER 133. Prior to the 1977 Act this action would have been brought in detinue, and its importance was that it was the first case of its type brought under the 1977 Act.

[189] There was no final decision; the matter was referred to a master for the calculation of the damages, on the criteria set out by the Court of Appeal.

[190] *Supra* fns 184-189 and text thereto.

[191] In *Radford* v *De Froberville* [1977] 1 WLR 1262, Oliver J assessed damages on the basis of the cost of cure at the time of the action, rather than the initial breach (the defendant was in continuing breach of a covenant to build a wall).

[192] The principles are discussed, and the requirements for the election established, in *United Australia, Ltd* v *Barclays Bank, Ltd* [1941] AC 1, the authorities being reviewed at pp 11ff. In a slightly different context in *Lipkin Gorman* v *Karpnale Ltd, supra* fn 12 Lord Goff observed (at p 573) that: "It is well established that a legal owner is entitled to trace his property into its product, provided that the latter is indeed identifiable as the product of his property". He cited *Taylor* v *Plumer* (1815) 3 M & S 562, as authority for this proposition.

other hand, the money remains identifiable in the defendant's hands,[193] the claimant may prefer to assert a proprietary claim to it. Apart from the advantage of the proprietary claim if the defendant is bankrupt, the claimant will also be able to claim any increase in value, for example if the money is advantageously invested.[194] Where, instead of being sold, the converted property is exchanged, the claimant should again obtain the benefit of any increase in its value up to judgment.

Waiver of tort cases can apparently over-compensate, especially if the sale or exchange has been at better than the market rate, or in the case of a sale, the defendant has profitably invested the proceeds. In these cases, the actual gain is disgorged, and indeed, in *United Australia*, Viscount Simon LC explained waiver of tort as, in reality, an election between tortious and restitutionary remedies.[195] Even if it is admitted that the waiver of tort is in a sense fictitious, however, since there would be no remedy at all in the absence of a tort, it seems generally to be accepted that it has as its basis the claimant's ability to ratify an otherwise unlawful transaction (for example, the sale of the chattel). That being so, he can reasonably be said to have lost the substitute (proceeds of sale), rather than the original chattel. Again, therefore, it is possible to analyse the remedy in loss-based terms. As has already been argued, my preference is for a loss-based analysis, if at all possible, since (absent deterrence) it is difficult to justify any remedy which has the effect of giving the claimant more than he has lost.

---

[193] At common law, it ceases to be identifiable once mixed with the defendant's money, or paid into a mixed bank account. However, a defendant who so mixes the money, with knowledge of the claimant's title to it, will become a constructive trustee, allowing further tracing in equity. In most situations, therefore, involving sale of a converted chattel, it will make no difference to the end result whether or not the proceeds are later mixed.

[194] *Trustees of the Property of FC Jones & Sons* v *Anne Jones* [1996] 3 WLR 703. Nourse LJ would have been prepared to arrive at the same result on money had and received grounds, but this looks incorrect in principle; a money had and received action assumes that property in the money passes to the recipient; the action is complete on receipt, and nothing that happens to the money subsequently ought to be relevant. See, for example, Millett, "Tracing the Proceeds of Fraud" (1991) 107 *LQR* 71 at p 79.

[195] *Supra* fn 192 at p 18. These remarks are *obiter dicta*, since the only issue was whether election had in fact occurred. He cited *Hunter* v *Prinsep* 10 East 378, however, as did Lord Atkin (at p 32), where it was clear that the effect of the election was not to waive any claim based on the wrongdoing of the other party. It is not an election between claims, in other words, but between remedies.

Defects and Repairs

The law appears to accord with the general principles argued above where a chattel is damaged. The principles are originally derived from cases involving defective contractual performance, but have been extended also to apply in tort.

If a chattel, for which there is a ready market, is damaged, mitigation principles allow that compensation will include cost of repair, only if that is reasonable in the light of the value of the repaired chattel; if the cost of repairs is greater than the difference between the market value of the repaired and unrepaired chattel, the claimant will be expected to replace the chattel in the market. If there is no ready market, the claimant cannot mitigate in this way, but reasonableness principles still apply, where the claimant claims cost of repair, or in the case of breach of contract, remedy of defects; he will be entitled to reinstatement, as opposed to diminution in value costs, where it is reasonable to do so.

The principles were originally derived from contract cases. In *The Alecos M*,[196] the owners of a 14-year old vessel contracted to sell it, along with a spare propeller, but in breach of contract failed to deliver the spare propeller. There was no market in propellers, so a spare would have had to be specially made up, in order to rectify the defect. The Court of Appeal, reversing Steyn J,[197] taking the arbitrator's view that the commercial value of a spare propeller in these circumstance was its scrap value, rather than it replacement cost, held that scrap value was accordingly the appropriate measure of damages. It would have been unreasonable for the purchasers to insist on remedying the defect, given that the vessel was usable without the spare propeller.[198]

---

[196] *Sealace Shipping Co Ltd* v *Oceanvoice Ltd, The Alecos M* [1991] 1 Lloyd's Rep 120. See also *Channel Island Ferries Ltd* v *Cenargo Navigation Ltd, The Rozel* [1994] 2 Lloyd's Rep 161.

[197] [1990] 1 Lloyd's Rep 82.

[198] *The Alecos M* was upheld by the House of Lords in *Ruxley Electronics and Construction Ltd* v *Forsyth* [1996] 1 AC 344. The House refused to award damages on a "cost of cure" basis, where a domestic swimming pool had been built to less than the contractual depth. There was no ready market, since as Lord Lloyd observed at p 371, nobody would reasonably move house merely to cure a minor defect. Both *Ruxley* and *The Alecos M* take the reasonableness principle beyond mitigation, to the more general question whether reinstatement is a reasonable option.

The Court of Appeal has recently applied similar principles in a negligence action in *Southampton Container Terminals Ltd* v *Schiffahrisgesellsch "Hansa Australia" Mgh & Co*,[199] where the claimants' crane was damaged. The equivalent type of crane was no longer generally available, but an equivalent could have been purchased, second-hand, from the United States, modified and shipped to the UK. The cost of so doing would have greatly exceeded the market value of the crane, and the Court of Appeal held that damages should be based on the resale value.[200] It was unreasonable to insist on the reinstatement of the position precisely as it was before the accident, since it was possible to replace the crane with another type, albeit less convenient, at a significantly lower cost.

It may therefore be inferred that if *The Alecos M* had been supplied with a spare propeller, in accordance with the contract, but the spare had been negligently destroyed, or converted and lost, the damages would have been the scrap, rather than the replacement value of the propeller.

Loss of Use Cases

The law has not developed so consistently in loss of use cases, as in cases where the issue has revolved around damage, and causes of action are still treated differently.

Trespass and Conversion. Loss of use can clearly arise as a result of conversion, for example where there is a continued detention of the chattel concerned. Early cases involved trespasses to land, however, the so-called wayleave cases, where the trespass caused no obvious financial loss to the plaintiff, but the court awarded as damages the market value of the defendant's gain.[201]

It seems that similar principles apply in conversion cases, where the goods are wrongly detained.[202] In *The Mediana*, a negligence case considered

---

[199] [2001] EWCA Civ 717.

[200] The claim was in fact brought by the underwriters, but the court also held, following *Taylor (Wholesale) Ltd* v *Hepworths Ltd* [1977] 1 WLR 659, that the insured value of the crane was irrelevant to the correct measure of damages.

[201] For example, *Livingstone* v *Rawyards Coal Co* (1880) 5 App Cas 25. Note that market rates are used; but evidence of the market rate was taken to be the royalty actually paid by the defendant for the surrounding coal field. See also *Whitwham* v *Westminster Brymbo Coal Company* [1896] 2 Ch 538.

[202] An alternative explanation for the position adopted in conversion is that the but for causation test has been held not to apply, in which case the defendant cannot

further below, Lord Halsbury used the following well-known illustration, in a case involving loss of use of a vessel:[203]

> What right has a wrongdoer to consider what use you are going to make of your vessel? More than one case has been put to illustrate this: for example, the owner of a horse, or of a chair. Supposing a person took away a chair out of my room and kept it for twelve months, could anybody say you had a right to diminish the damages by shewing that I did not usually sit in that chair, or that there were plenty of other chairs in the room?

This is, of course, an example of what was then detinue, and would now be conversion.

In *Strand Electric and Engineering Co Ltd* v *Brisford Entertainments Ltd*,[204] the Court of Appeal awarded as damages for detinue the full market rate of hire for the whole period of detention by the defendants, although the evidence suggested that such rate of hire would have been unlikely to be obtained by the plaintiffs in fact.[205] (The defendants, who owned a theatre, refused to return the plaintiffs' portable switchboards, fearing that without them, the theatre could not be let or sold.)

In both Lord Halsbury's example, and *Strand Electric*, the implication is that the damages awarded should not depend on the use of the chattel actually made by the plaintiff. In *Strand Electric*, Denning LJ, referring to the wayleave cases,[206] adopted a gain-based analysis. But Somerville LJ said:[207] "Why is not the plaintiffs' loss the value in the market of the user?"

Romer LJ refused to adopt a gain-based analysis, taking the view that it was immaterial that the defendants did not actively operate the

---

argue that the claimant would not have made profitable use of the chattel in any event, but for the conversion: *Kuwait Airways Corp* v *Iraq Airways Co supra* fn 21. The case involved two successive converters, and the Court of Appeal was anxious to prevent the second converter arguing no loss, because of the first conversion. It is not clear, however, that the analysis was intended to extend to what used to be detinue.

[203] [1900] AC 113 at p 117. See also *Watson, Laidlaw & Co Ltd* v *Pott, Cassels and Williamson* (1914) 31 RPC 104, *per* Lord Shaw at p 119, for a similar illustration.

[204] [1952] 2 QB 246.

[205] The evidence suggested that only about 75 per cent of the switchboards, which the plaintiffs let out as part of their business, would be out at any particular time, and that some were loaned *gratis*, or at reduced rents.

[206] *Supra* fn 204 at pp 253-254.

[207] *Ibid* at p 252.

switchboards.[208] The views of both Somerville and Romer LJ are therefore essentially in line with the loss-based principles argued at the start of this section.

It is probable that these principles operate in trespass cases, and conversion cases involving deprivation of user of the claimant's chattels. It is true that the land, and the chattels in *Strand Electric*, were profit-earning, but that would not seem to be true of the horse, or the chair, in Lord Halsbury's example, so there is no reason to suppose that the principles are necessarily limited to such chattels.

Contract. Loss of user can be the result of breach of contract, as much as it can of conversion. In *Penarth Dock Engineering Co Ltd* v *Pounds*,[209] the purchaser of a pontoon failed, in breach of contract, to remove it from the plaintiff seller's dock. Lord Denning MR (sitting as an additional Judge of the Queen's Bench Division) awarded the market hire rate for a similar berth for the pontoon, although the plaintiffs were planning to close the dock and would not have hired the space, even had the defendants removed the pontoon as the contract required. Adopting his own views from *Strand Electric*, Lord Denning MR adopted a gain-based analysis, but as we have seen, it is possible to reach the same result on loss-based principles.

In general, there is no doubt that contractual damages are compensatory in nature, so that even if the defendant has gained substantially from his breach, they will be small or nominal if the claimant has suffered no loss.[210]

Damages in Lieu Cases: Application to Chattel Misuse? There are cases involving property interests in land, which though possible to explain in compensatory terms, appear to give higher awards than would be available on any of the above principles. There are two different possible explanations for these cases. If they apply at all to chattel misuse, it is probably only to a very limited extent.

In *Wrotham Park Estate Co Ltd* v *Parkside Homes Ltd*,[211] the defendants deliberately breached a restrictive covenant prohibiting

[208] *Ibid* at p 256.

[209] [1963] 1 Lloyd's Rep 359.

[210] For a strong defence of adoption of a compensatory, rather than restitutionary principle to the award of contractual damages, even for cynical and deliberate breaches of contract, see *Surrey County Council* v *Bredero Homes Ltd* [1993] 1 WLR 1361, especially *per* Steyn LJ at p 1370.

[211] [1974] 1 WLR 798.

development on their land, in order to make a profit. The value of the plaintiffs' land was not thereby diminished at all. The plaintiffs sought an injunction, but were awarded damages *in lieu*. The *quantum* was such a sum as the plaintiffs might reasonably have demanded as a *quid pro quo* for relaxing the covenant had the first defendants applied to them for relaxation, which in the circumstances of the case, were assessed at five per cent of the reasonably anticipated profits from the development.

Wrotham Park was followed in *Bracewell* v *Appleby*,[212] where an injunction was sought preventing the defendants from using what they claimed was a right of way over the plaintiffs' land. As in *Wrotham Park*, the injunction was not awarded, but the plaintiffs obtained damages *in lieu*. As in *Wrotham Park*, these were based, not on the amount by which the plaintiffs' property had been reduced in value by the user, but on the amount the plaintiffs might reasonably be supposed to have accepted to relax the restrictions on the defendants' right of way. This was eventually calculated at £2,000.

Both these first instance cases were approved and followed by the Court of Appeal in *Jaggard* v *Sawyer*,[213] where the cause of action was breach of restrictive covenant and trespass. In none of these cases does the award appear, at any rate at first sight, to be justified in terms of the claimant's loss; indeed, no market loss was shown in *Wrotham Park*. On the other hand, nor are the awards obviously gain-based; in *Wrotham Park*, only five per cent of the reasonably anticipated profits were awarded, whereas in *Bracewell* v *Appleby*, the award of £2,000 should be contrasted with the defendant's market gain, which was assessed at about £5,000.[214]

Wrotham Park and *Bracewell* v *Appleby* were distinguished in *Surrey County Council* v *Bredero Homes Ltd*,[215] where a more traditional compensatory approach was taken to the award of contractual damages. The plaintiffs were two local authorities, who had sold land to a development company, the company covenanting not to build more than the 72 houses for which it had planning permission. In breach of covenant the company built 77 houses, and the Court of Appeal held that the plaintiffs were entitled to nominal damage only, having suffered no loss.

---

212 [1975] Ch 408.

213 [1995] 1 WLR 269, but see also *Wrotham Park Estate Co Ltd* v *Parkside Homes Ltd* [1974] 1 WLR 798; *Bracewell* v *Appleby* [1975] Ch 408.

214 *Ibid* at p 420.

215 [1993] 1 WLR 1361.

The case has been heavily criticised,[216] but analytically there are at least some similarities with *The Alecos M* or *Ruxley Electronics*, considered earlier.[217] The defendant's breach had occasioned no market loss, or indeed damage of any kind to any adjoining property owned or occupied by the plaintiffs, and obviously to demand full compliance with the contract would, at this stage (after the additional houses had been built), have been wholly unreasonable. *Bredero* is at least consistent, therefore, with principles already discussed.

If we assume, then, that compensatory damages, represent the norm, then we need to explain the *Wrotham Park* line of cases, which seem out of line. Yet though arguably the compensatory principle has been abandoned, the damages awarded do not necessarily represent the defendant's gain either; disgorgement damages were not awarded in any of these cases.[218] In *Bredero Homes*, Dillon L J distinguished the *Wrotham Park* cases on the basis that in those cases, but not *Bredero,* an injunction was sought and refused, but damages awarded *in lieu*.[219] The analysis seems to be in terms of compensating the claimant for the loss of the injunction itself. The claimant has lost his opportunity to bargain for the relaxation of the injunction, and the defendant has made a corresponding gain:[220]

> What the plaintiff has lost is the sum which he could have exacted from the defendant as the price of his consent to the development. This is an example of compensatory damages. They are damages for breach. They do not involve any concept of restitution and so to describe them is an error. The error comes about because of the assumption that the only loss which the plaintiff can have suffered is a reduction in the value of the dominant tenement.

The damages will again be objectivised, not necessarily representing the actual price that the claimant would have accepted or that the defendant

---

216 For example, Birks, "Profits of Breach of Contract" (1993) 109 *LQR* 518, from a restitutionary viewpoint. Even from a purely compensatory viewpoint the approach seems unduly narrow; for example, Dillon LJ expressly limited the application of the wayleave cases to actions in tort, yet as we have seen these can easily be explained in compensatory terms: *supra* fn 210 at p 1365.

217 *Supra* fn 181.

218 In both *Wrotham Park* and *Bracewell* v *Appleby, supra* fns 211-212 respectively, the award was significantly less than the defendant's gain.

219 *Supra* fn 215 at pp 1364 and 1368.

220 *A-G* v *Blake, infra* fn 251, *per* Lord Hobhouse at p 652. In *Jaggard* v *Sawyer* [1995] 1 WLR 269, Sir Thomas Bingham MR also adopted a compensatory analysis of *Wrotham Park*, and by implication, *Jaggard* v *Sawyer* itself: *ibid* at p 283.

would have paid.[221] It is, however, the value of the injunction that is objectivised; what would be the result of a reasonable bargaining process to discharge it. It is not compensation for an objectivised market loss for the property itself, as in the *Penarth Dock* case discussed above.

To analyse this situation in loss-based terms has been described as artificial,[222] but it no less artificial to adopt a gain-based analysis; the compensation is usually neither what the claimant would have been prepared to accept, nor what the defendant would have been willing to pay, the nature of a reasonable bargaining process being that you would expect to end up somewhere in between. As with the loss of use cases in contract and conversion, analysis in loss-based terms remains possible, and it is arguably as good an analysis as any.[223]

A more significant problem is that addressed by Steyn LJ in *Bredero.*[224] He was unconvinced "why ... the availability of a restitutionary remedy, as a matter of legal entitlement, [should] be dependent on the availability of the wholly different and discretionary remedies of injunction and specific performance", and it is difficult to argue against this viewpoint. He distinguished *Wrotham Park* and *Bracewell* v *Appleby* on the grounds that they were cases of invasion of property rights, restrictive covenants or easements, whereas in *Bredero* the plaintiffs had no relevant property to protect. If that is the correct explanation, then (although Steyn LJ did not himself accept this) *Wrotham Park* and *Bracewell* v *Appleby* can both be explained in compensatory terms. One of the attributes of a restrictive covenant or easement is that its owner can bargain it away; its market value

---

221 In *Jaggard* v *Sawyer*, *ibid* the plaintiff (who appears to have greatly disliked the defendant) would probably not have accepted any amount to relax the injunction. Similarly, in *Wrotham Park*, the plaintiffs would never have been willing to relax the covenant, the decision being that the defendants should pay by way of damages the sum which the plaintiffs might hypothetically have been willing to accept.

222 For example, Steyn LJ in *Bredero, supra* fn 215 at p 1369, referring to *Wrotham Park*: "[the] argument that the *Wrotham Park* case can be justified on the basis of a loss of bargaining opportunity is a fiction".

223 See, for example, Sharpe and Waddhams, "Damages for Lost Opportunity to Bargain" (1982) 2 *OJLS* 290. Note that what is being lost in these cases is the injunction itself, and the ability of the claimant to bargain with the defendant for its removal. This value is objectivised in the sense that it may be neither what the claimant would actually accept or the defendant actually be prepared to pay, but it is still the ability for those particular individuals to bargain with each other. It is quite different from the general market losses examined elsewhere in this chapter.

224 *Supra* fn 215 at p 1370. Note that (in this passage) he regards the remedy in *Wrotham Park* as restitutionary, not compensatory.

includes that attribute, whether or not the claimant intends to use it. If the right is infringed, then on the principles discussed earlier in this section, and consistently with *Strand Electric* and *Penarth Dock*, it is proper to compensate for loss of that attribute.

To what extent does any of this discussion apply to chattel misuse? If Dillon LJ's distinction is adopted, the principles of awarding damages *in lieu* of injunction are unlikely to apply to chattel misuse, except in most exceptional circumstances, simply because the injunction (or in post-Woolf terminology, freezing order) is not normally available.[225] Certainly, where there is a ready market, damages will be regarded as an adequate remedy for almost any conceivable contractual breach. For example, A who has contracted to sell a new Ford Fiesta car to B will not normally be restrained from selling, in breach of contract, to C, because B can go into the market and obtain a replacement elsewhere. It would be wholly inappropriate for B to seek an injunction, and to be compensated for the loss of being able to bargain with A for its removal. Similarly, if A supplies B with a defective Ford Fiesta, B is adequately compensated by damages, and there are in any case other obvious reasons why the award of an injunction would be inappropriate; the breach would be of a positive obligation.

The position might well be different with a unique chattel, however. Suppose, for example, A has contracted to sell a Constable painting to B, delivery date 1st October. B intends to use the painting purely for enjoyment, not for profit. A finds that he can profitably display the painting in an exhibition during October, and decides to delay delivery. B may seek an injunction to restrain user inconsistent with his contract. It may be, however, that if the delivery date is not really all that important to B (perhaps B is abroad during October, and cannot view the painting in any event), an injunction might be refused, but damages granted *in lieu.* It is arguable that B has suffered no loss (certainly, he had no intention profitably to display the picture himself), but he might be able to claim damages on *Wrotham Park* principles. In that case, the *Wrotham Park* line of cases have a limited application to chattel misuse.

If, on the other hand, Steyn LJ's distinction is correct, *Wrotham Park* does no more than compensate for an attribute of a property right infringed. It has no application to chattel misuse, because easements and restrictive covenants are not recognised outside land. It is not possible to conceive of

[225] However, Steyn LJ observed *ibid* that it might be available to restrain some charterparty breaches.

an equivalent property right, to be protected in a case involving only a chattel.[226]

Generally speaking, then, contract damages are compensatory, assuming the definition of loss argued at the start of this section. It is possible that where damages are awarded *in lieu* of an injunction, the value of the injunction itself, as a bargaining tool, forms a part of the remedy, but this has limited application for the purposes of this chapter.

Negligence. The law does not appear to have developed principles as clearly in negligence as it has in conversion and contract, perhaps because loss of use is less frequently an issue in negligence cases.

It is clear, however, that the owner of a chattel damaged by negligence can, in principle and subject to remoteness rules, recover in respect of the damage, and the damage can include consequential loss of profits.[227] This was established in *SCM* v *Whittall*,[228] where the plaintiffs, who had suffered damage to their materials and machines, as a result of the defendants' negligence, were also able to claim for consequent loss of production. In *Spartan Steel & Alloys Ltd* v *Martin & Co (Contractors) Ltd*,[229] the plaintiffs were held able to recover not only the damage negligently caused to the contents of their furnace, but also the loss of the profit they would have made on the "melt". However, limits were placed on this principle. Only foreseeable financial damage immediately consequential on the foreseeable physical damage to the metal in the furnace was recoverable; more remote economic loss was not.

With a profit-earning chattel, in *Spartan Steel* the contents of the furnace, it is clearly reasonable to regard its profit-earning ability as part of its value.[230] For damage causing longer-term loss of use, we suggested that replacement cost is a more appropriate measure, but replacement is clearly not an option on the timescale of *Spartan Steel*, so consequential loss of profits should be recoverable, as part of the value of a chattel which is damaged or destroyed. In *Spartan Steel*, the profits claimed were genuinely

---

226 *Port Line Ltd* v *Ben Line Steamers Ltd, supra* fn 132, disapproving contrary reasoning in *Lord Strathcona Steamship Co Ltd* v *Dominion Coal Co Ltd, supra* fn 129.

227 *SCM* v *Whittall, supra* fn 54.

228 *Ibid*, the Court of Appeal approving the earlier decision, of Lawton J, in *British Celanese Ltd* v *AH Hunt* (Capacitors) Ltd [1969] 1 WLR 959.

229 [1973] 1 QB 27.

230 This was effectively what the plaintiffs argued in *SCM* v *Whittall.*

lost by the plaintiffs, and there is no suggestion that they were at either over or under the normal market rates.

Where negligently-caused damage puts a profit-earning chattel out of use for a longer period, we have seen that it would normally be more appropriate to award replacement costs, on the assumption that it is possible to make similar profits with the replacement. It is reasonable to objectivise these losses, and expect the claimant to go into the market to hire a replacement. In *The Leisbosch*,[231] the plaintiffs' losses were unusually high because of their financial circumstances, but only a market rate was awarded. Actual costs of loss of use are clearly not conclusive, therefore, except perhaps in the absence of a ready market, when they might be the best evidence.[232]

Conversely, on the principle that the value of an attribute does not depend on whether the claimant actually uses it, there is a case for awarding replacement hire, whether or not the claimant chooses to hire a replacement, and whether or not the chattel is profit-earning. As we have seen, this happens in conversion and contract cases. In *The Mediana*, Lord Halsbury observed that:[233]

> I observe that it has been suggested that this was not an action for trover or detinue; but although those are different forms of action, the principle upon which damages are to be assessed does not depend upon the form of action at all.

This implies that the measure of damages should be the same, irrespective of the cause of action. This does not appear in fact to be the case, however, the principles not having been developed as clearly in negligence as elsewhere.

Most of the cases are about a century old, dealing with damage to ships. It was established in *The Greta Holme*[234] that damages can compensate

---

[231] *Owners of Dredger Liesbosch* v *Owners of Steamship Edison* [1933] AC 449.

[232] In *The Valeria* [1922] 2 AC 242, where a profit-earning ship was negligently damaged, compensation was assessed on the basis of recent earnings, which were the best evidence of present market rates. The loss was very short term, so actual replacement would probably have been impractical, but the much higher period charter rate the plaintiffs were actually paying for the vessel was disregarded, surely correctly so, since the plaintiffs could have replaced her at current market rates. Presumably the period charter had been entered into when the market was much higher. It must have been a demise charter, otherwise the plaintiffs would not have had a cause of action. See further *supra* fn 45.

[233] *Supra* fn 203 at p 118. He excepted punitive damages for trespass.

[234] [1897] AC 596.

for loss of use, even where the chattel is not profit-earning (in this case she was a dredger), and no direct financial loss was occasioned by the loss of use. However, *quantum* was not adequately examined, the House of Lords acting effectively as a jury. Although there was a commercial rate of hire for an equivalent dredger, a smaller sum was awarded. It was true that the plaintiffs, as a public body, would not have profited by letting the dredger, nor did they in fact hire a replacement dredger, but in principle I would argue that that should not affect their loss, especially as their work was in fact suspended because of the damage.

In *The Mediana*,[235] a distinction was drawn between special and general damage, special damage being provable loss, in the sense in which the losses in *SCM* v *Whittall* and *Spartan Steel* were provable. Special damage would be awarded as proved, but as in *The Greta Holme*, the plaintiffs had suffered only general damage, which was a jury question.[236] As in *The Greta Holme*, therefore, *quantum* issues were avoided, although recovery was held allowable in principle. As in *The Greta Holme*, the plaintiff was a public body, and the vessel was non-profit-earning (she was a lightship, negligently damaged). Unlike *The Greta Holme*, the plaintiffs' work was not suspended; they kept two additional lightships precisely for contingencies such as these, and simply replaced the damaged vessel with one of the backups. Thus (because they had made provision for the contingency that occurred) they did not incur any direct financial loss as a result of the loss of her use.

While these cases therefore established the principle of substantial damages for the loss of services, even where no directly quantifiable loss of profits was established, they laid down no principles as to quantification. As I have argued earlier, replacement hire ought normally to be the basis, but market profit-earning rates ought to be applicable (if different) until a replacement could reasonably be obtained. In the later case of *The Susquehanna*,[237] however, where a non-profit-earning oil tanker was replaced by another non-profit-earning tanker (there being more than enough such vessels in the fleet), the commercial hire value was not discarded, in favour of an award based on depreciation and interest. The House of Lords ostensibly followed *The Greta Holme*, but whether or not *The Greta Holme*

---

[235] *Supra* fn 203.

[236] For example, *per* Lord Halsbury *ibid* at p 118. The amount seems to have been agreed by the parties.

[237] [1926] AC 655.

had decided this issue, this surely amounted to under-compensation for the plaintiffs.

With profit-earning chattels, therefore, the law appears at award market replacement hire rates to compensate for loss of use, and also market loss of profit for short-term losses, where replacement is impractical. Higher rates, at least of replacement hire, do not seem to be awarded, even if incurred. With non-profit-earning chattels, the law will award substantial damages for loss of use, but the actual damages awarded have nearly always been at less than the commercial hire rate.

Some Conclusions

We started this section with the general principle that tort and contract damages are compensatory. Yet in cases such as *The Mediana*, and *Strand Electric*, the plaintiff appears to be compensated in respect of a profit not necessarily lost. Damages in this category are sometimes therefore described as gain-based or restitutionary. They are not, however, disgorgement damages,[238] but are objectivised, and therefore do not necessarily represent the gain to the defendant either. It would be very difficult to analyse *The Mediana* is gain-based terms. In *Strand Electric*, arguably the defendant has gained by the market hire rate, which otherwise he would have had to pay, but there was no enquiry whether he would actually have paid it, had he not converted the plaintiff's property. Moreover, there is nothing in the case to suggest that he would have been required to disgorge profits, had he been able to hire the property out himself, at above the market rate.

If (as has been argued) analysis in loss-based terms seems artificial, the same is therefore equally true of a gain-based analysis. In reality, the damages do not necessarily represent either the defendant's *actual* gain or the plaintiff's *actual* loss. Nonetheless, a loss-based analysis is possible, even if some might argue artificial. If, as must surely be the case, the value of a chattel does not depend on the use its owner makes of any particular attribute, that should apply equally to its ability to earn profits as to any other attribute. It is not unreasonable, therefore, to say that a loss has been suffered.

---

[238] Compare *A-G for Hong Kong* v *Reid supra* fn 157; *A-G* v *Blake infra* fn 251.

Deterrence Damages

There are some situations where damages are expressly awarded at above compensation rate. I have used the term "deterrence damages", because that is one of the justifications for them, and because the term "exemplary damages" applies only in tort.

Exemplary Damages

Exemplary damages are rarely awarded in tort cases, and the restrictions placed on such damages make it unlikely that they will often be awarded in chattel misuse cases. Since the economic torts require intention, even in some cases malice, and are activities the law sees as wrongful, exemplary damages will sometimes be awarded. However, it is difficult to think of realistic examples for the purposes of the present discussion.

The leading authority is *Rookes* v *Barnard*,[239] where Lord Devlin reluctantly felt bound by authority to accept the principle of exemplary damages, but also limited their application to three situations: (i) oppressive, arbitrary, or unconstitutional actions by servants of the government; (ii) conduct calculated by the defendant to make a profit which may well exceed the compensation payable to the plaintiff; (iii) where there is a statute expressly authorising exemplary damages. Only the second head is likely to be of any general application in chattel misuse cases, but it is not easy to think of real examples. One possibility might be a deliberate conversion, intending to profit from the wrongful use of the claimant's chattel. Another might be the deliberate destruction of a competitor's chattel, intending to put him out of business.[240] In each case, it is possible that the defendant's gain could exceed any damages awarded to the plaintiff,[241] and clearly these are activities that the law should discourage.

On the other hand, the first of these activities constitutes theft and the second criminal damage, and it is not easy to conceive of chattel misuse

---

239 *Loc cit* fn 2.

240 This has some similarities with *Bell* v *Midland Ry Co* (1861) 10 CBNS 287, a case involving wrongful obstruction of access to the plaintiff's wharf, for the purpose of extinguishing his trade and advancing their own profit.

241 In the first case, damages would be based on a market rate for the use, not the defendant's actual gain, which may be greater. *Supra* fns 202ff and text thereto. In the second case, the defendant's gain might exceed the claimant's loss if, for example, he had been enabled by the commission of the tort to gain a monopoly position in the industry.

cases falling within the *Rookes* v *Barnard* criteria, which do not fall within the criminal law.[242] There are certainly good arguments that the criminal courts are a better forum for deterring conduct regarded by the law as immoral than their civil counterparts, whose main function might be thought to achieve a fair distribution of losses. This was, for example, Lord Reid's view in *Cassell* v *Broome*,[243] arguing for a restrictive interpretation of the three categories. Among the arguments for preferring the criminal law are the greater safeguards accorded to the defendant, and that a windfall is not awarded to the claimant. In *Rookes* v *Barnard* itself, Lord Devlin took the view that:[244]

> I do not care for the idea that in matters criminal an aggrieved party should be given an option to inflict for his own benefit punishment by a method which denies to the offender the protection of the criminal law.

It is at least arguable, therefore, that where the conduct complained of is criminal, the courts should not award exemplary damages in a civil action. If so, then there will be very few cases involving misuse of chattels where an award of exemplary damages would be appropriate.

On the other hand, it is not certain that the courts would adopt so restrictive a view. Their Lordships were not of one mind in *Cassell* v *Broome*, the views of Lord Wilberforce, for example, being in sharp contrast to those expressed above.[245] The House of Lords has also recently, in a wholly different context, refused to restrict the development of exemplary damages in *Kuddus (AP)* v *Chief Constable of Leicestershire Constabulary*.[246] If a restrictive interpretation is not adopted towards the Devlin categories, then they may still have a limited application in the present context. It is arguable that the stigma of exemplary damages is less than that of a criminal conviction, but I would suggest that is an unconvincing argument in the above examples, where criminal stigma is clearly appropriate.[247]

---

[242] One possibility might be an unlawful threat against a dock company, unless a competitor's ship was detained, but this is a fairly fanciful example (of intimidation).

[243] [1972] AC 1027 at pp 1086-1087.

[244] *Supra* fn 2 at p 1230.

[245] *Loc cit* at p 1114.

[246] [2001] UKHL 29.

[247] Arguments for and against are rehearsed by Burrows, "Referring Exemplary Damages" in *Wrongs and Remedies of the Twenty-First Century* Birks (ed) (1996), Chapter 7. See also the Law Commission's Report on *Aggravated, Exemplary and*

Contract

A consequence of damages generally being loss-based is that it can, in certain circumstances, pay to break a contract, even accepting that damages are payable. It may, for example, pay a seller of a chattel to break the sale contract and sell to a third party, if that sale is on particularly lucrative terms. For example, the third party might agree to pay at well above the market value, if he needs the chattel particularly quickly, as where perhaps it is a part for a machine which he needs to keep going, to complete a lucrative supply contract.[248] Some argue that the law should discourage such cynical breaches, by allowing gain-based damages,[249] but it is surely more difficult to justify deterring breaches of contract, however cynical, than it is in the case of any tort. Indeed, the law positively discourages penalty clauses, which would have precisely this deterrent effect, and there is no equivalent in contract of the exemplary damages that can be used to deter tort actions. Indeed, in the particular example, it is far from clear to me that the seller should be discouraged from breaking the contract, and leaving the buyer to his remedy in damages.[250]

Exceptionally, account of profits may be awarded, even in the absence of a fiduciary relationship, in order specifically to deter a breach. However, the principles were limited in *A-G* v *Blake*,[251] and will hardly ever apply in chattel misuse cases. Blake's breach was deliberate and cynical, something that he had expressly contracted not to do, and there was a public interest in ensuring that he did not profit from it. (Blake, who was described by Lord Nicholls of Birkenhead as "a notorious, self-confessed traitor", who had been convicted and escaped from his imprisonment to the USSR, had sold his

---

Restitutionary Damages (1997) (Law Com No 247), which in Part V recommended that the availability of exemplary damages be extended for some torts.

[248] For example, the purchaser in *The Saudi Crown* [1986] 1 Lloyd's Rep 261 (the actual decision in which is not relevant to the present discussion) paid above the market rate for ricebran needed quickly to meet his commitments, when he had been let down by his supplier. Note that the contract breaker will not profit merely by selling at a higher price on a generally rising market, because the damages for breach will also be based on the higher market price.

[249] For example, Birks, "Profits of Breach of Contract" (1993) 109 *LQR* 518.

[250] In *Bredero*, Steyn LJ thought that restitutionary remedies in contract would create uncertainty and discourage economic activity *supra* fn 215 at p 1370. He also re-emphasised the undesirability of conferring a windfall on the aggrieved party, an argument that is also central to the views adopted in this chapter.

[251] [2000] 3 WLR 625.

story in breach of contract with his employer, the Crown. The House of Lords held him liable to account profits.) The undertaking broken was also very similar to a fiduciary undertaking, except that the information disclosed was no longer confidential.

Birks also notes that account of profits can be expressly provided for in the contract.[252]

Conclusion

"English law does not work in an analytical fashion."[253] The common law "is a maze and not a motorway."[254] Perhaps we should not expect too much logic, then, in this area of law. Certainly there are distinctions which are not easy to justify, for example between common law and equitable tracing of the proceeds, when the chattel has been wrongfully sold by the defendant, and (perhaps) on the availability of damages *in lieu* of an injunction.

Nonetheless, it seems generally to be accepted that deterrence, and moral crusades, are better suited to the criminal than the civil law. The claimant is generally not over-compensated, assuming a fairly wide view to be taken of compensation. More often, he is either under-compensated or not compensated at all. This is sometimes difficult to justify, especially in some of the negligence cases, involving loss of use. Nonetheless, I would suggest that the law often achieves a fair distribution of losses, or if preferred, allocates losses fairly as between first and third party insurers. This process involves consideration not only of the claimant's losses, but also the nature of the interest protected, the state of mind of the defendant, and the relationship between the parties. A single system is being asked to achieve a number of (often incompatible) objectives. It may not be surprising that it cannot do so ideally, and that compromise is sometimes inevitable.

In summary, however, I suggest that the following propositions can be advanced:

1. There is no automatic protection against misuse of chattels, whether that misuse be in the form of damage, or deprivation of use. Chattel misuse is about the law of wrongs, and if the claimant cannot point to a wrong, there is no remedy. Even legal ownership is not automatically

[252] *Supra* fn 249.

[253] *Cassell* v *Broome supra* fn 3 *per* Lord Wilberforce at p 1114.

[254] *Morris* v *Martin supra* fn 13 *per* Diplock LJ at p 730.

protected. It follows that those with interests in chattels are well-advised themselves to take steps to protect them.

2. The law protects some interests, such as legal ownership, better than others, such as contractual interests. Co-relatively, other people are under a greater obligation not to interfere with some interests in chattels than others.
3. Any interest in a chattel might be better protected against those who have entered into a voluntary relationship with the claimant than it is against strangers.
4. Generally speaking, and subject to a few exceptions, the law aims to compensate claimants for their losses, rather than deprive defendants of their gains.

7 Purchase Money Security Interests under the Revised Article Nine of the Uniform Commercial Code

KEITH MEYER

The Legal Context

Millions of transactions dealing with movable goods and services occur daily in the United States. Many are between businesses and many are between businesses and consumers. Some involve the sale of movable goods or intangibles; others are leasing arrangements. Still others involve loans or extensions of credit, with or without "security interests" (an interest that gives the creditor a claim to specific property of the debtor). Most transactions are completed without incident. However, when something goes wrong, the relevant legal rules must be determined and applied. Those rules are found in the Uniform Commercial Code (UCC).[1]

The UCC was conceived in 1940. The National Conference of Commissioners on Uniform State Laws (NCCUSL), an organisation of state governments started in 1892 whose purpose is to draft and secure enactment of uniform state laws on a wide variety of subjects, became interested in developing a single comprehensive commercial code covering all aspects of commercial transactions (contract, payment and credit).[2]

---

[1] The citations in this paper are to the 2000 version of the UCC. The source is Selected Commercial Statutes (West 2001). Unless otherwise indicated all cites are to Revised Article 9.

[2] The National Conference of Commissioners of state law (NCCUSL) is dedicated to ascertaining what private state law would benefit from model legislation. It drafts two types of proposed legislation: (1) Uniform acts which apply to legal problems common to all states and uniformity of treatment is very important; and (2) Model acts which involve problems common to all states but where uniformity is not important. Members who serve without compensation are called commissioners and come from 50 states plus the District of Columbia,

An established process exists for determining when NCCUSL will get involved. Initially, a study committee of Commissioners will be formed. This function is performed by the Permanent Editorial Board (PEB) of the UCC when an area covered by the Uniform Commercial Code is involved. Suggestions for changes can come from the PEB, individual Commissioners, the American Law Institute (ALI) or its members and third parties such as the American Bar Association. Once the Executive Committee of the NCCUSL and the ALI decide to proceed, a drafting committee is formed. This committee will have a Reporter who is a legal expert in the subject matter of the proposed statute. The product of the drafting committee is presented and must be approved by the membership of NCCUSL and also by the ALI membership when the UCC is involved. The ALI[3] is a private nonprofit corporation unlike NCCUSL. Its purpose is "to promote the clarification and simplification of the law and its better adaptation to social needs, to secure the better administration of justice and to encourage and carry on scholarly and scientific legal work".[4] The UCC

Puerto Rico and the Virgin Islands. Most are practising lawyers but some are judges and law professors. Each state normally sends 4 people. Each state's delegation, however, has only one vote on whether proposed acts should be approved by the Commission. Each commissioner *must* try to persuade his/her state legislature to adopt its proposals.

[3] The ALI has about 2,500 members (professors, judges and practising lawyers), who are elected for life. It is funded by gifts, dues, receipts from the sale of publications and returns on investments. NCCUSL conceived the idea of a Uniform Commercial Code and sought the help of the ALI who had and has a wider membership, greater prestige and more financial support. The ALI has formulated a comprehensive series of Restatements of common law. Examples are RESTATEMENT OF AGENCY, CONFLICT OF LAWS, CONTRACTS, JUDGMENTS PROPERTY, RESTITUTION, SECURITY, TORTS, TRUSTS. Many of these are in their third edition. Other areas covered include LAW GOVERNING LAWYERS, SURETYSHIP AND GUARANTY, UNFAIR COMPETITION, TRUSTS: THE PRUDENT INVESTMENT RULE. The ALI has been involved with codification projects, model acts and studies including the MODEL PENAL CODE, the UCC, Principles of Corporate Governance, a Federal Securities Code and various federal taxation proposals. For a general discussion of the process of Revised 9 see *infra* fn 6 and text accompanying *infra* fn 6. The ALI address is 4025 Chestnut Street, Philadelphia, PA 19104 and the internet address is http://www.ali.org and http://www.ali-aba.org. joined NCCUSL to sponsor the UCC project.

[4] ALI Bylaws Art I.

was born in 1951 when the UCC was approved by the ALI and the NCCUSL.

The UCC is a code but it does not have all of the characteristics of a civil code and reflects some common law concepts. Unlike ordinary statutes, the UCC contains a number of interpretive aids. For example, at the beginning of each Article is a section defining specific terms relevant to the Article. At the end of each section appears an official comment which identifies prior law, if any; explains on a section by section basis any changes or additions of new matter, and provides explanatory examples and cross-references to most other relevant sections. The hope of the drafters of the UCC was that bringing all of the basic commercial laws together in a comprehensive, integrated code would produce a number of positive results. This type of code should produce a document of common concepts, common terminology, internal consistency and a coherent philosophy. Accordingly, the UCC was designed to simplify the law, reduce uncertainty, diminish legal disputes and be adaptable to changing business situations and not need to be frequently amended. And, if the code were adopted by all of the states, a uniform body of commercial law would exist.

Uniform rules are needed among states for a variety of reasons. Commerce knows no state boundaries. Each state is independent in matters of legislation and judicature. Consequently, lawyers have to deal with court decisions and statutes of each state. The commonly accepted hypothesis is that the economy expands if more credit is available and uniform rules facilitate this effect. Transaction costs are minimised if parties in different states can rely on a known body of law when entering into a transaction and resolution of problems between the parties becomes easier if the outcome of litigation in whatever jurisdiction is reasonably predictable and uniform. Yet, traditionally in the United States, transactions involving movable property have been governed by state law not federal law, even though the federal government has the power to regulate them. The United States' form of government is designed to have a limited national government, with inherent powers retained in the states. The United States Constitution sets forth the powers of the national government. Congress is delegated certain powers in Article I, Section 8, including the so-called commerce power: to regulate commerce with foreign nations and among the states. The intent was to insure free national markets. This provision has been broadly interpreted to give Congress great power over commerce and to limit states' power to interfere with interstate commerce.[5] The sale of goods, the payment and the financing of the sale is within this power. If Congress chooses to regulate, Article VI of the U.S. Constitution, the so-called Supremacy Clause, applies. It states: "This Constitution and the laws of the United States ... and all treaties ... shall be the supreme law of the land; and the judges in every State shall be bound thereby, anything in the Constitution or laws of any State to the contrary notwithstanding". This means that anytime there is a conflict between federal and state law, the federal law controls, assuming that the federal law is constitutional.

The UCC facilitates the development of uniform laws without the involvement of Congress. For the UCC to become law, however, it must enacted by each individual state. Since 1944, NCCUSL and the ALI have been co-sponsors of the UCC and have worked to preserve and update it. The development process employed is designed to develop a national consensus that (1) the proposed statute is worthy of enactment by state legislatures and (2) uniformity is more important than refinements by individual state legislatures.[6] The change process can be slow. It normally

---

[5] For example, *New England Power Co* v *New Hampshire,* 455 US 331 (1982); *Katzenbach* v *McClung* 379 US 294 (1964); *Wickard* v *Filburn,* 317 US 111 (1942).

[6] Article 9 was substantially changed in 1972 (hereafter, F9) and was completely revised in 1999 (hereafter, R9). Previous drafts of R9 may be found on the Internet at http://www.law/upenn.edu/library/ulc/ulc.htm. Both NCCUSL & ALI work on revisions and both approve changes, but the NCCUSL alone directs the effort to get states to adopt the new version of the UCC. The ALI revision process typically starts with a study committee and a group of advisors. If changes are needed, a drafting committee is appointed. The drafting committee will contain academics, representatives of the various industries affected and consumer advocates. An attempt is made to develop a code that has broad appeal so that special interest groups will not derail states from adopting it. It must also be noted that currently the American Bar Association plays an important role in the development process. For a thorough discussion of the revision process of Article 9 of the UCC *see* Culhane, "The UCC Revision Process: Legislation you should see in the making" (1992-93) 26 *Creighton L Rev* 29. The creation process is not without its critics. Some have argued that the process is a closed society dominated by pro-business advocates and is too rigid in its approach to re-thinking uniform acts. *See* Patchel, "Interest Group Politics, Federalism, and the Uniform Laws Process: Some Lessons from the Uniform Commercial Code" (1993) 78 *Minn L Rev* 83; Rubin, "Thinking Like a Lawyer, Acting Like a Lobbyist: Some Notes on the Process of Revising UCC Articles 3 and 4" (1993) 26 *Loy L A L Rev* 743; Schwartz and Scott, "The Political Economy of Private Legislatures" (1995) 143 *U Pa L Rev* 595; Miller, "Realism Not Idealism in Uniform Laws - Observations

takes years for changes to be made, approved by the NCCUSL and the ALI, and for all of the states to adopt the changes. Yet, the uniform act has sections which contain alternative provisions giving states some choices and, state legislatures can and do change other sections as well as creating new provisions when enacting their UCC. Uniformity is dependent upon state legislatures adopting a Uniform Act without major changes and state courts' construction in a manner consistent with the UCC's purpose. Today, the UCC has been enacted with local variations in all fifty states. While some of the variations differ substantially from the uniform version, the basic rules prevail in all states. Of course, true uniformity could be achieved by Congress enacting the UCC.[7] In general, Congress has not exercised its power. Exceptions are bankruptcy and certain consumer legislation. If Congress federalized the UCC, litigation would be in federal courts and it would require more judges. However, special courts could be created to handle nothing but commercial law matters. Note that parts of Articles 3 and 4 dealing with check collection have already been federalised because of the need for uniformity. Yet, many oppose federalisation of Article 9 for a variety of reasons including creditor rights issues involve private law. Others argue for it, noting financing today is not confined to one state and large businesses operate in more than one state. Also, planning and transaction costs would be substantially reduced.

While the UCC was designed to be a comprehensive code, the drafters gave great latitude to parties as to agreements between[8] them and some latitude to judges. For example, section 1-102(2), which is applicable to all Articles of the UCC, sets forth the basic premises of the UCC:

> Underlying purposes and policies of this Act are: (a) to simplify, clarify and modernize the law governing commercial transactions; (b) to permit the continued expansion of commercial practices through custom, usage and agreement of the parties; and (c) make uniform the law among the various jurisdictions.

From the Revision of the UCC" (1998) 39 *S Tex LR* 707 (discusses the realities of the uniform drafting process).

[7] As indicated in the text, Congress has the power to enact legislation regulating commercial transactions under the Commerce Clause of the US Constitution because financing the sales of goods or loans for the purchase are within the definition of interstate commerce. US Constitution Article 1, § 8.

[8] While many provisions of the UCC may be varied by agreement, some cannot be. For example, obligations of good faith, reasonableness, diligence and care requirements cannot be changed. UCC § 1-102(3). Also see for example, §§ R9-602-03.

As to the role of judges, official comment 1 to § 1-102 states in part: "[The Act] is intended to make it possible for the law embodied in this Act to be developed by the courts in the light of unforeseen and new circumstances and practices. However, the proper construction of the Act requires that its interpretation and application be limited to its reason".[9] Also, § 1-103 recognizes non-UCC rules may apply. It states:

> Unless displaced by the particular provisions of this Act, the principles of law and equity, including the law merchant and the law relative to capacity to contract, principal and agent, estoppel, fraud, misrepresentation, duress, coercion, mistake, bankruptcy, or other validating or invalidating cause shall supplement its provisions.

The UCC is currently divided into eleven parts and its coverage is comprehensive. Article 1 includes general concepts and specific definitions of terms applicable to all Articles. Each Article, however, contains its own definitions, which if inconsistent with the general definitions, control.[10] Article 2 applies to "transactions in goods". It de-emphasises the title concept and includes a number of then novel provisions dealing with the formation of a sales contract, and creating different standards of conduct for merchants and non-merchants. Article 2A regulates all facets of leases.[11] Article 3 deals with payment methods concentrating on negotiable instruments and checks and other drafts. Article 4 deals with bank deposits and collections of checks and 4A deals with wire funds transfers. Article 5 deals with letters of credit. Bulk sales of the inventory of a business are covered in Article 6. Documents of title, including warehouse receipts and bills of lading, are the subject of Article 7. Article 8 articulates rules relating to investment securities such as stocks and bonds. Article 9 applies to all transactions intended to create a security interest in personal property or fixtures and to the sale of certain types of

---

[9] The general provisions affecting all parts of the UCC are in Article 1.

[10] Examples are found in Articles 2, 3 and R9 which have a more demanding definition of good faith than does Article 1. Compare UCC §§ 1-201(19) (honesty in fact in the conduct or transaction concerned), to 2-103(1)(b), 3-103(a)(4), 9-102(a)(43) (honesty in fact and the observance of reasonable commercial standards of fair dealing).

[11] A lease is "a transfer of the right to possession and use of goods for a term in return for consideration, but a sale, including a sale on approval or a sale on return, or retention or creation of a security interest is not a lease". UCC § 2A-103(j).

collateral that are considered to be financing arrangements.[12] The focus of this chapter will be Article 9.

Article Nine of the Uniform Commercial Code

Many of the transactions involving goods and services involve the extension of credit. This credit falls into two categories: unsecured and secured. If the debtor fails to pay for a good purchased on credit or fails to pay a loan when due, the unsecured creditor must file a law suit against the debtor, obtain a civil judgment and collect the judgment by having a law enforcement officer seize non-exempt property[13] and sell the property. This process is slow, expensive and not very productive. The secured creditor, however, contracts for an interest in specific property of the debtor and can often obtain the collateral quickly and without the expense of a law suit.[14] Further, an unsecured creditor's debt will be lost in bankruptcy, whereas a properly perfected secured creditor's security interest survives a debtor's bankruptcy.[15] Moreover, the secured creditor will in many instances prevail

---

[12] § F9-102 restricted coverage to sale of chattel paper and accounts. § R9-109(a)(3) broadens the coverage by adding the sale of payment intangibles and instruments but certain sales are excluded. See, for example, § R9-109(d).

[13] When the debtor is an individual, States and Congress have concluded that the public interest is not served by allowing the creditor to make the debtor a pauper. Accordingly, both state and federal law recognise that certain property of a debtor, who is an individual, is protected from the claims of a creditor seeking property *without the consent of the debtor*, that is, the property is exempt from involuntary seizure. Probably the most important property of a debtor is wages and this is protected under federal law as well as in some states. Consumer Credit Protection Act, 15 USC §§ 1671–77 (1994). Except for wages and outside of bankruptcy, state law defines what property cannot be seized by a creditor in the judicial debtor collection process. While state exemptions vary widely, some states exempt the following categories of property: the family residence and household furnishings, the clothing and personal effects of the debtor and the debtor's family, the family car, and the tools and other personal (movable) property used in the debtor's occupation. These protections do not apply to most consensual security interests given by the debtor.

[14] UCC § R9-609(a)(1).

[15] Bankruptcy law is federal law. 11 USC §§ 101-129 (1994, Supp IV 1998). The goal of bankruptcy is equal treatment for all creditors. The debtor's ability to make preferential transfers to creditors is considerably limited. After the filing of a bankruptcy petition, a creditor cannot improve its position *vis-à-vis* other

over other creditors and purchasers of the goods subject to a perfected security interest.

Article 9 governs secured transactions in personal or movable property. In the late 1940s, when the UCC was being drafted, the leading commercial states had separate and very different laws on chattel mortgages, conditional sales (retention of title), trust receipts, factors' liens and assignments of accounts receivable. In short, the law of chattel security was as provincial and nonuniform then as the law of real estate mortgages is today. The most radical innovation in Article 9 is its substitution of a unitary security device for the many security devices previously in use. The terms such as "mortgagee", "pledgee" and "conditional sale" do not appear in Article 9. Instead, the unitary security device is formulated in terms of four basic concepts: "secured party", "debtor", "collateral" and "security interest." In 1999, Article 9 was revised substantially, but the basic concepts were retained. Article 9 has a language all of its own. The person granting credit may become a "secured party" by contracting for a "security interest" in "collateral" to secure an obligation of the "debtor." The contract is a "security agreement". Security interest is defined to be "an interest in personal property or fixtures which secures payment or performance of an obligation".[16] Consider the following illustration. Suppose Farmer wants to borrow $40,000 from Bank to buy a new piece of equipment. Bank will only loan the money if the equipment is security for the loan. In Article 9 language, Bank is the secured party, Farmer is the debtor, the equipment is the collateral, Bank's interest in the equipment to secure payment is a security interest, and the agreement creating the security interest is the security agreement.[17] Because Bank is loaning Farmer the money to obtain the

---

creditors by seizing assets of the debtor. For individual debtors, bankruptcy provides the prospect of significant relief. This relief may take the form of relief from further personal liability for debts created prior to bankruptcy. A primary purpose of bankruptcy is to relieve honest debtors from oppressive debt and permit him/her a fresh start. While a secured creditor's debt will be discharged, a properly created security interest will remain and can be enforced against the property subject to the security interest after bankruptcy. Congress has in effect adopted the priority rules of Article 9. But see 11 USC §§ 547(b), (e)(3) & (c) (Supp IV 1998).

[16] UCC § 1-201(37).

[17] UCC §§ 1-201(3); R9-102(a)(73).

equipment, Bank's security interest is a special kind of security interest called a purchase money security interest (PMSI).[18]

The creation of an enforceable security interest requires more than an appropriate security agreement. The secured party must give value and the debtor must have rights in the collateral. Once these three requirements are satisfied, the security interest attaches to the specific property subject to the security interest and is enforceable against the debtor upon default. To achieve maximum protection, the secured party must "perfect"[19] its security interest. This normally requires some step beyond attachment such as the secured party filing a financing statement or taking possession of the collateral.[20] In general, depending on the type of collateral, perfection can

---

[18] § F9-107 provided:
"A security interest is a purchase money security interest (PMSI) to the extent that it is (a) taken or retained by the seller of the collateral to secure all or part of its price; or (b) taken by a person who by making advances or incurring an obligation gives value to enable the debtor to acquire rights in or the use of collateral if such value is in fact so used."
§ R9-103 (a-b) define a PMSI as:
"(a) [Definitions.] In this section:
(1) "purchase-money collateral" means goods or software that secures a purchase-money obligation incurred with respect to that collateral; and
(2) "purchase-money obligation" means an obligation of an obligor incurred as all or part of the price of the collateral or for value given to enable the debtor to acquire rights in or the use of the collateral if the value is in fact so used.
(b) [Purchase-money security interest in goods.] A security interest in goods is a purchase-money security interest:
(1) to the extent that the goods are purchase-money collateral with respect to that security interest;
(2) if the security interest is in inventory that is or was purchase-money collateral, also to the extent that the security interest secures a purchase- money obligation incurred with respect to other inventory in which the secured party holds or held a purchase-money security interest; and
(3) also to the extent that the security interest secures a purchase-money obligation incurred with respect to software in which the secured party holds or held a purchase-money security interest".
A PMSI holder in many instances is given special priority. See *infra* text accompanying fns 69-86, 95-97, 106, 109, 113, 125.

[19] § F9-303(1); § R9-308(a). Perfection is designed to give public notice of a security interest.

[20] § R9-308 defines perfection:
"(a) [Perfection of security interest.] Except as otherwise provided in this section and Section 9-309, a security interest is perfected if it has attached and all of the

occur in five different ways: secured party files a financing statement in a public office; secured party takes possession of the collateral; secured party obtains control; the security interest is noted on the certificate of title; and perfection can occur automatically upon attachment of the security interest under § R9-203(b).

Since the 1960s Article 9 has been changed significantly twice. Substantial amendments were made in 1972 and in 1999 Article 9 was completely revised. Although some references are made to the pre-1999 version which is referred to here as former Article 9 (F9), this chapter focuses primarily on Revised Article 9 (R9) which sets July 1, 2001 as the effective date. As of July 1, 2001, all fifty states had enacted R9 but a few have set the effective date later than July 1, 2001. While the core concepts of F9 such as scope,[21] attachment,[22] perfection,[23] priorities,[24] and default[25] are continued, significant changes have occurred. For example, instead of 55 sections there are now 135 with many sub-parts and changes were made to at least 25 other UCC sections. Most section numbers have been changed. Except for definitions which affect the whole code found in UCC section 1-201, R9s definitions are placed in one section, 9-102, which has 80 main parts with sub-parts. Revised Article 9 recognizes the electronic revolution by beginning to move away from the need of a signed piece of paper to establish an agreement as reference is made to "authentication" of a "record" instead of a signed writing.[26] Finally, consumer credit transactions are treated differently in many areas.[27]

---

applicable requirements for perfection in Sections 9-310 through 9-316 have been satisfied. A security interest is perfected when it attaches if the applicable requirements are satisfied before the security interest attaches."

[21] §§ R9-109.

[22] §§ R9-108, 9-203-04, 9-315(a). Also see *infra* fn 29.

[23] §§ R9-308–16, 9-501–07 and *supra* fns 19-20.

[24] For example, §§ R9-201, 9-317-39.

[25] §§ R9-601–24.

[26] See § R9-102(a)(7) and (a)(69). Also see *infra* fn 29 which discusses "authenticate" and "record."

[27] See for example, §§ R9-102(22-25), 9-108(b)(3) and (e), 9-612–16, 9-626(b) and cmt 4, 9-626(a)(3)(B), (4), cmt 3 and 9-626(b). A security agreement must describe the collateral in a way that reasonably identifies the collateral. Reasonable identification is defined differently for commercial transactions and consumer transactions. Revised section 9-108(b) provides, for example, that the identification of the collateral by type (inventory or request) is adequate for a commercial transaction but not for a consumer transaction. A description "all consumer goods" is not adequate. For other examples see 9-108(b) & (e). For a

This chapter will focus on the unique treatment of a purchase money security interest (PMSI) in Revised Article 9.

The Purchase Money Security Interest (PMSI)

Whether a security interest is a PMSI, as defined in § R9-103, is important in several contexts. One is perfection.[28] Most PMSIs in consumer goods are "automatically" perfected upon attachment,[29] that is no filing or possession by the secured party is required.[30] A number of special priority rules apply to conflicts between other creditors and PMSI holders. For example, a PMSI perfected by filing "before or within 20 days after the debtor receives delivery of the collateral"[31] has priority over certain buyers, lessees and lien creditors interests "which arise between the time the

---

definition of consumer goods see *infra* fn 117. Consumers have to be given a variety of special notices when a security interest is being foreclosed. See §§ 9-612-16.

[28] See *supra* fn 20 and accompanying text and § R9-309(1).

[29] § R9-203(b). Attachment requires the secured party give value, a security agreement exist and the debtor have rights in the collateral. Value is defined very broadly in § 1-201(44). Rights in general are not defined but 9-203(b)(2) provides the debtor must have rights or "the power to transfer rights in the collateral to a secured party". The debtor can obtain this power through any of the traditional bodies of law mentioned in § 1-103 or through specific Code provisions as in § 2-403(1)(b). The third requirement is that the debtor must have authenticated a security agreement unless the secured party has possession of the collateral or the collateral is a certificated security in registered form delivered to the secured party pursuant to a security agreement or the collateral is deposit accounts, electronic chattel paper, investment property or letter-of-credit- rights, and the secured party has control under 9-104, 9-105, or 9-107 pursuant to the debtor's security agreement. Security agreement is defined in 9-102(a)(73) and definition of agreement is in 1-201(3). Under R9, "authentication" of a "record" is the key not the signing of a piece of paper. Authenticate is defined in 9-102(a)(7) to mean: "to sign; or to execute or otherwise adopt a symbol, or encrypt or similarly process a record in whole or in part, with the present intent of the authenticating person to identify the person and adopt or accept a record". "Record", except as used in "for record", "of record", "record or legal title", and "record owner", means information that is inscribed on a tangible medium or which is stored in an electronic or other medium and is retrievable in perceivable form. 9-102(a)(69).

[30] § R9-309(1), 9-310(b), 9-313(a).

[31] § R9-317(e).

security interest attaches and the time of filing."[32] Another special rule applies to conflicts between PMSI holders and other secured parties. The normal priority rule dealing with more than one secured party claiming the same collateral is set forth in § R9-322 which provides that the first-to-file or perfect wins unless another rule applies.[33] Revised section 9-324 provides a number of exceptions to § R9-322. For example, a qualifying PMSI holder in equipment, inventory, or livestock may achieve priority over security interests perfected earlier in time of filing.[34] These special rules apply only if a secured party can qualify as PMSI holder. Thus, it is appropriate to first examine the definition of a PMSI.

PMSI Defined and the Tracing Requirement

A PMSI is a special type of security interest. This means the normal attachment[35] requirements as well as the special purchase money definitional elements in § R9-103 must be satisfied. In general, a PMSI can be obtained only in goods or software[36] and is created when a secured party provides the credit that enables the debtor to obtain the collateral. R9-103(1)(b) contains the basic definition which provides: "A security interest in goods is a purchase money security interest . . . to the extent that the goods are purchase-money collateral with respect to the collateral". "[P]urchase money collateral"[37] means goods or software that secure a "purchase money obligation" which is defined as "an obligation of an obligor[38] incurred as all or part of the price of the collateral," and those taken by a lender to secure an obligation "for value given to enable the debtor to acquire rights in or use of the collateral if the value is in fact so used".[39] Under these definitions, two types of PMSIs in goods or software

---

[32] *Ibid.* Also see *infra* fns 125-131 and accompanying text.
[33] §§ R9-322(a), (f)(1) and cmt 4. Also see *infra* fn 64 and accompanying text.
[34] See *infra* fns 68, 81, 96 and accompanying text.
[35] See § F9-203; § R 9-203. Also see *supra* fn 29.
[36] See § R9-103(a)(1).
[37] § R9-103(a)(1). See *supra* fn 18.
[38] Revised Article 9 uses two terms "debtor" and "obligor". Revised section 9-103 refers to an obligor. Obligor is defined in part to mean to be "a person that, with respect to an obligation secured by a security interest... (i) owes payment or other performance of the obligation..." § R9-102(a)(59). Debtor is defined in part to mean "a person having an interest, other than a security interest or other lien, in the collateral, whether or not the person is an obligor...". § R9-102(a)(28)(A).
[39] § R9-103(a)(2). See *supra* fn 18.

can exit. One is held by sellers to secure the buyer's obligation to pay and the other is held by a qualifying lender.

While a seller can normally establish the PMSI without difficulty, lenders must show that the loan "enabled" the debtor to acquire the good and the money was in fact used to purchase the good, that is, the funds have to be traced.[40] The tracing problem is solved by the lender issuing a cheque to the seller of the good or a joint payee (debtor and seller) cheque. The enabling requirement can occasionally be a problem if the debtor purchases the good before the loan is in fact made. For example:

July 1	A farmer has a tractor irreparably break during harvest and needs a replacement immediately. He calls his banker who tells him that bank will loan him the money but it will take about 5 days to process everything. After this conversation, Farmer purchases a new tractor from Dealer on an unsecured basis.
July 6	Farmer obtains a loan and signs the security agreement granting a security interest in the equipment as of July 6. Lender immediately issues Seller a cheque to pay for Debtor's purchase.

Did this loan enable the debtor to purchase the equipment? Would it make any difference if Farmer tells seller that bank would loan him the money for the purchase on July 1 but it would not be available until at least July 6?

Comment 3 to R9 provides:

> The concept of "purchase money security interest" requires a close nexus between the acquisition of collateral and the secured obligation. Thus, a security interest does not qualify as a purchase money security interest if a debtor acquires property on unsecured credit and subsequently creates the security interest to secure the purchase price.

Notwithstanding the above comment, it appears that the "enabling" requirement raises a question of fact to be determined on a case-by-case basis. Moreover, it should not be rigidly construed to exclude all transactions where the debtor first acquired the collateral on an unsecured basis. This is particularly true if the seller would not have made the sale without the lender's commitment to make the loan. Certainly, the nexus between the purchase and the loan must be very close, that is, months and years cannot pass. One of the architects of original Article 9, the late Grant

---

[40] See, for example, *MBank Alamo Nat'l Ass'n* v *Rayethon C,* 886 F 2d 1449 (Tex 1989); *In re Freeman*, 956 F 2d 252 (11th Cir 1992). See § R9-103 cmt 3.

Gilmore, argued in his treatise about Article 9 that: "If the loan transaction appears to be closely allied to the purchase money transaction that should suffice."[41] While it is not clear what kind of proof would be required to tie the loan and the sale together, it would seem that a lender should be able to make its case if the loan and sale were virtually contemporaneous and both the Seller and Debtor understood the sale would not happen without the loan.[42] Obviously, the lender should make the loan directly to the seller and before the acquisition.

Transformation and Dual Status

Under F9, questions arose concerning whether a properly created PMSI could be transformed into a non PMSI when a refinancing or consolidation of debts occurred. For example, consider a refinancing. Debtor in financial difficulty, gets the financing seller or lender to agree to reduce the amount of the monthly payments and extend the duration of debt. The refinancing is done by cancelling the original security agreement and substituting a new security agreement embodying the new terms. Some courts have held that a new loan was created and that the proceeds of the loan were not used to acquire rights in the collateral. Thus, no PMSI existed.[43] Others courts disagreed.[44] The transformation issue also arose when a seller who had a PMSI sold additional goods to debtor and the parties entered into a new security agreement covering the old and the new debts and old and new collateral (cross-collateralisation). Again, some courts have held a transformation occurred while others rejected the transformation rule in favor of a "dual status" doctrine which holds that the mere presence of a non PMSI does not destroy the purchase money aspect of the original transaction. Thus, a PMSI remained under the new security agreement to the extent that it secured the price of the original goods even though it

---

[41] Gilmore G, *Security Interests in Personal Property* II (1965) 782.

[42] § F9-107(b) had the same enabling requirement as § R9-103(a)(2) and therefore should be considered. See for example, *Valley Bank* v *Estate of Rainsdon,* 793 P 2d 1257 (1990) (loan not enabling because Rainsdon already owned the cows); *North Platte State Bank* v *Production Credit Ass'n,* 200 NW 2d 1 (1972) (loan month and a half after sale).

[43] For example, *In re Mathews*, 724 F 2d 798 (9th Cir 1984).

[44] For example, *In re Billings*, 838 F 2d 405 (10th Cir 1988).

secured the price of other items also.[45] Revised Article 9 deals with some of the transformation and dual status issues in *non consumer* transactions.

Revised Article 9 rejects the transformation rule in non consumer cases. First, the basic definition of a PMSI in § R9-103(b)(1) recognises the "dual status" in that it provides that a security interest in goods is a PMSI *"to the extent"* that the goods are purchase-money collateral, that is, to the extent that the good secures a purchase-money obligation incurred with respect to the good. And, § R9-103(f) rejects specifically the transformation rule in *non consumer* transactions. It states that a PMSI is not destroyed as such when the purchase-money collateral also secures an obligation that is not a purchase-money obligation or when collateral that is non purchase-money collateral also secures an obligation that is a purchase-money obligation or a purchase-money obligation has been renewed, refinanced or consolidated. Thus, a security interest in collateral may be *both* a PMSI and a non PMSI. This "dual status" which § R9-103(f) adopts may present application problems.

Jan 2	Lender holds a PMSI in Equipment#1 to secure an enabling loan of $100,000.
May 1	Debtor needs more money and refinancing. A new $50,000 loan is made, and a new security agreement reflecting the change is executed.
Dec 1	Debtor defaults with an unpaid debt of $150,000 and Equipment#1 is worth $150,000.

In the above scenario, § R9-103(b)(1) provides that the PMSI continues to the extent that the good secures a purchase-money obligation incurred with respect to the good. Of the obligations secured by Equipment#1, only $100,000 is a purchase money obligation under § R9-103(a)(2).[46]

The extent to which a PMSI remains can also arise when a debtor makes a payment on the new loan. Continuing the above example, if Debtor makes a $10,000 payment on the $150,000 debt, one must determine the extent to which the security interest remains is a PMSI. When the extent to which a security interest is a PMSI depends on the application of payments to a particular obligation, the payment must be applied in accordance with any reasonable method of application to which the parties agree (for example, FIFO, first in, first out).[47] In the absence of agreement, the payments are applied to obligations that are unsecured. If

---

[45] For example, *Pristas* v *Landaus of Plymouth, Inc*, 742 F 2d 797 (3d Cir 1984).

[46] § R9-103, cmt 7, discusses generally transformation and dual status. It must be noted that F 9 cases cited in fns 43-44 are consumer cases.

[47] § R9-103(e). See specifically § R9-103 cmt 7 b.

more than one obligation is secured, they are applied to obligations secured by purchase-money interests in the order in which those obligations were incurred. These rules apply only to *non consumer* transactions.[48]

Consumer Goods

Revised Article 9 specifically restricts the rules dealing with the dual status, transformation and cross-collateral rules to commercial transactions. Specifically § R9-103(h) states in relevant part "[t]he limitation of the rules . . . to transactions other than consumer-goods transactions is intended to leave to the court the determination of the proper rules in consumer-goods transactions. The court may not infer from that limitation the nature of the proper rule in consumer-goods transactions and may continue to apply established approaches".

Under F9, many of the cases involving the issue of whether a PMSI existed or had been transformed into a nonPMSI, involved consumer debt. Consumers filing a bankruptcy petition were interested in transforming a PMSI because current Bankruptcy Code section 522(f)[49] permits the debtor (person filing bankruptcy) to avoid (nullify) certain nonpossessory non PMSI's in consumer goods in certain exempt property.[50] Also, non PMSIs in household goods are unenforceable under certain other federal rules. For example, the Federal Trade Commission's Rule on Credit Practices make it an unfair act or practice for lenders or retail installment sellers to take a non PMSI in household goods.[51] Lenders are subject to similar rules.[52]

Purchase Money Security Interests in Software

While it was unclear under F9 what type of collateral was eligible to be made subject to a PMSI, § R9-103 provides specifically that a PMSI may only be created in goods, and in certain circumstances in software.[53] The software must be related to the good that is subject to a PMSI as specified in § R9-103(c). The debtor must acquire an interest in the software in an integrated transaction in which the debtor acquired an interest in the goods and the interest in the software must be acquired for the principle purpose

[48] *Ibid.*
[49] 11 USC § 522(f) (1994, Supp IV 1998).
[50] See *supra* fn 13.
[51] 16 CFR § 444.2 (a)(4) (2000).
[52] 12 CFR § 227.13 (2000) (Banks), 12 CFR § 535.2 (2000) (Thrifts).
[53] § R9-103(c).

of using the software in the goods. Thus, a creditor who finances the debtor's acquisition of the goods and the related software can obtain a PMSI in both.[54] An example would be the purchase of a computer with certain installed software. However, it is very important to note that a computer program "embedded" in the goods is considered part of the goods. Examples include the BIOS (Basic Input Output System) in a computer and the ABS brakes in most cars today. The definition of a good in § R9-102(a)(44) provides in relevant part:

> The term also includes a computer program embedded in goods and any supporting information provided in connection with a transaction relating to the program if (i) the program is associated with the goods in such a manner that it customarily is considered part of the goods, or (ii) by becoming the owner of the goods, a person acquires a right to use the program in connection with the goods. The term does not include a computer program embedded in goods that consist solely of the medium in which the program is embedded.[55]

Consignments

Revised section 9-102(a)(20) defines a consignment to be a transaction, regardless of its form, where: 1) a person delivers goods for sale to a merchant[56] who deals in goods of that kind under a name other than that of the person delivering; 2) the transaction does not create a security interest; 3) the merchant is not known by its creditors to be substantially engaged in selling the goods to others; 4) the aggregate value of the delivered goods is $1000 or more at the time of delivery; and 5) the goods were not consumer goods[57] immediately before delivery. Unfortunately, R9 fails to provide any guidance as to how one determines when a consignment-like transaction secures an obligation of the merchant, that is, a security interest

[54] The attachment and perfection requirements for both the good and software must be satisfied. See *supra* fn 29.

[55] Also see the definition of general intangible in § R9-102(a)(42) which states it includes software. Also see, § R9-102 cmt 5 d, and 25. Finally note that § R9-102(a) cmt 4 a states: "The definition of 'goods' and 'software' are mutually exclusive. Computer programs usually constitute 'software' and, as such, are not 'goods' as this Article uses the terms. However, under the circumstances specified in the definition of 'goods' computer programs embedded in goods are part of the 'goods' and are not software".

[56] UCC § R9-102(b), § 2-104.

[57] § R9-102(a)(23) and see *infra* fn 112.

is involved. This is surprising when one compares the elaborate provisions of § 1-201(37) defining when a lease creates a security interest.[58]

Once the transaction is determined to be a consignment, the consignor (deliverer) is considered to have a PMSI in the inventory of the consignee (possessor) for purposes of R9.[59]

PMSI Priority Rules when the Conflict is between a Prior Perfected Security Interest and a Perfected PMSI

The basic priority rule when two perfected secured creditors claim the same collateral is that the first secured creditor to file or perfect has priority over other subsequent secured creditors. Consider this example:

Jan. 1 SP#1 loans $ to D who grants SP#1 a security interest (SI) in all equipment D presently owns and any after-acquired equipment. D owned EQ#1. SP#1 perfected

---

[58] UCC § 1-201(37) provides in part:
"Whether a transaction creates a lease or security interest is determined by the facts of each case; however, a transaction creates a security interest if the consideration the lessee is to pay the lessor for the right to possession and use of the goods is an obligation for the term of the lease not subject to termination by the lessee, and (a) the original term of the lease is equal to or greater than the remaining economic life of the goods, (b) the lessee is bound to renew the lease for the remaining economic life of the goods or is bound to become the owner of the goods, (c) the lessee has an option to renew the lease for the remaining economic life of the goods for no additional consideration or nominal additional consideration upon compliance with the lease agreement, or (d) the lessee has an option to become the owner of the goods for no additional consideration or nominal additional consideration upon compliance with the lease agreement.
A transaction does not create a security interest merely because it provides that (a) the present value of the consideration the lessee is obligated to pay the lessor for the right to possession and use of the goods is substantially equal to or is greater than the fair market value of the goods at the time the lease is entered into, (b) the lessee assumes risk of loss of the goods, or agrees to pay taxes, insurance, filing, recording, or registration fees, or service or maintenance costs with respect to the goods, (c) the lessee has an option to renew the lease or to become the owner of the goods, (d) the lessee has an option to renew the lease for a fixed rent that is equal to or greater than the reasonably predictable fair market rent for the use of the goods for the term of the renewal at the time the option is to be performed, or (e) the lessee has an option to become the owner of the goods for a fixed price that is equal to or greater than the reasonably predictable fair market value of the goods at the time the option is to be performed."

[59] This is discussed below at pp 273-278.

by filing a proper financing statement in the proper place.

Feb. 1 D purchases EQ#2 with cash not supplied by any creditor.

Feb. 9 SP#2 loans $ to D who grants SP#2 a SI in EQ#1 and EQ#2. SP#2 perfected by filing a proper financing statement in the proper place.

Aug. 1 Debtor defaults on both loans.

Who has priority? SP#1 has priority as to both pieces of equipment. The basic priority rule when the conflict is between two perfected secured parties is that the first-to-file wins. This result is fair because SP#2 is deemed to know the first-to-file rule and could have learned of SP#1s interest by checking under Debtor's name the filed financing statements which are of public record. The first-to-file rule also applies to after-acquired property. Priority dates from the time of filing not perfection.[60]

PMSIs in certain circumstances are treated differently and given a priority often called a "super-priority." For example:

Jan. 1 SP#1 loans $ to D who grants SP#1 a security interest (SI) in all equipment D presently owns and any after-acquired equipment. D owned EQ#1. SP#1 perfected by filing a proper financing statement in the proper place.

Feb. 1 D purchases EQ#2 from seller who obtains a PMSI and files a proper financing statement in the proper place.

Aug.1 Debtor defaults on both loans.

Who has priority as to EQ#2? Assuming that seller can establish a PMSI, seller will defeat SP#1 even though SP#1 has a perfected security interest in EQ#2 and filed first.[61] In other words, the PMSI holder is given a super-priority. A variety of reasons are given for providing a purchase money creditor a super-priority over the first-to-file. The most common is that this priority makes it possible for the debtor to obtain additional secured financing and break the monopoly power of the first-to-file secured creditor who will not provide additional financing.[62] Another broad reason is that the super-priority really does not substantially impair the first-to-file

[60] See §§ R9-308, 9-203(b), 9-322 and *supra* fns 20 and 29.

[61] See §§ R9-322(a), (f)(1), and 9-324(a) *infra* fn 64.

[62] See, for example, Jackson & Kronman, "Secured Financing and Priorities Among Creditors" (1979) 88 *Yale L J* 1143, 1167.

secured creditors.[63] These creditors can bargain for and obtain from the debtor covenants and events of default that prohibit or restrict the debtor from obtaining PMSI financing. Also, the PMSI financier supplies new value that is in fact used to obtain a new asset. And, as we will see, the inventory financier must be given notice by subsequent PMSI holders. This notice enables the inventory financier to protect itself.

Regardless of the reasons, as under F9, R9 provides two ways to break the monopoly of the first-to-file or perfect rule:[64] a subordination agreement or proof of a PMSI. This part of the chapter will discuss § R9-324 which contains a set of rules that overrides the first-to-file or perfect rules.

Conflicts between a PMSI in Goods Other Than Inventory or Livestock and a Prior Perfected Security Interest in the Same Goods

Revised section 9-324(a) provides that a perfected PMSI in goods other than inventory or livestock has priority over a conflicting security interest in the same goods or their identifiable proceeds, *if* the PMSI was perfected when the debtor obtained possession or within 20 days of possession. Consider the following hypothetical:

Jan. 2 Dealer borrows $100,000 from Bank for working capital and grants a security interest in "all equipment now owned or hereafter acquired". Bank perfects by filing a financing statement with the secretary of state on Jan. 5.

Feb. 10 Dealer buys and takes delivery from ABC Manufacturing Co. a new machine to be used in its business and agrees to pay for it over four years. ABC obtains an enforceable security interest in the machine and files a proper financing statement in the proper place on Feb. 15.

If the dealer becomes insolvent it appears that under the first-to-file rule Bank would win because its security agreement covered after-acquired property and it filed first. However, ABC will win by utilizing § R9-

[63] Law and economics scholars support this view. See Kanda & Levmore, "Symposium on Revision of Article 9 of the Uniform Commercial Code: Explaining Creditor Priorities" (1994) 80 *Va L Rev* 2103.

[64] See §§ F9-312(5) and 9-316. Under Revised Article 9 the sections are 9-322(a) and 9-339.

324(a).[65] First, ABC must establish a PMSI under § R9-103. This can be done because the new machine is "purchase-money collateral" for a "purchase money obligation" the security interest secures Dealer's obligation to pay the purchase price.[66] The machine is being used in Dealer's business and therefore is classified as equipment not inventory.[67] ABC also filed 5 days after Dealer took delivery which is well within the 20 day grace period. Thus, ABC has priority as to the machine because all of the requirements are satisfied. What if the machine were to be exchanged for a new machine? ABC's super-priority continues in the new machine, which is identifiable proceeds,[68] assuming ABC's security interest in proceeds is perfected.[69]

Now assume the same basic facts of the above hypothetical except that ABC on February 10 delivered the machine to Dealer for it to test the machine to determine if it would work for Dealer. On March 1 Dealer decides to buy the machine and signs the installment contract and proper security agreement and proper financing statement. On March 15 ABC files the financing statement. The issue raised here is whether ABC can establish that it perfected its security interest within 20 days of debtor receiving possession. Possession is not defined in the UCC. This means that courts may look to common law rules as well as other provisions of the UCC to determine what is possession.[70]

---

[65] Revised Article 9-324(a) states:
"[General rule: purchase-money priority.] Except as otherwise provided in subsection (g), a perfected purchase-money security interest in goods other than inventory or livestock has priority over a conflicting security interest in the same goods, and, except as otherwise provided in Section 9-327, a perfected security interest in its identifiable proceeds also has priority, if the purchase-money security interest is perfected when the debtor receives possession of the collateral or within 20 days thereafter."

[66] See § R9-103(a)(2) and *supra* accompanying text fns 37-45.

[67] § R9-102(a)(44), (48), (33) and cmt 4a. Also see *infra* fn 118.

[68] Proceeds are broadly defined in § R9-102(a)(64) to include any property acquired upon the sale, lease, exchange or other disposition of the collateral. The proceeds can be either cash, § R9-102(a)(9), or noncash, § R9-102(a)(58). Subsection 9 defines cash proceeds to mean "proceeds that are money, checks, deposit accounts, or the like". Identifiable is not defined except as to commingled proceeds. See § R9-315(b).

[69] Perfection of proceeds is controlled by § R9-315(c-e).

[70] See UCC § 1-103 and, for example, § R9-313(cc) & (h).

The question of when the debtor obtained possession for purposes of starting the 20 day period running has been frequently litigated.[71] A fairly recent example is *Citizens Bank of Americus* v *Federal Financial Services, Inc.*[72] The court held that, notwithstanding the fact that debtor had had possession of the collateral for seven weeks, "possession" of the collateral is only established when the debtor acquired ownership of the collateral and executed a promissory note evidencing its obligation to pay the purchase price. Here Debtor obtained physical possession for demonstration purposes only and the collateral was not owned by the Debtor until the note and sale agreement were executed. This case represents the majority view that the key was not when the debtor received physical possession of the collateral but when did the person possessing the collateral become a debtor. Section F9-105(1)(d) defined a debtor to be a person who owes payment or other performance. While § R9-324(a) still provides that the 20 day grace period begins to run from the time the "debtor" receives possession, the term "debtor" is defined differently. A debtor is among other things "a person having an interest . . . in the collateral, whether or not the person is an obligor...".[73] Obligor means among other things "a person that, with respect to an obligation secured by a security interest in ... collateral, (i) owes payment or other performance of the obligation.... § R9-102(a)(59). Collateral is defined to mean " the property subject to a security interest . . . ".[74] Possession remains undefined. Comment 3 to § 9-324 recognises that a debtor may obtain physical possession of the good before deciding to buy the good on secured credit. It notes, a person can have possession of a good pursuant to a bailment or lease arrangement and neither a true bailment nor a true lease is governed by R9.[75] The comment goes on to specifically state: "Accordingly, the 20-day period in subsection (a) does not commence until the goods become 'collateral' . . . , that is, until they are subject to a security interest." UCC section 1-201(37) defines

[71] For example, *Brodie Hotel Supply, Inc* v *US*, 431 F 2d 1316 (9th Cir 1970); *Color Leasing 3, LP* v *FDIC*, 975 F Supp 177 (D RI 1997).
[72] 509 S E 2d 339 (Ga Ct App 1998).
[73] § R9-102(a)(28)(A).
[74] § R9-102(a)(12).
[75] The owner of property that is placed in the possession of another person should file a financing statement if there is the possibility that third parties could be misled. Then there is no problem if the relationship changes to creditor-debtor one. Former § 9-408 as well as § R9-505 authorises consignors, bailors and lessors to file a financing statement. However, if debtor-creditor relationship fails to develop the field financing statement needs to be terminated. § R9-513.

security interest to mean "an interest in personal property or fixtures which secures payment or performance of an obligation". Thus, it appears that the 20-day period does not begin to run until a debtor-creditor relationship is created and the creditor has obtained a security interest, which has attached under § R9-203. This means the debtor must have rights in the collateral, value is given and a proper authenticated agreement has been executed. The issue of when the 20 day period begins to run also arises if the debtor physically receives goods that must be assembled and/or be tested or when the debtor takes possession of goods in stages.[76]

In summary, on its face § R9-324(a) appears to be easily satisfied. The holder of a PMSI in noninventory who files within 20 days of the debtor receiving possession of the collateral can defeat a prior perfected secured creditor without having to search the records to discover earlier secured creditors or to provide any notice to these creditors. It is probably easy for sellers because they can easily control when the debtor obtains possession and file before transferring the good. Lenders, on the other hand, face some dangers. First, they must prove the advance was used to purchase the good and that the purchase of the good was made after the advance or substantially contemporaneously with it. Next, lenders must be certain when the debtor obtains possession of the goods and file within 20 days. This issue can be avoided by the lender filing a financing statement before it releases any funds. Finally, another possible problem that exists is the possibility of the previous secured creditor declaring the debtor in default when it learns of the lender's PMSI.

Inventory

Revised section 9-324 (b) states the requirements for a PMSI in inventory to obtain a super-priority. Like for noninventory, the person asserting a PMSI has the burden to prove that it has a PMSI in the appropriate inventory. Unlike under § R9-324(a), a PMSI holder must search the public

[76] Courts have struggled with this issue under former Article 9. Compare *In re Ultra Precision Indus, Inc* 503 F 2d 414 (9th Cir 1974) (time period did not begin to run until assembling and testing was complete) with *In re Michaels,* 156 B R 584 (Bankr D Vt 1989) (time period began when debtor had "physical control"). Revised Article 9's response to these cases is found in § 9-324, comment 3, which concludes that in the assembly and testing cases: the buyer "takes possession" within the meaning of subsection (a) when, after an inspection of the portion of the goods in the debtor's possession, it would be apparent to a potential lender to the debtor that the debtor has acquired an interest in the goods taken as a whole.

records and give an appropriate written notice to the creditor who has a perfected security interest in the debtor's inventory.[77] This written notice must be received by the prior perfected creditor within five years before the debtor receives possession of the inventory.[78] The PMSI holder must also perfect *before* the debtor receives possession of the inventory. If these requirements are satisfied, the PMSI holder will have priority as to the financed inventory as well as to certain proceeds of the inventory. Unlike for noninventory, the proceeds are quite limited. The proceeds include only identifiable cash proceeds[79] received by the debtor on or before delivery of the inventory to a buyer and chattel paper[80] or instruments[81] to the extent

---

[77] § R9-324(b) provides:
"[Inventory purchase-money priority.] Subject to subsection (c) and except as otherwise provided in subsection (g), a perfected purchase-money security interest in inventory has priority over a conflicting security interest in the same inventory, has priority over a conflicting security interest in chattel paper or an instrument constituting proceeds of the inventory and in proceeds of the chattel paper, if so provided in Section 9-330, and, except as otherwise provided in Section 9-327, also has priority in identifiable cash proceeds of the inventory to the extent the identifiable cash proceeds are received on or before the delivery of the inventory to a buyer, if:
(1) the purchase-money security interest is perfected when the debtor receives possession of the inventory;
(2) the purchase-money secured party sends an authenticated notification to the holder of the conflicting security interest;
(3) the holder of the conflicting security interest receives the notification within five years before the debtor receives possession of the inventory; and
(4) the notification states that the person sending the notification has or expects to acquire a purchase-money security interest in inventory of the debtor and describes the inventory".
The notice requirement is explained in Comment 4 to § R9-324.

[78] Comment 5 to § R9-324 makes it clear that a secured party that holds a PMSI in inventory does have to give notice prior to filing a proper financing statement. See *Kunkel* v *Sprague Nat'l Bank*, 128 F 3d 636 (8th Cir 1997).

[79] § R9-102(9) and (64). See *supra* fn 72.

[80] Chattel paper means a record or records that evidence both a monetary obligation and a security interest in specific goods, a security interest in specific goods and software used in the goods, or a lease of specific goods. The term does not include charters or other contracts involving the use or hire of a vessel. If a transaction is evidenced both by a security agreement or lease and by an instrument or series of instruments, the group of records taken together constitutes chattel paper. § R9-102(a)(11).

provided by § R9-330(b & e). If cash proceeds are deposited in a bank account, § R9-327 controls priority to the extent there is a conflict with the priority rules of § R9-324.[82] Under this new section, if the bank where the deposit account is located has a security interest in the deposit account, it will trump the PMSI holder.

The following hypothetical is designed to illustrate the basic application of § R9-324(b).

Jan. 1 Jane Doe owns and operates a business that sells all kinds of computers. Bank loans money to Jane and obtains a perfected security interest in all of Jane Doe's present and after-acquired inventory. Jane has 100 IBM computers.

Jan. 20 Apple Computer gives an appropriate written notice to Bank that Apple intends to sell five Apple computers to Jane Doe on credit and obtain a perfected security interest in them. Apple also files a proper financing statement covering the five Apple Computers in the proper place.

Feb. 1 Apple Computer Corp. sells Jane five Apple Computers on credit, and obtains from Jane a perfected security interest in the five and delivers the Apples to Jane's business.

Feb. 5 One Apple is sold to Joe who pays with a Visa credit card and another Apple is sold to Janet who pays by check.

Feb. 6 One Apple is sold to Sid on credit and Sid is given 90 days to pay.

Feb. 10 Jane defaults on both loans. Her inventory consists of 100 IBM computers and two Apple computers. She has a visa receipt showing the sale to Joe, Janet's check

---

[81] "Instrument" means for example, a negotiable instrument or any other writing that evidences a right to the payment of a monetary obligation, is not itself a security agreement or lease, and is of a type that in ordinary course of business is transferred by delivery with any necessary indorsement or assignment. The term does not include (i) investment property, (ii) letters of credit, or (iii) writings that evidence a right to payment arising out of the use of a credit or charge card or information contained on or for use with the card. § R9-102(a)(47).

[82] See § R9-324 cmt 8.

and a sales receipt showing the sale to Sid who was given 90 days to pay.

Bank claims priority to everything under § R9-322(a) because it filed first as to the inventory and this priority carried over to the proceeds.

In this scenario, the Bank is entitled to the 100 IBM computers because Apple does not have a security interest in the IBMs and a perfected secured creditor defeats an unsecured creditor.[83] Assuming both creditors have perfected security interests in the two Apples and that the check, Visa slip and Sid's obligation are proceeds, Bank will prevail unless Apple can utilise § R9-324(b). Revised section 9-324(b) applies inasmuch as the computers are inventory because they are goods held for resale.[84] Apple should win as to the two remaining Apples. Apple must establish a PMSI under § R9-103. This can be done because the Apple computers were "purchase-money collateral" for a "purchase money obligation" because the security interest secures Dealer's obligation to pay the purchase price.[85] Apple can also establish the other requirements. It filed a proper financing statement before debtor received possession of the inventory and it gave appropriate written notice before debtor received possession of the inventory. While Sid's obligation is a proceed of the inventory, it is classified as an account[86] under R9 and is not covered by § R9-324(b).

---

[83] See § R9-201(a). The negative inference from § R9-322(a)(2) and 9-317(a).

[84] Revised section 9-102(a)(48) defines "inventory" to mean goods, other than farm products, which:

"(A) are leased by a person as lessor;

(B) are held by a person for sale or lease or to be furnished under a contract of service;

(C) are furnished by a person under a contract of service; or

(D) consist of raw materials, work in process, or materials used or consumed in a business".

[85] See § R9-103(a)(2) and *supra* fns 35-42 and accompanying text.

[86] § R9-102(a)(2) defines the term account and subsection (i) applies here.

"Account", except as used in "account for", means a right to payment of a monetary obligation, whether or not earned by performance, (i) for property that has been or is to be sold, leased, licensed, assigned, or otherwise disposed of, (ii) for services rendered or to be rendered, (iii) for a policy of insurance issued or to be issued, (iv) for a secondary obligation incurred or to be incurred, (v) for energy provided or to be provided, (vi) for the use or hire of a vessel under a charter or other contract, (vii) arising out of the use of a credit or charge card or information contained on or for use with the card, or (viii) as winnings in a lottery or other game of chance operated or sponsored by a State, governmental unit of a State, or

Revised section 9-324(b) provides a super-priority only for identifiable cash proceeds which does not include an account. Cash proceeds "means proceeds that are money, checks, deposit accounts and the like".[87] Thus, the first-to-file rule of § R9-322(a) controls[88] and the Bank wins.

Revised Article 9 defines an account in relevant part to mean among other things "a right to payment of a monetary obligation, whether or not earned by performance . . . (vii) arising out of the use of a credit or charge card or information contained on or for use with the card . . . .". Thus if Jane has not received money for the Visa slip, it will be classified as an account and the super-priority rule of § R9-324(b) will not apply as the above discussion of Sid's obligation shows. It is not clear whether the drafters focused on the fact that defining the right to payment represented by the use of a Visa credit card as an account may substantially limit a PMSI holder's right to identifiable proceeds because many people use the credit card as cash. Moreover, the definition of cash proceeds covers checks which in many ways are not as close to true cash as an approved Visa card transaction is. It also must be noted that if the Visa card issuer has already transferred the payment to Jane's bank, the proceeds are now the deposit account. Arguably it is cash proceeds of the Apple, but was it received before delivery of the Apple to the buyer? No! In effect it is proceeds of an account. Moreover, R9 has added a new section dealing with priority issues dealing with deposit accounts.[89] Finally, if one of the buyers of an Apple had paid in part by trading in some good, the super-priority would not apply to the trade-in which is a noncash proceed.[90]

In summary, § R9-324(b) dealing with PMSIs in inventory is quite different from § R9-324(a)'s treatment of PMSI's in noninventory. First, there is no 20 day grace period for filing, the financing statement must be filed before debtor obtains possession of the inventory. Next, the secured

---

person licensed or authorised to operate the game by a State or governmental unit of a State. The term includes health-care-insurance receivables. The term does not include (i) rights to payment evidenced by chattel paper or an instrument, (ii) commercial tort claims, (iii) deposit accounts, (iv) investment property, (v) letter-of-credit rights or letters of credit, or (vi) rights to payment for money or funds advanced or sold, other than rights arising out of the use of a credit or charge card or information contained on or for use with the card.

[87] § R9-102(a)(9). See *supra* fn 67.

[88] § R9-322(a&b) and cmt 6, special rules are formed in § R9-322(c) when the first-to-file rules is in applicable to perfected security interests in proceeds.

[89] § R9-327.

[90] § R9-102(a)(9), (58). See *supra* fn 67.

party must give an appropriate written notice before delivery of the goods. Lastly, the treatment of proceeds is very different. The super-priority is in general limited to identifiable cash proceeds received on or before delivery of the inventory to a buyer.

Conflicts between PMSIs in Software and Prior Perfected Security Interests

As discussed earlier in the section dealing with the definition of a PMSI,[91] a PMSI can be obtained in a good and included software if the debtor acquires the software for the principal purpose for using the software in the goods. Thus, a creditor who finances the debtor's acquisition of the goods and the related software can obtain a PMSI in both, assuming the description in the security agreement covers the good and the software. Likewise a prior perfected creditor can obtain a perfected security interest in both the goods and software. Conflicts between the first-to-file and the subsequent PMSI holder are resolved under § R9-324(f). It provides the holder of a PMSI in software has priority in the collateral and identifiable proceeds to the extent provided for under the other relevant subsections of § R9-324. Thus, § R9-324(a) applies if the good containing the software is noninventory and § R9-324(b) would apply if the good containing the software was inventory to the debtor. If both creditors have a PMSI, § R9-324(g) (discussed below) applies. Again, the creditor must obtain a perfected PMSI in the both the good and the software.

PMSIs in Livestock and Prior Perfected Security Interests

Revised Article 9 changes the priority rule governing conflicts between a PMSI in livestock that are farm products[92] and prior perfected security

---

[91] In general, see the text accompanying *supra* fns 35-42 and specifically see text accompanying *supra* fns 54-56.

[92] § R9-102(a)(34) provides: "'Farm products' means goods, other than standing timber, with respect to which the debtor is engaged in a farming operation and which are:
(A) crops grown, growing, or to be grown, including:
(i) crops produced on trees, vines, and bushes; and
(ii) aquatic goods produced in aquacultural operations;
(B) livestock, born or unborn, including aquatic goods produced in aquacultural operations;
(C) supplies used or produced in a farming operation; or
(D) products of crops or livestock in their unmanufactured states."

interests. F9 treated livestock that were farm products as noninventory. Under R9-324(d) they are generally treated as inventory. R9-324(d) provides that a purchase money security interest in livestock that are farm products has priority over a conflicting security interest in the same livestock and in their identifiable proceeds (subject to the rights of a lender with a security interest in deposit accounts) and "identifiable products in their unmanufactured states." In order to qualify for the purchase money priority, there are several requirements which the secured party must meet: 1) the purchase money security interest must be perfected when the debtor receives possession of the livestock; 2) the purchase money secured party must send an authenticated notification to the holder of the conflicting security interest; 3) the holder of the conflicting security interest must receive the notification *within six months before* the debtor receives possession of the livestock; and 4) the notification must state that the purchase money secured party has or expects to acquire a purchase money security interest in the described livestock of the debtor.

The scope of this section is not absolutely clear. The collateral must be livestock that are farm products. The term "farm products" is defined. For a good to be a farm product, the debtor must be engaged in a farming operation and the good must be a crop, aquatic good produced in an aquacultural operation, livestock including aquacultural operations, supplies used in a farming operation or products of crops or livestock.[93] A farming operation is defined as "raising, cultivating, propagating, fattening, grazing, or any other farming, livestock, or aquacultural operation." Courts have struggled with determining what is a farming operation under F9, which defined farm products in the same way as R9 except there was no reference to aquaculture and the debtor had to have possession.[94] Some courts narrowly construed it as requiring a traditional farming operation while others have broadly defined it.[95]

---

§ R9-102(A)(35) states: "'Farming operation' means raising, cultivating, propagating, fattening, grazing, or any other farming, livestock, or aquacultural operation".

[93] *Ibid* cmt 4(a) to § R9-102 states that the terms crops and livestock are not defined. Revised section 9-102(34) defines farm products.

[94] See § F9-109(3).

[95] *Smith Enterprises* v *United Bank of Denver*, 28 UCC Rep 534, 2 B R 280 (Bankr D Colo 1980) (broad construction). For a bankruptcy case suggesting the *Smith Enterprises'* construction of farm products may be wrong, see *In re Blease*, 24 UCC Rep 450 (Bankr DNJ 1978). There the judge suggested that farming operations is a phrase to be narrowly construed and does not include farm related,

The term "livestock" is not defined. It clearly includes all types of cattle, such as, bulls, steers, heifers, cows, dairy cows, pigs, and sheep. But what about poultry, ostriches, domestic deer or exotic animals such as llamas?[96] The definition of farm products which refers to livestock including aquatic goods produced in aquacultural operations, suggests a broad definition of livestock was contemplated. The comments to F9 indicated that livestock included fowl.[97] Interestingly, most farmers would not use the term "livestock" to cover poultry. Comment 11 to § R9-324 discusses *aquatic* goods such as catfish raised on a catfish farm and includes some interesting language. It notes that, while catfish are farm products, within the definition of farm products, the "farm products" definition does not indicate whether they are crops or livestock. This

---

farm support or farm-like activities. Farm operations in the definition of farm products are to be defined in terms of a conventional farm operation. Another court holding "farming operations" is to be narrowly construed is *In re Collins*, 28 UCC Rep 1520, 3 B R 144 (Bankr DSC 1980). But see *In re Charolais Breeding Ranches, Ltd* 20 UCC Rep 193 (Bankr W D Wis 1976). Part-time farmers can operate a farming operation. See *In re Blease*, 24 UCC Rep Serv 450 (Bankr C DNJ 1978). See also the definition of a farmer in the Bankruptcy Code, which is based on percentage of income. See 11 USCA § 101(17) (1994) and for example, *Armstrong* v *Cornbelt Bank*, 55 B R 755 (D Ill 1985) (cash rent does not make lessor a farmer); *In re Dakota Lay'd* 57 B R 648 (Bankr D N D 1986). A number of courts have considered the farming operation issue. A tree and landscaping nursery is farming operation. *In re Houts*, 31 UCC Rep Serv. (ND NY 1981); *In re Frazier*, 16 BR 674 (Bankr N D Tenn. 1981). But note that in *Frazier* plants and shrubs in cultivation were farm products whereas mature and ready for sale stock was inventory. For cases dealing with breeding syndicators. See *In re Blankinship-Cooper, Inc*, 43 B R 231 (Bankr N D Tex 1984); *Northridge Farms, Inc* v *Trimble*, 37 UCC Rep Serv 1280 (Ky App 1983). Horse owners who race horses do not run a farming operation. *In re Bob Schwermer & Assoc*, Inc, 27 B R 304 (Bankr N D Ill 1983). For a general discussion of the term farm products, see Meyer, "The 9-307(1) Farm Products Puzzle: Its Parts and Its Future" (1984) 60 *NDL Rev* 401 at pp 412-15.

[96] Dictionary definitions of the term "livestock" vary. For example, the 1999 *Merriam-Webster's Collegiate Dictionary*, 10th Edition, defines livestock as "animals kept or raised for use or pleasure; *esp*: farm animals kept for use and profit". The 1984 *Webster's New World Dictionary* defines livestock as "domestic animals" and the number one definition of animals being "any living organism except a plant or bacterium" and with the second definition stating "any such organism other than a human being, esp. a mammal or, sometimes any four-footed creature".

[97] § F9-109 cmt 4.

question is to be resolved by the courts on a case-by-case basis. The negative inference is that courts will determine in all cases whether a farm product is a crop or livestock. In addition, comment 4(a) to § R9-102 specifically states that the terms "livestock" and "crops" are not defined.

The priority rule of § R9-324(d) expressly states that it applies only to livestock which are "farm products." Accordingly, it is implicit that livestock may yet be "inventory" under R9. This is the case if such livestock are held by a debtor other than a debtor engaged in farming operations.[98] While this is not as significant as it was under F9 in that inventory and livestock are treated generally the same, the devil is in the details. Revised section 9-324(b) and (d) differ as length of the effectiveness of the notice (5 years for inventory and six months for livestock). Proceeds are treated differently. The super-priority rule governing livestock extends to all "identifiable proceeds" which presumably would include amounts owed by a livestock processor to a debtor who has sold livestock but is paid after delivery of the livestock to the processor. The priority also extends to all identifiable products in their unmanufactured states. Conversely, the purchase money priority rule for inventory extends only to "identifiable cash proceeds . . . to the extent . . . received on or before the delivery of the inventory to a buyer....". And, a security agreement description or a financing statement description which

[98] While running a feedlot is a farming operation, cattle trading is not. *Security Nat'l Bank* v *Bellville Livestock Commission Co,* 619 F 2d 840 (10th Cir 1979); *Farmers State Bank* v *Webel,* 446 N.E.2d 525 (1983). See also *Swift & Co* v *Jamestown National Bank,* 426 F 2d 1099 (8th Cir 1970); *Burlington Nat'l Bank* v *Strauss,* 184 N W 2d 122 (Wisc Ct App 1971). Compare *Mountain Credit* v *Michiana Lumber & Supply,* 498 P 2d 967 (Colo Ct App 1972) (held logging operation not a farming operation); *In re Maike,* 77 B R 832 (Bankr D Kan 1987) (held puppy kennel was a farming operation). It should also be noted that once cattle cease to be classified as farm products and become part of the packer's inventory notwithstanding the fact that there was an oral agreement between the seller and the packer that the title would not pass and price would not be determined until carcass grade was determined. *First Nat'l Bank* v *Smoker*, 286 N E 2d 203 (Ind Ct App 1972). See also *In re Samuels*, 510 F 2d 139 (5th Cir 1975), rev'd, 526 F 2d 1238 (5th Cir 1976), *cert denied*, 429 U.S. 834 (5th Cir 1976). *In re Undertake* 1 UCC Rep Serv 2d 1723, 60 B R 705 (Iowa 1986). UCC § F9-109(3) defines farm products to include milk, and read together with Bankruptcy Code § 552(b) leads to the conclusion that a secured creditor has a continuing interest in the milk produced post-petition by laws which are security for creditor's loan.

described the collateral as all farm products would be fatally defective if the collateral is determined to be inventory.[99]

Purchase Money Security Interest in Crops

All types of crops such as grown, growing or to be grown are treated as personal property under the UCC.[100] Under § F9-312(2) it was possible for a creditor supplying the credit for the purchase of inputs including seed, fertilizer and chemicals to obtain a PMSI and a super-priority over a prior perfected secured creditor in limited circumstances. The crop production financier was required to have: 1) a perfected PMSI in the crops; 2) give new value in the form of a loan or credit sale to enable the debtor to produce the crops during the current production season; 3) the value must be given not more than 3 months before the crops become growing crops; and 4) the obligation owing to the prior perfected secured party must be overdue more than 6 months before the crops become growing crops.[101] This rule made it possible, in *limited* circumstances, for a farmer who is in default on a loan where lender has a perfected security interest in present and after-acquired crops, to obtain production financing for a new crop.

A number of groups such as farmers and the suppliers of inputs are unhappy with this rule. They in essence wanted a special purchase money rule for crop input financiers. The drafters decided not to add a special provision for creditors supplying production inputs because no consensus was reached regarding the appropriateness of a special priority for Production money financing. The drafters, convinced that § F9-312(2) was ineffective and difficult to understand and apply, eliminated it without replacing it. Consequently, under R9 the first-to-file rule applies to conflicts concerning crops even when a subsequent creditor could establish a PMSI in the crops.

---

[99] §§ R9-108 and 9-504. Also see *supra* fn 27.

[100] §§ R9-102(a)(44)(iv); 9-334(i); §§ F9-105(h), 9-203. *Moritz Implement Co* v *Matthews,* 265 Kan 179, 959 P 2d 886 (1998).

[101] A Kansas Bankruptcy court held that a production lender had priority over a prior perfected secured party to the extent of new value given to debtors for production costs and the 6 month requirement was satisfied because one of debtor's installment payments to the prior creditor was more than 6 months past due. *In re Cress,* 89 B R 163 (Bankr D Kan 1988). Also see *Salem Nat Bank* v *Smith,* 890 F 2d 22 (7th Cir 1989).

The drafters did create a so-called Model Provision for Production-Money Priority which is found in Appendix II to Revised Article 9.[102] While it was not included in the Uniform Act, there was sufficient interest in a scheme that provided special priority to production input suppliers that the drafter of R9 felt it appropriate to give states a suggested model provisions for states to consider. Kansas along with most states did not adopt Appendix II. It should be noted that Appendix II is much broader that F9-312(2) in that it does not require the debtor to be in default on a previous debt. The provisions are analogous to the PMSI rules for inventory and livestock under 9-324(b) and (d).

As to priorities, when a conflict between a prior perfected secured party that does not have a production-money security interest and a production-money security interest arises, the production-money security interest has priority in the production-money crops and in their identifiable proceeds if; 1) the production-money security interest is perfected by filing when production-money secured party first gives new value to enable the debtor to produce the crops and 2) the production-money secured party gives appropriate notice to all security interest holders, who have filed a financing statement, not less than 10 or more than 30 days before the production-money secured party first gives new value and the notice states that the production-money secured party has or expects to obtain a production-money security interest. The key is that notification gives the earlier party the opportunity to prevent subordination by extending credit. If two or more production-money secured parties, priority ranks according to time of filing, not the time of advance. If a prior perfected party supplies purchase money after a production-money secured party gives value, the prior secured party wins. If a person holds both an agricultural lien and a

---

[102] The following is a summary of the Production-Money priority provisions. A purchase-money obligation is an obligation incurred for new value given to enable the debtor to produce crops and the value is in fact used to produce the crops. Section 9-103A (c) provides that the production-money security interest definition encompasses the normal loan or credit sale concepts and does not lose its purchase money status even though: 1) Purchase money crops secure an obligation that is not a production-money obligation (living expenses?); 2) collateral other than crops secure the obligation; and 3) the production-money obligation has been renewed, refinanced or restructured. While the security interest does not lose its status because of one of the possibilities listed above, the production-money status is limited to the extent that it secured value that actually can be traced to direct production. Section 9-103A(d) places the burden of proof on the party claiming a production-money security interest.

production-money security interest in the same collateral, the agricultural lien priority rules apply. Thus, unless the statute creating the agricultural lien gives the lien holder priority over a perfected secured party, the lien holder loses to the first to file. However, the comments state that the holder of a production money security interest can waive its agricultural lien.

Conflicts between Two Perfected PMSI Holders

It is possible for this issue to arise in two situations where Debtor acquires a good subject to a PMSI. One transaction where this arises is when a seller and lender both have a PMSI. Consider this example:

Jan. 2 John Deere Dealer agrees to sell Farmer a $50,000 new tractor on terms calling for 20% down with the remaining $40,000 to be paid over four years. Bank files a proper financing statement in the proper place, issues a $10,000 cheque payable to Dealer and obtains a security interest in the tractor.

Jan. 4 Farmer signs the installment contract granting Dealer a security interest, Dealer files a proper financing statement in the proper place, and delivers the tractor to Farmer.

One year later, Farmer defaults on both the loan and the installment contract and the tractor is only worth only $40,000 and Bank is owed $10,000 and Dealer $40,000. Assume that both have a PMSI to the extent of the credit supplied.

Former Article 9 provided no clear answer to the issue of priority in respect of the above. While some argued that, upon sale of the collateral, the proceeds should be split on a *pro rata* basis, most courts[103] rejected this approach and used the first-to file on the theory that this was the default rule under § F9-312(5).[104] Revised Article 9 rejected both approaches and adopted a third found in § R9-324(g)(i) which provides that if one of the PMSIs is held by a seller, the seller PMSI gets priority over a lender PMSI. Thus, in the hypothetical above, Dealer gets 100 per cent of its unpaid debt satisfied and Bank gets nothing. Interestingly, the drafters in the Comment

---

[103] For example, *John Deere Co* v *Production Credit Ass'n*, 686 S W 2d 904 (Tenn Ct App 1984) (dispute between 2 PMSI's governed by the first-to-file or perfect rule).

[104] § F9-312(5) provided that unless otherwise provided conflicts between perfected secured creditors is controlled by the first-to-file or perfect rule.

13[105] rely on the Restatement (3d) of the Law of Property Mortgages to support this seller preferred rule notwithstanding the fact that Article 9 does not apply to pure real estate transactions.[106] The Comment states:

> The equities favor the vendor. Not only does the vendor part with specific real estate rather than money, but the vendor would never relinquish it at all except on the understanding that the vendor will be able to use it to satisfy the obligation to pay the price. This is the case even though the vendor may know that the mortgagor is going to finance the transaction in part by borrowing from a third party and giving a mortgage to secure that obligation. In the final analysis the law is more sympathetic to the vendor's hazard of losing real estate previously owned than to the third party lender's risk of being unable to collect from an interest in real estate that never previously belonged to it.

The other situation involving two PMSIs is where two lenders have a PMSI. Here the first-to-file applies.[107]

Conflicts between a PMSI in Fixtures and a Real Estate Encumbrancer or Owner of Real Estate

Except for construction mortgages,[108] a PMSI in fixtures has priority over a real estate encumbrancer or owner of real property if the debtor is in possession of the real estate or has an interest of record and the PMSI is perfected by a fixture filing[109] made before the goods become fixtures or within 20 days thereafter. Revised Article 9 defines a fixture to be "goods that have become so related to particular real property that an interest in them arises under real property law."[110] Thus, local law controls what is a

---

105 § R9-324 cmt 13. F9-312(4) applied to conflicts between two perfected secured parties - only one PMSI.

106 Article 9 does not apply to pure real estate transactions. See § R9-109(a)(1) and (d)(11). But see § R9-604.

107 § R9-324(g)(2).

108 § R9-334(h) and cmt 11.

109 § R9-102(a)(40) defines a fixture filing to mean:
"[T]he filing of a financing statement covering goods that are or are to become fixtures and satisfying Section 9-502(a) and (b). The term includes the filing of a financing statement covering goods of a transmitting utility which are or are to become fixtures".

110 § R9-102(a)(41).

fixture.[111] Common examples of fixtures include furnaces, built-in window air conditioners, built-in dishwashers, and curtain rods.

This conflict arises when a Debtor finances the purchase of a house by borrowing money from Bank and signs a properly recorded real estate mortgage granting Bank an interest in the house. A year after the purchase, the furnace fails and Debtor buys a furnace from seller pursuant to an installment sales contract. Debtor grants seller a PMSI in the furnace and a fixture filing is made before the furnace is installed. If Debtor defaults on both obligations, seller has priority to the furnace.[112] It must be noted that the requirement that a fixture filing be made before the good becomes a fixture or within 20 days must be satisfied. As to real property interests that arise subsequent to the goods becoming fixtures, the fixture financier will win so long as it has made a fixture filing any time before the subsequent real estate interest holder arises.

Another exception to the first-to-file rule is provided for a PMSI in readily removable replacements of domestic appliances that are consumer goods.[113] Under § R9-334(e)(2)(C) a perfected security interest in a fixture has priority over a conflicting interest in real property if before the goods become fixtures a security interest is perfected by any method permitted by R9 and the fixtures are replacements of readily removable domestic appliances that are consumer goods. This rule does not apply to original installations. The principal effect of this rule is that a secured creditor financing a consumer's purchase of a replacement appliance like a built-in dishwasher does not have to have to worry about prior recorded real estate interests. Moreover, assuming a PMSI in a consumer good, perfection is automatic upon attachment, that is, no financing statement needs to be filed.[114] Consider this illustration: Joe purchased a ten-year hold house. The house is a duplex, a two family dwelling. Joe lives in one part and leases out the other. The built-in dishwashers in both units have to be replaced. Joe purchased two dishwashers from ABC Appliances on credit and signed an installment sales contract. He also signs a proper security agreement granting ABC a security interest in both dishwashers. ABC does not make

---

[111] For cases dealing with the definition of fixtures see for example, *In re Park Corrugated Box Corp*, 249 F Supp 56 (D N J 1996); *Matter of Cliff's Ridge S King Corp* 123 B R 753 (Bankr W D Mich 1991); *Lewiston Bottled Gas Co* v *Key Bank Maine*, 601 A 2d 91 (Me 1992).

[112] § R9-334(d).

[113] Revised section 9-102(a)(23) defines consumer goods as "goods that are used or bought for use primarily for personal, family, or household purposes".

[114] See §§ R9-309(1), 9-310(b)(2), 9-334 cmt 8, and *see* § R9-203(b).

a fixture filing. The dishwashers were installed and became fixtures under local law. When Joe defaults, ABC discovers that the duplex is subject to a properly recorded real estate mortgage which was recorded before the dishwashers were installed.

To have priority over the real estate interest, ABC must establish that the dishwashers are fixtures that are readily removable replacements of domestic appliances that are consumer goods, and that before the dishwashers became fixtures, ABC's security interest was perfected by any method permitted by Article 9. The term "domestic appliances" is not defined. Comment 8 to § R9-334 clearly indicates that replacements of domestic appliances being used by a family are not to be considered permanent improvements. The dishwashers were clearly replacements and the one on the side Joe lived in would be considered a "consumer good" because it was being used for personal and family purposes.[115] ABC's security interest attached when Joe signed the security agreement and the purchase contract. ABC had a PMSI in this dishwasher because Joe's obligation was incurred to buy the furnace.[116] A PMSI in consumer goods is automatically perfected upon attachment.[117] Thus, ABC has a perfected security interest because the PMSI was in a consumer good[118] and has a super-priority. ABC does not have a super-priority as to the dishwasher installed in the rental unit because it is not a replacement of an appliance being used as a consumer good. This dishwasher is classified as equipment due to the fact that it is used in a rental unit, which is considered a business use.[119]

Priority Conflict between PMSI and a Buyer Not in the Ordinary Course (BNOC)

A buyer not in the ordinary course (BNOC) is basically a person who buys from someone who is not in the business of selling goods of that kind.[120]

---

[115] See *supra* fn 112.

[116] § R9-103 and see *supra* text accompanying fns 35-42.

[117] § R9-309(1) and see *supra* fn 20.

[118] See *supra* note 112.

[119] See § R9-102(a)(33) and cmt 4a. This comment indicates no intent to change Former Article 9's definition of equipment. § F9-109(2) defined equipment to be a good used or bought for use in business.

[120] UCC § 1-201(9) defines buyer in the ordinary course of business to mean a buyer who "buys goods in good faith, without knowledge that the sale violates the rights of another person in the goods, and in the ordinary course from a person,

Under F9, a BNOC defeated an unperfected secured creditor (no public filing) when the BNOC had given value, took delivery before the security interest was perfected and had no actual knowledge of the security interest.[121] Unless the BNOC was a transferee in bulk, the PMSI holder had to be perfected at the time of delivery, that is, there was no grace period for the PMSI holder to file. Revised Article 9 changes this rule. A PMSI perfected by filing "before or within 20 days after the debtor receives delivery of the collateral"[122] has priority over BNOC as well as a lessee[123] interest which arises between the time the security interest attaches and the time of filing.[124]

Priority Conflict between PMSI and a Lien Creditor

A lien creditor[125] is a creditor that has acquired a lien on specific property of the debtor by seizure, levy, or the like. This normally means an unsecured creditor obtains a judgment, a writ of execution and has a public official like a sheriff seize or take control of specific personal property of the debtor. A PMSI perfected by filing "before or within 20 days after the

---

other than a pawnbroker, in the business of selling goods of that kind". A person buys goods in the ordinary course if the sale to the other person conforms with the usual or customary practices in the kind of business in which the seller is engaged or with the seller's own usual or customary practices. A person that sells oil, gas, or other minerals at the wellhead or minehead is a person in the business of selling goods of that kind. A buyer in ordinary course may buy for cash, by exchange, of other property, or on secured or unsecured credit, and may acquire goods or documents of title under a pre-existing contract for sale. Only a buyer that takes possession of the goods or has a right to recover the goods from the seller under Article 2 may be a buyer in the ordinary course of business. A person that acquires goods in a transfer in bulk or as security for or in total or partial satisfaction of a money debt is not a buyer in ordinary course of business.

121 § F9-301(1)(c).

122 § R9-317(e).

123 *Ibid.* See also § R9-321.

124 § R9-317(e).

125 § R9-102(a)(52). "Lien creditor" means:

"(A) a creditor that has acquired a lien on the property involved by attachment, levy, or the like;

(B) an assignee for benefit of creditors from the time of assignment;

(C) a trustee in bankruptcy from the date of the filing of the petition; or

(D) a receiver in equity from the time of appointment".

debtor receives delivery of the collateral"[126] has priority over lien creditors' interests "which arise between the time the security interest attaches and the time of filing".[127]

Conclusion

While revised Article 9's treatment of PMSIs incorporates many of the key concepts from former Article 9, there are some important changes. A PMSI remains a special kind of security interest which is defined in R9-103. The basic definition in R9-103 is more complicated but it continues to recognise that a PMSI can be created in two basic ways. A seller, who sells on credit a good or software and retains a security interest to secure the buyer's payment, has a PMSI. Also, a lender who makes an advance or incurs an obligation "to enable the debtor to acquire rights in or the use of collateral"[128] and the money advanced is "in fact so used" has a PMSI. Unlike F9, R9 clearly limits a PMSI to goods and certain software and excludes intangibles.[129] A major reform is that R9 recognises that a security interest in nonconsumer collateral can be both a PMSI and a non-PMSI.[130] R9-103 also for the first time explicitly authorises cross-collateralisation of PMSIs in inventory.[131] And, a new section applying to nonconsumer transactions provides default payment rules if a PMSI depends on the application of a payment to a particular obligation and the parties could not agree upon a reasonable method.[132] Last, R9-103 expands the definition of a PMSI by making a consignor interest in nonconsumer goods consigned to a merchant a PMSI.[133] Whether a security interest in PMSI remains important in a number of areas. As under F9, most PMSIs in consumer goods are automatically perfected upon attachment.[134]

A number of special priority rules, some new and some old, apply to conflicts between a PMSI holder and other creditors or purchasers. For example, a PMSI perfected by filing "before or within 20 days after the

126 § R9-317(e).
127 *Ibid.*
128 UCC § 9-103.
129 R9-103(c), 9-102(a)(44 & 75).
130 R9-103(f).
131 R9-103(b)(2).
132 R9-103(e).
133 R9-103(d).
134 R9-309(1).

debtor receives delivery of the collateral"[135] has priority over certain buyers, lessees and lien creditors interests "which arise between the time the security interest attaches and the time of filing."[136] This changes prior law where there was no grace period for the secured party to file when the conflict involved a buyer not in the ordinary course or lessee. As to conflicts between two perfected creditors, like F9, R9 provides two ways for a creditor to break the monopoly of the first-in-time, first-in-right rule: a subordination agreement;[137] or establish a PMSI. R9-324 provides a number of exceptions to first-to-file or perfect whichever is earlier rule under R9-322. For example, a qualifying PMSI holder in equipment, inventory, livestock, software and fixtures may achieve priority over interests perfected earlier. The rules dealing with equipment, inventory and fixtures are essentially the same as F9. However, livestock that are farm products are now treated like inventory. If a secured creditor with a PMSI in livestock wants to obtain a super-priority, the secured creditor must perfect before the debtor obtains possession of the livestock and provide an appropriate authenticated notice to perfected secured creditors before the debtor obtains possession of the livestock. As to software, the PMSI holder has priority in the software and identifiable proceeds to the extent provided for under the other relevant subsections of section 9-324.[138] Section 9-324(a) applies if the good containing the software is noninventory and 9-324(b) applies if the good containing the software was inventory to the debtor. Another new PMSI priority rule governs priorities among competing PMSI holders. A PMSI for the price has priority over an enabling loan and multiple enabling loans rank in order of filing.[139] Finally, unlike F9, R9 has no special priority rule for crop production financiers.

As with much of revised Article 9, the section numbers dealing with PMSIs have been changed and the provisions dealing with PMSIs have become more complicated and represent an attempt to micro-manage credit transactions. Many of the changes are designed to resolve ambiguities and conflicts that existed under F9. Whether revised Article 9 will make secured transactions work more smoothly and without litigation remains to be seen.

---

135 R9-317(e).

136 *Ibid.*

137 R9-339.

138 R9-324(f).

139 R9-324(g).

PART II: CHOICE OF LAW RULES

8 International Insolvency, Security Interests and Creditor Protection

PAUL OMAR

Introduction

The purpose of this outline, featuring the relationship between insolvency, security and the protection of creditors' interests, is to first ask what constitutes the essence of the procedures, known collectively as insolvency, and to outline the role of the creditor in the process. This chapter then looks at the role of debt in the financing of enterprises and its primary use for the acquisition of assets as well as the means by which creditors seek to protect their interests by agreements with their debtor envisaging the use of security. It continues by analysing the nature of security and differences in legal cultures to the protection of the most fundamental of creditors' interests, the recovery of either physical assets the subject of the agreement or a sum representing the value of the debt.

This outline follows this by sketching some of the hurdles facing creditors seeking to protect their interests when the debtor-creditor relationship transcends national boundaries. Because this inevitably involves potential conflict between legal rules and courts asserting jurisdiction, this outline will illustrate specific aspects of the conflict, where choice of law rules have had to be adapted to the specificities of insolvency. This outline concludes by taking a look at the treaty framework that assists co-operation in international insolvencies and provides illustrations of conventions that govern security interests, whether specifically or as part of the creation of an overall case-management system. Lastly, a view will be taken of whether the development of a treaty framework permits the development of a culture of international co-operation from which creditors can benefit.

The Nature of Insolvency

Insolvency is an old subject at law though its reputation has not always been savoury. It has a long and antique history, the institutions of insolvency which were transmitted to the European commercial and legal worlds being derived from the medium of legal and business practice in the Northern Italian province of Lombardy. Insolvency has traditionally been a repressive regime, owing its institutions, laws and punishments to penal regimes. It was notable that the Roman Laws of the Twelve Tables provided that a debtor who failed to make good payments to his creditors could be cut into pieces (or "*in parti secanto*") or sold into slavery. It was comparatively rare that debtors were given any latitude in order to distinguish between those bankrupts who had committed frauds or wrongdoing from those who were insolvent due to misfortunes in trading. The first legislation in this area in England, the Statute of Bankrupts 1542, though providing for the collection and realisation of the debtor's estate, had an overall penal aim. In France, one of the first comprehensive ordinances on the subject was that promulgated in 1673 in the reign of Louis XIV. The codification of the rules relating to bankruptcy appeared in Title XI of this ordinance together with provisions detailing the amnesties to be offered to debtors by means of letters of pardon. This severity of approach continued to characterise the development of insolvency law until very recently, creating a stigma for the subject and making insolvency the subject of disdain by lawyers, lampoonery by authors and dread by the public. This infamy is still evident in press reporting of the vicissitudes of company affairs.

The impact of insolvency has often been felt at the international level over the centuries and incidentally illustrates the complexities of those trading and commercial links that have long been important for the lifeblood of nations. The rise of international commerce and the ease of setting up in more than one jurisdiction now mean that many companies have little difficulty in gearing their economic expansion to a global scale. Interaction between economic entities located in different countries, as a by-product of globalisation and the increasing dependence on new and powerful technologies that effectively "shrink" the world, has caused the delocalisation of business and the search for new markets to take companies throughout the world. Just as expansion has brought considerations of conflicts of law and choice of law in international contracts and litigation, so too the periodic downturns in the world economy have brought considerations of the rules in relation to insolvencies with an international dimension. Nevertheless, the nature of international insolvency is such as to raise a considerable number of issues, the attempted resolution of which may bring national systems into conflict.

The diversity of laws applicable to the transactions of a single company is nowhere more important than when their consequences are felt at the time of insolvency. During its lifetime, a company may have acquired assets in the country of its incorporation as well as elsewhere. The rules of law applicable to these assets will often be a matter for the law of the country in which they were acquired and may depend on the nature of the assets, whether real or personal property, moveable or immoveable, tangible or intangible. The disposal of the same assets may also be subjected to the same laws, as will the type of security that may be taken over these assets and the nature of execution available against these assets. Quasi-security arrangements will, of necessity, differ in their constitution and their impact depending on the principles of domestic law. Guarantees and support for security by means of registration or notice requirements will, without saying, differ from jurisdiction to jurisdiction. The nature of the protection afforded to creditors and the considerations they may need to take on board in any relationship with a potential debtor will rely on many of these factors.

Liabilities attendant on the use of these assets will also change with the jurisdiction in which the assets are located. For example, the company may have creditors pressing their claims in several jurisdictions. The laws applicable to these claims may raise issues of conflict of laws and the precise nature of the law applicable to the resolution of any dispute arising from the claim. These claims may be made more complex by the presence of qualifications, such as security, set-off and netting arrangements, and retention of title clauses. The identity of the creditors, including whether they are trade creditors, employees or shareholders may affect their treatment, with many national laws giving or refusing priority to certain categories of creditors. The priorities of these debts are also important. Certain creditors are given a statutory ranking, possessing a certain guarantee of payment from the assets of the insolvent company. Others may not have any guarantee, relying on the surplus after distribution is made to preferential creditors to meet their claims. By definition, the assets are never enough to meet all claims. Questions of how classes of creditors are to be treated fairly across all the jurisdictions where the insolvent company possesses assets are fundamental for efficient management of insolvency proceedings.

Indeed, of importance overall in the insolvency context will be the issues of efficiency and effectiveness of proceedings involving the company. Tied up with the questions of assets and liabilities will also be the matter of jurisdiction in respect of claims over the assets. This is especially important if it results in a restriction on the liquidator operating from another jurisdiction entering and claiming the assets in another jurisdiction when assets in any one country are set aside by order of court to meet the needs of the creditors in that jurisdiction before being made available to the rest of the company's creditors. The number of proceedings in existence involving the same insolvent company will have an impact on the assets left for distribution to creditors following the end of proceedings, not solely because of the absorption of fees by the management of the process in the courts but because of the lack of consensus between jurisdictions in dealing with fundamental issues of principle: including the identity and subjection of the debtor to proceedings, the qualification of the moment of insolvency, the availability of preservation measures over assets. It will be particularly important where the diversity of procedures available in different jurisdictions means that rescue procedures are not universally available, resulting in possible disadvantages and the loss of synergy across jurisdictions with regard to saving the company in financial difficulties.

Just as company law has evolved to take account of international business, insolvency law has had to cope with the effects the liquidation of a company may have at an international level. The phenomenon of cross-border insolvency has attracted academic, legislative and judicial attention. Courts have begun to evolve a spirit of co-operation with individuals called in to manage the insolvent company, which results from the realisation that the results of insolvency can have far-reaching consequences on the society whose interests the courts must take into account. Where the consequences of insolvency are felt in several jurisdictions, the attitude an individual court takes to assistance will influence the speed of the process of insolvency and may mean the difference between a swift solution to the problem or lengthy litigation, to the detriment of the company's and its creditors' interests. As will be discussed later, the benefits of negotiated treaty frameworks governing many of the issues previously dealt with by way of judicial discretion and principles of comity or assistance cannot be underestimated. This is particularly because it enhances the predictability of commercial arrangements and allows for creditors to plan their business relationships with their debtors.

The Role of Debt and the Agreement between Debtor and Creditor

Insolvency is fundamentally the inability to pay one's debts at the moment appointed for their settlement. Whether the test used is that of the "due debt" or the overall balance sheet picture of assets and liabilities, insolvency is a state that is defined at law, unfortunately often without regard for accounting conventions or methodologies, and brings with it a number of important consequences for the participants in the business. Nevertheless, the state of insolvency presupposes a debt, which itself presupposes an arrangement for the granting of credit. It may be a truism to say that debt is necessary for a company to initiate and expand business or that credit is indeed the lifeblood of commerce. Nevertheless, the business world does rely largely on the provision and availability of credit. For that reason, the management of credit and protection of creditors' interests are subjects dear to the hearts of all creditors. The giving of credit is normally the subject of express contractual arrangements between debtor and creditor that provide how the credit is to be repaid. Where the transaction foresees the acquisition of an asset for the needs of the business, the contract will often link in protection of the creditor's interest by making conditional, as alternatives exercisable on the occurrence of pre-determined events, either the repayment of the debt or the surrender of the asset representing the value of the debt.

Every year, an astonishing level of credit is supplied by financial lenders, usually banks, and by other institutions operating in the financial sector. Significantly as well, credit is often advanced through the provision of supplies, whether of goods or services, against future payment. These two forms of credit, usually called loan credit and sale credit, may be further complicated by the existence of mechanisms allowing for the presence of both forms of credit in the same contract or the linkage of a number of separate contracts into an overall framework governing transactions between the same debtor and one or more creditors. The sophistication of asset-financing techniques has led to specific financial instruments being created, nowhere more so than in the realm of high value assets, where syndication of the borrowing involving more than one lender is the norm. Whatever the nature of the instrument allowing for the formation of the obligation by the debtor *vis-à-vis* the creditor in return for the provision of credit, it is necessary to note that the success of the arrangement from the perspectives of both parties is primarily in the conclusion of the lending or supply arrangement with the satisfaction of the creditor in full.

The interest in insolvency is when the repayments are not made or goods and services are not paid for in full. In fact, the very nature of the lending arrangements might dictate such an outcome if the gearing or leverage, by which the ratio of borrowed funds to internally acquired funds is measured, is wholly unrealistic given the situation and needs of the debtor. This will not occur where business income from the use of supplies or credit is sufficient to service the credit agreement. It may, however, be a reality where business declines or becomes unprofitable and the costs of servicing the agreement exceed the available income of the business, thus inevitably pushing the business into a situation of financial instability. Although such situations are not wholly irremediable for the business, short-term solutions may be difficult to find without severely depleting the working capital or stripping the company of valuable assets in order to meet calls on cash flow. In the long term, severe asset reduction will affect the ability of the business to regenerate itself and reposition itself adequately to meet the challenge of new markets and new opportunities.

In situations such as these, commentators are united in stating that the prime purpose of an effective insolvency regime is to offer business the opportunity of reconsolidation if this is realistic. "Corporate rescue" as a concept is indeed a reflection of the ideal of saving the business on the brink of collapse. Nevertheless, considerations of efficiency would also dictate that businesses incapable of revival be dissolved as painlessly as possible. The view held in some quarters is that this is an expression of "Corporate Darwinism" by which only the fittest may continue successfully to adapt to changing niches and thus perpetuate their success. Whatever the truth of the above views, it is possible to suggest that insolvency offers an opportunity for the reassessment of business needs, one that is necessarily dependent on the participation of the creditors in the process, this being in part guaranteed by their desire to recover value from the credit arrangement. The attitude creditors take will, it goes without saying, depend on the amount of the indebtedness owed them, but may also rely on other intangible factors such as the business relationship, the importance of the debtor in a local economy and to the creditor who may wish to transact further business with the same debtor.

The assumption of risk is as much inherent in the debtor-creditor relationship as the notion of debt. The repartition of risk is, however, a delicate subject and likely to provoke many of the difficulties in the drafting of an agreement reflecting the interests of both parties to the transaction. With insolvency as a realistic prospect in mind, the interest comes in assessing how creditors meet the challenges posed by the risks of undertaking business, businesses fortunate enough to be financially well positioned, credit may be obtained often without terms other than the undertaking to repay. Prudence would dictate, however, that in a globalised economy subject to periodic downswings, no debtor is totally immune from the effects of insolvency, even where this is by virtue of the knock-on effect of third party insolvencies where these parties are themselves debtors of the borrowing company. This caution is often reflected in the standard terms of agreements and general conditions of lending applicable in the business sector to all businesses operating on the borrowing market. The ability of borrowers to negotiate individual terms may depend on the same intangible factors mentioned in the preceding paragraph, but is often severely circumscribed, even for companies demonstrating financial acumen and many of the indicia of reliability.

Beyond the immediate contractual arena, the mechanisms most frequently used to protect creditors' interests are varieties of security, by which is meant an interest in property or its equivalent, giving the creditor the choice to reclaim the indebtedness due represented in the form of a physical asset or a sum of money of corresponding value. It also enables greater certainty in connection with the enjoyment or enforcement of a right to be obtained. Security, of which more below, is as much a part of the bargain that is struck between debtor and creditor as the other terms of the agreement, many of which deal with conventional matters such as payment of interest, reflecting often an element of risk, redemption provisions or penalties as well as provisions governing the relationship of the agreement to other agreements (often called subordination). Nevertheless, the major clauses in any agreement will deal with the nature of the security, the assets reflecting the security, restrictions on modifying business activity or assets subject to the security as well as provisions governing the realisation of the security and creditors' remedies in the event of default exercisable directly over the affected assets.

Summary

To the extent that security is the linchpin around which borrowing arrangements revolve, it is necessary to understand that whether security attaches to the debt arrangement and what form this security takes may be a determining factor in creditors' attitudes to the insolvency process. Also of relevance to jurisdictions that allow private recovery measures such as receivership, the enforcement of contractually provided security will also dictate what insolvency measures may be available to the debtor. In any event, security is fundamental in that it will often also dictate the outcome for other creditors participating in the process because it allows for legitimate avoidance of the *pari passu* rule providing for equal treatment of all creditors. The general interest, it may be said, in insolvency for allowing for this rule to be bypassed is that creditors would not easily engage in lending arrangements without this guarantee that the indebtedness owed them could be recovered without having to compete with other creditors. This in turn affects the risk calculation in any lending transaction and allows for the perpetuation of a culture of lending at levels of interest accessible to most businesses.

The Concept of Security: The Common Law and Civil Law Traditions

Security usually attaches to assets. To the extent that there is a classification of assets into real or personal, security may be similarly categorised according to its use in connexion with specific types of assets. This is more usually the case in relation to real property, where the antiquity of security arrangements over this type of property often means that there is a more developed framework governing security in this context with, quite often, more formalities attendant on any transaction. As will be seen below, other forms of security may attach indifferently to groups of assets. Security in general may be divided into traditional security rights and modern types of security, created as a result of an acknowledgement that traditional rights may not be flexible enough to deal with the volume of business transacted by companies in this age and the impact of their trade levels on financing needs. Other considerations in relation to security that will be dealt with below include the attitude of lenders to debt resulting in constraints on the types of financing to which borrowers may have recourse.

The comparison in the section that follows will be largely between the laws of England and Wales, representing the common law position, and those of France, representing the civil law tradition. The protection of real property and other assets by the use of a security is of course intended to guarantee the debt owed to the creditor. There are two varieties of security in France which have traditionally been used by creditors to preserve their interests over particular assets belonging to their debtor and which are commonly found as a means of assisting business lending. These are the mortgage, commonly found in cases of specific protection of real property interests and the legal charge, which applies to all varieties of property. The equivalents in England and Wales are, on the one hand, the similarly titled mortgage and, on the other, the pledge and the contractual lien, which both have features akin to the legal charge in French law. In addition, the law in England and Wales also recognised the equitable charge, a form of security that, because of the differing legal histories of both jurisdictions, has no direct equivalent in French law. This separate development of equitable principles also affects the mortgage and lien, which have equitable equivalents. All of the above forms of security are termed true security to distinguish them from varieties of quasi-security and other rights aimed at boosting security interests but which do not amount to security in the classic sense. Later developments in France have also used traditional concepts for the development of what might be termed modern security methods.

Security Rights in the French Context

In France, as far as general security is concerned, it appears that the terminology and framework of security is still couched in the language of the early 19th century. It may be said with some justification that the values of security are still firmly linked to the ownership and enjoyment of real property interests. Although, in principle, the rights of a creditor *vis-à-vis* the debtor, where these are secured against property, are considered to be in the nature of personal rights, the nature of these rights can be equated to those existing in real property. Thus, although these rights are often dealt with as part of the section of the Civil Code that talks of special contracts, they may need to be registered and comply with the type of notice requirements more often found in the context of land so as to be fully effective against third parties. An example may be found in the case of leases, which because of their incidence on land come close to being interests in land, especially in the agricultural and business contexts.

The mortgage (or "*hypothèque*") is defined in Article 2114 of the Civil Code as being a physical right over real property which covers an obligation contracted by the debtor and may be created according to Articles 2116-7 by operation of law, by a decision of a court or by agreement between the parties. A mortgage may, nevertheless, only be taken out over property that can be subject to sale as part of a commercial transaction although Article 2118 does provide that a mortgage may extend to a right of enjoyment attaching to that property. Complex notice requirements govern the creation of mortgage rights which rank according to the date on which the mortgage was registered or, for registrations on the same date, according to the date of the contracts giving rise to the mortgage. The limitations of the mortgage are that it is to be found exclusively in the real property context and is limited to property already in existence, as mortgages may not by virtue of Article 2130 be created over future assets. Thus the availability of the mortgage as a financing tool is clearly seen as being restricted to those companies that already have a substantial asset base including real property elements.

In the French system, the legal charge (or "*nantissement*") exists in two varieties: the "*gage*" for moveables and "*antichrèse*" for immoveables and is a variation on the classical pledge. It is a security created by a deed in which the debtor provides, according to Article 2071, a specified asset to the creditor as security for his debt. It gives the creditor the right to be paid out of proceeds resulting from the use of the property, in preference to other creditors. The effectiveness of this type of charge is subject to it being created by deed, which must contain details of the property subject to the charge and, where the charge applies to incorporeal property, this deed must be the subject of express notification to the debtor. Although the effectiveness of a legal charge may be subject in certain instances to physical transfer of the property to the creditor or to a bailee, who holds it on behalf of the creditor, generally there is no need under Article 2076 for the debtor to be dispossessed of the asset over which security is enjoyed. It is thus an instrument that is found widely and is available also for creation of security over debts under Article 2081. Nevertheless, it is a cumbersome instrument, which must relate to a specified asset subject to the security and entails the creation of separate charges if types of property are considered distinct or come into existence at different times. This was very much the case in relation to the Eurotunnel project which is said to have required separate securities over rolling stock, bank accounts, intellectual property rights, receivables and equity in subsidiaries.

The difficulties with traditional security relate, in the case of the mortgage, to the limitation to real property already in existence and, in the case of the legal charge, to the need to specify the particular assets to which the charge relates. Given the absence of a generic charge that could relate to the totality of assets, it may be argued that French business has been considerably hampered in its ability to raise finance adequately. Nevertheless, an early law provided a partial solution to the problem by allowing the grant of a legal charge over the goodwill (or "*fonds de commerce*") of the business. The definition of goodwill outlined in Article 9 of the Law of 17 March 1909 was limited to the company name and trademark, furniture and machinery, client lists and any intellectual property rights, including copyrights, industrial designs and patents, associated with the business. A number of means have been used over the years to address this situation, notably by using the technique known in French as "debt-mobilisation" (or "*mobilisation de créances*"). This refers to the technique of using debts, to which the company is or becomes entitled, as a species of security against other loans granted usually by financial institutions. The use of a legal charge backed by a debt was one such method. Other techniques were also developed. Thus there were the examples of the use of bills of exchange guaranteeing payment at a fixed date as consideration for loans, the use of rediscounting by banks, the issue of bills by banks backed by debt and assignment of debt. In this last example, although the transfer of receivables to a third party was permitted, it was limited to instances where the debt was itself guaranteed by a mortgage or legal charge created over real property. In addition, there was a complicated procedure which involved using the services of a notary public and the execution of deeds. As a species of financing, with the costs frequently outweighing any advantage, it has rapidly lost popularity.

The needs of business were not really served until the early 1980s, when concerted lobbying by financial institutions and businesses alike inspired the Government to produce Law no. 81-1 of 2 January 1981, sponsored by Senator Dailly and which ever since has been referred to by his name. The law states as its purpose the facilitating of credit to business and contains in 16 relatively succinct articles a framework that has astonished commentators by the remarkable success it has experienced in the French business context. In brief, the law allows any financial institutions to have made in their favour and delivered a document of title (or "*bordereau*"), which will entitle the institution to any debt owed by a third party to the debtor. The document of title must include certain mandatory details permitting the identification of the parties and the debts to which the document relates. Failure to include these mandatory details is strictly sanctioned as the law renders any purported transfers void and ineffective. With the transfer, any security or guarantee attached to it is automatically transferred for the benefit of the financial institution. One point of note is that the law permits creditors to issue instruments on the back of receivables designed to allow the assignment of a part of eventual proceeds. This technique permits wider participation in the financing operation and spreads the risk attendant by regenerating cash flow for the credit institution. Assignments of title under this law are now very common and the use of the technique is widespread.

Security in the English and Welsh Context

In England and Wales, security in its essence developed from the use of real property as a means of representing to the creditor the availability of an asset to satisfy the loan. The extension of security to personal property, intangible property and collections of property are developments with which the common law is familiar, but which normally rely on the identification of the asset to be encumbered, often through incorporation by express reference in the contract. The institutions of the trust, floating charge and receivership, although deriving from original ideas associated with land law, have been reused in innovative and creative ways. In this context, the development of the floating charge, a species of charge capable of attaching to an indifferent collection of assets that may fluctuate in content during the currency of the charge, may be fairly described as allowing for the most flexible of all arrangements by which the debtor has full power to control and dispose of the assets subject to the charge provided the asset base does not diminish overall.

The position in England and Wales with regard to mortgages has some resonances with the French system, although the nature of the mortgage is wider in that it may be a conveyance of a legal or equitable interest in property generally, subject to a reconveyance of the property upon repayment of the loan. Sections 85-87 of the Law of Property Act 1925 apply special rules to the creation of legal mortgages of land and there are generally requirements of writing in relation to many forms of mortgages. Legal mortgages are broadly defined as mortgages where the formalities have been complied with in relation to the type of property in question. The equitable mortgage arises either because the interest is an equitable one in the property or because the formalities have not been complied with in full for the creation of a legal mortgage but it would be inequitable to deprive one of the parties concerned of the benefits of any arrangement. In substance, the mortgage is mostly found in the real property context and is similarly available to businesses with assets that are capable of being mortgaged as security for lending arrangements. The position in both jurisdictions may be fairly characterised, in relation to mortgages, as one that favours the borrower with a pre-existing asset base. The major difference in England and Wales is, however, that mortgages can extend to future assets and future indebtedness, thus greatly increasing its remit and making it a very widely used form of security.

The position in England and Wales with respect to other charges displays similarities to the French system. The pledge as a form of security is essentially the delivery of possession of the asset to the creditor without a transfer of ownership taking place, a situation the opposite to that of a mortgage. The requirement for delivery renders some assets, including land and those not subject to physical delivery, normally incapable of being pledged. The notion of physical delivery has, however, been mitigated by the categorisation of delivery as being constituted by actual or constructive delivery, allowing for the delivery of a representation that the assets are held to the benefit of the creditor by the debtor or a third party. The similarities to the types of legal charge in French law that require delivery up to the creditor are unmistakeable, perhaps a tribute to the common inheritance from Roman law principles. The lien, although it appears also at common law and in some statutory provisions, is primarily a contractual provision allowing for the right to retain property belonging to another until a debt has been satisfied. In its usual form, it is likened to a passive right of retention that continues only for so long as the creditor possesses the property. As a species of financing, the lien presents certain inconveniences, particularly because it is normally incapable of assignment. Insofar as the pledge and contractual lien may be comparable, a lien is in principle merely a power to detain property while the pledge carries with it an implied power of sale, allowing the creditor to deal with the property should the debtor default.

The position with regard to the equitable forms of security, which also include equitable liens, mortgages and charges cannot be compared to that prevailing in France. The equitable lien or mortgage represents the recognition of a right that would otherwise be held inadmissible because of some defect at common law that would render title otherwise incapable of enforcement. The equitable charge exists because it does not involve the transfer of possession, one of the hallmarks of the common law development of security interests, or of ownership. It merely represents the right of the creditor to have an asset belonging to the debtor dedicated to the settlement of the indebtedness, the discharge occurring when the debtor voluntary surrenders the asset or is forced to disgorge it by order of court. The right to appoint a receiver to recover the asset also serves to aid the discharge. The equitable charge is at the base the origin of the floating charge, this having developed by contrast to the fixed charge applying to nominated assets by extending to classes of assets constituting a fund. The interest of the floating as opposed to the fixed charge is in the nature of the creditor's participation, disposals under the fixed charge requiring consent, while those under a floating charge are normally at the disposal of the debtor until such time as the charge crystallises on the occurrence of a determining event. It may be argued that the development of the floating charge represents a considerable advance on earlier security methods that has avoided the need, as in France, for legislative intervention to adopt modern security techniques.

Summary

A number of conclusions may be drawn from the above outline. It may be said, firstly, that the French law of property is still firmly linked to the values associated with real property in a way that English and Welsh law has been able to move away from. If this view is the correct one, then it would follow that security and the protection of creditors' interests is similarly imbued with notions more properly associated with land and real rights and remains so despite the changing needs of business, thus creating a system that might be fairly described as static, and this despite later legislation introducing new security techniques. It is certainly true in all jurisdictions that new businesses, especially start-up and new technology enterprises, experience annual statistics of failure that are alarming. Some of these failures will be due to the ordinary risks inherent in conducting business in novel and untested conditions. Some, however, will undoubtedly occur because of the difficulties in securing adequate finance. Here, the underlying framework for security is of the utmost importance in facilitating methods for raising business finance. The best position for business is indeed where this framework contains a range of methods permitting finance to be tailored to the needs and situation of the business. In comparing both jurisdictions, the range of security seems to be wider in the English and Welsh context and allows for security to cater to a wide variety of assets. The flexible use of the mortgage and floating charge seem to especially assist this.

In this context, it may be argued that French law lacks the flexibility to adapt financing techniques because of the often very conventional setting for business in France. This situation is dictated for the most part by the orthodoxy of the security available and the attitudes of institutional lenders. The point must also be made that lenders in France may be subject to insolvency liabilities because of the development of principles governing the over- or under-supply of credit, leading to an orthodox approach in lending decisions because of greater risks attendant on the usual business of lending. Undoubtedly, there is a profound impact on business at large and the level of entrepreneurship and a consequent effect on the competitiveness of the French economy as a whole. Part of this impact may stem from macro-economic decisions as to the appropriate level of interest rates governing lending conditions, part lies at a more fundamental level where the interface between law and business operates. Without appropriate security methods, creditors and debtors cannot agree financing initiatives that lie outside the framework the laws of that jurisdiction provide, leading often to loans being negotiated across frontiers relying on more favourable techniques being available elsewhere. Nevertheless, this form of competition is ineffective if the assets available for security lie within the jurisdiction and remain subject to orthodox rules for recovery and debt-settlement.

It is for this reason that, independently of the recourse to financing and security that creditors and debtors may enjoy by being able to seek the most favourable conditions in other jurisdictions, the arguments around security still return firmly to considerations of domestic law. The examples afforded by the laws of these two jurisdictions of very contrasting antecedents and legal cultures illustrates in miniature the difficulties faced by creditors and debtors seeking the best arrangements for their financing initiatives. It may also be mentioned here for sake of completeness that both jurisdictions are familiar with quasi-security concepts, including the use of set-off and retention of title arrangements, and also have systems boosting security, for example the widespread use of personal and third-party guarantees covering indebtedness. Nevertheless, the systems for security acquisition in the two jurisdictions mentioned may be fairly taken as being at different parts of the spectrum in terms of facilitating business finance. Because domestic law is firmly at the heart of creating security, it should be firmly underlined that it also frequently determines the remedies to which creditors will be entitled in seeking to enforce their security. As the next section will demonstrate, the attitude of domestic courts to assisting creditors and claims from elsewhere will determine whether creditors have the best use of the security for which they may have contracted across national boundaries.

International Insolvency Considerations in Domestic Law

It is almost redundant to suggest that the transaction by an individual or business that crosses an international boundary will raise issues of conflicts of law and resolution of these conflicts by reference to the rules of private international law. It may also be superfluous to note that successful transactions often raise no such questions for resolution. It is only in cases of dispute that an attempt must be made to ascertain the proper law to apply and what the consequences are on the claim and the manner in which it may be raised, resolved or satisfied. As a species of private international law, international insolvency law exhibits many of the characteristics of this body of rules. Thus, international insolvency contains choice of law rules, jurisdiction rules as well as recognition and enforcement rules. Nevertheless, the competition in insolvency between jurisdictions, "unusually intense" as Professor Ian Fletcher argues,[1] has meant that the search for universal or common principles, through the rapprochement of domestic norms, has led to less success in international insolvency than in mainstream conflict of laws. This may be seen especially in relation to the doctrines of *renvoi* and *dépeçage*, which acknowledge possibilities for the use of the rules of other legal systems as the means to resolve disputes, either in conjunction with domestic rules or to their exclusion. It may be argued that this competition results from the economic nature of insolvency and its close relationship to state interests in proper management of the economy. Furthermore, this diversity in views may be said to make the task of harmonising legal rules more difficult because of the lack of a median rule or method for reconciling two obvious and contradictory extremes of position.

Apart from the general situation of conflict of laws, differences in domestic norms have a particular impact on the position of creditors and the priorities they assert in insolvency. Where the debtor faces creditors pressing their claims in more than one jurisdiction, this will inevitably raise issues of conflict of laws. The conflict may itself be made more complex by the presence of qualifications, including the presence of security, set-off and netting arrangements, retention of title clauses and other means of protecting title available to creditors in national laws. The treatment of creditors may also depend on their situation under domestic law and the adherence of the jurisdiction concerned to the principle of equality of treatment. Generally in insolvency systems, a variety of creditors exist. These include creditors given statutory ranking, possessing a certain guarantee of payment from the assets of the insolvent company, creditors without guarantee, relying on the surplus after distribution to preferential creditors to meet their claims. Many national laws also exist giving or refusing priority to certain categories of creditors. Furthermore, the

---

[1] Fletcher, *Insolvency in Private International Law* (1999) at p 10.

priorities of creditors' claims are also important because of the availability of enhanced protection in certain jurisdictions, for example, the institution of receivership in England and Wales, by means of which a creditor may enforce the security owed to him by the appointment of a manager over the debtor's assets. This may also happen where flexible methods of financing have been developed that are not dependent on the precise identification of assets, for example the floating charge.

As it is almost invariably the case that the insolvent will possess insufficient assets capable of satisfying all of the potential claims, the question of how classes of creditors are to be treated fairly across all the jurisdictions is fundamental for the efficient management of insolvency proceedings. Allied to this is how creditors are able to effectively participate in insolvency proceedings where these take place outwith their jurisdiction. Some of the difficulties faced by creditors in organising their participation have been catalogued by Professor Kurt Nadelmann.[2] These include rules discriminating in treatment between foreign and domestic creditors, the lack of prior notice to be able to comply with procedural requirements, the "race of diligence",[3] obliging creditors to pursue the execution of judgments and attachment of claims hurriedly to prevent competing interests from acquiring priority. Also counted as problems are forms of legal discrimination permissible when domestic proceedings are opened pending recognition of a foreign judgment, which often allows local creditors to obtain an advantage, as well as impediments within the recognition process conditional on special procedures being followed, for example the use of the "*exequatur*" procedure in France. Special problems exist for creditors who are unused to the types of remedy available in other jurisdictions and in cases where the debtor has more than one establishment leading to differences in treatment of the assets belonging to these establishments.[4] Finally, these problems are in addition to the ordinary problems attendant on international litigation such as the effect of time and distance, the costs attendant on making claims and the likely unfamiliarity with the foreign language and legal system.

The effects of decisions as to the assumption of jurisdiction to deal with all aspects of insolvency proceedings are generally classified according to whether the assets that are to be affected lie exclusively within the jurisdiction or include both these assets and all others located outside

---

[2] Nadelmann, "Legal Treatment of Foreign and Domestic Creditors" (1946) 10 *LCP* 696.

[3] *Ibid* at p 698.

[4] *Ibid* at pp 703-706.

the jurisdiction concerned. The presumption of control over these assets and the nature of the competence, whether exclusive or conjoint and arrogated by a court to itself, define to which school of thought that court belongs. Although these positions may seem, according to the definitions outlined below, mutually contradictory, the division between these viewpoints is not entirely clear-cut. Also subsumed into this debate is the question of unity or plurality of proceedings, also referred to as the problem of multiplicity of proceedings. Because this is the case, the question of whether courts adhere to the universality or territorialism principle has a bearing on the overall question of the conduct and efficiency of insolvency proceedings.

Territorialism

Territorialism may be defined as dealing with local assets for the general satisfaction of the claims of local creditors. Territorialism is still the norm in many jurisdictions, although very few territorial proceedings in modern times explicitly rule out participation by foreign creditors, in spite of this often being the case in earlier times. Nevertheless, participation by foreign creditors remains subject to the availability of knowledge and information, their ability to be diligent and to overcome procedural hurdles. In connection with the unity-plurality question, the adoption of the exclusive right to decide the fate of assets within the jurisdiction leads inevitably to the creation of more than one set of proceedings, especially where assets, establishments and obligations of the debtor are identified with more than one jurisdiction. This is not to say that a court applying the territorialism principle will not attempt to exercise some degree of control over these external assets, but the effect will be limited insofar as other courts purport to exercise exclusive jurisdiction over the same assets and will not allow conjoint control. The major advantage of territorialism will be from the local creditor's perspective where assets are held for the benefit of a smaller pool than might otherwise be the case. This would have an especial advantage for protected categories of creditors like employees, whose reliance on statutory guarantee schemes will lead to subrogation of these state bodies in their rights as against the employer in question. Nevertheless, localised benefit in this case is entirely dependent on the pool of assets available and creditors might find a disadvantage if the establishment or activity in their jurisdiction is minimal compared with elsewhere. The inability of creditors to predict what assets might be available would lead to uncertainty about the benefits of maintaining the territorialism rule.

The major disadvantages of territorialism are that reorganising the company or group of companies is difficult or impossible, as domestic proceedings are not normally geared to maximising the return other than for local creditors. Unless domestic rules specifically authorise this, insolvency officials are often unwilling to transfer domestic assets elsewhere in order to assist other operations involving the company. Quite often, there may be no specific statutory authority for co-operation and any transactions which could assist insolvency proceedings elsewhere may fall foul of domestic law. This factor would impede the likelihood of valuable domestic assets being sold as part of a parcel of assets or going concern where elements of the parcel or business derive from assets held in a number of countries. The net result of jurisdictions subscribing to the territorial rule is that liquidation, and not corporate rescue, becomes the norm when the principle is applied, despite the probability that the jurisdiction will possess quite a sophisticated rescue regime.

Territorialism also produces unequal results for creditors, despite the likelihood that domestic rules will subscribe to the *pari passu* principle of equal treatment of creditors. As noted above, although discrimination in practice at a procedural level against foreign creditors is rare, they may not be able to participate in their debtor's insolvency because of a lack of effective notice of proceedings and difficulties, especially with language and legal barriers, which may result in claims being processed late or out of time. The cost of collecting a debt across international boundaries and the uncertainty of litigation are also factors in denying creditors effective access to their debtor's insolvency. At a more substantive level, differing priority rules in each country will affect the overall distribution of dividends and surplus assets to creditors. Creditors may bear an unequal share of the risk element depending on what assets are available for the insolvency in any particular country. Local creditors will tend to benefit if there are assets in that jurisdiction and will be disadvantaged where assets have been dissipated or transferred out of the jurisdiction.

Shrewd debtors can utilise modern technology to transfer assets with rapid ease from one jurisdiction to another with view to benefiting preferred creditors or other persons. As insolvency practitioners are not always adept at tracing proceeds of insolvencies, creditors may have to pursue their own remedies but only very few creditors will be able to take advantage of multiple proceedings and prove debts in different countries, and then usually only because those creditors are themselves multinationals. This sophistication at the international level is not available to smaller domestic creditors. The results are that distributions are arbitrary and inconsistent and all of the factors of risk will end up being built into the cost of financing international transactions. Overall it might be contended that the net effect of maintaining a territorialism rule will be the consistent preference by creditors for financing arrangements reflecting this risk strategy and debtors seeking international financing will bear the burden of their jurisdiction's choice of legal rule.

Universality

Universality is used in two senses. First, in opposition to territorialism, it means the extension of jurisdiction to cover all of the assets of the debtor wherever situated. Second, in a narrower sense that has an impact on procedure, it refers to the co-ordination of what happens to the debtor's universal assets in a single procedure. Universality is almost always preferred to territorialism by commentators, both legal and academic, for reasons related both to the practical convenience of adopting the rule and the legal consequences of deference implicit in the recognition by other jurisdictions of the primacy of one set of courts. Thus following the acceptance of the forum as being competent, the universality principle allows for an effective choice of law to deal with all questions related to the debtor, thus resulting in a unified law for the purposes of the insolvency in question. Regardless of the aesthetic and convenient aspect of a single insolvency procedure, choice of a single law would avoid the problematic situation of conflict of laws.

The argument for universality is dealt with by Professor Jay Westbrook by reference to an economic analysis of competition outcomes. The argument here is that appointing the courts of one country as courts of universal jurisdiction produces two effects termed the Rough Wash and Net Gain. The first is an argument depending on the comparison of benefit from the local creditor's standpoint. A universality rule would even out any losses or gains for local creditors who would stand to obtain as much from the choice of the domestic court and acceptance of this fact by foreign courts (who would "defer" to the local court) in any one set of proceedings as where the converse occurs and the foreign court takes jurisdiction in another set of proceedings. The argument is called isolated by Professor Westbrook because it does not depend on whether there are benefits to commerce generally. Nevertheless, it is accepted that there would be a low incentive to maintain such a scheme without any positive benefits. Thus, the ideal outcome of the Rough Wash effect should be the creation of a net increase of value for creditors overall from the introduction of the system. The Net Gain argument takes the benefit argument further by stating that there would be a gain for commerce from lower transaction costs and the concomitant increase in trade because of the relative certainty that would be introduced by such a rule. Both arguments are however conditional on a high level of reciprocity built into the system. Professor Westbrook also points out an altruistic argument that he acknowledges is often touted as the leading argument for the adoption of the universality principle but contains serious weaknesses.[5]

Universality is not without its own criticisms. Chiefly, these revolve around the difficulties of organising the application of the rules of a single legal system to assets present in a number of jurisdictions. This is especially true in relation to "difficult" assets, notably real property encumbered with charges, intellectual property and intangible moral rights, other intangible assets such as shares, bonds and debentures, special property such as ships and aircraft and even ordinary assets where peculiarities attached to those assets make their negotiation and realisation difficult. The hurdles that universality faces also include the impact of sensitive areas of law, such as family law, which may impede seizure of a debtor's assets and the existence of mandatory or *ordre public* rules which may prevent effective recognition of the application and enforcement of laws in another legal system.

Practical Solutions

Advocates of a solution to the problem of international insolvencies look to reconciling the differences between the adoption of either a strict territorialism or universality principle.[6] In light of these arguments, many of the views on reconciliation comes through observation of the pragmatic attempts by courts and individuals to render the insolvency process more efficient and there are two essential types of practical solution that may be envisaged. The first, at the domestic level, requires recognition by the courts of the desirability of facilitating the administration of the debtor's assets through co-operative procedures. This method requires the evolution of principles of assistance and the eventual exercise of discretion in instances where the overall interests of the insolvency may demand an

---

5 Westbrook, "Global Insolvencies in a World of Nation States" *Current Issues in Insolvency Law* Clarke (ed) (1991) 26 at pp 32-33.

6 Fletcher, *op cit* fn 1 at pp 12-14.

abnegation of protection for the domestic creditor. Insofar as domestic law may allow latitude of manoeuvre, the domestic judge will be capable of achieving much by way of co-operation between courts called upon to administer the same insolvency. The second, examined in the next section, avoids the problems that may be caused by unhelpful domestic legislation by looking to the creation of supranational instruments, the negotiation of which will involve jurisdictions agreeing to common principles of co-operation and methods for resolving conflicts. This strategy has the advantage in most jurisdictions that adhere to the supremacy of written law by focusing the attention of judges called to enforce these rules to specific co-operation texts contained in the law. The pragmatic approach taken in the management of insolvencies has also led some scholars to attempt a classification of the methods of reconciliation by reference to the principles noted above. Professor Westbrook has noted that practice generally falls into two distinct forms: "secondary bankruptcies" or "modified universality".[7] Both of these practices modify the territorialism principle by allowing a single judicial forum access to other courts minded to co-operate in order to preserve and deal with assets belonging to the debtor for the benefit of the insolvency overall. Professor Fletcher also looks to the phenomenon of modified universality in discussing what he calls the "internationalist principle".[8]

In secondary or ancillary practice, a jurisdiction may distribute local assets to local creditors according to the priority system in force in that jurisdiction. The surplus from distribution would be remitted to the main or principal jurisdiction for distribution in accordance with its priority rules, which may differ in emphasis or content. This practice has received support from a variety of sources, not least in the creation of international initiatives seeking to settle methods of co-operation systems between subscribing states. Instances of this approach may be seen in conventions where the role of jurisdictions is firmly assigned by their being classified into main or ancillary jurisdictions. The effect of orders given in ancillary jurisdictions is thus limited to dealing with assets on an exclusively territorial basis. Commentators note the apparent contradiction in this strategy by pointing to the effect of such a system in effectively maintaining a 'grab-rule' for the benefit of local creditors while paying lip service to the notion of centralised administration of insolvency. This is because of the low probability that assets in any one jurisdiction will realise

---

7 Westbrook, "Choice of Avoidance Law in Global Insolvencies" (1991) 17 *BJIL* 499 at pp 516-517.

8 Fletcher, *op cit* fn 1 at pp 12-14.

a surplus adequate enough to meet the needs of unsecured creditors elsewhere as distribution according to priority rules of the main jurisdiction will still privilege secured and priority creditors only. In effect, unsecured creditors would only benefit by being present in the jurisdiction in question. As noted above, this position may be entirely arbitrary or fortuitous. While some instruments provide for creditors to account for dividends received in prior distributions where they also participate in other procedures, this is unlikely to affect all but the more mobile creditors, who will inevitably have the means of protecting their interests.

In the "modified universality" principle, jurisdictions accept the fact that a single court should manage the insolvency and offer such co-operation as they are able to give, bearing in mind the needs for reciprocity and procedural fairness in the treatment of creditors overall. The needs of local creditors may still form part of the considerations where it is intended that effect be given to orders by the single court in other jurisdictions, thus reserving some domestic control compatible with the overall co-operation framework. Professor Fletcher states that in effect this approach can complement the existing widespread adherence to the territorialism model by requiring co-ordination to the extent that the practical outcome is that the universality principle is attained *de facto*. By respect for the principle of collectivity and the existence of an entitlement to participation by all the creditors at some stage within the proceedings, all creditors will receive the fullest dividend possible. The "internationalist principle" he outlines is also predicated on the adoption of the modified universality principle as well as the realisation by jurisdictions of the need for a collaborative response to international insolvencies. This will take place through the evolution of rules of private international law in light of the reality of cross-border activities and the identification of common and flexible principles to regulate the management of such cases.[9]

Summary

The issues governing the organisation of insolvencies at international level raise complex and interesting questions, not just about the nature of the jurisdiction exercised by the courts but on how this has an impact on the position of participants in insolvency and their treatment. Traditional rules for approaching the problem of cross-border insolvency, which as noted above are divided into the territorialism and universality schools, are

---

[9] *Ibid* at p 14.

increasingly seen as inadequate to deal with what has become a significant phenomenon in the 1990s of the rise in international insolvencies. Nevertheless, which philosophical school of jurisdiction a court follows does not, in the opinion of commentators, matter when it comes to international insolvency organisation. If adhering to the universality principle, a court will still wish to ensure that its orders have effect beyond its borders. Even if other courts give this support voluntarily and always assuming reciprocity is not made a pre-condition, full and willing co-operation is only to be achieved through the existence of an appropriate international agreement. For countries adhering to the territorialism principle, the probability of a lack of reciprocity makes the conclusion of an international accord imperative. This view is given considerable credence by a host of commentators, writing on the phenomenon of international financial insolvencies. The failure of the Bank of Credit and Commerce International is held up as a particular example of the cogency of the need for international insolvency organisation.

Despite the questions asked by some commentators as to the necessity for international harmonisation of insolvency law, the consensus is that international organisation in the form of a treaty or other instrument remains the only method of ensuring "predictability, efficiency, equity and finality" in relation to cross-border instances. This is especially true where *ad hoc* solutions arrived at in the context of previous international proceedings are insufficient to ensure consistency of treatment in all instances in international insolvency cases. This may be seen in light of the very great differences between national laws relating to essential elements of the insolvency process. The questions of priorities, avoidance of preferences, avoidance of transactions generally, enforcement of revenue claims, equality between creditors and distributions and, crucial for creditors possessing security, asset recovery are only limited instances of areas where conflict between national laws is the norm. The focus on co-operation methods outlined above provides a partial solution to the differences that exist between the universal and territorial models but, as the next section will illustrate, are no substitute for proper organisation by means of international instruments designed to minimise or avoid conflicts of law.

The International Treaty Framework

International treaties in insolvency date from a very early period, some examples being found in the early Middle Ages, as witness the treaties between Verona and Trent in 1204 as well as that between Verona and Venice in 1304.[10] There exist also as examples of the early drive towards organisation of international proceedings a compact between two Dutch states in 1697 and a French ordinance of the early 18th century. Commentators have also added their voice to the debate. In 1825, Jabez Henry, a member of the English Bar and later judge, published a pamphlet titled "Outline of Plan of an International Bankruptcy Code for the Different Commercial States of Europe", in which he drew attention to the unequal treatment of and discrimination between creditors to justify the adoption of:

> ... something like a uniform system ... [to] place the subjects of each [state] on a footing of equality as to those rights which they are equally acknowledged to possess, whether as favoured nations by particular conventions or otherwise; and it would besides enable every man, when trading with a foreigner, to know his risk and remedy.[11]

Writing just before the turn of the 19th century, Josephus Jitta comments on the alternatives facing those seeking a solution to the evident violations caused by the application of contradictory rules emanating from different insolvency systems applied to the same set of facts.[12] He posits three solutions, the first being a world law, passed by a federal parliament assembled for that purpose, which he considers an unattainable objective. The second is the assimilation of bankruptcy rules through the elaboration of a common set of rules thereafter adopted by domestic legislators, which, although a more practical outcome, seems difficult to achieve. Lastly, he puts the case for a treaty, by which identical rules would be inserted in the laws of state parties.[13] As to the contents of any such treaty, he posits as the minimum rules on jurisdiction, publicity for proceedings, transactional avoidance and equality of creditors.

---

[10] Wood, *Principles of International Insolvency* (1995) at p 291.

[11] Graham, "Cross-Border Insolvency" (1989) *CLP* 217 at p 224 (citation).

[12] Jitta, International Bankruptcy Codification (1895) 7 *Jur Rev* 305.

[13] *Ibid* at pp 308-309.

One of the methods often used to attempt to achieve a consensus in insolvency law has been through the agreeing of conventions covering situations of conflict and providing for the allocation of jurisdiction and rules governing the resolution of differences in approaches for the management of insolvency proceedings. This approach has the advantage of avoiding a traditional obstacle, where national authorities agree to harmonise the conduct of insolvency proceedings across borders without, however, consenting to any substantial impact on domestic legal rules. Acceptance of this type of convention may in the long run create auspicious conditions for and lead towards gradual rapprochement of fundamental rules, but this is by no means a certainty, particularly between jurisdictions with very different legal ancestries and cultures. The experience of international conventions of this type is not uniform. Often, negotiated at bilateral or on a limited multilateral basis, the conventions have seemed to produce results by achieving cooperation between the courts of a few jurisdictions, often with shared legal cultures or close commercial relationships. In addition, some conventions have been negotiated on specific issues within the insolvency context or that have an insolvency-related dimension. A number of examples with relevance to the security context, including some at draft stage, will be outlined below.

Work leading to the adoption of instruments on a wider multilateral base has received mixed responses. In Europe, the convention in bankruptcy produced by the Hague Conference in 1925, which was never ratified by any signatory country, and the Benelux Convention on Private International Law, are examples of initiatives which have not met with any measure of success. This has also been the fate of the Council of Europe (or Istanbul) Convention 1990. Other examples of this type of convention elsewhere which have had limited effect include the Bustamante Code (Havana Convention) 1928 and the Nordic Convention 1933. Of more recent interest has been the successful conclusion of the European Insolvency Regulation 2000, which will be discussed below. A later evolution of the international form has been the utilisation of model laws. Chiefly found in the context of work by UNCITRAL, model laws are aimed at avoiding lengthy convention adoption and ratification procedures by leaving the enactment of provisions set out in model form to individual jurisdictions. These model laws are often accompanied by a guide to enactment covering the questions resolved by UNCITRAL working groups as to the interpretation of provisions with view to enactment. The advantage of model laws is also that they leave the format of adaptation to domestic legal systems a matter for domestic rules, thus respecting the individuality of legal traditions. Of relevance to this outline is the UNCITRAL Model Law on Cross-Border Insolvency 1997, the only initiative that may be said to have a truly global remit.

The UNCITRAL Model Law on Cross-Border Insolvency 1997

The United Nations Commission on International Trade Law (UNCITRAL) was established by the General Assembly in 1966 to act as the conduit by which the United Nations would play a more active role in reducing the disparities caused by domestic rules governing international trade. The general mandate of UNCITRAL is to harmonise and unify the law relating to international trade. UNCITRAL organised a Colloquium in Vienna in April 1994, co-sponsored by INSOL, at which suggestions were formulated for work in the insolvency arena by UNCITRAL. The first meeting of the UNCITRAL Working Group on insolvency in fact took place in Vienna in 1995 and four sessions were to go by before a definitive text was produced two years later. The format chosen for the text was that of a Model Law, which would allow countries to enact the measure rapidly as part of their domestic legislation and the final version was adopted by UNCITRAL in May 1997. This Model Law is a relatively brief document at only 32 articles. There are four key areas into which the document can be divided. These include the scope of the Model Law, rules for access by representatives of foreign insolvency proceedings, including the treatment of foreign creditors, and the effects of domestic recognition of foreign procedures. Finally, and most importantly, there are rules for co-operation and for co-ordination of simultaneous proceedings in several jurisdictions over the same debtor. These proceedings are divided into two types: "main" and "non-main" proceedings. The text is preceded by a preamble, a legislative form not often seen in common-law jurisdictions, and which is instructive as to the purpose of the Model Law. These are stated to be co-operation between courts, greater legal certainty for trade and investment, the protection of the interests of all creditors and the debtor, the protection and maximisation of assets in the insolvency and the ease in rescuing financially troubled businesses, thus protecting investment and preserving employment.

The Model Law enshrines the principle of creditor equality in four provisions: Articles 13, 14, 22 and 32. It provides in Article 13(1) that foreign creditors are to be treated in the same way as local creditors and gives them the same rights to commence and participate in domestic insolvency proceedings. This right is subject to one important qualification, in that the domestic jurisdiction can provide that local rules as to priorities and the ranking of claims will apply. Nevertheless, a safeguard against overt discrimination is provided in that the domestic jurisdiction must specify that foreign creditors will not be given a ranking lower than general non-preference claims unless local creditors in a similar position are similarly treated. This provision is included to avoid the claims of foreign creditors being ranked lowest, in contravention of the non-discrimination principle. The Model Law also irons out some of the disadvantages to which foreign creditors are subject by requiring notice to be given to them in any situation where domestic creditors are informed. Requirements under Article 14 provide that notice may be given individually or by any method the court deems appropriate and will include information on when proofs need be made, if these are required, and what form these are to take. With regard to secured creditors, this article also posits the rule that notification must also encompass whether secured claims must be filed, given that many jurisdictions do not have an express rule to this effect. Indeed, some jurisdictions may even discriminate against secured creditors by deeming filing to act as an explicit waiver of all or part of the security or other privileges attached to the credit while others deem a failure to file as being the equivalent of a waiver.

Although Article 19 allows for provisional relief, including stays of execution against the debtor's assets, and Article 21 sets out the varieties of relief that may be obtained, it is Article 22 that is integral to the procedures set out by the Model Law for the granting and modification of relief. This provision requires courts adjudicating on the issue of relief to be satisfied that the interests of creditors are protected, whether the relief is to be granted, terminated or its conditions altered in any way. Article 32 by way of conclusion inserts the "hotchpot" rule into the Model Law to provide for the equitable distribution of dividends to creditors. This is stated as being without prejudice to any secured claims or rights *in rem* enjoyed by creditors, the former category covering rights guaranteed by particular assets, the latter meaning those rights in relation to a particular property that may be also enforceable against third parties. In fact, to the extent that claims of secured creditors or creditors with rights *in rem* are paid in full, a matter entirely for the law of the enacting state, these claims are not affected by the "hotchpot rule". The rules governing co-ordination of simultaneous proceedings also have an impact on the situation of creditors. Article 20, which outlines the effect recognition of a main proceeding will have, states that recognition will stay execution against a debtor's assets and suspend any right to transfer, encumber or dispose of any assets.

Nevertheless, creditors still enjoy the right to bring proceedings necessary to preserve any right under a claim against the debtor. The availability of this moratorium provision is firmly stated in the Guide to Enactment accompanying the Model Law as being in order to prevent fraud and to protect the legitimate interests of the participants in the insolvency. Nevertheless, certain exceptions to the general stay rule may be provided by a state enacting the Model Law and may, as the examples in the Guide illustrate, include exceptions for secured claims, set-off and execution involving rights *in rem*.

The European Regulation on Insolvency Proceedings 2000

This regional project in the insolvency law field stems from the conclusion of a convention on 23 November 1995 by member states of the European Community (later Union) whose purpose was to construct a framework for handling cross-border insolvencies within the European Community. This draft seemed set to create a new framework for dealing with what had by then become a noticeable phenomenon of cross-border insolvencies. It ran, as the official story would relate, into a British Conservative Government that had withdrawn co-operation from European institutions in the wake of unresolved issues over the Bovine Spongiform Encephalitis crisis. One of the tactics used was to refuse to sign or adhere to instruments, of which this measure was one. As the signatures on the document were incomplete, the instrument failed to negotiate the final obstacle before entering into force. Despite this apparent setback, some member states of the European Community still desired the conclusion of an instrument in this area to govern the cross-border insolvency framework. After many years of speculation over the possibility of the convention project being revived, the project received a new lease of life through an initiative jointly proposed by Finland and Germany and submitted to the Council of the European Union on 26 May 1999. This has resulted in the production of the European Regulation on Insolvency Proceedings of 29 May 2000 (or "Regulation"). This Regulation incorporates, with some necessary textual amendments, the terms of the previous European Insolvency Convention. Nevertheless, because of the legal basis on which it has been adopted, Title IV of the EC Treaty provisions governing judicial co-operation in civil matters, the United Kingdom and Ireland were required to opt in to arrangements while Denmark remains outside the ambit of the Regulation.

The Regulation is intended to apply widely to a number of types of proceedings, irrespective of whether the debtor has incorporated status and whether the debt arises in the course of trade. Exceptions are contained, however, for a number of diverse bodies. These include insurance undertakings, credit institutions, investment undertakings holding funds or securities for third parties and collective investment undertakings. Legislation has, in fact, already appeared in the shape of two Directives of 19 March 2001 and 4 April 2001 covering the position of insurance undertakings and credit institutions respectively and there are further proposals mooted for the remaining bodies. The Regulation is intended to operate by allowing for the maintenance of simultaneous proceedings termed "main" and "secondary" proceedings. The definition in Article 3 of which proceedings are "main" or "secondary" is also of importance given that only "main" proceedings may include rescue-type proceedings, while "secondary" proceedings are limited to liquidation measures. As a basic rule, insolvency proceedings may be opened in the member state where the debtor has the centre of his main interests. Insolvency proceedings opened in this jurisdiction are deemed to have universal scope and encompass all the debtor's assets. In order to control the proliferation of proceedings, secondary jurisdiction to hear cases is qualified by limiting occasions when independent territorial proceedings may be opened to two specific instances: first, where proceedings are for the benefit of local creditors or creditors of a local establishment and, second, where main proceedings cannot be opened for any reason. This has the benefit of preventing territorial proceedings operating in order to further a localised grab-rule without some form of supervision or control. The Regulation also makes explicit the rule that the existence of main proceedings, once opened, results in all other territorial proceedings being converted to secondary proceedings.

Although the Regulation is intended generally to have a wide scope of application with many of the rules referring to co-ordination between proceedings, there is an acknowledgment in the text that widely differing laws apply across member states in relation to property. In practice, this makes it almost impossible to introduce insolvency proceedings with universal scope covering the totality of a debtor's assets in member states because of the difficulty in securing homogeneous treatment of assets. Drawing a line between the extreme positions of universality and territoriality, the Regulation recognises that strict application of the law of any member state where proceedings are opened to these assets would lead to insuperable problems and likely conflicts. The specific example cited in support of the framework the Regulation introduces is that of security interests. The distinction to be made with regard to select groups of creditors, principally those with preferential claims, also remains of fundamental importance. For that reason, in situations of particular conflict, these will be managed by special references to the relevant governing law. This will be the case of certain significant rights and legal relationships, rights *in rem* and contracts of employment being cited as examples. The Regulation acknowledges in its preamble the continuing competing principles and the attractiveness of territoriality by permitting the opening of domestic proceedings with coverage limited to locally situated assets alongside other principal proceedings with universal scope. The benefits heralded by the Regulation are chiefly to enable creditors to avoid over-centralisation of insolvency proceedings to their detriment by being able to rely on a locally created instrument evidencing rights. Despite the potential for fragmentation, the original draft Regulation stated that mandatory rules of co-ordination for all proceedings would avoid the tendency to over-centralisation of proceedings.

Creditors receive, besides the debtor and employees, explicit mention in the Regulation, confirming their central status to the success of any rescue arrangements. Information is felt to be the key to ensuring their active participation. The existence of the decision opening proceedings with regard to any debtor and its content must be notified in other member states. This is a mandatory requirement for the principal liquidator to fulfil. For business considerations, it may also, where there is an establishment in the member state concerned, be the subject of a ruling making notification compulsory. Prior notification is not, however, felt to be a pre-condition for recognition of foreign proceedings. This may not sit easily with the provision on protection of third parties also contained in the Regulation in situations where these parties are unaware of proceedings. This provision deems that persons acting in good faith effecting payment on account of any transaction with the debtor, where this payment should have been made to the liquidator, are taken to have been discharged from any further obligation in this respect. The difficulty for creditors here is that these payments, even if reintegrating the asset base, may by being subject to further claims fall outside those assets which are distributable.

In relation to how creditors may further assert their rights, all creditors, wherever domiciled in the Community, have the right to assert their individual claims in any of the insolvency proceedings that may be pending in relation to their debtor. This provision will also benefit tax authorities and social insurance institutions, which may extend their reach across national boundaries, and is an important departure from the practice in many jurisdictions with regard to the (non-) recognition of foreign penal and revenue laws. In practice, despite the notice requirements, only diligent creditors will be able to take advantage of these provisions and there well may be a cost-element prohibiting smaller creditors from participating in more than local proceedings. Nevertheless, in order to ensure equal treatment of creditors, there is an attempt to co-ordinate overall distribution of proceeds by requiring creditors to account for dividends received in other proceedings. Under this arrangement, the Regulation states that creditors may only participate in the distribution of total assets in other proceedings if creditors with the same standing have obtained the same proportion of their claims.

The Regulation does contain a number of exceptions to the general principle that the law of the "main" proceeding will govern the conduct of the insolvency. This is because the Regulation recognises that there will be cases in which strict adherence to this principle will interfere with the rules under which transactions are carried out in other member states and that parties' legitimate expectations and the overriding requirement for certainty of transactions in other member states will need to be met by providing for some exceptions from the general rule. The exceptions relate to particular rights, recognised as being useful in the insolvency context, to particular categories of transactions and to particular classes of participants in insolvency. Two forms of particular rights recognised as meriting exceptions from the general rule relate to rights *in rem* and the exercise of rights of set off, both considered as useful guarantees for the granting of credit. These rights are especially protected because they permit credit to be obtained in conditions not otherwise possible without the presence of a guarantee, even though the effect of this type of security is to insulate holders against the risks of insolvency affecting the debtor and interference by third parties with contractual arrangements governing the supply of credit.

In fact, the Regulation states in Article 5(1) that insolvency proceedings may not affect third party rights *in rem* in respect of any property situated in another member state at the time insolvency proceedings are initiated. Third party rights *in rem* are defined in Article 5(2) to include rights in relation to the disposal of assets under liens and mortgages, the right guaranteed by an assignment of security, the right to restitution from possessors or users in cases where use is contrary to the owner's wishes as well as rights *in rem* to the beneficial use of assets. As defined, these rights also include rights in relation to specified assets as well as collections of assets, as would be the case with the creation of a floating charge. Also included are any rights defined in Article 5(3) as being subject to registration on a public register for purposes of being enforceable against other parties. An exception is, however, provided, in cases where an action is brought on a point covered by Article 4(2)(m) relating to void, voidable and unenforceable rights. The proprietor of the right *in rem* can therefore continue to assert his right to separate settlement of his claim, which may rely on separation of the security on which the right depends from other assets. In order to more effectively deal with rights *in rem*, the liquidator may request the opening of secondary insolvency proceedings in the jurisdiction concerned if the debtor has an establishment there or deal with the security under preservation orders made in the context of principal insolvency proceedings. Proceeds from the sale of the security are first used to settle with the creditor, whose right *in rem* it is, before any surplus reverts to the asset fund.

As mentioned above, the situation of quasi-security is also covered with set-offs being expressly held in Article 6(1) as unaffected by the opening of insolvency proceedings where these set-offs would be recognised under the law applicable to the debtor's claim against the creditor. As a result, a creditor normally entitled to exercise this type of claim will be permitted to do so, even if it is not available under the law of the jurisdiction where proceedings are opened. The Regulation states that set off acquires as a result the status of a guarantee on which the creditor concerned can rely when the claim eventually arises. In cases of reservation of title, Article 7(1) provides that insolvency proceedings may not affect the rights of a seller where the assets are situated at the time proceedings are opened in another member state. Where it is the seller who is the subject of insolvency proceedings, Article 7(2) also states that this fact may not be used as grounds for the resolution of the contract and does not prevent the acquisition of title by the purchaser where the good are in another member state. Both set-offs and reservation of title clauses are also subject to the exception made for void, voidable and unenforceable acts.

The preservation of many domestic law rules is expressly stated in the Regulation as applying in cases of assets often found underlying security. For example, Article 8 provides that the law of the member state in which the property is situated expressly governs real property. The protection of specific interests, for examples those of contractual occupiers of property and general interests protected by the state where the property is found justifies this particular exception. Special rules are also provided in situations dealing with securities, which under Article 9 are determined by the law governing the financial market issuing the securities. The aim of this provision is to avoid any modification of the mechanisms for the regulation and settlement of transactions on organised financial markets so as to secure confidence in the integrity of payment or settlement systems. Furthermore, the law applying to rights over immovable property, a ship or aircraft that are subject to registration is under Article 11 that of the member state under whose authority the register is maintained. The same laws will also, according to Article 14, govern the disposal by the debtor of any property of these types. National rules are preserved in relation to issues governing acts detrimental to creditors, where these acts take place in another member state than where proceedings are opened. However, if the rules of that member state permit challenges to these acts, the main jurisdiction may also decide under Article 13 on the void nature, voidability or unenforceability of that act. The effect of insolvency proceedings on other litigation, however, is under Article 15 a matter exclusively for the member state where the lawsuit is pending.

Security-Specific Treaties and Proposals

Unidroit Convention on International Financial Leasing 1988. This convention, concluded in Ottawa on 28 May 1988, represents an early initiative dealing with the phenomenon of insolvency as ancillary to the main purpose of the text, to govern financial leasing transactions involving the conclusion of supply and leasing agreements for the supply of plant, capital goods or other equipment. The convention provides in Article 7 that the lessor's real rights in the equipment are to be valid as against a trustee in bankruptcy and other creditors, even where these creditors have already obtained attachment or execution over the assets of the debtor. The trustee, defined to include any liquidator, administrator or person appointed to administer the debtor's estate for the benefit of the general body of creditors, must therefore comply with any instruction by the lessor for the recovery of the property concerned. Nevertheless, where the exercise of any such rights by the lessor is conditional on certain formalities being complied with, for example the rules as to public notice, the trustee is not bound to take notice of any such rights that have not been notified according to any rules in force in the jurisdiction whose law is applicable. Nevertheless, where the provisions of any other treaty require as a matter of course that these real rights are to be recognised, these provisions will prevail. The law that may apply does differ according to the nature of the asset in question. In the case of a registered ship, the law is that of the state where registration has been effected in the name of an owner. As far as aircraft are concerned, the state of registration whose laws will apply is as defined in the Chicago Convention on Civil Aviation of 7 December 1944, while other mobile equipment, including for this purpose an aircraft engine, will have the law of the state where the lessee has its principal business apply. Cases not governed by any of the preceding definitions will in default have the law of the state where the equipment is situated apply. The rules in Article 7 are stated so as not to affect priority acquired by any creditor who has a consensual or non-consensual lien or security in equipment arising other than through attachment or execution as well as any rights of arrest, detention or disposal conferred as regards ships and aircraft by the rules of private international law. Two further provisions of the convention may be of application, the first contained in Article 4, stating that the convention rules do not cease to apply merely because the equipment has become a fixture to or incorporated in land, while leaving the matter of adjudication as to the fact of incorporation to the law of the land where the property is situated. The second is the general interpretation provision of Article 6(2), which requires that matters not settled within the convention or in accordance with the general principles addressed by the text are to be settled in conformity with the rules of private international law, thus opening the possibility for conflict between jurisdictions.

International Monetary Fund Report on Orderly and Effective Insolvency Procedures: Key Issues 1999. This report, produced by the legal department of the International Monetary Fund in May 1999, discusses major policy choices facing a country wishing to design or redesign an insolvency regime. It bases its conclusions on a comparative sampling from the laws of selected jurisdictions and identifies the advantages and disadvantages to possible solutions for issues deemed of universal importance. Of relevance to secured creditors, the report makes recommendations including some in relation to issues such as classes of creditors whose actions are to be stayed or prevented, quasi-security rights and the ranking of creditors for the purpose of distribution. In relation to security, the report states as a general principle that insolvency law should strike a balance between preventing secured creditors undermining the objective of maximising the value of the debtor's estate and protecting the interests of such creditors. It suggests that stays should be available not only in the case of unsecured creditors but also extend to secured creditors for a limited period of time so as to protect the asset base of the debtor for the benefit of creditors. Nevertheless, the interests of secured creditors would be protected by requiring that any automatic stay serve solely to allow the administrator a period for the identification and assessment of the debtor's estate. The administrator would only be permitted to seek an extension by demonstrating a cogent need. The protection of the value of a secured claim would also be effected by providing compensation for any depreciation in the value of the asset by providing collateral or period cash payments representing the value of the depreciation, interest, substitute equivalent collateral or by paying the full amount of the claim where the administrator seeks to sell encumbered assets. Alternatively, a valuation of the asset could be carried out at commencement of proceedings, including an assessment of the secured part of that value and a priority accorded for any subsequent distribution to creditors.

In relation to quasi-security, the report recognises the benefits of set-off to the banking system and acknowledges the reality of the lending environment where debtor-creditor agreements are likely to be concluded with financial institutions. The report concludes that a pre-commencement right to set-off should be protected during insolvency proceedings as well as any post-commencement right if the mutual claims arise from the same transaction, subject in any event to the usual rules governing avoidance provisions. Ranking and priorities are also dealt with in the report with recommendations for the establishment of rules providing for the maintenance of a system of priorities, deeming this important for facilitating the provision of credit, especially that credit which may be secured. The report states that priority rules should pay due regard to contractual terms allowing for security or subordination and provide that, when assets in the debtor's estate are encumbered. Proceeds should first be distributed to secured creditors to the extent of the value of their claim together with any compensation arising from the granting of a stay of attachment or execution to which the creditor was subject during proceedings. The report emphasises the need to ensure throughout the equality of treatment between domestic and foreign creditors. The report was considered by UNCITRAL in December 1999, together with recommendations put forward by other agencies such as the Asian Development Bank, the G22 Working Group on International Financial Crises and the World Bank, as possibly forming the base for a new working project in the insolvency field.

Unidroit Convention on International Interests in Mobile Equipment 2001

This proposal, authored by Unidroit over a period of some years, is expressed with a view to complimenting the Convention on Financial

Leasing, referred to above, and the Convention on Receivables Financing concluded on the same occasion. The proposal is considerably different in that it is proceeding in stages with the main convention having been enacted and various protocols dealing with specific examples of high-value mobile equipment being adopted at such times as negotiations on their content are finalised. The project overall is designed so that the main rules governing all categories of mobile equipment remain at a generalised level, with the protocols undertaking the task of containing rules specific to the types of equipment to be covered. The reason this method was chosen was to facilitate the early entry into force of one of the protocols, on which work in conjunction with the International Civil Aviation Authority had significantly advanced, dealing with the proposed new international regime for aircraft equipment. The participation of representatives of the aviation industry in the drafting of this protocol meant that the proposals met largely with the approval of the industry and in fact attracted considerable support for early enactment without waiting for the conclusion of the remaining protocols, which will deal with the specific rules governing space property and railway rolling stock, this latter being a collaboration between Unidroit and the Intergovernmental Organisation for International Carriage by Rail.

The convention states as its objective the facilitation of financing of the acquisition and use of high value or economically significant mobile equipment and the universal recognition and protection of interests in this equipment through the creation of an international registration system. The advantages of such a system will be to permit asset-based financing and leasing in the case of such equipment with lenders being assured of priorities in the case of insolvency of their debtor. Under Article 2(3), the main convention will apply for the moment to these specific categories of high-value mobile equipment, with the possibility being provided in Article 51 for the extension of the remit of the convention to other categories of high-value mobile equipment providing these possess the characteristic of unique identifiability. Both security and quasi-security are dealt with in the convention, the convention applying to all interests granted by a chargor under a security agreement, to any interest vested in a person deemed the conditional seller under an agreement containing a retention of title provision and any right enjoyed by a lessor under a leasing agreement. The provisions of Articles 18-26 sets out the registration system while Article 29 sets out the priority system once an interest has been registered over any subsequent registered interest or any unregistered interest, irrespective of whether the registration was obtained with actual knowledge of the existence of the other interest. Article 30 deals with the specific impact of insolvency by stating that an international interest is regarded as effective where prior to the commencement of insolvency proceedings the interest was in fact registered according to the provisions of the convention. The provision also states that it is not to derogate from a situation where the international interest has effect under the law applicable to the proceedings in question irrespective of its status under the convention. Furthermore, the fact that an international interest has been obtained does not affect insolvency law rules relating to the avoidance of transactions or transfers in fraud of creditors. It also does not act so as to prevent insolvency administrators from enforcing rights in property under their control or supervision. The same rules apply under Article 37 *mutatis mutandis* to instances where the assignor in an agreement providing for the transfer of an international interest becomes insolvent.

The equipment specific rules in the protocols are more complex with respect to the impact of insolvency. The aircraft equipment protocol, which was adopted at the same time as the convention, in fact contains alternative formulations in Article XI of the protocol setting out two very different schemes for insolvency administration. These are expressed in any event as not to apply unless a contracting state declares under Article XXX(3) of the protocol at the time of acceptance, approval, accession or ratification of the protocol which of the alternatives it will apply and which internal insolvency proceedings will be covered by the declaration.[14] The courts of the contracting state are subsequently obliged under Article XXX(4) of the protocol to take account of the declaration in administering insolvency proceedings. The first option, titled Alternative A, requires the insolvency administrator to give possession of the aircraft object to the creditor at the earlier of two dates, expressed as either the end of a waiting period specified in the declaration by the contracting state or the date when the creditor would have been entitled to possession were the provisions of the protocol not to apply. Until such time as the creditor indicates it is able to take possession, the insolvency administrator is required to preserve the aircraft object and maintain it so as to preserve its value under the agreement. This is without prejudice to the ability of the creditor to apply for other forms of interim relief. The creditor is assisted in this by the requirement for expeditious assistance by the relevant authorities following due notice being given by the creditor, subject to any applicable aviation safety rules. Furthermore, the insolvency administrator is also permitted to

[14] See below Stanford, "From Ottawa to Cape Town: Unidroit's Role in the Modernisation of the Law governing Leasing and the Taking of Security" Chapter 11.

use the aircraft object under any arrangement designed to preserve and maintain it or its value and may also retain the aircraft object where the debtor or the administrator is able to cure any defect that led to the default in the performance of the debtor's original obligations. No obligation of the debtor may be modified without the express consent of the creditor, although this is held not to affect any right the insolvency administrator may have to terminate the agreement. The priority scheme in insolvency proceedings is subject to any declaration made under Article 39(1) of the convention that allows a contracting state to promote a non-consensual right or interest before an interest registrable under the convention.

Alternative B in the aircraft equipment protocol differs in that the insolvency administrator or debtor may give notice at the request of the creditor that within a certain time the debtor or administrator will either cure all defaults and agree to perform all future obligations or give the creditor the opportunity to take possession of the aircraft object. Where the applicable law requires the creditor to take additional steps to obtain possession or provide a guarantee, the creditor is required to fulfil any such requirement and, further, to provide the court with evidence of its entitlement to claim and that an international interest has in fact been registered. Where the required notice has not been given to the creditor or the aircraft object has not been surrendered, the creditor is at liberty to apply to court for possession. This may be granted on such conditions as the court may order, which may also include the taking of any further procedural steps or the provision of a guarantee. In any event, the aircraft object may not be the subject of a sale without the consent of the court being obtained. The provision of the alternative formulations and the framework they introduce must also be read in light of Article XII of the protocol titled 'Insolvency Assistance.' This sets out as a requirement that the courts of a contracting state where the aircraft object is situated must co-operate, to the maximum extent permissible under the laws of that state, with any foreign court or insolvency administrator seeking to use the provisions of Article XI of the protocol. The protocol on space property, yet to be adopted, also contains alternative formulations similar to those in the aircraft equipment protocol, the relevant articles being Article XI (remedies on insolvency), Article XII (insolvency assistance), Article XXIV(4)-(5) (declaration and court application). Article XII of this protocol contains expanded jurisdictional bases, extending the requirement of co-operation to the courts of jurisdictions in which the property is situated, from which it is being launched into space, to which it is returning from space, from which it may be controlled, in which the debtor is located or which has a close connection with the space property.

The railway equipment protocol, yet to be adopted, is drafted using a similar clausal paradigm: Article IX (remedies on insolvency), Article X (insolvency assistance), Article XXV(1)-(2) (declaration and court application). By way of contrast, however, Article XXV(1) of the protocol allows for the exclusion of the protocol in the case of a purely domestic transaction covering rolling stock that is only capable of operation on a single railway system because the system displays the following characteristics: it has a different gauge system, it has differently designed elements or does not have a connection to any other railway system. Also in opposition to the framework set out in the two other protocols, an entirely different structure is provided for the management of insolvency proceedings. Under Article IX of the protocol, the application of the rules is subordinated to the occurrence of the earlier of two events: the first being the initiation of insolvency proceedings by the debtor or any other entitled party in a contracting state that is the primary insolvency jurisdiction of the debtor, the second being where the debtor has suspended or declared that it will suspend payments to creditors generally. A period of sixty days from this moment then commences during which the insolvency administrator may elect to cure any default and perform all future obligations or give possession of the rolling stock to the creditor, subject to any provisions expressly stated in the agreement and any related documentation as applying to the transfer. Until the creditor takes possession, the insolvency administrator is bound to preserve the railway rolling stock and its value, which arrangements may also include the continued use of the rolling stock. Retention of the rolling stock is also authorised where the debtor or administrator has cured any default in the performance of any obligations under the contract. Pending possession being taken by the creditor, the creditor may still exercise any other remedy available to it. No obligation of the debtor may be modified without the express consent of the creditor, although this is held not to affect any right the insolvency administrator may have to terminate the agreement. Similarly, the priority scheme in insolvency proceedings is subject to any declaration made under Article 39 of the convention that allows a contracting state to include a non-consensual right or interest among those interests registrable under the convention. Also the subject of an express mention in Article IX of the protocol is the fact that the protocol does not operate to modify the transactional avoidance provisions in Article 30 of the convention.

Summary

A clear conclusion that may be drawn from the outline above is that the international harmonisation of rules in the field of insolvency is certainly a desirable objective. The experience in many jurisdictions illustrates that, whether the rules develop from the civil or common law traditions, there is a common perception that insolvency is of prime interest to the creditors. Courts in all jurisdictions seek to preserve assets, define the interests at stake and regulate procedure. This has the effect frequently of also defining the relationship between domestic and foreign participants in insolvency. An element of discretion present in most jurisdictions allows courts to determine the extent to which assistance is given to other courts and insolvency participants from other jurisdictions as well as the articulation between the domestic procedure and any parallel foreign proceedings. Nevertheless, there is a measure of consensus internationally for equality of treatment for creditors and assistance is often given only in instances where there exists substantial reciprocity of treatment for creditors. Nevertheless, the difficulties placed in the path of creditors seeking to obtain remedies in jurisdictions unfamiliar to them cannot be underestimated. The common problems of any international litigation are well known: differences in language, laws and procedure and legal culture as well as the problems of time, distance and cost. To these must be added those peculiar to insolvency, not the least of which is that this is an area of law where courts have traditionally been slowest to develop principles of co-operation. Because creditors and the protection of their interests remain paramount in the process of developing international insolvency rules, the creation of an appropriate international framework remains a priority.

In this context, the adoption of the UNCITRAL Model Law represents for many the most important step taken in the emergence of a truly international framework for co-operation in insolvencies. The reputation of UNCITRAL as a promoter of harmonisation measures at the international level has done much to ensure that this text genuinely represents the concerns of national governments and domestic courts. It may be said with some conviction that the European Insolvency Regulation 2000 is an important part of the long history of international insolvency initiatives. As the most important of all the initiatives at regional level thus far, the Regulation may be seen as especially deserving of success, perhaps because of the very fate of its predecessors, the European Insolvency Convention 1995 and the related Council of Europe Convention 1990. It is likely that the lead given by the Regulation and its provisions will influence many future proposals in this field and may well lead to more acceptance for similar initiatives elsewhere. With regard to issue-specific conventions, there will always be a demand for clear and concise texts that regulate important facets of commercial life. The various conventions listed above have done much to promote acceptance of insolvency regulation as part and parcel of wholesale regulation in any subject area. In fact, the provisions on insolvency assistance may be said to reflect the current acceptance of co-operation as the norm in cases involving international elements. The impact of security arrangements and the need continually expressed by creditors and debtors operating in the financial lending arena for comprehensive yet user-friendly texts will undoubtedly create a climate for more proposals in this field, including some that may arise from work currently undertaken by UNCITRAL and other international bodies in connexion with the promotion of insolvency law reform at the global level.

9 Retention of Title Clauses and Non-Possessory Security Interests: A Secured Credit Regime within the European Union?

IWAN DAVIES

Introduction

A characteristic of sale of goods contracts is the mutuality of promises made between the seller and buyer whereby the former promises to deliver the goods and the buyer in return promises to pay the purchase price. The rationale of a retention of title clause is to secure the position of the seller where delivery of goods has taken place without payment having been made. Essentially, it is a contractual stipulation whereby the seller defers the transfer of property in the goods to the fulfilment of the primary obligations under the contract, notably, payment of the price.

The profusion of such clauses in Europe[1] is an indication of the law's inability in each jurisdiction to protect trade creditors. As Tepora has argued:

> The use of reservation of title (*reservatio dominii*) implies a reliance, through the incorporation of a proviso on the right of ownership, on the set of norms regulating rights of ownership, and on the corresponding legal conception of rights of ownership in cases where legislation has not provided any appropriate methods of satisfying the needs in question.[2]

---

[1] See below, pp 339-358.

[2] Tepora, "Reservation of Title as Security and in the Administration of Property" (1985) 29 *Scandanavian Studies in Law* 213.

An unsecured creditor will only recover after the shares of preferential and secured creditors are subtracted from the assets and, as Templeman LJ pointed out in *Borden* v *Scottish Timber Products Ltd*, a supplier in these circumstances receives a "raw deal".[3] The simplicity of retention of title clauses adds to their attraction in that often no formalities are necessary and validity can be guaranteed on the basis of contractual incorporation.[4] Moreover, several economic objectives are attained by the recognition of such clauses[5] which may be stated as follows: first, reduction in the "ripple effect" of chain bankruptcies because following a debtor's insolvency, the trade creditor, if he is not able to recover his goods, could be compromised financially perhaps leading to his own insolvency; second, trade creditors are given an incentive to continue supplying even a buyer in difficult economic circumstances which allows the latter to continue trading and possibly, thereby, preventing insolvency; third, such clauses give the buyer an incentive to pay early; lastly, if the trade creditor/seller repossesses the goods, he will have the advantage of turning them into profit by selling them elsewhere. These factors have contributed to making such clauses a phenomenon in Europe. In the UK, for example, one survey showed that 92 per cent of companies used some sort of retention of title clause.[6]

It could be argued that the legal phenomenon of retention of title facilitates the granting of credit which in turn promotes a market economy. As Drobnig has pointed out:

> Credit is the oil of an economy, especially a market economy. The more advanced a market economy becomes, the more it turns into a credit economy, as we all can observe ... Under present conditions, credit cannot as a rule, be granted without security.[7]

Security then is considered to be axiomatic to the development of a market economy. The more advanced the economy becomes the greater the demand for credit and in the wake of this, pressure is often exerted on legislators to extend the ambit of the law's recognition of non-possessory

---

[3] [1981] Ch 25 at p 42.

[4] See Bradgate, "Twenty-Five Years of *Romalpa*" *supra* Chapter 2.

[5] See Monti, Nejman, Reuter, "The Future of Reservation of Title Clauses in the European Community" (1997) 46 *ICLQ* 866.

[6] Wheeler, *Reservation of Title Clauses: Impact and Implications* (1991) at p 5. In one administrative receivership in the UK there were over 400 retention of title claims. See *Lipe Ltd* v *Leyland DAF Ltd* [1993] BCC 385.

[7] Drobnig, "Secured Credit in International Insolvency Proceedings" (1998) *Texas International Law Journal* 53 at p 54.

security interests.[8] Indeed as Goode has put it: "Without an adequate legal regime for personal property security rights, it is almost impossible for a national economy to develop".[9] However, within Europe, the most common and accepted model for the creation of security interests in movable property is the Roman law concept of *pignus,* that is, the possessory pledge.[10] The difficulty here is that where the transfer of physical possession is a necessary pre-requisite for a valid security interest this will prevent any economic use of the good by the debtor.[11]

All civilian codes continue to place an emphasis upon the pledge, although it has developed in different ways - it may be possessory or non-possessory, registered or unregistered. Essentially the pledge is a right *in rem* designed to guarantee the priority of the secured creditor on the insolvency of the debtor in respect of the asset charged. Historically, the dilemma for the pledge was its possessory nature: the collateral by being placed in the creditor's hands was unproductive and could not be used to repay the credit secured on it. It is significant that during the course of the twentieth century, civilian jurisdictions have sought to find ways of effectively using non-possessory security interests to achieve the same effect, notably through the development of the retention of title phenomenon. In contrast, the common law generally reflected a tolerance for the separation of possession and ownership. Indeed, this explains the distinction drawn by nineteenth century Victorian commercial lawyers between conditional sale and hire purchase[12] - the "owner" as distinct from the conditional seller's rights in the goods generally were held to be valid as against creditors of and purchasers from the debtor/hirer in possession.[13]

---

[8] The "credit prone" countries have been listed in the following order: US, Anglophonic Canadian Provinces, Germany, UK, France. See Drobnig, *ibid* at p 55. Compare Wood, *Comparative Law of Security and Guarantees* (1995) at pp 5-6.

[9] Goode, "Security in Cross-Border Transactions" (1998) 33 *Texas International Law Journal* 47.

[10] See s 451 ABGB (Austria); Art 2071-2076 Belgian Civil Code; s 236 Nr 1205 BGB (Germany); Art 669 Portuguese Civil Code; Art 1856 Spanish Civil Code.

[11] See Cuming, "The Internationalisation of Secured Financing Law" in *Making Commercial Law- Essays in Honour of Roy Goode* ed Cranston (1997) Chapter 22 at p 502.

[12] *Lee* v *Butler* [1983] 2 QB 318; *Helby* v *Matthews* [1895] AC 471.

[13] Factors Act (1889) s 9 (1); Sale of Goods Act (1979) s 25 (1). The hire purchase phenomenon can be criticised in that despite the fact that it is a method of

Such an approach makes it difficult to reconcile the frequently held notion that the common law abhorred "secret liens" and sought to protect third parties from the risk of misleading appearances.[14] Thus the nineteenth century bills of sale legislation did not essentially address the problem of ostensible ownership concerns arising from debtors retaining possession of goods charged, rather, the legislation was concerned to prevent over-exploitation by creditors of debtors.[15]

The main difficulty with the ostensible ownership doctrine is that it assumes that factual possession carries with it a suggestion of ownership. As assets become more and more encumbered and as the credit economy grows such an approach becomes less and less sustainable. Indeed, the prevalence of equipment leasing in the industrial sector demonstrates that possession by a user indicates a reasonable possibility that the equipment is leased and not owned. In the light of this are creditors and trade purchasers actually misled by factual possession? It can be persuasively argued that modern credit practices have outgrown the ostensible ownership doctrine.[16] As such, the real policy question posed by retention of title clauses as a form of non-possessory security device is the extent to which they adequately solve the practical problems which emerge in the sale of goods

---

financing the acquisition of goods it is still conceptualised as a bailment. This has necessitated the development of consumer protection regimes for the hirer. As Sykes and Walker have pointed out in *The Law of Securities* 5th ed (1993) at pp 541-542: "[A] major disadvantage of hire purchase is that it establishes an artificial transaction: when a third party financier is introduced, what is really a contract of loan upon security becomes in formal context first a sale, then a hiring contract with an option to bring into being a further sale. An 'equity' on the part of the purchaser has therefore had to be laboriously constructed. Perhaps the most basic defect is that there is no coherent body of common law and equity on which the house can be built". See also Giddins, "Rights of Ownership in Goods" *supra* Chapter 3.

[14] *Twyne's Case* 76 ER 809 (Star Chamber 1601). In this case the transfer of the goods without possession was made "pending the writ". However, as a matter of fact the creditor was in no way misled by the transfer and continued possession of the debtor. It should be noted that *Twyne's Case* was a criminal action involving imputed fraud and not ostensible ownership, as such.

[15] The Bills of Sale Act (1878) Amendment Act 1882 was aimed at the unscrupulous practice of moneylenders in enforcing their security. The 1882 Act laid down a prescribed form to which all security bills of sale had to confirm and outlawed powers of repossession by the grantee except for specified causes.

[16] See Dolan, "The UCC's Consignment Rules Needs and Exception for Consumers" (1983) 44 *Ohio State LJ* 21 at p 30.

process including the conflicting rights of the creditors of the buyer and seller in addition to those of the good faith purchaser. Significantly, under the European Directive on combating late payments in commercial transactions[17] between enterprises in the private sector and between such enterprises and the public sector, Member States are required to take the appropriate steps to ensure that all national legislation contain provisions according to which the seller can retain title to the goods sold until the buyer has made payment and, further, that the buyer should be able to recover them if payment is not made.[18]

In this chapter we shall examine the extent of the recognition and enforceability of such clauses within the main jurisdictions of Europe. Following this we shall consider whether a uniform approach to retention of title clauses is feasible so as to effectively facilitate the use and enforcement of these clauses within the European Union.

Retention of Title Clauses and the European Union: A Jurisdictional Approach

Austria [19]

Retention of title is not specifically regulated under the Austria Civil Code nor the Commercial Code. It is categorised as an expression of agreement between the parties so a unilateral retention of title clause is legally ineffective.[20] In some cases under Austrian law formalities are required for there to be an enforceable retention of title clause, for example, clauses incorporated into consumer contracts have to be in writing.[21] In the case of plant and equipment sales, if the reservation of title clause has not been recorded in the land registry the plant or equipment will be considered as

[17] Directive 2000/35/EC of the European Parliament and of the Council of 29 June 2000 on combating late payments in commercial transactions, OJ L200/35 (8.8.2000).

[18] *Ibid* art 4(1).

[19] See, generally, Davies (ed), *Retention of Title Clauses in Sale of Goods Contracts in Europe* (1999), Chapter 1.

[20] OBA, 1987, 51 and RdW 1987, 157.

[21] Article 21 (1) Austrian Consumer Protection Act.

part and parcel of the land and the owner of the land recorded in the land registry will be deemed to have good title in the plant and equipment.[22]

Belgium [23]

Under Belgian Law it is necessary for a reservation of title clause to be specifically inserted in the contract of sale.[24] In the context of bankruptcy, a retention of title clause must be evidenced in writing at the latest by the time the goods are delivered if this is to be enforced against the buyer and his creditors. Traditionally the issue of priority in bankruptcy is strictly controlled and is restricted to liens and mortgages including security interests in specific assets of the debtor.[25]

An important change to Belgian law was occasioned by the Bankruptcy Act 1997. Article 101 of that Act explicitly recognises the validly of the retention of title clause in the bankruptcy of the buyer[26] so long as the following conditions are satisfied: first, the clause must be evidenced in writing at the latest by the time of delivery of the goods; second, the goods must be in the possession of the buyer in their original state and have not become fixtures; third, the repossession claim must be made before the court has determined the claims filed in respect of the bankrupt's estate (*procès-verbal de vérification des créances*). It should be noted that the trustee in bankruptcy with the approval of the court might refuse the enforcement of a retention of title clause under Article 101

---

[22] Article 297a Austrian Civil Code.

[23] See, generally, Davies (ed) *op cit* fn 19, Chapter 2.

[24] The normal rule under Art. 1593 of the Belgian Code is that the contract is considered to be perfected as soon as the parties have reached an agreement as to price and subject matter.

[25] Special provision is made under Belgian law in respect of non-consumer finance leasing contracts by virtue of the Royal decree No 55, November 10, 1967 and further implemented by Ministerial Decrees of February 23, 1968 and December 24, 1976. Provided the operation qualifies as being "finance leasing" (which requires the rent to be calculated on the basis of the presumed duration of the economic life of the asset and the contract *includes* a purchase option) the owner/lessor can repossess the equipment even where the debtor/lessee is subject to bankruptcy proceedings or subject to a judicial settlement. However, it should be noted that specific approval from the Ministry of Economic Affairs is necessary to conduct finance leasing operations.

[26] Under the old law, Article 546 Bankruptcy Act 1851, the unpaid seller lost the benefit of a retention of title clause on the bankruptcy of the buyer.

provided it is in the interest of the other creditors and the agreed price including interest is paid by the trustee to the seller.

Denmark [27]

Under the Danish Sale of Goods Act, delivery of the goods to the buyer is deemed to complete the sale. However, the parties may by agreement alter this rule through a retention of title mechanism which is regulated by the Credit Agreements Act. In order for such a clause to be valid s34 provides: first that it must have been *agreed* at the latest upon delivery of the goods; second, the total amount payable must exceed a minimum amount; third, the purchase on credit must not have taken place according to a credit agreement with a variable loan amount. Furthermore, a buyer of goods subject to a retention of title clause is not normally allowed to resell the goods which constitute the subject matter of the clause. Where the buyer has wrongfully resold the goods, in principle, Danish law allows the original seller to repossess the goods from a later buyer. The Danish principle of *forhandlergrundsaetningen* is relevant, namely, a seller may not repossess the goods from a later good faith purchaser if the seller had handed over the object to a party whom he knew or ought to have known would resell it. Neither will the original seller prevail if he had been incautious or passive and in the English context an analogy can be drawn with voidable title concept. Thus, in one case a shopkeeper handed over silver cutlery without checking the customer's identity. The customer paid with a worthless cheque. It was held by the Court that the seller was incautious in the sale and could not thereby rely upon a retention of title clause against an innocent third party purchaser (an antique dealer) who had bought the cutlery from the rogue.[28]

Normally there is no registration requirement in respect of chattels under Danish law. However, as an exception to this rule, retention of title clauses covering motor vehicles, trailers as well as caravans have to be registered in the Registry of Cars *(bibogen)* if such a clause is to be effective against the buyer's creditors and purchasers. Even so, there is no requirement to register retention of title clauses in respect of vehicles subject to a consignment plan because the registration requirement is restricted to the point of sale from the dealer.

---

[27] See Davies (ed) *op cit* fn 19, Chapter 3.

[28] See U 1959 s 76 Ø.

France [29]

The French and German Civil Codes evince a different emphasis with regard to the question of the extent to which possession goes towards the *right* to possession and ownership. The approach under Article 2279 of the French Civil Code is that *possession vaut titre.* It is generally supposed that the French Code, following Savigny's possessory theory[30] emphasises the dual elements of *animus* and *corpus* whereas the German BGB (Civil Code) is more concerned with *corpus* following Jhering.[31] Thus the French Civil Code insists on an *animo domini* (*à titre de propriétaire*) together with factual possession which is defined as detention or enjoyment of a thing as distinct from a detention permitted by another.[32] Possession in French law goes towards acquisitive prescription, that is, it is *usucaptive.* This intention element is important so as to distinguish "normal" contracts such as deposit, hire or leave (*détenteur précaire*). In contract German law treats even the détenteur *précaire* as a possessor.[33]

To reserve title in goods is a derogation from the provision of Article 1583 of the Code Civile and, as such, it must be agreed between the vendor and purchaser. The principle of property transfer in France is by virtue of Article 1583, *solo consensu.* This rule provides that the sale is complete between the parties and properly transferred to the purchaser from the vendor once agreement has been reached on the subject matter of the contract even though the latter has not been delivered nor the price paid. However the rule is of "suppletive effect" and is not obligatory so the parties may derogate from the rule through, for example, the retention of title mechanism. However, Article 121 al 2 of *the Law of 25 janvier 1985* provides that it is for the person who wishes to avail himself of the clause to prove the existence of an agreement. As a consequence, in France, for a retention of title clause to be enforceable in an insolvency procedure it must be in writing although this does not mean that a special agreement has been signed by the parties. Thus, the *Law of 10 juin 1994* provides that the clause may be contained in a document dealing with a series of commercial

---

[29] See, generally, Davies (ed) *op cit* fn 19, Chapter 5.

[30] Savigny based his analysis on the dual Roman legal concepts of *possessio* and *detentio.* For a critique on this approach see Buckland W, *A Textbook of Roman Law* ed Stein at p 197.

[31] *Besitzville* cited by Buckland *ibid* at p 198.

[32] Article 1118 Code Civile.

[33] Section 854 BGB.

operations, that is, a standard form contract which governs the entirety of contractual arrangements between the parties.

In France, the enforceability of retention of title in insolvency was recognised in the *Law of 12 mai 1980*. This law confirmed that a reservation of title clause is enforceable where the purchaser of goods is subject to an insolvency procedure. The law was incorporated into Article 65 of the *Law of 13 juillet 1967*, which sets out in Article 121 the principles for reservation of title clauses. These dispositions were modified by a *Law of 10 juin 1994*, which was passed to extend and reinforce the effectiveness of reservation of title clauses so as to cover cases where the goods sold have become incorporated into other goods. Even so, there must still be a written memorandum "before" delivery so as to avoid fraud.

Germany [34]

In stark contrast to other civilian legal systems a reservation of title clause is not subject to a registration requirement under German law nor are there any other formal requirements. The retention of title clause provides a highly efficient means for securing the payment claims of a seller especially when compared with the pledge of movables because according to s 1205 of the BGB, (the German Civil Code), the pledgor must give up physical possession of the goods on the basis of the publicity or ostensible ownership principle (*Publizitätsprinzip*).[35]

The juridical basis of retention of title in s 455 of the BGB is the fact of agreement. Under the BGB a distinction is drawn between the contractual obligation which provides the legal basis for the obligation to transfer and the agreement to transfer the property. The effect of this is that although the purchaser does not become the owner of the goods so long as the purchase price is not fully paid he is, nevertheless, still in possession of the goods delivered and enjoys a right to possess. Accordingly, in terms of his right to possess the seller enjoys no more than indirect possession[36] whereas the purchaser is the (lawful) immediate possessor of the goods.

---

[34] See, generally, Davies (ed) *op cit* fn 19, Chapter 6.

[35] As a result in Germany the fact that a merchant has huge stocks of goods is almost irrelevant in respect of his true financial position. There is an argument that this is unjust from the point of view of the unsecured creditor but zero sum analysis suggests otherwise since the purchaser gets possession of the goods immediately which is in the interest of all creditors whether secured or not.

[36] Section 868 BGB.

The legal position of the original buyer is strong because the seller has the duty to transfer the property upon fulfilment of the purchase price being paid (*Verpflichtungsgeschäft*). When this is achieved not even the seller nor even the actual owner of goods can prevent this.

In Germany the law dealing with retention of title is essentially judge-made law developed by the courts. As such, the courts provide the purchaser with legal protection at an earlier stage than payment of the price under the principle of *Anwartschäftsrecht*, or inchoate ownership, thereby protecting the purchaser's expectation of acquiring title.[37] In many respects this can be analysed in terms of a minor form of ownership, for instance, it can be transferred independently (according to the rules which apply to the transfer of ownership) and even pledged. Like property, *Anwartschäftsrecht* is protected against dispossession and other invasions and if the seller is not the owner of the goods, the purchaser may acquire *Anwartschäftsrecht* in good faith by analogy to section 932 of the Civil Code which enshrines the principle of acquisition in good faith. In practical terms, this means that the purchaser who has acquired inchoate ownership (as a result of acquisition in good faith) becomes the owner of the goods even if he knows when paying the purchase price that the seller is not the true owner of the goods.[38] Even so, it should be noted that although the *Anwartschäftsrecht* works more or less like ownership, it is also predicated on the continuing validity of the contract of sale so it follows that it would cease if the contract were rescinded.

Holland[39]

The retention of title clause in Holland is a phenomenon of agreement, that is, a clause in a contract for the sale of goods pursuant to which the parties agree that the supplier will place the goods under the buyer's control, and that the supplier will remain the owner until the full purchase price is paid or certain other obligations are fulfilled. Prior to the introduction of the new Civil Code in 1992, there were no statutory provisions dealing specifically with retention of title and there were no restrictions on the obligations which a retention of title could secure. It was therefore possible for the seller to retain title until the buyer had fulfilled all his obligations to the seller on whatever legal basis such obligations arose, including, for example, the payment of damages in tort. However, Article 3:92 (2) of the

[37] BGHZ vol 20 p 88.

[38] BGHZ vol 10 pp 69, 70.

[39] See, generally, Davies (ed) *op cit* fn 19, Chapter 9.

Dutch Civil Code sets out an exhaustive list of the types of claims which may be secured by a retention of title.

Analytically, under Dutch law, both the supplier who retains title to goods sold and the buyer of such goods have a conditional ownership interest. The supplier is the owner subject to a condition subsequent that the buyer fulfils certain obligations: the buyer is the owner subject to a condition precedent that such obligations are fulfilled. The fulfilment of those obligations results in the supplier losing his (conditional) ownership rights and the buyer becoming the unconditional owner by operation of law without any further legal act being required. A retained title is neither a dependant not an accessory right, since it is not regarded as being so closely related to the supplier's claim that it cannot exist on its own. This means that a third party to whom the supplier assigns his claim against the buyer does not automatically acquire the supplier's retained title rights.

It is not possible to reserve title against sub-buyers of the buyer under Dutch Law. Likewise, a retention of title clause does not and cannot be made to extend to the proceeds of sale arising from sales by the buyer to sub-buyers or to the buyer's receivables arising from such sales. Where a buyer subject to a retention of title clause wrongfully sells the goods a good faith purchaser will acquire unconditional title thereto based upon Article 3.86 of the Dutch Civil Code, that is, a purchaser for value from a buyer in possession is protected provided that he neither knew nor should have known of the supplier's interest.

Greece [40]

Under Greek law the seller is obliged to transfer to the buyer the ownership of the goods sold which involves the transfer of possession with the intention that the latter becomes the owner of the goods, that is, acquisitive prescription. Article 532 of the Greek Civil Code provides that the seller can retain ownership in the good even though possession has passed. Such a clause is justified on the basis of freedom of contract - the contracting parties are merely agreeing on how the buyer will perform his obligations and when he will pay the agreed price. Formalities have to be respected to bind third parties, for example, the sale of cars requires the intervention of a notary.

---

[40] *Ibid*, Chapter 7.

Italy [41]

The sale of goods subject to retention of title has developed in the context of "registered movables" notably cars, whereby, if the seller's interest is to prevail against third parties it must be registered. Whilst as a matter of freedom of contract, Italian law recognises retention of title as a valid contractual mechanism,[42] it is not implied by law and must be expressly incorporated into the agreement. Moreover there is a publicity requirement under Article 1524 so that the clause can only be relied upon against the creditors of the buyer if it appears in a written document bearing "a certain date prior to the date of attachment". Further, Article 1524 states that in case of machinery[43] where the price exceeds 30,000 lire, the retention of title clause will prevail against third party interests including a buyer provided that it was registered in a special register kept in the office of the Clerk of the Court having jurisdiction over the place where the machinery is located. As far as newly manufactured goods and machine tools with a price of at least 500,000 lire is concerned, the so-called *Legge Sabatini* [44] provides that the machine must, in addition, display a plate in a prominent position with the name of the seller as owner and information identifying the machine if the reservation of title clause is to prevail against a third party acquirer.

Norway [45]

In Norway the retention of title concept is linked with that of a possessory lien. Thus where there has been delivery the right of detention is lost. In order for the seller in such a situation to be able to recover the goods he must have made a reservation to that effect. However, in terms of analysis, under Norwegian Law he is not exercising his right of retention but rather recovery of the object is made pursuant to other rules, notably, distraint or sales lien.

The principal requirement for the exercise of a retention right under Norwegian law is that of possession. Even so, the requirement of

---

[41] *Ibid,* Chapter 8.

[42] Article 1523 CC.

[43] The general position is governed by Article 1153 of the Italian Civil Code which protects the position of the *bona fide* purchaser and possessor of goods sold by the original buyer.

[44] *Law 18 November 1965, No 1329.*

[45] See, generally, Davies (ed) *op cit* fn 19, Chapter 10.

possession is not usually formulated so strictly that the creditor must have the object under his physical control. What is essential is that the owner, that is, the debtor has been deprived of control. The traditional formulation of this requirement is that the object in question must physically have been removed from the owner's sphere of control. It is possible under Norwegian law to exchange the object secured if the object originally detained is needed by the debtor. If the party retaining the object accepts the new object as security then few problems arise. Thus, provided the new security is equivalent to the original and the legal protection of the new right is established *before* the retained object is released then the transaction cannot be avoided under ss 5-7 of the Creditors Recovery Act. It should be noted that there are provisions, for example, under the Norwegian Sale of Goods Act which give the owner a right to enforce exchange of security where the value of the object is disproportionately great in terms of the sums secured.

An important requirement for a valid retention of title provision is that there must be a "natural" connection between the claim and what is being detained. Where the creditor wishes to extend legal title retention to cover other sums then this is dealt with in terms of possessary lien under Norwegian law. If and so long as the necessary possession exists, the right of retention is fully protected against the owner's creditors and later contract acquirers of the retained object. Acquisition in good faith cannot occur without the acquirer having had the object delivered and consequently the right of retention is safe so long as the object is in the possession of the person exercising it. In bankruptcy so long as the retained object in itself covers the claim, the right of retention provides full satisfaction of both principal and interest due.[46] Satisfaction of any balance due must be sought in the debtor's estate and will then give rise to a dividend.[47] Title retention does not convey any general sales right as does normally a mortgage. Still, the creditor may in some cases be granted a right of sale which may be in the form of an emergency sale where the owner cannot pay and the creditor risks being left with the object for an unfavourably long time. This is especially so in cases where the object is perishable such as fresh food.

It is worth noting that the credit and security law seen in Article 9 of the US Uniform Commercial Code which is replicated in Canada through

---

[46] Section 1-5b Liens Act, 8 February 1980, No 2.

[47] Section 8-17 Creditors Recovery Act, 8 June 1984, No 59.

Personal Property Security legislation is based on the non-possessory and possessory pledge. As can be seen from the above treatment, Norway has embraced this position and, in fact, is the only European country to have adopted this model in its civil law.

Portugal [48]

In the absence of a specific provision for retention of title in a sales contract, ownership of the goods is transferred to the buyer on delivery. The clause stipulating the retention of title must be expressly incorporated and formalities have to be respected. Thus in the case of real property or a registrable chattel, Article 409 of the Portuguese Civil Code provides that the retention of title clause must be included in the deed of registration if it is to bind third parties. Even where Portuguese law does not require the contract to be in writing it is preferable for reasons of legal certainty, to incorporate the retention of title clause in this way as such a clause is not lightly inferred by the courts. In any event, under the Code of Special Procedures for the Recovery of Companies and for Insolvency (1993), in order for the seller to achieve priority over all the creditors of the buyer the total value of the goods delivered subject to a retention of title must be stipulated in writing.

Spain [49]

The Spanish approach reflects the conventional civilian position, that is, where goods have been the object of a real or symbolic delivery, property will pass. Nevertheless, a retention of title clause incorporated into the sales contract can qualify the agreement so that law 50/1965 Sale of Goods by Instalments provides that the retention of title clause can be registered at the Special Registry and this was ruled by the Ministerial Order, 15 May 1982, to be effective against third parties so long as it was embodied in a written contract in accordance with Article 1227 and 1228 of the Spanish Civil Code. It is for this reason that some Spanish commentators have maintained that registration is necessary for any retention of title clause to be valid.

The capacity in which the buyer holds the goods subject to retention of title in the intermediate time between delivery and full payment is

---

[48] See Davies (ed) *op cit* fn 19, Chapter 11.

[49] *Ibid,* Chapter 12.

problematical under Spanish Law. Sometimes the buyer in the contract will be described as a simple commodatory but this is not appropriate because the *commodatum* is, in essence, a gratuitous contract and does not imply the purpose of transfer of property. On other occasions the buyer has been categorised as a precarist or simple tenant but the difficulty here is that by the very nature of the contract it is the buyer who decides the fulfilment of the obligations and, thereby, whether property passes under the contract. All of these positions are reflected in the Supreme court decisions of 10 June 1958 and 11 July 1983. In some cases the buyer has been categorised as a depositary as seen in the Supreme Court decisions of 26 January 1976 or 19 October 1982 but this approach can be criticised on the basis that it is inconsistent with the purpose of the contract which is that of a sale of goods. The buyer has also been identified with a lease tenant although the difficulty here is that the essence of a sale contract subject to a retention of title clause is that it is not merely the transmission of the use and enjoyment of a thing for a certain period. It is for this reason that some authors have categorised the position of the buyer as having an expectancy of property and that during the intermediate period he has a *sui generis* possession, in other words, a "special" possession as a future owner.

Sweden [50]

Under Swedish law, title is regarded as one of the most powerful rights *in rem*. Title includes the right to control and dispose of the property subject only to the restrictions the owner has voluntarily accepted or which have been imposed by legislation. The transfer of title is a matter of contractual intention under Swedish law. By virtue of s 54 of the Swedish Sale of Goods Act and s 40 of the Consumer Purchase Act a vendor may cancel the sale if the purchaser delays making payment and the delay constitutes a significant breach. If the buyer has already taken factual possession of the goods, the vendor may cancel the sale only if he has reserved the right to do so or the purchaser rejects the goods. An agreement incorporating the right for the vendor to reclaim the goods does not require any special form sent, although, in practice, it will normally be in writing. Further the agreement providing for retention of title must be entered into no later than the time the goods are handed over to the purchaser. Only simple retention of title clauses are recognised under Swedish law.

---

[50] See, generally, Davies (ed) *op cit* fn 19, Chapter 13.

There is no mandatory requirement for registration of retention of title clauses under Swedish law in contrast to other real rights, for example, floating charges which are registered in the court. In Sweden retention of title clauses have become popular precisely because of this. A trustee in bankruptcy of the buyer will take the goods subject to the retention of title clause and the original vendor may reclaim the goods from the bankrupt's estate. Third party purchasers of the goods, on the other hand, are bound only where they are not in good faith.

Switzerland [51]

Article 213 of the Swiss Code of Obligation provides that in the absence of a specific contractual clause to the contrary the purchase price becomes due and payable at the moment the buyer receives physical possession of the goods. However, Swiss law does provide for retention of title by virtue of Article 715 *et seq* of the Swiss Civil Code. Under these provisions retention of title is not implied by law and it must be expressly provided for in the contract between the seller and the buyer and properly registered with the Debt Collection Office at the domicile of the buyer. In the absence of a properly registered agreement between buyer and seller, Article 714 of the Swiss Civil Code provides that ownership of movable goods passes to the buyer with possession of these goods as provided for in Articles 922-925 of the Swiss Civil Code. These provide, as a general rule, that possession is transferred by the previous owner willingly giving the acquirer the means to freely dispose of the acquired goods.[52] Possession can also be transferred by proxy[53] and by way of transfer of documents giving evidence of possession and ownership of goods such as bills of lading.[54] In such cases the transfer of possession of documents of title to the buyer substitutes the transfer of possession of the goods themselves. However, Article 925, paragraph 2 of the Swiss Civil Code provides that if there is a conflict between the recipient of such documents and the recipient of the goods themselves the right of the recipient of the goods will prevail if both recipients were acting in good faith. Further Article 924 of the Swiss Civil Code provides that the acquirer of goods can obtain possession even if the goods themselves remain with the seller or are shipped to a third party by way of an express agreement (*constitutum possessorium*)

---

[51] See, generally, Davies (ed) *op cit* fn 19, Chapter 14.

[52] Article 922 Swiss Civil Code.

[53] Article 923 Swiss Civil Code.

[54] Article 925 Swiss Civil Code.

providing that the seller (or the third party) exercises possession on behalf of the buyer.[55]

The consequence of the rules of possession and ownership outlined above is that the protection offered to the seller by a retention of title clause is not absolute. If, for instance, the buyer breaches his contract with the seller and resells the purchased merchandise to a third party, he will acquire good title in the merchandise so long as he is acting in good faith.[56] The law therefore gives priority to the protection of a party acquiring goods based on the presumption that a person who has possession of movable goods also has title to these goods over and above any protection given to the seller by way of a retention of title clause. A retention of title clause creates an element of risk for third parties under Swiss law who conclude transactions with the buyer in reliance on the buyer's legal title to the goods in his possession. Without registration such third parties have no possibility to verify the title of their contractual partners in the goods they purport to own. This is especially the case in the event of commercial loans which are often extended in reliance upon the assets in the possession of the debtor. Therefore, Article 715, paragraph 1 of the Swiss Civil Code provides that a retention of title clause becomes valid only upon registration in a public register, the Retention of Title Clause Register (RTCR) which is maintained by the Debt Collection Offices in each Swiss region. Third parties can consult this register before extending credit or entering into other business relationships and therefore protect their interests.

The retention of title clause must be registered at the domicile of the buyer which, in the case of a company, means its main statutory domicile. In the event of a change of domicile, re-registration at the new domicile is necessary. The registration at the previous domicile expires after three months irrespective of the knowledge of the seller of the change of domicile. The seller must therefore carefully monitor the domicile of any parties who have possession of his goods under a retention of title clause and all buyers should, as a matter of contract, be obliged to report any change of domicile to the seller during the entire duration of the retention of title agreement. If the seller misses the deadline of three months, full

[55] Article 924 Swiss Civil Code.

[56] Article 714 para 2 in connection with Article 933 Swiss Civil Code.

title passes to the buyer; the seller may, however, regain title with effect as of the date of re-registration at the new domicile.[57]

Neither the Civil Code nor the Ordinance of the Federal Supreme Court contain provisions with regard to the time of registration. It has been consistently held by the Swiss Federal Supreme Court that the retention of title clause can be registered at any time before or after the transfer of possession of the goods. However, if possession is transferred before registration, full title passes to the buyer upon the buyer obtaining possession and the seller only has the right to re-obtain title in the goods with effect as of the later date of registration.[58] Registration has only the effect of "negative publicity", that is to say, any third party may rely in full on the non-registration of a retention of title agreement. Where a retention of title clause has been validly made and registered, the sale of goods by the buyer will constitute an embezzlement in accordance with Article 138 of the Swiss Federal Penal Code. This will be a small consolation to the seller since a retention of title clause does not prevent third parties from obtaining title to the goods so long as they are in good faith. Under Swiss Law a retention of title agreement between the buyer and seller will not protect the seller against the fraudulent acts of the buyer. The main purpose and effect of a retention of title clause is to protect the seller in the case of the insolvency of the buyer. In effect, a registered retention of title agreement gives the supplier a right to repossess the goods on bankruptcy or, if the goods are seized by the Swiss Debt Collection Office, they can be sold at auction *only* if a price is achieved which fully covers the claim of the seller to the outstanding amount of the purchase price.

United Kingdom and Ireland [59]

Retention of title is not a new phenomenon for the common law. Indeed the ingenuity of Victorian commercial lawyers led to the distinction being drawn between hire purchase, that is, a bailment of goods with the option to purchase and the conditional sale. Nevertheless it was the Irish High Court decision in *Re Interview*[60] and the Court of Appeal decision in the Scottish case of *Aluminium Industrie Vaasen BV* v *Romalpa Aluminium Ltd*[61] which

---

[57] Article 3 paras 1 and 3 of the Ordinance of the Swiss Federal Supreme Court regarding the Registration of Retention of Title Clauses.

[58] *BGE 93 111 104.*

[59] For a full discussion see Bradgate *op cit* fn 4.

[60] [1975] IR 382.

[61] [1976] 1 WLR 676.

alerted the commercial world to the protection afforded to a supplier who has sold goods subject to a retention of title clause. Such a clause can give suppliers the opportunity of obtaining priority over secured creditors in the event of the buyer's insolvency which in terms of legal categorisation arises out of the retained ownership interest. Whilst in terms of *economic effect*, a retention of title clause operates in the nature of a charge over the goods in favour of the seller. Nonetheless, its legal *form* is not that of a charge but merely a term of the contract of sale under which title is retained.

Typically there are three parts to the reservation of title clause. The first part is concerned with reserving ownership in the goods themselves. This is satisfactory so long as the buyer remains in possession, but is inadequate where, as so often happens, the buyer resells the goods to a third party who when acting in good faith and without notice of the clause will be protected by virtue of the buyer in possession exception to the *nemo dat* principle seen in the Irish Sale and Supply of Goods Act (1994) and the UK Sale of Goods Act (1979). Hence the second part of the clause concentrates not on the goods themselves but the proceeds due to or received by the buyer in the event of resale and seeks to create a trust in which the original buyer holds these proceeds on behalf of the original seller. The third part of the clause is concerned with the case where the goods have been delivered to the buyer and are then used in the process of manufacture: the device employed here is to declare the finished products as belonging to the seller.

In the case of the simple retention of title clause, the seller retains ownership in the goods delivered as against the buyer until the full purchase price for the goods has been paid. The effectiveness of such a clause is confirmed in the UK and Ireland as an expression of the sale of goods principle that property passes in accordance with contractual intention as distinct from conveyance. Significantly, current account and money clauses have been upheld in the UK and Ireland. This is where the seller retains ownership in the goods delivered as against the buyer until *all* debts or *other obligations* owed by the buyer to the seller have been paid. The imprimatur here is the House of Lords decision in ***Armour* v *Thyssen Edelstahlwerke AG***,[62] a decision on Scots Law, where Lord Keith acknowledged that such a clause did "in a sense give the seller security of title not by virtue of any right over his own property conferred by the

[62] [1991] AC 339.

buyer."[63] In Ireland an instructive case in this context is *Frigoscandia Ltd* v *Continental Irish Meat Ltd.*[64] The facts involved the sale of refrigeration equipment subject, *inter alia,* to a current account clause. Following default, the supplier sought to recover the goods on the basis of the retention of title clause. In reaching his conclusion, McWilliam J adopted the classic freedom of contract approach in support of his finding that the parties' intentions as expressed in the contract should be paramount. He concluded the matter as follows:

> The parties to a contract can agree to any terms they wish, and amongst others, they can agree that the property in the goods shall not pass to the purchaser until all the instalments of the purchase price have been paid.[65]

As we have discussed above,[66] insofar as a clause seeks to retain title as against a sub-buyer from the original buyer this is of limited value because of the well-established exceptions to the *nemo dat* principle.[67] The position of the sub-buyer is bolstered because he is not deemed to be on notice arising out of his knowledge of a generic retention of title clause not least because there are so many different types. Furthermore, the sub-buyer's knowledge of non-payment cannot be described as bad faith because this can hardly be considered a right "in respect of goods"; it is merely a personal right in respect of the contract of sale. This explains why an attempt is often made to extend a retention of title clause to the proceeds of resale of the goods supplied. As an equitable tracing right which arises by operation of law this is not registrable as a charge since such a right has not been conferred or created by the debtor company. Furthermore, if the

---

[63] *Ibid* at p 343. For a discussion here see McCormack, *Reservation of Title Clauses* 2nd ed (1997).
[64] [1982] ILRM 396.
[65] *Ibid* at p 398.
[66] See p 353.
[67] This is expressed in s 25(1) of the Sale of Goods Act (1979) which follows the Imperial Act of 1893:
"Where a person having bought or agreed to buy goods obtains, with the consent of the seller, possession of the goods or documents of title to the goods, the delivery or transfer by that person, or by a mercantile agent acting for him, of the goods or documents of title, under any sale, pledge, or other disposition thereof, to any person receiving the same in good faith and without notice of any lien or right of the original seller in respect of the goods, has the same effect as if the person making the delivery or transfer were a mercantile agent in possession of the goods of documents of title with the consent of the owner".

traceable funds are mixed then equity may declare a charge on the mixed fund. The point of principle is whether a fiduciary relationship can be established in relation to the proceeds, which, of course, depends upon the categorisation of the relationship as one of principal and agent. In England, the general approach has been hostile to such clauses and there has been a reluctance to find for a fiduciary relationship, even where the obligee is under an obligation to separate the proceeds of sales from other moneys and pass on all the rights relating to the sub-sales to the seller. Thus, in *Tatung (UK) Ltd* v *Galex Telesure Ltd,*[68] Phillips J found that despite elaborate contractual provision having been made which effectively fettered the obligee's ability to deal with the proceeds, nevertheless, this was categorised as a charge on the basis that the source of the plaintiff's rights was the contract and not equitable principles arising by operation of law. Such an approach does seem odd because it is tantamount to penalising the suppliers for being over-specific which would, if anything, suggest that they were acting as owners in relation to the process.[69]

The possibility of a retention of title clause constituting a charge over book debts was considered by Phillips J in *E Pfeiffer Weinkellerei-Weineinkauf GmbH and Co* v *Arbuthnot Factors Ltd.*[70] In this case, the contract between the plaintiff supplier and Springfield Wine Importers Ltd set out comprehensively the nature of the interest which the plaintiff was to have by way of security in respect of debts created by sub-sales. The retention of title clause was (translated from the original German) as follows:

> All claims that [the importer] gets from the sale ... with all rights including his profit amounting to his obligations towards [Pfeiffer], will be passed on to [Pfeiffer]. On demand the [importer] is obliged to notify the assignment of the claim to give [Pfeiffer] in writing all necessary information concerning the assertion of [Pfeiffer's] claims ... In case of cash sales, the money that has come from a third person immediately becomes [Pfeiffer's] ... this money has to be separated from other money, it must be booked correspondingly, and must be administered until called for.

Springfield had agreed to assign to the plaintiff the future debts owed by the sub-purchasers to Springfield up to the amount of Springfield's

---

[68] [1989] BCC 325.

[69] See also *Compaq Computer Ltd* v *Abercorn Group Ltd* [1993] BCLC 602.

[70] [1988] 1 WLR 150.

outstanding indebtedness to the plaintiff. Subsequently, Springfield then entered into a factoring agreement with the defendant which amounted to an assignment of the future debts. The approach taken by Phillips J is interesting in that he held that Springfield was not a bailee or any kind of fiduciary with respect to the plaintiff, and he found that the *Romalpa* case went the way it did because of the defendant's concession that it was a bailee of the plaintiff's goods. The normal implication Phillips J considered is that a buyer in possession, to whom title has not yet passed, when permitted to sub-sell in the ordinary course of his business does so for his own account. Such an approach is too extensive.[71]

In contrast to the approach taken in the *Arbuthnot Factors* case,[72] in the Irish case of *SA Foundaries du Lion* v *MV International Factors (Ireland) Ltd*,[73] the court found (Barrington J presiding) that the plaintiff supplier had a valid proceeds clause which prevailed over the defendant's factoring arrangement. The Irish cases are not consistent in this regard as seen, for example, in the Irish High Court decision of *Carroll Group Distributors Ltd* v *JF Bourke Ltd and Bourke Sales Ltd*.[74] In this case the retention of title clause provided that the property in the goods should remain in the plaintiff until the defendants had discharged all sums, but gave the defendants an express right to resell the goods. The clause further provided that, following resale, the defendants undertook to hold moneys received "in trust" for the plaintiff and to maintain an independent account of all sums received. It was held by Murphy J that the arrangement was in substance a charge on the proceeds of sub-sale because:

> ... the bargain made between the parties ... properly implemented would result in a bank account with the sums of money credited thereto which would probably be in excess of the amounts due by [the defendants] to [the plaintiff]. This would arise partly from the fact that the proceeds of sale would include some goods the cost price of which had been discharged and some had not. In other words the bank account would be a fund to which [the plaintiffs] could have recourse to ensure the discharge of the money due to them even though they would not be entitled to the entirety of that fund. Accordingly the fund agreed to be credited would possess all the characteristics of a mortgage or charge as identified by Romer LJ in *In Re George Inglefield Ltd* [1933] Ch 1 at 27-28.[75]

[71] See Bradgate *op cit* fn 4.

[72] See above.

[73] [1983] ILRM 66.

[74] [1990] ILRM 285.

[75] *Ibid* at p 289.

An important aspect of Phillips J's judgment in *Arbuthnot Factors* is the conclusion that a charge, by virtue of the proceeds clause, had been created over the book debt which required registration under s 395 of the UK Companies Act 1985. Of considerable commercial significance is the possibility of a fixed charge on book debts but in order to achieve this the company creating the charge must be limited in the manner in which it can deal with the debts.[76] In many instances the elaborate and restrictive provisions concerning the collection of the debts necessarily consequent on a fixed charge are not going to be commercially acceptable.

As well as horizontal extension of reservation of title clauses into debts arising between the trade creditor and debtor, there are also vertical extensions which seek to follow the goods supplied into a finished product or its proceeds. Such clauses are referred to as "aggregation clauses".[77] The obvious policy dilemma here is that of windfall because the supplier seeks to recover not only the buyer's processing efforts but also any new materials supplied by third parties. It is well established that parties cannot by their contractual stipulations alone alter the applications of the principles and rules of the law of property. Indeed the courts are reluctant to favourably construe a clause giving title to a supplier in products manufactured from his original goods and those of the buyer. It also appears clear that where goods of two third parties are combined in the manufacturing process, a retention of title clause purporting to accord title in the new goods to one of those suppliers will amount to a charge. This approach was confirmed in *Chaigley Farms Ltd* v *Crawford, Kaye and Grayshire Ltd*[78] where it was held that the identity of livestock was changed once it had been slaughtered by the buyer and the slaughtered animal could no longer be described as "livestock" under the retention of title clause.

An enforceable retention of title clause is a useful tool for a supplier of goods to include in a sale contract. Properly worded simple or all

---

[76] The principal authority in Ireland is *Re Keenan Bros Ltd* [1986] BCLC 242 whereas in England the seminal decision is *Siebe Gorman and Co Ltd* v *Barclays Bank Ltd* [1979] 2 Lloyd's Rep 142. For a review and discussion of the authorities see *Agnew and Bearsley* v *Commissioner of Inland Revenue and Official Assignee for the estate in bankruptcy of Birtwhistle* [2001] UKPC 28. In this case (more commonly referred to as *Brumark Investments*) the Privy Council held that the previous authority of *Re New Bullas Trading* [1994] BCC 36 was wrongly decided.

[77] For a discussion here see Davies *op cit* fn 19 at pp 115-119.

[78] [1996] BCC 957.

monies clauses have been upheld in the UK and Ireland. The more sophisticated forms of clauses, giving the seller rights to the proceeds of sub-sales or to new or mixed products developed from his own goods are vulnerable to being treated as registrable charges. Indeed, analytically there is no doubt that *any* retention of title clause performs a double function in that it contains both the elements of sale and of security. The emphasis on property reservation is that it allows the "owner" to seize the goods should the debtor fail on one of his primary obligations notably payment of the price. Since the purpose of the property retention is only to ensure *priority* the supplier is not essentially retaining the asset himself but rather the right to *use* the asset to gain repayment of the debtor's debt to him. It is for this reason that Robert Goff LJ held *obiter* in the Court of Appeal in *Clough Mill Ltd* v *Martin*[79] that the seller should retain the title to the material as trustee upon trust for sale accounting to the buyer for any surplus received.[80] Herein lies the heart of the dilemma inherent in the double function of the retention of title clause as both an expression of sales law and also the law of personal property security.

Retention of Title Clauses in Europe: an Overview

During the course of the twentieth century among the civilian family of law within Europe, the non-possessory pledge emerged by way of statutory regulation. The most extensive example of this is the Dutch Civil Code 1992[81] which regulates registered non-possessory pledges in general. Most of the other civil law countries have enacted specific statutes for specific categories of assets. Thus, as well as registries in respect of aircraft and ships, France and Italy, for example, have public registries in cars and also for machinery.[82] In Germany, non-possessory pledges are regulated in respect of even agricultural tenants' stock-in-trade, agricultural fruits and

---

[79] [1984] 3 All ER 982.

[80] *Ibid* at p 988. Compare *Welsh Development Agency* v *Export Finance Co Ltd* [1992] BCLC 148.

[81] *Nievuw Burgerlijk Wetboek (NBW)* arts 3:236-237. See also the new Quebec Civil Code 1994 arts 2665, 2696-2701 (movable hypothecs without delivery) 2702-2709 (movable hypothecs with delivery). See Drobnig, "Secured Credit in International Insolvency Proceedings" (1998) 33 *Texas International Law Journal* 53 at p 57.

[82] See above.

submarine cables.[83] One important effect of entry on the respective register is that the creditor has a right in the specifically identified asset although the scope of this will depend upon the terms and conditions of the purchase agreement.

The main difficulty with the above approach is that it is highly selective in terms of its effect and scope. In the light of this it is not surprising that civilian jurisdictions have resorted to ownership as a form of non-possessory security. Such a phenomenon can also be seen in common law jurisdictions. From a formal, economic functional perspective this represents a security interest for the buyer's trade credit. Indeed, the main dilemma with the retention of title mechanism is that ownership is such an unwieldy concept in that it provides too many rights to creditors. As Drobnig has pointed out:

> Ownership as the most comprehensive property right is dysfunctional for security purposes. It gives more rights to the secured creditor than are needed for the purpose of security. The counteracting interests of other persons, especially those of other creditors of the debtor, are so strong that the effects of the secured creditor's right of ownership must be limited.[84]

It is for this reason that the courts in both civilian and common law jurisdictions have sought to cut the scope of such clauses down[85] especially with regard to horizontal extensions into (general) debts or vertical extensions which seek to follow the goods supplied into a finished product or its proceeds.[86]

What clearly emerges from the above discussion is that the extent of the recognition of the validity of retention of title clauses and the formal requirements for establishing such clauses vary greatly from jurisdiction to jurisdiction. It is also obvious that the extent of the recognition of such

[83] See Drobnig, "Security Over Corporeal Movables in Germany" in *Security over Corporeal Movables* ed Sauveplanne (1974) at pp 187-192.

[84] *Op cit* fn 81 at p 60.

[85] German courts have treated the buyer's expectancy under a reservation of title as being equivalent to a right of ownership which can be transferred as security to another creditor. See Serick, *Security in Movables in German Law: An Outline* (1990) pp 30-35.

[86] See for example *Borden* v *Scottish Timber Products* [1981] Ch 25; *Tatung (UK) Ltd* v *Galex Telesure Ltd* (1989) 5 BCC 325; *Compaq Computer Ltd* v *Abercorn Group Ltd* [1993] BCLC 606; *E Pfeiffer Weinkellerei-Weineinkauf GmbH and Co* v *Arbuthnot Factors Ltd* [1988] 1 WLR 150.

clauses will pose significant difficulties if goods or equipment are moved from one country to another. As cross-border trade increases between the Member States of the European Union the dilemma can be simply stated: to what extent can a State come to terms with foreign contractual provisions (retention of title clauses) designed specifically to meet the policy requirements of the other legal system? We shall now consider this issue in greater detail.

The Challenge of International Secured Credit and Retention of Title

An attempt was made in the EEC Draft Directive in 1980[87] to harmonise the recognition of retention of title clauses within the (then) Member States of the Community. What was modestly proposed was the recognition of simple retention of title clauses and there was no attempt made to harmonise more extensive clauses. Since the time of the Draft Directive not much progress has been made within the European Union in harmonising the recognition of retention of title clauses within the Member States. There are two major explanations for this lack of progress: first, the process of harmonisation requires the identification of common assumptions[88] and in the case of the European Union, it has been easier to draft a directive harmonising rules on unfair terms in consumer contracts because of the similar importance of consumers to all Member States than having to deal with retention of title clauses;[89] second, it is not possible to adequately deal with retention of title clauses in isolation from other security interests. As Monti, Nejman and Reuter have pointed out:

> The drafting of a uniform retention of title clause directive could shatter the balance between the different security instruments with which the Member States now operate. It is truly chimerical to assume that it is possible to harmonise retention of title clauses at a European level. Retention of title clauses can be harmonised only if all security interests are also considered in a joint harmonisation effort.[90]

---

[87] Working Paper 111/D/278/80.

[88] Legrand, "European Legal Systems are not Converging" (1996) 45 *ICLQ* 52.

[89] See Monti, Nejman, Reuter, "The Future of Reservation of Title Clauses in the European Community" (1997) 46 *ICLQ* 866.

[90] *Ibid* at p 896.

In essence, the problem is that of balancing the different legal and business cultures within Europe and the need to promote effective secured financing so as to enhance the attractiveness of credit extension to the creditor by reducing risk.[91]

It is obvious that the various forms of security interests and the extent to which non-possessory security interests are recognised in different jurisdictions pose significant difficulties if collateral moves from one jurisdiction to another. Historically, two major techniques have been used to deal with cross-border movement of goods: first, an attempt is made to promote uniform conflict of law rules, that is, when goods move to ensure that the laws of the new jurisdiction are conceptually compatible with the law governing the transaction(s) at its inception; second, unification of substantive rules. We shall consider each of these possibilities in turn.

Conflict Rules

So long as goods or equipment are stationary there are unlikely to be problems in terms of the applicable law. However, as trade has increased between Member States and the process of globalisation has made national frontiers less important, the issue is increasingly one of the recognition in the new jurisdiction of a security interest validly created under the laws of the old jurisdiction. The conventional European position is that the law governing rights *in rem* in movables (that is, rights which directly affect third parties) is governed by the *lex situs*. Clearly there is an intuitive attractiveness in this approach not least because the physical location of a movable provides a clear and objective criterion. When the chattel moves to a new jurisdiction there are two possibilities: first, the security interest may be treated as valid in the new *situs* until it is displaced by a new title acquired in accordance with the law of the new *situs*;[92] second, the "transposition" approach,[93] that is, continued recognition depends upon

---

[91] As World Bank Studies have demonstrated the absence of efficient legal regimes governing secured transactions significantly diminishes the economic output of many nations. See for example, Office of the Chief Economist, Latin America and Caribbean Region, *How Legal Restrictions on Collateral Limit Access to Credit in Bolivia* (World Bank Report No 13873 - BO, 1994).

[92] Dicey and Morris, *The Conflicts of Law* (1999) rule 80.

[93] See Shilling, "Some European Decisions on Non-possessory Security Rights in Private International Law" (1985) 34 *ICLQ* 87.

whether it fits within the categories of rights *in rem* recognised by the law of the new *situs*.

Whichever of the above approaches is adopted in the relevant jurisdiction there are real difficulties posed for the foreign secured creditor. In the first place, even though the foreign security interest is recognised it may only be recognised as governing *inter partes* rights and not, thereby, bind third parties. Furthermore, the courts in the new *situs* in giving recognition to the foreign law will often seek to draw analogies with security interests recognised in the municipal law and this is particularly problematical where the analogies are only approximate. An example of this can be seen in *Re Reldtech Equipment Ltd*[94] where a German company delivered goods to an English Company subject to an extended retention of title clause validly created in Germany. This clause failed in England since it was analysed under domestic law as an attempt to create a charge which was held to be void for lack of registration.[95] Another reason why the *situs* rule poses problems for the foreign secured creditor is that the courts in the new *situs* may require the foreign security interest (if it is to have an effect *in rem*) to be subject to the same disclosure rules as the analogised right under domestic law. The obvious problem here is that the secured party may not become aware of these requirements until it is too late to comply with public notice requirements as the time limits will often have been set with only domestic security interests in mind.

The *lex situs* is not an appropriate mechanism for resolving the issue of recognising security interests in collateral not least because the *situs* of the collateral when the original security interest was created may be wholly fortuitous, for example, the supplier of goods may be in State A, the buyer may have its place of business in State B whereas the collateral is intended for use in State C. The fact that the collateral was originally located in A is not really significant in respect of validity issues for security interests which may arise in B, C or indeed any other state. Furthermore, in the light of the diversity of the recognition of non-possessory security interests in Europe there is a real risk where collateral moves between boundaries within Europe of the resolution of the dispute being dependent upon

---

[94] [1991] BCC 16.

[95] *Re Bond Worth* [1980] Ch 28. Compare *Armour* v *Thyssen Edelstahlwerke AG* [1991] 2 AC 339.

whether the jurisdiction has a liberal or a traditional approach to the recognition of the non-possessory security interest.[96]

In dealing with harmonising commercial security interests law within the European Union the differences in legal cultures and traditions pose a significant impediment. This can be illustrated by reference to the major conveyancing rules which apply notably, *possession vaut titre* and the exceptions to the *nemo dat* rule[97] arising out of ostensible ownership and/or apparent authority. These conveyancing rules reflect a domestic policy position, that is, the protection to good faith purchasers from loss at the hands of a prior undisclosed property interest in movables. One way of addressing this dilemma is the public disclosure of such security interests. This, of course, depends upon the sophistication of buyers or subsequent secured parties being able to identify (if the *lex situs* rule is not applied) the *lex loci debitoris*[98], that is, the state in which the executive office of the owner-debtor in possession of the mobile equipment is located and following on from this they must then determine what the public notice requirements are. If there are no public notice requirements, it follows that there is no way for the domestic buyer/creditor to discover the existence of the foreign security interest under the *lex loci debitoris* and, in this situation, the choice of law rule is not functional. Even where there is a public notice function in the location of the debtor, nonetheless, the choice of law rule is problematical because for policy reasons the state may not bind a buyer of equipment to this rule where the latter is not legally sophisticated enough to appreciate the need to conduct a search of the public notice system of the state where the debtor is located. Indeed, their dilemma can easily be illustrated by reference to the Unidroit Convention on International Finance Leasing.[99] At one stage during the preliminary

---

[96] See *Report of the Secretary-General: Study on Security Interests*, Yearbook of the United Nations Commission on International Trade Law (1977) Vol VIII part 2: 171 at pp 213-216.

[97] Sale of Goods Act 1979, ss 21-25.

[98] The North American approach to conflict of laws in mobile equipment is that the jurisdiction where the debtor is located governs the perfection and the effect of perfection and non-perfection of a security interest. See generally Cuming, "Recognition of Security Interests in Mobile Equipment: An International Approach" Chapter 6 in *Commercial and Consumer Law*, ed Cranston and Goode (1993) Chapter 6.

[99] Unidroit Convention on *International Finance Leasing* done at Ottawa 1988. This is fully set out in Appendix I below.

negotiations, the Study Group contemplated that the lessor should prevail over a good faith purchaser from the lessee. This was, however, objected to by civilian lawyers on the basis that it was contrary to the *possession vaut titre* doctrine which had implications beyond leasing. The solution was to limit the priority to creditors of the lessee subject to perfection of the lessor's title in accordance with the public notice requirement, if any, of the applicable law.[100]

The differences in legal culture and business practices become less significant where the businesses involved in a transaction share a common assumption. Thus attempts have been made through international conventions to address problems in respect of specific types of mobile equipment particularly aircraft and ships.[101] The only example of modest success here is the Geneva Convention on the International Recognition of Rights in Aircraft 1948.[102] This Convention recognises the inappropriateness of the *lex situs* for aircraft and its main purpose is to identify a constant source of law in order to reduce the risk for financiers. However, whilst it has unified the conflict of law rules,[103] it has failed to deal with the substantive law of security in aircraft so a state is free to refuse recognition of foreign types of security interests which do not fit into the domestic categories of security interests.[104]

---

[100] *Ibid*, Article 7.

[101] There are 3 major Conventions dealing with maritime mortgages and liens in 1926, 1967 and 1993. Only the 1926 Convention has come into force and of the parties to the Convention there is no common law country. The 1926 Convention is modest in terms of its effect in that it subordinates ship mortgages to listed maritime liens but it does not set down a conflict rule for priorities of completing mortgages. Whilst the 1967 and it successor 1993 Convention provides for ranking of mortgages and also a conflicts rule in terms of their effect on third parties - none have been implemented. See McGuiness, *The Law of Ship Mortgages* (2001).

[102] Signed at Geneva 19 June 1948, 310 UNTS 151, Art 1 (1).

[103] The Convention provides for the recognition of security interests such as mortgages or hypothecs provided that "such rights have been constituted in accordance with the law of the Contracting State in which the aircraft is registered as to nationality at the time of their constitution" and "are regularly recorded in a public record of the Contracting State in which the aircraft is registered as to nationality" (Article 1(1) (d) (i)-(ii)). The effect of the recording of such rights is determined according to the law of the State where the aircraft is registered (Article 2(2)).

[104] *Ibid,* Article 2(3). See Edmunds, "Mortgages of Aircraft" *supra* Chapter 4.

National conflict of laws rules are unsatisfactory not least because they amount to a domestic court applying to an international transaction a law designed primarily for domestic transactions. Since conflict of law rules vary, the reflection of the applicable law will depend upon the forum chosen and thus forum shopping is promoted. Whilst unifying conflict of law rules help in resolving this problem it does not deal with the efficacy of the security interest which is a matter of substantive law. The challenge then becomes one of developing substantive international credit and security law dealing with the validity of security interests, the public disclosure of such interests and clear priority rules in respect of competing claims.

Unification of Substantive Rules

The trend towards harmonisation of law in the twentieth century encompassed two distinct purposes: first to create a regime dealing with international transactions while preserving the identity of national laws implemented by an international Convention;[105] second, the creation of supranational entities where the focus of harmonisation was to progress a common market or political or economic grouping. In terms of the instruments available for harmonisation it is possible to identify the following: instruments which have the force of law subject to incorporation; instruments which deal with international commercial contracts and depend for their application on incorporation into contracts; a model law.[106] There are limits to the effectiveness of international proposals for contractual incorporation. By definition they are not mandatory and for them to have any realistic effect the commercial context must be such that there exists a considerable degree of homogeneity in practice as seen, for example, with performance bonds and documentary letters of credit.[107] Moreover, contractual mechanisms have, by definition, mainly an *inter-partes* dimension and, as such, are not apt for dealing with international security interests.

---

105 See, for example, the Vienna Convention on International Sales Law.

106 See, for example, the UNCITRAL Model Law on International Commercial Arbitration (1985). As a "model law" it is flexible in the sense that it can be enacted with changes.

107 See International Chambers of Commerce, *Uniform Customs and Practice Rules*.

During the twentieth century several attempts were made to achieve some degree of uniformity within the international community with respect to security interests. Initiatives were promoted by Unidroit and UNCITRAL as international intergovernmental agencies and they involved implementation by national governments through the adoption of an international convention or model law. These initiatives were noted[108] in a major study commissioned by UNICITRAL where Professor Drobnig was tasked to investigate the law of security interests in principal legal systems and to assess the need and also the prospects for harmonisation here. In this regard, Drobnig recommended a unified law on security interests and noted with approval Article 9 of the American Uniform Commercial Code as being "the most modernised, rational and comprehensive system of security interests in the present world".[109] Despite this, the Project was abandoned mainly because of the difficulty and complexity of the law and the refusal of receiving states to recognise security interests attached to mobile property before entering the receiving state.[110]

In the course of the last decade of the twentieth century a great change in attitude by legal policy makers can be seen to the challenge posed of recognising international security interests. To a large extent this new phenomenon can be explained as follows: first, the increasing globalisation of the world economy and the privatisation of state monopolies with the consequent conversion of sovereign risk to enterprise risk, that is, greater risk has brought into focus the need for an international framework of security interests; second, there has been a growing

---

[108] See United Nations Commission on International Trade Law, *Security Interests: Feasibility of Uniform Rules to be used in Financing Trade*, YB of the United Nations Commission on International Trade Law (1979) vol x, part 2, p 81; (1980) vol xi part 2 p 89; Fédération Bancaire EEC 1970, *Projet du convention relative aux effets extraterritoriaux des sûretés mobilieres sans dessaisissement* (1970); International Institute for the Unification of Private Law, *Study on Sales of Movables by Instalment and on Credit in Member Countries of the Council of Europe* (1968).

[109] See *Report of the Secretary-General: Study on Security Interests*, YB of the United Nations Commission on International Trade Law (1977) UN Doc A/CN 9/131.

[110] On the basis of the study undertaken the UNCITRAL Secretary, Professor Drobnig, reported that significant problems remained when receiving states refused to recognise security interests attached to mobile property before it entered the receiving state and also there were different registration laws making unification of laws overly complex. See United Nations Commission on International Trade Law, YB (1979) vol x part 2 (1) c at 81.

recognition of the standing of Article 9 under the US Uniform Commercial Code as being an appropriate model for reform[111] not least because it has itself been reformed to take into account modern technology and business practices.[112] The major characteristics of Article 9 are the bringing of all security devices under one regime accompanied by a functional/purposive definition of security interests with a simple perfecting priority mechanism linked to notice filing;[113] third, the collapse of the Soviet Block has resulted in the rewriting of the commercial laws of these emerging states so as to facilitate the development of a market company. The transition from one economic regime to another has provided an opportunity for fresh examination of the basic assumptions of other systems which are often taken for granted, notably, the facilitation of security interests;[114] fourth, the European Bank for Reconstruction and Development *Model Law on Secured Transactions* (1994) clearly draws its inspiration from Article 9 and this has also been evident in various World Bank initiatives;[115] lastly, the work of UNCITRAL in proposing a Convention on assignment of accounts receivable[116] and also the Unidroit Convention on International Interests in Mobile Equipment[117] are highly significant. It is noteworthy that both of these last initiatives deal with a specific type of secured transaction rather than secured transactions generally and, further, the

---

[111] This has been adopted throughout the Anglophone Provinces in Canada. It has also inspired reform in Australia and New Zealand.

[112] See Mooney and Harris, "How Successful Was the Revision of UCC Article 9? Reflection of the Reporters" (1999) 74 *Chicago Kent Law Review* 1357.

[113] Compare Janger, "Predicting When the Uniform Law Process will Fail: Article 9, Capture and the Race to the Bottom" (1998) 83 *Iowa LR* 569.

[114] See Drobnig, "The Conversion of a Socialist Economic System to a Market Economy: Legal Implications" *Commercial and Consumer Law* ed Cranston and Goode (1993) Chapter 15.

[115] The World Bank has linked many of its leading provisions to the reform of secured transactions law in debtor countries. See, generally, Head, "Evolution of the Governing Law for Loan Agreements of the World Bank and Other Multilateral Development Banks" (1996) 90 *Am J International Law* 214.

[116] The UNCITRAL Project would govern virtually any international assignment of a receivable and any assignment (domestic or international) of an international receivable, that is, a receivable for which the debtor and creditor are in different countries.

[117] Unidroit Convention on *International Interests in Mobile Equipment* done in Cape Town, November 2001. This is set out fully in Appendix II below.

adoption of these rules would not at least *prima facie* require domestic law changes to secured credit.

The International Interests in Mobile Equipment Convention[118] is innovative because the Convention is designed to provide a body of substantive law and an international registry for interests in certain specified high value goods that are taken across national frontiers. The scheme is unique because the intention is that the State parties to the Convention would treat it as displacing national law which would within national law constraints otherwise regulate the creation, registration and priority status of the security interest in equipment. As such, it is not a conflicts of law convention but it rather constitutes a form of international substantive law with its own default remedies including provisions for speedy interim judicial relief. Whilst the Convention has the potential to cover all categories of object so long as they are of high value and mobile, it was not possible to include within one instrument every detail required because these details were often equipment specific. The solution to this dilemma was to adopt a two instrument approach, that is, to keep the Convention applicable in general terms and to embody equipment-specific protocols notably, aircraft equipment, space property and rail rolling stock. This approach is flexible since it allows states to ratify the Protocols as they emerge in the light of the needs of particular industry sectors which, in turn, may require provisions of the Convention to be overridden. The overall approach therefore is to facilitate the objectives of asset-based financing.[119] Thus, it establishes through the international registry clear priority rules by the adoption of a notice filing mechanism. Indeed, tacking is envisaged so that the priority of the first registered interest over the later registered interest applies even as regards value given by the former with the actual knowledge of the latter's interest. The significance of filing is further bolstered by the priority rule that an outright buyer of the object will take subject to the registered interest notwithstanding his actual knowledge.[120]

---

[118] Early on in the drafting process the experts recognised that the functional approach to security interests anticipated under Article 9 of the Uniform Commercial Code was a step too far for those jurisdictions outside of North America. It is for this reason that the Convention applies to security interests, lease mechanisms and retention of title clauses. The issue of categorisation of the relevant interest is deferred by the Convention to the *lex fori.*

[119] See above.

[120] The priority rule is simple compared to the complexity of the newly drafted Article 9 of the Uniform Commercial Code. There is a special provision in respect of outright buyers which reflects the fact that their interests are not registrable.

The enforcement of bargains and an efficient recovery of assets are at the heart of an effective credit and security regime. A strong enforcement regime is essential to the rating of equipment receivables by rating agencies as well as lenders and lessors which, in turn, is pivotal in any securitisation issue.[121] However, whilst the Convention facilitates such a regime it is for the Protocol to specify which Convention rules apply. In the case of the Aircraft Protocol, for example, countries may permit self-help remedies, that is, repossession and realisation without judicial intervention.[122] Furthermore, the contracting country has the option of setting up a system of expedited relief.[123] Moreover, the Protocol promotes a responsive insolvency regime so countries can opt to adopt an international insolvency rule, notably, within a period specified after an act of insolvency where insolvency proceedings have been provoked, the equipment user must either cure all defaults under the transaction or return the equipment. In addition, the obligation of the equipment user to the financier/lessor may not be restructured, amended or modified in the context of insolvency proceedings without the consent of the financier/lessor. At the same time the Convention provides for a registration mechanism in respect of non-consensual rights and, thereby, the ranking of such rights, for example, various liens, pre-preferential creditors as provided by the national law. This mechanism provides notice to the secured lender of these interests and this allows the latter to calculate the costs and potential risks of the transaction.[124]

The Unidroit Convention only applies to commercial dealings in respect of equipment-specific matters of a particular value. This specific approach can be seen in the context of the previous work by Unidroit under the Factoring and International Leasing Conventions. Security interests in the Mobile Equipment Convention builds on the latter whilst the UNCITRAL proposed Convention builds on the former. Indeed this approach has led one commentator to state:

---

[121] See, generally, Goode, "The Protection of Interests in Movables in Transnational Commercial Law" [1998] *Unif LR* 453.

[122] Unidroit *Protocol to the Convention on International Interests in Mobile Equipment on Matters Specific to Aircraft Equipment* (the Aircraft Protocol), Article X.

[123] *Ibid* Article XXX.

[124] For a general discussion see below, Stanford, "From Ottawa to Cape Town: Unidroit's Role in the Modernisation of the Law governing Leasing and the Taking of Security" Chapter 11.

> So the field of commercial property rights is carved up slice by slice like a salami and when enough slices have been processed they can be reassembled to provide a corpus of law covering the whole.[125]

At the same time the drafters of the Mobile Equipment Convention realised that an elaborate provision in respect of after-acquired property[126] could lead to an extension of the Convention to assets quite different from those originally conceived which would lead to a potential conflict with the UNCITRAL Convention. It is for this reason that the scope of the Mobile Equipment Convention is restricted to those receivables which are asset specific or proceeds of insurance paid in consequence of loss or damage of equipment, that is, rights associated with interests in equipment. Indeed, this mirrors the function of the international registry which is organised on an asset basis and not by reference to the name of the debtor but rather to the unique identifiers of the relevant equipment.

The adoption of the Unidroit Convention will be significant because property enforcement rights, default remedies and insolvency issues will no longer be seen as exclusively domestic matters. What has been achieved under the Convention is a careful distillation between the problems posed by a single-asset security and security over a group of assets, between mobile and immobile assets, tangible and intangible security and between buyers and lenders.

Conclusion

The retention of title clause is a European phenomenon which is adopted by both civilian and common law jurisdictions as essentially a non-possessory security right. Under the common law, the buyer is deemed to have acquired no property interest other than that which is incidental to possession or which follows from statute. From a formal economic functional perspective what we have here is security for the buyer's trade credit. Analytically, the main difficulty with the legal form of retention of title is that ownership is an unwieldy concept - it provides too many rights

---

[125] Goode *op cit* fn 121 at p 460.

[126] It is possible to register a prospective interest but there are no provisions limiting the priority of future advances or giving special protection to holders of purchase money security interests.

to creditors - it is not surprising, therefore, that both the common law and civilian courts have sought to restrict the scope of such clauses.

The function of secured credit is to reduce risk for the financier.[127] At the same time, the efficacy of the security depends upon the willingness of the applicable legal regime to recognise the rights of the secured party when they come into conflict with various claims, for example, those of other creditors or a liquidator on insolvency. The problem becomes particularly acute when collateral moves from one jurisdiction to another and the issue then becomes the extent to which the laws of the new jurisdiction are conceptually compatible with the law governing the transaction of its inception. Two major techniques are used to deal with cross border movement of goods: first, to create elaborate uniform conflict of law rules; second, to seek unification of substantive rules. The former approach is not satisfactory because it does not offer a direct solution. Indeed, the difficulty with national conflict rules is precisely the diversity of the recognition of non-possessory security interests in Europe and there are, thereby, real risks in collateral crossing boundaries within Europe depending upon whether a jurisdiction has a liberal or traditional approach to the recognition of the non-possessory security interest. As we have seen, the recognition of the validity of retention of title clauses and the formal requirements for establishing such clauses vary greatly from jurisdiction to jurisdiction within Europe. These differences provide a significant obstacle "to a vivid international credit economy for which security upon movables is desired".[128] In any event, it is not possible to deal with retention of title clauses in isolation from other security interests.[129]

It is probably true to say that commercial law where this is defined as a legal regime facilitating the creation and enforcement of security interests in mobile assets "came of age" with the publication in the second half of the twentieth century of Article 9 of the Uniform Commercial Code. Whilst there is no evidence[130] to suggest that the drafters of Article 9 were

---

[127] For a general discussion see Baird, "Security Interests Reconsidered" (1994) 80 *Virginia LR* 2249.

[128] See Drobnig, "Secured Credit in International Insolvency Proceedings" (1998) 33 *Texas International Law Journal* 53 at p 70.

[129] See Monti, Nejman, Reuter, "The Future of Reservation of Title Clauses in the European Community" (1997) 46 *ICLQ* 866 at p 894.

[130] See generally Cuming, "Registration of Security Interests in Mobile Equipment: An International Approach", *Commercial and Consumer Law* Cranston and Goode (ed) (1993) Chapter 6.

consciously laying down principles which would form the basis for the harmonisation of secured financing regimes outside of the USA, nevertheless, the influence of Article 9 has been very great. An explanation for this may be the fact that Article 9 presents reformers with a system of law in that it brings all security devices under one regime by offering a purposive definition of a security interest which is meant to be all-embracing. The unified treatment of security seen in the USA is in stark contrast to that seen in Europe where there are separate regimes for particular types of transaction. These differences cause uncertainty especially in a commercial context where creditors are risk averse which may, therefore, prejudice the extension of credit whilst at the same time the uncertainty increases the transactional costs through higher legal fees as well as other internal creditor costs of time and effort.

During the twentieth century several attempts have been made to achieve some degree of uniformity within the international community with respect to security interests. The Unidroit Convention on International Interests in Mobile Equipment is innovative because it does not seek to harmonise international personal property security law but rather the focus is upon high value equipment as commercial assets moving between frontiers. The nature of this project is not merely to identify "good" law in a jurisdiction and then promote this as a "model law" to be adopted but rather to develop a secured financing law, that is, it represents the convergence of substantive rules of transnational commercial law: the law itself is international emanating from an international source which must be acceded to by national governments. In a real sense, the Unidroit Convention is designed to promote the objectives of asset financing by providing a mechanism recognising bargains, providing clear priority rules and facilitating a strong enforcement regime.

It is self-evident that as economic activity intensifies in the wake of the process of globalisation of the world economy, national frontiers have become less important. High cost equipment such as railway rolling stock, lorries, aircraft and construction equipment move across national frontiers even though they may be subject to security interests arising out of finance extended to the operator/debtor in another jurisdiction. The issue then revolves around the recognition in the new jurisdiction of such interests. In this regard, it is important to distinguish between equipment as commercial assets from mobile consumer goods not least because the public policy considerations involved in recognising foreign security interests are likely to be different. The process of harmonisation requires the identification of common assumptions. Thus, in the case of the European Union, it has been easier to draft directives harmonising rules in respect of consumer matters because of the similar importance of consumers to all Member States. In dealing with the harmonisation of commercial law and especially personal property security law, on the other hand, it is necessary to recognise that there are differences between legal cultures as well as business cultures. In the context of the Unidroit Convention on International Interests in Mobile Equipment, the differences in legal cultures between the common law and civil law are well known. The focus then becomes upon the extent to which businesses involved in the acquisition of and the financing of high value equipment moving between frontiers share a common business assumption both in respect of the Convention and also the appropriate Protocol. The success of the Convention and Protocols will be tested in their acceptance and adoption over time by the international community of what amounts to a new, discrete, international substantive personal property security law regime.

PART III: UNIFORM LAW

10 The Characterisation of Interests and Transactions Under the Convention of International Interests in Mobile Equipment, 2001

RONALD CUMING*

Introduction

The Convention on International Interests in Mobile Equipment (hereafter the "Convention") and an associated Protocol on Matters Specific to Aircraft Equipment was adopted at a diplomatic conference in November of 2001. When it comes into force, it will provide an international regime within which secured financing and leasing of high-value mobile equipment will occur. While the Convention addresses most of the legal issues that will arise out of these transactions, it is not a complete code of law. Peripheral issues are left to be determined under the relevant municipal law. This gives rise to the conflict of laws question as to what this law should be. In this chapter the author has identified some of issues in the context of which this question will arise, and has offered suggestions as to the approach to be used in identifying the most appropriate applicable law.

---

* Professor Cuming was the originator of the proposal for a convention on security interests in mobile equipment generally used in more than one state. He was a member of the Unidroit Study Group, a member of the Canadian Delegation to the three joint Unidroit-ICAO sessions of governmental experts and members of an ICAO Legal Sub-committee, chairperson of the Registration Working Group established at the first joint session, a member of the Canadian Delegation to the meeting of the ICAO Legal Committee on the Convention and Aircraft Protocol and a member of the Registry Task Force established at the second joint session.

Background

The basic structures of the Convention and Aircraft Protocol were developed by the International Institute on Unification of Private Law (Unidroit). Late in the development process, the International Civil Aviation Organisation (ICAO) became involved[1] because of the interest in the project demonstrated by the aircraft industry, including manufacturers, airlines and financiers.[2] Additional refinements were made at the meeting of the ICAO Legal Committee[3] and were approved by the ICAO Council. Drafts of the Convention and Aircraft Protocol were presented to the diplomatic conference in South Africa.

The problem that induced interest in a convention of this kind was the lack of recognition, priority or enforcement in one State of a security interest in mobile equipment created under the laws of another State.[4] The Convention is a body of international substantive law that addresses the central legal elements of secured financing and leasing of high-value

---

[1] Three Unidroit-ICAO co-sponsored meetings of governmental experts and members of an ICAO legal subcommittee were held in 1999 and 2000 at which the Unidroit proposals were further developed. See *Report of the First Joint Session of the Unidroit Committee of governmental experts and the Sub-Committee of the ICAO Legal Committee on the preparation of a draft Convention on International Interests in Mobile Equipment and a draft Protocol thereto on Matters Specific to Aircraft Equipment*, Unidroit CGE/Int Int/-Report; ICAO Ref LSC/ME/2-Report; *Report of the Second Session* (Dec 1999), Unidroit CGE/Int Int/2-Report; ICAO Ref LSC/ME/2-Report; *Report of the Third Session* (Mar 2000), Unidroit CGE/Int Int/3-Report; ICAO Ref LSC/ME/3-Report.

[2] The Convention has been designed to apply to a range of different types of mobile equipment. Article 2(3) lists three categories of equipment to which it will apply: aircraft objects (airframes, aircraft engines and helicopters), railway rolling stock and space property. Article 51 provides for the development and adoption of protocols dealing with other types of high-value mobile equipment. Because of the early participation of an Aviation Working Group formed by representatives of a wide range of organizations involved in the sale, financing and use of commercial aircraft with a mandate to work with Unidroit in the preparation of the Convention, the Aircraft Protocol was the first to reach full development. As a result, it was possible to address this protocol along with the convention at the diplomatic conference.

[3] See Legal Committee - 31st Session, Doc 9765-LC/191 (Nov 6/00).

[4] See, generally, Cuming RCC, "International Regulation of Aspects of Security Interests in Mobile Equipment" [1990-91] *Unif LR* 64 at pp 77-89, and Shilling, "Some European Decisions on Non-possessory Security Rights in Private International Law" (1985) 34 *ICLQ* 87.

mobile equipment: creation of interests, priority of interests, public disclosure of interests and enforcement following default.[5] In addition it provides for the extension of the registration and priority rules to "non-consensual rights or interests," such as repairers' or suppliers' liens, tax liens and wage liens, that a Contracting State elects to treat as consensual international interest.[6]

The location of the chargor, lessee or buyer in a Contracting State at the time of execution of the security agreement, lease or conditional sale is the factor that invokes application of the Convention.[7] The location of the secured party (chargee), lessor or seller is not relevant. Article IV of the Aircraft Protocol provides, however, that the Convention will apply to a transaction involving an aircraft if the aircraft is registered in a Contracting State or an agreement exits that the aircraft will be registered in a Contracting State. The Convention will apply to what in other contexts would be a transaction governed by national law because all or most of the factors relating to the agreement and the equipment are located in a single state. However, a limited exception is allowed. A Contracting State will be entitled to declare that the Convention will not apply to "an internal

---

[5] The Aircraft Protocol provides that the Convention's priority and registration provisions apply to sales of aircraft and aircraft engines. See Protocol, Article III and Convention, Article 41. While this will not provide a title registration system, it will have a similar force with respect to aircraft and engines purchased from manufacturers after the Convention and Protocol come into effect. A potential buyer will be able to search the "chain of ownership" from the manufacturer to the seller. A person who buys on the strength of this information will take free from an intervening transfer of ownership that has not been registered.

[6] The term "non-consensual right or interest" is defined in Article 1(s) as a right or interest conferred by law to secure the performance of an obligation, including an obligation to a State or State entity. Under Article 40, a State may declare that specified non-consensual rights or interests are to be treated as interests to which the Convention applies. The result is that these interests will be subject to the registration requirements and priority rules of the Convention and Protocol. An alternative approach is offered by Article 39. It provides that a State may make a declaration setting out a list of non-consensual rights or interests having priority under the national law of that State and that will have priority under the Convention. These rights or interests will not be subject to the registration requirement or priority regime of the Convention. The list of such interests will be kept on record at the International Registry. See Article 23.

[7] Articles 3 and 4. See also Article III, Aircraft Protocol.

transaction."[8] However, the effect of such a declaration will be limited since it will not exempt the transaction from the registration and priority rules of the Convention.[9]

The priority structure of the Convention is dependent upon an international registry for international interests and registerable non-consensual interests. Articles 15-27 of the Convention prescribe the basic features of the registries that will be established under protocols. They will be notice-based,[10] electronic systems.[11] The registry established under the Aircraft Protocol will be accessible for all purposes from any place in the world having facilities for transmitting registration data to the registry.

The priority rules of the Convention are very simple. Competing registered interests will rank in order of their registration,[12] and a registered interest will have priority over an unregistered interest. Knowledge of a prior unregistered interest will not affect the priority status of a holder of a registered interest.[13] Similarly, an unregistered international interest will be subordinate to the interest of a person who buys the property subject to an international interest from the chargor, lessee or conditional buyer. This is so whether or not the buyer's interest was acquired with or without actual

---

[8] Article 50. An "internal transaction" is defined in Article 1(n) as "a transaction ... where the centre of the main interests of all parties is situated, and the relevant object is located (as specified in the Protocol) in the same Contracting State at the time of the conclusion of the transaction and where the interest created by the transaction has been registered in a national registry of a Contracting State, which has made a declaration under Article 50".

[9] Article 50(2).

[10] A notice based system is one under which only specified data relating to transactions, not copies of contracts, are entered into the registry data base. In the context of the Aircraft Protocol, registration information relating to a transaction will be the type of agreement, the name and location of the chargee, lessor or seller, the name and location of the chargor, lessee or buyer and a detailed description of the aircraft object that is the subject-matter of the transactions. It will not include reference to the obligations of the chargor, lessee or seller or the terms of payment.

[11] Article 17(2)(i).

[12] Article 29(1). As to priority in the case of competing buyers, see Aircraft Protocol, Article XIV(1)-(2). The Convention does not affect the rights of a person in an item held prior to its installation on property to which the Convention applies if under the applicable law those rights continue after installation. Nor does it prevent the creation of rights recognised under the applicable law in such an item when it is installed.

[13] Article 29(2).

knowledge of the unregistered international interest. A registered international interest will have priority over a trustee in bankruptcy and execution or attaching creditors. Otherwise, an international interest will have the same priority in insolvency proceedings that it has under the law applicable to the proceedings.[14] If, under that law, the interest is valid against the trustee or administrator without registration, the lack of registration in the international registry will not be relevant.

A Regime of International Substantive Secured Financing Law

A report prepared for Unidroit[15] addressing the need for and feasibility of a convention on security interests in mobile equipment recommended a convention that would provide universally accepted choice of law rules supplemented by substantive priority rules.[16] The failure of a project undertaken by the United Nations Commission on International Trade Law[17] designed to develop a body of substantive international secured financing law induced the author to conclude that States were not willing at that time to accept such a radical step. In 1992 an exploratory working group of Unidroit composed of experts in secured financing of large equipment agreed that a project to develop a convention in this area was useful and feasible. However, the group concluded that the convention should not be based principally on choice of law rules but should provide a regime of substantive international secured financing law.[18] The Convention resulted from this approach.

The Convention is unprecedented in that it provides for a regime that in substantial measure will displace the municipal law of the Contracting States that would otherwise govern the types of transactions to which the Convention applies. It will implement a priority regime based on a single,

---

[14] Article 30.

[15] Cuming RCC, "International Regulation of Aspects of Security Interests in Mobile Equipment" *op cit* fn 4.

[16] *Ibid.*

[17] For a brief description of the UNCITRAL Project, see Cuming, *op cit* fn 4 at pp 123-132.

[18] See Unidroit 1992, Study LXXXII - Doc 5, *Report of the March 1992 meeting of the Restricted Exploratory Working Group to Examine the Feasibility of Drawing up Uniform Rules on Certain Aspects of Security Interests in Mobile Equipment.*

world-wide registry system designed to reduce dramatically the legal risk associated with acquiring interests in property subject to international interests. It will enable the parties to a secured financing transaction to use forms of agreements not recognised by the municipal law of many States. The result will be that persons located in Contracting States will have available to them a system of international law for the creation and regulation of rights even though the municipal law of these States does not provide for transactions of this kind.

While in most respects, interests arising under the Convention are *sui generis* and are governed by the Convention, the unprecedented approach contained in the Convention has resulted in questions that were not addressed by its drafters. Matters not specifically or implicitly controlled by the Convention will fall within the aegis of national law. A consistent approach to the choice of law that governs these issues will be an important factor in ensuring uniform application of the Convention.

The Structural Pattern of the Convention

The Convention "Security Interest"

Apart from the simple possessory pledge, there is no unitary concept of "security agreement" among the families of legal systems or among national legal systems belonging to the same legal family. Secured financing law is grounded in concepts of property, some of which are peculiar to particular families of law. This area of law embodies cultural attitudes and public policy choices that vary greatly among States or subdivisions of States with federal structures.[19] Civil law jurisdictions have only recently recognised formally in their codes the possibility of a non-possessory pledge. In several jurisdictions whose secured financing law was copied from England, traditional forms of agreements are used without formal recognition of their function as secured financing devices. This reality presented an important issue for the designers of the Convention. They realized that little would be gained by attempting to synthesize the concepts contained in the many national legal systems. This would result in a crazy-quilt of concepts and rules that would please no one, least of all

---

[19] See, generally, Cuming RCC, "The Internationalization of Secured Financing Law: The Spreading Influence of the Concepts of UCC, Article 9 and its Progeny" *Making Commercial Law - Essays in Honour of Roy Goode,* Cranston (ed) (1997) at p 22.

financiers and borrowers who have the greatest interest in an efficient international system for security interests in mobile equipment. A different approach was required.

While the Convention reflects some deference to national laws, generally, it eschews traditional formalism and employs a simple, functional approach to identification of the secured financing devices it recognises and regulates. Its focus is on the practical needs of parties to and persons affected by secured financing transactions, and not the conceptual structure of any particular national legal system. However, if one were forced to draw parallels to any particular national systems, it would be to those of the United States and Canada.[20] This is a product, not of a desire to force the conceptual structure of these systems onto the world, but of the similarity between the approach used to develop them and that used in the Convention. The North American systems represent a genuine attempt to have secured financing law that reflects the needs of the persons directly affected by it, and that, as much as possible, is free from traditional, outmoded legal concepts. The desire of the drafters of the Convention to design a system that would attract the support of the international financing community led to the use of a very similar approach. What is required is an efficient system that provides legal predictability and concomitant reduction in legal risk.

The Convention applies to, *inter alia*, a "security agreement" providing for a security interest[21] in kinds of mobile equipment specified in protocols. The term is defined in Article 1(ii) as "an agreement by which a chargor grants or agrees to grant to a chargee an interest (including an ownership interest) in or over an object to secure the performance of an existing or future obligation of the chargor or a third person". The nature and extent of the interest is not determinative, and how it arises is not important. The interest can be created by a transfer of ownership from the obligor (chargor) to the obligee (chargee) or through its simple recognition in the agreement. The chargor need not have an interest in the object at the date of execution of the agreement. However, as soon as an interest is

---

[20] See Uniform Commercial Code, Article 9; The Personal Property Security Act, R S S 1978, c P-6.2 (which is representative of personal property security law of most other Canadian provinces and territories) and Quebec Civil Code, Book Six, Title Three.

[21] "Security interest" is defined in Article 1(jj) as "an interest created by a security agreement". "Secured obligation" is defined in Article 1(hh) as "an obligation secured by a security interest".

acquired, the international interest arises without any specific step of appropriation on the part of the chargor or the chargee.

While the Convention is not explicit as to the nature of a security interest, it contains clues indicating what, in general terms, is involved. The use of the terms "chargor" and "chargee" in the English version of the definition of "security agreement" is instructive. While these terms indicate a hypothecation, the definition makes it clear that a transaction in the form of an English common law bill of sale by mortgage (chattel mortgage)[22] is within the scope of the Convention. The reference in the definition of "security agreement" to "grant" of an "interest" or agreement to grant an interest provides additional guidance.[23] It necessarily suggests that the chargor has or will acquire a property interest in an object that the chargor agrees is subject to or is to become subject to an *in rem* claim of the chargee. As a result of Article 7, an international interest cannot be created unless the equipment affected by it is "an object of which the chargor... has the power to dispose". This suggests that the chargor need not itself have a property right in the object, it is sufficient that it has the power under the applicable law to charge a property interest in the object. This power could be based on agency or, possibly, estoppel. What is clear, however, is that the charge affects property rights held by or under the control of the chargor.

National Security Interests under the Convention

The Convention permits the creation of an international security interest even though the nature and form of such an interest is unknown to the law of the jurisdictions in which the parties to the agreement creating it or the

---

[22] A fiduciary transfer of title such as the German *sicherungsubereignung* involves transfer of ownership by the debtor to the creditor. The purpose of the transfer is to secure an obligation of the transferee to the transferor. The transaction is based on statutory provisions dealing with ownership under which it is not necessary to give up possession of goods in order to transfer full title. See §§ 929 to 936 BGB (German Civil Code). Unlike a common law chattel mortgage, the debtor is not viewed as the beneficial owner of the collateral. Consequently, the transferee does not have a charge on the debtor's property; the transferee is the owner. Notwithstanding this, it would appear to fall within the specific wording of the definition of "security agreement".

[23] Article 2(2) provides that "an international interest in mobile equipment is an interest, constituted under Article 7, in a uniquely identifiable object of a category of object", set out in the Convention and designated in the Protocol.

subject-matter of security agreement are located. However, an international security interest may also be a security interest under the national law of one or both of the parties to the agreement. Most transactions that are security agreements under national law would fall within the generic definition of "security interest" in the Convention.[24]

As a practical matter, it is very likely that national forms of security agreements will be used to create national security interests that qualify as international security interests. Legal advisors will want to continue to use forms of transactions that are familiar to them and which will invoke national law to deal with perceived or suspected lacunae in the Convention regime.[25] The Convention will accommodate this practice. The parties are given a great deal of freedom to craft their agreement to meet their specific needs.[26] The writing requirements for an international security agreement are minimal and easily met.[27] The international registry will provide for the registration of a simple notice relating to an agreement or a prospective agreement and not a prescribed form of agreement.[28]

Characterisation of Interests under the Convention

While an international security interest arising under the Convention is *sui generis* and can exist without being recognised by the national law of the parties to the security agreement, it is not totally independent of that law. Whether it is viewed as a hypothecation or transfer of ownership, it is an *in rem* interest in property. The power of disposal referred to in Article 7 necessarily implies that the chargor has or acquires property to charge or has the power to charge property belonging to someone else. Given the

---

[24] If it is assumed that a security interest under the Convention is essentially a hypothec, transactions, other than those involving transfer of ownership to a creditor, that function as security agreements without having the characteristics of a hypothec may not be included. For example, a deferred "right of redemption" under Article 1756 of the Quebec Civil Code provides security to a seller. Article 1750 defines a sale with a right of redemption as one containing a resolutory condition by which the seller transfers ownership to the buyer while reserving the right to redeem it (that is, take it back).

[25] The use of an agreement in a form recognised by national law does not preclude the parties from asserting rights under the Convention that cannot be asserted under national law.

[26] Article 15.

[27] Article 7.

[28] Article 17(2)(i).

generic nature of a Convention security interest, there is no need to determine the nature of that interest other than to recognise that it is proprietary. However, since the draft Convention does not define what constitutes property for this purpose, it will be necessary to go to national law to get guidance in making this determination. Consequently, whether or not an international security interest exists may depend upon what national law is applied. The reason for this is that the concept of "property" is not uniform across families of law. For example, a lessee is viewed by the common law as having a special property interest in movable property in his or her possession.[29] It is not inconceivable that a lessee who holds mobile equipment under a long term lease would charge that interest in the equipment. However, a lessee is viewed as having only a possessory interest under most civil law systems and, consequently, does not have an interest that can support an international security interest.[30]

A very similar issue arises in the context of conditional sales agreements. Under the law of many jurisdictions, a buyer under a title reservation agreement does not acquire a property interest until the conditions of sale have been met and title passes. This is so even though the buyer has paid a substantial portion of the purchase price of the goods being purchased. Consequently, until full performance of the contract, the buyer has no interest to charge. However, under the law of other jurisdictions, the buyer is viewed as the owner of the goods and seller as having only a charge or security interest.[31] As owner, the buyer can create a second charge on its ownership interest. If the issue of enforcement of an international interest in a lessee's or buyer's interest arises, the determination of whether or not there is an international interest to enforce may depend upon the law applied to address the nature of the lessee's or

---

[29] See, generally, Cuming R and Wood R, *Alberta Personal Property Security Act Handbook* 4th ed (1998) pp 146-150; McDonnell J, "*Overview of Secured Financing, Chapter 2B: Rights in the Collateral*" in Coogan, Hogan, Vagts and McDonnell, *Bender's Secured Transactions under the Uniform Commercial Code* (2000) §§ 2B 05 and 2B 06.

[30] One way to eliminate any problems of this kind is to conclude that the Convention applies only to interests in objects and not to interests in limited interests in objects. There is some support for this approach in the definition of "security agreement" in Article 1(ii) which refers to the grant of "an interest... in or over an object to secure the performance" of an obligation. It is suggested, however, while this very narrow reading of the scope of the Convention may be etymologically justifiable, it was not the intention of the drafters.

[31] See text following fn 40, *infra*.

buyer's interest. If the court applies civil law concepts, it may well conclude no international interest exists that can be enforced. If, however, the matter comes before a court that applies the common law, an international interest would be found to exist and would be enforceable according to the terms of the contract and applicable provisions of the Convention.

Characterisation may affect priorities as well as enforcement issues. For example, assume a buyer under a conditional sales contract has given a "security interest" in its buyer's interest to a lender and the lender registered its interest in the international registry. The conditional seller's interest, which is an international interest under the Convention,[32] has not been registered. Whether the lender will have priority over the conditional seller will depend upon the characterisation of the lender's interest. If it is an "international interest" the priority rules of the Convention will apply giving priority to the lender.[33] If it is not, the Convention will not apply.[34]

Characterisation of Transactions under the Convention

The scope of the Convention is not confined to international interests created under security agreements. It extends as well to title reservations agreements and leasing agreements.[35] A "title reservation agreement" is defined in Article 1(ll) as "an agreement for the sale of an object on terms that ownership does not pass until fulfilment of the condition or conditions stated in the agreement." The seller is defined as a "conditional seller"[36] and the buyer as a "conditional buyer".[37] A "leasing agreement" is defined in Article 1(q) as "an agreement by which one person (a lessor) grants a right to possession or control of an object (with or without an option to purchase) to another person (a lessee) in return for a rental or other

---

[32] See text following fn 34, *infra*.

[33] Article 29.

[34] A sale by the conditional buyer would result in the buyer taking free from the conditional seller's interest. See Article 29(4). However, it does not follow from this that the conditional buyer has an interest that can be charged thereby creating an international interest.

[35] Article 2(2).

[36] Article 1(f).

[37] Article 1(e).

payment". The conditional seller's or lessor's ownership interests are international interests governed by the Convention.[38]

The approach contained in the Convention under which the three types of agreements are separately identified creates no difficulties for legal systems that rely heavily on formalism when categorising transactions. These include most national systems. However, a more complex approach is required in the context of the secured financing systems of the United States and the common law jurisdictions of Canada[39] that focus on function and reject formalism as a factor in characterising transactions as security agreements, leases or conditional sales contracts.[40]

The secured financing law of these jurisdictions defines conditional sales contracts as security agreements and not as transactions under which the conditional seller has ownership and the conditional buyer only possession with a contractual right to become owner upon fulfilling specified conditions. Under this approach, the conditional buyer is the owner of the goods and the conditional seller has a security interest or charge on those goods. Recognising that, functionally, leases are frequently used as secured financing devices in the United States[41] and Canadian common law systems, the secured financing law of these jurisdictions attaches little importance to form in the determination as to whether a particular transaction is a true lease or a security agreement in the form of a lease. The application of a function test to characterise lease transactions requires an examination of the relationship between the lessor and lessee in order to determine if, in that relationship, the standard indicia of a secured credit arrangement are to be found. The pertinent indicia are those that would be relevant to a person focusing on the economic significance of the

[38] No issue of characterisation of interests arises in this context. It is clear that the ownership of a lessor or a seller under a title reservation contract is an international interest under the Convention.

[39] The secured financing law of Quebec parallels that of the draft Convention. Neither a conditional sale nor a lease *(crédit-bail)* is treated as creating an hypothec. See generally, Quebec Civil Code, Articles 1745-1749 and 1842-1850.

[40] For example, Section 3 of the Saskatchewan Personal Property Security Act, 1993, *supra* fn 20 provides that the Act applies "to every transaction that in substance creates a security interest, without regard to its form and with regard to the person who has title to the collateral..."

[41] See Uniform Commercial Code, § 1-201(37) which sets out a list of factors a court should take into account when determining whether a transaction is a true lease or a security lease.

transaction.[42] If the practical effect of a transaction labelled a lease is to give the lessee most of the incidents of ownership though not legal title, the transaction is in substance a security agreement. Passage of ownership or title in a technical sense is not relevant. However, ownership in a non-technical sense is relevant. If the lessee is required to pay what is the equivalent of the lessor's capital investment in the leased asset plus a credit charge at the rate existing at the date of the agreement, there is strong but not conclusive evidence of a secured sale. A clause in a lease giving the lessee the option to purchase the goods at less than their expected market value (as determined at the date of execution) indicates that the lessee has acquired an equity in the goods not unlike that which would have been acquired under an instalment purchase contract. The economic reality is that it is quite predictable that the lessee will pay this amount to the lessor. Consequently, the transaction is likely to be characterised as a security agreement.

A transaction in the form of a title reservation agreement would be viewed very differently if the applicable law were the secured financing regime of the United States or a common law province of Canada than it would be if the applicable law were that of most other jurisdictions in the world. A transaction in the form of a lease that would be characterised as a lease in a jurisdiction that employs a formal test could be a security agreement under the law of a jurisdiction that applies a functional test.[43]

While the characterisation of a particular transaction as a security agreement rather than a lease or title reservation agreement does not affect the application of the priority rules of the Convention or its registration requirements, it does affect the remedies of a defaulting chargor, lessee or buyer. Under Article 9 the remedies of a lessor or conditional seller are those of an owner: simple recovery of the leased or sold object is permitted. Under Articles 7 and 8, the remedies of a chargee are those of a secured party. These remedies are designed to provide protection to the chargor's interest in the object.

---

[42] See §1-201(37) Uniform Commercial Code; and, Cuming RCC, "True Leases and Security Leases Under Canadian Personal Property Security Acts" (1982-83) 7 *Can Bus LJ* 251.

[43] This is not to suggest that in the United States or in the common law provinces of Canada all leases are treated as security agreements. If the transaction is functionally not a security agreement, it is treated as a "true" lease.

The Law that Governs Characterisation of Interests and Transactions under the Convention

It is clear that fundamental issues of characterisation could arise under the Convention. The final outcome of a dispute may well be affected by whether an interest is characterised as a property interest or a contractual right, or if a transaction is characterised as a lease or title reservation agreement, on the one hand, or a security agreement, on the other.

Article 2(4) provides that "the applicable law determines whether an international interest falls within" one or another of the three specified categories of interests set out in Article 2(2). Since the Convention offers no specific guidance on the question of what law governs characterisation of interests as being property interests or personal rights, this too must be determined under the applicable law. There are two difficulties associated with this approach. The first is that, because private international laws of nations are not uniform, different answers may be provided to the question of characterisation depending upon what is determined to be the applicable law. The second difficulty, at least in the context of common law jurisdictions, is that there is little helpful guidance in the case law as to what law governs characterisation of interests and transactions.[44]

Several possibilities might be considered. One of these draws inspiration from Article 42 of the Convention which provides a choice of jurisdiction rule. Subject to specified exceptions not relevant to this analysis, the "parties to a transaction" are free to choose by agreement the or courts of a Contracting State that will have exclusive jurisdiction "in respect of any claim brought under this Convention". The general rule is that a choice of jurisdiction is a strong indicator of an implicit choice of the substantive law applicable to the contract within which the choice is made.[45] A superficial analysis would lead to the conclusion that, by addressing the issue of jurisdiction, the parties have implicitly selected the law applicable to characterisation.[46] This view is not persuasive.[47] In the

---

[44] What is being addressed here is characterisation of interests and transactions and not characterisation of legal issues for the purposes of determining what set of rules apply to those issues. However, some of the same considerations are involved. See, generally, *Morris: The Conflict of Laws* by McLean, 5th ed (2000) pp 491-497.

[45] See, for example, *Hamlyn & Co* v *Talisker Distillery* [1984] A C 202 at p 212.

[46] Article VIII of the Aircraft Protocol provides that the parties to an agreement may agree on the law which is to govern their contractual rights and obligations under the Convention.

first place, Article 42 deals only with a choice of law by the parties to a transaction. Characterisation issues are not limited to *inter partes* matters. They affect third party rights to the extent that priority determinations are involved. Further, these issues are not purely contractual; they involve property or, at least, the determination of whether or not a property interest exists. The conception of property is a matter of general law, not private agreement. Consequently, characterisation cannot be a matter left to the choice of the parties to an agreement.

A second possibility is that the *lex situs* of the object at the date when the interest arose determines characterisation. The *lex situs* is often employed to address issues associated with interests in movable property.[48] However, this is equally problematic. Since the situs of highly mobile movable property at any particular time will, in many cases, be either casual or fortuitous, it is an inappropriate source of law applicable to substantive law issues associated with the property. Indeed, it was the failure of this approach that was the impetus for the Convention.[49]

In the absence of clear guidance on the matter, courts will be tempted to characterise interests and transactions according to their own law. As a result, the rights of the affected parties may differ significantly depending upon the jurisdiction in which the issue arises. This would be contrary to the purpose and spirit of the Convention.

It is the author's view that issues of characterisation are best determined under the law of the location of the chargor, lessee or buyer, as the case may be, at the time the international interest comes into existence.[50] The primary attraction of this approach is that this law is constant with respect to a particular transaction. It is the one source of law that produces the same result regardless of the State in which the issue of

---

[47] It is the author's view that the decision of the Ontario (Canada) Supreme Court in *Re Intex Moulding Ltd.* (1978), 38 D L R (4th) 111 in this respect is wrong. In this case the court held that characterisation of a lease as a security agreement was to be made under the proper law of the contract. See *contra, Gimli Auto Ltd* v *BDO Dunworthy Ltd* (1998), 160 D L R (4th) 373 (Alberta CA). In the context of United States law, the parties are free, as between themselves, to choose the law applicable to characterisation of transactions. However, this choice cannot affect issues involving priorities or third party rights. See § 1-105 Uniform Commercial Code and Official Comment 2 to § 9- 301 (1998).

[48] See Castel J-G, *Canadian Conflict of Laws* 4th ed (1998) p 81.

[49] See *supra* fn 4.

[50] In the great bulk of cases this will be the location of the chargor, lessee or buyer at the date the international agreement is executed.

characterisation arises.[51] This would provide predictability to secured parties, lessors and sellers when assessing the legal risk associated with entering into a transaction involving the types of property referred to in Article 2(3) of the Convention. They would know whether or not the interest being charged will be recognised as sufficient to support a charge under the Convention. They would know whether the transaction they enter into will be treated in all Contracting States as a security agreement, on the one hand, or a title retention agreement or lease, on the other. These are the same considerations that have induced experts to focus on the *lex situs* of goods that are not highly mobile.[52]

Experience has demonstrated that resort to the law of the location of the chargor at the time a security interest comes into existence is works very well where interests in highly mobile goods are involved. The statutory conflict of laws rules of Canadian jurisdictions[53] employ this approach to address issues of validity, priorities and the registration requirements relating to security interests in mobile equipment. Very few significant problems have been encountered with this approach in a much broader context than that addressed in this paper. There is no reason to

[51] Under Article 3 it is the connecting factor that determines whether or not the Convention applies to the transaction. It specifies the law (that is, the Convention) that applies to the central elements of the relationships associated with the transactions.

[52] The policy basis for choosing the *lex situs* of goods as the source of law to regulate issues of validity and priority of a security interest in goods is that "the physical location of a chattel constitutes an objective criterion, which is easily ascertainable, and the *lex situs* is the only law, the application of which people may reasonably be taken to expect. .... The *lex situs* is not only simpler and more convenient than any other to apply, but it is better suited to protect the interests both of the owner and of other parties". LaLive, *The Transfer of Chattels in the Conflicts of Laws* (1995) pp 114-115.

[53] See, for example, section 7, The Saskatchewan Personal Property Security Act, 1993, *supra* fn 20. This is representative of rules existing in all Canadian Personal Property Security Acts. See also Quebec Civil Code, Book Ten, Title One, Article 3102 *et seq.* The same approach was prescribed by former conflict of laws rules of states of the United States. See § 9-103, 1978 Official Text. However, a different approach which reflects a much more parochial view was employed in the 1998 Official Text of Article 9 of the Uniform Commercial Code. Under § 9-301, perfection of a security interest in goods is regulated by the law of the location of the debtor. However, priorities are determined by the law of the location of the collateral.

think the approach would not produce the desired result in the context of the Convention.

The prevailing jurisprudence in Canada indicates that characterisation of a transaction as being within or outside the scope of provincial Personal Property Security Acts is determined by the *lex fori*.[54] This is a reasonable approach where the question is the applicability of features of that law. For example, if the law of a jurisdiction requires that security agreements in the form of leases be registered, the policy basis for registration would be defeated if the issue whether an agreement relating to goods located in the forum is a security agreement or a true lease were to be determined under the law of a foreign jurisdiction that does not recognise the distinction between true leases and security leases. However, where the issue is the application of the Convention, to which the forum State is a party, the considerations are quite different. Resort by a court to the law of another State when addressing characterisation of interests or transactions otherwise governed by a convention that is part of the law of forum state would not involve frustration of the law of that State. Third parties in that State who have acquired competing interests to which the Convention applies are not prejudiced when their claims are in competition with international interests that draw some of their substance from the law of the location of the chargor, lessee or buyer. Their priority rights are governed by the Convention law. Even if, under the domestic law of that State, the secured party in the priority competition would not be viewed as having a charge on the object, persons who deal with the chargor, lessee or buyer in possession are protected through the registration requirements and priority rules of the Convention. In the context of characterisation of transactions referred to in Article 2(2) of the Convention, the forum court could not be unduly burdened by the requirement to treat a transaction as a security agreement rather than a lease or title reservation agreement.[55]

The Role of Article 5 of the Convention

Article 5(2) of the Convention provides that questions concerning matters governed by the Convention which are not expressly settled in it are to be

---

[54] See *Gimli Auto Ltd* v *BDO Dunworthy Ltd, loc cit* fn 47; *Jukes* v *Holiday Chevrolet Oldsmobile (1988) Ltd,* (1990) 82 Sask R 303 (Saskatchewan Queen's Bench). See also Quebec Civil Code, Book Ten, Title One, Article 3078.

[55] This requirement would extend only to matters addressed in the Convention. For practical purposes this is likely to involve enforcement only.

settled in conformity with the general principles on which it is based or, in the absence of such principles, in conformity with the applicable law. Article 5(3) provides that references to the applicable law are to the domestic rules of law applicable by virtue of the rules of private international law of the forum State.

Article 5(2) was copied from Article 7(2) of the United Nations Convention on the International Sale of Goods (1980) (Vienna Sales Convention).[56] Professor Honnold notes that Article 7(2) of the Vienna Convention is the product of a compromise representing a delicate balance between developing the Vienna Sales Convention's general principles and recourse to domestic law.[57] He cautions that the two aspects of the compromise should not be seen as being of equal relevance. Emphasis on the latter will threaten the *raison d'être* of the instrument - international uniformity of law. A "generous response"[58] to the invitation to develop the Vienna Sales Convention through the general principles upon which it is based is to be preferred.

The author's opinion is that application of the "general principles" on which the Convention is based leads to the law of the location of the debtor, lessee or buyer, as the case may be, when dealing with issues of characterisation. However, there is an impediment to the use of this approach when addressing the characterisation of agreements. As noted above, Article 2(4) provides that the applicable law determines whether a particular transaction is a security agreement, on the one hand, or a lease or conditional sale contract, on the other. As a result of Article 5(3), this law must be that applicable by virtue of the rules of private international law of the forum State. Consequently, a court is precluded from applying the "general principles upon which" the Convention is bases when determining the law applicable to the characterisation of a transaction unless, in the unlikely event, it also concludes that the Convention is an aspect of the private international law of the forum.[59]

---

[56] In turn, Article 7(2) was based on Article 17 of the Uniform Law of International Sales, 1964.

[57] Honnold, *Uniform Law For International Sales* 3rd ed at p 109.

[58] *Ibid* at p 110.

[59] The draft Convention presented to the Diplomatic Conference did not have this weakness. Article 2(4) of the draft provided that the "Convention does not determine" the characterisation of transactions referred to in Article 2(2). Under this formulation it would have been possible to apply the "general principles" of the Convention as a basis for the conclusion that the applicable law is that of the location of the debtor, lessee or buyer at the time the interest comes into existence.

However, there is nothing in the Convention to preclude application of Article 5(2) when characterising interests. Article 5(2) permits the use of the principles on which the Convention is based to deal with "questions concerning matters governed by the Convention which are not expressly settled in it". Characterisation of interests is governed by the Convention. Indeed, it is a matter that is fundamental to its scope of application. What is not expressly addressed is the method of determining the law that governs characterisation of interests. However, these principles call for the application of the *lex situs* of the debtor, lessee or buyer, as the case may be.

Summary

The principal goal of the drafters of the Convention was to provide a uniform international legal regime for the regulation of financing transactions involving mobile, high-value equipment.[60] A central feature of the Convention is its transcendence of the municipal law. However, since the Convention is not a complete code of law dealing with rights arising under international transactions that fall within its scope, some resort must be had to external law to address gaps in its regime.

The approach suggested in this article to the choice of law dealing with characterisation of interests and transactions would further the underlying policy of the Convention. If it were applied, there would be a significant reduction in the chances that different outcomes will be produced by the fortuitous event that an issue is litigated in one Contracting State and not another. If matters of characterisation are referred to the law the location of the chargor, lessee or buyer at the date the international interest comes into effect, legal predictability, so important to international secured financing, will be substantially enhanced.

It is not difficult to demonstrate that the general principles of the Convention dictate as much uniformity of law as is practicable in an international context. Uniformity is not possible if the approach to selection of the law applicable to characterisation is not itself uniform. In the light of this, it hard to understand why the drafter permitted the application of these general principles with respect to characterisation of interests but not characterisation of transactions.

---

[60] See Preamble.

11 From Ottawa to Cape Town: Unidroit's Role in the Modernisation of the Law governing Leasing and the Taking of Security

MARTIN STANFORD

Certain Preliminary Methodological Considerations

Efforts in the field of the international unification of law have up until relatively recently tended to be concentrated essentially on initiatives designed to unify existing rules of domestic law concerning activities of sufficiently transnational importance as to make the absence of uniform international rules a major source of legal uncertainty for commercial parties contemplating engaging in such activities. This was notably the case with Unidroit's two 1964 Hague Conventions on the International Sale of Goods[1] and its 1983 Geneva Convention on Agency in the International Sale of Goods. One of the principal drawbacks to such efforts has naturally been the difficulty encountered in persuading States to give up this or that rule of their domestic law in favour of a new uniform rule. However, this difficulty is often as nothing compared to the problems that arise when it comes to such States deciding whether or not to ratify or accede to such Conventions. It is a fact that the most successful efforts in the field of the unification of law have often occurred in those areas where uniform law serves the dual function of providing a uniform international legal framework for international manifestations of a particular type of commercial activity and filling a legal vacuum regarding such activity at

[1] The Convention relating to a Uniform Law on the Formation of Contracts for the International Sale of Goods and the Convention relating to a Uniform Law on the International Sale of Goods.

the domestic level. One of the most striking examples of such a phenomenon is the 1929 Warsaw Convention for the Unification of Certain Rules relating to International Carriage by Air, which, apart from governing international carriage by air for decades, has also provided the basis for the enactment of domestic carriage by air rules.

An area where developments in the international market place indicated that there was scope for the launching of a similar initiative in the 1970s, namely in respect of those novel contractual techniques developed by commercial parties, in particular among the financial community, to meet newly perceived market needs for which the existing range of contractual schemata had proven to be inadequate, was therefore seized upon with alacrity by the International Institute for the Unification of Private Law (Unidroit).[2] Thus it was in 1974 that Unidroit initiated work on the preparation of uniform rules for two such techniques. The first of these concerned that type of leasing which has since gone on to enjoy world wide success by reason of its ability to provide flexible financing terms and important cash flow benefits for small and medium-sized businesses, particularly in developing countries and countries with transition economies, for which lease finance will often represent the only source of funds permitting the acquisition of those categories of high-value capital equipment essential for them to modernise their means of production and thus to create vital new pockets of national wealth. The other initiative launched that same year by Unidroit concerned that type of factoring which has in recent years enabled more and more small- and medium-sized businesses, in return for assigning their debts, to obtain invaluable finance necessary to permit them to expand their production capacity.

---

[2] Unidroit is an intergovernmental Organisation with 59 member States drawn from all four corners of the world. It has its seat in Rome at Villa Aldobrandini. Its basic statutory objective is to prepare uniform private law rules, of a substantive nature, for adoption by States. Over its 75-year existence it has sponsored many international instruments, the most recent being the 2001 Cape Town Convention on International Interests in Mobile Equipment and Protocol thereto on Matters specific to Aircraft Equipment. Draft Conventions prepared by it have also served as the basis for many other international Conventions adopted under the auspices of other international Organisations, the most celebrated of which is perhaps the 1956 Geneva Convention on the Contract for the International Carriage of Goods by Road (commonly referred to as the CMR Convention). In recent years it has broadened the scope of its efforts to embrace such "soft law" exercises as the Principles of International Commercial Contracts, promulgated in 1994, and the Guide to International Master Franchise Arrangements, published in 1998.

Both these techniques presented the considerable advantage for initiatives directed toward the unification of law that they had almost entirely escaped the attention of national legislators, thus making the ground to be traversed effectively virgin territory. This however led some commentators to question the wisdom of treating leasing transactions independently of secured transactions in general. The thought here was that it might make more sense to treat one as a species of the other. The feeling within Unidroit at the time was however that, first, the formulation of a uniform legal framework for the *sui generis* type of leasing transaction need not necessarily bring the transaction under the scope of Article 9 of the Uniform Commercial Code of the United States of America and similarly inspired secured transactions legislation and, secondly, a security interest being closely tied to an underlying sale contract, the only potential security interest in the complex tripartite financial lease would be the purchase money security interest relating to the sale contract between the supplier and the lessor, while no security interest would arise under the agreement between the lessor and the lessee so long as there was no transfer of title to the latter.[3]

Ample confirmation of the accuracy of these conclusions was provided during Unidroit's preparation of what was to become the Unidroit Convention on International Financial Leasing. For continental Civil Law countries the lessor's ownership of the leased equipment under a financial lease was simply not negotiable: under no circumstances were they prepared to admit that a financial leasing transaction could be assimilated to a secured transaction. The ink was, however, barely dry on the Final Act of the diplomatic Conference at which the Unidroit Convention on International Financial Leasing was adopted when, in June 1988, the then Canadian member of the Unidroit Governing Council, Mr T B Smith, submitted a proposal to that body to the effect that "the success of efforts to develop the Convention on International Financial Leasing [having shown clearly] that, notwithstanding the great divergence of treatment accorded to security interests under the national laws of States, it is possible to address in the form of an international convention the subject of international regulation of aspects of this area of the law [and] that the Conventions on International Financial Leasing and International Factoring are only a first step toward providing comprehensive international harmonisation of laws relating to security interests in personal property [,] it is now open to

[3] Compare Stanford MJ, "Preliminary draft uniform rules on international financial leasing: explanatory report" in *Uniform Law Review* 1984/II, 77 at p 107.

consideration whether Unidroit should take another step in the movement toward this goal".[4] His proposal was for the Unidroit Governing Council to "consider a further project in the area of international regulation of aspects of personal property security law [to] be narrow in scope and ... be undertaken only if it can be demonstrated that there is a commercial need for further international regulation in this area".[5]

Past experience having demonstrated the inadvisability of framing the scope of initiatives for the unification of the law governing the taking of security in overly ambitious terms, Unidroit decided early on in its response to the call from Mr Smith to limit the scope of its efforts to the preparation of uniform international rules governing the taking of security in those categories of high-value mobile equipment which by their nature are likely to be moving either across or beyond national frontiers on a regular basis. The intention was, by concentrating on indisputably international situations, to reduce to a minimum potential objections on the ground of interference with rules of national law, the complexity of which has in some countries assumed the character of an "exasperated particularism".[6] At the same time it was nevertheless aware of the increasing recognition being accorded world wide to the existence of a direct link between the modernisation of national secured transactions legislation and the greater availability of much needed capital investment opportunities for the less developed economies of the world. Such was the message being conveyed in a whole range of initiatives for the modernisation of secured transactions legislation in such countries being promoted by the World Bank and the European Bank for Reconstruction and Development.[7]

When embarking on the preparation of uniform international rules governing the taking of security in high-value mobile equipment, Unidroit accordingly signalled its intention of not overlooking the potential usefulness of such rules as the basis for the modernisation of the law governing the generality of secured transactions. This it did by specifically

---

[4] Cited in Cuming RCC, "International regulation of aspects of security interests in mobile equipment" in *Uniform Law Review* 1990/1, 63.

[5] *Ibid.*

[6] Compare Ferrarini G, "Changes to Personal Property Security Law in Italy: a Comparative and Functional Approach" in *Making Commercial Law - Essays in Honour of Roy Goode,* Cranston (ed) (1997) 477 at p 485.

[7] Compare Stanford MJ, "A broader or a narrower band of beneficiaries for the proposed new international regimen?: Some reflections on the merits of the Convention/Protocol structure in facilitating the former" in *Uniform Law Review* 1999/2 pp 242-244.

envisaging the preparation in due course, once such uniform international rules had been adopted as an international Convention, of a model law on secured transactions in general, inspiration for which would be sought among the general principles informing said Convention.[8]

This chapter proposes to examine in turn the Unidroit Convention on International Financial Leasing and the Convention on International Interests in Mobile Equipment. As has been indicated above, the former should be seen as a necessary first step on the path toward the unification of law in the field of the taking of security.[9] As with the Warsaw Convention for the Unification of Certain Rules relating to International Carriage by Air and the Unidroit Convention on International Financial Leasing, the development of the Convention on International Interests has acquired special momentum from the perception that it will not only provide a new international regimen for the taking of security over equipment moving regularly across or beyond national frontiers but also has the potential to provide a model capable of filling the legislative vacuum that exists in this area of the law across whole areas of the globe.

The Unidroit Convention on International Financial Leasing[10]

Background

The Unidroit Convention on International Financial Leasing (hereinafter referred to as the Unidroit Convention) was opened to signature at the conclusion of a diplomatic Conference held in Ottawa on 28 May 1988.[11] Some 59 States were represented at the Conference. By 31 December 1990

---

[8] *Ibid.*

[9] It is moreover understood to be the intention of one major Government to ratify the Unidroit Convention on International Financial Leasing at the same time as the future Unidroit Convention on International Interests in Mobile Equipment. Compare Stanford MJ, "The Unidroit Convention on International Financial Leasing" *World Leasing Yearbook 2001*, 40.

[10] The part of this contribution dedicated to the Unidroit Convention on International Financial Leasing is based on the article "International Financial Leasing: The Status of the Unidroit Convention and an Analysis of its Provisions" contributed by the author to *Uniform Commercial Code Law Journal,* Vol 32, No 2 (Fall 1999) 182 *et seq.*

[11] The authentic texts of the Unidroit Convention are the English- and French-language versions adopted at the diplomatic Conference. The English-language version is reproduced in Appendix I hereto.

13 States had signed the Unidroit Convention (namely, Belgium, Czechoslovakia, Finland, France, Ghana, Guinea, Italy, Morocco, Nigeria, Panama, Philippines, United Republic of Tanzania, United States). In accordance with Article 16(1), the Unidroit Convention entered into force on 1 May 1995, pursuant to the deposit of an instrument of approval by France (on 23 September 1991) and the deposit of instruments of ratification by Italy (on 29 November 1993) and Nigeria (on 25 October 1994). Subsequently Panama too has ratified the Unidroit Convention (on 26 March 1997) and Hungary (on 7 May 1996), Latvia (on 6 August 1997), the Russian Federation (on 3 June 1998), Belarus (on 18 August 1998) and Uzbekistan (on 6 July 2000) have acceded thereto. Reliable information would seem to indicate that a number of other States, including the United States,[12] Colombia[13] and El Salvador,[14] intend becoming Parties to the Unidroit Convention in due course. In other States, for example Mexico, it is understood that the question of accession is being given favourable consideration by the relevant Government departments.[15]

---

[12] All the endorsements necessary for US ratification have been obtained, in particular those of the American Bar Association (ABA) and the Equipment Leasing Association of America. After recommending that the USA ratify the Unidroit Convention, the ABA Section of Business Law stated in its conclusion to the House of Delegates in February 1990 that "[t]he ratification of the Convention by the United States would, on the whole, further international leasing law and trade. Although the Convention may contain provisions which represent drafting choices different from those the group would have made, these provisions do not represent unfavourable deviations from the *status quo* and, in most instances, may be adequately addressed by the parties in their lease documentation, as is the current practice in the trade".

[13] The Colombian Federation of Leasing Companies in November 1993 formally called upon the Colombian Authorities to accede. A special committee subsequently set up by the Ministry of Justice to advise on the case for accession reported favourably. It is understood to be the intention of the Government to bring legislation providing for accession before Parliament in due course.

[14] Accession by El Salvador is planned as part of the legal framework for leasing currently being prepared under the direction of a project team manned by Government officials from the Central Bank and the offshoot of the latter *(Banco Multisectorial de Inversiones)* responsible for providing resources to the financial sector for development purposes.

[15] The Unidroit Convention was one of the principal topics under discussion at an international seminar *The Commercial and Financial Instruments of Unidroit and Uniform Law: The Mexican Challenge*, organised by the Ministries of Finance, Trade and Foreign Affairs of Mexico and the Institute of Legal Research of the National Autonomous University of Mexico (Mexico City, 6/8 November 2000).

In Sweden the Parliamentary Commission on Leasing in its final report[16] recommended not only that Sweden accede to the Unidroit Convention but also that it be taken as a model for the drafting of domestic Swedish legislation on leasing. In general, the Unidroit Convention has been recognised as providing a "useful model for countries in need of a legal framework in the domestic leasing arena".[17] In keeping with the fact that it was drafted with the needs of *inter alia* emerging lease economies in mind, it has been used as a drafting model in the preparation of domestic legislation in China, Ghana, Indonesia, Nigeria, Panama, the Russian Federation, Turkey and elsewhere.[18] Panama, for example, long before ratifying the Unidroit Convention, passed legislation designed to overcome the obstacles which had previously dogged the development of leasing there, which was heavily influenced by the Unidroit Convention.[19] In the United States internal personal property leasing law has been largely rewritten in the light of the principles underlying the Unidroit Convention.[20] The Unidroit Convention is also shaping law reform in this area. In the People's Republic of China the chapter on financial leasing (Chapter 14) of the Contracts Law which entered into force on 1 October 1999 was drafted in accordance with the provisions of the Unidroit Convention.[21] In Argentina consideration is being given by the Commission for the Reform of the Civil Code to the incorporation of its provisions in that country's Civil Code. Inspiration for regulation of inter-State leasing has also been sought in the Unidroit Convention, as may be seen in the Convention on Inter-State Leasing adopted by the Commonwealth of Independent States (CIS) in 1998.

---

[16] Compare SOU 1994:120.
[17] Compare Amembal SP, "Emerging lease markets" *World Leasing Yearbook 1999,* 16 *et seq.*
[18] *Ibid* at p 18.
[19] Compare Law no 7 of 10 July 1990.
[20] Compare Uniform Personal Property Leasing Act of 1985, subsequently re-written as Article 2A of the Uniform Commercial Code: Boss AH, "Statutory treatment of leasing transactions: the legislative history of Article 2A and the Unidroit Convention on International Financial Leasing" in *Equipment Leasing* (ed) Wong JJ (1998) § 2.09.
[21] Compare Yangpin S, "China Market Review" *World Leasing Yearbook 2001*, 168 at p 170.

Origins of Leasing

Leasing, notwithstanding the comparatively recent emergence of the technique currently associated with this term, has a long history. Historical evidence suggests its widespread use by the ancient Sumerians circa 5000 BC. Its modern development as a generally acceptable alternative to the outright purchase of capital equipment, though, is rather to be traced back to the development of the railways in the middle of the 19th century. The United Kingdom wagon leasing companies of the late 1850s were among the very first limited liability companies to avail themselves of the new corporate form. Although their activity spanned only a relatively short period of time, the wagon leasing companies made a vital contribution to the rapid development of railway freight. A similar pattern emerged in the United States where railroad companies pushing ahead with new routes tended to concentrate their financial resources on the provision of track and facilities, obtaining their rolling stock on leases initially known as "car trusts" but which later became better known as "equipment trusts".

It was, however, in the post-World War II period that leasing really began its spectacular growth, fuelled by the urgent need businesses had at that time to replenish their equipment. In the United States, for example, the conventional means of responding to this need, the conditional sale, was just not suitable, requiring almost invariably, as it did, a down payment of 15-20 per cent, a sum which many businesses simply did not possess at the time. Until the 1960s the use of leasing was thus principally confined in the United States to capital-poor, high-risk companies and the total annual volume of new equipment leases during the period in question probably did not exceed one billion US dollars. This situation changed, though, toward the end of the 1950s and with the advent of the 1960s with the acceptance of leasing by large industrial companies and public utilities, national banks and Governments, and the establishment of the first independent leasing companies, playing a role analogous to that of banks and financial institutions albeit with the significant difference that they set out to buy and then lease equipment to their clients rather than simply loaning them the necessary funds to buy it. While the first such companies saw the light of day in the United States, the pioneer among these being the United States Leasing Corporation, founded in San Francisco in 1952, the new technique was swiftly exported to both Europe and the Far East with the expansion of American leasing companies, and in particular US Leasing, overseas. This explains leasing's establishment of roots in the United Kingdom in 1960 (with the establishment of Mercantile Leasing), in the Federal Republic of

Germany in 1962 (with the establishment of Deutsche Leasing) and in Japan the same year (with the establishment of Orient Leasing). Manufacturer links provided the early impetus for this activity but leasing companies, whether or not linked to domestic financial institutions, soon began cultivating direct links with equipment users and leasing an ever wider variety of equipment to them.

Reasons for the Growth of Leasing

Leasing's popularity has led to the steady spread of leasing throughout the different parts of the world in the intervening years. A major contribution to its spread has undoubtedly been the work of the International Finance Corporation, from 1977 to date.[22] The IFC's activity in leasing has taken two forms. First, it has worked to promote the development of domestic financial markets through the introduction of leasing as an alternative source of equipment finance for industrial, agricultural and commercial enterprises. Second, it has set out to encourage competition and efficiency in the financial sector by participating in leasing companies the performance of which would serve to demonstrate the financial and economic viability of leasing. The IFC essentially acts as a project catalyst, bringing together domestic sponsors, foreign technical and financial partners and, where necessary, governmental authorities in order to ensure that the project is commercially viable and organised on sound management, operational and financial principles and will operate in a satisfactory regulatory environment. It provides both equity and loan finance to new ventures and helps new companies to arrange local funding. As of June 2000 it had approved investment in 92 equipment leasing companies in 47 countries. 34 of these companies were in Asia, 34 in Europe, the Middle East, North Africa and Central Asia, 13 in Sub-Saharan Africa and 11 in South America.

Apart from the major fiscal benefits accruing under leasing, IFC experience demonstrates that there are a number of non-fiscal advantages which leasing has over conventional borrowing. IFC finds that fiscal benefits are accorded to leasing for two principal reasons, first, in order to encourage investment in capital equipment and, secondly, to create a level playing-field with bank financing, since leasing companies recognise income earlier and receive both interest and repayment as taxable income.

---

[22] Compare Alemayehu M, "The IFC's leasing activities 1977-2000" *World Leasing Yearbook 2001,* 20 *et seq.*

IFC finds that the non-fiscal advantages of leasing are essentially five in number:

(1) *Availability:* In many countries with underdeveloped capital markets leasing may be the only source of medium- to long-term finance available for the procurement of capital equipment on suitable terms. For new or small companies leasing presents significant cash flow advantages. Leasing, moreover, permits them to borrow without the need for a prior business track record and for pre-existing assets to be offered as collateral.

(2) *Flexibility:* The pattern and size of lease payments may be better tailored to the particular needs of each lessee. In many countries lease payments do not have to appear on the balance-sheet, thus reducing the apparent leverage of the lessee.

(3) *Affordability:* The overall cost of leasing can be lower than conventional bank finance when the comparable collateral requirements, documentation, compensating balance requirements and the processing time are all taken into consideration along with the explicit interest rate, although it is true that in nominal terms interest rate spreads for leasing tend to be higher than for bank financing.

(4) *Coverage:* Leasing can cover up to 100 per cent of financing requirements, well above the typical coverage of bank loans and without the need to provide any collateral.

(5) *Security:* The lessor's ownership of the leased asset affords him a strong degree of security. Even where there are legal or practical restrictions on the lessor's ability to repossess in the event of the lessee's default, the lessor's position is no worse than that of a conventionally secured creditor.

Growth of Leasing

Equipment[23] leasing's steady growth, in particular in terms of its share of total investment, over the years 1978-1999 is eloquently reflected in the figures for the 50 leading national leasing markets collected by the London Financial Group.[24] These reveal that the total value of world leasing business increased ten-fold in U.S. dollar terms over that 21-year period, from US$ 40.8 billion in 1978 to US$ 473.5 billion by the end of 1999. Allowing for inflation, this means that the real volume of leasing business grew by 350 per cent over the period in question, giving a compound annual average real growth rate of some 7.5 per cent.[25] The sharpest growth came in the late 1980s in North America, Europe and Asia. Growth shows an uninterrupted pattern on a year-to-year basis with the exception of the two-year down-turn experienced between 1991 and 1993, which was almost entirely accounted for by a sharp drop in business in Europe, with a shortage of tax capacity in the United Kingdom coinciding with the onset of recession in continental Western Europe.

In terms of market penetration, that is leasing's percentage share of total investment, the story has again been one of inexorable growth, albeit at times punctuated by temporary reverses. Of the leading 50 national leasing markets at the end of 1999, those with the highest market penetration were Zimbabwe (32.6 per cent), the Czech Republic (30.5 per cent) and the United States (30 per cent). Other countries with high levels of market penetration at the end of 1999 were Australia (25.4 per cent), Portugal (25 per cent), Canada (22 per cent) and Estonia (20 per cent). Of these countries the market penetration of the United States' leasing market was far and away the most significant when seen in terms of the volume of that country's leasing business in 1999, namely US$226 billion. By comparison the volume of leasing business in Zimbabwe in 1999 amounted to only US$ 0.19 billion, in the Czech Republic to US$2.28 billion, in Australia to US$ 7.33 billion and in Estonia to US$0.22 billion. Leasing market penetration in the world's other two leading economies, namely

[23] The term "equipment" as employed in this context excludes real estate leases and leasing or hiring facilities to personal consumers rather than businesses. Compare Porter DJ, "Leasing penetration strengthens in 1999" *World Leasing Yearbook 2001,* 2 at pp 6-7.

[24] Compare Porter DJ *ibid* 2 *et seq.*

[25] It should however be noted that the increase in the total volume of equipment leasing world wide in 1999 represented an increase of 9.5 per cent over 1998 (compare Porter DJ *ibid* 2).

Japan and Germany, is nowhere as high as in the United States of America: in Japan it stood in 1999 at 9.5 per cent and in Germany at 14.8 per cent. In terms of volume of leasing business, these countries, nevertheless, rank next after the United States: leasing business in Japan in 1999 amounted to US$ 72.32 billion and in Germany to US$ 35.73 billion. Market penetration has increased steadily over the 1978-1999 period in the United States (from 15.6 per cent to 30 per cent) and, albeit in less dramatic proportions, Japan (from 4.8 per cent to 9.5 per cent).

Leasing volume is at the same time growing as a percentage of gross domestic product. The figures collected by the London Financial Group show that between 1998 and 1999 leasing volume registered a proportionate increase of 5.1 per cent when measured in these terms, rising from 1.56 per cent in 1998 to 1.64 per cent in 1999. It is interesting to note that three of the top five countries on this analysis are East European countries, the Czech Republic, where leasing volume represented 4.29 per cent of gross domestic product in 1999, Estonia, where it represented 4.22 per cent and Hungary, where it represented 2.86 per cent, and the other two countries of Sub-Saharan Africa, namely Zimbabwe, where leasing volume represented 3.33 per cent of gross domestic product in 1999, and South Africa, where it represented 2.74 per cent. In comparison, in the United States leasing volume represented 2.44 per cent.

Hallmarks of Leasing

The essential function of a lease, whether of real or personal property, is, on the one hand, to enable the lessee to obtain use and enjoyment without paying the full capital cost and, on the other, to permit the lessor to receive a return on its investment while retaining title and security in the goods or land. It thus involves the segregation of ownership and the right to beneficial use. The essential novelty of leasing in relation to the traditional concept of a lease lay in the way in which leasing companies set out to transfer to the lessee those rights and obligations, privileges and duties which, while traditionally vesting in the lessor, did not sit well with a lessor whose role was restricted to supplying the finance necessary to secure the lessee's use of the property.

While there have been many variants on the basic leasing pattern over the years, leasing facilities tend basically to take one of two forms, *operating leasing* or *financial leasing*. The fundamental difference between the two turns on the leasing company's ability to recover fully the cost of the equipment through the rentals.[26] The operating lease is that which differs least from the traditional lease. An operating lessor will rent the equipment for a period which is less than its useful economic life and for rentals which will amount to less than its purchase cost. Whereas an operating lease is normally bilateral in character, a financial lease will usually involve three parties, the supplier and lessee being joined by a lessor whose role is purely financial in character. The rentals payable over what is termed the "primary period"[27] of a financial lease will be sufficient to enable the lessor to recover the cost of the equipment, its financing costs and overheads and earn a return on its investment.

Reasons for Unidroit's Preparation of Uniform Rules

Unidroit's decision to embark on the preparation of uniform rules on leasing sprang from two not entirely unrelated factors, the one economic, the other legal. In economic terms, examples have been given of the extent to which leasing's potential as an investment tool has been realised at a national level. At the cross-border level, on the other hand, notwithstanding leasing's all too evident aptness to facilitate those injections of capital investment so sorely needed in so many parts of the world, its potential had very largely failed to be realised, with the exception of those occasional transactions the amount of money involved in which was felt to justify the investment of time and money in the structuring of a cross-border leasing facility.[28]

---

[26] Compare Goode RM, *Commercial Law,* 2nd ed (1995) at p 776, where he states that "[l]essors have coined a variety of labels to describe different leasing schemes. These have no *legal* significance, but are used to market particular leasing products, and reflect functional distinctions between one type of lease and another". Compare also Davies I, *Equipment and Motor Vehicle Leasing and Hiring Law and Practice,* (1997) pp 19-23.

[27] The primary period usually corresponds to between 50 per cent and 70 per cent of the estimated useful economic life of the equipment. At the end of this period the lessee may continue to use the equipment in return for the payment of a nominal rental.

[28] Compare Porter DJ, "European market soars, lifting world volume to record high" in *World Leasing Yearbook 2000,* 6 ("Even within the European Union, where there have been considerable efforts towards regulatory harmonisation, truly cross-border business remains inhibited by a variety of institutional barriers and 'knowledge gaps' concerning all the structuring steps necessary to set up a lease with a customer in a different jurisdiction from the lessor. The vast bulk of business is domestic, when viewed in terms of the lessor companies' countries of

In *legal terms*, the often vast differences in the legal treatment of leasing from one jurisdiction to another and the general failure of legislators to adopt a consistent attitude to the resolution of this problem were found to have played a major part in foiling leasing's efforts to reproduce at the cross-border level the success it had enjoyed at the domestic level. A handful of countries had sought to tackle the problem by legislation, starting with France in 1966, but in general most legal systems had simply tried to force leasing into the closest approximation amongst its existing range of contractual schemata, each jurisdiction invariably pursuing the internal logic of its own legal system. The confusion resulting therefrom was for a long time compounded by a reluctance on the part of the courts to recognise the inadequacy of applying to leasing precisely those neighbouring legal concepts the very limitations of which had led the financial community to develop leasing as an alternative in the first place.

In the United States, for example, the argument ran for a long time that leases could be adequately dealt with either under the traditional rules applicable to bailment or under the provisions of Article 9 of the Uniform Commercial Code, depending upon whether the particular lease was intended to be by way of security or not. Isolated voices were to be heard arguing for the inappropriateness of applying the remedies provisions of Article 9 to those leases which did not closely approximate to transactions traditionally handled as security devices; these voices were, however, still not willing to recognise the existence of a category of lease that was amenable to classification neither as a bailment nor as a security interest. It was therefore illustrative of the measure of the transformation which US thinking underwent on this issue through the participation of US experts in the preparation of Unidroit's uniform rules that in 1985 the National

---

residence, though increasingly international in terms of their corporate groups."). Compare also Clark TM, "The leasing phenomenon" in *Leasing Finance* (ed) Clark TM, 2nd ed (1990) 233 at pp 234-236, where the author indicated that, while the most highly publicised incentives for cross-border operations tended to be tax-based, cross-border lease facilities were also being written for a number of other reasons; first, in order to take advantage of the larger markets for the disposal of computers and other marketable assets; second, on account of the better security afforded by ownership of equipment as opposed to a mortgage or charge over the same; third, to avoid import and export restrictions and exchange controls; fourth, to enable multinationals, and in particular oil companies, to establish a separate ownership presence and reduce the political risk of sequestration and, fifth, to offset limited availability of two alternative major sources of international finance, namely export credit and sovereign lending.

Conference of Commissioners on Uniform State Laws saw fit to approve the text of an Uniform Personal Property Leasing Act, subsequently rewritten as Article 2A of the Uniform Commercial Code.

Purposes of the Unidroit Convention

The preamble makes it clear that the essential purposes of the Unidroit Convention are two-fold, first, to remove legal impediments to international financial leasing, while maintaining a fair balance of interests between the different parties to the transaction and, second, thus to enhance opportunities for international financial leasing. The preamble further clarifies the limited ambitions of the Unidroit Convention's authors, namely to provide only a minimal (as opposed to an exhaustive) legal framework for that *sui generis* type of lease commonly referred to as financial leasing. The technique which it employs to achieve this purpose consists in adapting the rules of law governing the traditional contract of hire to fit the distinctive triangular relationship set in motion by the financial leasing transaction (compare preamble). It was not the intention of the authors of the Unidroit Convention to affect thereby financial leasing's treatment for purposes other than its civil and commercial law treatment, for instance its accounting and revenue treatment (compare preamble).

Substantive Sphere of Application

A financial leasing transaction for the purposes of the Unidroit Convention is defined as a complex transaction involving the interaction of two contracts, a supply agreement and a leasing agreement. Article 1 describes this transaction as one in which the lessee selects the equipment from the supplier, essentially unassisted by the lessor, the lessor acquires that equipment in connection with a leasing agreement and the rentals payable under the leasing agreement are calculated in such a way as to take into account in particular the amortisation of the cost or at least a substantial part of the cost of the equipment to the lessor.

The granting to the lessee in the leasing agreement of an option to purchase the leased equipment is seen by some legal systems - essentially Civil Law jurisdictions - as a *sine qua non* of the *sui generis* type of lease encompassed by the Unidroit Convention. In other legal systems - characteristically Common Law jurisdictions - the granting of such an option would prevent the agreement from being qualified as a lease at all and would lead instead to its requalification as a hire-purchase or conditional sale. The divide on this issue proving to be unbridgeable, the Unidroit Convention simply provides that the granting of such options and the price at which they may be exercised are without effect on the Unidroit Convention's applicability. In common with other commercial law instruments, the Unidroit Convention is not intended to apply to consumer transactions. Whereas the rules of the Unidroit Convention in principle only apply to *equipment* leasing, the fact that the particular item of equipment leased has become a fixture to or incorporated in land does not mean that the Unidroit Convention's rules shall cease to apply in relation thereto. On the contrary, Article 4 extends the Unidroit Convention's application to such cases and provides that all questions regarding whether equipment has become a fixture to or incorporated in land and, if so, regarding the effect on the rights *inter se* of the equipment lessor and the real estate lessor are to be determined by the law of the State where the land is situated.

While the Unidroit Convention's application is nominally delimited by reference to *financial leasing* so that operating leases are in principle excluded, the authors of the Unidroit Convention were at pains to insist that a transaction was not intended to fall outside its sphere of application merely because the parties chose to denominate it an *operating lease;* in all cases it will accordingly be for those called upon to apply and interpret the Unidroit Convention to look at the substance of the transaction before deciding whether or not it meets the other criteria for a financial leasing transaction set out in Article 1, in particular the provisions of Article 1(2)(c). This is most important in view of the frequent intentional blurring of the distinction between financial leasing and operating leasing. The application of the Unidroit Convention extends to those sub-leasing arrangements common in international financial leasing transactions provided that the sub-lease is a financial leasing transaction otherwise subject to the Unidroit Convention. This is spelled out in Article 2 which makes it clear that the supplier for the purposes of the Unidroit Convention in the context of a chain of sub-leasing arrangements involving the same equipment is the person from whom the first lessor acquired the equipment. Thus, regardless of the number of sub-leasing arrangements involved in the chain, there will only ever be one *supplier* in relation to any sub-lessee, namely the original supplier.

The Unidroit Convention's application is also extended to *leveraged leasing* transactions, by virtue of Article 14. In leveraged leases, whereas title to the equipment - and hence entitlement to the tax indemnification benefits associated with ownership - vests in the lessor, the latter will, by reason of the huge amounts of money involved, put up only a part of the capital cost represented by the purchase of the equipment. For the rest of the cost it will have recourse to one or more lenders who will assure their position by requiring an assignment to themselves of the stream of rentals provided for under the leasing agreement. Article 14(1) accordingly permits the lessor to transfer any of its rights under the leasing agreement.

Territorial Sphere of Application

Given the reluctance of certain States to put their names to international instruments the effect of which would be to impinge on their domestic law, the Unidroit Convention is limited in effect to international financial leasing transactions. There would, however, be nothing to prevent its provisions being taken as a model for domestic law in those many jurisdictions where there is as yet a legislative vacuum in this area. This is in fact what was proposed by the Swedish Parliamentary Commission on Leasing. The drafters of the Unidroit Convention were at all times aware of the importance of clarifying the legal status of leasing at the domestic level in order for it to be able to realise its full potential at the transnational level.

The territorial sphere of application of the Unidroit Convention is defined in Article 3, by means of a formula modelled on Article 1 of the 1980 United Nations Convention on Contracts for the International Sale of Goods. The fundamental condition for the applicability of the Unidroit Convention is that the places of business of the lessor and the lessee should be situated in different States. The choice of the lessor's and lessee's places of business for the purpose of triggering the application of the Unidroit Convention reflects the fact that it is the agreement between these two parties which constitutes the fundamental legal relationship contained within the complex tripartite leasing transaction. For the Unidroit Convention to be applicable the States where the lessor's and the lessee's places of business *and also* the supplier's place of business are located must furthermore be Contracting States *or* the law applicable to both the supply agreement and the leasing agreement must be the law of a Contracting State. Whilst aware that such a move would necessarily considerably restrict the future application of the Unidroit Convention, the authors of the Unidroit Convention decided that it would be necessary to require that the supplier's place of business also be located in a Contracting State for the Unidroit Convention to apply in view of the impact of certain of its provisions, and in particular Article 10, on the supplier. The effect of

Article 3(1)(b) is that where lessor and lessee have their places of business in different States and, say, French law is the law applicable to both the supply agreement and the leasing agreement, then the Unidroit Convention is applicable, even though neither of the States where the parties have their places of business is a Contracting State.

Regulatory System of the Unidroit Convention

The regulatory system of the Unidroit Convention is analysed below from the point of view of, first, the duties imposed upon the lessor; second, the duties incumbent on the lessee; third, the rights of the lessee against the supplier; fourth, the position of the lessor in relation to third parties and, fifth, the extent to which the parties may exclude the application of the Unidroit Convention or derogate from its provisions.

Duties of the lessor. The Unidroit Convention basically treats the supplier as the most appropriate party from whom the lessee should seek redress. This is in line with the narrowly financial role recognised to the lessor and the correspondingly dynamic role in the selection of the supplier and the equipment played by the lessee. The only fundamental duty accordingly imposed upon the lessor in relation to the lessee is to ensure that the latter is placed in possession of the equipment.

1. Lessor's liability to the lessee for non-delivery, late delivery or a non-conforming tender.

   A notable exception to this rule is, however to be found in Article 12 dealing with the case where the equipment is not delivered, is delivered late or, upon delivery, fails to conform to the terms agreed. In such a case the lessee is to be treated as though it had agreed to *buy* the equipment from the lessor under the same terms as those of the supply agreement. The lessee may accordingly reject the equipment or terminate the leasing agreement. The lessor has, however, the right to cure the failure to tender equipment in conformity with the supply agreement, by ensuring that a conforming tender is made.

   This exception must, nevertheless, be seen in the context of the circumstances in which it was adopted, as a compromise solution between those delegations at the diplomatic Conference pressing for the embodiment of a rule expressly cutting off the possibility for the lessee to exercise its remedies against the lessor at the moment when it intimates acceptance of the equipment and those delegations opposed to such a rule. Article 12(2) enshrines the compromise solution. The first limb of this compromise was to make the provisions of Article 12, as indeed the vast majority of the provisions of the Unidroit Convention, subject to the parties' freedom of contract, thus making it possible for the parties to define in their contract the precise moment at which acceptance is to be deemed to occur and to provide that a lessee wishing to terminate the leasing agreement must first reimburse the lessor for any monies the latter may already have disbursed to the supplier. The second limb of the compromise was to make the question of the exercisability, and therefore also the losing of the lessee's remedies against the lessor under Article 12 subject to the law applicable to the supply agreement. The idea here was that, where, under this law, the buyer's acceptance would normally debar that party from subsequently seeking to reject or terminate as against the seller, as will be the case in many jurisdictions, then *so* will the lessee's acceptance debar it from subsequently rejecting or terminating as against the lessor.

2. Lessor's liability to the lessee in respect of the equipment.

Once the equipment has been accepted, the lessor cannot incur any liability for defects in that equipment. The only exception to this immunity is where the loss suffered by the lessee results from its reliance on the lessor's skill and judgment and intervention in the selection of the supplier or the specifications for the equipment. This reflects the fact that the Unidroit Convention only applies to international financial leasing transactions in which the lessee, in specifying the equipment and selecting the supplier, does not rely *primarily* on the lessor's skill and judgment. To the extent that the lessee abandons its technical neutrality in relation to the equipment, it follows that its immunity under Article 8(1)(a) should be proportionately reduced.

3. Lessor's warranty of quiet possession.

The Unidroit Convention provides that the lessor, as owner of the equipment leased, warrants that the lessee's quiet possession will not be disturbed during the currency of the lease by a third party having a superior title or right or claiming a superior title or right and acting under the authority of the court, save in those cases where the disturbance results from an act or omission of the lessee itself. This warranty of quiet possession is subject to the parties' freedom of contract but only to the extent that the disturbance of the lessee's quiet possession was not caused by an intentional or grossly negligent act or omission of the lessor. Where a broader warranty of quiet possession would be mandatory under the applicable law, then the lessor's liability is to be determined on that basis.

In addition, where the law of a Contracting State would not permit the lessor to exclude its liability for default or negligence, it will be for that State to indicate at the moment of its signature or ratification that it will apply its domestic law rules in preference to the rule set out in Article 8(3). This provision was added to accommodate those delegations attending the diplomatic Conference that took the view that the mandatory nature of Article 8(3) was too narrow and would infringe basic public policy rules of their jurisdictions.

Duties of the Lessee

1. Duty to take proper care of the equipment.

Apart from the lessee's duty to pay its rentals, it must also take proper care of the equipment, using it in a reasonable manner and keeping it in the condition in which it received it, subject to fair wear and tear. When the leasing agreement comes to an end and the lessee does not exercise an option to purchase the equipment or the renew the lease, the lessee must return the equipment to the lessor in a similar condition. The Unidroit Convention's exposition of the lessee's duties in this regard is framed in very broad terms and is intended to be filled out by the parties in their agreement and/or by the applicable law.

2. Duty to compensate the lessor in the event of its default.

Article 13, dealing with the consequences of the lessee's default, may be considered as setting out those elements of a liquidated damages clause not intended to be cut down under local law. It is, however, in no way intended to limit the parties' freedom to stipulate a liquidated damages clause of their own. It rather seeks to detail the measure of the lessor's loss and set out the rights and remedies which the lessor may exercise in the event of the lessee's default.

The lessor's remedies are divided into two categories, those that it may exercise in the event of any default by the lessee and those that it may only exercise where the lessee's default is *substantial.* Where the lessee's default is not substantial, the lessor is entitled to recover accrued unpaid rentals, together with interest and damages. Where the lessee's default qualifies as substantial, the lessor may either enforce an acceleration clause[29] in the leasing agreement or terminate that agreement and, following such termination, recover possession of the equipment and such compensation as will place it in the position in which it would have been had the lessee not defaulted.

The law governing liquidated damages clauses is in many countries considered a matter of public policy. The Unidroit Convention recognises this: it in no way seeks to oust the manifest right of the courts to review the bargain struck between lessor and lessee. Article 13(3) nevertheless invites the courts, in the event of a dispute, to have regard, in the first place at least, to the agreement of the lessor and the lessee as to the manner in which the compensation to be paid by the lessee upon default is to be computed. The courts nevertheless remain free to find on the facts that the compensation provided for would be excessive, the yardstick for this evaluation being the amount indicated in Article 13(2)(b), namely the sum needed to compensate the lessor for its loss of bargain. The limitation on the enforceability of the parties' liquidated damages clause provided for under Article 13(3)(b) is mandatory. Furthermore, in recognition of the injustice that would be wrought were a lessor who has already terminated the leasing agreement *also* to be able to enforce an acceleration clause, the lessor is obliged to

[29] A typical clause of leasing agreements, accelerating the lessor's entitlement to the payment of future rentals.

elect between the exercise of one or other of these remedies (compare Article 13(4)). This provision too is mandatory.

Rights of the Lessee Against the Supplier. The independent direct right of action of the lessee against the supplier instituted by Article 10(1) is one of the principal novelties of the Unidroit Convention in relation to pre-existing national law. The wide-ranging immunity in contract and tort granted to the lessor under Article 8(1) presupposed an alternative avenue of redress for the lessee where the supplier has failed to make a conforming tender. The problem that arises under many legal systems derives essentially from the absence of privity of contract between lessee and supplier, even if in actual fact their behaviour is akin to that of contracting parties, notably in the all important matter of providing the specifications for the equipment to be supplied. The proposed solution of a direct right of action, however, initially caused misgiving among those delegations which felt that their legal systems could achieve the same result by the lessor's assignment of its rights under the supply agreement. It was nevertheless recognised that an important drawback of the assignment solution was that it would not permit the lessee to recover from the supplier its own measure of loss, but only that of the lessor. The Unidroit Convention accordingly treats the lessee as a third party beneficiary of the duties undertaken by the supplier under the supply agreement. One necessary limitation was, however, placed on this independent right of action: failing the lessor's agreement, the lessee is not entitled to terminate or rescind the supply agreement itself, since otherwise title would revest in the supplier and the lessor would find itself deprived of the essential element of its security.

Position of the Lessor in Relation to Third Parties

1. Lessor's title.

One of the thorniest problems faced by the authors of the Unidroit Convention concerned how best to deal with the protection of the lessor's title to the equipment, on the one hand, and the protection of third parties dealing with the lessee, on the other. Failing public notice of the lessor's title to the equipment, third party creditors of the lessee might tend to believe they were dealing with the owner, rather than simply the lessee of the equipment. The vast majority of the authors of the Unidroit Convention were united in recognition of the desirability of a registration system as the only truly effective means of providing notice to third parties of the lessor's title. However, this recognition was tempered by realisation of the political impossibility at the time of imposing a system of registration on all Contracting States, all the more so for the sake of finance leases alone. The organisational and financial implications of such a system were acknowledged realistically to be such as to make the idea, however desirable, a non-starter. Moreover, the principle that a third party acquiring property in good faith should acquire good title thereto proved to be so entrenched a feature of certain Civil law systems that the authors of the Unidroit Convention recognised that it would be equally unrealistic to expect such States accepting a denting of this principle for the sake of financial leasing alone. It was recognised that the area where conflicts would in practice most often arise as between the lessor and third parties would be in cases where the lessee had gone bankrupt. The Unidroit Convention accordingly finally sought only to deal with the problem of the enforceability of the lessor's real rights[30] in the equipment in relation to unsecured creditors and the trustee in bankruptcy of the lessee.

The Unidroit Convention provides for the validity of the lessor's real rights in relation to these two categories of party. However, where the validity of the lessor's real rights in relation to such parties is made subject by the applicable law to the giving of public notice, the lessor will have to comply with such a public notice requirement for its title to be enforceable as against the lessee's trustee in bankruptcy and unsecured creditors. This proviso was however also intended as a diplomatic nod by the authors of the Unidroit Convention in favour of registration as the only effective solution in these matters.

The Unidroit Convention sets out detailed rules to determine which law is applicable to determine the question as to whether the lessor is going to have any public notice requirements to comply with. For the generality of equipment the Unidroit Convention points to the *lex rei sitae,* in line with the traditional conflicts of law rule applied in the matter of proprietary rights. The Unidroit Convention, however, recognises the inappositeness of the *lex rei sitae* to determine such matters in respect of equipment of a kind

---

[30] The employment of the term "real rights" was intended to cover not only those situations where the lessor was owner but also those cases where, say, in a sub-leasing arrangement, it might not be the owner.

normally moving from one State to another in the ordinary course of business and accordingly for this class of equipment points to the law of the State in which the lessee has its principal place of business.

The authors of the Unidroit Convention were naturally anxious to avoid creating any inference of a double registration requirement for those special categories of equipment, in particular ships and aircraft, already subject to registration pursuant to the law of a State. For registered ships, for example, the Unidroit Convention accordingly points to the law of the State in which it is registered in the name of the owner (a bareboat charterer being deemed not to be an owner for these purposes).[31]

2. Lessor's immunity from liability to third parties.

The lessor is granted immunity by the Unidroit Convention for any liability that it might otherwise incur, *in its capacity of lessor* (that is, as legal supplier of the equipment leased), to third parties for death, personal injury or damage to property caused by the equipment. The fact that this immunity in tort is stated only to extend to any liability that might attach to the lessor *qua lessor* means that it is not intended to affect any liability toward third parties that might be imposed upon the lessor in some other capacity, for example as owner or producer. The intention of this proviso was to avoid the Unidroit Convention running counter on this issue to that special body of international legislation, such as the 1969 International Convention on Civil Liability for Oil Pollution Damage adopted in Brussels in 1969 and amended in London in 1984 and the 1985 European Directive on the approximation of the laws, regulations and administrative provisions of the member States of the European Union concerning liability for defective products.

Ability of the Parties to Exclude the Unidroit Convention or Derogate from its Terms

In line with the generally accepted rule that Conventions in the commercial law field should not as a rule deprive the parties of their freedom to choose alternative rules to govern their agreement, the parties are free to exclude

[31] For aircraft registered pursuant to the 1944 Chicago Convention on International Civil Aviation the Convention points to the law of the State in which it is so registered.

the application of the Unidroit Convention altogether. However, so as to avoid the risk of two parties seeking to exclude its application to the detriment of the third party, such exclusion requires the agreement of all three parties.

Where the Unidroit Convention's application is not excluded *in toto* in accordance with Article 5(1), the parties may derogate from, or vary such of its provisions as they see fit with the exception of three provisions only. These exceptions are Article 8(3) (concerning the lessor's liability for disturbances of the lessee's quiet possession where such disturbances are the result of an intentional or grossly negligent act or omission of the lessor), Article 13(3)(b) (preserving the court's power to strike down a liquidated damages clause of the leasing agreement the effect of which would be to allow the lessor to recover compensation substantially in excess of the amount necessary to compensate itself for its loss of bargain) and Article 13(4) (preventing the lessor from *both* terminating the leasing agreement *and* enforcing an acceleration clause of the leasing agreement). The fact that these provisions of the Unidroit Convention were made mandatory reflected their public policy connotations for certain jurisdictions.

Conclusions

The Unidroit Convention set itself the task of removing certain legal impediments to international financial leasing with a view to opening new windows of opportunity for this remarkably successful innovation of the 1960s and 1970s. It is true that the Unidroit Convention has not to date had the success in terms of numbers of ratifications that the broad support from the world leasing industry on which it was based seemed to herald. Yet then again truly cross-border leasing transactions are still comparatively few and far between. Developed leasing markets have tended to be almost paranoid about anything in the way of legislation which seems to depart from the pattern of their standard contractual documentation. What little cross-border leasing is actually done is therefore invariably done on the terms of this documentation. It is not therefore surprising that many have seen the Unidroit Convention as having its greatest chances of success in those parts of the world without developed leasing markets and as a model for domestic legislation.

Cross-border leasing has always known how to maximise the opportunities offered by differing national regimes (as with the famous double dip lease) but these exceptions to the norm in fact only serve to bring into sharper relief the massive brake on the wider availability of such opportunities constituted by the general uncertainty as to the legal treatment of a financial leasing transaction from one jurisdiction to another.

The Unidroit Convention has supplied the cornerstone of international legal certainty regarding the *sui generis* type of leasing generally known as financial leasing. It for the first time provides a well-thought out legal framework distinguishing this *sui generis* lease from those neighbouring legal concepts in the shadows of which it grew to maturity. It is important to recall that this legal infrastructure has been designed as only a minimal framework to which the parties are free to add. Aware of leasing's well-proven ability to respond to changing market conditions, significantly it in no way seeks to impose a legislative straitjacket on these parties.

The importance of the role of the parties in making the Unidroit Convention live was recognised by the World Leasing Council in its decision to prepare a *Manual for Documentation of International Leasing Transactions under the Unidroit Convention on International Financial Leasing.*[32] The Manual, drafted by the late Mr Lawrence M Taylor, who represented the then American Association of Equipment Lessors on the Unidroit Committee of governmental experts that prepared the draft Convention submitted to the Ottawa diplomatic Conference and the World Leasing Council at the Conference itself, seeks to provide parties to international leasing transactions with a whole range of options to consider in drafting their contractual documentation, all of which are compatible with the Unidroit Convention. The Manual thus provides the parties with a blueprint for their exercise of the very broad measure of freedom of contract recognised to them under the Unidroit Convention. In doing so, it enables them to protect their essential interests as best they see fit.

As was noted earlier, leasing business continues to grow steadily throughout the world. This growth is necessarily a reflection of the urgent need of large parts of the world for new capital equipment as a means of modernising their industrial and agricultural infrastructures. However, the potential that this trend would seem to open up for wider use of cross-border leasing has still not been realised. The Unidroit Convention was, in the words of its preamble, designed to "make international financial leasing more available". The figures cited earlier for the world-wide growth in the use of leasing, in particular as a percentage of countries' gross domestic product, testify to the well proven credentials it has earned at the domestic

---

[32] Compare p 40 *infra*.

level. The increase in opportunities for cross-border lease financing that the Unidroit Convention was designed to facilitate continue to be thwarted whilst it awaits wider acceptance. Experts in various parts of the world, aware of the shortcomings of their domestic law regarding financial leasing, moreover continue to call for adoption by their Governments of the Unidroit Convention.[33] In the meantime, though, as has been shown, the Unidroit Convention is invariably taken as a model for the drafting of domestic legislation in this field and, albeit slowly, it continues to attract new ratifications and accessions. It is possible that renewed impetus may be given to this process with the development of a model law on leasing that is under consideration at the present time within Unidroit.[34]

The Convention on International Interests in Mobile Equipment

Introduction

The Convention on International Interests in Mobile Equipment (hereinafter referred to as the Cape Town Convention) and a Protocol thereto on Matters specific to Aircraft Equipment (hereinafter referred to as the Protocol) were opened to signature at the conclusion of a diplomatic Conference held in Cape Town on 16 November 2001.[35] Some 68 States were represented at the Conference, which was co-sponsored by Unidroit and the International Civil Aviation Organisation (ICAO); 20 States signed

---

[33] Compare Austin S, Schwartz R and Lenkowsky S, "Revision urgently required" *Asset Finance International* [1996] 22 at p 27.

[34] Compare Cuming RCC, "Model Rules for Lease Financing: a Possible Complement to the Unidroit Convention on International Financial Leasing" *Uniform Law Review* 1998/2-3, 371 *et seq.*

[35] The English-language text of the Cape Town Convention is reproduced in Appendix II hereto. The English-language text of the Protocol thereto on Matters specific to Aircraft Equipment is reproduced in Appendix III hereto. It should be noted that these texts are subject to verification by the Unidroit and ICAO Secretariats under the authority of the President of the Cape Town Conference within 90 days of their adoption (compare the authentic text and witness clauses of the Cape Town Convention and the Protocol). The decision to provide for the possibility of such verification was taken by the diplomatic Conference with a view to facilitating the complete conformity of the different language versions of the two instruments. The English, Arabic, Chinese, French, Russian and Spanish texts of the Cape Town Convention and the Protocol are all equally authentic (*ibid).*

the Cape Town Convention and the Protocol on 16 November 2001 (namely, Burundi, Chile, China, the Republic of the Congo, Cuba, Ethiopia, France, Ghana, Jamaica, Jordan, Kenya, Lesotho, Nigeria, South Africa, Sudan, Switzerland, Tanzania, Tonga, Turkey and United Kingdom). One additional State (Italy) has signed the two new international instruments since (on 6 December 2001).

The Cape Town Convention and the Protocol remain open to signature until such time as they enter into force (Article 47(1) of the Cape Town Convention and Article XXVI(1) of the Protocol). Both instruments are subject to ratification, acceptance or approval by signatory States (Article 47(2) of the Cape Town Convention and Article XXVI(2) of the Protocol) and non-signatory States may accede thereto at any time (Article 47(3) of the Cape Town Convention and Article XXVI(3) of the Protocol). The Cape Town Convention will enter into force on the first day of the month following the expiration of three months after the date of deposit of the third instrument of ratification, acceptance, approval or accession but only as regards a category of objects to which a Protocol applies; first, as from the time of entry into force of that Protocol; second, subject to the terms of that Protocol and, third, as between States Parties to the Cape Town Convention and that Protocol (Article 49(1) of the Cape Town Convention). The Protocol will enter into force on the first day of the month following the expiration of three months after the date of deposit of the eighth instrument of ratification, acceptance, approval or accession (Article XXVIII(1) of the Protocol).

Background

Legal and Economic Reasons for Unidroit's Preparation of Uniform Rules

As indicated above, the preparation by Unidroit of uniform rules on the taking of security over high-value mobile equipment grew directly out of the Unidroit Convention, and in particular Article 7 of that Convention which provides for the enforceability of the lessor's real rights against the trustee in bankruptcy and unsecured creditors of the lessee.[36] The success of that approach seemed to indicate the feasibility of extending the principle embodied therein to the enforceability of security rights in those special categories of high-value mobile equipment which, by reason of the fact that they are of a kind likely to be moving across or beyond national

[36] Compare pp 418-420 *supra*.

frontiers on a regular basis in the ordinary course of business, do not particularly lend themselves to the application of the law traditionally applied to questions regarding the validity, enforceability and priority ranking of such rights, the *lex rei sitae*. There was no doubt that the legal uncertainty resulting from the way in which a dispute concerning such questions might vary according to the jurisdiction in which the particular asset happened to be at the time when proceedings were brought tended to impact negatively on the willingness of banks and financial institutions to extend secured financing facilities in respect of such assets and, where they did, substantially to increase the cost of such facilities.[37]

This legal rationale was reinforced by economic reasons. The opportunities for asset-based financing of such categories of equipment have to date been restricted by the difficulties banks and financial institutions face in securing and collecting on loans granted for the acquisition of these categories of equipment by reason of the legal difficulties mentioned above. The special advantage of asset-based financing for high-value capital equipment resides in the reduction in costs that follows from the reduction in risk for the financier permitted by his ability to have prompt recourse to the value of the underlying asset in the event of default by the debtor.[38]

As also indicated above, there has never been greater recognition of the relationship between the modernisation of the law governing the taking of security and the increased flow of foreign capital investment. Both the World Bank and the European Bank for Reconstruction and Development have in recent years mounted major initiatives designed to put in place modern legislation governing secured transactions in their countries of operations. A World Bank team, comprising both economists and lawyers, has been advising the central banks of a number of jurisdictions in Latin America regarding the preparation of legislation designed to modernise their secured transactions laws. These efforts have to a large extent focused on widening the class of assets that may be offered as security for a loan. An European Bank team has prepared a Model Law on Secured Transactions, designed to provide a simple, efficient and modern legislative model for the granting of security over all types of property such as will encourage lenders from the industrialised world to finance the overhauling

[37] Compare Cuming RCC, "International regulation of aspects of security interests in mobile equipment" *op cit* fn 4.

[38] Compare Saunders A/Walter I, *Proposed Unidroit Convention on International Interests in Mobile Equipment as applicable to Aircraft Equipment through the Aircraft Equipment Protocol: Economic Impact Assessment* (1998) pp 4-11.

of the industrial and agricultural infrastructures of the countries of the Former Soviet Union and its Central and Eastern European satellite States.

A study on the likely economic impact of the Cape Town Convention and the Protocol prepared under the auspices of Insead and the Salomon Center of New York University[39] has concluded that, "to the extent adopted and effectively implemented, these proposed legal instruments will achieve significant economic gains. These gains will be widely shared among airlines and manufacturers, their employees, suppliers, shareholders, and customers, and the national economies in which they are located ... On conservative assumptions, the gains are estimated at several billion dollars on an annual basis".[40]

Working Methods Employed by Unidroit in the Preparation of the Cape Town Convention

Taking advantage of the particular working methods employed by Unidroit in the first stages of a unification of law project, its project for the development of uniform rules on the taking of security over high-value mobile equipment has from the very beginning benefited to an exceptional degree from input from the various business sectors involved in the financing of such equipment. Already during the initial Study Group stage, which over the four years between 1993 and 1997 was responsible for the preparation of the preliminary draft Convention which, following consideration by the Unidroit Governing Council in 1998 and subsequent fine-tuning by a steering and revisions committee set up by that body, was transmitted to Governments for finalisation, the world's two leading aviation manufacturers, Airbus Industrie and the Boeing Company, organised an Aviation Working Group, on which some of the world's leading aviation financiers also served, to monitor the development of Unidroit's preliminary draft Convention. This extraordinary pooling of resources by Airbus and Boeing, orchestrated by Mr J A Wool of Perkins Coie (Washington D C), permitted the identification for aircraft equipment of a whole range of novel solutions that often proved capable of extension to the generality of high-value mobile equipment and thus provided considerable impetus for the development of the preliminary draft Convention. In the final stages of the Study Group's work it also benefited

---

39 *Ibid.*

40 *Ibid* at p 32.

greatly from input from the International Air Transport Association (IATA) and its world-wide network of airlines.

In addition to these exceptional resources placed at the disposal of Unidroit's project by industry, it should be noted that the Unidroit Study Group, which was chaired by Sir Roy Goode, the British member of the Unidroit Governing Council and one of the world's leading experts in the field of the law relating to secured financing, also benefited greatly from the input of practising lawyers, such as Mr S Masuda from Mori Sogo (Tokyo), Mr S J McGairl from Freshfields (London), Mr G K Olufon from Continental Merchant Bank Nigeria Ltd. and Mr T J Whalen from Condon & Forsyth (Washington DC) who brought their considerable experience acquired over years of advising clients to enrich the process. Moreover, while the Study Group was creating the basis of the preliminary draft Convention, a Registration Working Group was at work identifying the requirements of the international registration system intended to underpin the future Convention. This Working Group was chaired by Mr RCC Cuming, a Canadian correspondent of Unidroit and one of the world's leading experts in the creation of personal property security registration systems.

When in 1998 the preliminary draft Convention was adjudged by the Unidroit Governing Council ready for transmission to Governments, it was moreover already accompanied by a preliminary draft Protocol on Matters specific to Aircraft Equipment that, building on the intensive participation of the aforementioned representatives of the world's aviation manufacturers and airlines in the work of the Unidroit Study Group, had been prepared by a special working group created at the invitation of the President of Unidroit, the core members of which were the Aviation Working Group, IATA and, by reason of its special competence for the development of the law relating to international civil aviation, ICAO This working group was chaired by Mr Wool, as co-ordinator of the Aviation Working Group.

The subsequent intergovernmental consultation process on the preliminary draft Convention and the preliminary draft Aircraft Protocol - over three sessions of a joint Unidroit Committee of governmental experts/Sub-committee of the ICAO Legal Committee held in 1999 and 2000[41] - was co-sponsored by Unidroit and ICAO, the latter however from the very beginning of this unique collaborative exercise having signalled

[41] The three joint Unidroit/ICAO sessions were followed by a separate session of the ICAO Legal Committee in accordance with the procedural requirements of ICAO in 2000: this session however expressly refrained from reopening the consensus reached by Governments over the three joint sessions.

that its involvement in the process extended only, in accordance with the delimitation of its statutory objectives, to aircraft equipment. These three joint sessions were chaired by Ms E Chiavarelli (Italy). Sir Roy Goode (United Kingdom) acted as Reporter.

In the meantime, following the preparation by another special working group created by the President of Unidroit, this time co-ordinated by Mr H Rosen (Zug, Switzerland), of a second preliminary draft Protocol, this time on Matters specific to Railway Rolling Stock and the Governing Council's approval in 2000 of the transmission of this text to Governments, a first joint session of a Unidroit/Intergovernmental Organisation for International Carriage by Rail (OTIF) Committee of governmental experts was held to consider this preliminary draft Protocol in 2001.[42] This first session was chaired by Mr K F Kreuzer (Germany) with Ms I Weinberg de Roca (Argentina) as Deputy Chairman. Ms Weinberg de Roca will chair future sessions of the Committee. The Unidroit Governing Council furthermore in September 2001 authorised the transmission to Governments of a third preliminary draft Protocol, on Matters specific to Space Assets, prepared by another working group created by the President of Unidroit, this time co-ordinated by Mr P D Nesgos (Milbank, Tweed, Hadley & McCloy, New York). This preliminary draft Protocol is already before the member Governments of the United Nations Committee on the Peaceful Uses of Outer Space (UNCOPUOS) for consideration as to the relationship between this instrument and the United Nations treaties on outer space.[43]

[42] Compare First Joint Session (Berne, 15/16 March 2001): report (prepared by the Secretariats of OTIF and Unidroit) (Study LXXIIH - Doc 5).

[43] Compare United Nations Committee on the Peaceful Uses of Outer Space/Legal Subcommittee (40th session: Vienna, 2-12 April 2001*): Draft convention of the International Institute for the Unification of Private Law on international interests in mobile equipment and the preliminary draft protocol thereto on matters specific to space property: report of the Secretariat and the secretariat of the International Institute for the Unification of Private Law* (A/AC105/C2/L225).

Principal features of the Cape Town Convention [44]

Dual Convention/Protocol Structure

As will already have been noticed, the Cape Town Convention has been given a quite unusual structure, namely that of a Convention with different companion Protocols. The original idea was to create a single instrument designed to carry not only the general rules common to all the categories of equipment falling within its sphere of application but also those special rules necessary to adapt and implement such general rules at the equipment-specific level. In 1996, however, the decision was taken by the Unidroit Study Group to delink the general and the special rules, with the former alone to be incorporated in the future Convention and the latter to be carried in equipment-specific Protocols. The immediate reason for this decision was to accommodate the aviation industry's desire to be able to enjoy the benefits of the new international regimen at the earliest possible opportunity, that is without having to wait for the formulation of the equipment-specific rules relating to categories of equipment other than aircraft equipment. The introduction of the Convention/Protocol structure was felt to accommodate this short-term desire of one equipment sector whilst at the same time adequately safeguarding the long-term benefits of uniformity for all the other categories of equipment to be encompassed by the future Convention's sphere of application.[45]

The provisions of the Cape Town Convention will accordingly apply indiscriminately to any of the categories of equipment to which it relates (by virtue of Article 2(3) of the Cape Town Convention) or may in future relate (under Article 51(1) of the Cape Town Convention). It will not however enter into force for any such category of equipment until such time as a Protocol, carrying the equipment-specific provisions relating to that category, has itself entered into force (Article 49(1)(a) of the Cape Town Convention) and is thereafter intended to take effect subject to the

---

[44] This contribution essentially concentrates on the Cape Town Convention, although, where appropriate, also refers to provisions of the Protocol. The author acknowledges his profound debt to the explanatory report and commentary on the draft Convention and the draft Aircraft Protocol drafted by Sir Roy Goode and finalised under the guidance of the Unidroit and ICAO Secretariats (DCME-IP/2) (hereinafter referred to as the *Explanatory Report*).

[45] Compare Stanford MJ, "A broader or a narrower band of beneficiaries for the proposed new international regimen?: Some reflections on the merits of the Convention/Protocol structure in facilitating the former" *op cit* fn 7 at p 244.

terms of that Protocol (Article 49(1)(b) of the Cape Town Convention). The Cape Town Convention and each such Protocol are to be read and interpreted as a single instrument (Article 6(1) of the Cape Town Convention) and, to the extent of any inconsistency between that Convention and such Protocol, the Protocol is to prevail (Article 6(2) of the Cape Town Convention).

Underlying Principles

The new international regimen is characterised by five underlying principles. These have been identified as follows: first, practicality in reflecting the salient factors characteristic of asset-based financing and leasing transactions; second, party autonomy in contractual relationships, reflecting the fact that parties to a high-value cross border transaction in equipment of the kind covered by the Cape Town Convention will be knowledgeable and experienced in such transactions and expertly represented, so that in general their agreements should be respected and enforced; third, predictability in the application of the Cape Town Convention, a feature which is specifically mentioned in the interpretation provisions of Article 5(1) and is reflected in the concise and clear priority rules, which give pre-eminence to certainty and simplicity and a rule-based rather than standards-based approach; fourth, transparency through rules which provide for registration of an international interest in order to give notice of it to third parties and which subordinate unregistered international interests to registered international interests and to the rights of purchasers; last, sensitivity to national legal cultures in allowing a Contracting State to weigh economic benefits against principles of national law considered of fundamental importance, and to make declarations to exclude, wholly or in part, select provisions of the Cape Town Convention it considers incompatible with these, for example, the exercise of extra-judicial remedies or the ready availability of judicial relief prior to a hearing on the merits.[46]

[46] Compare *Explanatory Report op cit* fn 44 at p 3 § 10.

Substantive sphere of application of the Cape Town Convention

1. Types of interest covered

The new international regimen applies to *international interests in mobile equipment*. The "international interest in mobile equipment" in question is an innovation of the Cape Town Convention. Whilst in most cases such an interest will at the same time constitute an interest in such equipment created under domestic law, the principal reason for proclaiming it an "international" interest was to ensure that it be recognised in all Contracting States as being autonomous, that is independent of the various categories of analogous national interest - even if the "domestic law of that State does not permit non-possessory (or indeed any) security interests in movable property",[47] - and thus to permit a creditor to invoke the remedies that it is granted under the Cape Town Convention, which will in most cases be stronger than those that it could invoke under domestic law.

Whereas the original intention was to create a unitary regimen for not only the classic security interest granted under a security agreement but also what are increasingly recognised by many as functional equivalents of such interests, namely the interest retained by a seller under a title reservation agreement and the interest vested in a person who is the lessor under a leasing agreement, it quickly became apparent that any attempt to assimilate these last-mentioned interests to security interests for all purposes in the future Convention would be to court the risk of its rejection by jurisdictions outside North America, the domestic law regimes of so many of which would not at this time be prepared to treat the interest retained by a conditional seller or a lessor as anything less than full ownership.[48]

The international interest created by the Cape Town Convention accordingly encompasses both the classic *security interest* (Article 2(2)(a) of the Cape Town Convention) and *the interest retained by a conditional seller* (Article 2(2)(b)) *or a lessor* (Article 2(2)(c)). On the other hand, the default remedies granted under the Cape Town Convention will differ according to whether

---

[47] Compare Goode RM, "The Unidroit draft mobile equipment Convention: confluence of legal concepts and philosophies", *Mélanges en l'honneur de Denis Tallon. D'ici, d'ailleurs: harmonisation et dynamique du droit* (1999) 69 at p 79.

[48] Compare pp 399-400 *supra*.

the international interest is created under a security agreement (Article 8 of the Cape Town Convention) or under either a title reservation agreement or a leasing agreement (Article 10 of the Cape Town Convention). Characterisation of the particular agreement is left to the applicable law as determined by the rules of private international law of the forum (Article 2(4) of the Cape Town Convention). This means that in those jurisdictions, like the United States of America, that would characterise title reservation agreements and certain types of leases as security agreements, the default remedies to be applied will be those provided for security agreements (that is, Articles 8 and 9 of the Cape Town Convention) whereas in those jurisdictions that would not treat title reservation agreements and leases as security agreements then the default remedies to be applied will be those provided for title reservation agreements and leases (that is, Article 10 of the Cape Town Convention). The practical effect of this will be to make the default remedies provided under the Cape Town Convention in respect of security interests to be of more limited application in countries outside North America than the default remedies provided for interests arising under title reservation and leasing agreements.[49]

The Cape Town Convention does not apply to outright sales, in that "these do not involve the assertion of any security or proprietary interest *vis-à-vis* the debtor".[50] Given, however, the keenness of aviation interests to see the benefits of the international registration system and priority rules of the Cape Town Convention extended to such sales, that Convention provides for the possibility of such extension in respect of a particular category of equipment under the relevant Protocol (Article 41 of the Cape Town Convention).[51]

States will at the moment of ratification or accession moreover have the possibility of making certain types of non-consensual interest, such as a repairer's lien, registrable in the same way as if they were international interests (Article 40 of the Cape Town Convention).

---

[49] Compare Goode RM, "The Unidroit draft mobile equipment Convention: confluence of legal concepts and philosophies" *op cit* fn 47 at p 76.

[50] Compare *Explanatory Report op cit* fn 44 at p 8 § 30.

[51] Thus for aircraft equipment compare Article III of the Protocol.

2. Types of property covered

The Cape Town Convention applies to international interests in three categories of mobile equipment and associated rights[52] secured by, or associated with an agreement creating or providing for such an interest (Article 2(1)). The three categories of high-value mobile equipment primarily envisaged by the Cape Town Convention are, first, airframes, aircraft engines and helicopters (Article 2(3)(a)) - generically referred to as "aircraft equipment" and, as such, the subject of the Protocol - second, railway rolling stock (Article 2(3)(b)) and, third, space assets (Article 2(3)(c)). For most of the gestation of the Cape Town Convention its sphere of application was delimited by reference to a non-exhaustive list of categories of equipment - aircraft equipment, containers, oil rigs, railway rolling stock, registered ships and space property - complemented by a residual category made up of any other categories of equipment of uniquely identifiable object. The requirement of unique identifiability was necessitated by the decision to underpin the Cape Town Convention with an asset-based (as opposed to a debtor-based) international registration system. The decision at a comparatively late stage to limit the ambit of the Cape Town Convention to just three categories of equipment was linked to the number of equipment-specific Protocols actively under preparation by Unidroit. There was nevertheless recognition of the desirability of leaving open the possibility of extending the application of the Cape Town Convention to other categories of uniquely identifiable high-value equipment in future (Article 51(1) of the Cape Town Convention). Considerable interest has for instance been expressed in the development of a future Protocol on mobile oil rigs.

The title of, and the preamble to the Cape Town Convention, as well as Article 2(1) and (2), indicate two additional criteria which determine the sphere of application of that Convention, namely that the equipment covered should be "mobile" and of "high value". Nowhere are these concepts defined and this was intentional. The criterion of "high value" will differ from one category of equipment to another and is therefore to be defined in the relevant Protocol. For aircraft engines, for example, this criterion is expressed in terms of

[52] "Associated rights" are defined as meaning "all rights to payment or other performance by a debtor under an agreement which are secured by or associated with the object" (compare Article 1(c)).

thrust or horsepower (Article I(2)(b) of the Protocol) and for airframes in terms of their carrying capacity (Article I(2)(e)).

The Cape Town Convention applies only to objects of a kind that are *uniquely identifiable* (Article 2(2)) and to associated rights capable of connection to a registered interest (Article 2(1)). The reason for this was, as indicated above, to facilitate the establishment of an asset-based registration system. Future property, which is not susceptible to registration, is accordingly excluded from the Cape Town Convention's sphere of application.[53] Neither does the Cape Town Convention apply to general proceeds - as opposed to money or non-money proceeds arising from total or partial loss or physical destruction or total or partial confiscation, condemnation or requisition of specific objects protected by registration (Articles 2(5) and 1(w)) - as for it to do so would broaden the ambit of that Convention in such a way that it would no longer be possible to limit its scope to objects capable of protection by registration and would involve dealing with perfection requirements and priority rules relevant to general asset and receivables financing detached from the underlying equipment.[54]

Territorial Sphere of Application and Formal Requirements

The only connecting factor provided for in the Cape Town Convention is that the debtor must be situated in a Contracting State at the time of the conclusion of the agreement creating or providing for the international interest (Article 3(1)). As indicated above, the Cape Town Convention is furthermore intended to apply to mobile equipment. The criterion of mobility, while nowhere defined, is intended to denote a category of equipment of a kind likely to be moving across or beyond national frontiers in the ordinary course of business, that is precisely those categories of equipment which do not particularly lend themselves to the application of the *lex rei sitae* for the settlement of disputes concerning the validity, enforceability and priority ranking of security rights.[55] However, the likelihood of such movement across or beyond national frontiers may not in a given case be realised. This raised the question whether the Cape Town Convention should govern such situations. Independently of whether a

[53] Compare Goode RM, "The Unidroit draft mobile equipment Convention: confluence of legal concepts and philosophies" *op cit* fn 47 at p 75.
[54] Compare *Explanatory Report op cit* fn 44 at p 20, *sub* comment 14.
[55] Compare pp 424-425 *supra*.

given State might find the Cape Town Convention's application in such a case desirable - some States argued that this might be seen as an unjustifiable degree of interference in the application of those States' domestic law rules - it is clear that, from a creditor's point of view, the link between such a creditor knowing in advance of lending funds against such an asset which law will apply in the event of his potential debtor's default and the ultimate willingness of that creditor to advance such funds will not alter in importance one iota in respect of such an asset so long as it remains possible that it may indeed move across national frontiers and, what is more, in a way that the creditor may have no means of ascertaining.[56] The view was taken that satisfaction of the criterion of mobility is to be sought in the nature of the category of equipment.

It is therefore quite possible that the Cape Town Convention may end up applying to a purely internal transaction. Those States not happy with the ouster of the application of their domestic law rules that this may involve are free, however, at the time of ratification or accession, to exclude the application of the Cape Town Convention, with the exception of certain provisions - essentially the registration provisions of Chapter V and the priority rules of Article 29 - in respect of a transaction which is an internal transaction[57] in relation to that State (Article 50 of the Cape Town Convention). It is envisaged that each Protocol may moreover require one or more additional connecting factors for any one of the categories of equipment covered by the Cape Town Convention. Thus a helicopter or an airframe pertaining to an aircraft [58] will be caught by the new international regimen where it is registered in the aircraft register of a Contracting State (Article IV(1) of the Protocol).

---

[56] This case was seen as arising in particularly acute form in the scenario of a railway train running round a circuit in Kansas. Compare Goode RM, "The Unidroit Mobile Equipment Convention" *Cross-border Security and Insolvency* (ed) Bridge and Stevens (2001) 225 at pp 232-233.

[57] An internal transaction is defined as "a transaction ... where the centre of the main interests of all parties to such transaction is situated, and the relevant object is located ... in the [State seeking to exclude the application of the Convention in respect of such transaction] at the time of the conclusion of the contract and where the interest created by the transaction has been registered in a national registry in that ... State, which has made a declaration pursuant to Article 50(1)" (compare Article 1(n) of the Cape Town Convention).

[58] The term "aircraft" is employed in the Protocol to refer to an aircraft as defined by the 1944 Chicago Convention on International Civil Aviation, that is either airframes with aircraft engines installed thereon or helicopters (compare Article I(2)(a)).

Formal Requirements. For an international interest to be validly constituted the agreement under which it is created or provided for has to meet certain formal requirements (Article 7 of the Cape Town Convention). These are relatively simple. First, the agreement in question must be in writing. Second, it must relate to an object of which the chargor, conditional seller or lessor has power[59] under the applicable law to dispose. Third, it must contain a description of that object sufficient to permit its identification. What for a given category of equipment will suffice for this purpose will be set out in the relevant Protocol.[60] Finally, in the case of a security agreement, the agreement must permit the determination of the secured obligations, although without the need to state the sum or maximum sum secured. Once these requirements are satisfied an international interest is created even if compliance with such requirements would not suffice to create a security interest under the otherwise applicable law and even if the international interest is of a kind not known to that law.[61]

Regulatory System of the Cape Town Convention

The regulatory system of the Cape Town Convention is analysed below from the point of view of, first, the default remedies available to the creditor; second, the international registration system; third, priority rules; fourth, the effect of the international interest in insolvency; fifth, assignments; sixth, jurisdiction and, finally, the extent to which the parties are free to derogate from provisions of that Convention.

Default remedies. The availability of adequate and readily enforceable default remedies was recognised as being of critical importance for the success of the Cape Town Convention, in particular for the realisation of its objective of making secured financing facilities more widely available and at lower cost. The creditor is accordingly armed under the Cape Town Convention with a set of *basic* default remedies that he may exercise in the event of the debtor's default.[62] Registration not being required for the

---

[59] For the creditor to have such a power it will not necessarily be the owner or the holder of a real right; it may have such a power by virtue of actual or ostensible authority from the holder of the object (compare *Explanatory Report*, p 25, *sub* comment 2 to Article 6).

[60] Thus for aircraft equipment compare Article VII of the Protocol.

[61] Compare *Explanatory Report op cit* fn 44 at p 25, *sub* comment 2 to Article 6.

[62] The creditor is granted two additional default remedies under the Protocol, namely to remove the aircraft's nationality registration under the 1944 Chicago

creation of an international interest - but rather to safeguard the priority of the holder of an international interest in relation to third parties - these remedies may be exercised even where the international interest in question has not been registered. And it should be noted that the remedies granted under the Cape Town Convention are not exhaustive: a creditor may also exercise such additional remedies permitted by the applicable law as are not inconsistent with the mandatory provisions of that Convention on default remedies (Article 12).

For the reasons given above,[63] the remedies granted under the Cape Town Convention will differ depending on whether the creditor is a chargee under a security agreement or a conditional seller or lessor. The remedies provided for chargees are more complex than those provided for conditional sellers and lessors: the remedies to be granted to a chargee must necessarily be more extensive because they involve the exercise of rights over another's property, whereas the remedies of a conditional seller or lessor simply involve his recovery of his own property.[64] In the case of a chargee, the remedies will be recovery of possession or control of the charged object (Article 8(1)(a)), sale or lease of the object (Article 8(1)(b)), collection or receipt of income or profits arising from the management or use of the object (Article 8(1)(c)) and vesting of ownership of the object in satisfaction of the debt (Article 9(1)). The first three of these remedies require the agreement of the chargor (Article 8(1)). With the exception of the last remedy - which requires a court order unless all interested persons, the chargor included, agree - they may all in principle be exercised by the chargee either with or without application to the court (Article 8(2)). However, States may, at the moment of ratifying or acceding to the Cape Town Convention, specify that such remedies may only be exercised with leave of the court (Article 54(2)). This safeguard was inserted for those States not familiar with self-help.

The chargor and other interested persons (for instance, subsequent chargees) are however provided with certain safeguards in the event of the chargee's exercise of his remedies, in addition, that is, to the safeguard mentioned above in relation to the remedy of vesting of the object in

---

Convention on International Civil Aviation (compare Article IX(1)(a)) and to procure the export and physical transfer of the aircraft object to the territory of another State (compare Article IX(1)(b)).

[63] Compare pp 431-432 *supra*.

[64] Compare Goode RM, "The Unidroit draft mobile equipment Convention: confluence of legal concepts and philosophies" *op cit* fn 47 at p 79.

satisfaction of the debt.[65] First, such remedies must be exercised in a commercially reasonable fashion (Article 8(3)). Second, notice of a proposed sale or lease must be given to interested persons (Article 8(4)). Third, States may, at the moment of ratifying or acceding to the Cape Town Convention, specify that the chargee may not grant a lease of the object whilst it is situated in, or controlled from their territory (Article 54(1)). Fourth, the default must be one which substantially deprives the creditor of what it is entitled to expect, unless otherwise agreed (Article 11(2)).

This last safeguard applies equally in respect of the remedies granted to conditional sellers and lessors. In the case of a conditional seller or lessor, these remedies will be termination of the title reservation or leasing agreement and recovery of possession or control (Article 10). Here again, as with a chargee's remedies under Article 8(2), these remedies may be exercised either with or without application to the court (Article 10(b)) and States will, at the moment of ratifying or acceding to the Cape Town Convention, have the opportunity of specifying that such remedies may only be exercised with leave of the court (Article 54(2)).

Of crucial importance for financiers in the context of asset-based financing of the categories of equipment covered by the Cape Town Convention is the power granted to the court, upon evidence being adduced as to default, to grant a creditor various forms of speedy interim relief, namely preservation of the object and its value (Article 13(1)(a)), possession, control or custody of the object (Article 13(1)(b)), immobilisation of the object (Article 13(1)(c)) or lease or management of the object and the income therefrom (Article 13(1)(d)). In respect of aircraft equipment an additional order may be granted by way of speedy interim relief, namely sale and application of the proceeds therefrom (Article X(3) of the Protocol).

This is one of a number of provisions of the Cape Town Convention and the Protocol which, albeit considered essential to the realisation of their commercial objectives - in so far as "[o]ne major impediment to true asset-based financing is the risk of protracted court proceedings following default",[66] - States will however, at the moment of ratification or accession, be free to opt out of.[67] This opt-in/opt-out approach commended itself to the authors of the Cape Town Convention as a means of balancing the

[65] Compare pp 436-437 *supra*.

[66] Compare Wool J, "The case for a commercial orientation to the proposed Unidroit Convention as applied to aircraft equipment" *Uniform Law Review* 1999/2 at p 299.

[67] *Ibid* p 294 *et seq.*

commercial and diplomatic objectives of the exercise, that is leaving it to the individual State to choose whether or not the anticipated economic benefits of that Convention, in terms of increased access to international capital market financing, justify the sacrificing of non-economic considerations (such as debtor protection concerns) or other economic considerations (such as bankruptcy reorganisation).[68]

International Registration System. At the heart of the Cape Town Convention lies the international registration system.[69] The international interest is registrable in an international registry (Article 16(1)). Different registries are contemplated for each category of equipment (Article 16(2)). Plans for the setting up of an international registry for aircraft equipment are already at an advanced stage. Meanwhile plans are also underway for the creation of an international registry for railway rolling stock. Registration serves a dual purpose. First, it serves to give public notice of the existence of the international interest. Second, it serves to preserve a creditor's priority and the effectiveness of the international interest in insolvency proceedings concerning the debtor (Article 30(1)).

An early decision was taken to go for an asset-based, as opposed to a debtor-based registry. The concept of a debtor-based registry was felt to raise particular problems at the level of languages. The idea of an asset-based registry, with assets being registered against currently owned and identified assets - as opposed to merely generic classes of asset - was considered to be greatly facilitated by the types of asset covered by the Cape Town Convention, namely specific types of property that lend themselves to unique identification, typically by manufacturer's serial number.[70] Registration is therefore against the object and not against the debtor.

Each international registry will be operated by a registrar (Article 17(5)) appointed by, and under the supervision of a supervisory authority (Article 17(2)(f)). The latter will enjoy international legal personality, where not already possessing the same (Article 27(1)). It will enjoy such immunity from legal or administrative process as is specified in the relevant

---

[68] Compare pp 425-426 *supra;* compare also p 443-444 *infra.*

[69] Compare Cuming RCC, "The registry system of the (draft) Convention on International Interests in Mobile Equipment and the (draft) Aircraft Equipment Protocol" (2001) 103 *Revue du Notariat* 33.

[70] Compare Stanford MJ, "Completion of a first draft of Unidroit's planned future Convention on International Interests in Mobile Equipment" *Uniform LR* 1996/2 274 at p 278.

Protocol (Article 27(2)). In this context, it should be noted that the immunity to be enjoyed by the supervisory authority of the international registration system for aircraft objects is to be that provided under the rules applicable to it as an international entity or otherwise (Article XVII(3) of the Protocol). The registrar, on the other hand, will, subject to three qualifications, be strictly liable for compensatory damages for loss suffered through errors or omissions attributable to either the registrar or his officers and employees or a malfunctioning of the international registration system (Article 28(1)). The registrar will not be so liable where the malfunctioning is caused by an event of an inevitable and irresistible nature, which could not be prevented by using the best practices in current use in the field of electronic registry design and operation, including those relating to back-up and systems security and networking (Article 28(1)). Furthermore, the registrar will not be liable for factual inaccuracies in the registration information received by it or transmitted by it in the form in which it received such information nor for acts or circumstances for which it is not responsible and arising prior to receipt of the registration information at the international registry (Article 28(2)) and the compensation payable by the registrar may be reduced to the extent that the person suffering loss has either caused or contributed to that loss (Article 28(3)).

The conferring of the functions of supervisory authority on an already existing intergovernmental body has to date been seen as an important guarantee of the credibility of the international registration system with prospective users.[71] The Council of ICAO on 22 November 2000 agreed in principle that ICAO should exercise these functions in respect of aircraft equipment[72] and the Cape Town Conference formally invited ICAO to accept the functions of supervisory authority upon the entry into force of the Cape Town Convention and the Protocol (compare Resolution No. 2 adopted by the diplomatic Conference). It is significant that OTIF has also indicated its keenness to exercise analogous functions in

[71] Compare Stanford MJ, "Unidroit's project for the creation of a new regimen governing the taking of security in high-value assets: a window of opportunity in the context of the privatisation and commercialisation of space" *Proceedings of the Workshop on Space Law in the Twenty-first Century* (organised by the International Institute of Space law with the United Nations Office for Outer Space Affairs) July 1999, 148 at p 150.

[72] Compare Stanford M J/De Fontmichel A, "Overview of the current situation regarding the preliminary draft Space Property Protocol and its examination by COPUOS" *Uniform LR* 2000/1 60 at p 62.

respect of railway rolling stock.[73] Unidroit and the Space Working Group have submitted to the United Nations Office for Outer Space Affairs and UNCOPUOS that the Secretary-General of the United Nations would moreover in principle be the most appropriate person to exercise such functions in respect of space property.[74]

By virtue of the fact that the international registration system is intended to be fully computerised, registrations and searches will be able to be made automatically from any point in the world. Provided that the asset against which a lender is contemplating advancing funds is the subject of an international interest that has been registered in the international registry, that lender will thus be able to find out, more or less instantaneously, the precise status of the asset in question. While there will be no direct reliance of the equipment-specific international registries on existing national registries or co-ordination between the two,[75] States will be able, where the relevant Protocol so provides, to use such existing national registries - for instance, those registration offices operated by civil aviation authorities under the 1944 Chicago Convention on International Civil Aviation, which are also used for registering interests recognised by the 1948 Geneva Convention on the International Recognition of Rights in Aircraft - as an alternative or the exclusive conduit for the transmission of registration information to the international registry (Article 18(5)). The holder of an international interest would thus be able to register his national interest and his international interest in the same asset simultaneously. The international registration system is designed to accommodate the registration of international interests, prospective international interests,[76]

---

[73] *Ibid.*

[74] Compare United Nations Committee on the Peaceful Uses of Outer Space/Legal Subcommittee (40th session: Vienna, 2-12 April 2001): *Draft convention of the International Institute for the Unification of Private Law on international interests in mobile equipment and the preliminary draft protocol thereto on matters specific to space property: report of the Secretariat and the secretariat of the International Institute for the Unification of Private Law* (A/AC 105/C 2/L 225), § 41.

[75] Compare Cuming RCC, "The registry system of the (draft) Convention on International Interests in Mobile Equipment and the (draft) Aircraft Equipment Protocol" *op cit* fn 69 at p 39.

[76] A "prospective international interest" is defined as "an interest that is intended to be created or provided for in an object as an international interest in the future, upon the occurrence of a stated event (which may include the debtor's acquisition of an interest in the object), whether or not the occurrence of the event is certain" (compare Article 1(y) of the Cape Town Convention).

registrable non-consensual rights and interests (Article 16(1)(a)),[77] assignments (Article 16(1)(b)), subordinations (Article 16(1)(e)) and certain other rights.[78]

It will be for each Protocol and the regulations to be promulgated thereunder[79] to specify the requirements for the effecting of registration (Article 18(1)(a)) and the searching (Article 18(1)(b)) of the international registry as also for ensuring the confidentiality of the information and documents of the international registry other than information and documents relating to a registration (Article 18(1)(c)).

Priorities. A registered interest has priority over both a subsequently registered interest and an unregistered interest (Article 29(1)). One of the prime concerns of the authors of the Cape Town Convention was to keep the priority rules as simple as possible. For this reason, the priority of the holder of a registered international interest will not be affected by the fact that he took with actual notice of an unregistered interest (Article 29(2)(a)) and, in a case where the security agreement covers future advances, the creditor will have priority as to such advances even if they were made with knowledge of a subsequent interest (Article 29(2)(b)).[80]

These priority rules suffer three exceptions. The first of these is that, since the interest of an outright buyer is not registrable under the Cape Town Convention, such a buyer takes free from an international interest not registered prior to his acquisition of such an interest (Article 29(3)). Second, since the interest or right of a conditional buyer or lessee is not registrable either under the Cape Town Convention, such a conditional buyer or lessee also takes free from an international interest not registered prior to the registration of the international interest held by its conditional seller or lessor (Article 29(4)). Third, the priority rules may be varied by agreement between the holders of competing interests (Article 29(4)).

---

[77] Compare pp 431-434 *supra*.

[78] In particular, notices of national interests, that is, notices of interests in purely internal transactions, will also be registrable in the international registry (compare Article 16(1)(d).

[79] The promulgation of such regulations, dealing with the operation of the international registry, will be the responsibility of the supervisory authority, in consultation with Contracting States (compare Article 17(2)(d)).

[80] Compare Goode RM, "The Unidroit Mobile Equipment Convention" *op cit* fn 56 at p 237.

Effect of the International Interest in Insolvency. An international interest is in principle effective in insolvency proceedings against the debtor provided that the interest was registered prior to the commencement of the insolvency proceedings in question (Article 30(1)). However, an international interest does not need to be so registered in order to be effective in the debtor's insolvency where it would already be effective for such purposes under the applicable law (Article 30(2)). And the effectiveness of the international interest in insolvency is in any case subject to any special rules of law applicable in insolvency proceedings relating to the avoidance of preferences and transfers in fraud of creditors and any rules of insolvency procedure relating to the enforcement of rights under the control or supervision of an insolvency administrator (Article 30(3)), for instance rules which restrict the enforcement of security with a view to facilitating a reorganisation of the debtor.[81]

Reflecting the fact that "[i]nsolvency laws that prevent or modify security-type and leasing rights result in greater risk to financial institutions that, in turn, pass on this risk to borrowers in the form of higher interest and leasing rates",[82] the Protocol contains special rules designed to strengthen the creditor's position *vis-à-vis* the insolvency administrator in the event of the debtor's insolvency. This it seeks to achieve by "ensuring as far as possible that the creditor either secures recovery of the object within a limited time or obtains from the insolvency administrator the curing of all past defaults and a commitment to perform the debtor's future obligations".[83] However, in recognition of the divide that opened up on this issue between those States prepared, on the model of Section 1110 of the American Federal Bankruptcy Code, to accept the idea of the court being precluded from exercising some of the powers it would normally have to stay proceedings or to modify the creditor's rights or remedies in such circumstances, in the interest of avoiding delay, and those States preferring to substitute "the court's discretion ... for the creditor's entitlement to take possession",[84] States will (under Article XXX(3)) have the choice, at the moment of ratification or accession, between a "hard" (Article XI, Alternative A) and a "soft" version (Article XI, Alternative B) of this special insolvency regimen. Alternatively, it will be open to States to opt for neither the hard rule nor the soft rule and in this case the issue will fall to be dealt with under the applicable law. This is thus another example of

[81] Compare *Explanatory Report op cit* fn 44 at p 8.
[82] Compare Wool J *op cit* fn 66 at p 298.
[83] Compare *Explanatory Report op cit* fn 44 at p 80, *sub* comment 1 to Article XI.
[84] *Ibid* p 12.

those provisions which, while judged "essential to the realisation of the commercial objectives"[85] of the Cape Town Convention and the Protocol, were felt to call in equal measure for the diplomatic reassurance afforded by the flexibility of the opt-in/opt-out technique.[86]

Assignment. Associated rights may be assigned (Article 31(1)) and such assignment registered in the international registry (Article 16(1)(b)). The formal requirements of a valid assignment follow those for the constitution of a valid international interest (Article 32(1)).[87] An assignment of associated rights will transfer to the assignee, to the extent agreed by the parties to the assignment, the related international interest and all the interests and priorities of the assignor under the Cape Town Convention (Article 31(1)). The assignee's priority with respect to associated rights and the related international interest the assignment of which has been registered covers not only purchase money/rental rights but also rights derived from cross-collateralisation (Article 36). The remedies exercisable by an assignee in the event of the assignor's default under an assignment by way of security (Article 34), the priority of competing assignments (Article 35) and the effect of the assignor's insolvency (Article 37) follow, *mutatis mutandis*, the rules laid down for the international interest itself.[88]

Jurisdiction. The fundamental principle of jurisdiction embodied in the Cape Town Convention is the respect of freedom of contract. Thus, subject to three exceptions, the parties to a transaction will be free to confer jurisdiction in respect of any claim brought under the Cape Town Convention upon the courts of any Contracting State and such courts will, unless otherwise agreed between the parties, have *exclusive* jurisdiction, even if the forum chosen has no connection with the parties or the transaction (Article 42).

The three exceptions to this rule concern insolvency proceedings, the making of orders against the registrar and the granting of speedy interim relief under the Cape Town Convention. First, the jurisdiction rules of that Convention will not be applicable to insolvency proceedings (Article 45). Second, the parties will not be able to confer jurisdiction to make orders against the registrar (Article 44(4)): the courts of the place in which the registrar has its centre of administration are to have *exclusive* jurisdiction to

---

85 Compare pp 436-439 *supra*.

86 *Ibid.*

87 Compare p 436 *supra*.

88 See *Explanatory Report op cit* fn 44 at p 8.

award damages or make orders against the registrar under Article 28[89] (Article 44(1)) and to make orders requiring the registrar in certain circumstances to discharge a registration (Article 44(2)). This rule is of especial significance in avoiding the possibility of the registrar finding himself faced with conflicting orders from courts of different States. Third, the courts of the Contracting State on the territory of which the object is situated are to have *concurrent* jurisdiction to make orders for interim relief under Article 13 other than orders for the lease or management of the object and the income therefrom[90] (Article 43(1)) and the courts of a Contracting State on the territory of which the debtor is situated are to have *concurrent* jurisdiction to make orders under Article 13(1)(d) for the lease or management of the object and the income therefrom (Article 43(2)). The distinction drawn between orders for interim relief under Article 13(1)(a), (b) and (c) and orders for interim relief under Article 13(1)(d) hinges on the fact that the former are seen as being *in rem* in nature and the latter rather as operating *in personam.*[91])

Ability of the Parties to Derogate from the Cape Town Convention's Terms. A good portion of the provisions of the Cape Town Convention are clearly not amenable to exercise of the parties' freedom of contract in that they affect third party rights. Subject to that limitation, though, the Cape Town Convention upholds the principle of freedom of contract, so firmly entrenched in international commercial law Conventions.[92] Thus the parties, in their relations with each other, are, with eight exceptions, free to derogate from or vary the effect of any of the provisions of Chapter III of the Cape Town Convention (Default remedies) (Article 15). The eight provisions of Chapter III that are mandatory are, first, those requiring the chargee to exercise the default remedies that he is granted under Articles 8(1)(a), (b) and (c) and 13 in a commercially reasonable manner (Article 8(3)); second, those requiring a chargee to give notice of an intended sale or lease (Article 8(4)); third, those requiring the chargee to apply any sum that he has realised by exercise of his remedies under Article 8(1) towards discharge of the amount of the secured obligations (Article 8(5)); fourth, those indicating how the chargee is to apply any surplus that he may have realised by exercise of his remedies under Article 8(1) (Article 8(6)); fifth, those restricting the grant of a vesting order (Article 9(3)); sixth, those

[89] Compare p 439 *supra.*
[90] Compare pp 436-439 *supra.*
[91] Compare *Explanatory Report op cit* fn 44 at p 59, *sub* comment 1 to Article 42.
[92] Compare pp 420-421 *supra.*

permitting the chargor to redeem the charged object so long as the chargee has not exercised his power of sale (Article 9(4)); seventh, those permitting the court, when granting orders for speedy interim relief under Article 13(1), to impose such terms as it deems necessary for the protection of interested persons[93] (Article 13(2)) and, finally, those requiring the remedies provided under Chapter III to be exercised in accordance with the procedure prescribed by the law of the place where the remedy in question is to be exercised (Article 14).

Conclusions

The Cape Town Convention has been dubbed "one of the most important commercial law conventions in the history of international private law".[94] The signs are unmistakably good for it and the Protocol entering into force very soon. Already 21 States have signed both instruments and it is significant that these are equally representative of both the developed and developing worlds and of the manufacturers, users and financiers of the categories of high-value mobile equipment encompassed by the Cape Town Convention. Other States, including the United States of America, have moreover signalled their intention to sign the two instruments shortly.

In choosing the venue for the diplomatic Conference Unidroit was particularly conscious of the special significance the proposed new international regimen holds for those countries so greatly in need of foreign capital investment for the development of their infrastructures. It is precisely the inadequacies of the laws of these countries relating to secured financing that so often acts as a brake on their ability to access international capital markets. By convening the diplomatic Conference in Cape Town, rather than the developed country venue that had become almost *de rigueur* in the past, it was *inter alia* the intention of Unidroit to signal its recognition that the key to the success of the end-product of the Conference was in many ways likely to turn on the extent of its acceptance by less developed countries. And the extent of its success with such countries may

---

93 "Interested persons" are defined as "(i) the debtor; (ii) any person who, for the purpose of assuring performance of any of the obligations in favour of the creditor, gives or issues a suretyship or demand guarantee or a standby letter of credit or any other form of credit insurance; (iii) any other person having rights in or over the object" (compare Article 1(m) of the Cape Town Convention).

94 Compare Goode RM, "The Unidroit draft mobile equipment Convention: confluence of legal concepts and philosophies" *op cit* fn 47 at p 81.

be judged by the considerable number already having becomes signatory States.

Other draft Protocols are well on the way to completion. The preliminary draft Rail Protocol, already before Governments,[95] corresponds to the "growing recognition at governmental level that creating a facility to enable railways to stand on their own feet financially is something that is not just politically desirable, and a budgetary benefit, but also an essential part of any revitalisation of the railway sector... and that...private capital should be a key component".[96] The preliminary draft Space Assets Protocol, which is already before member Governments of COPUOS,[97] is expected to "facilitate and expand space commerce"[98] through significantly facilitating asset-based financing of satellites and other space property at a time when more than 1,000 commercial communications satellites, valued at over US$5 billion, are due to be launched over the next ten years.[99] Member Governments of Unidroit have moreover indicated their interest in seeing the benefits of the Cape Town Convention extended in due course to other categories of high-value mobile equipment, in particular oil rigs.

A hallmark of the development by Unidroit of both the instruments considered in this chapter has been the active participation in all stages of their development by experts from the world of practice. This reflected Unidroit's concern, at a general level, to ensure that the results of its endeavours should respond to perceived market needs rather than abstract considerations of harmonisation of law and its consequent conviction, at a more specific level, that, given the unique extent to which the law in this area has tended to be shaped by the parties' contractual documentation, it would be unthinkable for any legislative initiative at the international level in this area to be mounted without due participation of experts working on a daily basis in the business sectors concerned. Thus, during both the initial study group stage and the final intergovernmental consultation process that led to the conclusion of the Unidroit Convention on International Financial Leasing, representatives of the world leasing industry took an active part in shaping the Convention. Their keenness to monitor the development of the

---

[95] Compare p 428 *supra*.

[96] Compare Rosen H, "Building a Railway to the future - Progress on the Draft Unidroit / OTIF Rail Protocol" in *Uniform Law Review* 2001/1, 50-52.

[97] Compare p 428 *supra*.

[98] Compare Panahy DA, Mittal R, "The prospective Unidroit Convention on international interests in mobile equipment as applied to space property" in *Uniform Law Review* 1999/2, 303 at p 312.

[99] *Ibid* at p 303.

Convention according to world-wide industry criteria even led the regional leasing company federations of five continents[100] to create an informal umbrella organisation grouping all five federations, the World Leasing Council.[101] The initial study group phase was moreover interrupted in order to permit a preliminary draft to be considered by leasing practitioners at a series of symposia held in different parts of the world.[102]

This process of industry involvement has reached new heights during the development of the Cape Town Convention. Not only has this work benefitted greatly from the input of experts from all the business sectors concerned, and in particular the Aviation Working Group organised jointly by Airbus Industrie and the Boeing Company, but responsibility for the preparation of first drafts of each of the draft or preliminary draft Protocols prepared to date has been undertaken - at the invitation of Unidroit - by working groups essentially made up of manufacturers, financiers and users or operators of the different categories of high-value equipment concerned, leavened admittedly by an admixture of expertise from the relevant sectorial international Organisations. The resulting products accordingly reflect industry consensus to an almost unprecedented degree and, to the extent that legislative exercises need, more than most, to be founded upon consensus if they are to prosper, then the chances of the Cape Town Convention attracting widespread acceptance must be considered to be excellent.

---

[100] North America, Latin America, Europe, Asia and Australasia.

[101] Compare p 422 *supra*.

[102] Three symposia, sponsored by the American Law Institute-American Bar Association Committee on Continuing Professional Education, Industrie-Leasing AG (the leasing subsidiary of the Swiss Banking Corporation) and Leasing Digest Conferences in conjunction with the Hong Kong Equipment Leasing Association, were organised in New York on 7 and 8 May 1981, in Zürich on 23 and 24 November 1981 and in Hong Kong from 10 to 12 January 1983 respectively.

APPENDICES

APPENDIX I

UNIDROIT CONVENTION ON INTERNATIONAL FINANCIAL LEASING

(Ottawa, May 1988)

THE STATES PARTIES TO THIS CONVENTION,

RECOGNISING the importance of removing certain legal impediments to the international financial leasing of equipment, while maintaining a fair balance of interests between the different parties to the transaction,

AWARE of the need to make international financial leasing more available,

CONSCIOUS of the fact that the rules of law governing the traditional contract of hire need to be adapted to the distinctive triangular relationship created by the financial leasing transaction,

RECOGNISING therefore the desirability of formulating certain uniform rules relating primarily to the civil and commercial law aspects of international financial leasing,

HAVE AGREED as follows:

Chapter I

Sphere of Application and General Provisions

Article 1

1. This Convention governs a financial leasing transaction as described in paragraph 2 in which one party (the lessor):

(a) on the specifications of another party (the lessee), enters into an agreement (the supply agreement) with a third party (the supplier) under which the lessor acquires plant, capital goods or other equipment (the equipment) on terms approved by the lessee so far as they concern its interests, and

(b) enters into an agreement (the leasing agreement) with the lessee, granting to the lessee the right to use the equipment in return for the payment of rentals.

2. The financial leasing transaction referred to in the previous paragraph is a transaction which includes the following characteristics:

(a) the lessee specifies the equipment and selects the supplier without relying primarily on the skill and judgment of the lessor;

(b) the equipment is acquired by the lessor in connection with a leasing agreement which, to the knowledge of the supplier, either has been made or is to be made between the lessor and the lessee; and

(c) the rentals payable under the leasing agreement are calculated so as to take into account in particular the amortisation of the whole or a substantial part of the cost of the equipment.

3. This Convention applies whether or not the lessee has or subsequently acquires the option to buy the equipment or to hold it on lease for a further period, and whether or not for a nominal price or rental.

4. This Convention applies to financial leasing transactions in relation to all equipment save that which is to be used primarily for the lessee's personal, family or household purposes.

Article 2

In the case of one or more sub-leasing transactions involving the same equipment, this Convention applies to each transaction which is a financial leasing transaction and is otherwise subject to this Convention as if the person from whom the first lessor (as defined in paragraph 1 of the previous article) acquired the equipment were the supplier and as if the agreement under which the equipment was so acquired were the supply agreement.

Article 3

1. This Convention applies when the lessor and the lessee have their places of business in different States and:

   (a) those States and the State in which the supplier has its place of business are Contracting States; or

   (b) both the supply agreement and the leasing agreement are governed by the law of a Contracting State.

2. A reference in this Convention to a party's place of business shall, if it has more than one place of business, mean the place of business which has the closest relationship to the relevant agreement and its performance, having regard to the circumstances known to or contemplated by the parties at any time before or at the conclusion of that agreement.

Article 4

1. The provisions of this Convention shall not cease to apply merely because the equipment has become a fixture to or incorporated in land.

2. Any question whether or not the equipment has become a fixture to or incorporated in land, and if so the effect on the rights inter se of the lessor and a person having real rights in the land, shall be determined by the law of the State where the land is situated.

Article 5

1. The application of this Convention may be excluded only if each of the parties to the supply agreement and each of the parties to the leasing agreement agree to exclude it.

2. Where the application of this Convention has not been excluded in accordance with the previous paragraph, the parties may, in their relations with each other, derogate from or vary the effect of any of its provisions except as stated in Articles 8(3) and 13(3)(b) and (4).

Article 6

1. In the interpretation of this Convention, regard is to be had to its object and purpose as set forth in the preamble, to its international character and to the need to promote uniformity in its application and the observance of good faith in international trade.

2. Questions concerning matters governed by this Convention which are not expressly settled in it are to be settled in conformity with the general principles on which it is based or, in the absence of such principles, in conformity with the law applicable by virtue of the rules of private international law.

Chapter II

Rights and Duties of the Parties

Article 7

1. (a) The lessor's real rights in the equipment shall be valid against the lessee's trustee in bankruptcy and creditors, including creditors who have obtained an attachment or execution.

   (b) For the purposes of this paragraph "trustee in bankruptcy" includes a liquidator, administrator or other person appointed to administer the lessee's estate for the benefit of the general body of creditors.

2. Where by the applicable law the lessor's real rights in the equipment are valid against a person referred to in the previous paragraph only on compliance with rules as to public notice, those rights shall be valid against that person only if there has been compliance with such rules.

3. For the purposes of the previous paragraph the applicable law is the law of the State which, at the time when a person referred to in paragraph 1 becomes entitled to invoke the rules referred to in the previous paragraph, is:

   (a) in the case of a registered ship, the State in which it is registered in the name of the owner (for the purposes of this sub-paragraph a bareboat charterer is deemed not to be the owner);

   (b) in the case of an aircraft which is registered pursuant to the Convention on International Civil Aviation done at Chicago on 7 December 1944, the State in which it is so registered;

   (c) in the case of other equipment of a kind normally moved from one State to another, including an aircraft engine, the State in which the lessee has its principal place of business;

   (d) in the case of all other equipment, the State in which the equipment is situated.

4. Paragraph 2 shall not affect the provisions of any other treaty under which the lessor's real rights in the equipment are required to be recognised.

5. This article shall not affect the priority of any creditor having:

   (a) a consensual or non-consensual lien or security interest in the equipment arising otherwise than by virtue of an attachment or execution, or

   (b) any right of arrest, detention or disposition conferred specifically in relation to ships or aircraft under the law applicable by virtue of the rules of private international law.

Article 8

1. (a) Except as otherwise provided by this Convention or stated in the leasing agreement, the lessor shall not incur any liability to the lessee in respect of the equipment save to the extent that the lessee has suffered loss as the result of its reliance on the lessor's skill and judgment and of the lessor's intervention in the selection of the supplier or the specifications of the equipment.

(b) The lessor shall not, in its capacity of lessor, be liable to third parties for death, personal injury or damage to property caused by the equipment.

(c) The above provisions of this paragraph shall not govern any liability of the lessor in any other capacity, for example as owner.

2. The lessor warrants that the lessee's quiet possession will not be disturbed by a person who has a superior title or right, or who claims a superior title or right and acts under the authority of a court, where such title, right or claim is not derived from an act or omission of the lessee.

3. The parties may not derogate from or vary the effect of the provisions of the previous paragraph in so far as the superior title, right or claim is derived from an intentional or grossly negligent act or omission of the lessor.

4. The provisions of paragraphs 2 and 3 shall not affect any broader warranty of quiet possession by the lessor which is mandatory under the law applicable by virtue of the rules of private international law.

Article 9

1. The lessee shall take proper care of the equipment, use it in a reasonable manner and keep it in the condition in which it was delivered, subject to fair wear and tear and to any modification of the equipment agreed by the parties.

2. When the leasing agreement comes to an end the lessee, unless exercising a right to buy the equipment or to hold the equipment on lease for a further period, shall return the equipment to the lessor in the condition specified in the previous paragraph.

Article 10

1. The duties of the supplier under the supply agreement shall also be owed to the lessee as if it were a party to that agreement and as if the equipment were to be supplied directly to the lessee. However, the supplier shall not be liable to both the lessor and the lessee in respect of the same damage.

2. Nothing in this article shall entitle the lessee to terminate or rescind the supply agreement without the consent of the lessor.

Article 11

The lessee's rights derived from the supply agreement under this Convention shall not be affected by a variation of any term of the supply agreement previously approved by the lessee unless it consented to that variation.

Article 12

1. Where the equipment is not delivered or is delivered late or fails to conform to the supply agreement:

   (a) the lessee has the right as against the lessor to reject the equipment or to terminate the leasing agreement; and

   (b) the lessor has the right to remedy its failure to tender equipment in conformity with the supply agreement,

   as if the lessee had agreed to buy the equipment from the lessor under the same terms as those of the supply agreement.

2. A right conferred by the previous paragraph shall be exercisable in the same manner and shall be lost in the same circumstances as if

the lessee had agreed to buy the equipment from the lessor under the same terms as those of the supply agreement.

3. The lessee shall be entitled to withhold rentals payable under the leasing agreement until the lessor has remedied its failure to tender equipment in conformity with the supply agreement or the lessee has lost the right to reject the equipment.

4. Where the lessee has exercised a right to terminate the leasing agreement, the lessee shall be entitled to recover any rentals and other sums paid in advance, less a reasonable sum for any benefit the lessee has derived from the equipment.

5. The lessee shall have no other claim against the lessor for non-delivery, delay in delivery or delivery of non-conforming equipment except to the extent to which this results from the act or omission of the lessor.

6. Nothing in this article shall affect the lessee's rights against the supplier under Article 10.

Article 13

1. In the event of default by the lessee, the lessor may recover accrued unpaid rentals, together with interest and damages.

2. Where the lessee's default is substantial, then subject to paragraph 5 the lessor may also require accelerated payment of the value of the future rentals, where the leasing agreement so provides, or may terminate the leasing agreement and after such termination:

   (a) recover possession of the equipment; and

   (b) recover such damages as will place the lessor in the position in which it would have been had the lessee performed the leasing agreement in accordance with its terms.

3. (a) The leasing agreement may provide for the manner in which the damages recoverable under paragraph 2 (b) are to be computed.

(b) Such provision shall be enforceable between the parties unless it would result in damages substantially in excess of those provided for under paragraph 2 (b). The parties may not derogate from or vary the effect of the provisions of the present sub-paragraph.

4. Where the lessor has terminated the leasing agreement, it shall not be entitled to enforce a term of that agreement providing for acceleration of payment of future rentals, but the value of such rentals may be taken into account in computing damages under paragraphs 2(b) and 3. The parties may not derogate from or vary the effect of the provisions of the present paragraph.

5. The lessor shall not be entitled to exercise its right of acceleration or its right of termination under paragraph 2 unless it has by notice given the lessee a reasonable opportunity of remedying the default so far as the same may be remedied.

6. The lessor shall not be entitled to recover damages to the extent that it has failed to take all reasonable steps to mitigate its loss.

Article 14

1. The lessor may transfer or otherwise deal with all or any of its rights in the equipment or under the leasing agreement. Such a transfer shall not relieve the lessor of any of its duties under the leasing agreement or alter either the nature of the leasing agreement or its legal treatment as provided in this Convention.

2. The lessee may transfer the right to the use of the equipment or any other rights under the leasing agreement only with the consent of the lessor and subject to the rights of third parties.

Chapter III

Final Provisions

Article 15

1. This Convention is open for signature at the concluding meeting of the Diplomatic Conference for the Adoption of the Draft Unidroit Conventions on International Factoring and International Financial Leasing and will remain open for signature by all States at Ottawa until 31 December 1990.

2. This Convention is subject to ratification, acceptance or approval by States which have signed it.

3. This Convention is open for accession by all States which are not signatory States as from the date it is open for signature.

4. Ratification, acceptance, approval or accession is effected by the deposit of a formal instrument to that effect with the depositary.

Article 16

1. This Convention enters into force on the first day of the month following the expiration of six months after the date of deposit of the third instrument of ratification, acceptance, approval or accession.

2. For each State that ratifies, accepts, approves, or accedes to this Convention after the deposit of the third instrument of ratification, acceptance, approval or accession, this Convention enters into force in respect of that State on the first day of the month following the expiration of six months after the date of the deposit of its instrument of ratification, acceptance, approval or accession.

Article 17

This Convention does not prevail over any treaty which has already been or may be entered into; in particular it shall not affect any liability imposed on any person by existing or future treaties.

Article 18

1. If a Contracting State has two or more territorial units in which different systems of law are applicable in relation to the matters dealt with in this Convention, it may, at the time of signature, ratification, acceptance, approval or accession, declare that this Convention is to extend to all its territorial units or only to one or more of them, and may substitute its declaration by another declaration at any time.

2. These declarations are to be notified to the depositary and are to state expressly the territorial units to which the Convention extends.

3. If, by virtue of a declaration under this article, this Convention extends to one or more but not all of the territorial units of a Contracting State, and if the place of business of a party is located in that State, this place of business, for the purposes of this Convention, is considered not to be in a Contracting State, unless it is in a territorial unit to which the Convention extends.

4. If a Contracting State makes no declaration under paragraph 1, the Convention is to extend to all territorial units of that State.

Article 19

1. Two or more Contracting States which have the same or closely related legal rules on matters governed by this Convention may at any time declare that the Convention is not to apply where the supplier, the lessor and the lessee have their places of business in those States. Such declarations may be made jointly or by reciprocal unilateral declarations.

2. A Contracting State which has the same or closely related legal rules on matters governed by this Convention as one or more non-Contracting States may at any time declare that the Convention is not to apply where the supplier, the lessor and the lessee have their places of business in those States.

3. If a State which is the object of a declaration under the previous paragraph subsequently becomes a Contracting State, the declaration made will, as from the date on which the Convention enters into force in respect of the new Contracting State, have the effect of a declaration made under paragraph 1, provided that the new Contracting State joins in such declaration or makes a reciprocal unilateral declaration.

Article 20

A Contracting State may declare at the time of signature, ratification, acceptance, approval or accession that it will substitute its domestic law for Article 8(3) if its domestic law does not permit the lessor to exclude its liability for its default or negligence.

Article 21

1. Declarations made under this Convention at the time of signature are subject to confirmation upon ratification, acceptance or approval.

2. Declarations and confirmations of declarations are to be in writing and to be formally notified to the depositary.

3. A declaration takes effect simultaneously with the entry into force of this Convention in respect of the State concerned. However, a declaration of which the depositary receives formal notification after such entry into force takes effect on the first day of the month following the expiration of six months after the date of its receipt by the depositary. Reciprocal unilateral declarations under Article 19 take effect on the first day of the month following the expiration of six months after the receipt of the latest declaration by the depositary.

4. Any State which makes a declaration under this Convention may withdraw it at any time by a formal notification in writing addressed to the depositary. Such withdrawal is to take effect on the first day of the month following the expiration of six months after the date of the receipt of the notification by the depositary.

5. A withdrawal of a declaration made under Article 19 renders inoperative in relation to the withdrawing State, as from the date on which the withdrawal takes effect, any joint or reciprocal unilateral declaration made by another State under that article.

Article 22

No reservations are permitted except those expressly authorised in this Convention.

Article 23

This Convention applies to a financial leasing transaction when the leasing agreement and the supply agreement are both concluded on or after the date on which the Convention enters into force in respect of the Contracting States referred to in Article 3(1)(a), or of the Contracting State or States referred to in paragraph l (b) of that article.

Article 24

1. This Convention may be denounced by any Contracting State at any time after the date on which it enters into force for that State.

2. Denunciation is effected by the deposit of an instrument to that effect with the depositary.

3. A denunciation takes effect on the first day of the month following the expiration of six months after the deposit of the instrument of denunciation with the depositary. Where a longer period for the denunciation to take effect is specified in the instrument of

denunciation it takes effect upon the expiration of such longer period after its deposit with the depositary.

Article 25

1. This Convention shall be deposited with the Government of Canada.

2. The Government of Canada shall:

   (a) inform all States which have signed or acceded to this Convention and the President of the International Institute for the Unification of Private Law (Unidroit) of:

      (i) each new signature or deposit of an instrument of ratification, acceptance, approval or accession, together with the date thereof;

      (ii) each declaration made under Articles 18, 19 and 20;

      (iii) the withdrawal of any declaration made under Article 21 (4);

      (iv) the date of entry into force of this Convention;

      (v) the deposit of an instrument of denunciation of this Convention together with the date of its deposit and the date on which it takes effect;

   (b) transmit certified true copies of this Convention to all signatory States, to all States acceding to the Convention and to the President of the International Institute for the Unification of Private Law (Unidroit).

IN WITNESS WHEREOF the undersigned plenipotentiaries, being duly authorised by their respective Governments, have signed this Convention.

DONE at Ottawa, this twenty-eighth day of May, one thousand nine hundred and eighty-eight, in a single original, of which the English and French texts are equally authentic.

APPENDIX II

CONVENTION ON INTERNATIONAL INTERESTS IN MOBILE EQUIPMENT

(Cape Town, November 2001)

THE STATES PARTIES TO THIS CONVENTION,

AWARE of the need to acquire and use mobile equipment of high value or particular economic significance and to facilitate the financing of the acquisition and use of such equipment in an efficient manner,

RECOGNISING the advantages of asset-based financing and leasing for this purpose and desiring to facilitate these types of transaction by establishing clear rules to govern them,

MINDFUL of the need to ensure that interests in such equipment are recognised and protected universally,

DESIRING to provide broad and mutual economic benefits for all interested parties,

BELIEVING that such rules must reflect the principles underlying asset-based financing and leasing and promote the autonomy of the parties necessary in these transactions,

CONSCIOUS of the need to establish a legal framework for international interests in such equipment and for that purpose to create an international registration system for their protection,

TAKING INTO CONSIDERATION the objectives and principles enunciated in existing Conventions relating to such equipment,

HAVE AGREED upon the following provisions:

Chapter I

Sphere of application and general provisions

Article 1 - Definitions

In this Convention, except where the context otherwise requires, the following terms are employed with the meanings set out below:

(a) "agreement" means a security agreement, a title reservation agreement or a leasing agreement;

(b) "assignment" means a contract which, whether by way of security or otherwise, confers on the assignee associated rights with or without a transfer of the related international interest;

(c) "associated rights" means all rights to payment or other performance by a debtor under an agreement which are secured by or associated with the object;

(d) "commencement of the insolvency proceedings" means the time at which the insolvency proceedings are deemed to commence under the applicable insolvency law;

(e) "conditional buyer" means a buyer under a title reservation agreement;

(f) "conditional seller" means a seller under a title reservation agreement;

(g) "contract of sale" means a contract for the sale of an object by a seller to a buyer which is not an agreement as defined in (a) above;

(h) "court" means a court of law or an administrative or arbitral tribunal established by a Contracting State;

(i) "creditor" means a chargee under a security agreement, a conditional seller under a title reservation agreement or a lessor under a leasing agreement;

(j) "debtor" means a chargor under a security agreement, a conditional buyer under a title reservation agreement, a lessee under a leasing agreement or a person whose interest in an object is burdened by a registrable non-consensual right or interest;

(k) "insolvency administrator" means a person authorised to administer the reorganisation or liquidation, including one authorised on an interim basis, and includes a debtor in possession if permitted by the applicable insolvency law;

(l) "insolvency proceedings" means bankruptcy, liquidation or other collective judicial or administrative proceedings, including interim proceedings, in which the assets and affairs of the debtor are subject to control or supervision by a court for the purposes of reorganisation or liquidation;

(m) "interested persons" means:

   (i) the debtor;

   (ii) any person who, for the purpose of assuring performance of any of the obligations in favour of the creditor, gives or issues a suretyship or demand guarantee or a standby letter of credit or any other form of credit insurance;

   (iii) any other person having rights in or over the object;

(n) "internal transaction" means a transaction of a type listed in Article 2(2)(a) to (c) where the centre of the main interests of all parties to such transaction is situated, and the relevant object located (as specified in the Protocol), in the same Contracting State at the time of the conclusion of the contract and where the interest created by the transaction has been registered in a national registry in that Contracting State, which has made a declaration pursuant to Article 50(1);

(o) "international interest" means an interest held by a creditor to which Article 2 applies;

(p) "International Registry" means the international registration facilities established for the purposes of this Convention or the Protocol;

(q) "leasing agreement" means an agreement by which one person (the lessor) grants a right to possession or control of an object (with or without an option to purchase) to another person (the lessee) in return for a rental or other payment;

(r) "national interest" means an interest held by a creditor in an object and created by an internal transaction covered by a declaration under Article 50;

(s) "non-consensual right or interest" means a right or interest conferred under the law of a Contracting State that has made a declaration under Article 39 to secure the performance of an obligation, including an obligation to a State, State entity or an intergovernmental or private organisation;

(t) "notice of a national interest" means notice registered or to be registered in the International Registry that a national interest has been created;

(u) "object" means an object of a category to which Article 2 applies;

(v) "pre-existing right or interest" means a right or interest of any kind in or over an object created or arising before the effective date of this Convention as defined by Article 60;

(w) "proceeds" means money or non-money proceeds of an object arising from the total or partial loss or physical destruction of the object or its total or partial confiscation, condemnation or requisition;

(x) "prospective assignment" means an assignment that is intended to be made in the future, upon the occurrence of a stated event, whether or not the occurrence of the event is certain;

(y) "prospective international interest" means an interest that is intended to be created or provided for in an object as an international interest in the future, upon the occurrence of a stated event (which may include the debtor's acquisition of an interest in the object), whether or not the occurrence of the event is certain;

(z) "prospective sale" means a sale which is intended to be made in the future, upon the occurrence of a stated event, whether or not the occurrence of the event is certain;

(aa) "Protocol" means, in respect of any category of object and associated rights to which this Convention applies, the Protocol in respect of that category of object and associated rights;

(bb) "registered" means registered in the International Registry pursuant to Chapter V;

(cc) "registered interest" means an international interest, a registrable non-consensual right or interest or a national interest specified in a notice of a national interest registered pursuant to Chapter V;

(dd) "registrable non-consensual right or interest" means a non-consensual right or interest registrable pursuant to a declaration deposited under Article 40;

(ee) "Registrar" means, in respect of the Protocol, the person or body designated by that Protocol or appointed under Article 17(2)(b);

(ff) "regulations" means regulations made or approved by the Supervisory Authority pursuant to the Protocol;

(gg) "sale" means a transfer of ownership of an object pursuant to a contract of sale;

(hh) "secured obligation" means an obligation secured by a security interest;

(ii) "security agreement" means an agreement by which a chargor grants or agrees to grant to a chargee an interest (including an ownership interest) in or over an object to secure the performance of any existing or future obligation of the chargor or a third person;

(jj) "security interest" means an interest created by a security agreement;

(kk) "Supervisory Authority" means, in respect of the Protocol, the Supervisory Authority referred to in Article 17(1);

(ll) "title reservation agreement" means an agreement for the sale of an object on terms that ownership does not pass until fulfilment of the condition or conditions stated in the agreement;

(mm) "unregistered interest" means a consensual interest or non-consensual right or interest (other than an interest to which Article 39 applies) which has not been registered, whether or not it is registrable under this Convention; and

(nn) "writing" means a record of information (including information communicated by teletransmission) which is in tangible or other form and is capable of being reproduced in tangible form on a subsequent occasion and which indicates by reasonable means a person's approval of the record.

Article 2 - The international interest

1. This Convention provides for the constitution and effects of an international interest in certain categories of mobile equipment and associated rights.

2. For the purposes of this Convention, an international interest in mobile equipment is an interest, constituted under Article 7, in a uniquely identifiable object of a category of such objects listed in paragraph 3 and designated in the Protocol:

   (a) granted by the chargor under a security agreement;

   (b) vested in a person who is the conditional seller under a title reservation agreement; or

   (c) vested in a person who is the lessor under a leasing agreement.

An interest falling within sub-paragraph (a) does not also fall within sub-paragraph (b) or (c).

3. The categories referred to in the preceding paragraphs are:

   (a) airframes, aircraft engines and helicopters;

   (b) railway rolling stock; and

   (c) space assets.

4. The applicable law determines whether an interest to which paragraph 2 applies falls within sub-paragraph (a), (b) or (c) of that paragraph.

5. An international interest in an object extends to proceeds of that object.

Article 3 - Sphere of application

1. This Convention applies when, at the time of the conclusion of the agreement creating or providing for the international interest, the debtor is situated in a Contracting State.

2. The fact that the creditor is situated in a non-Contracting State does not affect the applicability of this Convention.

Article 4 - Where debtor is situated

1. For the purposes of Article 3(1), the debtor is situated in any Contracting State:

   (a) under the law of which it is incorporated or formed;

   (b) where it has its registered office or statutory seat;

   (c) where it has its centre of administration; or

   (d) where it has its place of business.

2. A reference in sub-paragraph (d) of the preceding paragraph to the debtor's place of business shall, if it has more than one place of business, mean its principal place of business or, if it has no place of business, its habitual residence.

Article 5 - Interpretation and applicable law

1. In the interpretation of this Convention, regard is to be had to its purposes as set forth in the preamble, to its international character and to the need to promote uniformity and predictability in its application.

2. Questions concerning matters governed by this Convention which are not expressly settled in it are to be settled in conformity with the general principles on which it is based or, in the absence of such principles, in conformity with the applicable law.

3. References to the applicable law are to the domestic rules of the law applicable by virtue of the rules of private international law of the forum State.

4. Where a State comprises several territorial units, each of which has its own rules of law in respect of the matter to be decided, and where there is no indication of the relevant territorial unit, the law of that State decides which is the territorial unit whose rules shall govern. In the absence of any such rule, the law of the territorial unit with which the case is most closely connected shall apply.

Article 6 - Relationship between the Convention and the Protocol

1. This Convention and the Protocol shall be read and interpreted together as a single instrument.

2. To the extent of any inconsistency between this Convention and the Protocol, the Protocol shall prevail.

Chapter II

Constitution of an International Interest

Article 7 - Formal requirements

An interest is constituted as an international interest under this Convention where the agreement creating or providing for the interest:

(a) is in writing;

(b) relates to an object of which the chargor, conditional seller or lessor has power to dispose;

(c) enables the object to be identified in conformity with the Protocol; and

(d) in the case of a security agreement, enables the secured obligations to be determined, but without the need to state a sum or maximum sum secured.

Chapter III

Default Remedies

Article 8 - Remedies of chargee

1. In the event of default as provided in Article 11, the chargee may, to the extent that the chargor has at any time so agreed and subject to any declaration that may be made by a Contracting State under Article 54, exercise any one or more of the following remedies:

    (a) take possession or control of any object charged to it;

    (b) sell or grant a lease of any such object;

    (c) collect or receive any income or profits arising from the management or use of any such object.

2. The chargee may alternatively apply for a court order authorising or directing any of the acts referred to in the preceding paragraph.

3. Any remedy set out in sub-paragraph (a), (b) or (c) of paragraph 1 or by Article 13 shall be exercised in a commercially reasonable manner. A remedy shall be deemed to be exercised in a commercially reasonable manner where it is exercised in conformity with a provision of the security agreement except where such a provision is manifestly unreasonable.

4. A chargee proposing to sell or grant a lease of an object under paragraph 1 otherwise than pursuant to a court order shall give reasonable prior notice in writing of the proposed sale or lease to:

   (a) interested persons specified in Article 1(m)(i) and (ii); and

   (b) interested persons specified in Article 1(m)(iii) who have given notice of their rights to the chargee within a reasonable time prior to the sale or lease.

5. Any sum collected or received by the chargee as a result of exercise of any of the remedies set out in paragraph 1 shall be applied towards discharge of the amount of the secured obligations.

6. Where the sums collected or received by the chargee as a result of the exercise of any remedy set out in paragraph 1 exceed the amount secured by the security interest and any reasonable costs incurred in the exercise of any such remedy, then unless otherwise ordered by the court the chargee shall distribute the surplus among holders of subsequently ranking interests which have been registered or of which the chargee has been given notice, in order of priority, and pay any remaining balance to the chargor.

Article 9 - Vesting of object in satisfaction; redemption

1. At any time after default as provided in Article 11, the chargee and all the interested persons may agree that ownership of (or any other interest of the chargor in) any object covered by the security interest

shall vest in the chargee in or towards satisfaction of the secured obligations.

2. The court may on the application of the chargee order that ownership of (or any other interest of the chargor in) any object covered by the security interest shall vest in the chargee in or towards satisfaction of the secured obligations.

3. The court shall grant an application under the preceding paragraph only if the amount of the secured obligations to be satisfied by such vesting is commensurate with the value of the object after taking account of any payment to be made by the chargee to any of the interested persons.

4. At any time after default as provided in Article 11 and before sale of the charged object or the making of an order under paragraph 2, the chargor or any interested person may discharge the security interest by paying in full the amount secured, subject to any lease granted by the chargee under Article 8(1)(b). Where, after such default, the payment of the amount secured is made in full by an interested person other than the debtor, that person is subrogated to the rights of the chargee.

5. Ownership or any other interest of the chargor passing on a sale under Article 8(1)(b) or passing under paragraph 1 or 2 of this Article is free from any other interest over which the chargee's security interest has priority under the provisions of Article 29.

Article 10 - Remedies of conditional seller or lessor

In the event of default under a title reservation agreement or under a leasing agreement as provided in Article 11, the conditional seller or the lessor, as the case may be, may:

(a) subject to any declaration that may be made by a Contracting State under Article 54, terminate the agreement and take possession or control of any object to which the agreement relates; or

(b) apply for a court order authorising or directing either of these acts.

Article 11 - Meaning of default

1. The debtor and the creditor may at any time agree in writing as to the events that constitute a default or otherwise give rise to the rights and remedies specified in Articles 8 to 10 and 13.

2. Where the debtor and the creditor have not so agreed, "default" for the purposes of Articles 8 to 10 and 13 means a default which substantially deprives the creditor of what it is entitled to expect under the agreement.

Article 12 - Additional remedies

Any additional remedies permitted by the applicable law, including any remedies agreed upon by the parties, may be exercised to the extent that they are not inconsistent with the mandatory provisions of this Chapter as set out in Article 15.

Article 13 - Relief pending final determination

1. Subject to any declaration that it may make under Article 55, a Contracting State shall ensure that a creditor who adduces evidence of default by the debtor may, pending final determination of its claim and to the extent that the debtor has at any time so agreed, obtain from a court speedy relief in the form of such one or more of the following orders as the creditor requests:

   (a) preservation of the object and its value;

   (b) possession, control or custody of the object;

   (c) immobilisation of the object; and

   (d) lease or, except where covered by sub-paragraphs (a) to (c), management of the object and the income therefrom.

2. In making any order under the preceding paragraph, the court may impose such terms as it considers necessary to protect the interested persons in the event that the creditor:

    (a) in implementing any order granting such relief, fails to perform any of its obligations to the debtor under this Convention or the Protocol; or

    (b) fails to establish its claim, wholly or in part, on the final determination of that claim.

3. Before making any order under paragraph 1, the court may require notice of the request to be given to any of the interested persons.

4. Nothing in this Article affects the application of Article 8(3) or limits the availability of forms of interim relief other than those set out in paragraph 1.

Article 14 - Procedural requirements

Subject to Article 54(2), any remedy provided by this Chapter shall be exercised in conformity with the procedure prescribed by the law of the place where the remedy is to be exercised.

Article 15 - Derogation

In their relations with each other, any two or more of the parties referred to in this Chapter may at any time, by agreement in writing, derogate from or vary the effect of any of the preceding provisions of this Chapter except Articles 8(3) to (6), 9(3) and (4), 13(2) and 14.

Chapter IV

The International Registration System

Article 16 - The International Registry

1. An International Registry shall be established for registrations of:

   (a) international interests, prospective international interests and registrable non-consensual rights and interests;

   (b) assignments and prospective assignments of international interests;

   (c) acquisitions of international interests by legal or contractual subrogations under the applicable law;

   (d) notices of national interests; and

   (e) subordinations of interests referred to in any of the preceding sub-paragraphs.

2. Different international registries may be established for different categories of object and associated rights.

3. For the purposes of this Chapter and Chapter V, the term "registration" includes, where appropriate, an amendment, extension or discharge of a registration.

Article 17 -The Supervisory Authority and the Registrar

1. There shall be a Supervisory Authority as provided by the Protocol.

2. The Supervisory Authority shall:

   (a) establish or provide for the establishment of the International Registry;

(b) except as otherwise provided by the Protocol, appoint and dismiss the Registrar;

(c) ensure that any rights required for the continued effective operation of the International Registry in the event of a change of Registrar will vest in or be assignable to the new Registrar;

(d) after consultation with the Contracting States, make or approve and ensure the publication of regulations pursuant to the Protocol dealing with the operation of the International Registry;

(e) establish administrative procedures through which complaints concerning the operation of the International Registry can be made to the Supervisory Authority;

(f) supervise the Registrar and the operation of the International Registry;

(g) at the request of the Registrar, provide such guidance to the Registrar as the Supervisory Authority thinks fit;

(h) set and periodically review the structure of fees to be charged for the services and facilities of the International Registry;

(i) do all things necessary to ensure that an efficient notice-based electronic registration system exists to implement the objectives of this Convention and the Protocol; and

(j) report periodically to Contracting States concerning the discharge of its obligations under this Convention and the Protocol.

3. The Supervisory Authority may enter into any agreement requisite for the performance of its functions, including any agreement referred to in Article 27(3).

4. The Supervisory Authority shall own all proprietary rights in the data bases and archives of the International Registry.

5. The Registrar shall ensure the efficient operation of the International Registry and perform the functions assigned to it by this Convention, the Protocol and the regulations.

Chapter V

Other Matters Relating to Registration

Article 18 - Registration requirements

1. The Protocol and regulations shall specify the requirements, including the criteria for the identification of the object:

   (a) for effecting a registration (which shall include provision for prior electronic transmission of any consent from any person whose consent is required under Article 20);

   (b) for making searches and issuing search certificates, and, subject thereto;

   (c) for ensuring the confidentiality of information and documents of the International Registry other than information and documents relating to a registration.

2. The Registrar shall not be under a duty to enquire whether a consent to registration under Article 20 has in fact been given or is valid.

3. Where an interest registered as a prospective international interest becomes an international interest, no further registration shall be required provided that the registration information is sufficient for a registration of an international interest.

4. The Registrar shall arrange for registrations to be entered into the International Registry data base and made searchable in chronological order of receipt, and the file shall record the date and time of receipt.

5. The Protocol may provide that a Contracting State may designate an entity or entities in its territory as the entry point or entry points

through which the information required for registration shall or may be transmitted to the International Registry. A Contracting State making such a designation may specify the requirements, if any, to be satisfied before such information is transmitted to the International Registry.

Article 19 - Validity and time of registration

1. A registration shall be valid only if made in conformity with Article 20.

2. A registration, if valid, shall be complete upon entry of the required information into the International Registry data base so as to be searchable.

3. A registration shall be searchable for the purposes of the preceding paragraph at the time when:

    (a) the International Registry has assigned to it a sequentially ordered file number; and

    (b) the registration information, including the file number, is stored in durable form and may be accessed at the International Registry.

4. If an interest first registered as a prospective international interest becomes an international interest, that international interest shall be treated as registered from the time of registration of the prospective international interest provided that the registration was still current immediately before the international interest was constituted as provided by Article 7.

5. The preceding paragraph applies with necessary modifications to the registration of a prospective assignment of an international interest.

6. A registration shall be searchable in the International Registry data base according to the criteria prescribed by the Protocol.

Article 20 - Consent to registration

1. An international interest, a prospective international interest or an assignment or prospective assignment of an international interest may be registered, and any such registration amended or extended prior to its expiry, by either party with the consent in writing of the other.

2. The subordination of an international interest to another international interest may be registered by or with the consent in writing at any time of the person whose interest has been subordinated.

3. A registration may be discharged by or with the consent in writing of the party in whose favour it was made.

4. The acquisition of an international interest by legal or contractual subrogation may be registered by the subrogee.

5. A registrable non-consensual right or interest may be registered by the holder thereof.

6. A notice of a national interest may be registered by the holder thereof.

Article 21 - Duration of registration

Registration of an international interest remains effective until discharged or until expiry of the period specified in the registration.

Article 22 - Searches

1. Any person may, in the manner prescribed by the Protocol and regulations, make or request a search of the International Registry by electronic means concerning interests or prospective international interests registered therein.

2. Upon receipt of a request therefor, the Registrar, in the manner prescribed by the Protocol and regulations, shall issue a registry search certificate by electronic means with respect to any object:

   (a) stating all registered information relating thereto, together with a statement indicating the date and time of registration of such information; or

   (b) stating that there is no information in the International Registry relating thereto.

3. A search certificate issued under the preceding paragraph shall indicate that the creditor named in the registration information has acquired or intends to acquire an international interest in the object but shall not indicate whether what is registered is an international interest or a prospective international interest, even if this is ascertainable from the relevant registration information.

Article 23 - List of declarations and declared non-consensual rights or interests

The Registrar shall maintain a list of declarations, withdrawals of declaration and of the categories of non-consensual right or interest communicated to the Registrar by the Depositary as having been declared by Contracting States in conformity with Articles 39 and 40 and the date of each such declaration or withdrawal of declaration. Such list shall be recorded and searchable in the name of the declaring State and shall be made available as provided in the Protocol and regulations to any person requesting it.

Article 24 - Evidentiary value of certificates

A document in the form prescribed by the regulations which purports to be a certificate issued by the International Registry is prima facie proof:

(a) that it has been so issued; and

(b) of the facts recited in it, including the date and time of a registration.

Article 25 - Discharge of registration

1. Where the obligations secured by a registered security interest or the obligations giving rise to a registered non-consensual right or interest have been discharged, or where the conditions of transfer of title under a registered title reservation agreement have been fulfilled, the holder of such interest shall, without undue delay, procure the discharge of the registration after written demand by the debtor delivered to or received at its address stated in the registration.

2. Where a prospective international interest or a prospective assignment of an international interest has been registered, the intending creditor or intending assignee shall, without undue delay, procure the discharge of the registration after written demand by the intending debtor or assignor which is delivered to or received at its address stated in the registration before the intending creditor or assignee has given value or incurred a commitment to give value.

3. Where the obligations secured by a national interest specified in a registered notice of a national interest have been discharged, the holder of such interest shall, without undue delay, procure the discharge of the registration after written demand by the debtor delivered to or received at its address stated in the registration.

4. Where a registration ought not to have been made or is incorrect, the person in whose favour the registration was made shall, without undue delay, procure its discharge or amendment after written demand by the debtor delivered to or received at its address stated in the registration.

Article 26 - Access to the international registration facilities

No person shall be denied access to the registration and search facilities of the International Registry on any ground other than its failure to comply with the procedures prescribed by this Chapter.

Chapter VI

Privileges and Immunities of the Supervisory Authority and the Registrar

Article 27 - Legal personality; immunity

1. The Supervisory Authority shall have international legal personality where not already possessing such personality.

2. The Supervisory Authority and its officers and employees shall enjoy such immunity from legal or administrative process as is specified in the Protocol.

3. (a) The Supervisory Authority shall enjoy exemption from taxes and such other privileges as may be provided by agreement with the host State.

   (b) For the purposes of this paragraph, "host State" means the State in which the Supervisory Authority is situated.

4. The assets, documents, data bases and archives of the International Registry shall be inviolable and immune from seizure or other legal or administrative process.

5. For the purposes of any claim against the Registrar under Article 28(1) or Article 44, the claimant shall be entitled to access to such information and documents as are necessary to enable the claimant to pursue its claim.

6. The Supervisory Authority may waive the inviolability and immunity conferred by paragraph 4.

Chapter VII

Liability of the Registrar

Article 28 - Liability and financial assurances

1. The Registrar shall be liable for compensatory damages for loss suffered by a person directly resulting from an error or omission of the Registrar and its officers and employees or from a malfunction of the international registration system except where the malfunction is caused by an event of an inevitable and irresistible nature, which could not be prevented by using the best practices in current use in the field of electronic registry design and operation, including those related to back-up and systems security and networking.

2. The Registrar shall not be liable under the preceding paragraph for factual inaccuracy of registration information received by the Registrar or transmitted by the Registrar in the form in which it received that information nor for acts or circumstances for which the Registrar and its officers and employees are not responsible and arising prior to receipt of registration information at the International Registry.

3. Compensation under paragraph 1 may be reduced to the extent that the person who suffered the damage caused or contributed to that damage.

4. The Registrar shall procure insurance or a financial guarantee covering the liability referred to in this Article to the extent determined by the Supervisory Authority, in accordance with the Protocol.

Chapter VIII

Effects of an International Interest as Against Third Parties

Article 29 - Priority of competing interests

1. A registered interest has priority over any other interest subsequently registered and over an unregistered interest.

2. The priority of the first-mentioned interest under the preceding paragraph applies:

   (a) even if the first-mentioned interest was acquired or registered with actual knowledge of the other interest; and

   (b) even as regards value given by the holder of the first-mentioned interest with such knowledge.

3. The buyer of an object acquires its interest in it:

   (a) subject to an interest registered at the time of its acquisition of that interest; and

   (b) free from an unregistered interest even if it has actual knowledge of such an interest.

4. The conditional buyer or lessee acquires its interest in or right over that object:

   (a) subject to an interest registered prior to the registration of the international interest held by its conditional seller or lessor; and

   (b) free from an interest not so registered at that time even if it has actual knowledge of that interest.

5. The priority of competing interests or rights under this Article may be varied by agreement between the holders of those interests, but an assignee of a subordinated interest is not bound by an agreement to

subordinate that interest unless at the time of the assignment a subordination had been registered relating to that agreement.

6. Any priority given by this Article to an interest in an object extends to proceeds.

7. This Convention:

   (a) does not affect the rights of a person in an item, other than an object, held prior to its installation on an object if under the applicable law those rights continue to exist after the installation; and

   (b) does not prevent the creation of rights in an item, other than an object, which has previously been installed on an object where under the applicable law those rights are created.

Article 30 - Effects of insolvency

1. In insolvency proceedings against the debtor an international interest is effective if prior to the commencement of the insolvency proceedings that interest was registered in conformity with this Convention.

2. Nothing in this Article impairs the effectiveness of an international interest in the insolvency proceedings where that interest is effective under the applicable law.

3. Nothing in this Article affects:

   (a) any rules of law applicable in insolvency proceedings relating to the avoidance of a transaction as a preference or a transfer in fraud of creditors; or

   (b) any rules of procedure relating to the enforcement of rights to property which is under the control or supervision of the insolvency administrator.

Chapter IX

Assignments of Associated Rights and International Interests; Rights of Subrogation

Article 31 - Effects of assignment

1. Except as otherwise agreed by the parties, an assignment of associated rights made in conformity with Article 32 also transfers to the assignee:

   (a) the related international interest; and

   (b) all the interests and priorities of the assignor under this Convention.

2. Nothing in this Convention prevents a partial assignment of the assignor's associated rights. In the case of such a partial assignment the assignor and assignee may agree as to their respective rights concerning the related international interest assigned under the preceding paragraph but not so as adversely to affect the debtor without its consent.

3. Subject to paragraph 4, the applicable law shall determine the defences and rights of set-off available to the debtor against the assignee.

4. The debtor may at any time by agreement in writing waive all or any of the defences and rights of set-off referred to in the preceding paragraph other than defences arising from fraudulent acts on the part of the assignee.

5. In the case of an assignment by way of security, the assigned associated rights revest in the assignor, to the extent that they are still subsisting, when the obligations secured by the assignment have been discharged.

Article 32 - Formal requirements of assignment

1. An assignment of associated rights transfers the related international interest only if it:

   (a) is in writing;

   (b) enables the associated rights to be identified to the contract under which they arise; and,

   (c) in the case of an assignment by way of security, enables the obligations secured by the assignment to be determined in accordance with the Protocol but without the need to state a sum or maximum sum secured.

2. An assignment of an international interest created or provided for by a security agreement is not valid unless some or all related associated rights also are assigned.

3. This Convention does not apply to an assignment of associated rights which is not effective to transfer the related international interest.

Article 33 - Debtor's duty to assignee

1. To the extent that associated rights and the related international interest have been transferred in accordance with Articles 31 and 32, the debtor in relation to those rights and that interest is bound by the assignment and has a duty to make payment or give other performance to the assignee, if but only if:

   (a) the debtor has been given notice of the assignment in writing by or with the authority of the assignor; and

   (b) the notice identifies the associated rights.

2. Irrespective of any other ground on which payment or performance by the debtor discharges the latter from liability, payment or performance shall be effective for this purpose if made in accordance with the preceding paragraph.

3. Nothing in this Article shall affect the priority of competing assignments.

Article 34 - Default remedies in respect of assignment by way of security

In the event of default by the assignor under the assignment of associated rights and the related international interest made by way of security, Articles 8, 9 and 11 to 14 apply in the relations between the assignor and the assignee (and, in relation to associated rights, apply in so far as those provisions are capable of application to intangible property) as if references:

(a) to the secured obligation and the security interest were references to the obligation secured by the assignment of the associated rights and the related international interest and the security interest created by that assignment;

(b) to the chargee and chargor were references to the assignee and assignor;

(c) to the holder of the international interest were references to the assignee; and

(d) to the object were references to the assigned associated rights and the related international interest.

Article 35 - Priority of competing assignments

1. Where there are competing assignments of associated rights and at least one of the assignments includes the related international interest and is registered, the provisions of Article 29 apply as if the references to a registered interest were references to an assignment of the associated rights and the related registered interest and as if references to a registered or unregistered interest were references to a registered or unregistered assignment.

2. Article 30 applies to an assignment of associated rights as if the references to an international interest were references to an assignment of the associated rights and the related international interest.

Article 36 - Assignee's priority with respect to associated rights

1. The assignee of associated rights and the related international interest whose assignment has been registered only has priority under Article 35(1) over another assignee of the associated rights:

   (a) if the contract under which the associated rights arise states that they are secured by or associated with the object; and

   (b) to the extent that the associated rights are related to an object.

2. For the purposes of sub-paragraph (b) of the preceding paragraph, associated rights are related to an object only to the extent that they consist of rights to payment or performance that relate to:

   (a) a sum advanced and utilised for the purchase of the object;

   (b) a sum advanced and utilised for the purchase of another object in which the assignor held another international interest if the assignor transferred that interest to the assignee and the assignment has been registered;

   (c) the price payable for the object;

   (d) the rentals payable in respect of the object; or

   (e) other obligations arising from a transaction referred to in any of the preceding sub-paragraphs.

3. In all other cases, the priority of the competing assignments of the associated rights shall be determined by the applicable law.

Article 37 - Effects of assignor's insolvency

The provisions of Article 30 apply to insolvency proceedings against the assignor as if references to the debtor were references to the assignor.

Article 38 - Subrogation

1. Subject to paragraph 2, nothing in this Convention affects the acquisition of associated rights and the related international interest by legal or contractual subrogation under the applicable law.

2. The priority between any interest within the preceding paragraph and a competing interest may be varied by agreement in writing between the holders of the respective interests but an assignee of a subordinated interest is not bound by an agreement to subordinate that interest unless at the time of the assignment a subordination had been registered relating to that agreement.

Chapter X

Rights or interests subject to declarations by Contracting States

Article 39 - Rights having priority without registration

1. A Contracting State may at any time, in a declaration deposited with the depositary of the Protocol declare, generally or specifically:

   (a) those categories of non-consensual right or interest (other than a right or interest to which Article 40 applies) which under that State's law have priority over an interest in an object equivalent to that of the holder of a registered international interest and which shall have priority over a registered international interest, whether in or outside insolvency proceedings; and

   (b) that nothing in this Convention shall affect the right of a State or State entity, intergovernmental organisation or other private provider of public services to arrest or detain an object under the laws of that State for payment of amounts owed to such entity, organisation or provider directly relating to those services in respect of that object or another object.

2. A declaration made under the preceding paragraph may be expressed to cover categories that are created after the deposit of that declaration.

3. A non-consensual right or interest has priority over an international interest if and only if the former is of a category covered by a declaration deposited prior to the registration of the international interest.

4. Notwithstanding the preceding paragraph, a Contracting State may, at the time of ratification, acceptance, approval of, or accession to the Protocol, declare that a right or interest of a category covered by a declaration made under sub-paragraph (a) of paragraph 1 shall have priority over an international interest registered prior to the date of such ratification, acceptance, approval or accession.

Article 40 - Registrable non-consensual rights or interests

A Contracting State may at any time in a declaration deposited with the depositary of the Protocol list the categories of non-consensual right or interest which shall be registrable under this Convention as regards any category of object as if the right or interest were an international interest and be regulated accordingly. Such a declaration may be modified from time to time.

Chapter XI

Application of the Convention to Sales

Article 41 - Sale and prospective sale

This Convention shall apply to the sale or prospective sale of an object as provided for in the Protocol with any modifications therein.

Chapter XII

Jurisdiction

Article 42 - Choice of forum

1. Subject to Articles 43 and 44, the courts of a Contracting State chosen by the parties to a transaction have jurisdiction in respect of any claim brought under this Convention, whether or not the chosen forum has a connection with the parties or the transaction. Such jurisdiction shall be exclusive unless otherwise agreed between the parties.

2. Any such agreement shall be in writing or otherwise concluded in accordance with the formal requirements of the law of the chosen forum.

Article 43 - Jurisdiction under Article 13(1)

1. The courts of a Contracting State chosen by the parties and the courts of the Contracting State on the territory of which the object is situated have jurisdiction to grant relief under Article 13(1)(a), (b), (c) and Article 13(4) in respect of that object.

2. Jurisdiction to grant relief under Article 13(1)(d) or other interim relief by virtue of Article 13(4) may be exercised either:

   (a) by the courts chosen by the parties; or

   (b) by the courts of a Contracting State on the territory of which the debtor is situated, being relief which, by the terms of the order granting it, is enforceable only in the territory of that Contracting State.

3. A court has jurisdiction under the preceding paragraphs even if the final determination of the claim referred to in Article 13(1) will or may take place in a court of another Contracting State or by arbitration.

Article 44 - Jurisdiction to make orders against the Registrar

1. The courts of the place in which the Registrar has its centre of administration shall have exclusive jurisdiction to award damages or make orders against the Registrar.

2. Where a person fails to respond to a demand made under Article 25(1) or (2) and that person has ceased to exist or cannot be found for the purpose of enabling an order to be made against it requiring it to procure discharge of the registration, the courts referred to in paragraph 1 shall have exclusive jurisdiction, on the application of the debtor or intending debtor, to make an order directed to the Registrar requiring the Registrar to discharge the registration.

3. Where a person fails to comply with an order of a court having jurisdiction under this Convention or, in the case of a national interest, an order of a court of competent jurisdiction requiring that person to procure the amendment or discharge of a registration, the courts referred to in paragraph 1 may direct the Registrar to take such steps as will give effect to that order.

4. Except as otherwise provided by the preceding paragraphs, no court may make orders or give judgments or rulings against or purporting to bind the Registrar.

Article 45 - Jurisdiction in respect of insolvency proceedings

The provisions of this Chapter are not applicable to insolvency proceedings.

Chapter XIII

Relationship with other Conventions

Article 46 - Relationship with the Unidroit Convention on International Financial Leasing

The Protocol may determine the relationship between this Convention and the *Unidroit Convention on International Financial Leasing*, signed at Ottawa on 28 May 1988.

Chapter XIV

Final Provisions

Article 47 - Signature, ratification, acceptance, approval or accession

1. This Convention shall be open for signature in Cape Town on 16 November 2001 by States participating in the Diplomatic Conference to Adopt a Mobile Equipment Convention and an Aircraft

   Protocol held at Cape Town from 29 October to 16 November 2001. After 16 November 2001, the Convention shall be open to all States for signature at the Headquarters of the International Institute for the Unification of Private Law (Unidroit) in Rome until it enters into force in accordance with Article 49.

2. This Convention shall be subject to ratification, acceptance or approval by States which have signed it.

3. Any State which does not sign this Convention may accede to it at any time.

4. Ratification, acceptance, approval or accession is effected by the deposit of a formal instrument to that effect with the Depositary.

Article 48 - Regional Economic Integration Organisations

1. A Regional Economic Integration Organisation which is constituted by sovereign States and has competence over certain matters governed by this Convention may similarly sign, accept, approve or accede to this Convention. The Regional Economic Integration Organisation shall in that case have the rights and obligations of a Contracting State, to the extent that that Organisation has competence over matters governed by this Convention. Where the number of Contracting States is relevant in this Convention, the Regional Economic Integration Organisation shall not count as a Contracting State in addition to its Member States which are Contracting States.

2. The Regional Economic Integration Organisation shall, at the time of signature, acceptance, approval or accession, make a declaration to the Depositary specifying the matters governed by this Convention in respect of which competence has been transferred to that Organisation by its Member States. The Regional Economic Integration Organisation shall promptly notify the Depositary of any changes to the distribution of competence, including new transfers of competence, specified in the declaration under this paragraph.

3. Any reference to a "Contracting State" or "Contracting States" or "State Party" or "States Parties" in this Convention applies equally to a Regional Economic Integration Organisation where the context so requires.

Article 49 - Entry into force

1. This Convention enters into force on the first day of the month following the expiration of three months after the date of the deposit of the third instrument of ratification, acceptance, approval or accession but only as regards a category of objects to which a Protocol applies:

   (a) as from the time of entry into force of that Protocol;

   (b) subject to the terms of that Protocol; and

(c) as between States Parties to this Convention and that Protocol.

2. For other States this Convention enters into force on the first day of the month following the expiration of three months after the date of the deposit of its instrument of ratification, acceptance, approval or accession but only as regards a category of objects to which a Protocol applies and subject, in relation to such Protocol, to the requirements of sub-paragraphs (a), (b) and (c) of the preceding paragraph.

Article 50 - Internal transactions

1. A Contracting State may, at the time of ratification, acceptance, approval of, or accession to the Protocol, declare that this Convention shall not apply to a transaction which is an internal transaction in relation to that State with regard to all types of objects or some of them.

2. Notwithstanding paragraph 1, the provisions of Articles 8(3) and 9(1), Chapter V, Article 29, and any provisions of this Convention relating to registered interests shall apply to an internal transaction.

3. Where notice of a national interest has been registered in the International Registry, the priority of the holder of that interest under Article 29 shall not be affected by the fact that such interest has become vested in another person by assignment or subrogation under the applicable law.

Article 51 - Future Protocols

1. The Depositary may create working groups, in co-operation with such relevant non-governmental organisations as the Depositary considers appropriate, to assess the feasibility of extending the application of this Convention, through one or more Protocols, to objects of any category of high-value mobile equipment, other than a category referred to in Article 2(3), each member of which is uniquely identifiable, and associated rights relating to such objects.

2. The Depositary shall communicate the text of any preliminary draft Protocol relating to a category of objects prepared by such a working group to all States Parties to this Convention, all member States of the Depositary, member States of the United Nations which are not members of the Depositary and the relevant intergovernmental organisations, and shall invite such States and organisations to participate in intergovernmental negotiations for the completion of a draft Protocol on the basis of such a preliminary draft Protocol.

3. The Depositary shall also communicate the text of any preliminary draft Protocol prepared by such a working group to such relevant non-governmental organisations as the Depositary considers appropriate. Such non-governmental organisations shall be invited promptly to submit comments on the text of the preliminary draft Protocol to the Depositary and to participate as observers in the preparation of a draft Protocol.

4. When the competent bodies of the Depositary adjudge such a draft Protocol ripe for adoption, the Depositary shall convene a diplomatic conference for its adoption.

5. Once such a Protocol has been adopted, subject to paragraph 6, this Convention shall apply to the category of objects covered thereby.

6. The Annex to this Convention applies to such a Protocol only if specifically provided for in that Protocol.

Article 52 - Territorial units

1. If a Contracting State has territorial units in which different systems of law are applicable in relation to the matters dealt with in this Convention, it may, at the time of ratification, acceptance, approval or accession, declare that this Convention is to extend to all its territorial units or only to one or more of them and may modify its declaration by submitting another declaration at any time.

2. Any such declaration shall state expressly the territorial units to which this Convention applies.

3. If a Contracting State has not made any declaration under paragraph 1, this Convention shall apply to all territorial units of that State.

4. Where a Contracting State extends this Convention to one or more of its territorial units, declarations permitted under this Convention may be made in respect of each such territorial unit, and the declarations made in respect of one territorial unit may be different from those made in respect of another territorial unit.

5. If by virtue of a declaration under paragraph 1, this Convention and the Protocol extend to one or more territorial units of a Contracting State:

(a) the debtor is considered to be situated in a Contracting State only if it is incorporated or formed under a law in force in a territorial unit to which this Convention and the Protocol apply or if it has its registered office or statutory seat, centre of administration, place of business or habitual residence in a territorial unit to which this Convention and the Protocol apply;

(b) any reference to the situation of the object in a Contracting State refers to the situation of the object in a territorial unit to which this Convention and the Protocol apply; and

(c) any reference to the administrative authorities in that Contracting State shall be construed as referring to the administrative authorities having jurisdiction in a territorial unit to which this Convention and the Protocol apply and any reference to the national registry or to the registry authority in that Contracting State shall be construed as referring to the registry in force or to the registry authority having jurisdiction in the territorial unit or units to which this Convention and the Protocol apply.

Article 53 - Determination of courts

A Contracting State may, at the time of ratification, acceptance, approval of, or accession to the Protocol, declare the relevant "court" or "courts" for the purposes of Article 1 and Chapter XII of this Convention.

Article 54 - Declarations regarding remedies

1. A Contracting State may, at the time of ratification, acceptance, approval of, or accession to the Protocol, declare that while the charged object is situated within, or controlled from its territory the chargee shall not grant a lease of the object in that territory.

2. A Contracting State shall, at the time of ratification, acceptance, approval of, or accession to the Protocol, declare whether or not any remedy available to the creditor under any provision of this Convention which is not there expressed to require application to the court may be exercised only with leave of the court.

Article 55 - Declarations regarding relief pending final determination

A Contracting State may, at the time of ratification, acceptance, approval of, or accession to the Protocol, declare that it will not apply the provisions of Article 13 or Article 43, or both, wholly or in part. The declaration shall specify under which conditions the relevant Article will be applied, in case it will be applied partly, or otherwise which other forms of interim relief will be applied.

Article 56 - Reservations and declarations

1. No reservations may be made to this Convention but declarations authorised by Articles 39, 40, 50, 52, 53, 54, 55, 57, 58 and 60 may be made in accordance with these provisions.

2. Any declaration or subsequent declaration or any withdrawal of a declaration made under this Convention shall be notified in writing to the Depositary.

Article 57 - Subsequent declarations

1. A State Party may make a subsequent declaration, other than a declaration authorised under Article 60, at any time after the date on which this Convention has entered into force for it, by notifying the Depositary to that effect.

2. Any such subsequent declaration shall take effect on the first day of the month following the expiration of six months after the date of receipt of the notification by the Depositary. Where a longer period for that declaration to take effect is specified in the notification, it shall take effect upon the expiration of such longer period after receipt of the notification by the Depositary.

3. Notwithstanding the previous paragraphs, this Convention shall continue to apply, as if no such subsequent declarations had been made, in respect of all rights and interests arising prior to the effective date of any such subsequent declaration.

Article 58 - Withdrawal of declarations

Any State Party having made a declaration under this Convention, other than a declaration authorised under Article 60, may withdraw it at any time by notifying the Depositary. Such withdrawal is to take effect on the first day of the month following the expiration of six months after the date of receipt of the notification by the Depositary.

Article 59 - Denunciations

1. Any State Party may denounce this Convention by notification in writing to the Depositary.

2. Any such denunciation shall take effect on the first day of the month following the expiration of twelve months after the date on which notification is received by the Depositary.

3. Notwithstanding the previous paragraphs, this Convention shall continue to apply, as if no such denunciation had been made, in respect of all rights and interests arising prior to the effective date of any such denunciation.

Article 60 - Transitional provisions

1. Unless otherwise declared by a Contracting State at any time, the Convention does not apply to a pre-existing right or interest, which retains the priority it enjoyed under the applicable law before the effective date of this Convention.

2. For the purposes of Article 1(v) and of determining priority under this Convention:

   (a) "effective date of this Convention" means in relation to a debtor the time when this Convention enters into force or the time when the State in which the debtor is situated becomes a Contracting State, whichever is the later; and

   (b) the debtor is situated in a State where it has its centre of administration or, if it has no centre of administration, its place of business or, if it has more than one place of business, its principal place of business or, if it has no place of business, its habitual residence.

3. A Contracting State may in its declaration under paragraph 1 specify a date, not earlier than three years after the date on which the declaration becomes effective, when this Convention and the Protocol will become applicable, for the purpose of determining priority, including the protection of any existing priority, to pre-existing rights or interests arising under an agreement made at a time when the debtor was situated in a State referred to in sub-paragraph (b) of the preceding paragraph but only to the extent and in the manner specified in its declaration.

Article 61 - Review Conferences, amendments and related matters

1. The Depositary shall prepare reports yearly or at such other time as the circumstances may require for the States Parties as to the manner in which the international regimen established in this Convention has operated in practice. In preparing such reports, the Depositary shall take into account the reports of the Supervisory Authority concerning the functioning of the international registration system.

2. At the request of not less than twenty-five per cent of the States Parties, Review Conferences of States Parties shall be convened from time to time by the Depositary, in consultation with the Supervisory Authority, to consider:

   (a) the practical operation of this Convention and its effectiveness in facilitating the asset-based financing and leasing of the objects covered by its terms;

   (b) the judicial interpretation given to, and the application made of the terms of this Convention and the regulations;

   (c) the functioning of the international registration system, the performance of the Registrar and its oversight by the Supervisory Authority, taking into account the reports of the Supervisory Authority; and

   (d) whether any modifications to this Convention or the arrangements relating to the International Registry are desirable.

3. Subject to paragraph 4, any amendment to this Convention shall be approved by at least a two-thirds majority of States participating in the Conference referred to in the preceding paragraph and shall then enter into force in respect of States which have ratified, accepted or approved such amendment when ratified, accepted, or approved by three States in accordance with the provisions of Article 49 relating to its entry into force.

4. Where the proposed amendment to this Convention is intended to apply to more than one category of equipment, such amendment shall also be approved by at least a two-thirds majority of States Parties to each Protocol that are participating in the Conference referred to in paragraph 2.

Article 62 - Depositary and its functions

1. Instruments of ratification, acceptance, approval or accession shall be deposited with the International Institute for the Unification of Private Law (Unidroit), which is hereby designated the Depositary.

2. The Depositary shall:

(a) inform all Contracting States of:

(i) each new signature or deposit of an instrument of ratification, acceptance, approval or accession, together with the date thereof;

(ii) the date of entry into force of this Convention;

(iii) each declaration made in accordance with this Convention, together with the date thereof;

(iv) the withdrawal or amendment of any declaration, together with the date thereof; and

(v) the notification of any denunciation of this Convention together with the date thereof and the date on which it takes effect;

(b) transmit certified true copies of this Convention to all Contracting States;

(c) provide the Supervisory Authority and the Registrar with a copy of each instrument of ratification, acceptance, approval or accession, together with the date of deposit thereof, of each declaration or withdrawal or amendment of a declaration and of each notification of denunciation, together with the date of notification thereof, so that the information contained therein is easily and fully available; and

(d) perform such other functions customary for depositaries.

IN WITNESS WHEREOF the undersigned Plenipotentiaries, having been duly authorised, have signed this Convention.

DONE at Cape Town, this sixteenth day of November, two thousand and one, in a single original in the English, Arabic, Chinese, French, Russian and Spanish languages, all texts being equally authentic, such authenticity to take effect upon verification by the Joint Secretariat of the Conference under the authority of the President of the Conference within ninety days hereof as to the conformity of the texts with one other.

Annex

1. This Convention shall prevail over the UNCITRAL Convention on Assignment of Receivables in International Trade as it relates to the assignment of receivables which are associated rights related to international interests in aircraft objects, railway rolling stock and space assets.

2. The preceding paragraph shall be inserted into and constitute Article 45 *bis* of this Convention upon adoption by the United Nations General Assembly of the UNCITRAL Convention on Assignment of Receivables in International Trade.

APPENDIX III

PROTOCOL TO THE CONVENTION ON INTERNATIONAL INTERESTS IN MOBILE EQUIPMENT ON MATTERS SPECIFIC TO AIRCRAFT EQUIPMENT

(Cape Town, November 2001)

THE STATES PARTIES TO THIS PROTOCOL,

CONSIDERING it necessary to implement the Convention on International Interests in Mobile Equipment (hereinafter referred to as *the Convention*) as it relates to aircraft equipment, in the light of the purposes set out in the preamble to the Convention,

MINDFUL of the need to adapt the Convention to meet the particular requirements of aircraft finance and to extend the sphere of application of the Convention to include contracts of sale of aircraft equipment,

MINDFUL of the principles and objectives of the Convention on International Civil Aviation, signed at Chicago on 7 December 1944,

HAVE AGREED upon the following provisions relating to aircraft equipment:

Chapter I

Sphere of Application and General Provisions

Article I - Defined terms

1. In this Protocol, except where the context otherwise requires, terms used in it have the meanings set out in the Convention.

2. In this Protocol the following terms are employed with the meanings set out below:

(a) "aircraft" means aircraft as defined for the purposes of the Chicago Convention which are either airframes with aircraft engines installed thereon or helicopters;

(b) "aircraft engines" means aircraft engines (other than those used in military, customs or police services) powered by jet propulsion or turbine or piston technology and:

(i) in the case of jet propulsion aircraft engines, have at least 1750 lb of thrust or its equivalent; and

(ii) in the case of turbine-powered or piston-powered aircraft engines, have at least 550 rated take-off shaft horsepower or its equivalent,

together with all modules and other installed, incorporated or attached accessories, parts and equipment and all data, manuals and records relating thereto;

(c) "aircraft objects" means airframes, aircraft engines and helicopters;

(d) "aircraft register" means a register maintained by a State or a common mark registering authority for the purposes of the Chicago Convention;

(e) "airframes" means airframes (other than those used in military, customs or police services) that, when appropriate aircraft engines are installed thereon, are type certified by the competent aviation authority to transport:

(i) at least eight (8) persons including crew; or

(ii) goods in excess of 2750 kilograms,

together with all installed, incorporated or attached accessories, parts and equipment (other than aircraft engines), and all data, manuals and records relating thereto;

(f) "authorised party" means the party referred to in Article XIII(3);

(g) "Chicago Convention" means the *Convention on International Civil Aviation*, signed at Chicago on 7 December 1944, as amended, and its annexes;

(h) "common mark registering authority" means the authority maintaining a register in accordance with Article 77 of the Chicago Convention, as implemented by the Resolution adopted on 14 December 1967 by the Council of the International Civil Aviation Organization on nationality and registration of aircraft operated by international operating agencies;

(i) "de-registration of the aircraft" means deletion or removal of the registration of the aircraft from its aircraft register in accordance with the Chicago Convention;

(j) "guarantee contract" means a contract entered into by a person as guarantor;

(k) "guarantor" means a person who, for the purpose of assuring performance of any obligations in favour of a creditor secured by a security agreement or under an agreement, gives or issues a suretyship or demand guarantee or a standby letter of credit or any other form of credit insurance;

(l) "helicopters" means heavier-than-air machines (other than those used in military, customs or police services) supported in flight chiefly by the reactions of the air on one or more power-driven rotors on substantially vertical axes and which are type certified by the competent aviation authority to transport:

(i) at least five (5) persons including crew; or
(ii) goods in excess of 450 kilograms,

together with all installed, incorporated or attached accessories, parts and equipment (including rotors), and all data, manuals and records relating thereto;

(m) "insolvency-related event" means:

(i) the commencement of the insolvency proceedings; or

(ii) the declared intention to suspend or actual suspension of payments by the debtor where the creditor's right to institute insolvency proceedings against the debtor or to exercise remedies under the Convention is prevented or suspended by law or State action;

(n) "primary insolvency jurisdiction" means the Contracting State in which the centre of the debtor's main interests is situated, which for this purpose shall be deemed to be the place of the debtor's statutory seat or, if there is none, the place where the debtor is incorporated or formed, unless proved otherwise;

(o) "registry authority" means the national authority or the common mark registering authority, maintaining an aircraft register in a Contracting State and responsible for the registration and de-registration of an aircraft in accordance with the Chicago Convention; and

(p) "State of registry" means, in respect of an aircraft, the State on the national register of which an aircraft is entered or the State of location of the common mark registering authority maintaining the aircraft register.

Article II - Application of Convention as regards aircraft objects

1. The Convention shall apply in relation to aircraft objects as provided by the terms of this Protocol.

2. The Convention and this Protocol shall be known as the Convention on International Interests in Mobile Equipment as applied to aircraft objects.

Article III - Application of Convention to sales

The following provisions of the Convention apply as if references to an agreement creating or providing for an international interest were references to a contract of sale and as if references to an international interest, a prospective international interest, the debtor and the creditor were references to a sale, a prospective sale, the seller and the buyer respectively:

Articles 3 and 4;
Article 16(1)(a);
Article 19(4);
Article 20(1) (as regards registration of a contract of sale or a prospective sale);
Article 25(2) (as regards a prospective sale); and
Article 30.

In addition, the general provisions of Article 1, Article 5, Chapters IV to VII, Article 29 (other than Article 29(3) which is replaced by Article 14(1)), Chapter X, Chapter XII (other than Article 43), Chapter XIII and Chapter XIV (other than Article 60) shall apply to contracts of sale and prospective sales.

Article IV - Sphere of application

1. Without prejudice to Article 3(1) of the Convention, the Convention shall also apply in relation to a helicopter, or to an airframe pertaining to an aircraft, registered in an aircraft register of a Contracting State which is the State of registry, and where such registration is made pursuant to an agreement for registration of the aircraft it is deemed to have been effected at the time of the agreement.

2. For the purposes of the definition of "internal transaction" in Article 1 of the Convention:

   (a) an airframe is located in the State of registry of the aircraft of which it is a part;

   (b) an aircraft engine is located in the State of registry of the aircraft on which it is installed or, if it is not installed on an aircraft, where it is physically located; and

   (c) a helicopter is located in its State of registry,

at the time of the conclusion of the agreement creating or providing for the interest.

3. The parties may, by agreement in writing, exclude the application of Article 11 and, in their relations with each other, derogate from or vary the effect of any of the provisions of this Protocol except Article 9 (2)-(4).

Article V - Formalities, effects and registration of contracts of sale

1. For the purposes of this Protocol, a contract of sale is one which:

   (a) is in writing;

   (b) relates to an aircraft object of which the seller has power to dispose; and

   (c) enables the aircraft object to be identified in conformity with this Protocol.

2. A contract of sale transfers the interest of the seller in the aircraft object to the buyer according to its terms.

3. Registration of a contract of sale remains effective indefinitely. Registration of a prospective sale remains effective unless discharged or until expiry of the period, if any, specified in the registration.

Article VI - Representative capacities

A person may enter into an agreement or a sale, and register an international interest in, or a sale of, an aircraft object, in an agency, trust or other representative capacity. In such case, that person is entitled to assert rights and interests under the Convention.

Article VII - Description of aircraft objects

A description of an aircraft object that contains its manufacturer's serial number, the name of the manufacturer and its model designation is necessary and sufficient to identify the object for the purposes of Articles 7(c) and 32(1)(b) of the Convention and Article 5(1)(c) of this Protocol.

Article VIII - Choice of law

1. This Article applies only where a Contracting State has made a declaration pursuant to Article 30(1).

2. The parties to an agreement, or a contract of sale, or a related guarantee contract or subordination agreement may agree on the law which is to govern their contractual rights and obligations under the Convention, wholly or in part.

3. Unless otherwise agreed, the reference in the preceding paragraph to the law chosen by the parties is to the domestic rules of law of the designated State or, where that State comprises several territorial units, to the domestic law of the designated territorial unit.

Chapter II

Default Remedies, Priorities and Assignments

Article IX - Modification of default remedies provisions

1. In addition to the remedies specified in Chapter III of the Convention, the creditor may, to the extent that the debtor has at any time so agreed and in the circumstances specified in that Chapter:

   (a) procure the de-registration of the aircraft; and

   (b) procure the export and physical transfer of the aircraft object from the territory in which it is situated.

2. The creditor shall not exercise the remedies specified in the preceding paragraph without the prior consent in writing of the holder of any registered interest ranking in priority to that of the creditor.

3. Article 8(3) of the Convention shall not apply to aircraft objects. Any remedy given by the Convention in relation to an aircraft object shall be exercised in a commercially reasonable manner. A remedy shall be deemed to be exercised in a commercially reasonable manner where it is exercised in conformity with a provision of the agreement except where such a provision is manifestly unreasonable.

4. A chargee giving ten or more working days' prior written notice of a proposed sale or lease to interested persons shall be deemed to satisfy the requirement of providing "reasonable prior notice" specified in Article 8(4) of the Convention. The foregoing shall not prevent a chargee and a chargor or a guarantor from agreeing to a longer period of prior notice.

5. The registry authority in a Contracting State shall, subject to any applicable safety laws and regulations, honour a request for de-registration and export if:

(a) the request is properly submitted by the authorised party under a recorded irrevocable de-registration and export request authorisation; and

(b) the authorised party certifies to the registry authority, if required by that authority, that all registered interests ranking in priority to that of the creditor in whose favour the authorisation has been issued have been discharged or that the holders of such interests have consented to the de-registration and export.

6. A chargee proposing to procure the de-registration and export of an aircraft under paragraph 1 otherwise than pursuant to a court order shall give reasonable prior notice in writing of the proposed de-registration and export to:

(a) interested persons specified in Article 1(m)(i) and (ii) of the Convention; and

(b) interested persons specified in Article 1(m)(iii) of the Convention who have given notice of their rights to the chargee within a reasonable time prior to the de-registration and export.

Article X - Modification of provisions regarding relief pending final determination

1. This Article applies only where a Contracting State has made a declaration to that effect under Article 30(2) and to the extent stated in such declaration.

2. For the purposes of Article 13(1) of the Convention, "speedy" in the context of obtaining relief means within such number of working days from the date of filing of the application for relief as is specified in a declaration made by the Contracting State in which the application is made.

3. Article 13(1) of the Convention applies with the following being added immediately after sub-paragraph (d):

   "(e) if at any time the debtor and the creditor specifically agree, sale and application of proceeds therefrom",

   and Article 43(2) applies with the insertion after the words "Article 13(1)(d)" of the words "and (e)".

4. Ownership or any other interest of the debtor passing on a sale under the preceding paragraph is free from any other interest over which the creditor's international interest has priority under the provisions of Article 29 of the Convention.

5. The creditor and the debtor or any other interested person may agree in writing to exclude the application of Article 13(2) of the Convention.

6. With regard to the remedies in Article 9(1):

   (a) they shall be made available by the registry authority and other administrative authorities, as applicable, in a Contracting State no later than five working days after the creditor notifies such authorities that the relief specified in Article 9(1) is granted or, in the case of relief granted by a foreign court, recognised by a court of that Contracting State, and that the creditor is entitled to procure those remedies in accordance with this Convention; and

   (b) the applicable authorities shall expeditiously co-operate with and assist the creditor in the exercise of such remedies in conformity with the applicable aviation safety laws and regulations.

7. Paragraphs 2 and 6 shall not affect any applicable aviation safety laws and regulations.

Article XI - Remedies on insolvency

1. This Article applies only where a Contracting State that is the primary insolvency jurisdiction has made a declaration pursuant to Article 30(3).

Alternative A

2. Upon the occurrence of an insolvency-related event, the insolvency administrator or the debtor, as applicable, shall, subject to paragraph 7, give possession of the aircraft object to the creditor no later than the earlier of:

   (a) the end of the waiting period; and

   (b) the date on which the creditor would be entitled to possession of the aircraft object if this Article did not apply.

3. For the purposes of this Article, the "waiting period" shall be the period specified in a declaration of the Contracting State which is the primary insolvency jurisdiction.

4. References in this Article to the "insolvency administrator" shall be to that person in its official, not in its personal, capacity.

5. Unless and until the creditor is given the opportunity to take possession under paragraph 2:

   (a) the insolvency administrator or the debtor, as applicable, shall preserve the aircraft object and maintain it and its value in accordance with the agreement; and
   (b) the creditor shall be entitled to apply for any other forms of interim relief available under the applicable law.

6. Sub-paragraph (a) of the preceding paragraph shall not preclude the use of the aircraft object under arrangements designed to preserve the aircraft object and maintain it and its value.

7. The insolvency administrator or the debtor, as applicable, may retain possession of the aircraft object where, by the time specified in paragraph 2, it has cured all defaults other than a default constituted by the opening of insolvency proceedings and has agreed to perform all future obligations under the agreement. A second waiting period shall not apply in respect of a default in the performance of such future obligations.

8. With regard to the remedies in Article 9(1):

   (a) they shall be made available by the registry authority and the administrative authorities in a Contracting State, as applicable, no later than five working days after the date on which the creditor notifies such authorities that it is entitled to procure those remedies in accordance with the Convention; and

   (b) the applicable authorities shall expeditiously co-operate with and assist the creditor in the exercise of such remedies in conformity with the applicable aviation safety laws and regulations.

9. No exercise of remedies permitted by the Convention or this Protocol may be prevented or delayed after the date specified in paragraph 2.

10. No obligations of the debtor under the agreement may be modified without the consent of the creditor.

11. Nothing in the preceding paragraph shall be construed to affect the authority, if any, of the insolvency administrator under the applicable law to terminate the agreement.

12. No rights or interests, except for non-consensual rights or interests of a category covered by a declaration pursuant to Article 39(1), shall have priority in the insolvency over registered interests.

13. The Convention as modified by Article 9 of this Protocol shall apply to the exercise of any remedies under this Article.

Alternative B

2. Upon the occurrence of an insolvency-related event, the insolvency administrator or the debtor, as applicable, upon the request of the creditor, shall give notice to the creditor within the time specified in a declaration of a Contracting State pursuant to Article 30(3) whether it will:

   (a) cure all defaults other than a default constituted by the opening of insolvency proceedings and agree to perform all future obligations, under the agreement and related transaction documents; or

   (b) give the creditor the opportunity to take possession of the aircraft object, in accordance with the applicable law.

3. The applicable law referred to in sub-paragraph (b) of the preceding paragraph may permit the court to require the taking of any additional step or the provision of any additional guarantee.

4. The creditor shall provide evidence of its claims and proof that its international interest has been registered.

5. If the insolvency administrator or the debtor, as applicable, does not give notice in conformity with paragraph 2, or when he has declared that he will give the creditor the opportunity to take possession of the aircraft object but fails to do so, the court may permit the creditor to take possession of the aircraft object upon such terms as the court may order and may require the taking of any additional step or the provision of any additional guarantee.

6. The aircraft object shall not be sold pending a decision by a court regarding the claim and the international interest.

Article XII - Insolvency assistance

1. This Article applies only where a Contracting State has made a declaration pursuant to Article 30(1).

2. The courts of a Contracting State in which an aircraft object is situated shall, in accordance with the law of the Contracting State, co-operate to the maximum extent possible with foreign courts and foreign insolvency administrators in carrying out the provisions of Article 11.

Article XIII - De-registration and export request authorisation

1. This Article applies only where a Contracting State has made a declaration pursuant to Article 30(1).

2. Where the debtor has issued an irrevocable de-registration and export request authorisation substantially in the form annexed to this Protocol and has submitted such authorisation for recordation to the registry authority, that authorisation shall be so recorded.

3. The person in whose favour the authorisation has been issued (the "authorised party") or its certified designee shall be the sole person entitled to exercise the remedies specified in Article 9(1) and may do so only in accordance with the authorisation and applicable aviation safety laws and regulations. Such authorisation may not be revoked by the debtor without the consent in writing of the authorised party. The registry authority shall remove an authorisation from the registry at the request of the authorised party.

4. The registry authority and other administrative authorities in Contracting States shall expeditiously co-operate with and assist the authorised party in the exercise of the remedies specified in Article 9.

Article XIV - Modification of priority provisions

1. A buyer of an aircraft object under a registered sale acquires its interest in that object free from an interest subsequently registered and from an unregistered interest, even if the buyer has actual knowledge of the unregistered interest.

2. A buyer of an aircraft object acquires its interests in that object subject to an interest registered at the time of its acquisition.

3. Ownership of or another right or interest in an aircraft engine shall not be affected by its installation on or removal from an aircraft.

4. Article 29(6) of the Convention applies to an item, other than an object, installed on an airframe, aircraft engine or helicopter.

Article XV - Modification of assignment provisions

Article 33(1) of the Convention applies as if the following were added immediately after sub-paragraph (b):

"(c) is consented to in writing by the debtor, whether or not the consent is given in advance of the assignment or identifies the assignee."

Article XVI - Debtor provisions

1. In the absence of a default within the meaning of Article 11 of the Convention, the debtor shall be entitled to the quiet possession and use of the object in accordance with the agreement as against:

   (a) its creditor and the holder of any interest from which the debtor takes free pursuant to Article 29(4) of the Convention or Article 14(1) of this Protocol, unless and to the extent that the debtor has otherwise agreed; and

   (b) the holder of any interest to which the debtor's right or interest is subject pursuant to Article 29(4) of the Convention and Article 14(1) of this Protocol, but only to the extent, if any, that such holder has agreed.

2. Nothing in the Convention or this Protocol affects the liability of a creditor for any breach of the agreement under the applicable law in so far as that agreement relates to an aircraft object.

Chapter III

Registry Provisions Relating to International Interests in Aircraft Objects

Article XVII - The Supervisory Authority and the Registrar

1. The Supervisory Authority shall be the international entity designated by a Resolution adopted by the Diplomatic Conference to Adopt a Mobile Equipment Convention and an Aircraft Protocol.

2. Where the international entity referred to in the preceding paragraph is not able and willing to act as Supervisory Authority, a Conference of Signatory and Contracting States shall be convened to designate another Supervisory Authority.

3. The Supervisory Authority and its officers and employees shall enjoy such immunity from legal and administrative process as is provided under the rules applicable to them as an international entity or otherwise.

4. The Supervisory Authority may establish a commission of experts, from among persons nominated by Signatory and Contracting States and having the necessary qualifications and experience, and entrust it with the task of assisting the Supervisory Authority in the discharge of its functions.

5. The first Registrar shall operate the International Registry for a period of five years from the date of entry into force of this Protocol. Thereafter, the Registrar shall be appointed or reappointed at regular five-yearly intervals by the Supervisory Authority.

Article XVIII - First regulations

The first regulations shall be made by the Supervisory Authority so as to take effect upon the entry into force of this Protocol.

Article XIX - Designated entry points

1. Subject to paragraph 2, a Contracting State may at any time designate an entity or entities in its territory as the entry point or entry points through which there shall or may be transmitted to the International Registry information required for registration other than registration of a notice of a national interest or a right or interest under Article 40 in either case arising under the laws of another State.

2. A designation made under paragraph 1 may permit, but not compel, use of a designated entry point or entry points for information required for registrations in respect of aircraft engines.

Article XX - Additional modifications to Registry provisions

1. For the purposes of Article 19(6) of the Convention, the search criterion for an aircraft object shall be the name of its manufacturer, its manufacturer's serial number and its model designation, supplemented as necessary to ensure uniqueness. Such supplementary information shall be specified in the regulations.

2. For the purposes of Article 25(2) of the Convention and in the circumstances there described, the holder of a registered prospective international interest or a registered prospective assignment of an international interest shall take such steps as are within its power to procure the discharge of the registration no later than five working days after the receipt of the demand described in such paragraph.

3. The fees referred to in Article 17(2)(h) of the Convention shall be determined so as to recover the reasonable costs of establishing, operating and regulating the International Registry and the reasonable costs of the Supervisory Authority associated with the performance of the functions, exercise of the powers, and discharge of the duties contemplated by Article 17(2) of the Convention.

4. The centralised functions of the International Registry shall be operated and administered by the Registrar on a twenty-four hour

basis. The various entry points shall be operated at least during working hours in their respective territories.

5. The amount of the insurance or financial guarantee referred to in Article 28(2) of the Convention shall, in respect of each event, not be less than the maximum value of an aircraft object as determined by the Supervisory Authority.

6. Nothing in the Convention shall preclude the Registrar from procuring insurance or a financial guarantee covering events for which the Registrar is not liable under Article 28 of the Convention.

Chapter IV

Jurisdiction

Article XXI - Modification of jurisdiction provisions

For the purposes of Article 43 of the Convention and subject to Article 42 of the Convention, a court of a Contracting State also has jurisdiction where the object is a helicopter, or an airframe pertaining to an aircraft, for which that State is the State of registry.

Article XXII - Waivers of sovereign immunity

1. Subject to paragraph 2, a waiver of sovereign immunity from jurisdiction of the courts specified in Article 42 or Article 43 of the Convention or relating to enforcement of rights and interests relating to an aircraft object under the Convention shall be binding and, if the other conditions to such jurisdiction or enforcement have been satisfied, shall be effective to confer jurisdiction and permit enforcement, as the case may be.

2. A waiver under the preceding paragraph must be in writing and contain a description of the aircraft object.

Chapter V

Relationship with Other Conventions

Article XXIII - Relationship with the Convention on the International Recognition of Rights in Aircraft

The Convention shall, for a Contracting State that is a party to the *Convention on the International Recognition of Rights in Aircraft*, signed at Geneva on 19 June 1948, supersede that Convention as it relates to aircraft, as defined in this Protocol, and to aircraft objects. However, with respect to rights or interests not covered or affected by the present Convention, the Geneva Convention shall not be superseded.

Article XXIV - Relationship with the Convention for the Unification of Certain Rules Relating to the Precautionary Attachment of Aircraft

1. The Convention shall, for a Contracting State that is a Party to the *Convention for the Unification of Certain Rules Relating to the Precautionary Attachment of Aircraft*, signed at Rome on 29 May 1933, supersede that Convention as it relates to aircraft, as defined in this Protocol.

2. A Contracting State Party to the above Convention may declare, at the time of ratification, acceptance, approval of, or accession to this Protocol, that it will not apply this Article.

Article XXV - Relationship with the Unidroit Convention on International Financial Leasing

The Convention shall supersede the *Unidroit Convention on International Financial Leasing* as it relates to aircraft objects.

Chapter VI

Final Provisions

Article XXVI - Signature, ratification, acceptance, approval or accession

1. This Protocol shall be open for signature in Cape Town on 16 November 2001 by States participating in the Diplomatic Conference to Adopt a Mobile Equipment Convention and an Aircraft Protocol held at Cape Town from 29 October to 16 November 2001. After 16 November 2001, the Protocol shall be open to all States for signature at the Headquarters of the International Institute for the Unification of Private Law (Unidroit) in Rome until it enters into force in accordance with Article 28.

2. This Protocol shall be subject to ratification, acceptance or approval by States which have signed it.

3. Any State which does not sign this Protocol may accede to it at any time.

4. Ratification, acceptance, approval or accession is effected by the deposit of a formal instrument to that effect with the Depositary.

5. A State may not become a Party to this Protocol unless it is or becomes also a Party to the Convention.

Article XXVII - Regional Economic Integration Organisations

1. A Regional Economic Integration Organisation which is constituted by sovereign States and has competence over certain matters governed by this Protocol may similarly sign, accept, approve or accede to this Protocol. The Regional Economic Integration Organisation shall in that case have the rights and obligations of a Contracting State, to the extent that that Organisation has competence over matters governed by this Protocol. Where the number of Contracting States is relevant in this Protocol, the Regional Economic Integration Organisation shall not count as a

Contracting State in addition to its Member States which are Contracting States.

2. The Regional Economic Integration Organisation shall, at the time of signature, acceptance, approval or accession, make a declaration to the Depositary specifying the matters governed by this Protocol in respect of which competence has been transferred to that Organisation by its Member States. The Regional Economic Integration Organisation shall promptly notify the Depositary of any changes to the distribution of competence, including new transfers of competence, specified in the declaration under this paragraph.

3. Any reference to a "Contracting State" or "Contracting States" or "State Party" or "States Parties" in this Protocol applies equally to a Regional Economic Integration Organisation where the context so requires.

Article XXVIII - Entry into force

1. This Protocol enters into force on the first day of the month following the expiration of three months after the date of the deposit of the eighth instrument of ratification, acceptance, approval or accession, between the States which have deposited such instruments.

2. For other States this Protocol enters into force on the first day of the month following the expiration of three months after the date of the deposit of its instrument of ratification, acceptance, approval or accession.

Article XXIX - Territorial units

1. If a Contracting State has territorial units in which different systems of law are applicable in relation to the matters dealt with in this Protocol, it may, at the time of ratification, acceptance, approval or accession, declare that this Protocol is to extend to all its territorial

units or only to one or more of them and may modify its declaration by submitting another declaration at any time.

2. Any such declaration shall state expressly the territorial units to which this Protocol applies.

3. If a Contracting State has not made any declaration under paragraph 1, this Protocol shall apply to all territorial units of that State.

4. Where a Contracting State extends this Protocol to one or more of its territorial units, declarations permitted under this Protocol may be made in respect of each such territorial unit, and the declarations made in respect of one territorial unit may be different from those made in respect of another territorial unit.

5. If by virtue of a declaration under paragraph 1, the Protocol extends to one or more territorial units of a Contracting State:

   (a) the debtor is considered to be situated in a Contracting State only if it is incorporated or formed under a law in force in a territorial unit to which the Convention and Protocol apply or if it has its registered office or statutory seat, centre of administration, place of business or habitual residence in a territorial unit to which the Convention and Protocol apply;

   (b) any reference to the location of the object in a Contracting State refers to the location of the object in a territorial unit to which the Convention and Protocol apply; and

   (c) any reference to the administrative authorities in that Contracting State shall be construed as referring to the administrative authorities having jurisdiction in a territorial unit to which the Convention and Protocol apply and any reference to the national registry or to the registry authority in that Contracting State shall be construed as referring to the aircraft registry in force or to the registry authority having jurisdiction in the territorial unit or units to which the Convention and Protocol apply.

Article XXX - Declarations relating to certain provisions

1. A Contracting State may, at the time of ratification, acceptance, approval of, or accession to this Protocol, declare that it will apply any one or more of Articles 8, 12 and 13 of this Protocol.

2. A Contracting State may, at the time of ratification, acceptance, approval of, or accession to this Protocol, declare that it will apply Article 10 of this Protocol, wholly or in part. If it so declares with respect to Article 10(2), it shall specify the time-period required thereby.

3. A Contracting State may, at the time of ratification, acceptance, approval of, or accession to this Protocol, declare that it will apply the entirety of Alternative A, or the entirety of Alternative B of Article 11 and, if so, shall specify the types of insolvency proceeding, if any, to which it will apply Alternative A and the types of insolvency proceeding, if any, to which it will apply Alternative B. A Contracting State making a declaration pursuant to this paragraph shall specify the time-period required by Article 11.

4. The courts of Contracting States shall apply Article 11 in conformity with the declaration made by the Contracting State which is the primary insolvency jurisdiction.

5. A Contracting State may, at the time of ratification, acceptance, approval of, or accession to the Protocol, declare that it will not apply the provisions of Article 21, wholly or in part. The declaration shall specify under which conditions the relevant Article will be applied, in case it will be applied partly, or otherwise which other forms of interim relief that will be applied.

Article XXXI - Declarations under the Convention

Declarations made under the Convention, including those made under Articles 39, 40, 50, 53, 54, 55, 57, 58 and 60 of the Convention, shall be deemed to have also been made under this Protocol unless stated otherwise.

Article XXXII - Reservations and declarations

1. No reservations may be made to this Protocol but declarations authorised by Articles 29, 30, 31, 33 and 34 may be made in accordance with these provisions.

2. Any declaration or subsequent declaration or any withdrawal of a declaration made under this Protocol shall be notified in writing to the Depositary.

Article XXXIII - Subsequent declarations

1. A State Party may make a subsequent declaration, other than the declaration made in accordance with Article 31 under Article 60 of the Convention, at any time after the date on which this Protocol has entered into force for it, by notifying the Depositary to that effect.

2. Any such subsequent declaration shall take effect on the first day of the month following the expiration of six months after the date of receipt of the notification by the Depositary. Where a longer period for that declaration to take effect is specified in the notification, it shall take effect upon the expiration of such longer period after receipt of the notification by the Depositary.

3. Notwithstanding the previous paragraphs, this Protocol shall continue to apply, as if no such subsequent declarations had been made, in respect of all rights and interests arising prior to the effective date of any such subsequent declaration.

Article XXXIV - Withdrawal of declarations

Any State Party having made a declaration under this Protocol, other than a declaration made in accordance with Article 31 under Article 60 of the Convention, may withdraw it at any time by notifying the Depositary. Such withdrawal is to take effect on the first day of the month following the expiration of six months after the date of receipt of the notification by the Depositary.

Article XXXV - Denunciations

1. Any State Party may denounce this Protocol by notification in writing to the Depositary.

2. Any such denunciation shall take effect on the first day of the month following the expiration of twelve months after the date of receipt of the notification by the Depositary.

3. Notwithstanding the previous paragraphs, this Protocol shall continue to apply, as if no such denunciation had been made, in respect of all rights and interests arising prior to the effective date of any such denunciation.

Article XXXVI - Review Conferences, amendments and related matters

1. The Depositary, in consultation with the Supervisory Authority, shall prepare reports yearly, or at such other time as the circumstances may require, for the States Parties as to the manner in which the international regime established in the Convention as amended by the Protocol has operated in practice. In preparing such reports, the Depositary shall take into account the reports of the Supervisory Authority concerning the functioning of the international registration system.

2. At the request of not less than twenty-five per cent of the States Parties, Review Conferences of the States Parties shall be convened from time to time by the Depositary, in consultation with the Supervisory Authority, to consider:

   (a) the practical operation of the Convention as amended by this Protocol and its effectiveness in facilitating the asset-based financing and leasing of the objects covered by its terms;

   (b) the judicial interpretation given to, and the application made of the terms of this Protocol and the regulations;

(c) the functioning of the international registration system, the performance of the Registrar and its oversight by the Supervisory Authority, taking into account the reports of the Supervisory Authority; and

(d) whether any modifications to this Protocol or the arrangements relating to the International Registry are desirable.

3. Any amendment to this Protocol shall be approved by at least a two-thirds majority of States participating in the Conference referred to in the preceding paragraph and shall then enter into force in respect of States which have ratified, accepted or approved such amendment when it has been ratified, accepted or approved by eight States in accordance with the provisions of Article 28 relating to its entry into force.

Article XXXVII - Depositary and its functions

1. Instruments of ratification, acceptance, approval or accession shall be deposited with the International Institute for the Unification of Private Law (Unidroit), which is hereby designated the Depositary.

2. The Depositary shall:

(a) inform all Contracting States of:

(i) each new signature or deposit of an instrument of ratification, acceptance, approval or accession, together with the date thereof;

(ii) the date of entry into force of this Protocol;

(iii) each declaration made in accordance with this Protocol, together with the date thereof;

(iv) the withdrawal or amendment of any declaration, together with the date thereof; and

(v) the notification of any denunciation of this Protocol together with the date thereof and the date on which it takes effect;

(b) transmit certified true copies of this Protocol to all Contracting States;

(c) provide the Supervisory Authority and the Registrar with a copy of each instrument of ratification, acceptance, approval or accession, together with the date of deposit thereof, of each declaration or withdrawal or amendment of a declaration and of each notification of denunciation, together with the date of notification thereof, so that the information contained therein is easily and fully available; and

(d) perform such other functions customary for depositaries.

IN WITNESS WHEREOF the undersigned Plenipotentiaries, having been duly authorised, have signed this Protocol.

DONE at Cape Town, this sixteenth day of November, two thousand and one, in a single original in the English, Arabic, Chinese, French, Russian and Spanish languages, all texts being equally authentic, such authenticity to take effect upon verification by the Joint Secretariat of the Conference under the authority of the President of the Conference within ninety days hereof as to the conformity of the texts with one another.

Annex

FORM OF IRREVOCABLE DE-REGISTRATION AND EXPORT REQUEST AUTHORISATION

[Insert Date]

To: [Insert Name of Registry Authority]

Re: Irrevocable De-Registration and Export Request Authorisation

The undersigned is the registered [operator] [owner]* of the [insert the airframe/helicopter manufacturer name and model number] bearing manufacturers serial number [insert manufacturer's serial number] and registration [number] [mark] [insert registration number/mark] (together with all installed, incorporated or attached accessories, parts and equipment, the "aircraft").

This instrument is an irrevocable de-registration and export request authorisation issued by the undersigned in favour of [insert name of creditor] ("the authorised party") under the authority of Article 13 of the Protocol to the Convention on International Interests in Mobile Equipment on Matters specific to Aircraft Equipment. In accordance with that Article, the undersigned hereby requests:

(i) recognition that the authorised party or the person it certifies as its designee is the sole person entitled to:

(a) procure the de-registration of the aircraft from the [insert name of aircraft register] maintained by the [insert name of registry authority] for the purposes of Chapter III of the *Convention on International Civil Aviation*, signed at Chicago, on 7 December 1944, and

* Select the term that reflects the relevant nationality registration criterion.

(b) procure the export and physical transfer of the aircraft from [insert name of country]; and

(ii) confirmation that the authorised party or the person it certifies as its designee may take the action specified in clause (i) above on written demand without the consent of the undersigned and that, upon such demand, the authorities in [insert name of country] shall co-operate with the authorised party with a view to the speedy completion of such action.

The rights in favour of the authorised party established by this instrument may not be revoked by the undersigned without the written consent of the authorised party.

Please acknowledge your agreement to this request and its terms by appropriate notation in the space provided below and lodging this instrument in [insert name of registry authority].

[insert name of operator/owner]

____

Agreed to and lodged this
[insert date]

By: [insert name of signatory]
Its: [insert title of signatory]

____

[insert relevant notational details]

Index

abatement of rent 7-8
account of profits 184, 220-2, 224, 248-9
accounting 107
administration insolvency procedure 118, 120-3
administrative receivership 118-19, 120
Admiralty Courts 158
agency 85-6, 106
agriculture
  purchase money security interest (PMSI)
    crops 282-4
    livestock 278-82
aircraft
  mortgages 145-54
    form and content 148-50
    legal context 145-6
    registration 147-8, 150-4
  retention of title and 364
  Unidroit Convention on International Interests in Mobile Equipment and 330-2, 378, 423, 426, 509-37
Argentina 403
Australia
  leasing in 407
  retention of title in 86-9, 92
Austria, retention of title in 339-40

bailment, misuse of chattels and 217-20
bankruptcy 119, 294
Belgium, retention of title in 340-1
bill of sale 101, 146
bills of lading 203-4
bottomry 158, 161-2
breach of contract 182, 237

Canada 347-8, 383, 393
Cape Town Convention *see* Unidroit (Institution on Unification of Private Law), Convention on International Interests in Mobile Equipment
care of goods/equipment 8, 416
certainty 12
charges 34, 145-6, 301, 305
  floating charges 34, 306
  French concept of 302, 303
  retention of title and 40-3, 45-6, 49-51, 63, 65-6, 80-1, 87, 90, 93
  see also mortgages
charterparties 40-1
China 403
choice of law 4
civil law systems 3, 337
  see also individual countries
civil litigation 181
common law systems 3, 337-8
compensation *see* damages and compensation
computer software, purchase money security interest (PMSI) 266-7, 278
conditional sales 31, 41, 42, 47, 95-6, 102-3, 412
  Consumer Credit Act 1974 and 108-17
  insolvency and 119-25
  Unidroit Convention and 386-8
conflict of laws 308, 365
consignments, purchase money security interest (PMSI) 267-8
conspiracy 183, 211, 212-13
construction of agreements 43, 74
constructive notice 34, 72
consumer contracts 146
  ownership of goods and 108-17

consequences of wrongful possession 113-15
customer's right of termination of agreement 115-17
decision on granting return order 113
goods on premises 112, 113
hirer's right of termination of agreement 117
protected goods 111-12, 113
restrictions on repossession 109-11, 112
purchase money security interest (PMSI) 266
contract, misuse of chattels and 182, 223, 237, 248-9
contract of hire
Roman law 3, 4-5, 6, 27
Scots law 3-27
disguised security 23-6
essentialia 6-7
exclusion of lessor's duties 13-17
landlords and fixtures 20-3
legal context 3-12
lessee's duties 7-9
lessor's duties 9-11
modern finance or operating lease 12-26
naturalia 7-11
termination 17-20
contract of location 5
contract relationships, misuse of chattels and 223
conversion 112, 187-90, 191, 192, 211, 228, 231-2, 235-6
corporate insolvency 117-19
credit, provision of 297, 336
crops, purchase money security interest (PMSI) 282-4
cross-collateralisation 264
Crowther Committee 143
Czech Republic 407, 408

damages and compensation 181
liquidated damages 17-19, 104, 417-18
misuse of chattels and 212, 221
damages in lieu 237-42
deterrence and 182-3, 246
exemplary damages 246-7
gain-based 224, 229-30, 248
loss-based 224-9, 230-3
market values and 228-9
over-compensation 182-5
to lessor 417-18
debt 297
debt-mobilisation 303
default by lessee 417-18
default notice 109-10
defects 234-5, 415
warranty as to freedom from 10
delivery
lessee's duty 7
lessor's duty 9-10, 414-15
title to goods and 24
Denmark, retention of title in 341
dépeçage 306
destruction of goods 8, 10
see also misuse of chattels
deterrence 182-3, 221-2, 246
detinue 187, 189, 236
disguised security in modern finance or operating lease 23-6
droit de suite 169-70
duration of hire 7

economic loss, misuse of chattels and 193-201, 212
equity 3
charges 40-3, 45-6, 49-51, 63, 65-6, 80-1, 87, 90, 93, 305
equitable mortgages 145
liens 37-9, 40, 41, 44, 93, 305
redemption principle 159, 163
retention of title and 33-9
tracing 30, 33, 35-7, 51-7, 58-60, 84
Estonia 407, 408

European Bank for Reconstruction and Development (EBRD) 367, 400, 425
European Union
 regulation on insolvency 321-6, 333
 retention of title and 335-73
  Austria 339-40
  Belgium 340-1
  challenge of international secured credit and 360-70
  Denmark 341
  France 342-3
  Germany 342, 343-4
  Greece 345
  Ireland 352-8
  Italy 346
  Netherlands 344-5
  Norway 346-8
  overview 358-60
  Portugal 348
  Spain 348-9
  Sweden 349-50
  Switzerland 350-2
  UK 352-8
Eurotunnel 302
exclusion clauses 14-17
exemplary damages 246-7

fiduciary relationships
 misuse of chattels and 220-2, 224
 retention of title and 35-7, 58-9, 78-9, 82-3, 85-6, 87
finance leases 12-26, 96, 105-6, 107, 408-9
 disguised security 23-6
 exclusion of lessor's duties 13-17
 landlords and fixtures 20-3
 relief from forfeiture 131-8
 termination 17-20
 Unidroit Convention on International Financial Leasing 326-7, 363-4, 399, 401-23
  background 401-3
  purpose of 411
  reasons for preparation of 409-11
  regulatory system 414-21
  substantive sphere of application 411-13
  territorial sphere of application 413-14
fitness for purpose 10
fixtures 20-3, 285-7
floating charges 34, 306
foreclosure 165
forfeiture
 relief from 125-42
  case examples 127-38
  instalments already paid 139-40
  jurisdiction to grant relief 125-7, 128-9, 135-6
  policy argument for 127, 140-2
France 4
 concept of security in 300, 301-3, 306-7
 insolvency in 294, 317
 leasing in 410
 retention of title in 342-3
freezing orders 181

gain-based remedies 184, 224, 229-30, 248
Germany 12
 leasing in 405, 408
 retention of title in 342, 343-4
globalisation 294, 372
goodwill 302-3
Greece, retention of title in 345

hire
 contract of *see* contract of hire
 ownership of goods and *see* ownership of goods
hire purchase 31, 41, 47, 96, 102-3, 105, 106, 107, 352, 412
 Consumer Credit Act 1974 and

108-17
consequences of wrongful possession 113-15
customer's right of termination of agreement 115-17
decision on granting return order 113
goods on premises 112, 113
hirer's right of termination of agreement 117
protected goods 111-12, 113
restrictions on repossession 109-11, 112
perceived unfairness to customer 107-8
relief from forfeiture 125-31, 139-42
case examples 127-31
instalments already paid 139-40
jurisdiction to grant relief 125-7, 128-9, 135-6
policy argument for 127, 140-2
sale and hire-purchase back agreements 24-5, 26
Hungary 408
hypothec 20-1, 157, 172-3, 174

injunctions 181, 212
innominate contracts 6, 14
insolvency 97
international issues 293-334, 443-4
concept of security 300-7
domestic law and 307-16
English/Welsh concepts of security 300, 301, 304-6
French concept of security 294, 300, 301-3, 306-7
French law on insolvency 294, 317
nature of 294-300
practical solutions 313-15
territorialism 310-12
treaty framework 317-34
universality 312-13
ownership of goods and 117-25
retention of title and *see* retention of title
types of insolvency procedure 117-19
corporate 117-19
personal 119
insurance, insurance of ship mortgagee's interest 167-9
interference with contract 211, 212
interference with enjoyment 11
International Civil Aviation Organisation (ICAO) 378, 423
International Finance Corporation (IFC) 405-6
international issues
financial leasing 326-7, 363-4, 399, 401-23
insolvency 293-334, 443-4
concept of security 300-7
domestic law and 307-16
English/Welsh concepts of security 300, 301, 304-6
French concept of security 294, 300, 301-3, 306-7
nature of 294-300
practical solutions 313-15
territorialism 310-12
treaty framework 317-34
universality 312-13
retention of title and 360-70
conflict rules 361-5
unification of substantive rules 365-70
International Monetary Fund (IMF) 327-8
intimidation 183-4, 211, 213
inventory, purchase money security interest (PMSI) 273-8
Ireland, retention of title in 352-8
Italy
retention of title in 346

ship mortgages in 157

Japan, leasing in 405, 408
justice 12

land 98, 300
purchase money security interest (PMSI) and 285-7
landlords, fixtures and 20-3
leases 5, 20-3, 96
duties of lessee 7-9, 416-18
duties of lessor 9-11, 414-16
exclusion of 13-17
growth of 407-8
reasons for 405-6
hallmarks of 408-9
origins of 404-5
termination 17-20
third parties and 418-20
see also finance leases; operating leases
legal mortgages 145
droit de suite 169-70
legal title 98
lessee
default by 417-18
duties of 7-9, 416-18
rights against supplier 418
lessor
compensation to 417-18
duties of 9-11, 414-16
exclusion of 13-17
fixtures and 20-3
termination payments to 17-19
third parties and 418-20
title 418-20
leveraged leasing transactions 412-13
lex maritima 158
liens
contractual 301, 305
equitable 37-9, 40, 41, 44, 93, 305
maritime 162
purchase money security interest (PMSI) and 288-9
liquidated damages 17-19, 104, 417-18
liquidation 118, 119-20
livestock, purchase money security interest (PMSI) 278-82
loan credit 297
location, contract of 5
loss
misuse of chattels and
assessment of loss 224-49
economic loss 193-201, 212

Malta, ship mortgages in 157, 164, 167, 169, 177, 178
maritime liens 162
misuse of chattels 181-250
assessment of loss 224-49
defects and repairs 234-5
gain-based compensation 224, 229-30, 248
loss of use cases 235-45
loss-based compensation 224-9, 230-3
market values and 228-9
closer relationships 216-23
bailment 217-20
contract 223
fiduciary relationships 220-2, 224
economic loss 193-201, 212
interests less than full ownership 202-9, 211-16
example 213-16
by strangers 187-211
continuing damage 209-10
meaning of damage 210-11
protection of property interests 187-91
title to sue 191-209
mixed systems of law 3
mortgages 301, 304
aircraft 145-54
form and content 148-50
legal context 145-6
registration 145-6, 147-8, 150-4

spare parts 147-8
equitable 305
French concept of 300-2
goods/chattels 23-4, 101, 105, 106, 143
ships 155-80
bottomry distinguished from 158, 161-2
droit de suite 169-70
extent of security obtained 177-80
insurance of mortgagee's interest 167-9
legal context 155-8
legal framework 158-62
maritime liens distinguished from 162
mortgagee's powers 163-9
power of sale 163-5
prioritisation 174-7
problems caused by non-registration of mortgages on unregistered ships 170-4
registration 155, 156-8, 175-6
right to take possession 166-7

negligence 189-91, 242-5
continuing damage 209-10
title to sue 191-209
economic loss 193-201
interests less than full ownership 202-9
nemo dat quod non habet rule 72, 93-4
Netherlands, retention of title in 344-5
nominate contracts 6
essentialia 6-7
naturalia 7-11
lessee's duties 7-9
lessor's duties 9-11
Norway, retention of title in 346-8

operating leases 12-26, 97, 408-9, 412
disguised security 23-6
exclusion of lessor's duties 13-17
landlords and fixtures 20-3
relief from forfeiture 138-9
termination 17-20
oral contracts 7
ostensible ownership doctrine 338
ownership of goods 95-144
Consumer Credit Act 1974 and 108-17
consequences of wrongful possession 113-15
customer's right of termination of agreement 115-17
decision on granting return order 113
goods on premises 112, 113
hirer's right of termination of agreement 117
protected goods 111-12, 113
restrictions on repossession 109-11, 112
Insolvency Acts and 117-25
nature of respective interests of owner and hirer 97-100
relief from forfeiture 125-42
case examples 127-38
instalments already paid 139-40
jurisdiction to grant relief 125-7, 128-9, 135-6
operating leases 138-9
policy argument for 127, 140-2
retention of title *see* retention of title
use of security 100-8
example of different legal structures 104-7
hire purchase and conditional sale 102-3
mortgage of goods/bill of sale 101
pawn/pledge 100-1

perceived unfairness to customer 107-8
right to proceeds of resale 104

Panama 403
pawn 100-1
personal insolvency 119
pledge 100-1, 301, 305, 337
Portugal, retention of title in 348
prioritisation
conflict of laws 308, 365
purchase money security interest (PMSI) 268-89
retention of title and 361-5
ship mortgages 174-7
private finance initiative (PFI) 5
profit, account of profits 184, 220-2, 224, 248-9
property
equitable interests 34
liens 37-9, 40, 41, 44, 93
purchase money security interest (PMSI) 259, 261-90
buyer not in the ordinary course (BNOC) 287-8
consignments 267-8
consumer goods 266
crops 282-4
definition 262-3
inventory 273-8
liens 288-9
livestock 278-82
perfection 261-2
priority rules 268-89
real estate 285-7
software 266-7, 278
tracing requirement 263-4
transformation into non-PMSI 264-6

quiet enjoyment 11, 416

railways 332, 404, 428
receivership 118, 119, 120
redemption principle 159, 163
refinancing 264
registration
aircraft 147
aircraft mortgages 145-6, 147-8, 150-4
effect of 152-4
procedure 150-2
ship mortgages 155, 156-8
problems caused by non-registration of mortgages on unregistered ships 170-4
ships 155-6
Unidroit Convention on International Interests in Mobile Equipment 439-42
rent 6-7
abatement of 7-8
lessee's duty to pay 7-8
sequestration for 21
rental agreement 96
renvoi 306
repair
lessee's duty 8, 11
lessor's duty 11
misuse of chattels and 234-5
repossession
consequences of wrongful possession 113-15
debtor's remedies 114-15
protected goods 113-14
insolvency and 119-25
restrictions under Consumer Credit Act 1974 109-11, 112
ships 166-7
resale of goods 70-3
claims to proceeds of sale 43, 49, 73-89, 92, 104
residual value refund 106
restitution 184
restoration obligation 9
retention of title 29-94, 95
claiming 36-7
claims to original goods 43-57

identification and 51-7
processing/manufacturing and 57-70
claims to proceeds of sale 43, 49, 73-86, 92
Australian practice 86-9, 92
classification of transactions 40-3
equitable principles and 33-9
charges 40-3, 45-6, 49-51, 63, 65-6, 80-1, 87, 90, 93
claiming 36-7
liens 37-9, 40, 41, 44, 93
tracing 30, 33, 35-7, 51-7, 58-60, 84
European Union and 335-73
resale of goods 70-3
claims to proceeds of sale 43, 49, 73-89, 92
Unidroit Convention and 387-9
risk, insolvency and 298-9
Romalpa case *see* retention of title
Roman law 3, 54, 337
bottomry in 158
contract of hire in 3, 4-5, 6, 27
insolvency in 294
mortgage in 159, 160-1
specificatio 61-2

sale credit 297
sale and hire-purchase back agreements 24-5, 26
sale and lease-back agreements 26
Scots law
aircraft mortgages 150
contract of hire/lease in 3-27
disguised security 23-6
essentialia 6-7
exclusion of lessor's duties 13-17
landlords and fixtures 20-3
legal context 3-12
lessee's duties 7-9
lessor's duties 9-11
modern finance or operating lease 12-26
naturalia 7-11
termination 17-20
institutional writers 3
origins of 3
retention of title in 46
sequestration for rent 21
services, hire of 5-6
ships
mortgages 155-80
bottomry distinguished from 158, 161-2
droit de suite 169-70
extent of security obtained 177-80
insurance of mortgagee's interest 167-9
legal context 155-8
legal framework 158-62
maritime liens distinguished from 162
mortgagee's powers 163-9
power of sale 163-5
prioritisation 174-7
problems caused by non-registration of mortgages on unregistered ships 170-4
registration 155, 156-8, 175-6
right to take possession 166-7
slavery 4
software, purchase money security interest (PMSI) 266-7, 278
South Africa 408
space property 331-2
Spain, retention of title in 348-9
spare parts, mortgage of 147-8
specificatio 61-2
Sweden 403
retention of title in 349-50
Switzerland, retention of title in 350-2

tacking 176-7
taxation 107

termination of agreement
customer's right under Consumer Credit Act 1974 115-17
hirer's right under Consumer Credit Act 1974 117
termination of lease 17-20
where lessor does not seek termination payment 19-20
where lessor seeks termination payment 17-19
territorialism 310-12
third parties
lessor and 418-20
rights in contract 17
time order 113
title
legal 98
lessor's 418-20
passing of 24, 25
retention *see* retention of title
title to sue
misuse of chattels 191-209
economic loss 193-201
interests less than full ownership 202-9
tort
action in 111, 114-15
waiver of 232-3
tracing
purchase money security interest (PMSI) and 263-4
retention of title and 30, 33, 35-7, 51-7, 58-60, 84
treaty framework, international insolvency issues 317-34
trespass 112, 187, 235-7
trover 187, 188
trusts
commercial law and 34
misuse of chattels by trustees 220-2
retention of title and 87-9, 93
Scots law and 23

unfair contract terms 13-17
Unidroit (Institution on Unification of Private Law) 398-401
Convention on Agency in the International Sale of Goods 397
Convention on International Financial Leasing 326-7, 363-4, 399, 401-23
background 401-3
exclusion of or derogation from 420-1
purpose of 411
reasons for preparation of 409-11
regulatory system 414-21
substantive sphere of application 411-13
territorial sphere of application 413-14
text 451-64
Convention on International Interests in Mobile Equipment 328-32, 367, 368-70, 373, 377-95, 423-48
aircraft and 330-2, 378, 423, 426, 509-37
Article 5 of 393-5
assignment 444
background 378-81, 424-8
characterisation of interests under 385-7
characterisation of transactions under 387-9
derogation from 445-6
effect of international interest in insolvency 443-4
jurisdiction 444-5
law governing characterisation of interests and transactions under 390-3
national security interests under 384-5
principal features 429-46
priorities 442
reasons for preparation 424-6

registration system 439-42
regulatory system 436-46
remedies under 436-9
security interest in 382-4
structure 383-95, 429-30
substantive sphere of application 431-4
territorial sphere of application 434-6
text 465-508, 509-37
underlying principles 430
working methods in preparation of 426-8
Conventions on the International Sale of Goods 397
United Nations
Commission on International Trade Law (UNCITRAL) 318, 334, 366, 367, 381
Model Law on Cross-Border Insolvency 319-21, 333
Convention on the International Sale of Goods 394
United States of America 383, 403
leasing in 404, 407, 410
purchase money security interest (PMSI) 259, 261-90
buyer not in the ordinary course (BNOC) 287-8
consignments 267-8
consumer goods 266
crops 282-4
definition 262-3
inventory 273-8
liens 288-9
livestock 278-82
perfection 261-2
priority rules 268-89
real estate 285-7
software 266-7, 278
tracing requirement 263-4
transformation into non-PMSI 264-6
ship mortgages 162
Uniform Commercial Code 12, 23, 251-90, 411
Article 9 of 257-61, 347-8, 371-2, 399
legal context 251-7
universality 312-13
use
intended purpose 8
loss of 235-45
misuse *see* misuse of chattels

voluntary arrangements
corporate 118, 124-5
individual 119, 123

waiver of tort 232-3
World Bank 367, 400, 425
World Leasing Council 422

Zimbabwe 407, 408